**MIMESIS
INTERNATIONAL**

HISTORY
n. 10

THE INFLUENCE OF ITALIAN CIVIL LAW IN LATIN-AMERICA

80th Anniversary of the Codice Civile of 1942

Edited by
Francesca Benatti, Sergio García Long,
Mauro Grondona and Leysser León Hilario

MIMESIS
INTERNATIONAL

This book is published with the support of Edison S.p.a.

© 2024 – Mimesis International
www.mimesisinternational.com
e-mail: info@mimesisinternational.com

Isbn: 9788869774232
Book series: *History*, n. 10

© MIM Edizioni Srl
P.I. C.F. 02419370305

TABLE OF CONTENTS

PREFACE 9
Andrea Nicolussi

THE IDEA OF A LEGAL CODE AND THE MEANING OF CODIFICATION IN THE
POST-MODERN OPEN SOCIETY. PREMISES FOR A DISCUSSION 13
Mauro Grondona

L'INGIUSTIZIA DEL DANNO
INFLUENCES OF THE ITALIAN MODEL IN SOUTH AMERICAN CODES 31
Francesca Benatti and Nicolò Corvaglia

THE EFFECTS OF POSSESSION IN THE BOLIVIAN CIVIL CODE OF 1975
SUPPORTED UNDER THE INFLUENCE OF THE ITALIAN CIVIL CODE OF 1942 51
Juan Carlos Berrios Albizu

THE SEVERAL READINGS OF THE SOCIAL FUNCTION
OF PROPERTY AND ITS APPLICATION IN BRAZIL 73
Guilherme Calmon Nogueira da Gama and Patrícia Silva Cardoso

THE INFLUENCE OF THE ITALIAN LEGAL EXPERIENCE
ON THE PERUVIAN CIVIL CODE OF 1984 101
Juan Espinoza Espinoza

THE ITALIAN CIVIL CODE OF 1942 AND ITS INFLUENCE
ON BRAZILIAN CIVIL LIABILITY 117
Eugênio Facchini Neto

FORCE MAJEURE IN LATIN AMERICA AND THE CARIBBEAN
A LEGAL CARTOGRAPHY FOR IMPROVEMENTS IN NATIONAL LAWS 145
Sergio García Long

BETWEEN EXCUSABILITY AND RECOGNIZABILITY
THE 1942 *CODICE CIVILE* AND THE DISCIPLINE OF MISTAKE
IN THE 2002 BRAZILIAN CIVIL CODE   181
Elena de Carvalho Gomes

THE CENTRALITY OF THE PERSON FOR THE LEGAL SYSTEM.
REFLECTIONS ON THE PROTECTION OF THE UNBORN CHILD   197
Freddy Andrés Hung Gil

INFLUENCE OF THE ITALIAN EXPERIENCE ON THE NEW NOTION OF
NON-PECUNIARY DAMAGES IN LATIN AMERICA
(COLOMBIA, PERU AND VENEZUELA)   219
Milagros Koteich

THE ITALIAN CIVIL CODE AND ITS IMPACT ON ARGENTINE CIVIL LAW
(CONTRACTS IN GENERAL)   249
Luis F. P. Leiva Fernandez

THE FATE OF ITALIAN REGULATIONS ON UNJUSTIFIED ENRICHMENT IN
THE PERUVIAN CIVIL CODE
THE CHALLENGE OF SHAPING A NATIONAL LAW   271
Leysser León

NORMATIVE NEGOTIATING POWER AND PRIVATE AUTONOMY IN THE
FORMATION OF CONTRACT THEORY AND ETHICAL CONTRACT THEORY
SOME NOTES FROM ITALIAN AND URUGUAYAN CIVIL LAW   311
Juan José Martínez-Mercadal

NOTES ON THE INFLUENCE OF THE ITALIAN DOCTRINE ON
RIGHTS OF PERSONALITY [*DIRITTI DELLA PERSONALITÀ*] IN MEXICO   327
Jorge Eduardo Medina Villanueva

THE DEFINITION OF CONTRACT IN THE PRINCIPLES OF LATIN AMERICAN
CONTRACT LAW AND THE INFLUENCE OF THE ITALIAN CIVIL CODE   339
Pedro Mendoza Montano

CONTRACT LAW, PANDEMIC
AND THE PRINCIPLE OF SOLIDARITY IN THE ITALIAN LEGAL SYSTEM   363
Lorenzo Mezzasoma

LEGAL BRICOLAGE:
SOME THOUGHTS ON THE INFLUENCE OF THE *CODICE CIVILE*
ON THE PARAGUAYAN *CÓDIGO CIVIL*   381
Roberto Moreno

THE INFLUENCE OF ITALIAN CIVIL LAW IN VENEZUELAN CIVIL LAW
SUCCESSION LAW   449
Sheraldine Pinto Oliveros

REPERCUSSIONS OF ITALIAN LAW IN THE RE-READING OF THE
BELLO CODE CONCERNING BREACH OF CONTRACT   469
Lilian C. San Martín Neira

THE ITALIAN LEGACY IN PERUVIAN TESTAMENTARY LAW   493
Renzo E. Saavedra Velazco

THE REGULATION OF CHANGING CIRCUMSTANCES
THE INFLUENCE OF THE ITALIAN CIVIL CODE OF 1942
ON BRAZILIAN CIVIL LAW   517
Fábio Siebeneichler de Andrade

THE VOTING RIGHTS OF THE SHAREHOLDERS
OF THE MEXICAN CORPORATION, INFLUENCE OF ITALIAN LAW   539
Soyla H. León Tovar

Andrea Nicolussi
PREFACE

European and American legal Latinity as a common field of scholarly debate is a space that is still largely unexplored.

The richness of its potential is manifest. Take, for instance, the common linguistic roots and multiple cultural affinities that are accompanied by general affiliation with the codified legal tradition that radiated from Europe to Latin America in the nineteenth century. Or the common dogmatic method that supports the scientific-categorical construction of legal discourse.

This grandeur of possibility has resulted in a continuous and deeply rooted attention of Latin American legal culture to developments in Latin European law, which has often been characterized by a certain one-sidedness since the attention paid by the Latin Americans has often not been matched by an equal attention on the part of the Europeans. Moreover, with few exceptions, it is individual European legal systems that are usually considered in comparison with individual Latin American legal systems.

A new frontier, or rather a frontier still heuristically pregnant, is represented by a more conscious broadening of the debate, as well as the deepening of the *cercanias y lejanias* that legal experience is capable of highlighting in the broader space of legal Latinity as a whole.

Of course, it is unquestionable that, in addition to *cercanias*, there are also *lejanias*—due to historical, social, economic, and ethnic differences, which are also evident and relevant. Nevertheless, they can expose the relativity of certain legal categories or rules. In such cases, the problem-system relationship can be expressed in very different ways, suggesting various keys of interpretation for a rule that could be formulated as identical or quite similar. Even the socio-economic datum may suggest a remarkably peculiar consideration of classical disciplines, such as the relationship between property and possession. Consider, for example, the issue of enrichment or, according to a certain aquiliano-centric perspective, of damages *in re ipsa* for the unlawful occupation of real estate. In particular, although the latter has recently "occupied" Italian jurisprudence, other countries (such as Brazil) experience the opposite problem; i.e., the need to avoid protection of large landlords (perhaps *latifundist*) at the detriment of poor people in need of housing. Similarly, some scholars purport that adhering to a strict liability regime for enterprises potentially hinders the development of weaker companies operating in Latin American to the benefit of foreign entities that are better positioned to cope with the costs arising from such a liability scheme. Clearly, these issues are mentioned merely for descriptive purposes – to provide examples of topics which are both problematic (which, as such, must be considered) and capable of offering diverse perspectives from which to elaborate a more informed and advanced discourse – and will not be addressed in the context of this work.

However, apart from some *lejanias*, most legal issues are well-known. Accordingly, the method should remain familiar, albeit in the different nuances of its application. Written law's shared authority as both the fundamental source of law and dogmatic tradition is given the opportunity to continue and to be renewed in the broad space of legal Latinity. Admittedly, contemporary jurisprudence has for some time been emerging from the abstractions of a technicality that compromises the relationship between law and reality, just as the new dogmatics have become aware of the hermeneutic dimension that has been reversed, especially in the sometimes uncontrolled expansion of judge-made law. However, this exuberance, which at times even tests the systematic hold of law, is often nourished by a loss of rigor in legal discourse, as well as in a certain methodological renunciationism that, in sum, weakens the legal dimension itself. Hence the flight into justicialism, remedialism, or functionalism, which sometimes views the experience of judge-made law as a form of liberation from constraints that are poorly understood and, perhaps for that reason, poorly endured. Indeed, any experience of law, whether it places the law or the judge at its center, cannot ignore the principle of certainty and thus the constraints of legal discourse. The response of Sir Edward Coke to the vague claims of William I is too famous to repeat here by recalling the artificial reason of law. It goes without saying, then, that to imagine a space of debate extended to European and American legal Latinity is not only to shy away from provincialism in the most banal sense of the narrowness of a local perspective, but above all from a scientific provincialism that does not know how to make good use of the international dimension of law, even from the perspective of the scientific scope of legal categories and their differences as instruments of knowledge, from the legal point of view, of reality. Whether legal Latinity can be a voice capable of enriching the international legal debate will also depend on its self-awareness, which includes the ability to use a Latin language without embarrassment. The question of why English was chosen for this volume is therefore not meaningless. It is to be hoped that English was conceived as a means of signifying the opening up of that same legal Latinity, which does not wish to abandon its linguistic characteristics, but which at the same time presents itself as a voice aware of its scholarly responsibility in a debate that cannot fail to be open and global.

Mauro Grondona
THE IDEA OF A LEGAL CODE AND THE MEANING OF CODIFICATION IN THE POST-MODERN OPEN SOCIETY
Premises for a discussion

1. This book would not be possible without the remarkable commitment and perseverance of fellow editors, as well as the prompt and generous adhesion of numerous colleagues. Indeed, such efforts have come together to form a work capable of attracting a significant group of Latin American jurists who are eager to examine the relationship between Latin America and Europe from a very different lens compared to the past. Furthermore, as manifest from the diverse ideological propensities of the various authors, as well as for historic reasons (which must always take precedence), this shift in viewpoint has occurred relatively recently. Thus, against a book that offers readers (who are hopefully eager to go beyond mere learning and to reflect critically on the many problems and questions that the book helps to raise) an extremely rich text of assorted topics and a fresh perspective, this book presents clear potential for further research in dozens of areas. At the same time, the variety and richness of approaches makes it almost impossible, and perhaps even unnecessary, to include in these introductory pages an analytical account of the peculiarities that each essay represents and expresses. I would otherwise be doing the work of a 'halved reader' (moreover, culturally biased, as a European), and I do not intend to take on this task.

In maximum summary, then, I would say that each writing gives voice to a legal reconstruction in the perspective of that more or less remote dialogue (especially since, nowadays, Europe and Latin America are much closer than in the relatively recent past, for reasons that will be briefly addressed in the upcoming chapters) between the Italian civil code (and therefore Italian legal culture, which is undoubtedly not embodied only in the civil code) and the legal decisions of the Italian courts (which, as living law, express a fundamental component of a legal system's culture) subsequent its entry into force in 1942, and the Latin American codifications that have looked to the Italian Civil Code as a technical reference—first for design during the formation stage, and then, depending on the historical moment, the political conditions, and the general cultural context, as a dogmatic reference for its application. In other words: as happens during the process of applying social mechanisms, 'contextual' elements (generically understood) are fundamental for the functioning of the legal mechanism. And this is especially true when the social dimension can be expressed within a political context ascribable to the concept of 'open society', understood as the plurality of individual perspectives that quickly take on a significant social, and therefore political and legal, consistency (as I will attempt to explain below); after all, the passage from a *pluralist* to a *plural* society efficiently expresses the sense of maximum social and ordinamental openness. Thus, such transition reinforces the line between society, politics, and law that underpins those perpetually evolving ideas of juridicity at the heart of every liberal legal and political culture.

Ergo, this volume represents a traceable fragment of the cultural history of codification—which is very different from the codification of culture—in Latin America, where living law has been filtered in light of the greater or lesser influence or incidence of the Italian civil code. And it is precisely from this perspective that this volume must be placed: within the phenomenon of the progressive opening up of legal systems. It must moreover be noted that such aperture stems from the gradual opening up of society to both political pluralism and social plurality. Hence, a cultural perspective of history requires understanding manifestations of culture as comprehensive expressions of the spheres of the individual, and thus of society.

For this reason, times of 'crisis' are prone to match times of profound methodological innovation, of profound critical renewal. Although this process often involves reclaiming the past, or certain traditions thereof, without reverence for chronological sequence (especially if one considers the concept of time as a mere 'human constant', and therefore 'present' and 'past' to be linked by an underlying continuity precisely because they are 'constants of humanity'), it is profoundly necessity to reconsider certain starting points and certain theoretical assumptions hitherto presented as obvious or as necessitated. Indeed, this phenomenon of 'recycling' (recovering, adapting, transforming) the human experience leads to the gradual opening up of legal systems, which is the physiological effect of that indispensable 'cultural fine-tuning' that occurs over time and that, albeit partially and in a necessarily limited perspective, every scientific discipline has the institutional task of carrying out.

Consequently, the aim of this project is essentially two-fold: (i) to briefly discuss the topic of current civil codification and (ii) to read the topic of codification in the current liberal-democratic, legal-political perspective, thus expressly considering the legal dimension of today's postmodern open society. Naturally, this will be done through the collective voice of the editors (and beyond any differences in perspectives among them, which do not in any case invalidate the general need for a renewed civilian dialogue between Europe and Latin America[1]), and with particular thanks to Francesca Benatti, who not only came up with the grand idea of assembling this collection but who also had the tenacity to oversee the ambitious and exceptionally difficult execution and completion phases.

2. Let us start with some concise remarks on codification. Although, the most recent and significant literature[2] (including this volume, albeit based on different assumptions and having

---

[1] On the not-so-friable trail of T. Ascarelli, *Experiências de viagens jurídicas - Direito civil e Direito comercial* (1948 - the title of the paper is in Portuguese but the text is in Italian), in Id., *Ensáios e pareceres*, São Paulo, Edição Saraiva, 1952, pp. 401-408.

[2] See the essays collected in M. Graziadei & L. Zhang, *The Making of the Civil Codes. A Twenty-First Century Perspective*, Berlin, Springer, 2023, https://link.springer.com/book/10.1007/978-981-19-4993-7.

different objectives) holds codification to be a topical theme, this volume chronicles the phenomenon's unfolding though a synthetic, multi-voice dialogue that accounts (also critically) for the incidence of the 1942 Italian Civil Code in the so-called 'Latin American civilian legal experience'. This approach intentionally broadens the long-distance dialogue between Italy (and, to some extent, Europe) and Latin America beyond the limited codification space (especially since Latin American civil codes reflect various political-cultural and technical-legal authorities) precisely because these forces are then manifest (beyond their express and formal transposition within a given code or codification project) in different ways. And while such multiplicity is eventually rendered unitary in the perspective of living law, that is, of applicable law (the centrality of which, one might add, reinforces the ordering function typical of law), such consolidative effect is no longer exclusive of the code, as will be explained in greater detail below.

The purpose of codification, and thus the success of the 'code idea', lies in the need give order to phenomenological reality (i.e., what occurs empirically). Within the legal field, this need is practically ineliminable from the mental purview of the jurist and the law. More generally, however, the need for order (as a stabilizing factor between individuals and society) is a central aspect of human existence: order is at the core of civil society, of collectivity, of plurality of persons, ideas, groups, aggregates. In short, given the notion of individual freedom is increasingly broad, order is above all central to today's open society. This problem is also a fundamental tenant of the legal dimension, which requires empirical order that respects certain theoretical requirements in order to provide adequate solutions for the liberal-democratic society which it governs.

Therefore, the idea of 'order' is inconsequential to the discussion of codification (and especially that of the civil code), as law is and always has been an indubitably ordering instrument. However, delving into the order of this instrument (i.e., law) raises more complex issues. More specifically, one might question: Is legal order necessarily imposed by a legislator upon political delegation from the represented community, or is it an order that tends to be spontaneous and assert itself thanks to progressive adjustments that first manifest through mainly jurisprudential interventions and subsequently (as well as eventually, rather than necessarily) enforced through legislation (i.e., codicistic consecration)? In this sense, a legal order is the expression of those jurisprudential novelties accepted within a given system, irrespective of their codification or legislative formalization. Thus, insofar as they are sufficiently consolidated, these judicial mutations are fundamental for social stabilization.

From here, then, emerges the second problem, within which one might identify a so-called 'problem of the ordering of order', understood as an equally anthropological need, political requirement, conceptual premise, methodological opportunity, and applicative outlet.

More specifically, this second problem reflects the question of whether the 'order' is static and stable or mobile and volatile. That is, is it an open or closed order?

I would say that the answer offered by contemporary law (i.e., the law of postmodernity, understood as a convenient formula for a minimal periodization and beginning in the 1970s when interdisciplinary discourse was taken seriously and applied, albeit excessively and erroneously) is indisputable: order is forever open, that is, it is constantly transforming.

The current order is 'stability in mobility', then.

Herein lies the radical difference between modern and postmodern law: the multiplication of sources of law and, moreover, juridicality. In fact, juridicality is a far broader concept than law, not least because it escapes and even questions law's classic formalism, starting with the idea of hierarchy of sources. On a related note, it may be added that statutory formalism characterizes the legal dimension of conviviality; it is a way of being in society. That is, legal formalism is not only an inherent feature of the legal phenomenon or a methodological attitude of interpreters. It is that too, but it is also an effect of collective mentality, and thus of a way of being and thinking about society and life therein—as individuals, as part of groups, as a collective.

The moment the social perception of the individual changes, all those phenomena and relationships that were previously united (e.g., the idea of hierarchy, expressive form, canon) necessarily change. Furthermore, the proximity between legal and literary theories, even with respect to the current conception of democracy, becomes obvious[3].

Therefore, it is against this background that law – which is as much a social science as a humanistic discipline – can be put to good use and its full potential realized. Likewise, it is evident that the specific legal theme is precisely that of the general theory of the sources of law, in addition to the division of powers, linked to the universal allegiance to the *rule of law* principle.

But this legal declination is only one aspect (and effect) of the much broader phenomenon that is still used to qualify, via the term 'postmodernism', the notion of order. And through such qualification the notion of order is also (and continues to be) transformed (which, to be clear, is fundamental for both the purpose of the law and its very existence), going from a static order, understood as an ideal model to strive for (with the prevalence of ought-to-be over being), to a dynamic one, understood as a society where individual (and thus social needs) is paramount despite such attainment is rendered impossible by the very events occurring in society. Indeed, the speed at which postmodern society changes is the real problem posed by contemporary open society as – on closer inspection, thanks precisely to the mass acceptance on a global scale, within the limits of the 'democratically possible' – the expression of the pluralistic paradigm (and as such applicable to every sphere of liberal-democratic societies).

Therefore, the need for order remains firm, but the search for order and the ways of achieving such order necessarily change compared to the past.

---

3   See, for example, G. Mazzoni, *The novel, human sciences, democracy*, https://italianacademy.columbia.edu/sites/default/files/content/Guido%20 Mazzoni,%20Novel,%20human%20sciences,%20democracy%20 Italian%20academy.pdf.

In other words (at the risk of stating what is very well known), pluralism is intrinsic to the social dimension and characteristic (and to some extent also problematic)[4] of what may undoubtedly be qualified as postmodern liberal-democratic society. Moreover, according to some, this postmodern liberal-democratic society may also be called – albeit not without posing a series of political-philosophical questions that can only be briefly mentioned at here – a 'plural society', understood as a postmodern model of the Popperian open society, despite, however, this model responded to the anthropological logic of modernity and not to postmodernity; in fact, Popper died in 1994 and 'The Open Society and Its Enemies' was published in 1945. We are therefore within a time frame that can certainly be read from the perspective of modernity, which, if not coincidental, certainly has points of contact with the idea of 'ordered order', and not, as has been the case since the 1970s, with the idea of 'ordering order', i.e. dynamically performing its ordering function. In the postmodern open society there is no longer an ideal order, an ideal model, an ideal type in the Weberian sense, with its obvious repercussions in terms of legal reasoning by facts. Instead, there is the need for an order that becomes progressively such by proceeding in parallel with the same ordering need; order as the consequence of the exigency itself, not its premise. This social-political pluralism, as previously stated, becomes foundational of the whole 'social experience', that is, of all the modes and manifestations through which human beings tend to act, because of context. This means that both pluralism and order must be adapted to diverse backgrounds. However, it is clear that all contemporary liberal-democracies, as plural societies, are challenged by the progressive construction of an order that, precisely because it is plural, cannot but be open, flexible, and, moreover, adapted to the circumstances; the plural character of the postmodern

---

[4] In more recent literature, see, for example, M.J. Sandel, *Democracy's Discontent. A New Edition for Our Perilous Times*, Cambridge (MA, US)-London, The Belknap Press of Harvard Univ. Press, 2022.

open society is necessarily expressed in a contextual key – hence a primary and very delicate problem of legitimation precisely of those essential political readings in a contextualist sense – in order to avoid an excessive flexibility of the open order leading to the rupture of the very order that was intended to be adapted to the context.

3. Applying these brief and elementary considerations to the topic of codification it is apparent that the general sense of codification must change as well. More specifically, it must be endowed with a pluralistic afflatus or, even better, that legal polyvalence that arises from that same context that nevertheless requires at least some form of order. That is not to say that such shift alters the notion of the code as an 'ordering order,' but rather that such order is considered as such in terms of 'ordered order' (i.e., as static) where it is a necessarily dynamic order.

The difference is decisive: if the code is a static order then it must be read, first and foremost, according to a conservative approach, or one which remains as faithful as possible to the literal meaning of the words used by the legislature.

From this perspective, in order to ensure the code's order is truly an 'ordering order' (since it is already ordered), legislation, doctrine, and judges should collaborate to ensure the code remains as unaltered as possible over time. This reading (which, as I see it, does not represent reality, neither theoretically nor practically, and therefore, as it does not facilitate the search for that order indispensable to the individual and society, must be abandoned in favor of an order suitable for understanding the present context and not an anachronistic order) essentially suggests that the order of the code governs all relations pertaining to the private law sphere, and it does so in an exclusively attractive and conformist fashion; in this sense it also simplifies, as monism (whatever its declination) is less complex than pluralism precisely because it denies *in radice* the very legitimacy of complexity. Here, too, we are facilitated by reference to the notion of canon, which is similar to that of code to the extent they are both semantic and *tout se tient* (recalling *et pour cause*, the famous *dictum* of Ferdinand de Saussure[5], a celebrated linguist). In this way we allude to the affinities (more than structural in a strict sense, systematic in a broad sense) between language and law—language and law to be understood as mobile, open systems. The problem, of course, is not the destruction of the canon or code, but of their reform, including the very delicate process of determining new content and related issues of legitimacy and legitimation. In any case, even from this perspective, legal and literary theories, though often unconsciously, proceed in parallel.

Nevertheless, returning to the discussion at hand, in this space we continue to reason according to a static order—which, by definition, is not very ductile, malleable, or flexible, and not at all multipurpose—and predetermined principles, values, and detailed rules that are waiting to be applied. That is, our behavior is based on a legal instrument (i.e., a civil code) that is necessarily characterized by a prefixed ordering that does not always correspond to the social reality requiring ordering.

Of course, sometimes the problem arises from certain codified precepts (i.e., principles), whereas other times issues may arise from the absence of explicit principles which are only subsequently communicated in doctrine—the constructor of legal concepts. But the substance of the reasoning does not change: there is a constituted order of law (a 'constituted' in a twofold sense, there being a constituted order and a constituted law; hence, the ordering force of law understood precisely as an order), which looks at stability from the perspective of fixedness. In this regard, the constituted order of law is a necessarily static order.

However, the very idea that the code is an ordering tool has changed in recent decades. Nowadays, instead of being understood as a tool containing an ordered order, the code is

---

5 See E.F.K. Koerner, *Noch einmal on the History of the Concept of Language as a «Système où tout se tient»*, in *Cahiers Ferdinand de Saussure*, 1998, No. 51 (1998), pp. 203-221.

considered an instrument to facilitate the constantly search for order; order is realized through its own construction. Searching for order means progressively constructing an order that turns out to be contextually adequate.

Still, this case is not a question of general order (as with the order of constituted law mentioned above) of actions. Rather, it is a matter of the order (i.e., of individual orders) in relation to the specific problem that invokes a solution. Hence, we are dealing with an order closely linked to the idea of justice in the specific case. Furthermore, every legal system contains (at least potentially) elements that are not *ex ante* necessarily disruptive of the order but that nevertheless can be traced to a 'second system' such that a dual system[6] (with one system being more flexible than the other) may be identified; one which, on closer inspection, may avoid the self-extinction of an overly rigid system (albeit overly open systems also risk self-destruction).

If we think in the terms just indicated, the change of perspective with respect to the function of the code (an ordering but not authoritarian function, so to speak) entails a parallel change of perspective with respect to the ordering content of the code. Accordingly, it becomes possible to overcome the code's ideological-cultural authoritarianism (implicit in certain legislative technique), but not at the expense of its operational rule.

Thus, such shift yields fewer detailed rules, more elastic criteria, more provisions containing open cases, and more general clauses. In short, everything that, from the standpoint of legal technique, lends itself to ductile and flexible use in search of such desired order (which, in this sense, is the product of interpretive work that links the problem to the system), with the *caveat* (perhaps unnecessary or overabundant at this point) that by system (and one could at most substitute the term with the less ambiguous 'whole') we do not mean a closed legal order. On the contrary, with the term 'system' we suggest an open legal

---

6   This has been sharply observed by T. Ascarelli, *Experiências de viagens jurídicas, supra* note 1, p. 404.

order that allows for that progressive adaptation not only to social novelties but to those individual conducts that move under the banner of liberal pluralism. Moreover, this liberal pluralism, on the one hand, marks the centrality of individual freedom (which affects the content of juridicality in no small way) and, on the other hand, fixes the need (in my opinion increased to the limit and not diminished, and this is by no means a paradox) to construct an order of actions. It is important to note, then, that order of actions is not synonymous with general order of society, which is absorbed by social pluralism, coinciding with the latter. Specifically, society is imbued with social pluralism, and it legitimizes as many orders of actions as there are freedoms that seek, in concrete cases, the road to the turn of a juridicization (becoming of legal relevance), which will then be attributed, not by the legislator but by the judge, along that earlier referenced path of a jurisprudential law that constantly rewrites (more or less extensively) the civil code and thus of that fragment of the overall juridicity that is reflected therein.

Against this background of the open legal order, the civil code is essentially the legal *substratum* on which (prevailing) elements interact—all of which can all be considered, collectively, aspects of the new problem that arises and that will serve as a fragment of a legal order, not necessarily parallel or alternative to that of the code, but integrating the latter, in the idea (in this sense postmodern and therefore more liberal) that the concrete legal order has a greater prescriptive force and regulatory effectiveness than the abstract legal order.

For the avoidance of misunderstanding, since the polemic (at least in Italy) is quite insistent and repeated (although controversial with weak foundation), it must be clear that reference to the concrete legal order (i.e., the dimension of the order that arises from the need to solve a problem), is not intended to indicate an authoritarian (or, worse, totalitarian) perspective that endows judges with such discretion that their weight may be comparable to political authority, and in this sense a sovereign and therefore arbitrary power.

Instead, emphasizing the concrete dimension of the legal order (i.e., on the legal order that is established in practice, that is constructed progressively with respect to the specific cases, and namely the facts, that must be resolved) has rendered the same self-executing (or, at any rate, widely accepted) as nowadays it is necessary to uphold, first and foremost in theoretical terms, a vision of law that seeks to protect to the fullest an individual freedom that itself becomes an instrument of juridicity—a juridicity that is not arbitrary, either directly, by force of social actors, or indirectly, by court intervention; it is a juridicity appreciable, in evidence, only within a philosophical-political context (which is the one present today, in postmodern society, and which in my opinion must be defended against claims aimed at the reaffirmation of a pre-established juridical order), which has at its center individual freedom, that is, the action of the human being, in this sense a dialectical factor of an equally dialectical juridical-political order.

4. Moving toward conclusion, if we were to connect the scattered and fragmentary statements made – in relation to the idea of the code (including its structure and function), to the concept of codification, of an open legal order, of a legal order in progressive construction, of the code not as a limiting but as a balancing tool that simultaneously represents a propulsive ordinal factor precisely because it is an institutional tool from which and on which to work in an attempt to introduce into the order that which society requires a response in necessarily ordering terms – it is possible identify one aspect in particular which purpose is both unifying and harmonizing, and thanks to which the order – and therefore also the code (or especially the code, that is, the codes) – becomes the product of the social cooperation that makes it precisely harmonious in the context in which it will then be called upon to operate.

I am referring to purposeful cultural globalization, which is a significant and steadily growing feature of postmodernity, in this sense strengthened and hardened by the penetration of technology within intellectual work. This has hugely facilitated the knowability of sources and their retrievability (and for that matter, this volume itself could not have been born, or would have been born in a different perspective, outside of technological globalization). Still, the knowledge, or at any rate the knowability, of sources brings with it, almost naturally, interest or curiosity in comparison, and hence greater ease (even against the recent past) of dialogue between different legal systems, as well as different social, economic and partly political contexts, in addition to greater ease of mutual listening. Here is the link (denied or otherwise opposed by many, but that is a mistake) between technology and culture: there is no mutual exclusion but, on the contrary, one works fruitfully on the other.

Moreover, cultural globalization (in which technology holds a strong point) has created a genuine need to develop, in the full political sense, and adopt certain solutions already tried elsewhere. Adoptable solutions that were indeed eventually adopted, but not because (as was frequently the case in the past, albeit involuntarily, that is, even in the absence of specific culturally colonizing aims[7]) they were imposed, even by the mere cultural force (i.e., for reasons of prestige) of the model, by one order on another. However, this view is no longer proposable today and is in any case anachronistic. In this sphere, the beneficial renewal generally comes from *cultural studies*, and specifically from *cultural legal studies*[8], which both have had and retain the merit of having brought scholars' attention to the centrality of that perspectivism (which, as is well known, has multiple declinations in the philosophical sphere, but which here, in our limited legal sphere, can be considered above all in reference to its use by a leading personality who contributed greatly to comparison, in a very broad and certainly transdisciplinary

---

[7] On this topic, see L. Salaymeh & R. Michaels, *Decolonial Comparative Law: A Conceptual Beginning*, in *Rabel Journal of Comparative and International Private Law (RabelsZ)*, Vol. 86, No. 1, pp. 166-188, January 2022, DOI: 10.1628/rabelsz-2022-0007, Max Planck Private Law Research Paper No. 22/1, Available at SSRN: https://ssrn.com/abstract=4014459.

[8] See J.L. Schulz, *What is Cultural Legal Studies?*, in *Manitoba Law Journal*, vol. 44, No. 2 (2021), pp. 143-150.

sense. I refer, of course, to the great Erich Auerbach[9] who was, as is well known, a jurist by training[10] before devoting himself entirely to the field of Romance philology and, more generally, to the history of ideas).

I recalled the need to adopt certain solutions already worked out within a 'foreign' legal system precisely because the postmodern open society does not reason in terms of localisms and compartmentalization, but in universalistic terms. This *viaticum* is met, specifically, with the transformative force of individual freedom. That is, each human being – insofar as they are free and within the limits of the freedom available to them – is an autonomous producer of juridicality. In this sense, the dimension of subjectivity and, even more generally, subjectivism as a conceptual category, explain the speed of an increasingly meaningful law in a transnational, and thus increasingly homogeneous, key—if only within those liberal-democratic legal-political spaces. And also in this respect everything holds, in the sense that a *quid pluris of* freedom entails a *quid pluris* of liberal-democracy, and the reciprocal is true. In other words, the opening of society, and thus the expansion of freedom, is a positive-sum game - subject to the problem of time, that is, the speed of change (which is, as I also mentioned above, the real problem of contemporary liberalism[11]).

---

9   See in particular E. Auerbach, *Letteratura mondiale e metodo* (It. transl.). Con un saggio di Guido Mazzoni, Milano, nottetempo, 2022, as well as R. Castellana, *Il metodo di Auerbach*, in *Allegoria/56*, 2007, pp. 52-79 https://www.allegoriaonline.it/126-sul-metodo-di-auerbach. However, for the Italian-speaking reader, the very recent translation of P. Casanova, *La Repubblica mondiale delle lettere*, a cura di C. Benaglia, con postfazione di Franco Moretti, Milano, nottetempo, 2023, should now be seen in a different perspective.

10   E. Auerbach, *Die Teilnahme den Vorarbeiten zu einem neuen Strafgesetzbuch*, Berlin, Juristische Verlagsbuchhandlung Dr. jur. Frensdorf, 1913.

11   See P. Barrotta (ed.), *Soggettivismo, tempo ed istituzioni – a partire dalla Scuola Austriaca*, Soveria Mannelli (CZ), Rubbettino, 2005; G.P. O'Driscoll, Jr. & M.J. Rizzo, *Austrian Economics Re-Examined. The economics of time and ignorance*, London-New York, Routledge, 2015.

Moreover, the sense of the transformative and, as such, legal-political force of subjectivity does not conflict with the idea of the state.

Simply put, the extension of individual freedom should not be seen as antagonistic to the state. Indeed, the contemporary open society as a postmodern society is necessarily one that moves (politically) under the banner of liberal-socialism, understood as individual freedom to be reconciled with social justice. This is, and remains, a fixed point in any order. Therefore, the role of states remains firmly in place and, to some extent, expanding (with respect to certain social policies). But equally firm remains the fact that the progressive construction of the order (i.e., of law) is a collective enterprise[12], thus finding its main driving force in the individual freedom of every human being (and, moreover, increasing the general sense of the inherently universalistic character of law).

---

12 This aspect (obviously connected to the universalistic dimension of law, in this sense to be favored and not opposed) is very clear in Tullio Ascarelli, who in fact looked, rightly, with great confidence to comparative law as a universalizing tool (and the adjective 'universal' in him meant above all peace and freedom, and therefore prosperity, individual and social - and then the mind immediately goes, because of the evident Crocianism, in both of them, with respect to the dimension of historicity that makes sense and is rooted in the present, to the famous pages of A. Momigliano, *Peace and Liberty in the Ancient World: The Cambridge Lectures 1940*, Cambridge, Cambridge Univ. Press, 2013): T. Ascarelli, *Concetti giuridici e interpretazione*, in Id., *Ensáios e pareceres*, *supra* note 1, pp. 409-415, at 414: «È su questo terreno [i.e. that of comparative law] che ritroveremo il perché della stessa diversa teoria delle fonti e dell'interpretazione nei vari diritti e che l'interpretazione a sua volta ci apparirà come parte della struttura costituzionale di ogni paese, volta appunto alla rinnovazione e all'integrazione di ogni diritto costituito e insieme elemento di connessione tra ogni norma data e una più compiuta esperienza giuridica, nella quale ritroverai la storia diversa di stati e popoli, la diversità di esperienze politiche e di fedi religiose, di strutture economiche e condizioni ambientali, in quella complessa diversità delle genti nell'unità fondamentale del genere umano, che permette di intendere e comprendere, data la comune unità, le diversità e nei cui confronti il diritto torna ad essere manifestazione di coltura e civiltà collettiva. Questo mondo concettuale, cui accennavo, è invero creazione collettiva, creazione dei giuristi come tecnici elaboratori e creazione anche di tutti i consociati; è insieme strumento di interpretazione e applicazione delle norme e condizione della loro stessa espressione».

From this perspective, the state fulfills the social function of making not only abstractly possible but concretely operative the legal force of individual freedom with emancipatory policies to be adapted naturally to the socio-economic context of reference[13].

Let us return, however briefly, to Erich Auerbach, who, indeed, is a sure guide capable of accompanying us with ease within that (already evoked) legal perspectivism that rejects the idea of an iron legal logic because deductive logic descending from unquestionable assumptions written in a text (which in this sense is unduly sacralized - moreover, the sacralization of a text, that is, the predicate sacred nature of a text should never lead to hermeneutical paralysis, through which, of course, the text is killed and certainly not enlivened)[14], such as the civil code, welcomes instead with open arms, and with the utmost hermeneutical confidence[15], an inductive legal logic; a logic that is constructive and reconstructive, rooted in the dynamics of conflicting interests, that is, in society, understood as an aggregate of forces and drives that always bring out an axiologically orienting, and therefore ordering tendency.

A liberal ordering in the postmodern sense cannot fail to take note of this tendency, not least because, in this way, there is a spontaneous reconciliation, in a non-authoritarian sense, between liberal subjectivism and liberal ordering. The order has been fully liberalized thanks to a subjectivism which, having operated as a source of legal transformation, at least in part has necessarily objectified itself in that exact order on which it has affected in a modifying sense; an order which, at this point, is

---

13 On this topic, see the perspective of R.M. Unger, *False Necessity. Anti-Necessitarian Social Theory in the Service of Radical Democracy*, London-New York, Verso, 2004 (1st ed. 1987).
14 Cf. C. Ginzburg, *La lettera uccide*, Milano, Adelphi, 2021.
15 Cf. T. Greco, *La legge della fiducia. Alle radici del diritto*, Roma-Bari, Laterza, 2021 (in 2022, the highly successful volume reached its third reprint. Every jurist will be well pleased, vigorously defending what the author agreeably calls the 'fiduciary paradigm,' and beneficially oriented on the cooperative side. But, specifically, law is nothing but regulatory cooperation, i.e., social cooperation in a regulatory key. There is also a Spanish translation of the volume: T. Greco, *La ley de la confianza. En las raíces del Derecho*, Madrid, Dykinson, 2023).

then ready to be rechallenged by new individual-based drives, which is then the perfect physiological legal-political dynamic of the open society.

In this respect, it should be added that the speed of transposition also functions as an effective tool to just as quickly point out what that transposition has produced in terms of social suboptimality, if only at that particular historical moment, that is, with respect to that general context. But the limit always comes after and not before the action; otherwise, we fall back into that authoritarian order which is itself incompatible with the current legal-political meaning of the open society[16].

In conclusion, the legal-political ordering of open societies (in that postmodern sense alluded to several times using a noun and adjective sometimes much criticized for their relativistic scope; when there is one, of course – but this is only one of the possible meanings of the term postmodernism) has on its side the notable advantage of allowing a sharp caesura, on the legal front (and really on all fronts, as extensive multidisciplinary research attests), between the notion of a closed legal order and one of an open legal order, between the idea of a juridicity that is pre-existing because it is predetermined by a state power, juridically legitimate and politically legitimized by popular consensus, and a juridicity that is successive, or constantly under construction, equally legitimate and legitimized by that individualistic-based subjectivism that then goes on to result in a legal order that is capable of constant renewal precisely because it is open.

This, I would argue, is the favorable legal-political context to which to trace the idea of code and the current meaning of codification today.

---

[16] And, thus, a space opens up for rethinking the precautionary principle as an instrument of spontaneous social cooperation in the sign of an advanced liberalism and not as a preventive limit, paralyzing action. For many interesting and acute considerations see C.R. Sunstein, *Laws of Fear. Beyond the Precautionary Principle,* Cambridge, Cambridge Univ. Press, 2005.

FRANCESCA BENATTI* AND NICOLÒ CORVAGLIA**
L'INGIUSTIZIA DEL DANNO
Influences of The Italian Model
in South American Codes

1. *The peculiarities of the Italian liability model*

Extra-contractual liability has always been a subject in search of a difficult balance. While it has often been considered the most suitable and immediate instrument capable of attributing legal value to economic loss, this quality is met by the opposing need to avoid using this institution to attribute relevance to injuries unworthy of compensatory relief. The European civil law landscape offers two primary civil liability models: the French model, characterized by a marked generality whereby the obligation to "repair" damage[1] is triggered by any intentional or negligent act, and the German model, characterized by an analytical typification of the legal assets that, if prejudiced, give rise to the obligation to compensate the aggrieved party. In the former system, liability arises merely from a voluntary and/or negligent human action causing a personal, certain, and direct injury, without regard for any other condition. Thus, the dismissal of claims for compensation on the grounds that other requirements have not been met is against the positive datum[2]. The Italian Civil Code of 1942 (c.c.It.), having renounced

---
* Professor of Comparative Law, Università Cattolica del Sacro Cuore.
** Master's Degree in Law, Università Cattolica del Sacro Cuore
1 On the concept of damage in Italy see A. Nicolussi, Voce "Danno", in Diritto civile, (Milano : Giuffrè Editore) 2011, p. 533.
2 P. le Tourneau and L. Cadiet, *Droit de la responsabilité*, 2nd edn (Paris: Dalloz, 1998), par. 654: "Des lors, il conviendrait de réparer tout préjudice, sans porter un jugement de valeur sur la conduite de la victime, appréciation forcément subjective et variable. La position inverse conduit au singulier

slavish imitation of French law in favor of the German example, represents a sort of "middle ground" between these two models. Indeed, this mix resulted in a successful mediation between unbridled generality and excessive taxation, consecrated in the expression "unjust damage".

On these words, there would later be a definitive divide in the legal doctrine. On the one hand, there are theorists of the general clause advocating the judge's task to attribute significance to the syntagma introduced for the first time by Article 2043 c.c.It.[3]. And on the other hand, there are scholars who, instead, argue "injustice" must be determined by the injury of subjective legal situations identified, *ex ante* and exclusively, by the law[4]. Moving from Stefano Rodotà's intuition (already advanced in Piero Schlesinger's prolusion at the Catholic University of Milan), subsequent authors have elaborated new and autonomous interpretations. However, while agreeing that civil liability identifies which of the two conflicting interests is more deserving of protection, these interpretations nevertheless differ on the criterion by which to sanction the pre-eminence of one or the other subjective legal situation[5]. With his enlightening

---

    résultat de faire bénéficier l'auteur d'un dommage d'une irresponsabilité qui, de son côté, ne se justifie en aucune façon".

[3] S. Rodotà, *Il problema della responsabilità civile*, 1st edn (Milano: Giuffrè, 1964), p. 138: "Introducing one or more general clauses into a system does not mean that the judge, with regard to the issues governed by these clauses, can adjudicate according to his particular sentiment about the needs of the society and time in which he lives. In fact, the judge's decision must always be based on legal criteria, even when the practical establishment of those conditions requires a reconstruction that reflects current reality".

[4] C. Castronovo, *Responsabilità civile*, 4th edn (Milano: Giuffrè, 2018), p. 131, in which the author discusses "a subjective situation of mere power as a sufficient qualification of relevance, as a perceptible index in positive law of the protection accorded to an interest" and criticizes Rodotà's reading by resolving it "in the judge's power to deem worthy of compensation a patrimonial loss that although not anchored to a subjective situation i.e., to an interest already reputed worthy of protection by the system".

[5] F.D. Busnelli and E. Navarretta, 'Abuso del diritto e responsabilità civile', in N. Irti, G. Visintini, A. Luminoso, C. Mazzoni, A. Gentili, M. Sesta (eds.), *Studi in onore di Pietro Rescigno*, V (Milano: Giuffrè, 1998) p. 77, affirm that the scheme of abuse of rights is applicable to liability, the existence of which must be verified by considering "a possible misuse [of the right] by

lucidity, Pietro Trimarchi warns that it is not possible to reconstruct a unitary tort theory but only to generally indicate which operations the interpreter must perform when required to determine whether a situation not expressly governed by the law is "unlawful". These are criteria related to the delimitation of what the law can address, aimed at coordinating freedom of action with the necessary preservation of what is due to each person and ensuring the efficient functioning of justice. Therefore, it is necessary to consider not only the interests of the parties in immediate conflict, but also the interests of third parties indirectly involved. That is, it means contemplating not only the immediate result of the individual case, but also the consequences of the repeated application of the rule of law[6].

After an initial period of difficulty in interpreting the new "unjust damage" formula introduced in 1942, which finds no match in the past literature[7], Italian legal scholars clearly distinguished the injustice of the damage from the unlawfulness of the conduct[8] and have focused on whether the latter should be considered a constituent element of liability. The French, albeit without the comfort of the positive datum[9], include unlawfulness

      judging *a posteriori* the modalities and the result of the extrusion of the same potentiality inherent in the *facultas*, not in an absolute perspective [...] but in a relative, 'relational' and especially legal perspective [...]. While it is true that the injustice of the harm highlights the locus of a conflict of interest, it does not say what its solution should be and whether it can consist in an *a posteriori* comparison. This notion, on the contrary, can be inferred from the prohibition of abuse, which on the other hand is an indispensable principle for reconstructing the possible rules of such *a posteriori* comparison".

6   P. Trimarchi, *La responsabilità civile: atti illeciti, rischio, danno*, 3rd edn (Milano: Giuffrè, 2021), p. 51.

7   A. Fedele, *Il problema della responsabilità del terzo per pregiudizio del credito*, 1st edn (Milano: Giuffrè, 1954), p. 117, in which the author attributed the qualification of "unfair" to the behavior and not to the damage, thus equating it with "unlawfulness".

8   This distinction between injustice that pertains to the harm and unlawfulness that refers instead to the conduct is well present in Rodotà, *Il problema della responsabilità civile*, (n 2), pp. 110–11.

9   F. Piraino, "'Ingiustizia del danno" e antigiuridicità', Europa e diritto privato, II (2005), p. 703 argues that "the notion of unlawfulness has entered under the guise of *faute*".

among the conditions that make a claim for compensation admissible, speaking cogently of "*préjudice licite*" and stating that "*l'intérêt lésé ne doit pas être illégitime*"[10]. The same considerations then seem to apply to the German legal system, which expressly mentions this requirement in Article 832 of the BGB. In Italy, there seems to be a shift from considering such a conduct requirement as a founding prerequisite of civil liability[11], although very often the thin line separating injustice and unlawfulness is absent-mindedly crossed, and the latter thus ends up becoming a requirement for compensation[12].

It should be noted how the Italian model has shaped very few Latin American countries. Most Latin American codes seem to be mainly influenced by the *Code Civil*, and only two of them (i.e., the Argentine and Bolivian codes) show a significant trace of the Italian model in current legal provisions. The reason is clearly grasped by Guido Alpa, according to whom the flexibility of Article 2043 c.c.It. (which represents an almost "flight to becoming", open to the protection of new situations and interests without, however, opening itself to their proliferation) makes the rule complex for foreign jurists who do not fully understand

---

10 Le Tourneau and Cadiet, § 654.
11 Cfr. Piraino's detailed analysis, '"Ingiustizia del danno" e antigiuridicità', (n. 7), p. 721.
12 P. Schlesinger, 'La ingiustizia del danno nell'illecito civile', Jus (1960), pp. 342–44. "In Article 2043 a general principle is codified, apt to represent an instrument sensitive to the need for the protection of the most varied interests [...] the fundamental duty of *alterum non laedere*, the very general duty not to cause harm to others, a duty released from the individual provisions of other cases of tort, and precisely for this reason apt to provide protection to every kind of interest deserving of protection. [...] Injustice means *unjustified* harm, done without the injurious act being authorized by a rule, without the injurious conduct being enacted in the exercise of a faculty concretely conferred by the law. The traditional requirement of *iniuria* should, therefore, be understood not in the contra *ius* sense of contrariety to a protected right or interest of the injured party, but in the historically more correct sense of *non iure*. [...] In order to exclude the injustice of a harm, the generic lawfulness, due to the lack of a specific prohibition, of the harmful conduct is not sufficient, but it is necessary that the legislator, because of some particular social need, authorizes the act even at the cost of another's sacrifice. Therefore, the general principle that 'unjust' is any harmful conduct not enacted in the exercise of a right may well be upheld".

its scope[13]. Therefore, most Latin American codes lean toward distinctly French legislative solutions: the prevalence of the general clause finds definite confirmation in Article 1833 of the Paraguayan Civil Code[14], in Article 1645 of the Guatemalan text, and also in Article 1045 of the Costa Rican code[15].

However, besides the fact that these data are insufficient to understand the real influence of Italian law, it seems appropriate to make some observations. It should first be noted that the Italian influence is limited to the 1942 code. For example, since the Italian Civil Code of 1865 influenced the Venezuelan codes of 1916 and 1922 and the Venezuelan legal landscape was not yet developed, Pedro Manuel Arcaya proposed looking to Italian doctrine and jurisprudence to improve the codes' application and reduce the differences between the two models[16]. On the other hand, for what concerns the section on obligations, the Venezuelan Civil Code of 1942 is deeply indebted to the 1927 Italian-French Project and is left almost identical in the 1982 code.

It then appears necessary to ask, "which code circulates?"[17]. It has, in fact, been pointed out that the Italian code of 1942 has

---

13 G. Alpa, *Nuevo Tratado de la Responsabilidad Civil* (Lima: Jurista, 2006), p. 458.

14 Article 1833: "*El que comete un acto ilícito queda obligado a resarcir el daño. Si no mediare culpa, se debe igualmente indemnización en los casos previstos por la ley, directa o indirectamente*". It should be noted, however, that the subsequent Article 1834 takes care to define "*los actos voluntarios [que]sólo tendrán el carácter de ilícitos*" in a manner reminiscent of par. 823 of the BGB. This choice also seems interesting because the Paraguayan code was strongly influenced by the Italian model.

15 Article 1645 of the Guatemalan code states, "*Toda persona que cause daño o perjuicio a otra, sea intencionalmente, sea por descuido o imprudencia, está obligada a repararlo, salvo que demuestre que el daño o perjuicio se produjo por culpa o negligencia inexcusable de la víctima*", while Article 1045 of the Costa Rican text states, "*Todo aquel que por dolo, falta, negligencia o imprudencia, causa a otro un daño, está obligado a repararlo junto con los perjuicios*".

16 M.C. Domínguez Guillén, 'Curso de derecho civil III', Revista Venezolana de Legislación y Jurisprudencia, CA. (2017).

17 M. Graziadei, 'Il Codice civile in Italia e all'estero', Rivista italiana per le scienze giuridiche (speciale 2022), pp. 535–69.

ambiguous premises between liberalist instances and dirigiste tendencies that probably facilitated its first circulation in Latin America[18]. However, subsequent evolution has led to overcoming those premises in order to align the code with Constitutional, European, and supranational legislation[19]. This second phase of Italian law has not affected all countries in the same way.

Another aspect concerns the different areas of civil law, which degree of acceptance may vary by system. While there are some 300 references to Italian law in the Argentine Civil Code[20], the Italian influence in other systems is either more nuanced or is limited to certain subjects.

Moreover, the circulation of the Italian model has been primarily scientific. Italian legal doctrine has long been closely linked[21] to Latin American legal doctrine, including through amicable relations[22]. Indeed, Italian law is recounted in these systems through the perspectives and voices of individual scholars, and many Italian authors are cited in jurisprudential decisions almost as a source of law. For instance, Francesco Messineo was a chief authority in the first half of the 20th century, and Guido Alpa during the second — with their names reoccurring in the literature almost as much or more than those of national jurists. This relationship with Italian doctrine has continued over time, albeit tempered by new generations' now evident affection for the North American model. Despite academics still travel to Italy to study and conduct research, there has been a noticeable change,

---

18 Graziadei, 'Il Codice civile in Italia e all'estero'.
19 That is stressed by Guido Alpa, *La responsabilità civile. Parte generale*, (Torino: Utet, 2010).
20 D.F. Esborraz, 'L'influsso del diritto italiano sul nuovo Progetto di "Codice civile e commerciale" della Repubblica Argentina', in S. Lanni, P. Sirena (eds.), *Il modello giuridico – scientifico e legislativo – italiano fuori dell'Europa* (Napoli: Esi, 2013), p. 127.
21 The influence of Emilio Betti, Tullio Ascarelli and Enrico Tullio Liebmann is well known.
22 Consider the cases of Fernando Hinestrosa, Carlos Fernandez Sessarego. Very interesting is L. León Hilario, *40 años del Código Civil peruano, entre la influencia del derecho civil italiano y la búsqueda de una identidad propia, presso* https://laley.pe/2024/01/12/codigo-civil-peruano-influencia-derecho-civil-italiano/.

which partially depends on the perceived decline of the Italian academy: the great legal scholars reputed to be "*auctoritas*" have been replaced by authoritative scholars who are nevertheless viewed as close and with whom one openly confronts.

Otherwise, Italian jurisprudence is not considered in the writings of Latin American jurists. However, this has brought about a piecemeal view and transposition of the model, especially regarding civil liability, which has evolved primarily through case law. In the legal scholarship, this aspect is addressed in depth by only a few authors.

2. *Peru*

In the area of civil liability, the Peruvian legal system contains a general clause in Article 1969 of the *Código Civil* (c.c.p.), clearly evidencing the influence of the French model[23]. This caused a split in the doctrine, which was already divided between those that did not consider unlawfulness a constitutive element for indemnity and those that, through a systematic interpretation of the phenomenon, came to the opposite conclusion[24]. For the latter, Article 1971 c.c.p. is the cornerstone of the entire system of liability. In fact, reasoning *a contrariis*, if it is true that this provision excludes the obligation to repair harm when the fact occurs in certain circumstances that render the conduct lawful (i.e., *iure*), it can be inferred that unlawfulness is in all respects a prerequisite of liability. It should also be pointed out that this condition was (at least initially) reconciled with a principle of typicality, thus defining unlawful conduct as that which is punishable (i.e., prohibited by the legal system) despite not necessarily constituting a criminal offense[25]. Nowadays, there seems to be a general consensus that liability is

---

23 Article 1969 c.c.p. states, "*Aquel que por dolo o culpa causa un daño a otro está obligado a indemnizarlo. El descargo por falta de dolo o culpa corresponde a su autor*".

24 L. Taboada Còrdova, '¿Es la antijuridicidad un requisito fundamental de la responsabilidad civil extracontractual?', Advocatus, (1994) p. 54.

25 Taboada Còrdova, p. 55.

based on an atypical scheme of unlawfulness[26]. This is also evident from Article 1985 c.c.p., which, by requiring an adequate causal link between fact and damage, implicitly admits that any conduct (and not only those explicitly listed *ex ante* as *non iure*) can become a source of liability[27]. However, if unlawfulness is atypical, it is necessary to identify a criterion on the basis of which a fact is contrary to the law. In this regard, the meaning of unlawfulness can be surmised from Article V of Introductory Title of the Civil Code[28] (which refers to the violation of provisions of public order and morality) as well as by making use of a *"criterio de valoración social en una determinada sociedad y en un momento histórico determinado"*[29].

Nonetheless, this view (which appears relevant in the Peruvian landscape[30]) is opposed by another orientation that, invoking a more rigorous and literal reading of Article 1969 c.c.p., avails of the authoritative reflection of Leysser Léon to highlight how the provision does not require any requirements other than malice or guilt and the creation of harm[31]. In fact, "the categories of wrongful act and unlawfulness cannot always be understood as synonymous with damage-generating fact"[32]. Once the causal link between fact and damage is established, it is no longer necessary to qualify man's behavior as lawful or unlawful as civil liability may also arise from so-called "neutral facts", such as driving a vehicle, not connoted by unlawfulness[33]. This leads to strong and

---

26 Schlesinger, (n. 10), p. 344; cfr. Trimarchi, (n. 4), p. 82.
27 Taboada Córdova, (n. 13), p. 56.
28 Taboada Córdova , p. 57. Article V *"Es nulo el acto jurídico contrario a las leyes que interesan al orden público o a las buenas costumbres"*.
29 Taboada Córdova , p. 57.
30 A careful reconstruction can be found in E. Buendia de los Santos, "Responsabilidad, concepto, funcion y estructura", forthcoming.
31 L. León Hilario, *La responsabilidad civil. Lineas fundamentales y nuevas perspectivas*, 2nd edn (Lima: Jurista, 2007), p. 189: *"siempre en el terreno jurisprudencial, es preocupante que nuestros jueces, muy frecuentemente, efectúen de forma mecánica el 'juicio de responsabilidad', incluso asumiendo que en el ordenamiento jurídico peruano existen presupuestos de la protección resarcitoria que la legislación no requiere"*.
32 G. Fernández Cruz, *Introducción a la responsabilidad civil. Lecciones universitarias*, 1st edn (Colección lo esencial del derecho, 2018), p. 123.
33 Fernández Cruz, p. 124.

effective criticism of case law that goes beyond the textual datum to accommodate scholarly arguments and introduce elements not strictly provided for in Article 1969 c.c.p.[34].

But even some of these authors, while reluctant to envelop the concept of damage in the *"camisa de fuerza del hecho ilícito"*, nonetheless manage to delimit its uncontrolled expansion by implicitly attaching to it the adjective "injusto"[35]. Mere pecuniary loss alone has long since ceased to be sufficient to speak, in a technical sense, of damage; on the contrary, it must be the consequence of an injury to a personal status that is relevant under the law[36]. Authors arrive at this conclusion by no longer looking only at the solutions adopted by individual national codes, but also at the common European experience summarized in the *Principles of European Tort Law* (specifically, Article 2:101) and thus end up tacitly incorporating injustice into the very concept of damage.

To determine which injury is worthy of Aquilian protection, the judge is called upon to carry out a balancing of interests through a so-called *juicio de resarcibilidad*. This decision, which performs the same delimiting function that the injustice of the injury has for us, is not limited *tout court* to cases of abuse of right.[37] Rather, taking a closer look, it compels the interpreter to perform a more strenuous task, consisting of three steps: *"(i) predisponer un reconocimiento de los intereses protegidos por la cláusula normativa general; (ii) identificar las técnicas de protección de tales intereses; y, (iii) examinar cuál de estas técnicas se adapta mejor a la naturaleza de nuestro ordenamiento y a las exigencias de la praxis"*[38]. Those weighing the two positions must decide by following normative indices but also, in the absence of these, by looking at other criteria

---

34 León Hilario.
35 Fernández Cruz, p. 125: *"hoy por hoy, la responsabilidad civil es una reacción al daño injusto"*.
36 H.A. Campos García, 'El juicio de resecabilidad en el ordenamiento jurídico peruano', Ius et Veritas (2012), p. 215, recuperado a partir de https://revistas.pucp.edu.pe/index.php/iusetveritas/article/view/11999 states that *"esta forma de entender el daño, es decir, como 'lesión de un interés jurídicamente relevante' ha sido recogida por solo referido al daño resarcible"*.
37 Cfr. Campos García, (n. 23), p. 222.
38 Campos García, p. 223.

according to an approach that seems typically Italian[39]. Public policy or imperative provisions are examined only residually[40].

The two main theories of tort liability that are opposed in the Peruvian legal system both draw important cues from Italian doctrine. As for the first, which sees unlawfulness as an inescapable condition for the arising of the indemnity obligation[41], one cannot help but be reminded of Piero Schlesinger's famous prolusion that overcame[42], in the most convincing manner, the purported two-faced nature of "injustice" by resolving it simply in *non iure* (although the majority of Italian doctrine seems to have now stopped considering the latter as a prerequisite of Article 2043 c.c.It.[43]). Other similarities may instead be found with the thinking of the proponents of the second thesis. For these, proponents of a civil liability freed from unlawfulness, the Italian model of reference is the one theorized by Stefano Rodotà and refined, albeit with significant ramifications, in Italian legal science[44]. In this perspective, the reflection that Article 1969

---

39 Trimarchi, (n. 4), p. 51: "the criterion by which the interests at stake are compared is a criterion of general utility, understood as a synthesis or coordination of the interests of the consociates".

40 Campos García, (n. 20), p. 226: "*la fuente de los criterios para decidir la prevalencia no puede sino encontrarse en el ordenamiento considerado en la totalidad y globalidad de sus valores y sus principios, de sus estándares valorativos, de sus reglas y normas generales, así como de sus disposiciones particulares y casuales, que son posibles de deducir sea del sistema formal o real del derecho, así como de la praxis del mismo derecho. Esto implica que debe tenerse en consideración variables como el respeto a las normas imperativas, normas de orden público o buenas costumbres, al momento de determinar si los intereses en conflicto deben o no ser amparados, frente a la lesión que puedan sufrir por la tutela resarcitoria*".

41 J. Espinoza Espinoza, 'Sobre los denominados Actos ilícitos dañosos', Ius et Veritas (2015), p. 117.

42 Schlesinger, pp. 342–44.

43 Cfr. however G. Tucci, 'La risarcibilità del danno da atto lecito nel diritto civile', Rivista di Diritto Civile, (1967), I, p. 252, which notes that "in the interpretation given instead by the doctrine, injustice is not a selective criterion of the damages resulting from the intentional or negligent act, to which legal relevance should be attributed, but stands to indicate the peculiar essence of unlawfulness, which by its nature represents a judgment of ought-to-be referable only to the act of man".

44 C. Salvi, 'La responsabilità civile', in G. Iudica and P. Zatti (eds.), *Trattato di diritto privato*, 3rd edn (Milano: Giuffrè, 2019), p. 81.

c.c.p. is a "general *normative clause*"[45] is illuminating. There is a sense, therefore, of how the injustice of the damage penetrates the damage itself until it becomes a whole: the damage referred to in Article 1969 c.c.p. cannot but be unjust. On the basis of Rodotà's influence, the relevance of the injury will take place through the *juicio de resarcibilidad* with which the judge weighs the two legal situations (that of the injurer and that of the injured party) to determine which of the two is, in the concrete case, deserving of compensatory legal protection[46]. The adjudicator called to this task, however, is urged by a part of the doctrine to make broader inquiries: the analysis of the interests of the two parties is only the first step in the *juicio de resarcibilidad*, but the general legal perspective and the practical requirements will also be taken into account. This approach reveals the influence of Pietro Trimarchi's studies[47] and the juseconomic perspective.

On the other hand, the thesis that resolves civil liability in the abuse of rights does not seem accepted. While it is true that this reading would appear to comply with the dictate of Article 1971 c.c.p., it is also true that, in adhering to it, certain facts (believed by some authors to be capable of giving rise to civil liability) would be excluded from the scope of Article 1969 c.c.p.[48].

3. *Argentina*

If the influence of the Italian model in the Peruvian legal system has been primarily expressed at the scholarly rather than statutory level, by contrast, Argentine legislation appears to have

---

45   L. León Hilario, (n. 18), p. 183.
46   Salvi, p. 89: "The exercise of a right does not constitute, in civil liability (unlike in criminal liability), an exception in the proper sense, since establishing whether the harmful act is to be considered the exercise of a right is possible only through a comparative assessment with the prejudiced interest, which is the very substance of the judgment concerning the qualification of injustice of the damage".
47   Trimarchi, (n. 4), p. 51.
48   Cfr. Campos García, n. 20: "*el ejercicio de un derecho no es per se e in se un supuesto que determine en todo caso la irresponsabilidad*".

specifically adopted, in its code, several uniquely Italian solutions[49]. This impact is evident in the definition of compensable damage contained in Article 1737 of the Argentine Civil Code (c.c.a.). It is barely necessary to point out that the Argentine legislature, in an attempt to systematically unify civil liability provisions, intended to merge both contractual and extra-contractual liability in a single macro-institute, thus creating a truly peculiar model that has aroused numerous criticisms[50]. For the purposes of our investigation, however, we will focus primarily on non-contractual liability. It should also be pointed out that the Argentine code has made the functions of the institution explicit at the statutory level by including not only the traditional compensatory function but also the preventive/dissuasive and punitive purposes[51]. Such a choice does not seem destined to remain a mere statement of principle and is not without practical repercussions, especially if one considers its impact both on the extent of compensable damage and on the concept of damage itself.

After these necessary premises, it is appropriate to analyze the Argentine model. An initial reconnaissance of the doctrinal panorama provides an account of how civil liability has been traversed, along the lines of the Peruvian experience, by an important discussion on its constituent elements. While those authors that adhere to a more restrictive view of the institution did not recognize unlawfulness as a constitutive element of the case[52], others affirmed its fundamental role within liability even considering constitutional principles[53]. In

---

49 Cfr. in this regard D.F. Esborraz, 'Nuovo Codice civile e commerciale della Repubblica Argentina (circolazione del modello giuridico italiano nel)', Digesto delle discipline privatistiche italiane (2016), p. 574 (attributing this influence primarily to a linguistic issue consisting in the fact that Italian is more similar to Spanish and therefore the "language barrier" is very reduced).
50 M.J. Lòpez Mesa, 'El nuevo Código Civil y Comercial y la responsabilidad civil (de intenciones, realidades, concreciones y mitologías)', Revista Anales de la Facultad de Ciencias jurídicas y Sociales (2016), p. 58.
51 B. Masci, 'Evolución de la responsabilidad civil en el derecho argentino y español', Revista Anales de la Facultad de Ciencias Jurídicas y Sociales. Universidad Nacional de La Plata (2019), p. 112.
52 López Mesa, (n. 37), p. 59.
53 M.G. Burgueño Ibarguren, 'La vigencia de la antijuridicidad en el Derecho de Danos', Responsabilidad civil y Seguro (2015), p. 30 refers to Article 19

fact, the second thesis emphasized the necessity for the obligation to pay damages to arise from a breached legal obligation, as otherwise it would be unfair to impose such a remedial duty upon individuals. The dispute, of which the lawmaker was likely aware, was resolved ultimately settled along the lines of the latter by Article 1710 c.c.a., which imposes on all citizens the duty to avoid causing a "*daño no justificado*". It follows that unlawfulness has now become part of the case for civil liability, as confirmed by the definition set out in Article 1717 c.c.a. These authors structure the concept of unlawfulness in purely objective terms without any regard for the subjective element; unlawfulness translates to the mere failure to comply with the duty of *alterum non laedere* in the absence of a valid legal exception[54].

Therefore, unlawfulness has remained central to the Argentine compensatory system, although its incidence seems destined to be attenuated by a new provision (i.e., Article 1737 c.c.a.) that has been greatly affected by Italian influence[55]. The determination of unlawfulness, *rectius* of compensability, is thus supplemented by an important new element (i.e., the harm), which becomes the basis of a compensatory assessment[56]. Aquilian relief can no longer be granted regardless of the existence of harm, which the expressly law defines for the first time as "injury to a right or interest not repudiated by the legal system". It is within the framework of this new focus on injury that we find the most significant influences of Italian *scientia iuris*: for the first time, damage is no longer merely a generic product of unlawful conduct but is identified with words that cannot but sound familiar to Italian jurists. While the national

---

of the Argentine Constitution according to which "*Ningún habitante de la Nación será obligado a hacer lo que no manda la ley, ni privado de lo que ella no prohíbe*".

54 Burgueño Ibarguren, p. 38. Cfr., however, also F.R. Posteraro, 'Nuevos perfiles de la antijuridicidad en materia de responsabilidad civil en el Código Civil y Comercial', El Derecho, n. 14619 (2019), p. 1, for a reconstruction of the vicissitudes of *antijuridicidad* in Peruvian doctrine.

55 Código Civil y Comercial de la Nación Argentina, Article 1737. Concepto de daño: "*Hay daño cuando se lesiona un derecho o un interés no reprobado por el ordenamiento jurídico, que tenga por objeto la persona, el patrimonio o un derecho de incidencia colectiva*".

56 Burgueño Ibarguren, (n. 40), p. 39

matrix that inspired the Argentine legislature is all too evident, it is not as easy to reconstruct which of the many ideas and nuances of the doctrine were transfused or at least influenced the drafters of the code. The reference to the injury of a legally relevant right or interest inevitably echoes Stefano Rodotà's expression[57], but as discussed in the introduction, it is precisely from this insight that the great rift between theorists of the general clause and supporters of an unjust damage was generated; a rift that, while endowed with a certain elasticity, was routed within the banks of the law to avoid any arbitrariness on the part of the judge.uQdd

Argentine doctrine, and perhaps the design of the code itself, seems to generally lean toward an open tort model and thus closer to the general clause. However, in the doctrinal landscape we find different readings of the phenomenon enriched by further nuances due to these authors' confrontation with a positive datum that is still different from the Italian one. However, some scholars explicitly refer to the injustice of the damage, thereby acknowledging and confirming what we assumed: the Italian model has penetrated, albeit summarily, the new code[58]. Nevertheless, it is argued that a system hinging only on unjust damage would be insufficient to restore all the injuries that can occur in modern society[59]. This argument is especially submitted by authors who identify in the new civil and commercial code the consecration of unlawfulness as a constituent element. Unlawfulness is hence proposed as an enhancement or sophistication of the pure Italian model. Yet, as admitted by the proponents of the thesis themselves, the two systems end up operating in the same way since, to deem the duty of "not harming

---

57 Cfr. n. 2 p. 139.
58 Burgueño Ibarguren, (n. 40), p. 38 speaks of the *"custom of the daño injusto"*.
59 Burgueño Ibarguren, p. 39: "*el daño injusto se limita a daños patrimoniales, no a los morales que tienen un régimen propio, y limitado a los ilícitos criminales, en el artículo 2059 del Código Civil italiano; mientras que en Argentina la noción de daño y de antijuridicidad atrapa a todo tipo de daño. En segundo lugar, y lo más importante, en el futuro Código argentino, se receptó expresamente la antijuridicidad; por lo que la injusticia o ilicitud se tiene en cuenta por la conducta y violación al deber de no dañar a otros; mientras que en Italia hubo un desplazamiento de un sistema como el nuestro a otro que enlaza la injusticia con el daño no con el hecho dañoso (34), sin haber reconocimiento expreso del elemento 'antijuridicidad'*".

the other" violated and consequently to determine the presence of unlawful behavior, it is sufficient to analyze damage according to the criteria established under Article 1737 c.c.a.[60].

Part of the doctrine, on the other hand, exhibits a certain predilection for the Italian model by placing greater emphasis on Italian theories of unjust damage. For these scholars, such syntagma has two requirements: damage (understood as prejudice, or the difference between the previous/better legal situation and the current/worse one) and its qualification as unjust. The latter characteristic, however, cannot be reduced to a mere *flatus vocis*, nor can it be made to coincide *tout court* with unlawfulness: "*la calificación de injusticia reclama un juicio valorativo, que no puede prescindir de la situación del dañador u del dañado*"[61]. Thus, the result of this value assessment (conducted by the judge on a case-by-case basis) may determine whether the injuries caused to the legal sphere of the injured party are worthy of compensatory protection. However, the judge should not interpret extracontractual liability too literally as Article 1737 c.c.a. provides for a certain elasticity of tort liability, which refers to a generic injury to an interest not repudiated by the system. Therefore, all those "*que la sociedad y los valores comúnmente aceptados, muestran que son dignos y respetables aun cuando no están incorporados en las normas en forma expresa*" should be considered as legally relevant interests. *Lo jurídico no se agota en lo legal*[62].

Hence, the reform of Argentine civil law is ultimately appreciated despite there being no shortage of opinions (especially regarding civil

---

60 Burgueño Ibarguren, p. 39, where it states that "*Con esto ya hay suficiente antijuridicidad a los fines de la función resarcitoria.*"
61 V. Moreno, 'Evolución y actualidad de la responsabilidad civil', Revista Anales de la facultad de Ciencias Jurídicas y sociales. Universidad nacional de LA Plata (2018), p. 193.
62 Moreno, p. 203. Cfr. also F.A. Ubirìa, *Derecho de Daños en el Código Civil y Comercial de la Nación*, 1st edn (Buenos Aires: Abeledo Perrot, 2015), p. 120: "*según la época y las circunstancias, la línea divisoria entre un interés merecedor de tutela y otro que no, resulta bastante delgada, y es el ordenamiento a través de la recta interpretación de la jurisprudencia y la doctrina la que le confiere carácter resarcible a un daño*".

liability) that underline how the much proclaimed systematization of the law of private individuals has ended up leaving numerous pockets of asystematicity[63]. These positions are supported by a minority part of the doctrine that has also opposed the use of civil liability as an instrument of social engineering which purpose is both redistributive and punitive. Accordingly, this line of thought proposes a return to a strict use of law, pointing out that the function of the institution under consideration can only be, first and foremost, limited to compensation[64]. The interpreter, and especially the judge, plays a key role also at this juncture. That is, it is the interpreter/judge who has the final say in determining whether the interest is worthy of compensation. But in this

> *particular labor de traducción o adaptación, el juez debe verificar las consecuencias que produce en el caso concreto su propuesta hermenéutica a priori de la regla general. Si los resultados que produce son absurdos, ello quiere decir que el trabajo judicial es incompleto, erróneo o arbitrario.*[65]

The natural elasticity of civil liability cannot be exploited to render it a generic tool for conflict resolution; ultimately, it is always the law to which the judge must refer and thus, we understand, even when he or she must determine which interests are legally relevant.

The analysis of these positions appears to reveal that Italian doctrine, so rich in differences and nuances, has left several legacies in Argentina. Those who affirm the pre-eminence of unlawfulness, comforted moreover by the codistic innovations, evidently draw on the positions of Schlesinger, who had first equated unjust damage with unlawfulness (damage caused *non iure*). Moreover, this is the interpretation that best reconciles unlawfulness with the new element of the injustice of harm without having to radically alter

---

63   Lopez Mesa, (n. 39), p. 64 speaks of "*auténtica confesión de asistematicidad*".
64   Lopez Mesa, p. 70: "*Lo que exceda de ello [dal danno provocato], y que extienda ad infinitum el deber indemnizatorio, prescindiendo de todo reproche al pagador del siniestro — que ya no podría ser técnicamente llamado responsable — podrá ser otra cosa, pero no un sistema de responsabilidad civil, ya que claramente desborda sus notas esenciales*".
65   Lopez Mesa, p. 71.

the framework of their assumptions and even managing to affirm a substantial equivalence, at least in functional terms, between the Italian and Argentine models.

However, not everyone views the legislator's choice as devoid of practical repercussions. That is, some positions have seriously analyzed the new textual datum and have turned to the "source" order of the unjust damage to give meaning to the imported syntagma. Rodotà's approach, however nuanced, seems to be dominant among these positions, as it should be given the traditional tendency to invest both compensatory and redistributive functions in civil liability. In particular, Rodotà notes that the general clause, due to its elasticity, allows the judge not to remain anchored to the law, but to periodically assess whether the interest deduced in court is worthy of compensatory protection not only in the light of positive law but also of case law and social feeling. Incidentally, the same positions lend themselves to extra-legislative considerations that are also closer to the readings proposed by Trimarchi (e.g., the situation of both the tortfeasor and the injured party must be considered, the effects of which also fall on other individuals).

Finally, there are more rigorous and conservative positions that have little tolerance for the contention that civil liability may be used generically as a tool of social engineering or a means of righting every wrong, or even as a sanctioning instrument or one to implore greater rigor in the institution's application.

4. *Bolivia*

The Bolivian code (c.c.b.) is certainly the legislative text that has been most inspired by the Italian model. In fact, Article 984 c.c.b. and Article 2043 c.c.It. are functionally identical, as Article 984 c.c.b. reads, "*quien con un hecho dolso o culposo, ocasiona a alguien un dano injusto, queda obligado al resarcimento*". The very wording of the Article alone is enough to denote the great influence the Italian model had on the Bolivian legislature. In no other Latin American code can one find such an express transposition of the provision of Article 2043 c.c.It.

Some authors believe that Article 984 c.c.b. is "*màs amplitud que otros artìculos de legislaciones similares lationamericanas*", as well as faithful to the Romanist tradition. Furthermore, because of its "*amplitude*," it contains an integral analysis of "*los hechos*"[66]. Such a reading thus seems to obliterate the scope, however delimiting, of the term "unjust" and, consequently, the doctrinal *querelle* that arose in relation to the meaning attributed to it as a result of Italian influence. A very similar position also seems to be shared by another orientation according to which "*la ley no exige ninguna particularidad en cuanto a este* [*el daño*]*, solo dice: que quien ocasione dano a otro està obligado a resarcirlo*"[67].

Still, the landscape appears to be complex and varied even in Bolivia. If the Italian influence appears clear in the legislative text, it cannot be limited to this or to doctrinal references. In fact, the jurisprudence indicates citations of authorities such as Messineo, whose thoughts are quoted in an explanatory statement to define tort as

> *Messineo señala: "...se entiende por acto ilícito (civil), un acto (unilateral), de ordinario, humano que origina daño a otro y que genera, a cargo del agente (Autor del daño), una responsabilidad, la cual consiste en la obligación de resarcir dicho daño" (Derecho Civil y Comercial Tomo VI).*[68]

5. Conclusions

Although the French tort model is certainly the most popular among South American legislative texts, the Italian system also

---

[66] J.G. Bustamante Morales, 'Responsabilidad extracontractual del Estado boliviano en el caso LaMia, un breve análisis jurídico', Revista *Ratio* Juris, 14, 29 (2019), p. 259.

[67] F. Remmy Camacho, 'La responsabilidad civil en el Derecho romano y en el Derecho civil boliviano', in A. Díaz-Bautista Cremades; J.G. Sánchez (eds.), *Fundamentos romanisticos del Derecho contemporaneo*, 1 edn (Burgos: : Asociación Iberoamericana de Derecho Romano : Boletín Oficial del Estado, BOE), 2002, p. 873.

[68] M.R. Delgadillo Pacheco. c/ Serapio Espada Lascano, TSJ Sala civil, No. 325/2013.

seems to have influenced the legislature and doctrine of some Latin American countries. Bolivia has accepted the de facto dictate of the 1942 code without making any changes to it. Argentina has incorporated Rodotà's teaching at the legislative level. In Peru, the closeness to Italian authors has even managed to permeate the interpretation of a positive datum of undoubtedly French origin. Among the many theories of extracontractual liability circulating in Italy, there is no doubt that the most popular one in the Latin American countries is that which invokes the idea of the general clause; this notion is often integrated with the most recent findings of the Italian school (e.g., the work of Pietro Trimarchi). Moreover, the continuing success of many Argentine and Peruvian authors with regard to unlawfulness means that many scholars look to Italian doctrine, and especially the positions of Piero Schlesinger (undoubtedly the most influential voice that has welded injustice and unlawfulness together).

Nonetheless, it is certain that the Italian theses, though viewed with respect and attention, have never been unquestionably adopted by the legal systems examined herein. The doctrines of the various countries have skillfully filtered these Italian notions such that only to those which were compatible with the local legal experience would enter the system. For instance, Italian doctrine notes how the wording of Article 927 of the Brazilian Civil Code on liability for dangerous activity is better than that of Article 2050 c.c.It. In this regard, it should be noted that the Brazilian provision is based on Article 493 of the Portuguese Civil Code of 1966, according to which "[w]hoever causes damage to others in the course of an activity that is dangerous by its nature or by the nature of the means employed is obliged to compensate for the damage, unless it is proved that he has adopted all the measures required by the circumstances to avoid it". In turn, the Portuguese rule was influenced by 2050 cc.It.

The numerous original theses that have derived from this influence (and recollected in this concise analysis) certainly suggest that Latin American doctrine is aware of its acceptance of the Italian experience, paying proper attention to incorporate it flexibly and thus allowing such doctrine to open not only to new horizons and perspectives for these legal systems, but also to address the various unique needs of their countries.

Although the relationship between the Latin American and European worlds has long been mistakenly considered a simple imitation or passive admiration on the part of the former towards the latter, the situation has always been more complex and today there can be no doubt that it is a true dialogue of equals. Several factors (not just legal ones) contribute to this[69]. In a multipolar and fragmented society, one cannot help but detect traces of European stagnation offset by Latin American effervescence, albeit amidst lingering social and political economic challenges. This broad trend results in a shift in the understanding of law, connoted by global pluralism, in which comparative law (itself with diverse traits) plays a key role. While Rodolfo Sacco already realized the importance of looking beyond Europe and North America, the doctrine is now aware that

> similar comparisons in our epoch are no longer confined within the boundaries of the Western legal tradition; they will be even less limited in the future. Obviously "problems without a passport" — like global warming and environmental protection — will maintain their centrality in this perspective... But, beyond this, there will be more comparative contributions coming from a variety of new voices from many parts of the world, and more collaborative comparative law work, which is just beginning to show its promising future.[70]

One might question whether Latin American legal systems will take on a configuration of their own such that they can be considered an independent legal family or will retain their eclectic pluralism, albeit in a more fruitful dialogue with each other, within the civil law family. However, it is conceivable that they will play a more influential role, and this is not surprising because, as noted in 1971, the Latin American world can always be considered "every comparatist's dream"[71].

---

[69] A. Nicolussi, 'Latinità e diritto privato: il diritto civile italiano in Perù', Europa e diritto privato, 2019, p.1189-1194

[70] M. Graziadei, 'What Does Globalisation Mean for the Comparative Study of Law?', The Journal of Comparative Law, 16 (2), (2021) p. 532.

[71] K.S. Rosenn, 'Teaching Latin American Law', The American Jour. Comp. Law, 19 (1971), p. 692.

Juan Carlos Berrios Albizu *

THE EFFECTS OF POSSESSION IN THE BOLIVIAN CIVIL CODE OF 1975

Supported under the Influence of
the Italian Civil Code of 1942

1. *Concept*

Possession is considered an institution in various legal systems, and its approximate concept depends on the perspective developed within each normative framework.

In Bolivia, since the implementation of the Civil Code of 1975[1], in force since April 2, 1976 (later referred to as the Bolivian Code, national legislation or domestic legislation), Article 87 describes possession as the power exercised over a thing through acts that denote the intention of having property rights or other real rights over it. This definition evokes the requirement of two elements, one objective and one subjective.

It is described as the corpus, and when it refers to the subjective element, to a person's intention regarding the thing. That is, how a person acts with respect to the thing. In Latin it's called the "animus". This latter element differentiates with respect to the way in which the possessor behaves, since the material appropriation of the thing can be carried out by a contract between the owner of the thing (i.e., a good). In that case, there will be detention and not possession.

Detention is understood as that material control of the thing granted by its owner with the intention of being returned to the owner, be it in any of its contractual expressions: lease, deposit, antichresis, loan, etc. In detention, the detainer does not behave as the owner of the thing. On the contrary, the detainer exercises

---

* Judge of the Tribunal Supremo de Justicia de Bolivia
1 República de Bolivia, Gaceta CODCIV, 1 de enero de 1975.

his right in full recognition of lack of ownership. That's the difference.

2. *Legal nature of possession*

When the nature of possession must be defined, it's about defining whether it's considered a fact or a right. This debate is understood to have been generated by the Romanists Paulo and Paniniano, as described by José Luis Lacruz Berdejo and others[2]. Paulo maintained that possession is only a fact and not a right, whereas Paniniano stated that possession is a right and not a fact. The doctrinaires continue to submit that, according to the Romanists of the last century, possession was considered a fact in classical law, and that during Justinian times there was a tendency to highlight its legal value[3].

For his part, Pedro Alejo Cañón Ramírez[4] summarizes the subjective and objective theories. For the first, possession is considered a mere fact because it is based on a material circumstance. However, Ramírez also attributes the quality of law to it, since this fact gives rise to consequences that are protected by law. For the second, contrary to the above, Ramírez qualifies possession as a right, since he considers that one doesn't own a thing, but a right *in rem* that one has over the thing. The author explains that this last theory leads to the thesis according to which possession is a provisional right, since it is qualified as a *de facto* power exercised over things and protected with real actions. It is a provisional *de facto* power of attorney.

It's understood that both subjective and objective theories recognize the parameters of a factual situation with legal

---

[2] J.L. Lacruz Berdejo, F. de Asís Sancho Rebullida, A. Luna Serrano, J. Delgado Echeverría, F. Rivero Hernández and J. Ramos Albasea, *Elementos de Derecho Civil III; Derechos Reales; Posesión y Propiedad*, 1st edn, I (Dykinson, 2000), p. 30.

[3] Lacruz Berdejo, de Asís Sancho Rebullida, Luna Serrano, Delgado Echeverría, Rivero Hernández and Ramos Albasea.

[4] P.A. Cañón Ramírez, *Derecho civil; Bienes-Derechos Reales*, I (A, B and C, 1985), pp. 96–99.

consequences. In accordance with Article 87 of the Bolivian Civil Code, it is understood that possession is a *de facto* situation that generates legal effects, since possession by itself, even in bad faith, is protected by law.

3. Legislative background

3.1. Santa Cruz Civil Code

The Civil Code was promulgated on October 18, 1830 and came into force on April 2, 1831. This code was designed by the lawyers Manuel María Urcullu, Casimiro Olañeta, Manuel José de Antequera and José María de la Lloza, and influenced by the Napoleonic Civil Code of 1804 and Castilian Law (the Seven Legal Items of Alfonso, the wise man, the Newest Compilation of 1805, the Laws of Toro and those of style) — although it's understood that the French code had greater impact.

On possession, Article 1517 of the original text (Article 1530 of the ordered text with the reforms introduced) describes possession as the detention or enjoyment of a thing or a right, which one has or exercises by himself or by others[5]. This nomenclature is complemented by Article 1718 of the same legal body (Article 1531 of the text ordered with the reforms), which distinguishes between natural possession and civil possession.

For the purposes of acquisition of property rights, doctrinaire Rafael Canedo[6] submits that the detention indicated in Article 1517 (Article 1530, according to the text ordered with the reforms) is not just any detention. Instead, to acquire ownership, the detainer must exercise his right with the intention of becoming the owner or portraying himself as the owner of the thing. Canedo states that possession, even if it's annulled, is nothing more than a fact and never a right. He further argues that the legal effects

---

5 República de Bolivia, Gaceta, Decreto octubre 28 de 1830.
6 R. Canedo, *Código Civil Boliviano; Comentado, Concordado y Anotado*, 2nd edn (Cochabamba, 1989), pp. 630–31.

are improperly attributed to possession, having their origin in the property it represents.

As can be seen, this conclusion shows that only possession in good faith may be recognized, i.e., possession which emerged from a right that was not consolidated. Alternatively, an action *in rem* has a time bar of thirty years, as indicated in Article 1565 of the aforementioned Code.

3.2. *Bolivian Civil Code of 1975*

The Bolivian Civil Code, drafted during the transition from a *de facto* government, entered into force on April 2, 1976. This Code was elaborated through the works by a commission made up of lawyers Hugo Sandoval Saavedra, Pastor Ortiz Mattos, Raúl Romero Linares, and Oscar Frerking Salas — all appointed by Supreme Decree 10575 of November 10, 1972[7] for the purpose of complementing the previously established commission.

According to the references of the new Code, shared with different Bolivian doctrinaires, it's understood that the Bolivian Civil Code of 1975 was the product of three legal systems: the Italian, the French and the Spanish, with the first being the most influential.

4. *Importance and usefulness of possession in the Bolivian Civil Code and the influence of the Italian Civil Code of 1942*

It has been said that possession is a factual situation that generates legal consequences. Such explains the presumptions, the legal action available in defense of possession, and the effects that possession entails. For example, when a person obtains possession through a specific title and proves, even after several years, to still possess the property, there is a legal presumption of so-called "intermediate possession". If during that period the

---

[7] República de Bolivia, Gaceta, Decreto Supremo 10575 de 10 de noviembre de 1972. Edición 637.

possessor has improved the property, at the time of handing the property over to the rightful owner, he is entitled to compensation for improvements made. If the possession is long enough, the possessor can even acquire ownership through usucapion.

Each of these aspects together with their normative reflections will be addressed in the following paragraphs.

5. *Presumption of possession*

According to the Royal Spanish Academy[8], the presumption refers to aspects that are considered certain under the law without the need for the fact in question to be proven. In accordance with the orientation described in our legal system of private law, it is understood that the presumption is a mean of proof that has different qualifications for the named and the unnamed. For the former, there are presumptions that don't admit evidence to the contrary, and others that do. For the latter, they leave it to the discretion of the Judge.

Without delving into dogmatic positions on this institution, it is sufficient to note that the presumption, as Juan Collareta[9] points out, is the result of a logical operation through which, starting from a known fact, another unknown fact is found to exist. In other words, via the presumption, a fact is considered certain for the purpose of determining legal consequences, such as when the possession is in good or bad faith.

The institution of possession also contains presumptions. Article 88 of the Bolivian Civil Code, for example, envisages three instances in which a legal presumption exists:

I. The possession of the person currently exercising power over the thing is presumed unless it is proven that the possessor began to exercise such power as a simple holder.

---

8 Real Academia Española, *Diccionario de la Lengua Española*, 22nd edn, II (Madrid: Grafinor 2001), p. 1829.
9 J.V, Collareta Gil, *Derecho Civil; parte general; personas*, 1st edn (Oruro: Latinas Editores, 2005), p. 218.

II. The current possessor who proves to have possessed the thing also in the past is presumed to have possessed the thing continuously unless proven otherwise.

III. Current possession doesn't presume previous possession; however, if the possessor has the thing by way of a title that supports the possession and there is no evidence to the contrary, it is presumed that the thing has been possessed continuously since the date of the title.

In accordance with the first paragraph, it's understood that the law protects the current possessor regardless of whether his possession has a legitimate or illegitimate origin. Obviously, as a *iuris tantum* presumption, this provision admits evidence to the contrary. The following is presumed under the cited article: a) the possessor is he who currently has the material availability of the thing, b) the current possessor who demonstrates to have previously possessed the thing is presumed to have exercised possession also in the interim, and c) current possession doesn't presume previous possession, but if the existence of a title that protects the possession is justified, it's presumed that he has possessed continuously since the date of the title.

On the other hand, it should also be considered that Bolivian law distinguishes between possession in good faith and possession in bad faith.

The first is recognized in Article 93 of the Code. According to this provision, a person possesses the thing in good faith when he believes to have acquired the thing or right from the true owner. This nomenclature comes from Article 1147 of the Italian Civil Code of 1942 (referred to herein as "Model Code", "Source Code", "Italian Code", or "Legislative Source"), which establishes that a possessor in good faith is one who possesses an object without knowing that his possession harms another's right.

Reference under Bolivian law to the acquisition of the right from the object's true owner illustrates a common scope with that of the same rule established in the Source Code, which regulates the possessor who is unaware that the thing belonged to another person. More specifically, in the Bolivian system, the possessor's mindset plays a fundamental role in qualifying possession as being in good or bad faith, as "bad faith possession" is that in which the possessor knew that the thing belonged to another person. It follows, then, that "good faith possession" exists when the possessor is unaware that the object is owned by another person. This is consistent with a similar provision contained in the Italian Code, which states that the possessor is in good faith when he is unaware that the object he possesses infringes the right of another person.

There is a presumption under Bolivian law of good faith possession, just as there is in the Model Code. Both sources contemplate the existence of concurring factors that affect the legal qualification of possession. That is, the Bolivian Code requires bad faith be proven, whereas the Source Code (in excluding the existence of good faith possession merely because the possessor is unaware that the object belongs to somebody else when such ignorance is attributable to the possessor's gross negligence) implicitly requires the possessor to ascertain, via a sort of "due diligence," the status of the person from whom he acquires possession. The presumption of good faith possession is also provided elsewhere in the Source Code. It follows that whether gross negligence exists is a circumstance that must be proven, either by the current possessor (reversal of the burden of proof) or by the person seeking restitution of the object in question

The last part of the precept is the most controversial in terms of the effects of possession. The Bolivian Civil Code states that possessory effects arise only in cases of initial good faith. This provision is similar to the Italian rule, which establishes that good faith is presumed and must exist only at the time of taking possession.

This orientation gives rise to different positions regarding its consequence since, like the transformation from possession to detention, possession can transform from good faith to bad faith. The possessor's awareness about the quality of the possession that he exercises can vary. Take, for example, the case in which the current possessor, after having acquired the object from the person he believed to be the rightful owner, loses ownership of the thing due to a court order in favor of another party. In this case, by maintaining possession of an item he knows to belong to somebody else, the possessor becomes a bad faith possessor — even if possession was originally in good faith. In other words, the possessor knows he has not acquired title to the item from the item's rightful owner, and he knows that he is infringing someone else's right. This produces different consequences with regard to the acquisition of the fruits, for example, for which there is a distinction between good faith and bad faith possession in terms of the extent of fruits that must be returned to the owner.

6. *Possessory actions*

Possession as a fact generates legal consequences. One of them is that, depending on whether the possessor is in good faith or in bad faith, he cannot be deprived of the object except by court order. This complies with the apothegm of the prohibition of justice by one's own hand.

The Fifth Book of the Bolivian Code describes the actions available to protect possession against whoever disturbs or threatens the exercise of this situation or deprives the possessor of the object. These remedies are embodied in the action to recover possession (restitution), the action to retain possession, the new construction claim and the feared damage claim.

6.1 *Action to restore possession*

Through this action, the possessor deprived of property or a right *in rem* can file a lawsuit to recover the object connected to such right. This precept allows a possessor who has been stripped of his possession to recover the relevant object. It is further understood that the deprivation must have been in fact, i.e., without judicial authorization. Thus, as explained in previous paragraphs, when the possessor has been materially deprived of the asset, he is allowed to recover such (stolen) object via the remedy providing for restitution pending a judicial decision on the legitimacy of the possession.

This provision, too, mimics Article 1168 of the Model Code, which scope is to re-establish possession of the object in question. The law is clear in identifying the person entitled to file this action, i.e., the person who has been violently or secretly dispossessed.

Likewise, by comparing the two sources of law (i.e., the Bolivian rule with the Italian one) it is observed that Article 1169 mentions that reintegration (restitution) can be requested from the person who currently possesses the object in a private capacity, who would have been aware of the dispossession that occurred. This means that the new owner must have been aware of the dispossession of the property that he currently owns. The precept under analysis doesn't refer to whether the dispossession was performed by the same person who delivered the object, his employee or whether it was done on behalf of the person who transferred possession. In any case, unless the current owner was unaware of the dispossession, property cannot be restituted under the provision. In practice, this aspect would be difficult to prove, since the person claiming reintegration would have to inquire about the legal, family and/or affective relationships between the new possessor and the dispossessor, such that it would make protection unfeasible. Moreover, the situation is aggravated in the event of collusion between the dispossessing person and the new possessor. It is considered that with this legal formula the reintegration action, in the terms indicated in Articles 1168 and 1169, would have little impact if the action is attempted against the new acquirer of possession.

This is also true in the Bolivian case, as Article 1461, first paragraph, the last part, of the Bolivian Code states that the action may be brought against the dispossessor or his universal heirs, as well as against parties that have acquired the object by way of particular title despite being aware of the dispossession. This last sentence means the dispossession can be consolidated in civil impunity, since the spirit of the provision is that the possessor cannot be dispossessed except through a judicial decision. This confirms that the dispossessing party can assign the good to a new possessor, in whose favor the party delivering possession must guarantee that delivery (e.g., by way of sale, lease, antichresis or other) is made in good faith and no circumstance exists by way of which possession may be disturbed or interrupted. In such a situation (as previously stated) it would be difficult for the previous (dispossessed) possessor to demonstrate that the current (new) possessor has indeed become aware of the dispossession. Otherwise, it would be important to consolidate civil impunity, reserving criminal proceedings for other types of purposes, and this is not what is sought in restitution ("reintegration") proceedings.

Although the Bolivian legislator has had several opportunities to amend the private law system, the possibility of making such a change has not been considered. Such a situation is apparent in view of the latest special rule on the matter, i.e., the Civil Procedure Code (in force since February 6, 2016) in its entirety.

6.2 *Action to maintain possession*

This action protects against material disturbance of possession and differs from the previous action in that: (1) there must be deprivation of possession (i.e., an expropriation or dispossession) and (2) it only aims protect against acts of disturbance, meaning that the action protects the possessor against the owner or third parties whose actions or claims threaten the possessor's situation. This is how Article 1462 of the Bolivian Civil Code describes it: A rule that also states that this action does not cover those who obtained possession in a violent or clandestine manner, unless a year has elapsed since the violence or secrecy has ceased.

This action mimics Article 1170 of the Italian Code of 1942, which envisages the availability of a so-called "maintenance action" (providing for the maintenance of possession) in favor of those who have been disturbed in their possession of property, a right *in rem*, or the universal disposition of goods. The provision protects those who are threatened with material acts or acts that are aimed at stealing possession.

Although the provision does not establish the duration of protection, it is understood that the possessor-applicant's situation shall be maintained until a judicial decision defines the right or possession.

The last section of Article 1170 of the Source Code sets out that possession is restored to those who have suffered a non-violent or clandestine dispossession. This last formula is considered to have been absorbed by Article 1168 of the aforementioned Code, since otherwise it would distort the scope of Article 1170 (which aims to maintain an already established possession).

For the rest, both systems deny protection to those whose possession is illegitimate (i.e., because possession was obtained in a violent or clandestine manner, unless such violence or clandestineness had ceased within a year of the new possessory claims). This rule is consistent with the reasonable term position and goes against the intangibility of the beginning of possession, which (as stated in the previous points analyzed), in accordance with the last part of Article 93 of the Bolivian Civil Code, for the purposes of possession will only be considered the initial good faith.

6.3 *Complaint of new construction*

Under this action, the possessor may lodge a complaint related to a new work that is detrimental to his interests when there is an effective risk that such work will cause material damage or in any case impact the rights of the applicant. However, there are very few cases in which this remedy is effectively actionable. For example, it applies in cases in which injury derives from non-compliance with laws on light pollution, hindrance of views, or failure to maintain adequate distance between the new construction and the existing property (including excavations and/or planting of trees, bushes, or other greenery). That is, the danger must relate to a material impact on the infrastructure or a potential consequence for the holder's estate. It is thus unactionable merely because the new construction prevents or restricts access by clients to a business located on the adjacent property. In any case, the remedy has a temporary effect, consisting in the suspension of works or the provision of guarantees.

Article 1171 of the Source Code states this action is available to the owner or the possessor of the thing, as well as the holder of a right of enjoyment on the thing. The availability of the remedy extends to a possessor whose *nomen iuris* is found outside the chapter on "actions in defense of possession", forming part of a title called "denunciation of new work and feared damage". The assumptions for the source-provision are the same as those of the Bolivian rule: both require a threat of damage caused by the work to the property where the owner/possessor/right holder is located, and that the action must be filed before the work is completed.

6.4 *Imminent hazard complaint*

An imminent hazard complaint allows the possessor to defend the object in possession from neighboring property (e.g., a building or accessory thereto) that represents a potential source of harm. More specifically, the law protects the integrity of the threatened asset by allowing the claimant to request the demolition or repair of the building, removal of the tree, or other measures to avert harm. Like the previous case, this action is considered a precautionary measure or demand.

In the Italian system, this remedy is found in Article 1172, which establishes the complaint of imminent hazard can be filed by the owner or possessor of an object, as well as the holder of a right of enjoyment of the thing. Moreover (consistent with what is referenced in the previous section), unlike in the Bolivian system, this article is found in a special title on "complaints of new construction and imminent harm" and is not part of the actions in defense of possession.

Under Bolivian law (contrary to the Italian case, which attributes status to the owner, possessor, and holder of a right *in rem*), only the holder is entitled to seek this action. Due to the issue of derivative possession or detention, it can be concluded that in the case of the national system, the owner can also make claims whether he has a delegate in possession, since he possesses the object through his ownership title.

The Bolivian legislator has not made changes to this institution contained in the 1975 Civil Code, despite having implemented a new Procedural Code.

7. *Of the fruits and works done by the possessor*

The good (thing), depending on its nature and the owner in possession, can generate natural fruits (e.g., plantations) or civil fruits (e.g., legal business and income). Likewise, the holder of a good can modify it according to his tastes or the utility he wishes to derive from its economic exploitation.

In these cases, the law specifically regulates the treatment of the fruits and the improvements and/or constructions. These cases are the ones that will be considered below.

7.1 *Fruits*

It is important to recall that possession is a *de facto* power exercised over a thing by means of which the exercise of property rights or other real rights is denoted.

While the good is in his possession, the possessor (especially the one in good faith) may modify, improve and/or make additions to the property. It is understood that, in the case of the bona fide possession, the possessor believes he has acquired the right from the object's rightful owner. On the other hand, the bad faith possessor knows that the good he holds does not belong to him and that there has been no agreement between him and the previous holder regarding the current possession being exercised. Thus, whether possession is connotated by good or bad faith is of great importance when determining the extent and source of compensation for the fruits received by the owner and for the useful improvements and/or repairs that the possessor would have implemented with respect to the property.

It turns out that the changes, modifications, and implementations, when generated in the form of real estate, if they are attached to the land, belong to the owner of the land. If the holder is defeated in a lawsuit in which the ownership of the property is attributed to another person or if he recognizes in an out-of-court agreement the property belongs to another, in both cases, he is entitled to compensation for the improvements and extensions to the good.

In the Bolivian system, Article 94 governs the situation of the fruits. The provision establishes that the possessor in good faith enjoys the natural and civil fruits produced until the day he is served noticed of demand and is only obliged to return those fruits acquired after such service. This provision only applies to the possessor in good faith, who can enjoy the natural and/or civil fruits, but not the possessor in bad faith, who is liable for the value of the fruits consumed or enjoyed.

This normative description has its source in Article 821 of the Italian Code, which states that natural fruits belong to the owner of the thing that produces them unless such benefits are attributed to others. This is analogous to the situation of the possessor in the Bolivian Code, which describes the good faith possessor, and that of the Italian system, which envisages the good faith possessor as the owner of the thing or the derivative possessor (holder).

7.2 *Repairs, improvements and/or extensions*

The Bolivian rule refers to improvements and extensions in Article 97 of the Civil Code, which establishes the holder is entitled to compensation for useful and necessary improvements. If the holder is in good faith, he is entitled to compensation in the amount equal to the increased value of the object due to such improvements and/or extensions. If, on the other hand, the possessor is in bad faith, he is entitled to the lesser amount between the expense and the increase in value. It does not describe the concept of repairs, improvements, and extensions.

Article 96 sets out that the possessor, referring to both categories (in good or bad faith), is entitled to be reimbursed for the costs of extraordinary repairs estimated at the date of reimbursement. This description refers to the expenses necessary for its conservation.

Arguments submitted in legal proceedings have rarely mattered in terms of the qualification of what has been introduced to the property since, if the works had the purpose of repairing the property, it is understood that they prevented its deterioration or destruction. Not much factual or evidentiary argument is seen in the case law on this situation. In a generic way, after the dispossession, it is only a matter of making a claim on what has been invested in the asset due to possession, whether in good faith or bad faith.

These reparations have their normative source in Article 1150(I) of the Source Code. Said provision establishes that the holder, even in bad faith, is entitled to reimbursement of expenses incurred for extraordinary repairs. The difference between the systems lies in the amount: in the Bolivian system, the extent of the amount owing to the possessor is determined according to the date of reimbursement; in the Italian system, it is not specified whether the extent owed should be determined according to the time the works were made or at the time of compensation.

Having clarified the situation of expenses for repairs, it is now necessary to point out the concept of improvements and/ or extensions described in Article 97 of the Bolivian Civil Code. This article does not define improvements and/or extensions; however, it can be inferred from the text that improvements consist of all the works performed on a certain infrastructure (i.e., on what is already built).

It is not always straight forward whether and to what extent an improvement may be classified as a repair versus a sumptuary. This is because absent works that clearly fall within the category of repairs, it must be debated whether the work can be qualified as a useful improvement or sumptuary. The first (repair) gives rise to compensation for any holder. The second (useful improvement) gives rise to its compensation, varying in amount depending on if the possessor making the improvement is in good or bad faith. The third (luxury improvement or mere recreation) is not compensable.

To establish an orientation on useful improvements, it is appropriate to cite the doctrinal contribution of Nestor Jorge Musto[10] who understands that useful improvements are those that are of manifest benefit to any possessor. This position describes that the improvement must serve any possessor and implies that the qualification must be made according to the criterion that any person can be satisfied with the improvement. A different result is produced in the event the improvement only satisfies the party who implemented it; in that case, it is entered and qualified as sumptuary.

As said before, much depends on the quality/type of the improvement made, and especially whether it can be considered useful or serving a third-party. On the contrary, if the improvement is not going to satisfy a third-party interest, its usefulness is limited to the person who implemented the improvement. In this case, the works are considered a sumptuary or mere recreational improvement.

This distinction is important for determining the extent of compensation since, unlike in the case of repairs, a sumptuary entitles the improving party to a different amount than if he were to have made a mere recreational improvement. In both, the useful improvement will be recoverable to the possessor irrespective of his good or bad faith, with the same difference in recoverable amount as specified above.

The Bolivian Code also describes extensions as works made to what is already built (part of the doctrine calls them "additions") and treats them in a manner analogous to improvements.

It is also noteworthy that under Bolivian law sumptuary improvements are not recoverable, as it is understood that this type of improvement is made by the owner. However, sumptuary improvements are not qualified as repairs or useful improvements, either, as they only satisfy the implementer.

---

10   N.J. Musto, *Derechos Reales*, I (Argentina: Astrea, 2000), p. 254.

The Source Code, in its Article 1150, sets out that the possessor, even in bad faith, is entitled to be reimbursed for extraordinary reparations made (i.e., those made to avoid the destruction or ruin of the thing). It is understood that this thesis was adopted in the Bolivian system.

The Italian system of 1942 distinguishes between improvements and additions, the latter being described in Bolivian legislation as implementations (or additions). The Source Code does not describe the difference between useful and sumptuary improvements. Instead, it establishes rather generally that improvements are subject to compensation, with the only difference being the amount to be reimbursed to the possessor who made such improvements depending on whether he acted in good or bad faith.

Absent any restriction, it appears that the Italian Source allows many kinds of improvements to be reimbursed — unlike the Bolivian system.

7.3 *Right of retention*

According to the Royal Academy of the Spanish Language[11], the term "retaining" means preventing something from leaving, moving, being eliminated or disappearing. In the legal field, this definition suggests that a person is entitled to prevent something from moving or leaving his possession.

In accordance with the provisions of section IV, Article 14, of the Political Constitution of the Plurinational State of Bolivia[12], in the exercise of rights, no one will be forced to do what the Constitution and the laws do not mandate, nor to deprive themselves of what these do not prohibit. This tenet, considered in the doctrine as the principle of freedom, allows the performance of acts described in the Constitution and the laws. With regard to the latter, Article 98 of the Bolivian Civil Code entitles the possessor in good faith to retain the thing until

---

11 Real Academia, *Española Diccionario de la Lengua Española*, II, p. 1963.
12 Estado Plurinacional de Bolivia, Gaceta Oficial de Bolivia Constitución Política del Estado, Edición primera, 2009, p. 3.

the indemnities are paid and the aforementioned expenses are reimbursed, referring to the repairs and useful improvements. This retention right also governs several other legal relationships, such as mandates, deposit agreements, usufructs, etc.

In the case of possession, the rule allows the asset to be retained pending payment for the expenses incurred to carry out the implementations on the asset, irrespective of whether they are repairs and/or useful improvements. Obviously, this qualification may be made consensually or judicially.

This right of retention has its source in Article 1152 of the Italian Code, which states that the possessor can retain the thing pending payment of compensation owed, provided that a request has been made for payment during the relevant legal proceedings.

This formula suggests that compensation is only payable in the context of legal proceedings. However, the provision must be understood broadly (and not literally) as it applies to all types of actions involving property or possession and not only the latter.

The Bolivian Code governs the right of retention in favor of the *bona fide* possessor, i.e., the person who believes he has acquired the item from its rightful owner. However, it only establishes that the possessor has the right to retain the item until the expenses generated by the repairs and improvements, as well as useful additions, are paid.

The Source Code further protects the possessor by establishing a legal guarantee pursuant to which he cannot be evicted or deprived of possession until he has been reimbursed for expenses incurred for repairs, improvements and/or additions to the object in question. This right of retention can be exercised at the holder's option since, by the delivery requirement, bona fide possession would already be called into question, impairing the possibility of receiving the civil and natural fruits of the property. Accordingly, when cost of maintenance or ordinary expenses is high, it is understood that the holder will have little interest in retaining the object since such expenses will be deducted from the economic value of the asset, given that only repairs (extraordinary expenses), improvements and useful additions are compensable.

8. *The seizure*

Possession entails effects regarding the implementations that would have been made on the thing as well as those regarding the possession exercised for a certain time. If possession exceeds the term established by law, this permanence allows the possessor to acquire ownership (i.e., title or the property right) in the absence of consent or an express transfer agreement between the possessor and the thing's rightful owner. In this sense, inactivity, lack of use, or the owner's inertia is punished.

8.1 *Real estate seizure*

One of the ways a person acquires ownership pursuant to Article 110 of the Bolivian Civil Code (and in accordance with the doctrine) is through usucapion. The acquisition of property under this institution differs depending on whether ownership relates to movable or immovable property. This way of acquiring property rights is known in foreign doctrine and legislation as acquisitive prescription or positive prescription.

In the Bolivian system, two modes of seizure of real estate have been identified: the ten-year (extraordinary) seizure and the five-year (ordinary) seizure.

In the first case (ten-year usucapion), the law provides for acquisition of the property right through ten-year or extraordinary usucapion. This means that possession is only required for ten years for title to transfer. Article 138 of the Bolivian Civil Code does not specify whether the possession must be in good faith. That is, it does not require the possessor to have obtained possession from who he believed to be the rightful owner of property; the article only requires possession, meaning that the possessor must merely consider himself the owner of the item, thus performing acts of lordship, by which he would be able to demonstrate the elements of ownership (corpus and animus) described in the doctrine.

This way of acquiring property has its source in Article 1158 of the Italian Code, which clarifies that ownership of real property and other rights *in rem* are acquired by virtue of continuous possession for twenty years. This provision, in establishing only that possession must be continuously exercised for a period of twenty years, differs from the Bolivian rule in terms of time necessary for usucapion passage of title (with the latter only requiring ten years). Likewise, the source code governs how other rights *in rem* are acquired, albeit in a generic way. Conversely, the Bolivian chapter on usufruct simply establishes that ownership may be acquired through usucapion, without any distinction between property rights and other rights *in rem*.

In the second case (five-year usucapion), the applicable rule (i.e., Article 134 of the Bolivian Civil Code) states that the person who, by virtue of title suitable to transfer ownership, acquires property in good faith from someone who is not the owner may usucapate the property. The provision also requires registration of title and possession for five years. Essentially, this form of acquisition does not result in the acquisition of property, but rather perfects an acquisition that has defects. This form of acquisition is described as that which occurs when a person obtains ownership of property from someone who was not, in fact, the rightful owner, or when another person has previously acquired the property and recorded such title prior to the successor claiming ownership through usucapion. If ownership is disputed, the law settles the conflict by recognizing the ownership of the first person who registers title. In that case, the current holder loses his right based on a title with a defective registration. It is understood that the right must be granted to the one person who exercises possession of a thing, and this aspect can only be achieved only through the action of usucapion; with this, the owner who has a predecessor with defects in his title is allowed.

As usucapion extinguishes the property right of the owner who has abandoned the property or has not shown interest in exercising the right, the term for usucapion is reduced to five years in cases where the possessor-usucaptor has acted in good faith. It is also required that the title of the property subject to usucapation is transcribed in the Land Registry. The requirement of good faith serves to protect a person who acted in good faith, for if the purchaser knew that the property had another owner or that the seller was in dispute with the previous owner, he could not be assumed to be in good faith in acquiring the property rights. This thesis is also found in Article 1154 of the Italian Model.

The context of this institution is provided by Article 1159 of the Source Code, the content of which (as mentioned in this section) turns out to be similar to that of Article 134 of the Bolivian Code. However, with some differences.

8.2 *The seizure of movable property*

In the case of usucapion of movable property not subject to transcription, it is established that the bad faith possessor can acquire ownership through possession for ten years. In this case, it is further understood that stolen things are considered found, provided there has been no claim for the object by its owner. Likewise, this legal presumption provides that he who exercises possession over an abandoned object, even knowing the true owner, can acquire ownership of movable property through usucapion pursuant to Article 149 of the Bolivian Civil Code.

In the case of usucapion of movable property subject to transcription, the Code determines that the owner of such property acquires ownership by mere possession for three years, starting from the date title was registered. This type of *usucapión* is similar to the five-year usucapion of immovable property.

Both cases are inspired by the Italian Source. The first case is influenced by Article 1161 of the Italian Code, with the difference that the Italian Model distinguishes between possession in good faith and possession in bad faith. Unlike in the Bolivian Code, the Italian Model requires bad faith possession for twenty years for usupacion of immovable property to occur, whereas ownership of movable property may be acquired after ten years of good faith possession.

This turns out to be a variant of the forms of possession. More specifically, the Bolivian system only addresses possession in bad faith and not possession in good faith. Instead, the Source

Code clarifies that difference, allowing the good faith possessor to acquire the property right in less time than the bad faith possessor.

9. *Conclusions*

In terms of rights *in rem*, the Bolivian Civil Code has been inspired by the Italian Civil Code of 1942.

For more than 45 years, the institutions of the possession system and its effects have been maintained. This is also true in the national jurisprudence, as evidenced by the 2014 decision of the Bolivian Supreme Court, Civil Division (order No. 567 /2014 of October 9, 2014), in which the Court, called upon to rule on a case of modification (interversion) of possessory title, referred to the Argentine doctrine as a source of authority despite its domestic source of law is similar to Article 1164 of the Italian Civil Code of 1942, both with regard to content and orientation (i.e., they both modify the status of the possessor into owner).

The effects of possession have served to determine the extent of monies to be remitted to a possessor for expenses incurred in connection with possession of a certain good, as well as restitution for its fruits, the actions to defend its possession and the acquisition of ownership through usucapion.

Despite the evolution of legal and regulatory systems, the institution of possession has remained consistent.

Guilherme Calmon Nogueira da Gama*
Patrícia Silva Cardoso**

THE SEVERAL READINGS OF THE SOCIAL FUNCTION OF PROPERTY AND ITS APPLICATION IN BRAZIL

1. The various readings of the social function in Italy

The definition of the legal nature and the content of the social function clause is closely related to the conception of property that one intends to defend. There are practically two starting points: either property is associated with a subjective right, or it is considered a function or a relative power, limited by Public Law. In the middle ground is the doctrinal current that holds that it is a subjective right conditioned to its social function. In summary:

> [...] three conceptions of the right to property are modernly affirmed: one that attributes it to the individual as such, basing it on human nature; one that denies it to the individual as such; one that recognizes it to the individual not as a natural right, but as a form of social or civil duty.[1]

The traditional position affirms the incompatibility between the subjective right and the social function or, at best, admits only its merely external interference. The opposite current holds that property cannot be seen as a subjective right, but rather as a duty-power, so that the owner's interest is conditioned to the satisfaction of non-owner interests, that is the general or social interest. In Italian doctrine, the two poles are represented by Widar Cesarini Sforza and Enrico Finzi. The origin of the divergence

---
*   Full Professor of Civil Law UERJ.
** Associate Professor of Civil Law UFF.
1   W. Cesarini Sforza, 'Proprietà ed espropriazione', Educazione fascista, 2 (1929), 108–21. F. D'Urso. *La proprietà: un dibattito di primo Novecento* (Napoli: Editoriale Scientifica, 2012), note 3, p. 1.

lies in the foundation of property: while Widar Cesarini Sforza understands that the justification of property must be sought in the human will, prior to the State, assuming a subjective position; for Enrico Finzi its foundation lies in the collective interest, in the greater common advantage that the goods are used with full freedom by the citizens[2], hence the need for the social function.

The theme of property is constant in Widar Sforza's writings and goes through three phases in his law production: 1) the first begins in the late 20s of the 20th century and has as its inaugural landmark the essay "Proprietà ed espropriazione" (1929), the year in which his best known work, "Il diritto dei privati," is published; 2) the second period runs from the 1930s until the civilist codification of 1942 and encompasses the writings that most reflect the scholar's position; 3) the last phase brings texts defending subjectivism in the face of state interventionism in the economy and the constitutionalization of the social function of property.[3]

In the first essay, Widar Sforza analyzes the theme of the relations between Public Law and Private Law in the property issue and also faces the problem of corporate relations arising from the "Carta del Lavoro", which brings a new approach to the relation between property and production, as well as the theme of the owner and entrepreneur (one of the tendencies of the Italian Constituent Assembly was to associate property as linked to business or to define property as a business) of the fascist regime. He notes the crisis of the traditional model and defends the return to subjectivism as a solution, which he considers adequate to

---

2 Finzi goes so far as to state that property is a social function: "[...] la proprietà, riprende ad essere, oltre che un diritto soggettivo, una funzione sociale. La giustificazione di essa non si ricerca più nella volontà divina od umana, bensì nell'interesse collettivo, nel maggior vantaggio comune a che i beni vengano utilizzati in piena libertà dai singoli cittadini" (*[...] property, once more becoming, in addition to being a subjective right, a social function. The justification for it is no longer sought in the divine or human will, but in the collective interest, in the greater common advantage of goods being used in full freedom by individual citizens*). E. Finzi, *L'officina delle cose. Scritti minori* (Milan: Giuffrè, 2013), p. 21.

3 D'Urso, p. 113.

preserve property from the constant attacks it has been suffering from special legislations that deprive it of its essential content.

Enrico Finzi brings two main contributions to the study of property[4]: the first is the inaugural lecture of the academic year 1922–1923, at the Royal Institute of Social Sciences "Cesare Alfieri", entitled "Le moderne trasformazioni del diritto di proprietà" (1922); the second is a lecture given at the First National Congress of Agrarian Law, entitled "The Agrarian Law and the discipline of production". Moreover, his best-known work – "Il possesso dei diritti" (1915) – is the background of his reflections directed against the dogmatics of the 18th century and its objective imposition of law.

In a certain way, the discussion between Sforza and Finzi is anticipated by Romagnosi and Laurent, which Ferdinando Bianchi[5] described as in "a polemic on the legal limits of private property" in a work published in 1885 on the subject — that is, before the insertion of the clause on the social function of property in the Italian Constitution.

Romagnosi argues that the general interest should only prevail in case of true necessity, in order to provide the least possible sacrifice in the owner's individual right. Laurent criticizes this thesis and argues that the individual right may be restricted whenever a social right is at stake. In turn, Bianchi, when describing the controversy, takes an intermediate position, stating that it is not possible to establish a priori a hierarchy or priority among rights, since this depends on the particular economic, social and moral conditions of each country.

Resuming the polemic between Sforza and Finzi, the proposals of each of the scholars will be briefly described in order to compare them and propose a solution[6]. The two authors embody

---

4 D'Urso, p. 113.
5 F. Bianchi, *I limiti legali della proprietà nel diritto civile* (Macerata, 1885), pp. 31–37. Apud F. Negro, *La storia economica e sociale della proprietà* (Bologna: Forni Editore, 1970), p. 293.
6 The divergence among doctrines is exposed by Francesco D'Urso, in a book dedicated to the main moments of the debates on the right to property in the Italian contexto. D'Urso, pp. 113–15.

two different ways of looking at the phenomenon of ownership: property as the potestas of the owner versus property as an instrument of economic organization[7].

Two models of Private Law are confronted: one, classical, aimed at guaranteeing the exercise of private autonomy by the subjects, as well as respect for their civil liberties as citizens; the other, objectified, understood as the law of property and of the economy, in which the individual finds little space. Sforza's which view represents the greatest Italian exponent of the doctrine, who considers there to be an insurmountable contradiction between the notions of right and function. Finzi, on the other hand, defends an objective conception of property and maintains that the objective transformations of the domain have led to a change in the subjective pole, displacing the pertinence of the individual to the collectivity (understood more or less broadly)[8].

Sforza starts from the classical jusnaturalist notion, which treats property as a projection of the subject itself, reason for the protection granted by the legal system and center of the system of subjective rights and Private Law. Finzi's analysis is strongly influenced by Economics and by the corporative principles introduced by the Fascist State; therefore he maintains that property is considered not only as the property of the individual, but should be treated as the basis of the social structure and the center of the legal system[9].

The different views of the gravitational center of the legal system have repercussions on the approaches to property and its social function. If, for Sforza, property is an excrescence within the Private Law system, because subjective rights are definitely incompatible with the social function of the law; for Finzi, it is the very basis because property is no longer considered a subjective

---

7 The two trends in the examination of property are pointed out by P. Grossi, *L'inaugurazione della proprietà moderna* (Napoli: Guida Editori, 1980), p. 52.
8 Finzi, *L'officina delle cose. Scritti minori*, p. 37.
9 Cfr. I. Stolzi and E. Finzi, 'Il Contributo italiano alla storia del Pensiero', in *Treccani Enciclopedia – Diritto* (2012). Available at ☐http://www.treccani.it/enciclopedia/enrico-finzi_(Il_Contributo_italiano_alla_storia_del_Pensiero)_Diritto)/☐. Accessed on May 17, 2016.

right and is transformed into a discretionary power, modeled by Public Law. The remodeling of property by Public Law and its qualification as a discretionary power, along the lines of Administrative Law, transforms the owner from a dominus into a manager[10], and he starts to enjoy a public duty, which allows his actions to be shaped so that the solution that best serves the public interest can be adopted.

Finzi's proposal aims to reconcile private law with public law, as well as the coexistence of freedom and duty within the same legal instrument. Such discretionary power would be equally free and binding: autonomy applies only to the choice of means for achieving productive results, which are determined by the State in view of the common interest[11]. The qualification of property as a discretionary power makes space for two new possibilities in the study of the theme: a) the excess and misuse of power in the exercise of property; b) the insertion of the social function in the structure of property and the verification of the protection of legitimate interests that are outside the ownership circle[12].

Finzi was an enthusiast of the social doctrine to the point of preaching the remodeling of private law by it. Sforza is positioned at the opposite extreme and attacks both the "socialist"[13] doctrine and the social doctrine: he accuses the former of attacking the fundamental rights of the individual; as for the latter, he says that it is a tangle of confused ideas that end up undermining the protection of property[14].

Here lies the fundamental point of all the criticism developed by Sforza: any intervention of the State in property — either to

---

10 In a shrewd critique, Giovanni Tarelo points out the change that has occurred in private property, citing that the proposal to abandon it as a subjective right in order to propose it as a power-duty to be exercised not in benefit of the owner, but of society as a whole would have made the owner assume the garb of an owner-functionary. G. Tarello, *La disciplina costituzionale della proprietà* (Genova: ECIG, 1973) pp. 26–32.
11 Cfr. Stolzi and Finzi, 'Il Contributo italiano alla storia del Pensiero'.
12 Cfr. D'Urso, p. 207.
13 The word is put in quotation marks to indicate the multiplicity of socialist doctrines. The nomenclature is used interchangeably only to emphasize the author's opposition to them.
14 Sforza, 'Proprietà ed espropriazione', p. 112, apud D'Urso, p. 208.

restrict the faculties of ownership or to impose duties to meet social interests — does not have the power to change its legal nature, which remains of Private Law. This can be affirmed even in the case of expropriation for public or social interest. In such situations, the property right does not change its features to become a duty or a function; what occurs is its substitution by another that arises to compensate the owner for the loss. In summary: the social function is exercised by the State and, on account of its supremacy over the private individual, private property may yield under exceptional circumstances, in which the interest is undoubtedly present, giving rise to the right to compensation.

The mentioned author defends the individual vector of private property in a context extremely unfavorable to his proposal, of growing State intervention in the economy and the birth of the corporate phenomenon in Italy. His central line of reasoning can be summarized in two topics: a) property is the relationship between the individual and the thing and, as such, it is essentially subject-oriented, the engine of Private Law; b) the denial of the functionalization of property, which would be totally incompatible with the nature of the subjective right.

He maintains that the concept of property remains centered on the traditional cores of absolutism and exclusivity, exactly as formulated by modern property theorists, so heavily criticized by contemporary doctrinaires[15]. In view of the centrality of the subject, property must be considered on the basis not of itself, but of the subject, and the perspective of Private Law must be maintained and reinforced as the regulator of the legal sphere of the individual. The proposals that consider the subject as a function of property, as proposed by Finzi, must be set aside. For Sforza, it is precisely in this objectivist perspective, of the

---

15 Among them: S. Rodotà, *Il terribile diritto. Studi sulla proprietà privata e i beni comuni* (Bologna: Il Mulino, 2013); P. Grossi, *História da propriedade e outros ensaios*, tr. L. Ermani Fritoli and R.M. Fonseca (Rio de Janeiro: Renovar, 2006).

prevalence of the thing over the subject, that the "Trojan horse" of the social function of property is hidden[16].

Thus, he strongly fights the understanding that property would be dynamized or enriched by the insertion of a social element in its core; on the contrary, he understands that this ends up emptying it because the social function would only be "a comfortable slogan", without any real content. The nature of property demonstrates said incompatibility: since it is a relationship between the subject and a thing, there is no question of imposing obligations on third parties, who are alien to it, in addition to being an original right, prior to the State, indissolubly linked to the human personality and freedom, a synthesis between two opposing concepts being impossible.

According to Sforza, either property is individual and private or it cannot be considered as such and, therefore, its socialization is not admissible[17]. What may occur is the suppression of property for the sake of social or collective interest — as in the case of expropriation for public and social utility — but not the insertion of duties in the internal content of the right. If the owner's powers are confused or reduced to duties, in reality, the right itself disappears and it loses its ownership status.

Despite the sharp criticism, the author seems to make a concession to the conception of the social function as an external limit by defending the split between property and production, and consequently between the owner and the producer. The owner of an asset that is outside the production process does not have any obligation; however, when such asset enters the production process, he becomes a producer (or entrepreneur) and duties may arise that are foreign to ownership[18].

---

16   W. Cesarini Sforza, 'Codice Civile e Carta del lavoro nella definizione della proprietà', in *Stato e diritto* (Roma: Studium Urbis, 1941); W. Cesarini Sforza, *Vecchie e nuove pagine di filosofia, storia e diritto*, Vol. II, Ricerche storiche e questioni giuridiche (Milan: Giuffrè, 1967). Apud D'Urso, note 28, p. 123.
17   D'Urso, p. 131.
18   D'Urso, p. 137.

All things that are objects of production will be objects of the property right, but not all things that are objects of property are involved in the productive process. He does not conceive property as an instrument of production, but as a subjective right, granted in favor of the individual. However, he considers that the act of production has in itself a social function, but only in its external aspect, without the subjective and voluntarist elements being attacked. Property is subjective, but production is considered as a center of interest, an activity directed to a social end from an objective point of view. When an individual uses a good, introduces it into the productive process, therein lies a social function.

Within its logic, the subjectivist conception allows analysis of the legal system as a complex of rights and obligations. Conversely, the objectivist conception introduces the notion of the State's will as the only source of law. Returning to the pluralist view of the legal system, which originated with Santi Romano[19], he proposes the difference between Private Law — which emanates from the State's normative source — and the law of private parties, which is the law that private parties create to regulate collective interests in the absence or insufficiency of State laws[20].

To understand his fight against the social function, it is important to better understand the distinction he makes between Private Law and the Law of private parties[21]. In Private Law, there is a necessarily inter-subjective relationship and a general

---

19 Cfr. M. Cerinioni, 'Prime riflessioni sull'autonomia privata', Annali della Facoltà Giuridica dell'Università di Camerino, 1 (2012), p. 135. Available at ☐http://d7.unicam.it/afg/sites/d7.unicam.it.afg/files/CERIONI_prime_riflessioni_fonti.pdf☐. Accessed on May 20, 2016.
20 Cerinioni., pp. 131–69.
21 The author starts from the premise that there is a State Law, responsible for stating Public Law and Private Law, and the Non-State Law, within which fits the law of the private parties "complex of norms that emanate from non-state authorities to regulate certain legal relations between persons subject to them", citing as examples the ethical and deontological codes, a notion associated with the idea of groups organized around a common goal. His entire work is permeated by dualisms: state and non-state law; public and private law; rights and duties; subject and object, property and company.

dimension, since people are linked by a common interest or bond. In property law, the relationship is between the subject and the thing, and there is no inter-subjective relationship. Property is an original right and prior to the State, and it precedes both Private Law and the Law of Private Individuals.

In contrast, Finzi points out that the right to property cannot be reduced to the relationship between the individual and the thing, this being only its internal aspect, alongside which is the external aspect, represented by the faculty of exclusion of the use of the thing by third parties. The emergence of the social function generates the internal fusion between the individualistic nature of the right to property and its social function. This is because the objective is transposed to the content of the right itself, giving it a new conformation and generating positive duties to the owner, who can be obliged to make a use of it that is in conformity with the collective interest[22].

Within this logic, the social function belongs to the structure of property. For this reason, right and function cannot be considered as opposing concepts, but rather as elements of the same institute. The limits on property should not be reduced to the imposition of a negative duty not to harm anyone (the *neminem laedere* principle), because the insertion of the functional element generates duties for the owner, previously considered only social duties that eventually become legal duties.

He also maintains that the decline of the absolutism of ownership is linked to the protection that this right receives, protection that was appropriate in a context in which the conservation of use was fundamental, especially for real estate. With the changes introduced in the economy by the circulation of values, the utility of goods became greater the more they were used for exchange. This is reflected in the very protection granted to the owner, which, traditionally, was represented by the action

---

These dualisms are used to demarcate the characteristics not only of the branches of Law, but also of its concepts.

22 E. Finzi, 'Le moderne trasformazioni del diritto di proprietà', in *Archivio giuridico* (Modena: Società Tipografica Modenese, 1923), 52–72. Apud D'Urso, note 189, pp. 171–72.

of claim the property. For him, "the property ceases to be simply the active legitimation of the action of claim and becomes passive legitimation of several private and public claims: social function, therefore, right conditioned to duties, duties in retribution of the diffuse interest"[23].

Finzi argues that the value of property is positively linked to the likelihood the goods will be sold and, therefore, in the interest of the owner, there must be a tempering in the absolutism of the traditional defense of property. Sforza, on the contrary, contends that the maximum protection of the right to property should be guaranteed as a way to protect the individual and ensure the defense of his legal positions, in relation to the State and to third parties. Thus, the classical mechanisms of defense of property, as a subjective right, must have supremacy before other non-property interests, since property remains an institute essentially of Private Law.

For Finzi, Private Law tends to crumble, but it will have to be rebuilt on a new basis, with an objective character, no longer being the ordering of the subject, but the ordering of goods. Property continues to be at the center of the patrimonial system, but an objectified property, the expression of a social function, in which he mentions the ideals of the "Carta del Lavoro", that determines that private autonomy in the field of production is the most useful instrument in the interest of the Nation[24].

Property must be refounded by the nature of the thing because goods are endowed with a new economic-social meaning: they are no longer considered only as objects of private ownership, but as the basis of social organization, which points to the centrality of the thing to the detriment of the subject[25].

Having said this, we now intend to verify, among those who sustain the existence of a social function in property, what is the content that should be attributed to it and, thus, we will start

---

23   D'Urso, p. 207.
24   Finzi, *L'officina delle cose. Scritti minori*, p. 41.
25   A view also held by P. Grossi in his writings.

with the lessons of Italian doctrine[26]. Regarding the extent and legal nature of the social function of property, there are several meanings, among which the following are proposed[27]: i) social function is a polysemic expression, of variable content, whose meaning can only be deduced from the systematic interpretation of article 42 of the Italian Constitution; ii) social function cannot be verified in the abstract, but must be fulfilled by the principle of solidarity, applied concretely; iii) social function is an external limit to the right to property, which must continue to be qualified as a subjective right; iv) social function means link between property and person; v) social function is social utility, a notion linked to economic freedom; vi) social function is an internal limit to the right to property.

Within the first current, which in fact is an amalgamation of several others, it is assumed that the social function is in fact a semantic problem. The phrase admits an infinite number of meanings, varying according to ideological trends or the constitutional provision with which it is associated. A first possibility is to attribute to it a mathematical logical meaning that property, as an institute born in society, is social, and thus it has an innate a "social function", an expression that would be a pleonasm. Another semantic possibility is to understand the expression "social function" as the function of being an instrument to preserve society, so that the law should be aimed at guaranteeing the property as a social foundation. It is also possible to understand that the social function qualifies the means of acquisition, use and limits (including quantitative ones) that the legislator should give to the right of property.

Each of these meanings is articulated with a line of interpretation of articles 2, 3, and 4 of the Italian Constitution, in conjunction with section 3 of article 41 of the Constitutional text, as well as with article 42, which deals with the social function. Accordingly, in order to clarify the meaning of the expression "ensure its

---

26 The theme has been discussed in the doctrine since the 1960s, and has gone through several phases of concretization in Italy.
27 The various currents are systematized by G. Alpa and A. Fusaro, *Metamorfosi del diritto di proprietà* (Antezza: Matera, 2011), pp. 336–56.

social function and make it accessible to all", provided for in the Constitution, we must proceed with a succinct analysis of the possible connections with the aforementioned constitutional provisions.

One of the interpretations, with a more liberal content, articulates art. 42 with art. 41, item 3, of the Italian Constitution, to conclude that the expression "make it accessible to all" (right after the social function clause) should be interpreted to protect against the suppression of property, in attention to the achievement of a private law equality that guarantees free initiative and the operation of a market economy[28]. Property has an intrinsic virtue that, by itself, would justify its legal recognition and protection by the legal system.

Another side argues that the guarantee of development of each individual's personality does not refer to the protection of patrimonial legal positions, but rather to existential legal situations with particular attention to the solidarity demands laid out in the Constitution. Hence, property has no intrinsic justification, unlike labor, but only an absolute subjective patrimonial situation. A supporter of this line of thought is Pietro Perlingieri[29], for whom the systematic approach leads to the conclusion that salary is a fundamental right[30], unlike property, which does not enjoy its own protection, but only as an instrument for the realization of constitutional objectives. Such reading is confirmed by the topographical location of article 42, inserted in title III of the Italian Constitution, which deals with economic relations. Labor, inserted in the same title, enjoys greater protection than property, since it "is protected in

---

28 Cfr. Tarello, *La disciplina costituzionale della proprietà*, pp. 26–32.
29 P. Pierlingieri, *Introduzione alla problematica della proprietà* (Napoli: Edizioni Scientifiche Italiane, 2012).
30 Art. 36. Il lavoratore ha diritto ad una retribuzione proporzionata alla quantità e qualità del suo lavoro e in ogni caso sufficiente ad assicurare a sé e alla famiglia un'esistenza libera e dignitosa (*Workers have the right to remuneration commensurate with the quantity and quality of their work and in any case sufficient to ensure a free and dignified existence for themselves and their families*). Available at ☐https://www.senato.it/documenti/repository/istituzione/costituzione.pdf☐. Accessed on June 8, 2016.

all its forms and applications"[31]. In this way, property can yield before other non-property interests that fulfill the constitutional dictates, and therein lies the social function of property. This implies that the legal discipline of property does not touch only the owner, but also all other legitimate interests that may come into its sphere.

For Michele Costantino[32], the social function of property refers to the modes of attribution and use of property. Property has an external justification and, thus, all its legal discipline must be interpreted so as to ensure such function, whether in its allocation or in its exercise. Based on this, the ownership of the property right does not matter, but the concrete verification of its social utility, its modes of acquisition and use, which do not enjoy legal protection per se, must be confronted with the other legitimate interests[33] that gravitate around the interest of the owner. Likewise, there is no aprioristic supremacy relationship between the subjective right and the legitimate interest: the greater or lesser protection granted to each of them depends on the nature of the concrete situation under analysis.

This position holds that the social function is not merely a semantic issue, but a new element that modifies the traditional structure of property, both public and private, and the way of coordinating the interests of individuals with the general interest. Its inclusion in the content of property would have renewed the individualistic concept by imposing a new integrative content, which goes beyond the powers of the holder of the subjective right.

It should also be noted that there are doctrinal constructions that continue to associate property with individual freedom. But the existence of a social function, which can be understood as economic freedom or social utility, is recognized even in these

---

31   Art. 35. La Repubblicatutelaillavoro in tutte le sue formeedapplicazioni. Avaiable at □https://www.senato.it/documenti/repository/istituzione/costituzione.pdf□. Accessed on June 8, 2016.
32   M. Costantino, 'Capitolo unico. Il diritto di proprietà', in P. Grossi, *Mitologie giuridiche della modernità* (Milan: Giuffrè, 2001), pp. 252–53.
33   G. Alpa and M. Bessone, *Poteri dei privati e statuto della proprietà. I. Oggetti, situazioni soggettive, conformazione dei diritti* (Padova: CEDAM, 1980), p. 177.

cases. One of these notions, which associates property with the individual, holds that the problem of social function does not arise in the concrete level of the use and exercise of the faculties inherent to the domain, but mainly in the sphere of "having", arising from the constitutional requirement of making property accessible to all[34]. Property is seen as a projection of the person, and legislative interventions should be aimed at realizing this principle, which is turned to the future, being a criterion to guide future interventions by the legislator, as well as to concretely value the owner's actions in order to verify if there is any trace of antisocial behavior. This is the tendency to identify the social function with the interests of a special category of subjects that has been protected in the Constitution or in sparse laws[35].

In turn, another conception that also starts from the assumption of property as an expression of the person (and his individual freedom) defends that the social function should be understood as social utility, understood as a limit to the freedom of economic initiative that can be established by law. The social function is not the foundation of private autonomy, but a constitutional limit and, for this reason, the legislator may establish limits to the economic utility in favor of the social function[36].

It is worth noting that the above trends are closely linked to the concept that considers the social function is an intrinsic limit or a component of the content of the right to property, as opposed to those that classify it as an extrinsic limit, or that understand property only as an expression of individual freedom. Santoro-Passarelli is a great advocate of the trend that defines the social function is an external limit of the right to property, which continues to be so considered. The doctrinaire clarifies that the defense of property as a subjective right is not the result of a conceptual preciosity and, indeed, it is a fundamental operation

---

34 Alpa and Fusaro, p. 343.
35 Cfr. A. Prata, *A tutela constitucional da autonomia privada* (Coimbra: Almedina, 1980), p. 176, note 323.
36 Alpa and Fusaro, p. 348.

to establish what still resides in the structure of property, despite so many innovations that limit and change it[37].

This must be done rationally and without great illusions about the social function. For him, in addition to the need for conceptual clarity, it is also necessary to establish the practical effects of the changes that have occurred and to dimension them within the structure of property, which "is power and not function, freedom and not discretion, autonomy and not control"[38]. To this end, it should not be overlooked that the constitutional provision of private property has a broader meaning than that contained in the Civil Code and comprises several legal positions, among them public property and private property.

Public property differs substantially from private property by the nature of the interest that animates it and is configured as a power linked to a function. Private property, on the other hand, is a subjective right, since the private subject is free to exercise it, unlike the public subject, who has a duty. Therefore, the social function of property must be read in different ways, depending on whether the property is public or private: the idea of internal limit only applies to public property, which itself has a social function; for private property, it must be understood as an extrinsic limit, set by law in view of the social interest.

Antonio Gambaro supports the uselessness of the social function formula, which would be doomed to disappear for lack a concrete content[39]. The doctrinaire points out that this formula was elaborated to regulate the grounds for attributing property, as a guideline for the choices that the legal system must make when attributing property to each one (and its status). For this reason, when applied separately from the attributive choices of each legal system, that is, applied when property is already in the hands of each individual — at a time after the recognition of

---

37 Alpa and Fusaro, p. 342.
38 Alpa and Fusaro, p. 342.
39 A. Gambaro, 'Note introduttive', in *XXV Conferenza Internazionale dell'Osservatorio "Giordano Dell'Amore" sui rapporti tra diritto ed economia. Fra individuo e collettività. La proprietà nel secolo XXI* (Milano: Fondazione Cariplo, 2012), p. 11.

private property — it brings more problems than solutions, given the lack of precise determination of its content.

At the theoretical level, the construction would be useful to indicate the removal of the absolute conception of property rights. But, as a formula that generates legal rules, it cannot play an effective role[40]. The attribution of individual property to someone already results from a choice made by the legal system, which considers a certain appropriation or specification worthy of protection. Therefore, if the property has already been attributed to the individual through the constitutional recognition of a subjective right, it is not possible to proceed to a new conformation, under penalty of violation of legality and the very constitutional guarantee of private property.

In the same sense, Giovanni Pellerino maintains that, despite the various contents and proposals intended to fill the formula of social function, the impossibility of establishing a univocal meaning to the concept ends up demonstrating its uselessness. The essence of the concept of property does not pass through the social function, but through the role that property occupies in society today. Therefore, it would be more appropriate to speak of a structural function of property. The legal formatting of property as a subjective right gives to the economy the assumptions that allow it to function, and to the law the criteria to make choices, based on the binomial "to have or not to have".

In view of the role it plays in today's society, the author proposes that the concept be left aside in favor of a structural function, indicating the function it plays in the social context. Legally, the mentioned binomial presents itself with three structural dimensions, each with a different choice[41]: i) material dimension: definition of what may be object of the right of property; ii) temporal dimension: to attribute legality to the expectations and powers of the owner, guaranteeing him protection; iii) social dimension: the social pacification generated by the institutionalization of the consensus about the

---

40 Gambaro, p. 11.
41 G. Pellerino, *L'idea di proprietà. Storia come evoluzione* (Lecce: Pensa Multimedia, 2004), p. 217.

"meum" and the "tuum" (consensus between the owner and the non-owners about the property).

2. The social function of property in Brazil: some considerations

Because of the difficulties in the elaboration of a unitary concept of social function, in Europe, a good number of jurists propose its suppression, sustaining that it is an outdated question that brings more problems than solutions in view of the absence of a concrete content[42]. As pointed out, in Italy, a country that has had the social function clause inserted in its Constitution since 1948, even today no consensus has been reached on its scope, there being a myriad of currents that seek to define it[43].

However, if elsewhere the concept is considered worn out or despicable, in Brazil the question is faced with enthusiasm[44], for having been foreseen in the Magna Carta of 1988, which was confirmed by the Civil Code that followed it[45]. Please note that the 1988 Constitution was not the first Brazilian Constitution to consecrate the functionality of property. The pioneerism must be attributed to the 1934 Constitution, which included property in

---

42 By all: Gambaro, 'Note introduttive', p. 8.
43 Cfr. G. Alpa, who reports in his work on property at least six different currents on the content of the social function of property, especially in Italy, a country in which, more than 50 years after the insertion of the clause in the Constitution, no consensus has yet been reached on its content. Alpa and Fusaro, pp. 335–56.
44 Among the numerous works that address the theme, one can cite: J.I. Pilati, *Propriedade e função social na Pós-modernidade* (Rio de Janeiro: Lumen Iuris, 2011); M. Alcino de Azevedo Torres, *Property and possession: a confrontation around the social function*, 2nd end (Rio de Janeiro: Lumen Iuris, 2010).
45 The Brazilian Civil Code, published on January 10, 2002, had a long vacatiolegis period, and came into force one year after its publication. This is the wording of article 1,228 §1 of the Civil Code: "The right of property must be exercised in accordance with its economic and social purposes and in such a way that the flora, fauna, natural beauty, ecological balance and historic and artistic heritage are preserved, as well as to avoid air and water pollution". Available at http://www.planalto.gov.br/ccivil_03/leis/2002/L10406.htm. Accessed on May 10, 2016.

the chapter of the individual rights and guarantees and provided that such right could not be exercised against the social or collective interest, as determined by law. The 1937 Constitution only established that the right to property was guaranteed to all and that its content and limits would be those set by law. The issue came back to light in the 1946 Constitution, which guaranteed the right to property and dictated that its use would be conditioned to social welfare, so that the law could promote its fair distribution, with equal opportunity for all.

The 1967 text and Constitutional Amendment no. 1 of 1969 introduced the social function of property as a principle of the economic order, also foreseeing indemnity in public debt bonds in case of expropriation of rural property. The aforementioned Constitutions are fruits of the institutional context of the 1960s, a period in which there was a flurry of laws that sought to concretize the social function of agrarian property: Law no. 4132/62, defining the cases of expropriation for social interest; and Law no. 4504/64, the so-called Land Statute, dealing with the organization and functioning of the Brazilian Institute for Agrarian Reform.

The 1988 Constitutional text reinforces the notion of property as a constitutional guarantee and determines that it is a fundamental right that will fulfill its social function, while defining it as an element of the economic order. It also brings diverse specifications for rural and urban properties. As to the former, it establishes that rural property that does not fulfill its social function is subject to expropriation for agrarian reform purposes, and soon afterwards states that productive property cannot suffer such sanction. The social function of the urban real estate property is based on the fulfillment of the city planning requirements foreseen in the Master Plan prepared by the Municipality and, in case of non-compliance, successive sanctions can be imposed that interfere with the property owner's faculties. These sanctions are: i) compulsory parcelling or compulsory building; ii) progressive urban property tax over time; iii) expropriation-sanction with payment through public debt bonds.

The recognition of property as an individual right endowed with a collective function, in addition to the fact that such function can be fulfilled in different ways that relate to the nature of the asset in question, creates difficulties. Such compatibility between the individual and the social cannot be achieved without some doctrinal effort to concretize its content. It is also up to the Judiciary to give it the appropriate conformation in the litigations that are submitted to its appreciation.

Despite the optimistic view, the problem of conceptual indefiniteness remains, with the formula "social function of property" being used as a comprehensive expression with the vocation of sheltering the most diverse interests. In view of the difficulties pointed out above, especially by scholars from countries that have more recently established the social function of property, who have tried unsuccessfully to give it a concrete content, it seems useful to draw lessons from concrete experience, added to the doctrinal efforts of systematization.

With this, it is intended to avoid the "panacea of the social function", that is, its not very careful application, since the formula, despite its rhetorical beauty, can have a great variety of meanings, which can weaken not only its legality, but also the very guarantee of private property.

These are important considerations so that the foreign models may enrich the Brazilian juridical discussion, but are not imported in a hurried way, without the analysis of the adequacy to the particular circumstances and to the concrete development of the property right in Brazil. The property system is not immutable, just like any other institution or institute of social life, in view of the wide variety of concrete forms that property has taken throughout the history of societies. It develops in a particular way in each context, and it is up to positive law, based on local needs, to demarcate individual property.

A first observation concerns the constitutional qualification of the guarantee of property in each of the sovereign States. The Brazilian Constitution includes property as a fundamental right and element of the economic order; the Italian Constitution includes the guarantee in the list of economic rights and, for this reason, it is common in the doctrine of this country the consideration of property as an economic concept, which can present several legal conformations[46]. Such understanding has opened space for the questioning of property as a subjective right and its understanding as a legitimate interest, that is, a legally protected interest that must be weighed against other non-property interests that are at stake in the concrete case.

Furthermore, in Brazil, the problem of land distribution and the need for land title regularization are extremely serious and cannot be ignored. The high number of irregular occupations makes the need for greater research on the legal nature and content of the social function of property urgent, without neglecting the constitutional contours brought to rural and urban properties. By way of example, two emblematic judgments from Brazilian jurisprudence will be presented: the cases of "Favela Pulmann" and "Fazenda Primavera", which reflect the situation of property and ownership in Brazil, cases that would hardly be imaginable in the European context.

The Superior Court of Justice (STJ), in the emblematic case of the Pulmann Slum[47], a situation of serious conflict of possession, applied the social function clause to legitimize the possession of families who occupied a partially built piece of land, whose construction had been paralyzed for a long period. The Court

---

46 By all: Alpa and Bessone, *Poteri dei privati e statuto della proprietà*, p. 177.
47 STJ Judgment. Resp. 75. 659. Date of Judgment: 6/21/2005. CIVIL AND PROCEDURAL. ACTION FOR VINDICATION. LANDS OF SUBDIVISION LOCATED IN A SLUM AREA. PERISHING OF THE PROPERTY RIGHT. ABANDONMENT. CC, ARTS. 524, 589, 77 AND 78. MATTER OF FACT. REEXAMINATION. IMPOSSIBILITY. PRECEDENT NO. 7-STJ.
I. The property right assured in article 524 of the former Civil Code is not absolute, and its loss is caused by the abandonment of land in a subdivision that has not been concretely implemented and that has gradually become slumized over time, with the disfiguration of the originally planned fractions and layout, consolidating a new social and urbanistic reality at the site, consubstantiating the hypothesis foreseen in articles 589 c/c 77 and 78, of the same substantive law.
[...] III. Special appeal not cognizable. Available at http://www.stj.jus.br/SCON/jurisprudencia/doc.jsp?livre=75659&b=ACOR&p=true&l=10&i=3. Accessed on May 16, 2016.

applied the technique of weighing interests and recognized that possession with a social function should prevail over property that does not fulfill this same function, based on the following grounds: a) the right to property was exercised in an antisocial manner, since the owners left the land in complete abandonment for over twenty years; b) the physical removal of the families would be unfeasible and would violate the existential interests of the people involved; c) because of this, the *jus reivindicandi* is paralyzed by the principle of the social function of property, without, however, prejudice to the right to compensation from the state for indirect expropriation.

In the "Primavera Farm"[48] decision, the Court held that land occupied by the Landless Workers' Movement (MST) should be expropriated for failure to fulfill its social function, as evidenced by the fact that it was in debt to the Federal Government. The company Agropecuária Primavera had entered into a leasing contract with the company Merlin and had been developing its activities regularly. The property was productive and had cultivated land and land being prepared for cultivation, as well as improvements, when it was invaded by members of the Landless Workers Movement (MST). They began to occupy the farm and use the vehicles contained therein, and also invaded the company's offices, destroying goods and equipment.

The Court of Justice of the State of Rio Grande do Sul understood that, in spite of the existence of agricultural productivity, the property was not fulfilling its social function due to tax debts that culminated in a lien in favor of the INSS (National Institute of Social Security). The STJ, reexamining the decision, recognized the occurrence of direct expropriation and the consequent obligation of the State to indemnify the property owner[49]. The social function of the property was used as an argument to legitimize the violent occupations carried out by the

---

48 G. Tepedino and A. Schreiber, 'O papel do Judiciário na efetivação da função social da propriedade', available at http://www.tepedino.adv.br/wp/wp-content/uploads/2012/09/biblioteca5.pdf. Accessed on August 30, 2016.

49 The invasion prompted a request for federal intervention in the State of Paraná, a request that was denied by the STJ. Available at http://stj.jusbrasil.

MST and productivity was evaluated taking into consideration the criterion of default with the tax authorities, and not the income and agricultural products produced.

The examples exposed above demonstrate, in an incipient way, the framework of the application of the social function of property in Brazil and make clear the need to define guidelines. If, on the one hand, the reality of irregular occupations in the country and the need to protect the less favored classes is clear, it should not be forgotten that the stimulation of private property contributes effectively to the social order and progress of the nation, as Law 14382/22 sought to stimulate. Having said this, it is understood that the discussions on the social function of property elsewhere can help in the development of its doctrinal bases.

When it comes to the social function in Brazil, there are two opposing inclinations[50]. There are polarized tendencies that understand the social function in two ways: the first, positivist in nature, has justified the social function by answering the question in terms of its paradigm of productive use of property, under the direction of the State. Another trend, of a political-social nature, considers in this clause a mandate from the legislator for the distribution of wealth, linked to the objectives of the Republic to ensure the dignity of the human person and a free, just, and solidary society.

---

com.br/noticias/130467428/stj-rejeita-intervencao-no-parana-e-mantem-ocupacao-de-fazenda-pelo-mst. Accessed on August 30, 2016.

[50] Among them: G.C. Nogueira da Gama and A.L. Ribeiro de Oliveira, 'Função social da propriedade e da posse', in G.C. Nogueira da Gama (ed.) *Função social no Direito Civil* (São Paulo: Atlas, 2007), 39–67; A. Osório Gondinho, 'Função social da propriedade', in G. Tepedino, (ed.), *Problemas de direito civil-constitucional* (Rio de Janeiro: Renovar, 2001); E. Roberto Grau, *A ordem econômica na Constituição de 1988*, 9th edn (São Paulo: Malheiros Editores, 2004); R. Reis Mazzei, 'A função social da propriedade: uma visão pela perspectiva do Código Civil de 2002', in R.M. de Andrade Nery (ed.), *Função do Direito Privado no atual momento histórico* (São Paulo: Editora Revista dos Tribunais, 2006), 377–410; Pilati, *Propriedade e função social na Pós-modernidade*, p. 67; G. Tepedino and A. Schreiber, 'A garantia da propriedade no direito brasileiro', Revista da Faculdade de Direito de Campos, 6 (2005), 101–19 (p. 105).

Questions have been raised about the nature of the social function and its qualification as a principle of social solidarity, oriented towards stimulating economic activity, or as a subjective right of the collectivity. There are still two other ways of conceiving the social function: 1) as a general clause that permits the verification of proprietary behavior a posteriori by the Judiciary branch; 2) the conception that holds that the law is the instrument par excellence for fulfilling the social function, so that its content would be determined by it.

The prevailing thesis is that the social function is an a posteriori component to be analyzed against the owner's behaviour in order to verify whether he has exercised his right in an antisocial manner. Such an orientation leads to a rupture with the traditional property schemes, leading the discourse to a social dimension that has repercussions on the rights of the owner, who must conform his actions in search of the satisfaction of general interests.

However, it should be pointed out that the definition of a right in rem refers primarily to the relationship of lordship and power that is established between the owner and the property, proposing that the dimension of exclusion of third parties is external and not part of the right. The social function, precisely because it concerns the owner in his dealings with third parties, cannot be configured as an internal element.

It is an element that is not part of the law because property is the relationship between a person and his work, a relationship between a person and a good, a relationship that arises from an ordering of reason stemming from the natural law of "not to steal"[51] and from the dictates of justice that intend to attribute to each what is his. The theological meaning is extrinsic to property

---

51   For St. Thomas Aquinas, the promotion of the common good requires respect for private property by the respective right. The usurpation of another's good against the will of the owner is theft, and any form of unjustly retaining another's good, even if in accordance with civil law, violates the commandment not to steal. In the Summa Theologica, theft and robbery are inserted in the "Subjective Parts of Justice", when the vices opposed to commutative justice are presented. L. Rampazzo, 'Capitalist property versus human property: the reflection of St. Thomas taken up by Mounier', available

— it is outside the relationship between the person and the good, placing itself between the person and the collectivity. Therefore, the social function cannot be qualified as an intrinsic content to the right to property, because, in this respect, what exists is the relationship between subject and object, the relationship with third parties appearing in its external aspect, the only aspect in which it would be possible to insert a supposed social function of property as a limit.

Another fundamental point is to know at what moment such teleological meaning must be verified. Analyzing it a posteriori, based on the behavior of the owner weighed against other legitimate interests that arise under the concrete circumstances, weakens the security provided by the recognition of property as a legal institution, since its content can be filled in a varied way, according to the events of the moment.

Considering property is a fundamental right under the Brazilian Constitution and the characteristic vagueness of the formula of social function, it is noted that the latter can easily be used to favor the most diverse interests, including to weaken the protection of property. The question traverses not only the structure of the right to property and its very definition, but also touches on private autonomy and State intervention.

Property is associated with freedom, which makes it a fundamental right worthy of protection and grants the owner the possibility of doing everything that is not forbidden by law. Therefore, conditioning it to the fulfillment of a social function annihilates the subjective aspect of the right itself, which is essentially individual.

It is a subjective right that has an indissoluble link to the human person. On the other hand, it is true that private autonomy can be limited — both in the ways of using and disposing of things that are objects of property rights — in cases where there are sufficiently strong reasons that justify the supremacy of the public or collective interest. However, the content of the social

---

at http://www.publicadireito.com.br/artigos/?cod=1e9b64527e41c736. Accessed on August 31, 2016.

function should not be fulfilled in such a way as to annul the essential characteristics of property, which occurs when the social function is insisted upon as an internal element of private property, in which case the social function transforms property: from *ius* to *munus*, making it a contradiction.

A *munus* is understood as a set of functions that are the obligation of an individual and end up being imposed on the owner, who is then called an "owner-functionary". Such procedure mischaracterizes it, transforming it into a Public Law institute, increasingly subject to State intervention, which constitutes a violation of the constitutional guarantee of private property. The Constitution of the Federative Republic of Brazil provides for urban and rural properties and, in its core, several ways of accomplishing the respective social functions through various parameters imposed by the Constituent himself, which are spread out to the ordinary legislator[52].

The defense of the social function as a conforming element of the right to property is associated with the concept of differentiated properties, according to which the definition of property would vary according to the conformation given to it by the social function. Therefore, it is not unimportant to inquire whether the "theory of plurality" of proprietary types is applicable (and has repercussions in the establishment of several social functions) or if there remains only one social function for any type of property established in the national legal system.

Thus, according to the destination of the goods, the restrictions may vary, being admitted in different degrees, according to the nature and destination of the goods. This is what occurs in the Brazilian constitutional text. Article 186 establishes the requirements of rural property must observe in order to fulfill its social function; while article 184 provides the guidelines for the definition of sanctions for the property that does not fulfill this function. Furthermore, the Constitution establishes requirements

---

52   Cfr. L. da Silva Santana, *A propriedade privada e sua função social: uma análise da situação proprietária* (Dissertação, Mestrado em Relações Sociais e Novos Direitos – Programa de Pós – Graduação em Direito, Faculdade de Direito, da Universidade Federal da Bahia, Salvador, Bahia, 2012), p. 759.

for expropriation on the grounds of social interest for agrarian reform purposes, which led to the promulgation of Law 8629/96, which establishes criteria for verifying rural productivity and provides for expropriation in the event of non-compliance with the social function.

Article 182 does the same for urban property, shifting the verification of the social function to compliance with the requirements of the Master Plan of each municipality. The City Statute (Law no. 10257/01) materializes the constitutional requirement and sets criteria for the exercise of property rights, deriving from Urbanistic Law, applied with a view to promoting a more adequate and rational ordering of cities.

The reference to the constitutional provisions is not exhaustive, in the sense of analyzing all the criteria provided in a detailed manner, but only aims to demonstrate that each of the provisions brings specific requirements to be met by the property, depending on whether it is qualified as urban or rural, and that the provision of different limits does not affect the unity of the concept. The essence of property is the same, whether the property is urban or rural: it is the strongest right that exists over an asset, whose ratio iuris is private utility.

Starting from the premise that the social function is an extrinsic limit to property, it can be stated that there are several conceptions of social function, according to the destination and nature of the property, which does not threaten the unity of property and the constitutional guarantee; on the contrary, it refers to the unity and also the elasticity of the right to property. The structure of property is constant and the social function, as an extrinsic limit, is a criterion imposed on the legislator that refers to the specificities of the property or subjects in question.

Since the social function is an extrinsic element, it does not qualify the property, only the limitations that fall upon it, whether positive or negative, to define whether they are admissible. Consequently, each type of property may be restricted by different measures, depending on the subjects and assets involved[53]. The admissible restrictions vary, established according to the characteristics or destination of the property[54], but without losing sight of the fact that the protection of property, in the last analysis, concerns the protection of people and of private autonomy, which creates the imposition of limits before State intervention.

It is interesting to note how the influence of Italian law is present in the shaping of the notion of the social function of property in Brazilian law. All the intense debate carried out in the light of the Italian legal system is also found in the Brazilian legal reality, as we sought to demonstrate in the course of developing this work.

3. Concluding remarks

Having seen the controversies about the content of the social function, and having demonstrated the limits of dogmatics in the elaboration of a concept of socially adequate property, it is understood that, given the impossibility of defining its content, the formula should be read in the following terms: a private property fulfills a social function due to its recognition in the constitutional text, as well as the ways of appropriation of goods and the attribution of real ownership by the Civil Code[55]. Therefore, the limitations imposed by the social function, being external to the concept, do not have the power to change the right of property.

The social function, first of all, is a prius in relation to the recognition of property and not only a posterius in relation to

---

53 J.L. de los Mozos, *El derecho de propiedad: crisis y retorno a la tradición jurídica* (Madrid: Edersa, 1993), p. 215: "To speak in these cases of 'propiedades' is to abuse the words, since the most that can be reached is to speak of 'functional estates', singularized by their agrarian or urban destination. Thishas no bearing whatsoever on the nature of the right, real or personal, that falls on the thing, but only on the peculiarities of the object on which it falls, as we have previously stated".
54 Cfr. Gambaro, 'Note introduttive', p. 8.
55 Gambaro, p. 8.

its exercise, which means that in the attribution of ownership by the Constitution is the recognition of its social function. This is clearly supported by the fact that the Brazilian Civil Code contains the same diction, because its content is limited to preventing the antisocial use of the property, being a negative and extrinsic limit, arising from the requirements of the common good, and not the imposition of positive duties on the owner, under penalty of serious violation of his freedom.

It is argued that the recognition of private property brings in itself a social function, arising from the constitutional guarantee. In light of this, the potential restrictions should be as few as possible, so as not to limit individual freedom and entrepreneurship: laws that are too restrictive of this right are illegitimate and go against free enterprise as the foundation of the economic order. As far as private property is concerned, the function of appropriation in general terms is the same, but the legal regime may change depending on the legal good in question. Once the social function is recognized at the moment of the attribution of ownership, after its distribution and qualification as private, public or collective, one can speak of a greater or lesser state action, a matter related to private autonomy.

Juan Espinoza Espinoza*

THE INFLUENCE OF THE ITALIAN LEGAL EXPERIENCE ON THE PERUVIAN CIVIL CODE OF 1984

1. *The Ligurian presence in Peru*

In my childhood, and in most people's in Peru, when our mothers made steak-topped "green pasta" for lunch, it was like a holiday. Many years later, when I first traveled to Genoa, I was surprised to find that *pesto trofiette* was a typical Ligurian dish. The pasta is in fact shorter, it is a main course, and it is heresy to eat it as a side dish. The culinary surprises went even further: our *pastel de acelga* was their *torta pasqualina* [aka giant green pie], and *menestrón* was *minestrone* (for the record, soup is called *minestra* in Italian). Likewise, *fugasa* is no more than a Spanish version of *fügassa* in the local dialect (called *focaccia* in Italian). I therefore realized that many "Peruvian" dishes are *specialità tipica della cucina genovese*. The reason for such a delicious Italo-Peruvian fusion is the Ligurian presence in Peru.

Why is this so? Because most Italians arriving in Peru are Ligurian; and they came not only after the second half of the 19th century and the years after the Italian Unificacition, but also at the end of the century and the beginning of the 1900s, long after the first migratory wave had taken place, bringing Venitian farmers on crowded ships to southern America[1]. It is undeniable that the Italo-Peruvian fusion is the love child of the Ligurian influence in Peru.

---

* Professor of Civil law at the Universidad Nacional Mayor de San Marcos and Pontificia Universidad Católica del Perú.
1 G. Chiaramonte, 'La migración italiana en América Latina. El caso peruano', Apuntes. Revista de Ciencias Sociales, 13 (1983), pp. 15-36 (p. 17).

But such presence has not only influenced our food — it has also had an impact on our law.

2. *The Peruvian Civil Code of 1984*

The Peruvian Civil Code of 1984 [PCC] is a kind of "New Testament" crafted by several apostles. In 1965, the government created the Commission for the Study and Revision of the (still applicable) Peruvian Civil Code of 1936, chaired by Professor Carlos Fernandez Sessarego. Later on, the Commission for the Review of said project was created; and in 1984 the current Civil Code was finally enacted. In 1965, the most renowned Peruvian legal experts were summoned and, in 1976, each one of them was entrusted with the task of drafting a Project of a Book for the Code[2]. The drafting of the great 19th century Latin-American codes were all entrusted to one person. The Argentinean Civil Code of 1869, penned by Dalmacio Velez Sarfield and based on the draft of the Brazilian Civil Code by Augusto Texeira de Freitas, is one example. Another includes the Chilean Civil Code, written by Andres Bello. Even though the current Pevuvian Civil Code is the result of the contributions of highly respected legal experts, its systematic interpretation is troubled by the fact that each of its [so-called] books follows different legal models that do not always coincide. Returning to our opening metaphor, each gospel has a different perception of the divine.

The PCC — particularly in Book I, Personal Rights (for which Fernandez Sessarego was the rapporteur and main contributor)[3],

---

2   For further information on the members of and consultants to the reform committee, see F. Vidal Ramírez, *El Derecho Civil en sus conceptos fundamentales* (Lima: Gaceta Jurídica, 1992), pp. 93–8.

3   In fact, it is stated that, "when drafting the Project for the Book of the Right of Legal Subjects, the 1984 codifier relied on Italian scholarship, and to a lesser extent on jurisprudence than the 1942 Civil Code, which has been brilliantly commented upon and abundantly and eloquently criticized". C. Fernández Sessarego and C. Cárdenas Quirós, 'Estudio preliminar comparativo de algunos aspectos del Código civil peruano de 1984 en relación con el Código

and in Book VII, Sources of Obligations (which includes contract law) — has taken its essence from the Italian *Codice Civile* of 1942. The book of Legal Act (in the context of the Peruvian legal experience), however, deserves special attention, as it was inspired by the Book of Contracts of the Italian code — specially in its treatment of such concepts as formalities, representation, interpretation, condition, term, deceit and invalidity (which includes nullity and annullability), error, intent, and coercion, among others. That is why reference to the Italian Civil Code, as well as scholarship and jurisprudence (which explain and enrich it), is required to interpret national legislative models.

3. *Carlos Fernandez Sessarego: a solid bridge that started the contemporary Italian legal experience in Peru*

Apart from the translations of the texts of Francesco Messineo, Domenico Barbero and some others, the Peruvian civil law landscape in the 80s had very little knowledge of the contemporary Italian legal experience. Fernandez Sessarego built bridges: his carefully thought-out production introduced the most recent theoretical, legistative and jurisprudential trends in Italian civil law. Mr. Fernandez' making the Italian Civil Code [ICC] known, which can be seen in the PCC and his legal papers, can be confirmed in his extensive oeuvre.

a) Making the unborn deserving of rights (art. 1 PCC), in fact:

> [A]mong others, the brilliant opinions of Bianca, Busnelli, Oppo, Biscontini, and Traverso should be kept in mind as they have all contributed to the outline of a realistic idea of the legal status of the unborn.[4]

b) The legal treatment of the right to privacy (art. 14 PCC), thus:

---

civil italiano de 1942', in *El Código civil peruano y el Sistema jurídico latinoamericano* (Lima: Cultural Cuzco, 1986), p. 107.

4 C. Fernández Sessarego and C. Cárdenas, p. 109.

[T]he right to privacy or reserve has been widely discussed by Italian scholarship and jurisprudence, and article 14 has mostly drawn inspirations from the latter. There are many Italian scholars who have treated the subject:Ravá, Ligi, Pugliese, De Cupis, Vassalli, Rodotà, Rescigno, Palladino, De Mattia, Galli and Franceschelli.[5]

c) The legal treatment of entities, in which:

[T]he important contribution of the ample Italian scholarship on the matter is quite noticeable. There are many experts whose views on entities have somehow contributed to the different approaches adopted by the Peruvian Civil Code. Among many others are Ascarelli, Catalano, D'Alessandro, Magni, De Giorgi, Frosini, Galgano, Giannini, Orestano, Rescigno, Scarpelli, Bianca, Zatti.[6]

d) In the 90s, in Latin America, Mr. Fernandez Sessarego was the first to speak for the recognition and protection of the right to one's identity. He did very thorough research into the legislative, theoretical and jurisprudential influences of the Italian legal experience[7].

e) Mr. Fernandez Sessarego drew from the writings of Paradiso, De Giorgi, Bonillini, Rotondi, De Cupis, Messineo, Rescigno, Busnelli and the Italian court predecents to the introduce the term personal damage in the PCC and the Latin-American legal system[8].

Considereing the fact that the influence of the ICC on the Peruvian legal system is quite extensive, I will focus on select legal figures to show that the Peruvian code is no unreflected-upon copy of its source, the Italian one, but the product of a

---

5   C. Fernández Sessarego and C. Cárdenas, p. 112.
6   C. Fernández Sessarego and C. Cárdenas, p. 117.
7   C. Fernández Sessarego, 'El derecho a la identidad personal', in *Tendencias actuales y perspectivas del Derecho Privado y del Sistema Jurídico latinoamericano* (Lima: Cultural Cuzco, 1990), 55–102.
8   C. Fernández Sessarego, 'El daño a la persona en el Código Civil de 1984', in *Libro Homenaje a José León Barandiarán* (Lima: Cultural Cuzco, 1985), pp. 163–222.

happy "fusion" with particular touches that have enriched the circulation of the Italian model in our country.

4. The scope of civil liability in professional commitments or technical issues of extreme difficulty

Drawing from article 2236[9] of the ICC, article 1762 of the PCC establishes that:

> If the rendering of a service includes solving highly difficult professional issues or technical problems, the party rendering the service is not liable except when there is intent or gross neglicence.

When the article was first subjected to analysis and commentary, scholars pointed out that:

> [I]n the application of scientific rules, those applying the rules are liable only on the grounds of intent and gross negligence, an example of which would be ignorance of such rules or their poor application due to gross negligence; but there is no liability in an honest mistake made by the one rendeing the service when the mistake is due to a lack of ordinary diligence in solving technical issues of special difficulty.[10]

Let us note the following:

i. The code refers to the obligee (the renderer of the service) and not just to the professional.

ii. Much emphasis is placed on the solution of highly difficult technical issues.

---

9 Which reads "Liability of a party rendering a service. If the rendering of a service includes solving highly difficult technical problems, the party rendering the service is not liable except when there is intent or gross negligence".
10 M. de la Puente y Lavalle, 'Exposición de Motivos y Comentarios. Prestación de Servicios', in *Código Civil VI. Exposición de Motivos y Comentarios* (Lima: Okura Editores, Commission in charge of the Study and Revision of the Civil Code, edited by D. Revoredo de Debakey, 1985), p. 446.

I remember that the scope of this article was debated at the International Seminar on the Civil Liability of Professionals, which took place on November 19th and 20th, 1991, and was attended by Atilio Anibal Alterini. Other noteworthy participants included Max Arias Schreiber Pezet[11], Carlos Cardenas Quiros, Carlos Fernandez Sessarego, Fernando Vidal Ramirez and Lizardo Taboada Cordova, the first of whom raised his concerns about article 1762 on the grounds that its wording could cause confusion, thus unjustly benefiting [freelance] professionals over other types of obligees to a contract. Mr. Cardenas then suggested that the "or" in article 1762 should be understood to affect both parts of the sentence, thus meaning "highly difficult professional issues" or "highly difficult technical issues", a stance that I embraced at the moment. It can be seen that the Peruvian legislator's contribution to the Italian model was "professional issues", and consequently, its "highly difficult" nature should be common to both[12].

In accordance with the aforementioned, it is stated that:

> [T]he way article 1762 should be interpreted is that the professional rendering services of special technical difficulty is to be considered liable only on the grounds of intent or gross negligence, which amounts to saying that if the service rendered can be considered a normal one in the course of a professional activity, the rules to apply are the general ones.[13]

---

11 M. Arias Schreiber later confirmed his stance and warned this article "is highly questionable". M. Arias Schreiber Pezet, *Luces y sombras del Código Civil* (Lima: Studium, 1991), vol. II, p. 130.

12 J. Espinoza Espinoza, 'Responsabilidad Civil de los Profesionales', Revista de Derecho y Ciencias Políticas UNMSM, 49 (1991–1992), p. 325. Likewise, G. Fernández Cruz, 'Responsabilidad civil médica', Diálogo con la Jurisprudencia, 1 (1995), p. 63.

13 W. Gutiérrez Camacho, 'Paciente o consumidor: el contrato de servicio médico y la responsabilidad del médico', Diálogo con la Jurisprudencia, 22 (2000), p. 67.

The above suggests that ordinary negligence, as governed by article 1329[14] of the PCC and defined by article 1320[15] thereof, is to be presumed in professional services or technical issues of no special difficulty. It can be deduced from the foregoing that, when dealing with a breach [of contract], article 1762 (as well as article 2236 of the Italian code) regulates a special treatment that partially derogates the ordinary rules of contractual liability, and the obligor is given a burden of proof whose weight mirrors the negligent professional rendering of the service[16].

The scope of article 1762 should not be understood as reduced or circumscribed only to professional service agreements, as such an interpretation would clearly clash with the system designed by the PCC. Indeed, article 1756 (contained in Book VII, Sources of Obligations; Part IX, Rendering of Services; Chapter One, General Rules) establishes:

> The forms of nominate service rendering are:
> a) The provision of services
> b) The manufacturing agreement
> c) The agency contract
> d) Bailment
> e) Sequestration

Even though article 2236 of the ICC is systematically placed within the intellectual services contract (article 2230) as a sub-type of a manufacturing contract, article 1762 of the PCC is found within the general rules, and thus applicable, for instance, to the manufacturing contact. In fact, the decision (dated 4.15.2013) rendered in arbitration proceedings before processed at the Camara de Comercio de Lima, held (page 185) as follows:

---

[14] Which prescribes that "it is presumed that failure to comply with an obligation, or the belated, partial o defective compliance thereof, is due to the obligor's slight negligence".

[15] Which reads "whoever fails to act with due diligence as expected by the nature of the obligation and as dictated by the personal, temporal and local circumstances thereof incurs slight negligence".

[16] G. Musolino, 'Contratto d'opera professionale', in F. Busnelli (ed.), *Il Codice Civile. Commentario* (Milano: Giuffrè Francis Lefebvre, 2020), p. 562.

> There is no doubt that the contract between X and Y leading to this arbitration meets the requirements established in article 1762 of the Civil Code: on the one hand it is a *construction contract for a plant*, which is a kind of service rendering (article 1756); on the other, it is clear that [the contract] involves specially complex technical aspects that go beyond average professional or technical preparation[17]

(emphasis added).

Even though this legislative model was originally created only considering freelance professions, its scope (not only because of its location in the PCC, but also because service rendering has undeniably evolved) reaches those professions of special complexity going beyond the average expertise expected in every case.

Therefore, the party providing the service can be either a person or an entity. In the latter case, when it comes to "highly difficult professional issues or technical problems", article 1762 should be interpreted in light of article 1325, as the entity will use a "third party" (an employee) to render the service and will be objectively liable as the obligor to a contract for its employees' actions (while acting on its behalf). As a result, it must be understood that the party rendering the service will be objectively liable when gross negligence can be invoked on the entity's employees if they do not use the right caution or when it is obvious they do not have or apply the knowledge that every expert in such a field should have[18]. When providing a technical service, it is important to keep in mind an aspect of negligence that can be defined as incompetence, which is assessed using the rules of a specific field; while, in order to assess the degree of diligence (attention, care, zeal and goodwill) and good judgement, only the ordinary standards are used[19].

Article 1319 defines gross negligence as inexcusable negligence (a concept matching grave negligence), and it is

---

17 No more information can be provided due to the confidentiality duty imposed by article 43 of the Camara de Comercio de Lima's arbitration rules.
18 G. Musolino, p. 582.
19 G. Musolino, p. 582.

rightly stated that "negligence is 'the legal assessment' of diligence"[20]. Therefore, gravity does not refer to the normative aspect of negligence; rather, it concerns its very essence, as assessed case-by-case by the judge (or arbiter), concurrently with other subjective actions, under the umbrella of diligence[21]. Thus, the judge (or arbiter) can assess negligence as greater or lesser in relation to the circumstances surrounding the subject's actions[22]. On the other hand, the idea of intent matches "the doer's willingness to cause harm"[23] as described in article 1318 apropos of nonperformance [of an obligation].

A typical case of gross negligence occurs when a doctor amputates the wrong leg, or when a contractor does not use steel when building a high structure, thus making it vulnerable. On the other hand, defective equipment or components requiring repair or replacement would probably qualify as slight negligence, as such problems can occur in the course of a construction even when reasonable precautions have been taken.

Limiting liability to gross negligence does not grant unreasonable immunity as it does not mean that the minimum competence expected automatically calls for only minimal diligence and good judgement. The first allows for indulgence during the assessment of a service rendering, but the assessment of the remaining two should be carried out on formally severe criteria. Gross negligence also includes experimental temerity and all instances of recklessness reflecting superficiality and disregard for the primary goods that the service provider is entrusted with. We can finally conclude that through the limitation of this special kind of liability to the *culpa lata*, yields, on the one hand, more certainty in the assessment; and on the

---

20 C. Maiorca, 'Colpa civile (teoría generale)', in *Enciclopedia del Diritto* (Milano: Giuffrè, 1960), vol. VII, p. 577.
21 C. Maiorca, p. 581.
22 C. Maiorca, p. 581.
23 R. Scognamiglio, 'Responsabilità Civile', in *Novissimo Digesto Italiano* (Torino: UTET, 1968), vol. XV, p. 640. Intent is also defined as "the doer's plan and willingness to harm though his own behaviour". C. Salvi, 'Responsabilità extracontrattuale (diritto vigente)', in *Enciclopedia del Diritto*, (Milano: Giuffrè, 1988), vol. XXXIX p. 1223.

other, a more uniform assessment as gross negligence is easier to identify[24].

We can therefore state that article 1762 of the PCC is not a mere copy of article 2236 of the ICC — the former has widened the latter's scope and allows for new interpretive horizons undoubtedly enriched by case law and Peruvian and Italian scholarship.

5. *Personal damage*

The members of the Commission for the Revision of the 1984 code (more out of distraction than conviction) "bought into" the Italian jurisprudential experience (starting in the 70s) of having to create a term different from moral damage to free themselves from the interpretive straight jacket imposed by article 2059 of the ICC. Likewise, as scholarship accurately states, biological damage became a sort of "blanket clause" for personal damage[25]. If civil liability has indeed become a first-rank institution and maybe unbearably affirming of new rights among individuals, damage to health represents the most advanced protection of the person. It follows that any physical injury, no matter the extent, immediately calls for monetary compensation. Thus, the expresion "biological damage" or "damage to health" seems to have taken on the role of a jurisprudential blanket clause, the resource that bridges the gap towards compensatory legal relevance[26].

Although the Italian Constitutional Court has already overcome this impasse, it maintains the distinction between personal damage (also known as biological damage or damage to health) and moral damage.

Along these lines, article 1984 of the PCC first states that:

---

24 G. Musolino, p. 583.
25 C. Castronovo, *Danno biologico. Un itinerario di diritto giurisprudenziale* (Milano: Giuffrè, 1998), p. 151.
26 C. Castronovo, pp. 151–52.

Moral damage is compensated for keeping in mind its magnitude and the damage sustained by the victim and his/her family.

Article 1985 then states:

> The compensation addresses the consequences arising from the action or failure to act that causes the damage, including lost profit, personal damage and moral damage, there needing to be a cause-and-effect relationship between the [failure to] act and the damage sustained. The amount of the compensation incurs interest as of the date of the damage.

There is no unified opinion among Peruvian scholars on the meaning of the terms "personal damage" and "moral damage". Some say they are the same, others say they are different. It is stated that, "moral damage is non-monetary damage and it is inflicted upon personality rights or values that fit better in the realm of affectivity than in the economic reality"[27]. Other scholars notice a difference, stating that, "on this issue we can clearly see that scholarship and general jurisprudence have traditionally considered moral damage as 'pain, a feeling of sadness, suffering, emotional distress'"[28]. In conclusion, even though moral damage and personal damage are identical in their non-monetary content, they differ in scope. However, in the field of civil liability, they usually overlap.

The way our civil code was put together allows for subjective or non-monetary damage (not affecting the subject's property) to include personal damage, understood as a wrong to the

---

27 F. Osterling Parodi with the collaboration of C. Cárdenas Quirós, in *Exposición de Motivos y Comentarios al Libro VI del Código Civil (Las Obligaciones)* (Lima: Okura Editores, Commission in charge of the Study and Revision of the Civil Code, edited by D. Revoredo de Debakey, 1985), p. 449. Likewise, some subscribe to "the tendency to consider moral damage opposite to monetary damage (and somehow related to morality); that is, understanding it [moral damage] in its broadest conceptual dimension, which encompasses the traditional *pretium doloris* and all the non-monetary possibilities a person has to have a fulfilling life and achieve his projects". R. Jiménez Vargas-Machuca, 'Los daños inmateriales: una aproximación a su problemática', Themis, 50 (2005), 273–82 (p. 277).

28 C. Fernández Sessarego, 'El daño a la persona en el Código Civil de 1984', p. 213.

existential and non-monetary rights of all subjects of law (be they individuals or entities), and moral damage defined as the "ephimeral and temporary"[29] anxiety, distress, physical or mental suffering sustained by the victim. Given this definition, entities would not be able to justifiably sue for moral damages.

Concerning "personal damage" it has been said that:

> [I]t would be more appropriate to call the damage sustained by a person "subjective damage" instead of "personal damage" as the latter seems too narrow to encompass all posible situations. Subjective damage would be complemented by non-subjective damage, thus placing the subject of law at the very core of the difference between both kinds of damage. The foregoing would also help us distance ourselves from the monetary and non-monetary damage definition, whose focus is the property of the subject of law.[30]

In fact, part of Peruvian scholarship has long discussed and questioned the introduction of the term "personal damage". The Explanatory Memorandum [to the PCC] states that it is difficult to understand why article 1985 uses "personal damage"[31], deems it "unnecessary"[32], and believes its inclusion was "relevant"[33] to reflect the humanistic ideology of the civil code. However, I would like to point out as "common ground" between this stance

---

29 As stated by the Italian Constitutional Court in its ruling of 07.14.86 No. 184, in *Giurisprudenza di Diritto Privato*, noted by G. Alpa (Torino: Giappichelli, 1991), vol. I, p. 5.
30 C. Cárdenas Quirós, 'Apuntes sobre el denominado Daño a la Persona', Aequitas, Revista de Derecho y Ciencia Política, 1 (1989), p. 78.
31 J. León Barandiarán, 'Exposición de Motivos y Comentarios. Responsabilidad Extracontractual', in *Código Civil*, VI, *Exposición de Motivos y Comentarios* (Lima: Okura Editores, Commission in charge of the Study and Revision of the Civil Code, edited by D. Revoredo de Debakey, 1985), p. 807.
32 F. de Trazegnies Granda, *La responsabilidad extracontractual* (Lima: Fondo Editorial de la PUCP, 1988), p. 107, who states that "personal damage is not a sub-type of moral damage". Likewise, L. León Hilario, *La Responsabilidad Civil. Líneas fundamentales y nuevas perspectivas* (Lima: Normas Legales, 2004), p. 290.
33 J. Pazos Hayashida, 'Indemnización del daño moral, Comentario al art. 1322 C.C.', in *Código Civil Comentado* (Lima: Gaceta Jurídica, 2004), vol. VI, p. 926.

and that accepting a difference between moral and personal damage that all the civil codes following in the footsteps of the French legal model use "moral damage" and understand it to mean non-monetary damage. Therefore, (almost) all of us can agree that there is a damage outside the monetary sphere that should be conpensated. The discussion does not focus on the object of the protection but on the *nomen juris* to be used. Respected peruvian scholars have firmly stated that personal damage should be undestood as meant by its Italian roots[34].

It is important to point out, though, that there is an article (art. 1322) in the chapter dealing with the non-compliance with obligations that reads: "Upon its infliction, moral damage leads to compensation".

When dealing with civil liability for non-compliance with obligations, the PCC adopts a broader concept of moral damage, whereas said concept is "restricted"[35] in the law of torts. As we can clearly see, this article only recognizes moral damage and not personal damage. Nevertheless, this apparent contradiction can be sorted out by *a simili* and systematically interpreting articles 1322 and 1985. In addition, stating that personal damage is only possible in torts but not in contractual liability cases obvioulsy violates the principle of equality among victims [those sustaining a damage], which principle has been safeguarded (as a right) in article 2.2 of Peru's 1993 Constitution.

Can we just eliminate the term "personal damage" and subsume it in "moral damage"? The answer is necessarily "yes", but there are at least two reasons for which the conceptual difference should be maintained.

a. The term "personal damage" is not only regulated in article 1985 of the PCC. It could also be found in article 32 of the [now-

---

34 G. Fernández Cruz, *Introducción a la Responsabilidad Civil. Lecciones Universitarias* (Fondo Editorial PUCP, 2019), p. 104.
35 D. Ugarte Mostajo, 'Apuntes sobre la noción de "daño moral". A propósito del caso Asociación de afectados españoles por el Costa Concordia 2012 c. Costa Crociere S.P.A.', Actualidad Civil, 32 (2017), p. 58.

defunct] Consumer Protection Law, in the section dealing with civil liability arising from defective products (next to moral damage), and it is now found in article 103 of the Consumer Protection and Defense Code, (apropos of compensationable damages). It can also be found in artcicle 345-A of the new PCC, which refers to "personal damage" in its second paragraph; and in legistative decree 1029, which modified article 238 of the General Administrative Procedure Law, which recognized personal damage (along moral damage) in order to indemnify those sustaining damages whose provenance is public administration or services it provides.

b. I do not find it accurate to say that the term "personal damage" is unknown to jurisprudence. My research on the matter has, sadly, shown that lawyers sue for and courts grant compensation for all kinds of reasons, and the same could be said about "moral damage". Also, I have been able to establish that the same opinions found in local scholarship can be found in the limited jurisprudence that itemizes non-monetary damages.

On 03.18.11, the Peruvian Supreme Court issued the *Tercer Pleno Casatorio Civil* (apropos of article 400 of the Civil Prodecure Code) pointedly calling it court precedent, where the court establishes that "moral damage can be compensated and is included in personal damage". It is stated that:

> It is worth pointing out that personal damage should include moral damage. The latter is the tribulations, distress, affliction and psychological suffering, and depressive states of a person. In the case unde review, it is the most affected spouse who basically experiences the above, but the other spouse can also experience them at a lesser degree.

Well, the fact that moral damage is included in personal damage does not mean that the damages should not be customized. Whoever is seeking damages must provide evidence of the facts leading to personal damage (for example, loss of reputation) and of those leading to moral damage (pain, suffering, sadness, affliction) and the damaging consequences of said facts. That is why the court cited scholarship stating that psychological damage "can be diagnosed by a medical profesional".

These legislative models have resonated throughout Latin America. That is why in the Explanatory Memorandum to the Preliminary Draft of the Argentinian Civil and Commercial Code of 2012, the commission has expressed that "Latin American law has extensively quoted the PCC, which has two texts"[36]: such texts are articles 1984 and 1985.

The legal system designed by the civil code, which differentiates between "personal damage" and "moral damage", has been circulating among our legal operators for almost forty years. And whether we like it or not, it has seeped into them. Whatever the coordinates established in the PCC, reality shows that scholarship and jurisprudence admit both stances. The foregoing reveals that the name given to non-monetary damage is not a problem; the problem is that legal operators should internalize the right and effectively seek its protection. Evidence thereof includes a well-known medical malpractice case from 2010 in which doctors amputated the wrong leg of the patient. The arbitration panel awarded (dated 06.19.12) the 86-year-old victim compensation for non-monetary damages in the amount of S/ 1,100,0000 (S/100,000 for subjective moral damage and 1,000,000 for personal damage).

Scholarship has also defined personal damage as:

> [T]he harm to one's physical or mental integrity [in the course of a person's life] that is not an abstract and unifom damage experienced equally by all human beings, but a damage of varying consequences that must be assessed according to each victim's circumstances (age, gender, health conditions, etc).[37]

It has also been said that, "in this context, moral damage, excluding a human being's psychological and physical integrity, is a harm to the feelings wherever posible, which leads to

---

36 Preliminary draft of the Civil and Commercial Code of the Republic of Argentina, fundamentals, 2012, 232.
37 J. Retamozo Escobar, 'Daño a la persona y daño moral: un paso adelante...', Actualidad Civil, 11 (2015), p. 203.

pretium doloris"[38]. I will finally emphazise the fact that personal damage should be undertood as that which negatively affects the rights or the legitimate non-monetary interests of both people and entities[39].

6. *Quick note*

Going back to the gastronomic world, I find it necessary to reflect upon the fact that stating that article 1762 of the PCC is a mere copy of art 2236 of the ICC, or that "personal damage" is equivalent to the Italian "danno biologico", is like stating that "green pasta" is the same as pesto *trofiette*...

---

[38] F. Escobar, p. 203. On the contrary, following Colombian scholarship stating that, "in order to indemnify personal damage [...] it has to be put in the category of moral damage". R. Morales Hervias, 'Manifiesto contra el daño al proyecto de vida', Gaceta Civil & Procesal Civil, 80 (2020), p. 88. An opposing view responds that "it would unnecessarily curtail the true meaning and scope of personal damage and would ignore the fact that the term has been expressly adopted by the law and domestic jurisprudence". C. Calderón Puertas, 'Nuevamente sobre el daño a la persona y el daño moral. A propósito de una reciente sentencia proveniente de un juzgado penal', Gaceta Civil & Procesal Civil, 80 (2020), p. 117.

[39] For that reason, I prefer C. Fernández Sessarego's first definition, which states "personal damage, as defined by contemporary scholarship and adopted by current jurisprudence, is a wrong inflicted on a person's right, value or interest as such. [The damage] affects the person [as the wronged element] has no monetary-economical connotation". C. Fernández Sessarego, 'El daño a la persona en el Código Civil de 1984', p. 214.

Eugênio Facchini Neto[*]

THE ITALIAN CIVIL CODE OF 1942 AND ITS INFLUENCE ON BRAZILIAN CIVIL LIABILITY

1. Introduction

This chapter analyzes the possible influence of the Italian Civil Code on Brazilian civil liability, addressing both the direct legislative influence and the influence of Italian jurisprudential development.

As this is a work substantially aimed at a non-Brazilian audience, it was understood that the foreign reader may be interested in some brief information about the formation of Brazilian law in general, the influences received, and its traditions, before delving specifically into the subject of civil liability. The articles of the Italian Civil Code on civil liability were then analyzed in numerical order in an attempt to identify any influence on the Brazilian situation.

2. Sources of Brazilian civil law

Brazil was colonized by Portugal, starting in the first decades of the 16th century. During the entire colonial period until Brazil's independence on September 7, 1822, the country was governed

---

[*] PhD in Comparative Law (Florence/Italy), Master in Civil Law (USP). Full Professor of the Master's and Doctorate Courses in Law of PUC/RS (Pontifícia Universidade Católica do Rio Grande do Sul). Professor and former director of the Escola Superior da Magistratura/AJURIS. Associate Justice at the Court of Justice of the State of Rio Grande do Sul, Brazil.

by Portuguese law. After independence, a law was passed stating that the sources of Portuguese law would remain in force in the country, especially the Ordinances of the Portuguese Kingdom, until amended or revoked.

Subsequently, the imperial Constitution of 1824 reinforced the purpose of drafting a civil code, for which there were several attempts throughout the 19th century. As a preparatory step, in 1855, the imperial government commissioned Augusto Teixeira de Freitas to draft a "Consolidation of Civil Laws", aiming to organize the "sparse, contradictory, disorderly and numerous" Brazilian civil legislation. The work was published in 1857, consolidating all the private legislation in 1333 articles, preceded by a monumental introduction and enriched by detailed notes. The work had great persuasive authority, albeit no legal value.

Between 1860 and 1865, the same Teixeira de Freitas published parts of an 'Esboço de Código Civil' (*Civil Code Draft*) which, despite having a total of 4908 articles, was incomplete. Over the next three decades, different jurists were hired to write the preliminary draft of the new code — Nabuco de Araújo, in 1872, Joaquim Felício dos Santos, in 1881, and Coelho Rodrigues, in 1890 — but none succeeded.

In April 1899, Clóvis Beviláqua, a professor at the Recife Law School, was hired to draw up a new draft, which was presented in October of the same year. After a long debate in Congress, the new Civil Code was promulgated on January 1, 1916, and came into force a year later. The code was inspired by the structure of the German BGB, although it had also been influenced, in many institutes, by French doctrine and jurisprudence from the second half of the 19th century[1].

---

[1] According to Pontes de Miranda, however, the Italian Civil Code of 1865 had an important influence on the content of some rules of the Beviláqua Code. According to the author, "of the Codes, the one that quantitatively contributed the most was the Civil Code, 172 [...]. Then came the Portuguese, 83; the Italian, 72; the German Projects, 66; the Privatrechtliches Gesetzbuch für den Kanton Zürich, 67; the Spanish, 32; the Swiss Law of 1881, 31; the Austrian BGH, 7". F. Cavalcanti Pontes de Miranda, *Fontes e evolução do direito civil brasileiro*, 2nd edn (Rio de Janeiro: Ed. Forense, 1981), p. 93.

In September 1942 the "Law of Introduction to the Brazilian Civil Code" came into force, inspired by the provisions on laws in general, contained in the Italian Civil Code, published six months earlier.

When the First Republic (1889–1930) came to an end, with the subsequent deflagration of the so-called "Estado Novo", a movement began aiming to reform the civil code. In 1941, Orozimbo Nonato, Hahnemann Guimarães and Philadelpo Azevedo elaborated a "First Project of Code of Obligations", where they proposed the unification of the civil and commercial law of obligations[2], inspired by what had occurred in Switzerland and Poland. The project, however, did not succeed.

Other attempts at recodification occurred in 1963, when Orlando Gomes presented a Draft of the Civil Code and Caio Mário da Silva Pereira presented a Draft of the Code of Obligations[3]. The projects did not succeed either.

In 1969, the ruling military junta appointed a "Revising and Elaborating Commission" for the Civil Code, chaired by Professor Miguel Reale. Created to review the preliminary draft of Orlando Gomes, the Commission, in fact, elaborated a new code. After receiving criticism and suggestions from the jurists, the draft was revised and presented to the national Congress in 1975, and finally promulgated in 2002, entering into force in January 2003.

---

2   In fact, Teixeira de Freitas, in his 'Esboço do Código Civil', had already proposed the unification of private law. An analysis of his precocious intuition can be found in O. de Carvalho, 'Teixeira de Freitas and the unification of private law', in S. Schipani, (ed.), *Augusto Teixeira de Freitas e il diritto latino-americano. Atti del Congresso Internazionale del centenario di Augusto Teixeira de Freitas. Collana di Studi Giuridici Latinoamericani* (Padova: CEDAM, 1988), pp. 101–53.

3   On the history of efforts of brazilian recodification, see R. de Figueiredo Marcos, C. Fernando Mathias and I. Noronha, *História do Direito Brasileiro* (Rio de Janeiro: Forense, 2014), pp. 571 ff.

3. Characteristics of the Brazilian Civil Code of 2002

From a structural point of view, the Reale Code remains faithful to the Germanic tradition, divided into a General Part and a Special Part. The General Part is comprised of three Books: "On Persons", "On Assets" and "On Juridical Acts". The Special Part has five books: "Law of Obligations", "Business Law", "Law of Things", "Family Law", and "Law of Succession". At the end, there is a "supplementary book", intended for the transitional provisions.

The new code greatly reflected the projects of Orland Gomes and Caio Mario. It also incorporated suggestions made in the doctrine, as well as solutions offered by the case law. During its passage through Congress, the project underwent changes inspired by the legislation that came after the Bill, especially the Federal Constitution. According to Miguel Reale, the Code was inspired by the values of *ethics*, *sociality* and *operability*[4]. Its openness to change is revealed by the increase in the number of general clauses. A discipline of the rights of personality was adopted (arts. 11 to 21) and the law of obligations was unified.

Some influences of the Italian Code can be detected on Brazilian law, such as art. 13 of the Brazilian C.C. ("Except for medical requirements, it is forbidden to dispose of one's own body when it causes a permanent impairment of physical integrity or is contrary to good morals"), which was inspired by art. 5 of the Italian C.C. ("The acts of body disposal are forbidden when they cause a permanent impairment of physical integrity or are otherwise contrary to law, public order or good morals")[5].

---

4   M. Reale called them "fundamental principles" in *História do Novo Código Civil* (São Paulo: Ed. Revista dos Tribunais, 2005), pp. 37–42, and called them "fundamental directives" in *O Projeto de Código Civil – Situação atual e seus problemas fundamentais* (São Paulo: Ed. Saraiva, 1986), pp. 3–13, where he adds the "systematic guideline".

5   On the Portuguese (mainly) and Italian (occasionally) influences on the configuration of the protection of personality rights by the Brazilian Civil Code, see P. Mota Pinto, 'Direito de personalidade no Código Civil português e no novo Código Civil brasileiro', in A. Calderale (ed.), *Il nuovo codice civile brasiliano* (Milan: Giuffrè, 2003), pp. 17–61.

Diego Corapi[6] points to the influence of the *Codice* in the Brazilian option for the unification of the law of obligations (although without also covering labor law, as occurred in the Italian Code), emphasizing that articles 966 and 1142 of the Brazilian Code, when defining the entrepreneur and the establishment, respectively, correspond almost entirely to what is stated in articles 2082 (*imprenditore*) and 2555 (*azienda*) of the Italian Code.

We will now examine in greater detail the main characteristics of civil liability in the current Civil Code.

4. Features of civil liability in the Brazilian Civil Code of 2002

The main function of civil liability is to transfer the damage suffered by one party to another party. To do so, it is necessary to identify which damages should be transferred and which should remain with the party that suffered them, as well as to indicate the criteria that should govern the choice of such damages and define to whom they can be imputed. In almost all countries, all these tasks essentially fall to doctrine and jurisprudence, given the laconicity of the legislative texts on this subject[7]. It has not been any different in Brazil.

Civil liability, as systematized in the Civil Code of 2002, presents important characteristics, some of which are highlighted below[8].

a) It maintained fault[9] as an important foundation of civil liability, as can be seen in the general clause of the new art. 186;

---

6   D. Corapi, 'L'unificazione del codice di commercio e del codice civile in Brasile', in A. Calderale (ed.), *Il nuovo codice civile brasiliano* (Milan: Giuffrè, 2003), p. 8.

7   P.G. Monateri, *Trattato di Diritto Civile. Le Fonti delle Obbligazioni*, Vol. III: La Responsabilità Civile (Turin: UTET, 1998), p. 16.

8   E. Facchini Neto, 'Da Responsabilidade Civil no Novo Código', in I. Wolfgang Sarlet (ed.), *O Novo Código Civil e a Constituição*, Vol. I, 2nd edn (Porto Alegre: Livraria do Advogado, 2006), pp. 171–234.

9   However, in contrast to the "psychological" fault of earlier times, a more objective conception of fault is now adopted ("objective fault", sometimes

b) At the same time, however, it has strengthened the tendency to increase no-fault liability — already announced by special legislation and reflected in the jurisprudence, although often camouflaged with the label of presumption of fault. On one hand, it innovated materially by establishing new cases of liability without fault. At other times, the innovations were merely formal, transforming certain jurisprudential developments into legal provisions. Even more relevant was the creation of three general clauses of strict liability, such as abuse of right[10], the strict liability for created risk[11], and products liability[12].

Besides these general clauses, the new code created or established new specific rules of strict liability, as is the case of the direct responsibility of the incapacitated (art. 928), though subsidiary and by equity, the vicarious liability (art. 932[13] c/c art. 933[14]), responsibility for damages caused by animals (art.

---

referred to as normative fault or fault against legality). This tendency towards objective (and not purely psychological) fault is universal, according to M. Bessone, 'Tipicità e atipicità dell'illecito, colpa e responsabilità oggettiva come formule di politica del diritto', in F. Macioce (ed.), *La responsabilità civile nei sistemi di Common Law*, Vol. I: Profili generali (Padova: CEDAM, 1989), p. 214.

10   Art. 187. The holder of a right that, in exercising it, manifestly exceeds the limits imposed by its economic or social purpose, good faith or good customs, also commits an illicit act.

11   Art. 927, sole paragraph: There will be an obligation to repair the damage, independently of fault, in the cases specified by law, or when the activity normally developed by the author of the damage implies, by its nature, risk to the rights of others.

12   Art. 931. Except in other cases provided by special law, individual entrepreneurs and companies are liable independently of fault for damages caused by products put into circulation.

13   Art. 932. The following are also liable for civil reparation I – parents, for minor children who are under their authority and in their company; II – the guardian and the curator, for the orphans and wards, who are in the same conditions; III – the employer or principal, for their employees, servants and agents, in the exercise of their work, or because of it; IV – the owners of hotels, inns, houses or establishments where lodging is provided for money, even for educational purposes, for their guests, residents and pupils; V – those who have freely shared in the proceeds of the crime, up to the same amount.

14   Art. 933. The individuals listed in items I to V of the previous article, even if they are not at fault, will be held responsible for the acts carried out by the

936[15]). Other hypotheses of strict liability were also maintained (arts. 929[16], 937[17], and 938[18], for example). As a result, the more attentive doctrine began to submit that there is no longer one foundation — fault or risk — that prevails over the other: what exists is a "dualistic model" that adopts "diverse technical processes aimed at repairing the damages suffered"[19], with fault being "only one of the possible criteria for imputation of responsibility"[20].

c) The new civil code maintained the atypicality of extra-contractual civil liability found in the Latin tradition, moving away from the Germanic model of semi-typicality but without perfectly aligning itself with the pure French model of atypicality. In fact, the former enshrines three small general clauses that specify the interests that, if harmed, would give rise to compensation. The French model, on the other hand, in the general clause of art. 1382 (formula rearranged to the current art. 1240 of the CC, with the 2016 reform), does not specify the protected interests, nor does it indicate requirements to trigger the duty to repair damages other than causation and guilt: *"tout*

---

third parties mentioned therein.
15 Art. 936. The owner, or keeper, of the animal will compensate the damage caused by the animal, if he does not prove guilt on the part of the victim or force majeure.
16 Art. 929. If the injured person, or the owner of the thing, in the case of clause II of art. 188, are not guilty of the danger, they will have the right to compensation for the damages they have suffered.
17 Art. 937. The owner of a building or construction is responsible for the damages resulting from its ruin, if the ruin was caused by a lack of repairs whose necessity was manifest.
18 Art. 938. Whoever inhabits a building, or a part thereof, is responsible for the damage resulting from things that fall from it or are thrown in an improper place.
19 G. Tepedino, A. de Miranda Valverde Terra and G. Sampaio da Cruz Guedes, *Fundamentos do Direito Civil*, Vol. IV: Responsabilidade Civil (Rio de Janeiro: Forense, 2020), p. 7.
20 A. Schreiber, *Novos Paradigmas da Responsabilidade Civil. Da Erosão dos Filtros da Reparação à Diluição dos Danos* (São Paulo: Ed. Atlas, 2007), p. 46.

fait quelconque de l'homme, qui cause à autrui un dommage, oblige celui par la faute duquel il est arrivé, à le réparer"[21].

The line followed by the C.C. of 2002 ("Art. 186. Whoever, by voluntary action or omission, negligence or imprudence, violates a right and causes damage to another, even if exclusively moral, commits an illicit act") seems to follow the path adopted by the Portuguese Civil Code, in the first part of its art. 483(1). Both formulas distance themselves from the Germanic model, but at the same time they move away from the French normative model, by requiring the unlawfulness of the conduct. However, the Brazilian model is more flexible, since the general clauses of the civil law diploma allow the judiciary to "promote the extended construction of the right to damages"[22, 23].

d) As with all human endeavor, it is possible to glimpse deficiencies in the new Brazilian civil liability system. However, in comparative judgment it can be said that the new code is among the most advanced models. The technique of general clauses will allow great jurisprudential developments, correcting eventual

---

21 Although it is known that the issue is much more complex than the simplicity of the legal enunciation might indicate. This is because the notion of fault, in the mentioned legal provision, also encompasses the notion of unlawfulness. And then other requirements must be present for the duty to repair to arise. On this mismatch between normative simplicity and operational complexity in French law, see the classic work of P.G. Monateri, *La sineddoche. Formule e regole nel diritto delle obbligazioni e dei contratti* (Milan: Giuffrè, 1984).

22 J. Martins-Costa and G.L. Carlos Branco, *Diretrizes Teóricas do Novo Código Civil Brasileiro* (São Paulo: Ed. Saraiva, 2002), p. 129. The acceptance of general clauses of strict liability encounters some resistance, as is the case of Ponzanelli, who understands that it should be up to the legislator, not the judge, to define the cases of no-fault liability. G. Ponzanelli, 'Regole di responsabilità oggettiva e rimedi disponibili a favore del soggetto danneggiato', in L. Vacca (ed.), *La responsabilità civile da atto illecito nella prospettiva storico-comparatistica* (Turin: Giappichelli, 1995), p. 321.

23 Sinde Monteiro refers that the Brazilian Code consecrated the compensability of moral damages without providing any type of criteria for its identification, not even emphasizing the need for a minimum of objective gravity of the damage, as required in the Portuguese Code (art. 496, no. 1). J. Sinde Monteiro, 'Responsabilidade civil: o novo Código Civil do Brasil face ao direito português, às reformas recentes e às actuais discussões de reforma na Europa', in A. Calderale (ed.), *Il nuovo codice civile brasiliano* (Milan: Giuffrè, 2003), p. 314.

insufficiencies present in the legislative work. Even because, as pointed out by Prof. Miguel Reale, "the hermeneutic structure is a natural complement to the normative structure", which is why "the Code arises with the idea of leaving something to the doctrine and the jurisprudence, which will come to give a living content to the rules"[24].

We now analyze the main characteristics of civil liability in the Italian Civil Code of 1942, mentioning some of its influences on Brazilian law.

5. Characteristics of civil liability in the Italian Civil Code of 1942

Italian tort law was halfway between the French model (atypical, for property damage) and the German model (typical, for non-property damage)[25]. According to Trimarchi, the wording of art. 2043 broadens the list of unlawful acts, adding that "in a system of this nature, the interpreter has the task of specifying the concept of 'wrongful damage' in order to determine the concrete figures of unlawful acts"[26].

For a more didactic understanding, this topic will be divided according to the normative provisions contained in the Civil Code regarding liability (arts. 2043 to 2059).

5.1. The general opening clause of art. 2043 of the Civil Code

Di Majo recalled that the *Codice*'s Explanatory Memorandum (*Relazione*, no. 797) states that the expression *danno ingiusto* was included in art. 2043[27] to give greater precision in relation to

---

24 M. Reale, *O Projeto de Código Civil. Situação atual e seus problemas fundamentais* (São Paulo: Saraiva, 1986), pp. 12 and 9, respectively.
25 A.P. Mirabelli di Lauro and M. Feola, *La Responsabilità Civile – Contratto e Torto* (Turin: Giappichelli, 2014), p. 108.
26 P. Trimarchi, *Istituzioni di Diritto Privato*, 11th edn (Milan: Giuffrè, 1996), p. 126.
27 Article 2043 (Compensation for wrongful act). Any intentional or negligent act, which causes unjust damage to others, obliges the one who committed

the previous model, departing from the broad generality of the French regime, in order to clarify that fault and wrongfulness are distinct concepts, and that therefore, in addition to the conduct being intentional or negligent, it would be necessary that there be injury to the legal sphere of others[28].

Initially, the expression *danno ingiusto* (unjust damage) was interpreted as referring to an absolute subjective right, or entitlement[29]. Later, however, it was expanded to also include relative subjective rights (paradigmatic, in this regard, was the judgment of the "Meroni case" — Cass., January 26, 1971, no. 174) and to legally protected interests distinct from entitlements (with the famous Cass. decision no. 500, *Sezioni Unite*, July 22, 1999[30]), especially in light of constitutional principles.

---

the act to compensate for the damage.

28 A. Di Majo, *La tutela civile dei diritti,* Vol. III; Problemi e metodo del diritto civile, 3rd edn rev (Milan: Giuffrè, 2001), p. 176.

29 G. Alpa explains that the limitation of the indemnity of damages only to absolute subjective rights reflected the values dear to the bourgeois society of the 19th century, especially property, also avoiding a worrying expansion of the indemnifiable damages, to the detriment of nascent companies. G. Alpa, 'Tradition Revisited: Tort', in G. Alpa, *What is Private Law?*, trans by A. Lordi (Pisa: Pacini, 2022), p. 87.

30 The case involved the liability of the public administration for an unlawful act that had damaged a legally relevant interest, without the characteristics of a subjective right. The evolution of the concept of *danno ingiusto* was described. It was recalled that, at times, in the eagerness to recognize the reparability of some damages, situations that did not fit comfortably into this category were elevated to the category of "subjective right", such as the idea of "right to the integrity of the patrimony" or "right to free negotiable determination". To include legitimate interests within the scope of art. 2043, the magistrates referred to the fact that said legal provision does not constitute a *secondary rule* aimed at sanctioning a conduct prohibited by another (primary) rule, but that art. 2043 itself is a *primary rule* aimed at guaranteeing compensation for damage unjustly suffered by someone as a result of someone else's conduct. Consequently, it is affirmed that it is not possible to establish, *a priori*, which interests are worthy of protection, and that it must be considered unfair "the damage that the legal system cannot tolerate to remain the victim's responsibility, and must be transferred to the author of the fact, as long as it is harmful to a legally relevant interest." On this important decision, see F.D. Busnelli and S. Patti, *Danno e responsabilità civile*, 3rd edn (Turin: Giappichelli, 2013), pp. 283–90.

Part of the Italian doctrine states that the notion of unjust damage has also served to displace the focus of civil liability from the unlawful act that caused the damage, to the damage suffered by the victim[31]. Thus, it is said, for example, that nowadays "the problem of civil liability lies in reacting to an unjust damage and no longer to an unlawful act"[32].

The fact is that, more than any other sector, Italian civil liability law has undergone the renovating influence of the 1948 Constitution, aimed at protecting the inviolable rights of the individual and founded on the undeniable duties of political, economic and social solidarity[33]. So much so that the Constitutional Court, with decision no. 184, of July 14, 1986, interpreted the provisions of art. 2043 of the civil code in light of art. 32 of the Constitution (which consecrates a generic right to health), and affirmed that art. 2043 c.c. includes compensation not only for patrimonial damage but also all damage that constitute an obstacle to the full realization of the human person, including biological damage[34].

Although the Brazilian Civil Codes of 1916 and 2002 did not use the expression "unjust damage", and Brazilian doctrine and jurisprudence have not deepened the discussion about the

---

[31] Busnelli and Patti, *Danno e responsabilità civile*, p. 405.
[32] In those terms, M. Comporti, *Esposizione al pericolo e responsabilità civile* (Napoli: Edizioni Scientifiche Italiane, 2014), pp. 41 and 40, respectively.
[33] D. Cavicchi, 'L'ingiustizia', in P. Cendon (ed.), *Responsabilità civile*, Vol. I (Milanofiori Assago: UTET Giuridica, 2017), p. 219.
[34] It cannot be said that, eighty years after the *Codice Civile* came into force, the meaning and scope of the expression *danno ingiusto* has already been consolidated, because sometimes this topic comes back to be debated, as happened in the emblematic case *Cir vs. Fininvest* (21255/2013), judged by the Court of Cassation in 2013. The judgment resulted in the confirmation of the conviction of Berlusconi's giant holding company Fininvest to pay 500 million euros for having bribed and corrupted a magistrate of the *Corte d'Appello di Roma* to rule in favor of the company in an important case that took place in the early-90s, involving the acquisition of the publishing company Mondadori by the Fininvest group's company Mediaset. For more information, see the articles published and later inserted in C. Scognamiglio, *Ingiustizia del danno, contatto sociale, funzione del risarcimento (Saggi sulla responsabilità di diritto civile)* (Turin: Giappichelli, 2021), pp. 3–15 and 17–29.

meaning of the adjective attached to the noun damage, the fact is that this expression is frequently mentioned in both Brazilian doctrine and jurisprudence[35].

In the following articles (2044 and 2045), the code successively disciplines self-defense and the state of necessity as causes of exclusion or reduction of civil liability. Although the Brazilian Civil Code also mentions these circumstances as "licit" activities (art. 188 of the C.C.), it does not do so in a way similar to, or impacted by, Italian law, which is why this issue will not be addressed.

The same occurs with the issue of imputability, addressed by art. 2046 c.c., since Brazilian law does not recognize the distinction existing in Italian law between a natural capacity (discernment and the ability to act accordingly), dealt with in

---

[35] As an example (nine judgments from the Superior Court of Justice (STJ) were found whose summaries mention "unfair damage") the following decisions from the STJ: "SPECIAL APPEAL. CIVIL LIABILITY [...] UNJUST DAMAGE. OBJECTIVE GOOD FAITH. SOCIAL AND ECONOMIC PURPOSES. OFFENSE TO GOOD MORALS. [...]. 1 – One of the most important trends in civil liability is the displacement of the illicit fact, as the central point, to come closer and closer to repairing the unjust damage. Even if a certain act has been performed in the exercise of a recognized right, there will be unlawfulness if it was in manifest abuse, contrary to good faith, the social or economic purpose of the right [...]" (STJ, Fourth Panel, REsp no. 1.555.202/SP, Reporting Minister Luis Felipe Salomão, judged on December 13, 2016); "[...] ACTION FOR RECOVERY OF MATERIAL DAMAGE CUMULATED WITH COMPENSATION FOR MORAL DAMAGE. PAWNED JEWELRY. IMPOSSIBILITY OF RESTITUTION [...] 3. The Brazilian system of civil liability is oriented towards the reestablishment of the economic-legal equilibrium broken by the occurrence of unjust damage. (STJ, Third Panel, REsp no. 1.320.973/PB, Reporting Judge Nancy Andrighi, issued on March 18, 2014).

Even in Federal Supreme Court (Supremo Tribunal Federal) itself, the Brazilian constitutional Court, the expression "unfair damage" has also been used: "CIVIL LIABILITY. COMPENSATION. UNLAWFUL ACT [...]. BY RAISING, IN AN INADEQUATE MANNER, CIRCUMSTANCES THAT PREVENT THE APPLICABILITY OF ART. 159 OF THE CIVIL CODE, WITHOUT DEFINING THE REGULAR EXERCISE OF RIGHTS, OR OTHER EXISTING CIRCUMSTANCES OF CIVIL LIABILITY FOR UNJUST DAMAGE CAUSED TO OTHERS, THE VENERABLE APPELLATE DECISION DOES NOT DESERVE TO STAND. [...]." (STF, First Panel, RE 91860, Reporting Justice Rafael Mayer, j. on February 8, 1980).

this article, to be assessed by the judge for purposes of Aquilian responsibility, and the legal capacity, fixed in art. 2 of the *Codice* at eighteen years of age, for business purposes. In Brazilian law, the treatment of imputability is the same, both for the assessment of business responsibility and for Aquilian liability, i.e., at the age of eighteen, with few exceptions (like art. 928).

5.2. Direct liability of incapacitated persons

The first part of art. 2047[36] of the Italian Civil Code establishes that for damages caused by an incapacitated person, those responsible for his/her surveillance and supervision shall be liable, that is, normally the parents or whoever acts on their behalf. This is a formally presumed-fault liability, in view of the possibility of removing responsibility if there is proof that they were unable to avoid the damage. However, Italian jurisprudence is particularly strict in admitting such proof. This part of the legal provision substantially announces the provisions of the following article, in which the persons responsible for the incapacitated are listed.

Of interest here is the second part of art. 2047c.c.[37] which provides for the possibility of direct responsibility of the incapacitated person for the damage caused by him, subject to the conditions established therein, i.e., that the victim has not succeeded in obtaining compensation from the person responsible for the incapacity. This is a subsidiary and mitigated liability, which influenced the Portuguese Civil Code[38] and, through the latter,

---

36 Art. 2047, first part: "In the case of damage caused by a person who is incapacitated, compensation shall be payable by the person who is responsible for the supervision of the incapacitated person, unless he proves that he could not prevent the fact".
37 Art. 2047, second part: In the event that the injured party has been unable to obtain compensation from the supervisor, the court, taking into consideration the economic conditions of the parties, may order the perpetrator of the damage to pay equitable compensation.
38 Article 489 (Compensation by a non-attributable person) 1. If the act causing the damage has been committed by a non-attributable person, the latter may, on grounds of equity, be ordered to repair it, in whole or in part, provided that it is not possible to obtain due compensation from the persons responsible for

the Brazilian Civil Code[39]. In essence, the three codes provide for a direct, but subsidiary, liability of the incapacitated person, to be activated only if it is not possible to obtain reparation for the damage from the person responsible for him. And in all three models the principle of full compensation is set aside, allowing for an equitable determination of the compensation, lower than the amount of the damage suffered by the victim, taking into account the economic situation of the parties, especially if the economic conditions of the injured party are better than those of the incapacitated party. This is the only provision of the Italian Civil Code in which the economic conditions of the parties may be taken into consideration in setting the quantum of compensation[40].

In Art. 2048, the Italian Civil Code regulates the liability of parents, guardians, tutors and teachers in terms very similar to those already contained in the Code of 1865, inspired, in turn, by the French model of 1804. Since there is no influence of this discipline on Brazilian law, we will not discuss it.

5.3. *The liability of employers and principals for damages caused by their employees and agents*

Art. 2049 of the Italian Civil Code regulates the liability of employers and principals in a very laconic manner[41], stating that

---

its supervision. 2. Compensation shall, however, be calculated in such a way as not to deprive the non-attributable person of the necessary food, according to his state and condition, nor of the means indispensable to fulfill his legal duties of maintenance.

39   Art. 928. The incapacitated person is liable for the losses he causes, if the persons responsible for him do not have the obligation to do so or do not have sufficient means. Sole Paragraph. The indemnification provided for in this article, which must be equitable, will not take place if it deprives the incapacitated person or those who depend on him of what is necessary.

40   Marco Comporti, *Il Codice Civile. Commentario. Fatti illeciti: la responsabilità presunte*. Artt. 2044-2048 (Milano: Giuffrè Ed., 2012, 2nd edn), p. 202/203.
About this article, see Manuela Rinaldi, Il danno cagionato dall'incapace. In: Paolo Cendon (dir.). *Responsabilità civile*, Vol. III (Milanofiori Assago: UTET Giuridica, 2017), p. 3.926.

41   Art. 2049. (Liability of masters and principals). Masters and principals are liable for damage caused by the wrongful act of their servants and committed

they are liable for unlawful acts committed by their employees or agents in the performance of the duties assigned to them.

The wording of the final part of the provision gave doctrine and jurisprudence room to identify the need for a necessary causal connection (*nesso di occasionalità necessaria*[42]) between the duties and the damage. Once the nexus is established, the liability of employers and principals for damages caused by their employees and agents is objective and may be excluded only by proof of the fortuitous event, but not by simple proof of the absence of their fault[43].

As to the purely formal aspect, the Italian text is more restricted than the Brazilian one. This is because the former only provides for the liability of employers and principals if the harmful act has been committed in the performance of the employee's or agent's duties, whereas the Brazilian code provides for the liability of employers and principals, including for damages caused by employees or agents not only in the performance of their duties, but also "due to such duties" (art. 932, III). However, apart from the formal data, Italian jurisprudence, as mentioned, has long applied the aforementioned provision in a broad manner, so as to cover harmful conduct that is not included in the strict exercise of the employee's or agent's duties. This is the case when the employee causes damage by deviating from the activity specifically assigned to him; or when he causes damage on the occasion of spontaneous activities performed outside his working hours or during vacation periods; or when he maliciously practices damaging acts in the interest of the employer, even if such initiatives have not been authorized, or even have been forbidden; extending liability even to the case in which the damage caused by the employee has been practiced in his own interest, provided it is closely connected with the exercise

---

in the performance of the duties to which they are assigned.

42 Among so many, Cass. Civ., sec. III, June 06, 2014, no. 12828.

43 In these terms, P. Trimarchi, *La responsabilità civile: atti illeciti, rischio, danno* (Milan: Giuffrè, 2017), pp. 287–88. Between pages 306 and 323 the author analyzes extensive case law involving the application of employers' and principals' liability.

of his functions and notably facilitated by this circumstance[44]. According to Franzoni, the nexus of *occasionalità necessaria* exists when the functions performed by the employee or agent have facilitated or made possible the wrongdoing and the damaging event, even when acting beyond the limits of their powers, or even transgressing orders received[45].

Although the corresponding Brazilian provision (art. 932, III, c.c.) does not contain the expression "necessary occasionality", this concept is frequently mentioned in jurisprudence to extend the liability of employers for harmful acts committed by their employees, revealing the influence of Italian law on Brazilian theory[46] and jurisprudential practice[47].

5.4 *Liability for the exercise of dangerous activities*

Art. 2050 of the Italian Civil Code disciplines the "liability for the exercise of dangerous activities", stating that "whoever causes damage to another in the exercise of a dangerous activity, due to its nature or the nature of the means used, is obliged to repair it, if he does not prove to have taken all appropriate measures to avoid the damage".

---

44 Having cited all these precedents, Trimarchi concludes that employers' liability for the harmful acts caused by their employees requires only that they have been facilitated by the exercise of their duties. Trimarchi, *Istituzioni di Diritto Privato*, pp. 154 and 155. In the same sense, A. Torrente and P. Schlesinger, *Manuale di Diritto Privato*, 14th edn rev (Milan: Giuffrè, 1995), p. 637.
45 M. Franzoni, *Trattato della Responsabilità Civile*, Vol. I: L'illecito, 2nd edn (Milan: Giuffrè, 2010), p. 821.
46 I refer to W. Melo da Silva, *Da responsabilidade civil automobilística* (São Paulo: Saraiva, 1974), p. 203; W. de Barros Monteiro, *Curso de direito civil. Direito das obrigações* – I, 5th edn (São Paulo: Saraiva, 1975), p. 422; P. de Miranda, *Manual do Código Civil Brasileiro de Paulo de Lacerda*, Vol. XVI, 3rd Part, Vol. 1, (São Paulo: Intellectus, 1974), p. 373; A. Lima, *A responsabilidade civil pelo fato de outrem* (Rio de Janeiro: Forense, 1973), p. 236.
47 Superior Tribunal de Justiça, Third Panel, REsp 623040/MG, Reporting Justice Humberto Gomes de Barros, j. on November 16, 2006; STJ, Third Panel, REsp 1787026/RJ, Reporting Justice Paulo de Tarso V. Sanseverino, j. em October 26, 2021.

This is an important general clause of strict liability, necessary to solve problems that arose throughout the 20th century, as intrinsically dangerous instruments, devices and activities became part of peoples' lives. Many of these activities are lawful, although potentially harmful. It fell to the legislator, then, to identify the situations in which damage should be compensated, distinguishing them from those which harm should be borne by the victim.

The similar general clause of strict liability foreseen in art. 927 of the Brazilian C.C.[48] was inspired by art. 2050 of the Italian Civil Code[49], although presenting important formal differences. In the Brazilian formula, the responsibility is expressly no-fault, while the Italian formula points to a presumed fault liability[50]. However, in jurisprudential practice, they are practically equivalent, given the rigor with which Italian jurisprudence evaluates the proof that all suitable measures to avoid the damage have been adopted. Such proof is practically never considered satisfactory, which leads to a *de facto* strict liability. According to Trimarchi, proof of having adopted the measures reasonably related to a diligent conduct is not enough: proof of having adopted all the safety measures offered by technology is required, regardless of their cost — that is, there is liability for any damage that is objectively avoidable, given the current state of technology[51].

---

48 Art. 927, sole paragraph: "There will be an obligation to repair the damage, regardless of fault, in cases specified by law, or when the activity normally developed by the author of the damage implies, by its nature, risk to the rights of others".

49 Art. 2.050. Whoever causes harm to others in the performance of a dangerous activity, either by its nature or by the nature of the means employed, shall be liable for compensation unless he proves that he has taken all appropriate measures to avoid the harm.

50 It would be a kind of "recrudescence of the criterion of fault", an idea that has been superseded by "a constant jurisprudence that, when it has held the dangerousness of the activity from which the damage resulted, has always affirmed not reached the proof that the author of the dangerous activity took all measures suitable to avoid it". In these terms, C. Castronovo, *Responsabilità Civile* (Milan: Giuffrè, 2018), pp. 33 and 34.

51 Trimarchi, *Istituzioni di Diritto Privato*, pp. 157–58.

Since the enactment of the Code, the majority Brazilian doctrine has hastened to affirm that the expression "activity", contained in the sole paragraph of art. 927 of the C.C., should be interpreted as a set of acts, organized for an economic purpose, and not as an isolated act[52]. Thus, this provision would only apply, substantially, to business activities and not to isolated conducts (such as driving a vehicle, known to be an inherently dangerous conduct).

According to Trimarchi[53] and Bessone[54], this would also be the situation in Italy, since the liability for risk only performs its function if applied to the exercise of economic activities. But this position is not unanimous, for Visintini states that the rule, by using the expression "*chiunque*" (whoever), does not distinguish between business activities and that of a private individual who organizes a dangerous non-profit activity. And she states that although case law is more voluminous in relation to business activities, there are also cases involving private individuals, such as hunters[55] and those who practice some dangerous sports activities[56].

Dangerous activities are those in which statistical observation and experience indicate that they produce relevant damage to third parties. This category includes not only those activities whose harmful potential is deduced from the frequency of accidents caused, but also by the magnitude or severity of the damage caused, even if less frequent[57].

---

52 By all, S. Cavalieri Filho, *Programa de Responsabilidade civil*, 11th edn rev (São Paulo: Ed. Atlas, 2014), pp. 217–18.
53 P. Trimarchi, *Rischio e Responsabilità Oggettiva* (Milan: Giuffrè, 1961), p. 43.
54 M. Bessone, 'Problemi attuali della responsabilità civile', in F. Macioce (ed.), *La responsabilità civile nei sistemi di Common Law*, Vol. I: Profili generali (Padova: CEDAM, 1989), p. 28.
55 From whom you are even required to take out a civil liability insurance policy (Law No. 157, dated February 11, 1992).
56 G. Visintini, *Cos'è la responsabilità civile – Fondamenti della disciplina dei fatti illeciti e dell'inadempimento contrattuale*, 2nd edn (Napoli: Edizioni Scientifiche Italiane, 2014), p. 207.
57 M. Comporti, *Esposizione al pericolo e responsabilità civile* (Napoli: Edizioni Scientifiche Italiane, 2014), p. 173.

The Italian case study of the application of art. 2050 involves some clearly dangerous activities, such as the production and distribution of gas cylinders; electric power distribution; crane operation, whether in construction or in port loading and unloading operations; pharmaceutical activity; activity that generates toxic residues; pyrotechnic activity; railway transportation, among others. But the provision has also been applied to other less obvious situations, such as management: of an amusement park; of sports or recreational facilities; of a hotel with an elevator; of a bakery activity; of a "mechanical bull", among others[58].

Brazilian jurisprudence has also applied this general clause of strict liability to situations that do not fit easily into the legislative framework[59], as has occurred with Italian jurisprudence.

In art. 2051, the Italian Civil Code regulates liability for the custody of the thing (or for the fact of the thing, or fact of property) in a generic way, something that does not exist in Brazilian law. The specific cases foreseen in the Brazilian Civil Code (arts. 937 and 938) were influenced by French law, not by Italian law, which is why they will not be discussed here. The same occurs in relation to the liability for damage caused by animals, disciplined by art. 2052 of the Italian Civil Code and art. 936 of the Brazilian Civil Code, because the Brazilian provision is broader than the Italian one and was not influenced by it.

The liability for damage arising from the ruin (however partial) of a building is regulated by art. 2053 of the Italian Civil

---

58 All these cases are taken from the work of Franzoni, *Trattato della Responsabilità Civile*, pp. 416–19, which provides the data for each of the decisions.

59 STJ, Second Section, REsp NO. 1197929/PR and REsp 1199782/PR, Reporting Justice Luis Felipe Salomão, judged on August 24, 2011 (liability of banks for damages suffered by someone due to the use of forged documents by third parties, with whom they performed banking transactions); STJ, Third Panel, AgRg nos EDcl no AREsp 210505/SP, Reporting Justice Sidnei Beneti, j. on October 16, 2012 (liability of an industry for damages suffered by the structure of a house, due to shaking caused by the frequent passage of trucks in front of it); STJ, Second Panel, REsp 1869046/SP, Reporting Justice Herman Benjamin, j. on June 9, 2020 (State liability for the murder of a lawyer on the premises of the forum, caused by his client's opposing party).

Code in a manner that goes back to the provision of art. 1386 of the French Civil Code. The same occurs with Brazilian law (art. 937), which, in this aspect, has not been influenced by Italian law.

Italian law contains a specific discipline of liability for damages arising from the circulation of vehicles (art. 2054), considered a particular type of generic liability for dangerous activities. The Brazilian Civil Code, however, does not contain a particular provision, which is why this hypothesis will not be analyzed here either.

5.5 *The liability for non-pecuniary damage*

Art. 2059 c.c. states that "non-pecuniary damage must be compensated only in cases determined by law (Cod. Proc. Civ. 89; Cod. Pen. 185, 598)". It therefore moved away from French regime.

At the time of the Italian Civil Code of 1865, its art. 1151, a substantial translation of art. 1382 of the French Code, referred to "damage" as being indemnifiable, without any adjectives. Some interpreters thus argue that its scope was generic, covering any type of damage. The jurisprudence, however, was more cautious, applying art. 1151 only to patrimonial or pecuniary damage.

According to Mirabelli di Lauro and Feola[60], the legislator of 1942 departed from the French model[61] and conditioned the Aquilian protection of the human person to the existence of a crime. But this option could not survive the advent of the Republican Constitution, which had introduced a system of values based on the unconditional protection of the human

---

60 Mirabelli di Lauro and Feola, *La Responsabilità Civile – Contratto e Torto*, pp. 111 ff.
61 Whose jurisprudence, since the beginning of the 20th century, had set itself to indemnify "any damage", caused by "any fault", without requiring the objective element of fault, that is, wrongfulness. H. Mazeaud and L. Mazeaud, *Traité Théorique et Pratique de la Responsabilité Civil Délictuelle et contractuelle* (Paris: Sirey, 1931), p. 31

person (art. 2), of his or her psychophysical integrity (art. 32), and of his or her dignity.

The attack on the rigid conditions of art. 2059 began in the 1970s, with decisions by Genoan judges[62]. The interpretation was the following: since the Italian Constitution guarantees the right to health (art. 32: "The Republic protects health as a fundamental right of the individual") as one of the fundamental rights of the Italian citizen, it was understood that if someone's physical integrity were harmed, the absolute constitutional right to health itself would be injured. This would constitute an "unjust damage" under art. 2043 of the Italian Civil Code, which guarantees compensation regardless of the presence of a crime. The leading case on this new type of damage was the decision of the *Tribunale di Genova* in the case *Rocca vs. Ferrarese*, handed down on May 25, 1974[63].

Italian jurisprudence soon embraced this thesis, which was accepted by the entire judiciary, including the Court of Cassation (when it judged the case *Ferrante vs. Lisi*, in 1981) and the Constitutional Court (with the cases *Repetto vs. AMT di Genova* and *Saporito vs. Manzo,* handed down in 1986), with the support of the doctrine.

Later the protection of biological damage was moved from art. 2043 to art. 2059, which now encompasses the much broader category of fundamental human rights[64].

The notion of biological damage was gradually extended to include not only physical integrity, but also psychological integrity and disturbances of all kinds, including damage to relationships, various somatizations, aesthetic damage, damage

---

[62] Vito Monetti and Giancarlo Pellegrino, who also doctrinally spread their thought: 'Proposte per un nuovo método di liquidazione del danno alla persona', Foro it., 1974, V, c. 159 ff.
[63] *Giurisprudenza Italiana*, 1975, I, 2, 74.
[64] This understanding has been expressed in several decisions: Cass., civ., sez III, May 31, 2003, no. 8827 e 8828; Cass. Civ., sez. I, January 15, 2005, no. 729; Cass. Civ., sez. III, October 20, 2005, no. 20323; Cass. Civ., sez. III, June 14, 2007, no. 13953; Cass., civ., sez III, August 6th, 2007, no. 17180.

to the sexual sphere, etc. In other words, a diffuse and multiform conception of "health" has been adopted[65].

In 2003, the Court of Cassation (decisions nos. 8827 and 8828, decided on May 31, 2003) and the Constitutional Court (decision no. 233, decided on July 11, 2003) consolidated this jurisprudential evolution. As a consequence, the rights of personality have been valued, whose violation has come to be considered "damage to the person", converging in a disordered way in the scope of biological damage. In other words, in an attempt to offer more effective civil protection to rights of personality, and considering the narrowness of the Italian codified system, the practical solution found was to consider as biological damages also the violations of almost all rights of personality, in a dysfunctional way. These decisions were important because they also confirmed the presence of a new kind of damage, the existential damage.

5.5.1. *Existential damage*

The so-called Triestina School (of the University of Trieste) is responsible for its origin, especially Paolo Cendon, seconded by Patrizia Ziviz[66], who, analyzing the jurisprudence on biological damages, identified several cases that, strictly speaking, could not be decided under that label. In doctrinal articles written in 1993 and 1994, they coined the expression *danno esistenziale* to group certain types of damages that were neither subjective moral damages in the usual sense (characterized by transitory pain and suffering) nor biological.

In the mid-90s Italian jurisprudence began to adopt this nomenclature, abandoning the threefold classification of

---

65 Eugênio Facchini Neto, 'A tutela aquiliana da pessoa humana: os interesses protegidos. Análise de direito comparado', *THEMIS – Revista da Faculdade de Direito da Universidade Nova de Lisboa*, Year XII, no. 22/23. (Coimbra: Almedina, 2012), pp. 70/72.

66 A history of the evolution of the Italian system regarding the reparation of non-pecuniary damage is found in P. Zivis, *Il danno non patrimoniale - Evoluzione del sistema risarcitorio* (Milan: Giuffrè, 2011).

compensable damages adopted by the Constitutional Court in decision no. 184 of 1986. It was substituted by a fourfold classification, according to which, besides property damage, there would be a genus of non-pecuniary damage, which would include subjective moral damage (characterized by temporary disturbance of the victim's state of mind), biological damage (consisting of medically proven damage to the person's psychophysical integrity) and existential damage. The notion was first recognized by the Italian Court of Cassation in 2000 (Cass., June 7, 2000, no. 7713).

Some years later, the *Sezioni Unite* of the Court of Cassation, in decision no. 6572, issued on March 24, 2006, clarified that

> existential damage is understood as any damage that a wrongful conduct causes to the non-economic activities of the subject, altering his life habits and his way of living socially, seriously disturbing his daily routine and depriving him of the possibility of expressing and realizing his personality in the external world. On the other hand, the existential damage is based on the nature of the damage that is not merely emotional and internalized (typical of moral damage) but can be objectively verified through evidence of life choices that are different from those that would have been made if the harmful event had not occurred.[67]

In addition to the distinction between subjective moral damage and existential damage, biological damage is now restricted to the presence of a physical or psychological injury, or a health impairment, identified by an expert.

Once this type of damage was admitted, there was a natural expansion and abuse of its invocation, accepting a series of "*danni bagatellari*" (bagatelary damages), such as: a bride's claim for having broken the heel of her shoe during the wedding ceremony; time lost due to a delay in air travel; a woman's discomfort due to a wrong haircut; loss of the opportunity to watch a soccer match on television due to a power cut or interruption of cable TV signal.

---

[67] Free translation of the partial reproduction of the judgment, reproduced by Gregor Christandl, in his work *La Risarcibilità del Danno Esistenziale* (Milan: Giuffrè, 2007), p. 326.

Due to the abusive invocation of existential damages, the Court of Cassation, through the *Sezioni Unite*, on November 11, 2008 (decisions nos. 26972, 26973, 26974 and 26975), affirmed that such figure does not constitute an autonomous sort of damage, but a kind of non-pecuniary damage, reparable whenever it violates a fundamental right of the person.

Thus, it was affirmed that non-pecuniary damage constitutes a unitary category that cannot be subdivided into subcategories. The reference to certain types of damage (moral, biological and existential) would respond only to descriptive requirements and would not imply the recognition of distinct categories of damage.

The November 2008 decisions denied that compensable damages could be defined as mere inconvenience or discomfort: "It is not worthwhile to invoke completely unimaginable rights, such as the right to quality of life, to the state of well-being, to serenity: in short, the right to be happy" (ruling no. 26972). It was also affirmed that the duty of social solidarity towards the victim must coexist with the duty of tolerance that we all must have towards certain nuisances and disturbances that life in society imposes, assessable by the judge according to parameters provided by the social conscience at a given historical moment.

However, this decision did not put an end to the existential damages saga, since subsequent jurisprudence, including that of the Court of Cassation, continued to refer to this category[68], and it also continued to be the object of intense academic production[69].

In Brazil, the first mention of "existential damages" was made in a scholarly article published in 2005[70] and the first book was

---

68 Mirabelli di Lauro and Feola, *La Responsabilità Civile – Contratto e Torto*, pp. 282 ff., with ample jurisprudential reference.
69 Serve as an example the almost one thousand pages of the book coordinated by P. Russo (ed.), *La responsabilità civile – I danni esistenziali* (Milanofiori Assago: UTET, 2014), containing long articles related to the topic, written by about thirty diverse authors.
70 A. Alves Almeida Neto, 'Dano existencial: a tutela da dignidade da pessoa humana', Revista de Direito Privado, 24 (2005), pp. 21–53.

published in 2009[71], both inspired and influenced by the Italian experience.

The first judicial decision that made reference to existential damages was from the Court of Justice of Rio Grande do Sul (Ap. civ. 70044580918, of October 19, 2011). In the labor courts, the first decision was issued by the *Tribunal Regional do Trabalho* — TRT of the 4th Region (RO no. 0000105-14.2011.5.04.0241, from March 2012), involving excessive working hours. Since then, especially in the labor courts, the category of existential damages has been widely invoked and applied, especially in situations of excessive working hours and without regular vacation time, with drastic reduction of time to live the other dimensions of life[72].

But there is another Italian doctrinal and jurisprudential development that has influenced Brazilian civil liability: damages derived from injury to the right to identity, addressed below.

5.5.2. *Damages to the right to identity*

Sometimes called right to image-attribute (different from portrait-image), the right to personal identity consists of the right that the social projection of one's personality does not suffer distortions, even without affecting one's honor, derived from the erroneous attribution of ideas, opinions, or behavior different from those that the individual has always manifested in any aspect of his relationship life.

In Italy, this figure was already addressed in the 1950s by Adriano de Cupis (*Tutela assoluta dell'individualità personale* [1955] and *Tutela giuridica contro le alterazioni della verità personale* [1956]). In 1981, it was Antonio Gambaro's turn

---

71 F. Rampazzo Soares, *Responsabilidade civil por dano existencial* (Porto Alegre: Livraria do Advogado, 2009), a master's thesis written under my supervision.
72 So intense was the acceptance in the labor jurisprudential sphere that the labor reform carried out in 2017 expressly included the figure of existential damage in the list of damages subject to compensation (art. 223-B of the CLT – Consolidation of Labor Laws).

to speak on the subject[73], mentioning the North American experience[74]. More recently, G. Pino addressed the issue in a book[75].

The leading case began with the judgment of the Praetor of Rome, on May 6, 1974, which in 1985 reached the *Corte di Cassazione* (*Veronesi Case* – Cass. June 22, 1985, no. 3769). Subsequently, the right to personal identity was the object of some jurisprudential refinements (Cass. February 7th, 1996, no. 978; *Corte Costituzionale*, no. 297/1996).

Although Brazilian law does not contain any express legal provision on this figure, the Italian conception of the right to identity (much more than the almost ignored North American origin) has also influenced the Brazilian law on civil liability, as can be seen from published works[76] and judgments that refer to it[77].

---

73 A. Gambaro, 'Falsa luce agli occhi del pubblico', Rivista di diritto civile, 27 (1981), pp. 84–135.
74 From the legal point of view, it is customary to indicate an article by Prosser (*Privacy*), published in 1960, as being the germ of the right to identity. In this article, Prosser distinguished four kinds of privacy protection: intrusion; public disclosure of private facts; appropriation (right of publicity); *false light in the public eyes*. The notion of identity protection was linked to the latter species (later incorporated in the Restatement of the Law – Torts – Second). However, Brazilian doctrine and jurisprudence was influenced by the Italian developments of the right to identity, not by the North American matrix.
75 G. Pino, *Il diritto all'identità personale – Interpretazione costituzionale e creatività giurisprudenziale* (Bologna: Il Mulino, 2003), p. 9.
76 The first of which was the doctoral thesis of R. Cleber da Silva Choeri, *O Direito à Identidade na Perspectiva Civil-Constitucional* (Rio de Janeiro: Renovar, 2010).
77 In Brazil, there is a casuistry in this regard, although sometimes under the denomination of violation to the right to image-attribute: REsp 1630851 / SP, dated April 27, 2017, Reporting Justice Sanseverino; REsp 1393195/ MG, dated September 27, 2016, Reporting Justice Marco Buzzi; REsp 1374778/RS, dated June 18, 2015, Reporting Justice Moura Ribeiro. Marco Buzzi; REsp 1374778/RS, dated August 6th, 2015, Reporting Justice Moura Ribeiro; the earliest mention of the "right to identity" in the STJ occurred on September 9th, 2002, in the judgment of REsp 358598/PR, Reporting Justice Barros Monteiro. In state courts, the following case may be cited: "CIVIL APPEAL. CIVIL LIABILITY. ACTION FOR DAMAGES [...]. DAMAGE TO THE IMAGE. SPECIES OF DAMAGE THAT DOES NOT APPLY TO

6. Final considerations

In concluding this analysis, it is clear that civil liability in the Brazilian legal system has been influenced by Italian law, whether inspired directly by the text of the 1942 Civil Code or through the jurisprudence of the last eighty years.

Direct textual influence is evident by the similarities between Italian art. 2050 and Brazilian art. 927, sole paragraph, albeit mediated by the Portuguese experience. Another repercussion resided in the reverberation of the discussions on what constitutes unjust damage, although the Brazilian code does not use such an expression. But perhaps the greatest repercussion is attributable to the doctrine and case law involving the saga of existential damages, given the enormous invocation of this institute in the Brazilian forensic sphere, especially in the labor courts.

THE CASE AT HAND [...]. The right to image-attribute, also called right to personal identity, is the right that a person has to be identified within his social relations by his own personal characteristics and exactness. It covers, consequently, the right to oppose that his image is distorted, attributing to him characteristics that are not his [...]" (Civil Appeal, No. 70069378206, 9th C.C., Court of Justice of RS, judged on August 24, 2016).

Sergio García Long[*]

FORCE MAJEURE IN LATIN AMERICA AND THE CARIBBEAN
A Legal Cartography for Improvements in National Laws

1. *Introduction*

This essay is intended to serve as a report on *force majeure* in Latin America and the Caribbean according to Civil Codes, as well as a Peruvian national report on *force majeure*. These two reports are interesting because the first one shows the French influence in Latin American and the Caribbean while the second shows the French-Italian influence in Peru regarding *force majeure*. With these reports, English translations of national legal provisions on *force majeure* are provided, which will be useful for the English-speaking community.

Also, *force majeure* models in Latin America and the Caribbean can be compared with international law instruments and *force majeure* clauses in international contracting. The new Civil Code of the People's Republic of China, which contains a modern and updated regulation compared to other national models, is also taken as a reference.

The above review will show that national laws in Latin America and the Caribbean are outdated with respect to the usages of *force majeure* in contracting. In view of this, international instruments and *force majeure* clauses may be used as guides

---

[*] Pontifical Catholic University of Peru (J.D. *summa cum laude*). Lecturer in Private and Corporate law at Pontifical Catholic University of Peru. LLM International Business and Commercial Law at the University of Manchester (ongoing). Member of the Civil Law Advisory Council of the Lima Bar Association. Expert in contracts, corporation, finance and arbitration. Email: sergio.garcial@pucp.edu.pe.

to complement the application of domestic law and for a future legislative reform. In general, the possibility to freely derogate national laws is the best solution for improvements without the need for legal reform.

2. *International law as supplement of domestic laws*

International law instruments are the result of various initiatives aimed at achieving consensus across nations. While it is true that each jurisdiction will have its own law by virtue of its own culture, when it comes to cross-border transactions such nationalism can generate inconveniences. In order to reduce transaction costs and facilitate the performance of international contracts, organizations such as UNCITRAL[1] or UNIDROIT[2] have developed international law instruments (hard and soft law) that, taking into account national differences, propose a coherent body of rules that would allow a French and German, or a Dutch and English lawyer, to reach an agreement regardless of differences in domestic law or legal families.

To achieve uniformity, international instruments regulate how their text is to be interpreted. The CISG[3] is taken as a starting point, not only because it dates back to 1980 and is one of the most successful international initiatives, having been ratified to date by 94 states of different legal traditions, but also because it is the predecessor of other important instruments.

Article 7(1) CISG governs the autonomous interpretation of the Convention's provisions, and states that when interpreting its text (i) regard is to be had to its international character, (ii) the need to promote uniformity in its application, and (iii) the observance of good faith in international trade[4]. This provision

---

1   United Nations Commission on International Trade Law.
2   International Institute for the Unification of Private Law.
3   United Nations Convention on Contracts for the International Sale of Goods.
4   See F. Ferrari, 'Uniform Interpretation of the 1980 Uniform Sales Law', Georgia Journal of International and Comparative Law, 24 (1994), pp. 183–228; A.S. Komarov, 'Internationality, uniformity and observance of good

has been replicated in other instruments, such as article 1.6(1) PICC[5], article 1:106(1) PECL[6], Preamble of the OHADAC Principles[7], article I.1.7 TransLex Principles[8], and article 4 PLACL[9].

> Article 7
> (1) In the interpretation of this Convention, regard is to be had to its international character and to the need to promote uniformity in its application and the observance of good faith in international trade.
> (...)

The scope of article 7(1) CISG is to set the guidelines for international sales law to develop as a truly autonomous body of law, independent of national law. To that end, criteria are provided for it to be detached from domestic legal concepts. A clear example of this is provided by the regulation under article 79 CISG of *force majeure*, which uses the disguise of "impediments" to avoid employing a term from domestic law (in this case, French law).

Although in principle this could lead us to think of a dissociation between national and international law, this is not the case. International law is not limited to cross-border transactions, but serves to feed back into domestic law. Even if we are dealing with a domestic case that must be resolved by applying domestic law, this does not mean that the sources of international contract law cannot be considered. It may happen that national law has a gap or is ambiguous on a certain legal matter and that the answer is found in an international instrument (which in its elaboration reviewed and took into account national laws), and as such, it is considered even if it is not directly applicable to the national case. This is how international instruments can be used to

---

faith as criteria in interpretation of CISG: some remarks on article 7(1)', Journal of Law and Commerce, 25 (2005), pp. 75–85.
5   UNIDROIT Principles of International Commercial Contracts.
6   Principles of European Contract Law.
7   OHADAC (Organisation pour l'Harmonisation du Droit des Affaires dans le Caraïbe), Principles on International Commercial Contracts.
8   Principles on Transnational Law.
9   Principles of Latin American Contract Law.

understand, interpret and complement domestic laws. As stated in the Preamble to the PICC:

> PREAMBLE
> *(Purpose of the Principles)*
> (...)
> They may be used to interpret or supplement domestic law. They may serve as a model for national and international legislators.[10]

Article 1:101 PECL also states as follows:

> Article 1:101: Application of the Principles
> (...)
> (4) These Principles may provide a solution to the issue raised where the system or rules of law applicable do not do so.[11]

---

[10] Comment 6 states: "6. The Principles as a means of interpreting and supplementing domestic law. The Principles may also be used to interpret and supplement domestic law. In applying a particular domestic law, courts and arbitral tribunals may be faced with doubts as to the proper solution to be adopted under that law, either because different alternatives are available or because there seem to be no specific solutions at all. Especially where the dispute relates to an international commercial contract, it may be advisable to resort to the Principles as a source of inspiration. By so doing the domestic law in question would be interpreted and supplemented in accordance with internationally accepted standards and/or the special needs of cross-border trade relationships."
On the application of the PICC to interpret and complement domestic law, see M.J. Bonell, 'The UNIDROIT Principles and Transnational Law', Uniform Law Review, 5 (2000), pp. 199–218; M.J. Bonell, *An International Restatement of Contract Law. The UNIDROIT Principles of International Commercial Contracts*, 3rd edn (New York: Transnational Publishers, 2005); K.P. Berger, *The creeping codification of the new lex mercatoria*, 2nd edn (London: Kluwer Law International, 2010). Also M.J. Bonell, 'Symposium Paper: The *UNIDROIT Principles of International Commercial Contracts*: Achievements in Practice and Prospects for the Future', Australian International Law Journal, 17 (2010), pp. 177–184.

[11] Comment F states: "F. *The filling of Gaps*. Even if the contract is subject to a specific national legal system, because of the parties' choice of law or by virtue of the objective connecting factors of the conflict of laws, the Principles may perform a function. Paragraph (4) envisages the case where a national legal system does not contain a rule for the solution of a specific issue. In such a case the court or arbitral tribunal is invited to use the Principles as a source of law from which to fill the gap. Such recourse to the Principles is in line with the practice of many courts to use foreign decisions or legal writings if confronted with a novel problem. A set of rules elaborated on the

Also see article 2 PLACL:

Article 2. Functions
(1) These Principles apply to interpret international uniform law instruments and domestic law governing the contract.
(2) These Principles may also be used as a model for national or international legislators.[12]

---

basis of a careful and comprehensive comparative study of the legal systems of all the Member States may carry at least the same persuasive authority as cases or writings from an individual country." O. Lando and H. Beale (eds.), *Principles of European Contract Law, Part I and II* (London: Kluwer Law International, 2000), p. 97.

[12] The Presentation states: "At the outset, we were also able to note that contract law in Latin America is quite unequal. It is easy to see the diversity not only of sources, but also of periods to which national laws respond. Hence, the objective could not be limited to proposing a model Code or an idea of uniformity of contract law. Therefore, the objective was that the Principles should serve as a model for reforms in countries that merit it, for example, the Chilean and Colombian cases. These largely maintain the rules of the original codes of the nineteenth century, structured in terms of contracts in a contractual relationship based on a thing of kind or certain body, with a gravitating importance of the property and the idea of contracting parties arranged in a situation of equality that enabled them to decide what was best for them at the time of contracting. The urgency of reform in this type of law is pressing, which has led judges, influenced by the doctrine, to gradually transform the law of contracts by way of praetorian law. In other cases, on the other hand, it is believed to be pertinent to inspire better solutions by the courts or arbitration judges as *lex mercatoria*. This is what we wanted to reflect in Article 2 which contemplates the functions in the following terms. "(1) These Principles apply to interpret international uniform law instruments and domestic law governing the contract. (2) These Principles may also be used as a model for national or international legislators." The aim is thus to contribute to the formation of a Latin American contract law based on these Principles, giving shape to a modern formulation of what we understand should be the current law governing contracts. It is not, therefore, about something necessarily existing or, in other words, it does not seek here to reflect a common law already established in the region that allows us to see the consensus on the matter, but rather, based on certain shared solutions, it proposes a model of what it is thought should be the future of contract law in the countries of the Latin American region. Therefore, there is no Code here, which seemed to us an unwieldy and chimerical work, but we deliver here a more modest but realistic work that contemplates principles or general rules beyond the casuistry."
C. Pizarro Wilson, 'Presentación', in *Los Principios Latinoamericanos de Derecho de los Contratos* (Madrid: Agencia Estatal Boletín Oficial del Estado, 2017), pp. 16–17.

One case where national law is not clear in Latin America and the Caribbean is on *force majeure* and acts of God, and one way to clarify this difference is to look at international contract law. As shown by international contracting, it makes no sense to distinguish between those two concepts. Also, international instruments and *force majeure* clauses provide a more complex and adequate contractual structure, which addresses aspects omitted by national laws (many specific duties) and formulates more clearly the conditions to meet in order to claim *force majeure*.

3. *Force majeure in Europe*

The concepts of "fortuitous event", better known as act of God, and *"force majeure"*, were initially used in France under the original articles 1147 and 1148 of the *Code Civil* 1804, which referred expressly to *cause étrangère* (extraneous or external cause), *cas fortuit* (fortuitous event) and *force majeure*[13].

> Article 1147. A debtor shall be ordered to pay damages, if there is occasion, either by reason of the non-performance of the obligation, or by reason of delay in performing, whenever he does not prove that the non-performance comes from an external cause which may not be ascribed to him, although there is no bad faith on his part.
>
> Article 1148. There is no occasion for any damages where a debtor was prevented from transferring or from doing that to which he was bound, or did what was forbidden to him, by reason of *force majeure* or of a fortuitous event.

---

13 On *force majeure* in French law before the 2016 reform, see J.D. Smith, 'Impossibility of performance as an excuse in French law: The doctrine of force majeure', Yale Law Journal, 45 (1936), pp. 452–67; S. Litvinoff, 'Force majeure, failure of cause and théorie de l'imprévision: Louisiana law and beyond', Louisiana Law Review, 46 (1985–86), pp. 1–64; H. Beale, 'Partial and temporary impossibility in English and French Law', in *Mélanges en l'honneur de Denis Tallon. D'ici, d'ailleurs: Harmonisation et dynamique du droit* (Paris: Société de Législation Comparée, 1999), pp. 19–32; B. Nicholas, 'Force majeure in French law', in E. McKendrick (ed.), *Force majeure and frustration of contract*, 2nd edn (New York: Informa Law from Routledge, 2013), pp. 21–31.

After the 2016 reform by Ordonnance 2016-131, the *Civil Code* dropped the distinction between extraneous cause, act of God and *force majeure*, and now only uses the term *force majeure* according to articles 1218 and 1231-1 of the *Civil Code 2016*, in harmony with contractual practice and international instruments[14].

> Article 1218. In contractual matters, there is *force majeure* where an event beyond the control of the debtor, which could not reasonably have been foreseen at the time of the conclusion of the contract and whose effects could not be avoided by appropriate measures, prevents performance of his obligation by the debtor.
>
> Article 1231-1. A debtor is condemned, where appropriate, to the payment of damages either on the ground of the non-performance or a delay in performance of an obligation, unless he justifies this on the ground that performance was prevented by *force majeure*.[15]

Article 1470 of the Civil Code of Québec also abandoned the distinction between act of God and *force majeure* (mentioning only the latter), and refers to the extraneous cause and the unforeseeability and irresistibility of *force majeure*.

> Article 1470. A person may be relieved of liability for injury to another person if he proves that the injury resulted from *force majeure*, unless he has undertaken to make good the injury.
> *Force majeure* is an unforeseeable and irresistible event, including an extraneous cause with the same characteristics.

---

14 On French law after the 2016 reform, see S. Rowan, 'The new French law of contract', International & Comparative Law Quarterly, 66 (2017), pp. 805–31; R. Cabrillac, 'El nuevo derecho francés de los contratos', Themis, 70 (2016), pp. 56–66; E. Savaux, 'El nuevo derecho francés de obligaciones y contratos', ADC, 69 (2016), pp. 715–41; B. Fauvarque-Cosson, 'The French contract law reform and the political process', European Review of Contract Law, 13 (2017), pp. 337–54; P. Sirena, 'The new design of the French law of contract and obligations: an Italian view', in J. Cartwright and S. Whittaker (eds.), *The Code Napoleón Rewritten. French contract law after the 2016 reform* (Oxford: Hart Publishing, 2017), pp. 339–60.

15 From the English translation of J. Cartwright, B. Fauvarque-Cosson and S. Whittaker. See https://www.trans-lex.org/601101/_/french-civil-code-2016/.

The Civil Code of Spain 1889 contains a general clause for *force majeure* under its article 1105, which does not mention act of God or *force majeure* specifically. However, these concepts are found in other provisions, whether by reference only to an act of God (e.g. 1129, 1136, 1183, 1488) or jointly with *force majeure* (e.g. 1602, 1625)[16].

> Article 1105
> Outside the cases expressly mentioned in the law, and those in which the obligation should require it, no one shall be liable for events which cannot be foreseen or which, being foreseen, should be inevitable.[17]

The Italian *Codice Civile* 1942 does not use the terms act of God and *force majeure* in its articles 1218 and 1256, but of a "supervening impossibility" (*impossibilità sopravvenuta*) caused by a "non-attributable cause" (*causa non imputabile*), although it is understood that it refers to the act of God and *force majeure* of the French legislator[18].

> Article 1218. Liability of the debtor
> A debtor who fails to follow exactly the performance due is liable for compensation unless he proves that the non-performance or delay was

---

16 On Spanish law, see recently C. Lepín Molina (ed.), *Caso fortuito o fuerza mayor en el derecho. Estudios a partir de la pandemia del Covid-19* (Valencia: Tirant lo Blanch, 2020).

17 See the English translation in https://www.icj.org/wp-content/uploads/2013/05/Spain-Spanish-Civil-Code-2012-eng.pdf.

18 On Italian law, see G. D'Amico, 'La responsabilità contrattuale: attualità del pensiero di Giuseppe Osti', Rivista di Diritto Civile, 1 (2019), pp. 1–24; P. Sirena, 'L'impossibilità ed eccessiva onerosità della prestazione debitoria a causa dell'epidemia di COVID-19', in *Derecho de los Desastres: Covid-19*, Vol. II (Lima: Facultad de Derecho de la Pontificia Universidad Católica del Perú, 2020), pp. 1325–38; O. Clarizia, 'Coronavirus ed esonero da responsabilità per inadempimento di obbligazione ex art. 1218 C.C.: Impossibilità sopravvenuta oppure inesigibilità della prestazione?', Actualidad Jurídica Iberoamericana, 12 (2020), pp. 352–65; C. Amato, 'Responsabilità da inadempimento dell'obbligazione', in E. Navarretta (ed.), *Codice della responsabilità civile* (Milan: Giuffrè, 2021); G. Andreotti, 'Lo "spazio" normativo della colpa nell'art. 1218 c.c.', Giustizia Civile, 11.10.2021 (https://giustiziacivile.com/obbligazioni-e-contratti/approfondimenti/lo-spazio-normativo-della-colpa-nellart-1218-cc).

caused by impossibility of performance resulting from a cause not attributable to him.

Article 1256. Definitive impossibility and temporary impossibility
An obligation is extinguished when, due to a cause not attributable to the debtor, performance becomes impossible.
If the impossibility is only temporary, the debtor, as long as it lasts, is not liable for the delay in performance. However, the obligation is extinguished if the impossibility continues until, in relation to the title of the obligation or the nature of the object, the debtor can no longer be held obligated to perform or the creditor no longer has an interest in achieving it.

In contrast to French speaking jurisdictions, in Germany acts of God and *force majeure* are particularly regulated. Section §275 BGB deals with *Unmöglichkeit* (impossibility), with a particular regulation in its second paragraph for cases that go beyond physical impossibility, and in parallel, section §313 BGB with the doctrine of *Geschäftsgrundlage* (basis of the contract) or German hardship[19].

Section 275. Exclusion of the duty of performance
(1) A claim for performance is excluded to the extent that performance is impossible for the obligor or for any other person.
(2) The obligor may refuse performance to the extent that performance requires expense and effort which, taking into account the subject matter of the obligation and the requirements of good faith, is grossly disproportionate to the interest in performance of the obligee. When it is determined

---

19 On German law, see T. Rauh, 'Legal consequences of force majeure under German, Swiss, English and United States' Law', Denver Journal of International Law and Policy, 25 (1996), pp. 151–72; R. Zimmermann, 'Remedies for non-performance. The revised German law of obligations, viewed against the background of the Principles of European Contract Law', Edinburgh Law Review, 6 (2002), pp. 271–314; B. Markesinis, H. Unberath and A. Johnston, *The German Law of Contracts*, 2nd edn (Oxford: Hart Publishing, 2006); P. Ridder and M.-P. Weller, 'Unforeseen Circumstances, Hardship, Impossibility and Force Majeure under German Contract Law', European Review of Private Law, 22 (2014), pp. 371–92; I. Kokorin and J. van der Weide, 'Force majeure and unforeseen change of circumstances. The case of embargoes and currency fluctuations (Russian, German and French approaches)', Russian Law Journal, 3 (2015), pp. 46–82; H. Can Aksoy, *Impossibility in Modern Private Law. A Comparative Study of German, Swiss and Turkish Laws and the Unification Instruments of Private Law* (London: Springer 2014).

what efforts may reasonably be required of the obligor, it must also be taken into account whether he is responsible for the obstacle to performance.

(3) In addition, the obligor may refuse performance if he is to render the performance in person and, when the obstacle to the performance of the obligor is weighed against the interest of the obligee in performance, performance cannot be reasonably required of the obligor.

(4) The rights of the obligee are governed by sections 280, 283 to 285, 311a and 326.

It is important to note the wording of the European legal provisions on *force majeure* and Act of God, as several of them were copied by Latin jurisdictions — in some cases under a single perspective (such as Chile with France), while in others under a mixed one (such as Peru with France and Italy). This explains some of the complications arisen in national jurisdictions.

4. *Force majeure in Latin America and the Caribbean*

Latin America and the Caribbean, strongly influenced by the French tradition and the *Code Civil* 1804, include several jurisdictions (besides Peru) that recognize the concepts of act of God and *force majeure*, albeit the law does not distinguish between them.[20]

For South America, let us consider Chile, Ecuador, Colombia, Venezuela, Paraguay, Uruguay, Brazil, and Argentina. Peru will be mentioned later in a separate section.

Act of God and *force majeure* are mentioned in article 45 of the Civil Code of Chile:

> Art. 45. A *force majeure* or act of God is an unforeseen event that cannot be resisted, such as a shipwreck, an earthquake, the seizure of enemies, acts of authority exercised by a public official, etc.

Article 30 of the Civil Code of Ecuador defines act of God and *force majeure* in the same way:

---

[20] For Latin America and the Caribbean, see E. Muñoz, 'Impossibility, Hardship and Exemption under Ibero-American Contract Law', The Vindobona Journal of International Commercial Law and Arbitration, 14 (2010), pp. 175–92.

Art. 30. A *force majeure* or act of God is an unforeseen event that cannot be resisted, such as a shipwreck, an earthquake, the capture of enemies, acts of authority exercised by a public official, etc.

Act of God and *force majeure* are also so defined in article 64 of the Civil Code of Colombia:

Article 64. *Force majeure* or act of God
A *force majeure* or act of God is an unforeseen event that cannot be resisted, such as a shipwreck, an earthquake, the capture of enemies, acts of authority exercised by a public officer, etc.

Article 1272 of the Civil Code of Venezuela regulates acts of God and *force majeure* as follows:

Article 1272
The debtor is not obliged to pay damages when, as a consequence of an act of God or *force majeure*, he has failed to give or do that to which he was obliged or has executed that which was prohibited.

Article 426 of the Civil Code of Paraguay refers to an act of God and *force majeure* in the following terms:

Art. 426. The debtor shall not be liable for the damages and interest caused to the creditor for non-performance of the obligation, when these are the result of an act of God or *force majeure*, unless the debtor has assumed responsibility for the consequences of the act of God, or this has occurred due to his fault, or he has already incurred in default, which was not caused by an act of God or *force majeure*.

Article 1343 of the Civil Code of Uruguay also mentions acts of God and *force majeure*:

Art. 1343. Damages are not owed when the debtor has not been able to give or do the thing to which he was obliged or has done what was forbidden, yielding to *force majeure* or due to an act of God.
The following cases are not included in the aforementioned rule:
1. If one of the parties has taken upon himself especially the act of God or *force majeure*.
2. If the act of God has been preceded by some fault on his part, without which the loss or non-performance would not have taken place.
3. If the debtor had fallen into default prior to the occurrence of the act of God; the provisions of Chapter VI, Title III, Part One of this Book shall be observed.

Article 393 of the Civil Code of Brazil refers to acts of God and *force majeure* as follows:

> Art. 393. The debtor is not liable for the damages resulting from acts of God or *force majeure*, if he has not been expressly held responsible for them.
> Sole Paragraph. The act of God or *force majeure* is verified in the necessary fact, whose effects could not be avoided or prevented.

In Argentina, act of God and *force majeure* are mentioned in articles 955 (contracts) and 1730 (torts) of its Civil and Commercial Code, and it is even expressly stated that such terms are synonymous. This suggests that the legislator was aware that the distinction had no practical relevance, but on the other hand, wanted to respect tradition and did not dare to use only one concept.

> Article 955. Definition. The supervening, objective, absolute and definitive impossibility of the performance, produced by act of God or *force majeure*, extinguishes the obligation, without liability. If the impossibility occurs due to causes attributable to the obligor, the obligation modifies its object and becomes that of paying compensation for the damages caused.

> Article 1730. Act of God. *Force majeure*. An act of God or *force majeure* is an event that could not be foreseen or, having been foreseen, could not be avoided. Act of God or *force majeure* exempts from liability, except as otherwise provided.
> This Code uses the terms "act of God" and "*force majeure*" as synonyms.

For the Caribbean, let us consider Costa Rica, Cuba, El Salvador, Guatemala, Honduras, Nicaragua, Panama, Puerto Rico and Domincan Republic.

Articles 702 and 703 of the Civil Code of Costa Rica states as follows:

> Article 702. The debtor who fails to fulfill his obligation, either in substance or in manner, shall be liable for the same fact for the damages caused to his creditor, unless the failure arises from the fact of the latter, *force majeure* or act of God.

Article 703. The debtor is not bound by an act of God, except when he has contributed to it or has expressly accepted such liability.

Article 99.1 of the Civil Code of Cuba notes that:

Article 99.1. No civil liability shall be incurred by the perpetrator for damages caused:
a) in legitimate defense, in a state of necessity, or in fulfillment of a duty, assessed in accordance with the provisions of the criminal legislation;
b) by *force majeure* or act of God, or if the conduct of the author had been provoked by the victim of the damage; and
c) by performing a lawful act with due diligence.
Civil liability shall not be excluded if the act that caused the damage or injury was caused by the author in a state of mental derangement, transitory mental disorder or mental development retarded by error or driven by insurmountable fear. In the latter case, the person who caused the fear is also jointly and severally liable.

Article 43 of the Civil Code of El Salvador establishes that:

Art. 43. A *force majeure* or act of God is an unforeseen event that cannot be resisted, such as a shipwreck, an earthquake, the capture of enemies, acts of authority exercised by a public official, etc.

Article 1426 of the Civil Code of Guatemala reads as follows:

Article 1426. The debtor is not liable for the non-performance of the obligation due to an act of God or *force majeure*, unless at the time of its occurrence he was in default.

Article 1363 of the Civil Code of Honduras is particular. Many jurisdictions, starting with Chile and its followers, have a general clause for *force majeure* as well as other specific provisions. Honduras does not have a general clause similar to Chilean article 45; rather, it has a specific article (i.e. article 1363) on the consequences of non-performance, including act of God (this article resembles article 1547 of the Civil Code of Chile).

Article 1363
The debtor is liable only for ordinary fault in obligations which by their nature are useful only to the creditor; he is liable for slight fault in obliga-

tions contracted for the reciprocal benefit of the parties; and for slightest fault in obligations in which the debtor is the only one who brings benefit.

The obligor is not liable for the act of God, unless he is in default (being the fortuitous event of those that would not have damaged the thing owed, if it had been delivered to the obligee), or that the fortuitous event has occurred by his fault.

The proof of the diligence or care is incumbent on the one who should have used it; the proof of the fortuitous event is incumbent on the one who alleges it.

All which, however, is understood without prejudice to the special provisions of the laws, and of the express stipulations of the parties.

Article 1864 of the Civil Code of Nicaragua sets out the following:

> Article 1864. Apart from the cases expressly mentioned in the law, the debtor shall not be liable for the damages and interests caused to the creditor for non-performance of the obligation, when these are the result of an act of God or *force majeure*, unless the debtor has assumed responsibility for the consequences of the act of God or *force majeure*, or this has occurred through his fault, or he has already been in default, which is not caused by events that could not have been foreseen, or which, if foreseen, were unavoidable.

Article 34-D of the Civil Code of Panama is unusual because it proposes some definitions as follows:

> Article 34-D. *Force majeure* is the situation produced by acts of man, which it has not been possible to resist, such as acts of authority exercised by public officials, seizure by enemies, and others similar.
>
> An act of God is that which arises from events of nature that could not have been foreseen, such as shipwrecks, an earthquake, a conflagration and others of the same or similar nature.

Article 1166 of the Civil Code of Puerto Rico has a general clause for acts of God, although *force majeure* is also mentioned next to act of God in other legal provisions (e.g., articles 1369 and 1376), but also alone (e.g., articles 732 and 1541).

> Article 1166. Act of God
> Apart from the cases expressly mentioned in the law and those in which the obligation so declares, no one is liable for those events which could not have been foreseen, or which, foreseen, are unavoidable.

However, acts of God are for the account of the obligor until delivery is made, if:
(a) he is in default in an obligation to give, unless the act of God had also occurred, the thing due being in the creditor's possession, without prejudice to his duty to indemnify the default; or
(b) is bound to deliver the same thing to two or more persons.

Article 1148 of the Civil Code of Dominican Republic is a copy of article 1148 of the *Code Civil* 1804.

Art. 1148. Damages do not apply when, as a consequence of *force majeure* or act of God, the debtor was unable to give or do what he is obliged to do, or has done what he was forbidden to do.

Finally, we can consider two Latin American harmonization projects.

On the one hand, attention is drawn to the proposal of article 89 PLACL, which is entitled "*Force majeure* or acts of God". This legislative option is innovative in the international field, as this distinction is absent in other international law instruments — such as the CISG, PICC, PECL — that prefer the use of a single term ("impediment" or "*force majeure*"). Apparently, the PLACL chose to follow the prevalent tradition in Latin America.

Article 89. *Force majeure* or acts of God
Force majeure or an act of God is an event beyond the control of the obligor that temporarily or permanently impedes it from performing an obligation at no risk to it and the occurrence and effects of which it could not have avoided.[21]

If the PLACL are intended to be applied in Latin America, and most jurisdictions there recognize acts of God and *force majeure*, then there would already be a certain "uniformity". As such, it would make sense to insist on the distinction, although the PLACL themselves point out in their comments that both concepts are used interchangeably: "And article 89, without

---

21 R. Momberg and S. Vogenauer, 'The Principles of Latin American Contract Law: text, translation, and introduction', Uniform Law Review, 23 (2018), pp. 144–70 (p. 164).

making a distinction, defines *force majeure* or act of God (...)"[22]. Again, the label is insisted on but no distinction is made in substance.

On the other hand, article 56 of the Code of Obligations for Latin America of GADAL (Group for the Harmonization of Law in Latin America) has abandoned the distinction and only uses *force majeure*:

> Article 56. *Force majeure*. *Force majeure* is an event that is unforeseeable, irresistible, beyond the control of the obligor, which prevents performance.
>
> The fact of the third party, the acts of authority and the fact of the creditor, which comply with the elements of *force majeure*, shall be equated to the latter.
>
> If the *force majeure* is temporary, the effects of the obligation are suspended until the impossibility of performance is overcome, unless the suspension entails the loss of the creditor's interest, in accordance with article 53.
>
> If the *force majeure* is definitive, the obligation is extinguished by impossibility of performance in accordance with Chapter V of this Title.
>
> The obligor must notify the creditor of the *force majeure* within a reasonable time. Otherwise he is liable for damages arising from the lack or delay in giving notice.
>
> The creditor must notify the obligor, within a reasonable time, of the loss of its interest in the performance in order for the *force majeure* to be considered definitive.

Note 31 on article 56 clearly states that "It is accepted the equation between act of God and *force majeure*, as well as the preeminence that the latter has assumed in practice over the former"[23].

The results of this legal mapping on *force majeure* in Latin America and the Caribbean are as follows:

---

[22] I. de la Maza Gazmuri and Á. Vidal Olivares, 'El contenido: una primera aproximación', en *Los Principios Latinoamericanos de Derecho de los Contratos* (Madrid: Agencia Estatal Boletín Oficial del Estado, 2017), p. 54.

[23] See 'Código Marco de Obligaciones para América Latina', in A. Saccoccio and S. Cacace (eds.), *Europa e America Latina due continenti, un solo diritto. Unità e specificità del sistema giuridico latinoamericano*, Vol. I (Turin-Valencia: G. Giappichelli & Tirant lo Blanch, 2020), p. 441.

- The distinction between act of God and *force majeure* is still used, but national laws mention both indistinctly. Only in exceptional cases, such as Panama, is a definition proposed for each concept; however, the rule is that the same old examples are used to explain both acts of God and *force majeure*, as in Chile and its followers.
- The three traditional conditions (externality, unforeseeability and irresistibility) according to French law are either not all expressly regulated or are regulated differently across national laws.
- The legal provisions on acts of God and *force majeure* are very old and this can be easily evidenced in the legislative technique of using examples of natural disasters.
- National laws are outdated in comparison to international instruments, especially on the formulation of the general three conditions, as well as in comparison to *force majeure* clauses which include important duties such as notification, mitigation of damages, best efforts, renegotiation, among other aspects, which are absent in national laws.

5. *Force majeure in international law instruments*

Despite knowing that *force majeure* is the standard term in international practice, the CISG preferred a neutral term. As *force majeure* comes from French law, the term "impediment" was chosen in order to avoid the use of French or other national law in the application of the rules on exemption from breach of contract under the CISG[24].

> Section IV. Exemptions
> Article 79

---

24 B. Audit, 'The Vienna Sales Convention and the Lex Mercatoria', in T.E. Carbonneau (ed.), *Lex mercatoria and arbitration* (Cambridge: Kluwer Law International, 1998), pp. 173–94 (p. 179); C.M. Germain, 'Reducing legal babelism: CISG translation issues', in L.A. DiMatteo (ed.), *International Sales Law. A Global Challenge* (Cambridge: Cambridge University Press, 2014), pp. 51–62 (p. 54).

(1) A party is not liable for a failure to perform any of his obligations if he proves that the failure was due to an impediment beyond his control and that he could not reasonably be expected to have taken the impediment into account at the time of the conclusion of the contract or to have avoided or overcome it, or its consequences.

(...)

This legislative technique has been replicated by other international instruments which have also opted for the use of the term "impediment" as the sole term such as the PECL (article 8:108) and DCFR (article III. – 3:104). Considering the well-known use of *force majeure* clauses at international contracting, other instruments, such as the PICC (article 7.1.7), OHADAC Principles (article 7.1.8) and TransLex Principles (article No. VI.3), also mention *force majeure,* albeit as a synonym of "impediment". These international instruments do not propose two distinct terms or differences.

It is important to note, however, that according to the CISG Advisory Council Opinion No. 7 of 2007, the wording of article 79 is so broad and neutral when referring to the term "impediment" that it is not limited to *force majeure*, and as such, article 79 may be invoked for hardship cases[25]. Additionally, and more recently, the CISG Advisory Council Opinion No. 20 of 2020 has clarified the scope of application of hardship under the CISG and has set the consequences of claiming hardship[26], which are similar to those of *force majeure* (no renegotiation neither court intervention in the contract)[27].

---

[25] CISG-AC Opinion No. 7, Exemption of Liability for Damages under Article 79 of the CISG, Rapporteur: Professor Alejandro M. Garro, Columbia University School of Law, New York, N.Y., USA. Adopted by the CISG-AC at its 11th meeting in Wuhan, People's Republic of China, on 12 October 2007.

[26] CISG-AC Opinion No. 20, Hardship under the CISG, Rapporteur: Prof. Dr. Edgardo Muñoz, Universidad Panamericana, Guadalajara, Mexico. Adopted by the CISG Advisory Council following its 27th meeting, in Puerto Vallarta, Mexico on 2–5 February 2020.

[27] See the debate in I. Schwenzer and E. Muñoz, 'Duty to renegotiate and contract adaptation in case of hardship', Uniform Law Review, 24 (2019), pp. 149–74; L.A. DiMatteo, 'Legal tradition bias in interpreting the CISG: hardship as case in point', in F. Benatti, S. García Long and F. Viglione

On the other hand, a major achievement of international instruments has been the standardization of the requirements of *force majeure*.

In national law, the wording of what constitutes an act of God or *force majeure* is debated, to the extent that it affects the significance of the single term. For instance, if it is said that the event must be "extraordinary", it opens the discussion as to what is extraordinary. For this reason, the choice of international law was to formulate the requirements in a more extensive manner in order to avoid different interpretations (e.g. beyond the control, or even beyond the reasonable control).

Most international instruments set out the same three general conditions that must be met for an impediment (*force majeure*) to excuse performance of the contract. There is also a fourth condition, although it appears only in some international instruments. Apparently, it goes without saying. Nonetheless, it should be noted that the fourth requirement is formulated in the same or a very similar manner in order to avoid different and possibly contradictory interpretations.

The three general requirements contained in article 79 CISG, including the way they have been formulated, are the same as those found in article 7.1.7 PICC, article 8:108 PECL and

---

(eds.), *The transnational sales contract. 40 years influence of the CISG on national jurisdictions* (Milan: Wolters Kluwer – CEDAM, 2022), pp. 124–60; S. García Long, 'A single theory of impediments under the CISG: A Latin-American perspective', in F. Benatti, S. García Long and F. Viglione (eds.), *The transnational sales contract. 40 years influence of the CISG on national jurisdictions* (Milan: Wolters Kluwer – CEDAM, 2022), pp. 219–67; M.L. Kubica, 'Exemption of liability for damages: hardship and the rule from art. 79 of the Vienna Convention', in F. Benatti, S. García Long and F. Viglione (eds.), *The transnational sales contract. 40 years influence of the CISG on national jurisdictions* (Milan: Wolters Kluwer – CEDAM, 2022), pp. 415–57; P.J. Mazzacano, 'CISG article 79 at 40: 'Impediments' to uniform interpretation?', in F. Benatti, S. García Long and F. Viglione (eds.), *The transnational sales contract. 40 years influence of the CISG on national jurisdictions* (Milan: Wolters Kluwer – CEDAM, 2022), pp. 487–509; B. Zeller, 'Covid-19 and article 79 – A revisit', in F. Benatti, S. García Long and F. Viglione (eds.), *The transnational sales contract. 40 years influence of the CISG on national jurisdictions* (Milan: Wolters Kluwer – CEDAM, 2022), pp. 601–19.

article III. – 3:104 DCFR. The affected party is not liable if it proves that the impediment: (1) was beyond its control, (2) could not reasonably be expected to have taken the impediment into account at the time of the conclusion of the contract, and (3) could not reasonably have avoided or overcome the impediment or its consequences. Additionally, a fourth condition is that the risk must not have been assumed by the affected party. This is expressly stated by TransLex Principles, OHADAC Principles and PLACL.

6. *Force majeure in Peru*

6.1 *The black letter of the law and the French–Italian influence*

The Peruvian experience shows that the legislator has a certain taste for importing concepts, but above all for mixing concepts from different jurisdictions. The legislative techniques of the French and Italian legislators were not incorporated alone; rather, they were introduced jointly such that articles 1314, 1315, 1316, 1317, 1431 and 1433 of the Peruvian Civil Code 1984 include four concepts that must be considered: "act of God" (*cas fortuit* or *caso fortuito*), "*force majeure*" (*fuerza mayor*), "non-attributable cause" (*causa non imputabile* or *causa no imputable*), and "supervening impossibility" (*impossibilità sopravvenuta* or *imposibilidad sobrevenida*).

> Article 1314. Whoever acts with the ordinary diligence required is not attributable for the non-performance of the obligation or for its partial, late or defective performance.
>
> Article 1315. Act of God or *force majeure* is the non-attributable cause, consisting of an extraordinary, unforeseeable and irresistible event, which prevents the performance of the obligation or determines its partial, late or defective performance.
>
> Article 1316. The obligation is extinguished if the performance is not executed for a cause not attributable to the obligor.
> If such cause is temporary, the obligor is not liable for the delay as long as it lasts. However, the obligation is extinguished if the cause that

determines the non-performance persists until the obligor, according to the title of the obligation or the nature of the performance, can no longer be considered obliged to perform it; or until the obligee justifiably loses interest in its performance or it is no longer useful to him.
An obligation which can only be partially performed is also extinguished if it is not useful to the obligee or if the obligee has no justified interest in its partial performance. Otherwise, the obligor is bound to perform it with reduction of the consideration, if any.

Article 1317. The obligor is not liable for damages resulting from the non-performance of the obligation, or from its partial, late or defective performance, due to <u>causes not attributable</u> to him, unless otherwise expressly provided by law or by the title of the obligation.

Article 1431. In contracts with reciprocal performances, if the performance to be made by one of the parties <u>becomes impossible</u> without fault on the part of the contracting parties, the contract is terminated by operation of law. In this case, the discharged obligor loses the right to the consideration and must return what he has received.
However, the parties may agree that the risk shall be borne by the obligee.

Article 1433. The rules of articles 1431 and 1432 are applicable when performance of the obligation <u>becomes partially impossible</u>, unless the obligee expresses to the obligor his agreement to partial performance, in which case a proportional reduction in the consideration due must be made.
The contract is terminated when the reduction is not possible.
(Emphasis added)

This mixed legislative technique is not the most appropriate.

First, the concept of "non-attributable cause" is broad enough to cover the cases of absence of fault (article 1314) as well as the occurrence of an act of God and *force majeure* (article 1315).

Second, if act of God and *force majeure* are regulated, it is unnecessary to add a third concept of "non-attributable cause" to be used indistinctly. Why add a third concept to be used as a genus of the other two? It could even be said that there are four terms to refer to the same thing, since according to article 1315 an act of God or *force majeure* is the non-attributable cause which is an event.

Third, article 1315 mentions non-attributable cause, act of God, and *force majeure*, without distinguishing them, since in the end what matters is that such concepts comply with the conditions of exteriority, unforeseeability and irresistibility.

Fourth, to explain the cause-effect relationship, a single term was considered sufficient to define the cause and another for the effect. However, while it is clear that the effect is the supervening impossibility, three (or four) terms are proposed to refer to the cause, which is unnecessary.

Fifth, the requirement of irresistibility is understood as a synonym for supervening impossibility, which is another unnecessary synonym to take into account.

The problem of the formulation of several concepts can be solved in practice if they are used indistinctly. However, given Peruvian law does not distinguish between them, doctrine and case law propose similarities and differences that do not facilitate their practical application. Recently, in the Plenary Chamber Session No. 018-2020 dated December 2, 2020, the Members of the Court of the National Superintendence of Health – SUSALUD unanimously adopted a binding precedent on act of God and *force majeure* as grounds for exemption from liability for administrative violations. The Plenary Chamber proposed a table of similarities and differences, which is contrary to the letter of article 1315 of the Peruvian Civil Code[28].

The example of the French legislator's 2016 reform should be followed. Although it was the French who began to speak of *cause étrangère*, *cas fortuit* and *force majeure*, they also recognized that it made no sense to have three concepts if they were to be used interchangeably. Therefore, it was preferred to use only *force majeure*. The same option was implemented in Quebec and China.

---

[28] See S. García Long, 'Por qué no debemos distinguir entre "caso fortuito" y "fuerza mayor". Reflexiones desde el derecho contractual transnacional', Gaceta Civil & Procesal Civil, 93 (2021), pp. 21–48 (pp. 22–23).

6.2 Debates on Peruvian law

Article 1315 of the Peruvian Civil Code states that an act of God or *force majeure* must meet three conditions: (a) exteriority, (b) unforeseeability, and (c) irresistibility.

Peruvian commentators have discussed the following: (1) how each of such conditions should be understood, and (2) whether for an event to qualify as an act of God or *force majeure* the concurrence of the three conditions indicated by law must be verified[29].

First, there is usually a discussion about the extraordinary nature of the event, whether it is an internal or external risk, an extraneous or foreign cause, an event that occurs without the fault of the affected party, an exceptional event, an event beyond the control of the debtor, whether the event would affect any person or only the debtor in its particular position, among other interpretations.

---

29 For the general discussion on *force majeure* in Peruvian law for contracts and torts, see F. Osterling Parodi, *Las obligaciones* (Lima: Fondo Editorial de la Pontificia Universidad Católica del Perú, 1988); F. de Trazegnies Granda, *La responsabilidad extracontractual* (Lima: Fondo Editorial de la Pontificia Universidad Católica del Perú, 2001); G. Fernández Cruz, 'El deber accesorio de diligencia y la responsabilidad derivada del incumplimiento de las relaciones obligatorias', in F. Escobar Rozas, R. Morales Hervias, L.L. León and E. Palacios Martínez (eds.), *Negocio jurídico y responsabilidad civil. Estudios en memoria del Profesor Lizardo Taboada Córdova* (Lima: Grijley, 2004), pp. 583–625; G. Fernández Cruz and L. León Hilario, 'Caso Fortuito y Fuerza Mayor. Artículo 1315', in *Código Civil Comentado por los 100 mejores especialistas*, Vol. VI (Lima: Gaceta Jurídica, 2004), pp. 875–90; J. Espinoza, *Derecho de la responsabilidad civil*, 7th edn (Lima: Rhodas, 2013); M.A. Ortega Piana, 'Consideraciones sobre la imposibilidad prestacional', in M.A. Torres Carrasco (ed.), *Los Contratos. Consecuencias Jurídicas de su Incumplimiento* (Lima: Gaceta Jurídica, 2013), pp. 191–207; M. Castillo Freyre and G. Rivas Caso, 'La diligencia y la inejecución de las obligaciones', Ius et Veritas, 48 (2014), pp. 130–41; J.A. Beltrán Pacheco, 'Imprecisiones en torno al caso fortuito y la fuerza mayor', Lumen, 13 (2017), pp. 21–35; L. Barchi, 'Reflexiones jurídicas en tiempos del Covid-19: "la fuerza mayor se hizo viral"', Ius et Praxis, 50–51 (2019–20), pp. 61–79; García Long, 'Por qué no debemos distinguir entre "caso fortuito" y "fuerza mayor". Reflexiones desde el derecho contractual transnacional', pp. 21–48; G. Fernández Cruz, *Limitación de responsabilidad, exoneración y liberación del deudor* (Lima: ARA Editores, 2022).

Although such formulations may seem synonymous, their differences are better appreciated when applied to a concrete case. For example, a strike may be exceptional but not an external risk for an employer, and could even be deemed as an event occurring through the fault of the employer to the extent it is motivated by the latter's failure to comply with labor and occupational health and safety standards. On the other hand, the Covid-19 pandemic seemed to be an external, strange and alien, risk that occurred without the fault of the affected party. It was also exceptional and had the potential to affect any person — not only the debtor in its particular position. However, perhaps the same cannot be said of a second or third wave of contagions.

Regarding unforeseeability, it is often discussed whether it should be understood in the abstract or in the concrete, whether it should be reasonable, and whether it should focus only on the affected party or on both parties. For example, the closure of the Suez Canal could be reasonably unforeseeable in concrete terms and only with respect to the party that had to transport goods, while the Covid-19 pandemic seems reasonably unforeseeable in abstract terms and for both parties.

Regarding irresistibility, it is considered synonymous with impossibility, since it is irresistibility that ultimately confirms the debtor's inability to overcome the event that prevents it from performing. In view of this, it is discussed whether irresistibility must be analyzed from the perspective of any person or from the position of the obligor in its particular position in relation to the efforts and measures to implement to avoid or overcome the event, and whether it can be qualified by a criterion of reasonableness.

Second, it is discussed whether all three conditions must be met both for an act of God and *force majeure*, despite the law clearly requires those three conditions for an exception to apply. Following the French tradition, the act of God has its emphasis in being a cause alien to the parties, or external. Therefore, it deals with typical natural disasters, such as hurricanes, avalanches, storms, floods, eruptions, tsunamis, earthquakes, tidal waves, among other situations that cannot be attributed on anyone but God. These events, given their magnitude and amplitude, would also be irresistible. However, it can be questioned whether they are really unpredictable, both in the abstract and in the concrete. For example, since Peru is in a seismic zone, buildings are constructed with this risk in mind. As such, it would be difficult for a builder who sees his work destroyed by an earthquake to prove that the event that affected him was unforeseeable. On the other hand, *force majeure* has its emphasis on being an "act of the Prince" (*fait du prince*) or act of state authority. As such, if the Prince says something, it must be obeyed. Within this context, irresistibility stands out. Eventually, it could be questioned whether it would also be an extraordinary event, as well as unforeseeable.[30]

From this conceptual perspective, Peruvian doctrine may question why the Peruvian legislator enunciated three general conditions for both an act of God and *force majeure*, when conceptually there are differences that would justify formulating different conditions for each one. However, the option of the Peruvian legislator, and of most of Civil Codes, is that both concepts are subject to the same conditions. Thus, the distinction between act of God and *force majeure* does not generate a distinction between conditions for practical purposes.

7. *Force majeure clauses in international contracting*

It is necessary to pay attention to the contractual structure of *force majeure* clauses in international contracts to see why they are different and better than the regulation of national laws[31].

---

[30] See recently C. Pizarro Wilson, 'El "hecho del príncipe" como circunstancia sobreviniente durante la ejecución de los contratos', in *Derecho de los Desastres: Covid-19*, Vol. II (Lima: Facultad de Derecho de la Pontificia Universidad Católica del Perú, 2020), pp. 1121–35.

[31] On *force majeure* clauses, see W. Swadling, 'The judicial construction of force majeure clauses', in E. McKendrick (ed.), *Force majeure and frustration of contract*, 2nd edn (New York: Informa Law from Routledge, 2013), pp. 3–18; M. Furmston, 'Drafting of force majeure clauses — some general guidelines', in E. McKendrick (ed.), *Force majeure and frustration of contract*, 2nd edn (New York: Informa Law from Routledge, 2013), pp. 57–62; A. Berg, 'The detailed drafting of a force majeure clause', in E. McKendrick (ed.), *Force majeure and frustration of contract*, 2nd edn (New York: Informa Law from

First, the inclusion of a *force majeure* clause aims at overcoming the debates and differences with respect to national laws. Therefore: (i) the only term used is *"force majeure"* and as a synonym for "impediment", (ii) the conditions are better formulated, and (3) all requirements must be met.

Second, the *force majeure* clause seeks to overcome the traditional Civil Law view of supervening impossibility, which is seen as an objective, absolute and definitive event, and as such, which generates a natural effect that is the automatic termination of the contract. On the contrary, a *force majeure* clause is focused on managing or administering the impediment in order to regulate the conduct of the parties for the duration of the impediment and the possibility of overcoming it in order to resume the performance of the contract. Therefore, the first effect of the *force majeure* clause is the exoneration from liability for the duration of the impediment; specifically, no liability for damages (or penalties) and no claim for specific performance of the contract can be made while the contract is affected, without prejudice to the exercise of other remedies by both parties. In practical terms, the affected party has the possibility of "suspending" its performance for the duration of the event. Termination will only be exercised on a residual basis and if the impediment cannot be overcome within a certain period of time. In this way, any impediment is treated as if it were temporary.

Routledge, 2013), pp. 63–118; F. De Ly, 'Chapter 4. Analyzing the ICC Force Majeure Clause 2003', in F. Bortolotti and D. Ufot (eds.), *Hardship and Force Majeure in International Commercial Contracts. Dealing with Unforeseen Events in a Changing World* (Paris: ICC Publishing, ICC Dossier, 2018), pp. 113–22; E. Erdem, 'Chapter 5. Revision of the ICC Force Majeure and Hardship Clause', in F. Bortolotti and D. Ufot (eds.), *Hardship and Force Majeure in International Commercial Contracts. Dealing with Unforeseen Events in a Changing World* (Paris: ICC Publishing, ICC Dossier, 2018), pp. 123–36; K.P. Berger, 'Chapter 6. Force majeure clauses and their relationship with the applicable law, trade usages and general principles of law', in F. Bortolotti and D. Ufot (eds.), *Hardship and Force Majeure in International Commercial Contracts. Dealing with Unforeseen Events in a Changing World* (Paris: ICC Publishing, ICC Dossier, 2018), pp. 113–22; J.H. Robinson, J.C. Selman, W. Steineker and A.G. Thrasher, 'Use the force? Understanding force majeure clauses', American Journal of Trial Advocacy, 44 (2020), pp. 1–34.

Third, the introduction of a *force majeure* clause is the opportunity to supplement aspects on which national laws are silent. For instance, a standard *force majeure* clause contains the conditions for invoking *force majeure*, the duty to give notice of the impediment, exoneration as the first effect, an extension of time for the same period as the duration of the impediment, the duty to mitigate damages, the duty to use best efforts to overcome the impediment, the duty to renegotiate the contract, termination as a remedy and last effect, who is entitle to termination, and the possible intervention of an expert or a judge or arbitrator, when such intervention may take place, and what they could do. The *force majeure* clauses of the ICC, ITC and World Bank are among the leading model clauses.

8. *Force majeure in China*

It is relevant to note the recent Civil Code of the People's Republic of China of 2020 which, among its innovations, regulates *force majeure* following the improvements proposed by international instruments and *force majeure* clauses in international contracting[32]. Articles 180, 563 and 590 of the Chinese Civil Code state as follows[33]:

---

[32] On *force majeure* in Chinese law, see L. Ross, 'Force majeure and related doctrines of excuse in contract law of the People's Republic of China', Columbia Journal of Asian Law, 5 (1991), pp. 58–95; D.L. Grace, '*Force majeure*, China & the CISG: Is China's new contract law a step in the right direction?', San Diego International Law Journal, 2 (2001), pp. 173–208; B. Olson, '*Force majeure* in China', Columbia Journal of Asian Law, 33 (2020), pp. 295–345; K. Fung Tsang, 'From coronation to coronavirus: Covid-19, *force majeure* and private international law', Fordham International Law Journal, 44 (2020), pp. 187–232; Q. Liu, 'Covid-19 in civil and commercial disputes: first responses from Chinese courts', The Chinese Journal of Comparative Law, 8 (2020), pp. 485–501; J. Henri Herbots, 'Covid-19 and contracts in China and Europe', China-EU Law Journal, 8 (2022), pp. 1–9; S. Li, P. Nai, G. Yang and T. Yu, 'Force majeure and changed circumstances during the Covid-19 pandemic: the case of sports service contracts and judicial responses in China', The International Sports Law Journal, 22 (2022), pp. 259–70.

[33] See the English translation in L. Chen, J. Ge, J. He, Q. Liu, Z. Wu and B. Xion (eds.), *The Civil Code of the People's Republic of China. English translation*

Article 180
One does not bear civil liabilities for failure to perform civil duties merely because of *force majeure*, except as otherwise provided by law.

Force majeure are unforeseeable, unavoidable and insurmountable objective situations.

Article 563
The parties to a contract may terminate the contract under any of the following circumstances:
(1) where it is rendered impossible to achieve the purpose of the contract due to an event of *force majeure*;
(2) where prior to the expiry date of performance, the other party expressly states, or indicates through its conduct, that it will not perform its principal obligation;
(3) where the other party delays performance of its principal obligation, and fails to perform within a reasonable period after the demand;
(4) where it is rendered impossible to achieve the purpose of the contract due to the delayed performance of the obligations or other breach of contract by the party;
(5) other circumstance as provided by law.
A contract requiring the successive performance of the obligations without a term may be terminated by a party at any time, provided that the other party is notified within a reasonable period.

Article 590
Where a party is unable to perform the contract due to a *force majeure* event, the party shall be exempted from liability, in part or in whole, on the ground of the impact of the *force majeure* event, except as otherwise provided by law. Under such a circumstance, the party shall timely notify the other party to mitigate the losses caused to the other party and provide evidence within a reasonable period of time.

If a *force majeure* event occurs after a party delays its performance, this party shall not be exempted from liability for breach.[34]

Two remarks on the Chinese regulation for Latin lawyers. First, impossibility of performance is linked to the frustration of purpose according to paragraph (1) of article 563. In hindsight, this was particularly relevant in times of pandemic. It was discussed whether contracts had become impossible or excessively onerous due to the consequences of the Covid-19 pandemic. However, it seemed that these two excuses did not fit easily. In response,

---

(Boston: Brill Nijhoff, 2021).
34   See articles 94, 117 and 118 of Contract Law (1999).

frustration of the purpose was considered because it seemed to explain more simply why a contract should not be performed during the pandemic, e.g., it was said that if a tenant could not use the business premises because of the lockdown, he would be entitled to terminate the contract because its purpose would have been frustrated. Therefore, among Latin lawyers, the need to import the English doctrine of frustration of purpose was again seriously considered[35]. In view of the above, it is interesting to pay attention to the Chinese model. While English lawyers distinguish between impossibility of performance (or physical impossibility) and impossibility of purpose, Chinese article 563 mixes both cases and considers that the affected party may be released from the contract if it will not be possible to achieve the purpose of the contract due to a *force majeure* event. This legislative model, which is careful to link *force majeure* with the frustration of the purpose, shows that it is not urgent to import a foreign figure if national law already contains the tools to yield a solution (e.g. a broad regulation on *force majeure* would be sufficient).

Secondly, the Chinese provision expressly refers to the duties of notification, evidence and mitigation of damages. These duties, as well as other specific ones, are fundamental with respect to *force majeure* when one understands that it is the management of the impediment that is important. Indeed, unlike the old laws in Latin America and the Caribbean, *force majeure* clauses in international contracting present a more complex contractual structure that includes what should the parties do from the occurrence of the impediment, during its duration, and what should be done to overcome the impediment, or in any case, how to proceed in case nothing can be done by the parties. For this reason, *force majeure* clauses include different specific duties, such as the duty to notify the impediment, the duty to prove what

---

35 See the background and debate over this English importation in S. García Long, 'El injustificado entusiasmo civilista por la frustración del propósito del contrato (frustration of purpose)', in *Dogmática y práctica del derecho privada moderno. Estudios jurídicos en homenaje a Gastón Fernández Cruz*, Vol. I (Lima: ARA Editores, 2022), pp. 461–513.

happened, the duty to mitigate damages for the duration of the impediment, the duty of best efforts to overcome the impediment, the duty to renegotiate, the duty of good faith, among others. Clearly, the structure of the *force majeure* clause will depend on the transaction, but in general, the duties of notification, evidence and mitigation of damages are — and should be — agreed upon in any *force majeure* clause. Therefore, Chinese article 590 stands out for expressly including these three duties, which may serve as a precedent and guide for a future reform to update the Civil Codes in Latin America and the Caribbean.

9. Force majeure *and the Covid-19 pandemic*

During the Covid-19 pandemic, special attention was paid to *force majeure* in comparative and international law[36]. It was

---

[36] See K.P. Berger and D. Behn, '*Force majeure* and hardship in the age of corona: a historical and comparative study', McGill Journal of Dispute Resolution, 6 (2019–20), pp. 78–130; C. Twigg-Flesner, 'A comparative perspective on commercial contracts and the impact of COVID-19 — Change of circumstances, *force majeure*, or what?', in K. Pistor (ed.), *Law in the time of COVID-19* (New York: Columbia Law School, 2020), pp. 155–65; S. García Long, 'Contratos en cuarentena: pandemia y cambio de circunstancias', in *Derecho de los Desastres: Covid-19*, Vol. I (Lima: Facultad de Derecho de la Pontificia Universidad Católica del Perú, 2020), pp. 151–87; K.A. Adams, 'Force majeure in the time of coronavirus', in *Derecho de los Desastres: Covid-19*, Vol. II (Lima: Facultad de Derecho de la Pontificia Universidad Católica del Perú, 2020), pp. 1223–33; D. Philippe, 'Coronavirus: force majeure? Hardship? Deferral of obligations? Some practical elements. Advice for the analysis and redaction of clauses', in *Derecho de los Desastres: Covid-19*, Vol. II (Lima: Facultad de Derecho de la Pontificia Universidad Católica del Perú, 2020), pp. 1277–93; C. Jerez, M. Kubica and A. Ruda, 'Covid-19, fuerza mayor y contrato, en el amplio panorama del Derecho de los Desastres', in *Derecho de los Desastres: Covid-19*, Vol. II (Lima: Facultad de Derecho de la Pontificia Universidad Católica del Perú, 2020), pp. 1475–98; A. Janssen and C.J. Wahnschaffe, 'Covid-19 and international sale contracts: unprecedented grounds for exemption or business as usual', Uniform Law Review, 25 (2021), pp. 1–30; E. Muñoz, 'Covid-19 and related Public and Private Measures as an Impediment to performing CISG Contracts', Texas International Law Journal, 57 (2021), pp. 61–83; O.N. Ravi, 'Force majeure in commercial contracts', CMR University Journal of Contemporary Legal Affairs, 3 (2021), pp. 59–79; V.V. Palmer, 'Excused

considered that many contracts could not be performed because had become impossible, especially due to supervening illegality or acts of the Prince. However, the pandemic presented certain particularities. Usually, when one thought of *force majeure* events, one took as a reference events of surprise and of consequences that could not be avoided or overcome. While it is true that the pandemic was a surprise event, its consequences have extended over time for several years, and it is this passage of time that generates the paradox of unpredictability: over time, the unpredictable becomes foreseeable[37]. If a *force majeure* event occurs, the invoking party may benefit from the exonerating effect. However, can the same be said of a second or third wave? Will the unforeseeability requirement still be met? It is for this reason that many *force majeure* clauses have had to be adjusted in order to derogate the traditional conditions, in particular, unforeseeability.

Indeed, it was common to observe that *force majeure* clauses generally derogated the unforeseeability condition so that it was understood that a *force majeure* event could be raised even for a foreseeable event as long as it could not be avoided or overcome. The intention of the clause was to make *force majeure* more flexible in favor of the claimant. In this regard, it is worth recalling the model of the Spanish legislator which states in article 1105 of the Spanish Civil Code that "no one shall be liable for those events which could not have been foreseen, or which, foreseen, were unavoidable".

Another alternative was to expressly include the term "pandemic" in the list of specific events that would qualify as *force majeure*. Thus, the conditions of exteriority and unforeseeability were ruled out. As shown from the 2020 ICC *force majeure* model clause, the incorporation of a specific event presumes the verification of all conditions except irresistibility.

---

performances: *Force majeure*, impracticability, and frustration of contracts', The American Journal of Comparative Law, 70 (2022), pp. 70–88.

37 See Á. Carrasco Perera, 'Reivindicación y defensa de la vieja doctrina "rebus sic stantibus"', Revista Cuadernos Civitas de Jurisprudencia Civil, 98 (2015), pp. 175–206.

The parties also began to include a specific clause so that the affected party could invoke the effects of *force majeure* even if the consequences of a second or third wave were foreseeable. In a case of a contract for the sale of real estate, the construction company indicated that the delivery date of the apartment was tentative and could be postponed if new governmental measures were implemented for the pandemic, which was to be expected. If it were not for this clause, the construction company could not claim *force majeure* to exonerate itself from the delay in the delivery date. Note that the intention of the clause was to emphasize that the most important thing is that the claiming party cannot avoid or overcome the event, and not the lack of foresight.

International contracting shows that the most important condition for *force majeure* is the irresistibility of the event or its consequences. For instance, the ICC Force Majeure Clause 2020 (Long Form) regulates in its first paragraph the three traditional requirements of *force majeure* (a, b and c), while the third paragraph contains a list of specific events. According to the comments to this third paragraph, these events are presumed to cause *force majeure*. However, it is a presumption in relation to the conditions that the event is beyond control (a) and could not reasonably have been foreseen at the date of the contract (b), so that it would still remain to be proved that the event or its consequences could not have been avoided or overcome (c)[38].

Paragraph 3 (e) states as presumed events "plague, epidemic, natural disaster or extreme natural event", and not expressly "pandemic". It should be noted that the 2003 model, in the same paragraph 3 (e), referred to "act of God" and included a list of events that could be subsumed under "natural disaster": "(e) act of God, plague, epidemic, natural disaster such as but not limited

---

[38] The 2020 model is similar to the 2003 one since both have nine paragraphs, but the 2020 model makes some improvements, for example, it adds headings to all paragraphs, states that the duty of notice also functions as a burden for the affected party (paragraph 5), and indicates that if the impediment lasts up to 120 days either party may terminate the contract. See the clause in https://iccwbo.org/publication/icc-force-majeure-and-hardship-clauses/.

to violent storm, cyclone, typhoon, hurricane, tornado, blizzard, earthquake, volcanic activity, landslide, tidal wave, tsunami, flood, damage or destruction by lightning, drought". Also, section 2 of clause 33 of the 2005 Mineral Development Agreement between the Republic of Liberia and Mittal Steel Holdings N.V., specifically included as *force majeure* "epidemics" but not "pandemics". But this changed after the Covid-19 outbreak. For instance, the BIMCO Force Majeure Clause 2022 expressly includes plague, epidemic and pandemic as presumptive *force majeure* events in its paragraph (b)(v).

It is interesting to analyze whether the pandemic qualifies as a natural disaster from a legal point of view. It is discussed whether we should focus on the outbreak of the pandemic itself which can occur due to natural or mixed causes, or on the spread of the virus due to human-to-human activity. This is relevant when drafting *force majeure* clauses, and namely to decide if it is sufficient to include "natural disaster", or if "pandemic" must be expressly provided.

The revised wording of the MAC/MAE clause in corporate agreements is also noteworthy. The rule is that the MAC/MAE can only be invoked to terminate the contract in the face of unknown risks, as has been widely established by Delaware courts[39]. So, if there is knowledge of the risk of a pandemic, one would expect the MAC/MAE definition to include pandemic as an exception so that the clause cannot be claimed for a known risk. While some contracts were not clear on this issue, others were. For instance, while the LVMH's acquisition of Tiffany & Co., announced on November 24, 2019, had an MAE that among its exceptions only referred to "other natural disasters"[40], the announced acquisition of E*Trade Financial Corporation by Morgan Stanley on February 20, 2020 had an MAE clause that expressly excluded Covid-19, unless it created

---

[39] On MAC clause in Delaware case law, see S. García Long, *Un big MAC, por favor: la cláusula MAC en fusiones y adquisiciones* (Lima: Facultad de Derecho de la Pontificia Universidad Católica del Perú, 2016).

[40] https://www.sec.gov/Archives/edgar/data/98246/000119312519299997/d840067dex21.htm.

a disproportionately adverse effect. In other words, since the risk was known, Covid-19 was agreed as an exception so that it would not constitute a MAE, but at the same time, an exception to the exception was agreed so that it would constitute a MAE if it would have a disproportionately adverse effect relative to other companies in the same industry[41]. Likewise, on February 20, 2020, the transaction between Sycamore Partners and L Brands Inc. (owner of Victoria's Secret) was announced, whose MAE clause excluded the existence, occurrence or continuation of pandemics[42].

In this context, a study conducted by Jennejohn, Nyarko and Talley in 2020, consisted of a review of contracts announced between 2003 and 2020, which included 1702 MAC clauses. The objective was to identify terms that could be related to a pandemic, from general terms such as "act of God" or "*force majeure*", to more specific ones such as "epidemic", "pandemic" and "public health". Within the MAC, these terms were used as exceptions to the buyer's right to terminate the contract, although in certain cases an exception to the exception was included. The following table summarizes the terms used and their frequency[43]:

---

41 https://www.sec.gov/Archives/edgar/data/1015780/000119312520044851/d886839dex21.htm.
42 https://www.sec.gov/Archives/edgar/data/701985/000095010320003347/dp121693_ex0201.htm.
43 The table is found specifically in M. Jennejohn, J. Nyarko and E. Talley, 'Covid-19 as force majeure in corporate transactions', in K. Pistor (ed.), *Law in the time of Covid-19* (New York: Columbia Law School, 2020), pp. 141–54 (p. 144), however, the full study should be reviewed because it contains other statistical data of relevance. That study has its background in E. Talley and D. O'Kane, 'The Measure of a MAC: A Machine-Learning Protocol for Analyzing Force Majeure Clauses in M&A Agreements', Journal of Institutional and Theoretical Economics, 168 (2012), pp. 181–208.

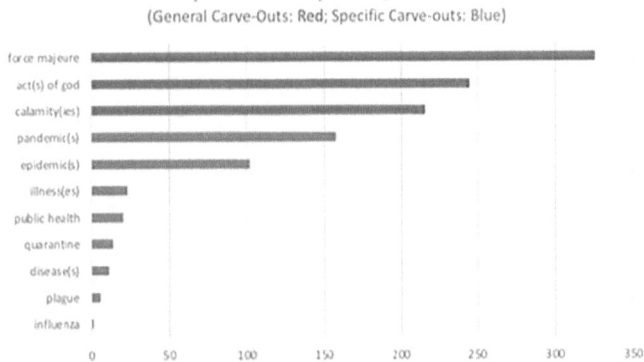

As evidenced by contractual practice, parties have adapted their contracts to better function in a pandemic environment, and these improvements should be considered for future reform in national laws, specifically, Civil Codes.

10. *The need to improve Civil Codes in Latin America and the Caribbean*

With the aim of achieving uniformity and better contract law to facilitate both domestic and cross-border negotiations, various international instruments have taken as their starting point the differences that exist in national jurisdictions and proposed improvements in various areas, including *force majeure*. These improvements are not only useful in the context of international transactions, but also for domestic transactions and legislative reforms, since the aim is that the international instruments are also used to interpret and supplement national law, especially where there are gaps or inefficiencies.

The improvements formulated in transnational contract law on *force majeure* that should be taken into account by national laws, especially in Latin America and the Caribbean, are the following:

- No distinction should be made between act of God and *force majeure*. Only one term should be used. One should only refer to "impediment" or *force majeure*; and in any case, if the distinction between act of God and *force majeure* is insisted upon out of respect for tradition, legal professionals should use them indistinctly and as synonyms, without formulating similarities or differences between them.

- The conditions for an impediment to qualify as *force majeure* and excuse non-performance are four: (1) that the impediment is beyond reasonable control, (2) that it is not reasonable to expect that the impediment was taken into account at the time the contract was entered into, (3) that it is not reasonable to avoid or overcome the impediment or its consequences, and (4) that the risk of occurrence of the impediment or its consequences has not been assumed by the affected party.

- All of the four conditions must be met. To consider that this should not be so is based on the premise of insisting on the distinction between act of God and *force majeure*, and on the believe that some conditions should be more relevant than others in some case. On the contrary, if no difference is recognized, all conditions must be met in any case.

- It is advisable to pay attention to the contractual structure of *force majeure* clauses to identify those aspects that are not considered by national laws, but that can be included by agreement. For instance, national laws do not expressly regulate specific duties such as the duties of notification, evidence, mitigation, best efforts, renegotiation, good faith, and others.

Transnational contract law does what is sometimes not a priority in national laws: it facilitates the application of the law instead of creating conceptual categories that are only useful in law schools, but not in national and international contractual practice.

Elena de Carvalho Gomes[*]
BETWEEN EXCUSABILITY AND RECOGNIZABILITY
The 1942 *Codice Civile* and the Discipline of Mistake in the 2002 Brazilian Civil Code

1. The Roots of the import of Italian models in Brazilian civil law

The influence of Italian law in the Brazilian system[1] is not a novel phenomenon, as illustrated, for instance, by the frequency with which the Italian doctrine is cited in manuals and scientific works, as well as legal decisions. Evidence of such authority is found in various fields of law. Civil law was the segment most clearly influenced by Italian doctrine and law. While such sway was already discernable in the first half of the 20th century, it became increasingly apparent and intense after World War II until becoming finally manifest at the beginning of the current century, with the introduction of the present Civil Code of 2002.

Following Brazil's independence from Portugal and a series of unsuccessful attempts to pass unified legislation, the first Brazilian Civil Code was finally enacted in 1916[2]. Its author,

---

[*] Associate Professor of Civil Law at the Federal University of Minas Gerais, in Belo Horizonte, Brazil. Ph.D. from the Scuola Superiore Sant'Anna di Studi Universitari e di Perfezionamento, in Pisa, Italy.
The Author thanks Nina França for the help with the translation of the paper

[1] E. de Carvalho Gomes, 'Conteúdo da *Obligatio*: Federico Procchi em Paráfrase', Estudos Sociais e Políticos, 17 (Belo Horizonte: Revista Brasileira de Estudos Políticos, 2005), 17–38, p.17.

[2] The 1824 Constitution of the Empire of Brazil, enacted by Emperor D. Pedro I after the declaration of independence from Portugal, established that the lawmaker should "organize", "as soon as possible", a civil code and a criminal code, "founded on the solid bases of Justice and Equity." Throughout the 19th century, there were several attempts at codifying civil law. It seems worth referring to the "incomplete monument" by Augusto Teixeira de Freitas, known as *Esboço*, an unfinished work of 4,908 articles, which strongly influenced the Argentinian codification of 1869. J.P. Schmidt,

Clovis Bevilaqua, availed of several sources to draft the first code. The BGB and the *Code Civil* were especially influential, although the experience of previous attempts at codification also inspired the 1916 Civil Code's development, as well as the *Codice Civile* of 1865 (known as "*Codice Pisanelli*"), albeit to a limited extent[3].

Throughout the 20th century, Italian Private Law doctrine became increasingly influential among Brazilian jurists. Various circumstances can be conjectured to explain why Italian law specifically emerged as an important reference point for the Brazilian Private Law doctrine. First, it is significant that several Italian jurists, immigrated to Brazil during World War II to escape ethnic persecution. That was the case of Enrico Tullio Liebman — who, to be clear, was a proceduralist — and of Tullio Ascarelli, both of whom taught at the University of São Paulo. The presence of such jurists whose works were already acknowledged at the time has very likely contributed to the diffusion of the Italian doctrine[4] in Brazil. There is no doubt, however, that the formation of an intellectual elite in tune with the ideas of Italian nationalism in the interwar period represented a fundamental factor for a definitive proximity between Brazilian jurists and Italian civil law. To this elite belonged precisely the one who would become, so to speak, the *father* of the Brazilian Civil Code currently in force: Miguel Reale[5].

The son of an Italian immigrant, Miguel Reale was an already recognized natural law philosopher and publicist when he assumed the position in 1969 of coordinator of the commission

---

Zivilrechtskodifikation in Brasilien (Tübingen: Mohr Siebeck, 2009), p. 33. Teixeira de Freitas's importance to Latin-American law can be measured by the important volume that was dedicated to him by the *Centro Interdisciplinare di Studi Latinoamericani* of Tor Vergata University of Rome: S. Schipani (ed.), *Augusto Teixeira de Freitas e il Diritto Latinoamericano* (Padova: CEDAM, 1988).

3 Pontes de Miranda, *Fontes e Evolução do Direito Civil Brasileiro*, 2nd edn (Rio de Janeiro: Forense, 1981), p. 93.
4 De Carvalho Gomes, p. 17.
5 Schmidt, p. 68.

in charge of drafting a civil code[6]. This was a surprising choice for the Brazilian legal environment, and not only because of Reale's field of education. Despite being undeniably one of the most important Brazilian jurists of the 20th century and already widely celebrated back then, in a country so well-represented by accomplished authorities on Private Law, Reale's appointment was perceived as faintly disparaging of the field (subordinating it to Public Law) and thus unthinkable[7]. It should be noted, however, that Brazil was under a military regime at the time — a circumstance that somehow made the choice for Miguel Reale less surprising.

Throughout his lifetime, Miguel Reale was regularly involved in Brazilian politics, especially in his home State of São Paulo where he occupied several public positions in different fields. For the current discussion, his involvement with the Brazilian integralist movement (which he joined in 1933) seems particularly interesting. The so-called *Integralismo*, of which Reale soon became a prominent figure, was a movement created in 1932 that aimed to lay the foundation for a Brazilian form of nationalism, following the model of Italian fascism. However, the movement lost momentum following the ban in 1938 of the Brazilian Integralist Action, the group in charge of promoting such ideas, and Miguel Reale subsequently distanced himself from the campaign[8]. Nevertheless, it is arguable that many of the ideas and concepts of *Integralismo* continued through the thoughts and works of Miguel Reale.

Since the beginning of his education, Reale always exhibited special preference for the Italian legal science, having been strongly influenced by it[9]. Such partiality is very clearly revealed

---

[6] The project that would become the 2002 Civil Code was submitted by Miguel Reale to the Brazilian Government in 1975. For several reasons, mostly political, the project was merely converted into law — with many changes from the original text — in 2002. For this reason, the 2002 Civil Code is critiqued for containing archaic provisions. For articulated remarks on the legislative process of the 2002 Civil Code, see Schmidt, p. 90.

[7] Schmidt, p. 67.
[8] Schmidt, p. 69.
[9] Schmidt, p. 67.

in the 2002 Civil Code, which the Jurist — as the Code's "key figure" (*Schlüsselfigur*)[10] — drafted in such a manner that it is impossible to understand without knowledge of of his way of thinking. Indeed, the extensive influence of the Italian doctrine and the 1942 *Codice Civile* represent one of Reale's most significant marks on the current Brazilian Civil Code.

Such imprinting is revealed at several levels, including through the Code's principles and its interventionist character (which is very focused on the role of general clauses and their implementation by judges)[11], as well as provisions pertaining to specific institutions which rules are often based on mere translations of the *Codice Civile*. That is the case of mistake, a circumstance which taints intent, as will be discussed below.

2. *The Codice Civile in the General Part (*Allgemeiner Teil*) of the 2002 Brazilian Civil Code*

If it is true that the current Brazilian Civil Code was largely inspired by the 20th century Italian doctrine and the *Codice Civile*, it is also correct that these were not the sole sources of inspiration of the Brazilian lawmaker. Indeed, the 2002 Civil Code is anything but a mere reproduction of the Italian codification. Its division into a General Part and a Special Part — a established dichotomy of Pandectist origin — denies this conclusion, as does the provision of the *legal transaction* (*Rechtsgeschäft*), as opposed to the *legal act* (*acte juridique*), as the main category of legal facts. This is further confirmed by the documented influence of the Portuguese Civil Code[12] and the inexplicit yet unequivocal incorporation of norms from other legal systems[13]. Nevertheless, the *Codice Civile* undeniably

---

10   Schmidt, p. 68.
11   Schmidt, p. 70.
12   J.C: Moreira Alves, *A Parte Geral do Projeto de Código Civil Brasileiro* (São Paulo: Saraiva, 1986), p. 98.
13   This is the case, for example, of article 11 of the 2002 Civil Code, which is directly inspired by article 5 of the Peruvian Civil Code.

represents one of the fundamental paradigms of the Brazilian codification of 2002, sufficing to recall the references made thereto by José Carlos Moreira Alves, the author responsible for the General Part, for whom the Italian Code represents a "model of the legal technique" and which, moreover, would have been very useful to the Portuguese lawmaker[14].

Several provisions of the 2002 Civil Code are rooted in the *Codice Civile*, especially in the General Part. For example, mirroring article 5 of the Italian Civil Code[15], article 13[16] generally prohibits acts of disposal of one's body that may permanently impair physical integrity or are contrary to "good customs" (understood as public decency). This is also the case of article 93, which substantially defines the *pertenças*, a category absent from the 1916 Civil Code, according to the same criteria set out in article 817 of the Codice Civile, although the Brazilian discipline differs from the Italian one[17].

The provisions governing mistake, a circumstance which taints one's intent to participate in a legal transaction, also clearly illustrate the influence of the 1942 Italian codification experience on the 2002 Brazilian Civil Code. In fact, breaking

---

14   Moreira Alves, p. 24.
15   Art. 5. "(Atti di disposizione del proprio corpo). Gli atti di disposizione del proprio corpo sono vietati quando cagionino una diminuzione permanente dell'integrità fisica, o quando siano altrimenti contrari alla legge, all'ordine pubblico o al buon costume".
16   This is the wording of article 13 of the 2002 Brazilian Civil Code: "Art. 13. Salvo por exigência médica, è defeso o ato de disposição do próprio corpo, quando importar diminuição permanente da integridade física, ou contrariar os bons costumes. Parágrafo único. O ato previsto neste artigo será admitido para fins de transplante, na forma estabelecida em lei especial".
17   The definition of the *pertenças* is basically the same, so that article 93 of the 2002 Civil Code essentially represents a translation of article 817 of the *Codice Civile*: the *pertenças* would be things destined, in a lasting way, towards the service or embellishment of something else. This institute's regime, however, is shown to be distinct because, while in the Italian system, unless otherwise stipulated, the legal transactions that concern the main asset also include the *pertenças* (*Codice Civile*, art. 818), according to article 94 of the 2002 Civil Code, the presumption is precisely the opposite, that is, the legal transactions that pertain to the main asset, in principle, do not include the *pertenças*.

with the traditional view on the Brazilian institution, the current discipline is founded on provisions of the *Codice Civile* translated into Portuguese. At the same time, if it is true that the regulation in question represented a novelty in Brazilian law, inspired in particular by a Civil Code then considered technically superior, it cannot be denied that the Brazilian doctrine was not yet fully prepared to abandon the parameters that had always oriented the treatment given to the subject matter. This still happens today, albeit with less intensity.

3. Excusability *in the Discipline of Mistake in Brazilian Law*

The laws governing mistake have always highlighted the limits of legal transactions being founded exclusively and in radical terms, on the intention of the parties. That is, circumstances affecting intent have generally fallen within the scope of the rules on mistake. This is because if *consent* were the determining criteria, it would be flawed to assert that such acceptance had been formed according to an erroneous assumption relating to the object or the person whom the declaration of intention referred[18]. In other words, if the validity of a transaction were to depend on the correspondence between the will and its outward expression (i.e. declaration of intent), then acts that did not reflect the party's express intent must be considered flawed, resulting in their invalidation as a consequence of mistake[19]. At best[20] one could require the mistake be relevant, that is, one without which the party would not have entered into the contract. Thus, the legal relevance of mistakes in spite of which the transactions would have been nevertheless celebrated, even if in some other way,

---

18 In this sense, J.B. Villela, 'Da *Razón* para Errar de Vélez Sarsfield à *Conocibilidad* do Novo Código Civil Peruano: Tendências Latino-Americanas a uma Teoria Objetivista do Erro', in S. Schipani (ed.), *Dalmacio Vélez Sarsfield e il Diritto Latinoamericano* (Padova: CEDAM, 1991), pp. 331–39, p. 331.
19 Villela, p. 332.
20 Villela, p. 332.

the so-called "accidental mistakes", would be withdrawn. Even so, under the "primacy of the intention", the acknowledgement of the mistake as a vitiating factor depended exclusively on proving the divergence between what was declared based on a false perception of reality and what would have been declared if there were no mistake. Ultimately, the validity of the declaration of intention remained subordinated to circumstances related only and exclusively to the mistaken party, which thus made irrelevant the position of the counterparty, who could only "accept" the outcome of the legal transaction.

Throughout the 20th century, the discipline of mistake was criticized for, among other things, providing broad protections for the mistaken party. More specifically, as the Brazilian Civil Code of 1916 only required the mistake be substantial for the declaration of annulment of acts resulting therefrom[21], a transaction could be invalidated for the mere existence of a mistake without regard for any other circumstances. Thus, the law could potentially reward those whose mistake was the result of carelessness or inattentiveness. This seemed illogical and was further inconsistent with the rules found in authoritative doctrine, such as Teixeira de Freitas's *Esboço*, that excluded the possibility of annulment whenever the mistake was a consequence of negligence or imprudence; in other words, when it was not excusable[22]. In this context, despite the absence of a singular and specific provision, the Brazilian doctrine — with exceptions[23], although few — began introducing, in addition to the standard of substantiality, the standard of *excusability* as a requirement for the invalidation of one's declaration of intention[24]. Thus, an additional requirement was established, although not textually by

---

21 That was what article 86 prescribed: "Legal transaction are voidable when the declarations of intention come from a substantial mistake".
22 Art. 466. "Ignorance or factual mistake will not benefit the agents, whenever there has been negligence or imprudence on their part, without which the illicit act would not have been done": A. Teixeira de Freitas, *Código Civil – Esboço* (Brasília: Ministério da Justiça 1983), p. 171.
23 For the exceptions, Villela, p. 332, n. 7.
24 In this sense, E.C. Silveira Marchi and others, *Comentários ao Código Civil Brasileiro* (São Paulo: Atlas, 2013), p. 134.

law. It was argued, however, that this requirement was implicit in the legal text, as Silvio Rodrigues defended, among others:

> The law does not expressly require the excusability of mistake in order to admit it among the vitiating factors of the legal act. So that, if the interpreter sticks to mere literal legal exegesis, it is enough for the mistake to be substantial to make the act voidable.
>
> Such interpretation, in my opinion, is inadmissible. [...] The omission of this premise in the law stems from the fact that the lawmaker understands that it can be found implicit in the concept of the mistake, it thus being superfluous to insist.
>
> It appears to be effectively impossible to imagine that the law can authorize the undoing of a legal act for the benefit of those who promoted it, based on an inexcusable mistake.[25]

Those in favor of the standard of excusability (uncontemplated by the law) argued that such requirement was necessary to protect the reliance of the counterparty on the mistaken party's declaration of intention[26], noting that the former should not have to bear the consequences of an error (i.e., invalidity of the transaction) caused by the lack of attention or precaution of the mistaken party. That is, when the mistake was such that "it wouldn't be committed by an individual of common intelligence"[27]. It seems, however, that proponents of this solution were less concerned with protecting the counterparty as, to some extent, punishing the careless mistaken party by preventing the annulment of the act, with the view that "an inexcusable mistake [is] equivalent to bad faith"[28]. Accordingly, it seems relevant that "excusability" was commonly defined in "negative terms", as the inexistence of a "good" reason for making the mistake. As explained by Caio Mário da Silva Pereira, one of the greatest Brazilian jurists of the 20th century:

---

25 S. Rodrigues, *Direito Civil: Parte Geral*, I, 25th edn (São Paulo: Saraiva, 1995), p. 189.
26 O. Gomes, *Introdução ao Direito Civil*, 18th edn (Rio de Janeiro: Forense, 2001), p. 417.
27 C. M. da Silva Pereira, *Instituições de Direito Civil*, I, 17th edn (Rio de Janeiro: Forense, 1995), p. 329.
28 Gomes, p. 417.

The doctrine also adds that the mistake is to be considered excusable, not affecting the transaction, only when the agent proceeds without the normal precautions, that is, such that an individual of common intelligence would not make it.[29]

4. The Codice Civile and the criteria of the recognizability of mistake in the 2002 Brazilian Civil Code

Excusability constituted a fundamental reference point in the Brazilian discipline of mistake when the 2002 Civil Code entered into force, after more than twenty years of proceedings in the National Congress. The legal discipline set out in the new Code governing cases of mistake was expected to be oriented by this element, which had been an established standard in the Brazilian doctrine and case law since the 20th century absent an explicit legal reference. After all, it represented an important indicator of the comprehension of the category by the national doctrine. This was not, however, what happened. Instead, the 2002 Civil Code adopted a model that, at least at a first glance, seemed incompatible with the requirement of excusability: the one from the *Codice Civile*.

The definition of the legally relevant mistake, found in article 138 of the 2002 Civil Code, composes a synthesis of articles 1428[30] and 1431[31] of the Italian Civil Code. That is not a mere coincidence. The jurist responsible for writing the Brazilian Civil Code's General Part, José Carlos Moreira Alves, never hid its direct inspiration[32]. Nevertheless, he always argued that article 138 of the 2002 Civil Code should be read bearing in mind that, for it to be legally relevant, the mistake should be excusable —

---

29 S. Pereira, p. 329.
30 Art. 1428. Rilevanza dell'errore. "L'errore è causa di annullamento del contratto quando è essenziale ed è riconoscibile dall'altro contraente".
31 Art. 1431. Errore riconoscibile. "L'errore si considera riconoscibile quando, in relazione al contenuto, alle circostanze del contratto ovvero alla qualità dei contraenti, una persona di normale diligenza avrebbe potuto rilevarlo".
32 Moreira Alves, p. 50.

a feature absent from the foundation of the Italian discipline of 1942.

Indeed, according to articles 1428 and 1431 of the *Codice Civile*, a contract may only be annulled if the mistake is substantial *and recognizable* by the other party, understood as able to be perceived by an "ordinarily diligent person" in light of the circumstances of the contract or the quality of the contracting parties. Hence, the fact that the mistaken party had a reason to commit an error is not necessarily relevant for the purpose of establishing the existence of a vitiating factor, and therefore does not alone entitle the mistaken party to annul the legal transaction; it is fundamental that the mistake be susceptible to objective acknowledgement. That is why it is said that the *Codice Civile* adopts, in terms of subject matter, the criteria of the recognizability of the mistake.

According to the Italian doctrine, the 1942 lawmaker sought to promote the protection of justified reliance[33] through the adoption of recognizability. The idea is basically as follows: on the one hand, the mistake renders the relevant transaction inadequate to its intended function, i.e., to act as an instrument for people to autonomously carry out their economic plans, providing structure for their interests; on the other hand, the mistaken party does not act alone[34]. More specifically, legal transactions typically involve a party, who through his/her declarations sets the tone of the negotiating structure, and a counterparty, who relies on and behaves according to those statements, expecting certain effects. Furthermore, just as the expressions of the mistaken party must be taken into account, so must the expectations and reliance arising therefrom[35]. In an attempt to balance the different interests at stake, the Italian lawmaker provided that legal transactions tainted by mistake may to be annulled, but not

---

[33] A. Trabucchi, *Istituzioni di Diritto Civile*, 49th edn (Milan: Wolters Kluver – CEDAM, 2019), 148; E. Navarretta, 'Capitolo Quarto', in U. Breccia and others, *Diritto Privato*, 1st part, 2nd edn (Torino: UTET, 2010), p. 281.

[34] P. Trimarchi, *Istituzioni di Diritto Privato*, 19th edn (Milan: Giuffrè, 2011), p. 175.

[35] Trimarchi, p. 176.

at the expense of the counterparty's reliance. In other words, the lawmaker does not place the risk of annulment on the party that relied upon the validity of the act, unless it, having acted with the ordinary diligence required by law, could have perceived the other party's mistake[36].

It follows, then, that the Italian Civil Code bases the legal relevance of the mistake on a requirement unrelated to its "excusability", which traditionally characterized the Brazilian discipline of the subject in the 20th century. So, while requiring the excusability of the mistake focuses, fundamentally and exclusively, on the behavior of the mistaken party (irrespective of the counterparty's interest and reliance on the validity of the transaction), requiring the mistake to be recognizable shifts the attention to the counterparty, who is penalized via the undoing of the transaction for failing to detect a mistake that could have been noticed by an ordinarily diligent person.

Since the 2002 Civil Code was inspired by the Italian rules on mistake, one would think that the same considerations on the recognizability of the error would be found also in Brazil, thus excluding the relevance of the mistake's excusability for the annulment of the legal transaction. That did not happen. Moreover, it is surprising that José Carlos Moreira Alves himself supported the coexistence of both criteria[37]. This was apparently the rule contained in the Draft[38], a provision that was harshly criticized by another member of the Commission, Clóvis do Couto e Silva, who did not share the view that excusability *and* recognizability should be relevant for the invalidation of a legal transaction tainted by mistake[39].

According to Moreira Alves, "maintaining both requirements" was justified for two reasons. First, despite the law's silence, it was customary in practice to consider whether a mistake was

---

36 Navarretta, p. 281.
37 Moreira Alves, p. 49.
38 Art. 146: "Legal transactions are voidable when the declarations of intention emanate from a substantial mistake, as long as it is excusable and recognizable by the other party." Moreira Alves, p. 47, n. 12.
39 Moreira Alves, p. 47, n. 12.

excusable. Second, echoing article 1428 of the *Codice Civile* was not sufficient per se to justify the annulment of a legal transaction based only on the recognizability. Moreover, according to the Author, "combining the two requirements would make it harder — and less damaging to the counterparty — to annul a legal transaction on the grounds of mistake which, as Prof. Couto e Silva acknowledges, is a tendency of modern law"[40].

Moreira Alves' observation is indubitably accurate since requiring both conditions would make it drastically more difficult to annul legal transactions tainted by mistake. Indeed, the mistaken party is effectively faced with a double burden: on the one hand, s/he must prove the mistake was excusable (i.e., committed without fault); on the other, s/he must demonstrate that such mistake should have been noticed by the counterparty. Therefore, a solution providing the mistaken party with "total helplessness" is only available if both conditions are met[41].

In the end, the Commission abandoned the requirement of "excusability of the mistake" in favor of unequivocal protection of the counterparty's reliance, as illustrated by the requirement of recognizability contained in the current article 138[42]. Furthermore, if the lawmaker intended to render the regime of the mistake useful and practical, no alternative requirement would have been suitable.

5. *End of discussion?*

Considering article 138 of the Brazilian Civil Code, inspired by the *Codice Civile*, subordinates the annulment of the legal transaction to the mistake's ability to be perceived by a person of normal diligence and in light of the circumstances, it is conceivable that Brazilian law would exclude the relevance of excusability despite its historical importance (especially during

---

40 Moreira Alves, p. 52.
41 J. Casillo, *O Erro como Vício da Vontade* (São Paulo: Revista dos Tribunais, 1982), p. 69.
42 Casillo, p. 69.

the 20th century). Indeed, much of the doctrine recognizes that the 2002 Civil Code favored recognizability over excusability in order to protect reliance[43]. This position was also explicitly acknowledged in an interpretation of the Civil Code, approved in 2002 at the Civil Law Workshops (*Jornadas de Direito Civil*), sponsored by the Center of Legal Studies of the Federal Justice Council. According to the interpretation, "In the purview of article 138, it is irrelevant whether the mistake is excusable, because the legal provision adopts the principle of the protection of reliance"[44].

Surprisingly, the voices that manifested in favor of maintaining the requirement of excusability were not few, as if the 2002 Civil Code had not promoted a deep reform of the discipline of mistake, inspired by the Italian codification[45]. For instance, some scholars, such as José Carlos Moreira Alves, argued that

---

43 A.A.A.M. Magalhães, *O Erro no negócio Jurídico* (São Paulo: Atlas, 2011), 102; S. de Salvo Venosa, *Direito Civil: Parte Geral* (São Paulo: Atlas, 2001), p. 348; C. Chaves de Farias and N. Rosenvald, *Curso de Direito Civil: Parte Geral e LINDB*, I, 13rd edn (São Paulo: Atlas, 2015), p. 544.

44 R. Rosado de Aguiar Júnior (ed.), *Jornadas de Direito Civil I, III e IV: Enunciados Aprovados* (Brasília: CJF, 2007), p. 18. The "Civil Law Workshops" (*Jornadas de Direito Civil*) were an initiative sponsored by the Center of Legal Studies of the Federal Justice Council, central organ of the federal Brazilian legal structure. The goal of the event, whose first edition happened precisely in 2002, in the period of *vacatio legis* of the 2002 Civil Code, consisted in promoting the discussion about the new diploma, aiming to elaborate interpretative statements that could help with the task of applying the law. The proposals for statements were discussed and voted by groups composed of representatives from different legal careers and civil law scholars, who could approve or refute them. R. Rosado de Aguiar Júnior, 'Apresentação', in R. Rosado de Aguiar Júnior (ed.), *Jornadas de Direito Civil I, III e IV: Enunciados Aprovados* (Brasília: CJF, 2007), p. 9. While being in the wider aspect of the theory of the sources of law, the interpretative statements fit into the category of doctrinal sources of law, they have an enormous importance in Brazilian law, in which they are frequently invoked as rules of legal nature.

45 P. Stolze Gagliano and R. Pamplona Filho, *Novo Curso de Direito Civil: Parte Geral*, 11th edn (São Paulo: Saraiva, 2009), p. 348. Also, C.R. Gonçalves, *Direito Civil Brasileiro*, I, 6th edn. (São Paulo: Saraiva, 2008), p. 368, although he considers the wording of article 138 "defective", he affirms it cannot be said with certainty that the 2002 Civil Code has adopted the criterion of recognizability.

both requisites — excusability and recognizability — should be relevant. However, while the latter advocated the express provision of both conditions in the legal text, despite the wording of article 138 of the 2002 Civil Code, current supporters of this "hybrid position" insisted (and continue to insist) that a mistake must in any case be "excusable" for it to invalidate the legal transaction; provided it is also established that the mistake could have been perceived by a person of normal diligence, in light of the transaction's circumstances[46].

As discussed above, the black letter of article 138 does not allow for such interpretation, which significantly distorts the scope of the provision and renders the mistake practically an allegorical figure, given it is virtually impossible for the mistaken party to invoke the condition. It seems that part of the Brazilian doctrine insists on maintaining the criterion of excusability (despite the legal context is entirely hostile to it) for reasons related to the prestige that this requirement has always enjoyed, whose acknowledgement has always dispensed explicit legal acceptance. Why should it be different with the 2002 Civil Code?

The difference lies precisely in the paradigms adopted by the two lawmakers to provide for the annulment of the legal transaction by mistake. While the Civil Code of 1916 did not impose great onuses on the mistaken party (a circumstance that indeed made it necessary to introduce an additional requirement, even if not written) to invalidate the act, the 2002 Civil Code tracked a different path. In the wake of the Italian model, the current Brazilian codification had already opted for this additional requirement, having passed over the need to prove the excusability of the mistake in favor of recognizability. Once one is elected, there is no space for another. *Tertium non datur*. This was, moreover, defended in Italy, as noted by Torrente and Schlesinger:

---

46 C. Fiúza, *Direito Civil: Curso Completo*, 18th edn (São Paulo: Saraiva, 2015), p. 304; F. Menke, 'Art. 138', in G.E. Nanni (ed.), *Comentários ao Código Civil: Direito Civil Contemporâneo* (São Paulo: Saraiva, 2019), p. 228.

It is discussed whether, besides the requirements of essentiality and recognizability, it would be necessary for the mistake not to depend on the mistaken party's fault. Such requirement was considered necessary by the doctrine formed under the repealed code, which justified it with recourse to the aforementioned theory of responsibility. Since the current code has been inspired by a different theory, that of recognizability, which gives importance to the reliance of those the declaration of intention is directed at, the excusable or inexcusable character of the mistake does not seem to have any relevance (*see* Cass. 13 marzo 2006, n. 5429).[47]

6. Conclusion

Although the Brazilian legal doctrine's interest in Italian law is not recent, it was undoubtedly renewed with the arrival of the 2002 Civil Code. Indeed, the Italian *Codice Civile*, considered a "model of legal technique", has inspired Brazilian law in many aspects. One example is provided by the rules on mistake, a condition that taints intent, which, compared to the previous regime, gradually began to favor the requirement of recognizability over excusability as grounds for annulling a legal transaction that had been concluded as a result of error.

The unmistakable change of the legal paradigm was not sufficient to alter the way mistake was understood, which is still somehow interpreted in Brazil according to the 1916 Civil Code. Thus, the evolution of the legal discipline of mistake confirms that legal transplant does not, per se, translate to effective social and economic reform if the local environment does not provide the "suitable cement" in which such provisions and/or solutions can prosper[48]. Something that, when it comes to mistake, does not seem to have happened.

---

47   A. Torrente and P. Schlesinger, *Manuale di diritto privato*, 23rd edn (Milano: Giuffrè, 2017), p. 566.
48   The image comes from L. Léon Hilario, *La responsabilidade Civil: Lineas fundamentales e nuevas perspectivas*, 3rd edn (Breña: Instituto Pacífico, 2017), p. 168.

Freddy Andrés Hung Gil[*]
THE CENTRALITY OF THE PERSON FOR THE LEGAL SYSTEM
Reflections on the Protection of the Unborn Child

I. *The person and its centrality for the legal system*

The person, which undoubtedly constitutes one of the basic notions for legal science and especially for Civil Law, does not belong exclusively to these as it is a polysemic and transdisciplinary notion. This is evidenced by the fact that, alongside the legal concept, there are non-legal meanings of "person" that are relevant to other spheres of human knowledge. Numerous disciplines use the term "person" as a category, each attributing their own meaning and theoretical scope. From a legal point of view, the concept of person does not attempt to explain its essence as a reality or phenomenon beyond the legal sphere. Rather, as submitted by Recaséns Sichés, it attempts to clarify what this legal qualification[1] consists of — which is not limited to men and women considered generically or individually, but extends to other realities: the non-individual legal person.

The legal concept of person, in its essence, takes the human being as its point of reference. The notion of man precedes that of person and, the latter, appears as an allusion in the forensic language of the authors of classical antiquity and even outside it, to the legal dimension or aspect of the human being. The concrete notion of *homines* (which is the basis of the Roman abstraction of *humanitas*) is strongly linked to other legal concepts such as *liberi, servi, cives romani, ingenui* and *qui in utero sunt,* among

---

[*] Full Professor of Civil Law, Faculty of Law, University of Havana, Cuba. Notary Public.
[1] L. Recaséns Sichés, *Filosofía del Derecho*, 14th edn (México: Porrúa, 1999), p. 261.

others. For the ancient Latin jurists, according to Catalano, "the notions of *homo* and *persona* evidenced different aspects of the same concrete reality: man"[2]. However, it should be stressed that for Roman private law, individuality is not conceived as a primordial idea (although it will become so after a gradual process which does not even culminate in the work of Justinian). The *ius privatum* will take as its primary reference point the family group and, within this, a privileged subject will have primacy: the *pater familias*[3].

The influence of Roman law, and particularly the theory of the three states (*libertatis*, *civitatis* and *familiae*), is notable in the subsequent reworking of the concept of the person. From Justinian Law and up to the Renaissance, through the work of the medieval canonists, the principle that *persona est homo in status quondam consideratus*[4] remained effective, despite in some sources the term is used in a way similar to the modern notion of legal capacity[5]. The concept of the person inherited from the Justinian tradition underwent modifications from the 16th century onwards, which tended to break down the notions of man and person. Another notable tribute to the doctrinal construction of the modern notion of person is introduced by the contributions of various German schools (especially in the 19th century), under which new concepts such as personality, capacity, and the legal fiction to regulate the capacity of the *nasciturus*, among others, were formulated[6].

The theories of Ferrara and Kelsen have contributed to the consolidation of the position described above. Ferrara, in his "Theory of legal persons", states that the person is a merely

---

[2] P. Catalano, *Diritto e persone*, tomo I – *Studi su origine e attualità del Sistema Romano* (Torino: Giappichelli, 1990), p. 169.

[3] J. Iglesias, *Derecho Romano*, 12th edn (Barcelona: Ariel, 1999), p. 327.

[4] Cfr. J.G. Heinecio, *Recitaciones del Derecho Civil según el orden de la Instituta*, 2nd edn, I, trans. by L. de Collantes (Paris: Librería Salvá, 1847), p. 57.

[5] Cfr. Nov. Theod. II, 17,1, Inst. 1,16,4.

[6] M. Gayosso y Navarrete, *Persona: naturaleza original del concepto en los derechos romano y náhuatl* (Veracruz: Ediciones Universidad Veracruzana, 1992), pp. 50–52.

formal legal concept that does not presuppose corporeality or spirituality in the invested subject, so that man holds this status by the force of the legal system. For Kelsen, the person (both individual and non-individual) is a person as a center of normative imputation, not a reality but a concept immanent to the legal order, constructed by it and which does not find its ultimate meaning beyond the legal sphere[7].

In recent decades, the doctrine has debated the legal nature of the person, resulting in an abundance of literature on the topic under consideration, with the corresponding appearance of scientific theories, including[8]:

1) Formalist theory, which groups together those who maintain that the person is a legal category imputable to man or to another type of reality, as provided for by the legal system;

2) Realist theory, which contrary to the formalist theory, affirms that the category of person refers to a natural reality which is a *prius* with respect to the Law;

3) Eclectic theory, according to which the nature of man and the legal recognition thereof as a formal category complement rather than exclude each other.

Espinoza adds to the theories analyzed, the so-called "three-dimensional theory", whose main exponents are the Spanish civilists, Díez- Picazo and Gullón, who state:

> What does it mean in the legal order to recognize man as a person? We believe that it is not enough to recognize his aptitude to be the subject of rights and obligations or, if you like, of legal relations, as this would be to minimize it. It means above all that legal rules must be given and developed taking into account the dignity of man as a person and his attributes.

---

7 H. Kelsen, *El método y los conceptos fundamentales de la Teoría pura del Derecho*, 1st edn (Madrid: Revista de Derecho Privado, 1933), p. 43; G. Radbruch, *Filosofía del Derecho* (Granada: Editorial Comares, 1999), p. 167.

8 C. Fernández Sessarego, *La noción jurídica de la persona*, 2nd edn (Lima: Fondo editorial de la Facultad de Derecho de la Universidad Nacional Mayor de San Marcos, 1968); J. Espinoza Espinoza, *Derecho de las personas*, 5th edn (Lima: Editorial Rodhas SAC, 2006), pp. 165–66.

The existence, therefore, of the recognition of the person conditions the very production of the person and his development.[9]

The three-dimensional theory, although manifesting certain features of eclecticism, is noteworthy because, far from focusing on a controversy between iusnaturalist and iuspositivist positions — which, moreover, is of no real practical significance at present, since the States recognize the status of every human being as a person — it alludes to the axiological dimension of the person[10]. The apparently irreconcilable tension between both positions can lead to another solution which is not merely eclectic — and this demonstrates the validity of the theory defended by the Spanish civilists — but more centered on man as the ultimate reason, together with social life, for Law. Law can be conceived as a set of rules and canons in which man is merely the necessary piece for the functioning of the enormous machinery, when it should be quite the opposite. In this way, a remarkably humanistic vision of the legal phenomenon is achieved, which cannot be alien to it.

II. *Reflections on the protection of the unborn child. Theories on the legal status of the unborn child. The legal status of the extracorporeal embryo*

The word *nasciturus* is the Latin word that identifies the conceived human being still in the maternal womb, differentiating it from *natus*, which is already born. *Nasciturus* is the future participle of the verb *nascor*, which means to be born. In the Spanish language there is no equivalent of this term,

---

9   L. Díez-Picazo and A. Gullón, *Sistema de Derecho Civil*, I (Madrid: Editorial Tecnos, 1992), p. 223. Cfr. F. De Castro y Bravo, *Derecho civil de España*, II (Madrid: Instituto de Estudios Políticos, 1952; reedición facsímil, Editorial Civitas, 1984), pp. 32 ff., M. Alonso Pérez, 'Reflexiones sobre el concepto y valor de la persona en el "Derecho Civil de España"', Anuario de Derecho Civil, XXXVI, 3 (octubre-diciembre, 1983), p. 1117 ff.

10 Universal Declaration of Human Rights Article 6. See the content of the interventions at the SISDiC Sicily Conference ("La personalità umana nell'ordinamento giuridico" di Pietro Perlingieri, cinquant'anni dopo) LUMSA Palermo, 5-6 novembre 2021.

so the doctrine continually uses the Latin word or other Spanish variants such as *"concebido"* or *"el que habrá de nacer"* (the one who will be born)[11].

In terminology, there is a line of continuity — as Catalano points out — that goes from the Roman Republic to the Principate and extends to the 18th century, in which the technical term to identify the unborn child is based on the Latin locution, *"qui in utero sunt"*. Other expressions such as *conceptus, liberi nondum nati, qui nasci speratur*, are less frequent or come from later sources[12]. The *Siete Partidas* refer to the state in which men can be found to "born or to be born" (Prologue to T. XXIII, P. IV) or expressly allude to "the creature in its mother's womb" (P. IV, T. XXIII, L. III). Modern Civil Codes use terms that reflect, to a certain extent, the previous legislative tradition: *"concebido"* in the Spanish Civil Code of 1888 and in the Cuban Civil Code of 1987; *"ungeborne kinder"* in the Allgemeines Landrecht and in the Austrian Civil Code; *"concepito"* in the Italian Civil Code of 1942; and *"nascituro"* in the Brazilian Civil Code of 2002, to cite but a few examples.

The traditional doctrine admits a generic category (*nasciturus*), and this category contains two species: *conceptus* (to be conceived) and *concepturus* or *nondum conceptus* (that which is to be conceived). The *conceptus* can be defined as follows: it is the human being during the period of gestation from conception to birth. Despite being united to the vital support provided by the mother's body, it is genetically individualized and receives special protection from the legal system, regardless of whether it is recognized as a person[13].

One of the most controversial aspects within the scientific doctrine that studies the unborn child is that relating to its

---

11 T.J. Aliste Santos, 'Derecho y concebido no nacido: el problema de la subjetividad jurídica del nasciturus', Revista Conocimiento y Cultura Jurídica, Monterrey, México, 2, (julio-diciembre, 2007) 147.
12 Catalano, pp.196–97. Roman law used other expressions to refer to the conceived human being, as follows: *venter* (D. 35, 2, 9,1), *partus* (D. 11, 8, 2) and *postumus* (D. 38, 16, 3, 9).
13 Espinoza Espinoza, pp. 55–57.

legal status. Adopting a position on this important issue has, in addition to its theoretical scope, a normative projection that translates directly into the protection conferred by legal systems on the unborn child. The following is a critical review of the most relevant theoretical approaches to the issue under debate[14].

Portio mulieris *theory*

The interpretation of the theory of *portio mulieris*, deriving from some Roman texts cited by traditional Roman and civil doctrine, suggests that the conceived is part of the woman or her viscera, a simple organ of the mother. The *Digest* — also known as the *Pandects* — states in this respect: "*partus antequam edatur mulieris portio est vel viscerum*" (D. 25, 4, 1, 1), "*partus nondum editus homo non recte fuisse dicitur*" (D. 35, 2). The thesis put forward is also based on the affirmation of the jurisconsult Gaius that the conceived child is not yet in *rebus humanis, in rerum natura*[15].

The thesis of *portio mulieris*, defended on the basis of a fragment of Ulpianus' opinion in D. 25, 4, 1, 1, 1, can be categorically challenged based on an analysis of the complete text of the above cited quote[16]. The quote from Ulpianus corresponds to the Title "On the inspection of the womb and the custody of childbirth" and refers to the inappropriateness of the recognition of unborn children, because as long as the birth has not taken place they are bound to the mother's body. The close connection between the notions of *homines* and *qui in utero sunt* is set aside by taking as a reference the fragment of a classic commentary that solves a case in which the divorced woman

---

14   Espinoza Espinoza, p. 68.
15   D. 30,24.
16   "It appears most evidently from this Rescript, that the senateconsults on the recognition of children had no application, if the woman concealed that she was pregnant, or even denied it; and not without reason, because the childbirth, before [the child] is delivered, is part of the woman or of her entrails; but after the child has been delivered by the woman, the husband can already claim in his own right by interdict either that the child be exhibited to him, or that he be allowed to take it away, extraordinarily".

claims not to be pregnant and the ex-husband refutes this and, for obvious reasons, the recognition or the exhibition of the child *in utero* does not proceed[17]. Both the quote under analysis and that contained in the *Partidas*, rather than dealing directly with a definition of *qui in utero est*, direct their attention to the solution of the concrete cases in which, after the divorce or the death of the husband, the pregnancy can be hidden or simulated. These regulations, on the other hand, did not neglect the protection of the integrity of the woman[18].

Today, the basis of this theory is weak for obvious reasons. For instance, although during the period of gestation the unborn child depends on the life support provided by its mother, it cannot be said that it is part of the mother's body[19], as it is genetically separate and has its own anatomical structures which differ substantially from those of the mother. Nevertheless, the theory of *portio mulieris* has served as a cornerstone for some constructions that attempt to explain the legal status of the *nasciturus* in Roman law and even beyond.

Fiction theory

The theory of fiction also finds its basis in classical Roman sources and has been accepted in numerous civil codes that admit the Latin principle, "*nasciturus pro iam nato habetur quotiens de comodis eius agitur*". In this respect, the *Corpus Iuris Civilis* states, "*Partus dum in ventre portatur speratur*" (Code, L. VII, T. V, L.14), from which it is inferred that the child conceived before birth is simply a hope of man. Referring to the protection granted to the *nasciturus*, Paulus states, "*qui in utero est perinde ac si in rebus humanis esset, custuditur, quoties dex conmodies ipsius partus quaeritur quam alli, antequam nascatur nequam prosit*"[20]. The *Partidas* take up the tradition present in the Roman texts by expressing that, "as long as the child remains

---

17 P. VI, T. VI, L. XVII.
18 Catalano, pp. 169–72.
19 D. 1, 5, 5, 2.
20 D. 1, 5, 7; Lex Iulia et Papia Liber XI, 50, 11, 153; D. 38, 16, 7.

in its mother's womb, whatever is done or said for its benefit will benefit it, just as well as if it were born" (p. iv, t. xx). (P. IV, T. XXIII, L. III).

The fiction by which status is granted to the *nasciturus* is owed to Savigny. For this eminent jurist, the legal status of the natural person begins at birth, after the newborn has completely separated from its mother's womb. Consequently, the merely conceived being becomes capable of inheriting *mortis causa* by means of a fiction by which the status is attributed to the conceived being ahead of and in expectation of birth[21]. The fiction theory considers the conceived being as born for the purpose of acquiring eventual rights. The legal status of the *nasciturus* is equated to that of the born, but the acquisition of rights is subject to a suspensive condition: the birth of the new being with the requirements demanded by law so that personality can be attributed to it.

At present, as Catalano asserts, two schools of thought can be clearly seen with regard to the legal status of the unborn child. The first, of Justinian inspiration, is present in much of the Iberian area (perhaps, more precisely, Ibero-American). The second is strongly influenced by German pandects studies, which also finds expression in the Italian Codice Civile of 1942[22]. The Roman tradition adopted by Spanish historical law and, subsequently, by some Latin American legal systems (the contributions of Teixeira de Freitas and Vélez Sarsfield are significant) leads to an equivalence between the *nasciturus* and the newborn for the purposes of the effective protection of the interests and of the "person" itself of the unborn child. This equation has suffered the onslaught of the Germanic doctrines of the 19th century (in particular, the Savignian theory that grants capacity to the *nasciturus* through a fiction and the appearance

---

21 F.C. De Savigny, *Sistema de Derecho Romano actual*, I (Madrid: F. Góngora y Cía. Editores, 1878), pp. 278 ff.
22 P. Catalano, 'Observaciones sobre la "persona" del concebido a la luz del Derecho Romano', in *La persona en el Sistema Jurídico Latinoamericano*, 1st edn, Universidad Externado de Colombia, 1995, pp. 139 ff.

of abstract concepts alien to the sources of Roman Law[23]) so that some legal systems with deep Roman roots have set aside the previous tradition, in terms of the legal consideration of *qui in utero est*, to accept the thesis of the fiction[24].

The civil law doctrine of the last centuries, strongly influenced by the abstract notions and concepts developed by German pandectistics, has been characterized by a certain rigidity on the topic under consideration. The theory of fiction, despite its apparently undisputed and indisputable veracity (an infinity of treatises and manuals seem to confirm it, as well as its normative reception), has been severely criticized on the basis of technical-legal[25] and historical[26] considerations.

The theory of fiction has been accepted by numerous civil codes, especially by those that emerged in the heat of the 19th century Germanic doctrines of refined legal technique. This theoretical direction, despite the criticisms it has received from recent civil doctrine, was an effective way of protecting the *nascituri* in the historical moment in which it arose[27]. Some of the Latin American civil codes (Paraguayan, Peruvian and Brazilian, for example) protect the conceived in terms similar to the Roman tradition and distance themselves from the legal fiction, although

---

23 G. Margadant, *La segunda vida del Derecho Romano*, 1st edn (México: Porrúa, 1986), p. 335.
24 E. Arroyo I Amayuelas, *La protección al concebido en el Código Civil* (Madrid: Editorial Civitas, 1992), pp. 39–48. Similarly, the break of the Italian Codice Civile with the Roman tradition with regard to the legal consideration of the unborn child (see Article 1) is overwhelming, to the point of becoming — in the words of Catalano — anti-Roman. P. Catalano, 'Il concepito "soggetto di diritto" secondo il sistema giuridico romano', in *Memorias del XV Congreso Latinoamericano de Derecho Romano*, Morelia, Michoacán, México, 16-18 de Agosto de 2006, p. 13.
25 See M.J. García Garrido, 'Sobre los verdaderos límites de la ficción en derecho romano', Anuario de Historia del Derecho Español (1957–1958), 338 ff. Catalano, p. 203. Gayosso y Navarrete, p. 60.
26 T.J. Aliste Santos, 'La protección histórica al concebido y su proyección en el Derecho Civil español actual', Actualidad Civil, 4, (febrero de 2008), 398.
27 A. Ollero Tassara, 'El estatuto jurídico del embrión humano', in J. Ballesteros and E. Fernández (eds.) *Biotecnología y Posthumanismo*, 1st edn (Thomson–Aranzadi, 2007), p. 342.

they accept abstractions such as status and subjectivity[28]. The Cuban Civil Code of 1987 is inserted in the Roman tradition by admitting the principle of *commodum*; however, like its Spanish predecessor, it admitted the theory of fiction. In this continuity of the Iberian doctrine, as concerns the legal status of the unborn child (fortunately the legislator did not take into account the viability requirements demanded by the Spanish Code in its *pristine wording*, currently modified)[29], there are examples of the premature obsolescence of some of the institutions of the last Latin American Civil Code of the last century[30].

Theory of personality

The aforementioned theory is based on the consideration of the legal personality of the conceived being. The theory of personality finds its genesis in Roman Law and has a line of continuity in the Iberian and Latin American legislative traditions.

Catalano in Italian doctrine and the Mexican Romanist Gayosso y Navarrete, who closely follow Orestano's reflections, affirm the existence of an evident ontological parity in the Roman sources of the classical and Justinian periods between *qui in utero est* and *natus*. This analogy between conceived and man (which leads back to the notion of person) is obscured under the influence of the pandectistic and civilistic doctrines that emerge from the end of the 18th century, as well as by the appearance of abstract concepts, which contributes to the negation of the ontological parity on the normative level[31].

---

28 See Peruvian Civil Code article 1, Paraguayan Civil Code article 28, Brazilian Civil Code article 2.
29 Article 30 of the Spanish Civil Code as amended by the third final provision of Law 20/2011, of 21 July, on the Civil Registry. ("B.O.E." 22 julio).
30 L.B. Pérez Gallardo, 'De la Codificación Civil', in C. del C. Valdés Díaz (ed.), *Derecho Civil Parte General* (La Habana: Editorial Félix Varela, 2002), p. 69.
31 R. Orestano, *Il problema delle persone giuridiche in Diritto Romano* (Torino: Giappichelli, 1968); Catalano, pp. 169–72; 195–221; Gayosso y Navarrete, pp. 49–75, 56, 97–115.

In Roman law, despite the variety of its sources, there is a vocation for giving legal form to questions of concrete social life. This is particularly evident in the edicts of the magistrates and the senateconsults[32]. The eminently casuistic and practical character of Roman law can also be seen in the definitions of *qui in ventre est* that have survived to the present day, which are more focused on providing a solution to a particular case than on pure dogmatic theorization[33].

As regards the legal consideration of the *nasciturus*, there is a conceptual continuity in the Iberian area. Thus, the work of Alfonso X, the Wise[34], specifies that in terms of their status and condition, men can be "free or servants, born or to be born" (P. IV, T. XXIII). The *Partida* itself, Law III, refers to the status or condition in which "the creature is while in its mother's womb".

On the legal consideration of the unborn child, the Justinian-Iberian tradition can be seen in the work of Teixeira de Freitas in Brazil (*Consolidação das Leis Civis*, 1858; and *Esboço*, 1860) and of Vélez Sarsfield, in Argentina (*Código Civil*, 1869). For these eminent jurists, the *nasciturus* is already a person and they make this clear by using the concept of "*pessoas por nascer*" (Teixeira) and "*personas por nacer*" (Vélez). These authors consider that the conceived person is not a future person or a mere hope, but an unborn person who already exists in the mother's womb[35]. In Teixeira's work, a line of continuity can be seen with respect to the concepts and principles of Justinian Roman Law. Thus, the

---

32   F.C. Savigny, *De la vocación de nuestro siglo para la legislación y para la Ciencia del Derecho* (Madrid: La España Moderna), p. 44.
33   J.C. Costa, 'Protección al concebido. Vigencia de los principios rectores del Derecho Romano en la legislación argentina', in *Memorias del XV Congreso Latinoamericano de Derecho Romano*, Morelia, Michoacán, México, 16 al 18 de Agosto de 2006, p. 3.
34   J.M. Castán Vázquez, 'La Recepción en las codificaciones americanas de la tradición romana justinianea sobre el comienzo de la existencia humana', in *La persona en el Sistema Jurídico Latinoamericano*, 1st edn, Universidad Externado de Colombia, 1995, pp. 167 ff.
35   S. Cifuentes, *Elementos de Derecho Civil – Parte* General, 4th edn., Firdt published 1999 Buenos Aires (Buenos Aires: Astrea, 1999), pp. 104 ff; J.J. Llambías, *Tratado de Derecho Civil*, I, 16th edn (Buenos Aires: Abeledo Perrot, 1995), pp. 251 ff.

Consolidação das Leis Civis is close to the Latin tradition since, in its article 1, it accepts the discipline present in D. 1, 5, 7 and 26; in 50, 16, 129 and 231, and in the *Esboço,* it follows this precept in open criticism of the Savignian theory on the capacity of the *nasciturus*[36]. The Argentine Civil Code of Vélez, inspired by the work of Freitas, establishes in Article 70 the beginning of the existence of persons (using conception as a reference point) and establishes the possibility of the acquisition by the *nasciturus* of certain rights. This acquisition is conditioned by a resolutive condition: live birth, even if only for a short period of time. The European tradition, strongly influenced by 19th century pandectics, in the opposite direction to the line described above, has accepted numerous abstract concepts that lead to the suppression of the ontological parity between man and person and give way to an "exceptional legislative equalization"[37].

The criticism of the theory of the personhood of the unborn child is based on the fact that it assimilates the concepts of human life and human person, not necessarily equivalent, according to its detractors[38]. On the other hand, the nature of the rights granted to the unborn child (rights subject to a condition) and the obvious contradiction in the legislative solution historically adopted by Article 74 of the Argentine Civil Code of Vélez, is paradigmatic in terms of the admission of this thesis. It considered that the unborn child who dies before complete separation from the

---

36 Catalano, p. 208. Article 1 of the Consolidation provides that: "*As pessoas considerao-se como nascidas, apenas formadas no ventre materno; a Lei lhes-conserva seus direitos de sucessão para o tempo do nascimento. A Lei lhes-conserva seus direitos para o tempo do nascimento, contanto que nascão vivos. Eliminem-se as palavras – de sucessão –, porque, além deste direito, ha outros que a Lei lhes-conserva*".

37 Catalano, p. 205.

38 D.H. D'Antonio, *Actividad jurídica de los menores de edad*, 3rd edn (Buenos Aires: Rubinzal–Culzoni Editores, 2004), pp. 22–25. See A. Orgaz, *Personas Individuales* (Buenos Aires, 1946), pp. 251–53; Cifuentes, (n 36) pp. 103-106; Guillermo A Borda, *Tratado de Derecho Civil*, tomo I, (Buenos Aires: Abeledo Perrot, 1999), pp. 225 ff.; C. Casonato, 'Introduzione al Biodiritto. La Bioetica nel Diritto Costituzionale comparato', Università Degli Studi di Trento, Quaderni del Dipartimento, 57 (2006), pp. 30 ff.

maternal body is considered as if it had never existed, are at the center of the debate[39].

Theory of subjectivity

The notion of subject of law, which is central to the theoretical constructions coming from 19th century German pandectics, is widely reflected in modern doctrine, which has even equated it with the concept of person. The category "subject of law" has also been accepted in the legislative sphere, as the Peruvian Civil Code of 1984 recognizes it and applies it to specific legal categories (e.g., individual person, collective person, *nasciturus*, organizations of unregistered persons)[40].

Part of current scientific doctrine has noted the existence of certain entities which, although they lack legal personality, are attributed rights and duties. The classic and apparent equivalence between "person" and "subject of law" seems to be severed by the existence of certain "subjects" that hold certain rights and obligations despite not technically being considered persons. This reality has led to a broadening of the theory of legal subjects to include non-personal entities. In this way, the theory of subjects not only groups together entities with personality – natural and legal persons — but also entities without personality[41].

Numerous legal systems establish that the personality of the human being arises from birth, which does not prevent specific measures from being established for the defense and protection of the conceived person. However, part of recent civil doctrine has not hesitated to affirm the legal subjectivity of the unborn

---

39 Article 21 Còdigo Civil y Comercial: "Los derechos y obligaciones del concebido o implantado en la mujer quedan irrevocablemente adquiridos si nace con vida. Si no nace con vida, se considera que la persona nunca existió".
40 Espinoza Espinoza, p. 74. A. Guzmán Brito, 'Los orígenes de la noción de sujeto de derecho', Revista de Estudios histórico-jurídicos, XXIV (2002).
41 M. Montoya Osorio and G. Montoya Pérez, *Las Personas en el Derecho Civil. Las personas y otros sujetos*, 2nd edn (Bogotá: Editorial Leyer, 2007), pp. 239–41.

child, even though it is not yet considered a person[42]. Conceived beings who are not recognized *strictu sensu* legal personality are in a special situation as centers of normative imputation[43]. During this period, the legal systems protect the unborn child as the object of the so-called "favorable effects" (*commodum*). The special protection granted to the unborn child makes it the center of legal imputation during gestation and, therefore, a subject of special or privileged law[44].

The protection of the unborn child, a mix of concepts that are similar to its essence without perfecting conforming to its real nature, is in a sort of legal limbo[45] that can only be clarified on the basis of a special category — not yet enunciated by the doctrine — or, as Aliste Santos considers, through a "situation of transit" between these categories, as an explanatory theoretical construction of the protection of a notably atypical subject[46].

The theory of subjectivity comes from an abstraction typical of modern Law and in the theoretical insufficiency that is predicated of the constructions that explain the attribution of eventual rights in favor of an entity without legal personality[47]. Recognizing the subjectivity of the conceived child is fully sustainable as an explanatory theory of its legal status especially if one also accepts the unborn child will eventually, unquestionably, acquire legal personality. It is a subject of Law in which — in the words of Aliste Santos — the essence of the person germinates[48].

---

42 Montoya Osorio and Montoya Pérez, p. 240. See Espinoza Espinoza, p. 74; B. Ubertazzi, 'La Ley reguladora de la subjetividad del nasciturus', Anuario de Derecho Civil, LXI, 3 (julio-septiembre de 2008, Madrid, 2009) pp. 1361–87.
43 H. Kelsen, *Teoría Pura del Derecho* (México: Ediciones UNAM, 1982), p. 183.
44 Espinoza Espinoza, pp. 74–78.
45 Aliste Santos, 'La protección histórica al concebido y su proyección en el Derecho Civil español actual', p. 402.
46 Aliste Santos 'Derecho y concebido no nacido: el problema de la subjetividad jurídica del nasciturus', pp. 146–47.
47 M.D. Vila-Coro Barrachina, *El concebido no nacido en el orden jurídico* (Edición facsímil, Editorial de la Universidad Complutense de Madrid, Madrid, 1991), pp. 189–90.
48 Aliste Santos, 'Derecho y concebido no nacido: el problema de la subjetividad jurídica del nasciturus', pp. 146–47.

The legal status of the extracorporeal embryo

The legal status of the extracorporeal embryo differs considerably from the traditional considerations on the conceived, for different reasons. On the one hand, the direct reference to the mother's womb disappears — at least for a more or less long period of time. On the other hand, and this is the most important, the legal protection of the extracorporeal conceived raises new dilemmas that have not been resolved by historical legal regulations[49]. Traditional protection focuses on the patrimonial aspects of remedies for the unborn child, leaving the protection of its integrity to the criminal sphere[50]. In the *sui generis* conditions in which the unborn child is found outside the woman's body (as it will only be born through specialized interventions) and the increasing utilitarian reification to which it can be subjected as a contribution to research and therapeutic purposes, a regulation appropriate to the conditions described is required.

The dizzying development of biomedical sciences in recent decades, and in particular the biotechnological advances related to assisted human reproduction techniques, have raised new questions about the early stages of embryonic development and the regulation of the treatment of human embryos[51]. Alongside the profound legal issues, at the heart of which is the status of the *in vitro* embryo and the protection to be afforded to it, other questions of a markedly ethical nature have also arisen. The

---

49 The legal protection of the conceived child — as Arroyo I Amayuelas asserts — can be approached on the basis of different models, known as casuist and globalist. According to the casuist models, protection is not structured on the basis of a general principle that can be applied to cases not covered by the rule but which are congruent with its spirit, but is based on certain specified areas. The globalist formulations, on the other hand, embrace the principle of commodum (i.e., of the effects that are favourable to it) in a broad and open way to new situations not expressly provided for by the legislator. Arroyo I Amayuelas, pp. 145–61.
50 J.J. Castiella Rodríguez, *Instituciones de Derecho Privado*, I, 2 (F. Delgado de Miguel Coord, 1th edn, Thomson–Civitas, 2003), p. 36.
51 J.J. Castiella Rodríguez, pp. 23 ff. Ollero Tassara, 'El estatuto jurídico del embrión humano', p. 340; Espinoza Espinoza, pp. 64 ff.

emergence of new biotechnological interventions with a direct impact on prenatal human life imposes limits on the validity of the theories that have been accepted as fair and effective in terms of the protection of the conceived and makes it necessary, perhaps urgently, to re-read this protection in the light of current realities.

Central to the discussion on the legal status of the embryo lies the questions of, put bluntly, how the extracorporeal embryo should be legally qualified and, consequently, what protection should be granted. The answer to the first question inevitably leads the law to provide a coherent answer to the second or, at least, to start down the path of contradiction. The embryo is not a person — this question seems to be settled in those legal systems that consider that personality begins after birth — but it is not precisely for that reason that it should be understood to be a thing. Nor, however, does the embryo receive a protection similar to that of the physical person, which is based on the dignity of man. The solution must not be evaded, let alone placed at the complete disposal of science, which can lead to the equation of what is technically possible with what is legally admissible[52].

III. *Towards a reinterpretation of the legal protection of the unborn child in the extra-patrimonial sphere*

Effectively protecting the interests of the unborn child beyond the economic sphere is a subject on which there is no consensus in traditional civil law doctrine and for which many jurisdictions express a marked reservation. For those legal systems that admit casuistic solutions for the protection of the unborn child, restricting such protection to the sphere of patrimonial rights may appear to be a direct consequence of the application of legal rules that favor the regulation of specific situations in which certain

---

52 Ollero Tassara, 'El estatuto jurídico del embrión humano', pp. 348–50, A.M. Azzaro, 'Diritto al figlio e diritti del figlio', in *Procreazione Assistita e Diritti della persona. Problemi attuali del Diritto di Famiglia* (Urbino: Edizioni Scientifiche Italiane, 2000), p. 127.

rights of this nature are attributed. There is nothing to prevent special protection being given to the life of the conceived through the criminalization of abortion or its regulation, the existence of rules protecting maternity, and so on. On the other hand, for those systems that resort to globalist protection based on the principle of *commodum* or favorable effects, the contradiction becomes very clear when delving into the debated aspect.

The predominance of the patrimonialist interpretation as regards the content of the favorable effects can be motivated, firstly, by the patrimonialization of the institutions of private law in the civil codification of the 19th century, born under the auspices of liberal-bourgeois thought[53]. On the other hand, the protection of the conceived is set against the interests and expectations of other subjects, which contributes also to the indirect protection of those of other subjects. Finally, the erroneous consideration of the patrimonial and the personal as watertight compartments tends to make it difficult to admit the protection of the conceived once the frontiers of patrimonial rights have been crossed, in view of the constant that is evident in many legal systems of establishing that birth determines the acquisition of legal personality.

Despite the reluctance of part of the doctrine to admit the existence of a guardianship of the unborn child in the extra-patrimonial sphere[54], the following rights are mainly, but not exclusively, recognized in favor of the unborn child:

---

53 Ollero Tassara, 'El estatuto jurídico del embrión humano', p. 342.
54 See by the author of this research in: 'La persona nell'ordinamento giuridico cubano', in A. Barenghi, M. Proto and L.B. Pérez Gallardo (eds.), *Costituzione e diritto privato. Una riforma per Cuba* (Napoli: Editoriale Scientifica, 2019); 'Un acercamiento a la tutela jurisdiccional de los intereses y derechos eventuales del nasciturus', in J. Mendoza Díaz (dir.) and J. Manso Lache (ed.), *Los retos del debido proceso ante los nuevos paradigmas del Derecho Procesal* (La Habana: Ediciones ONBC, 2019); 'El estatuto jurídico del embrión extracorpóreo. Implicaciones civiles y familiares', in A.A. Estancona Pérez, G. Berti de Marinis and A. Gallardo Rodríguez (eds.), *Los nuevos retos del derecho de familia* (Valencia: Tirant Lo Blanch, 2021); *Per omnia. La protección jurídica del concebido no nacido en el Derecho Civil* (Santiago de Chile: Ediciones Olejnik, 2018).

1. Right to life and right to be born.

2. The conceived person who is born alive has the right to have his maternal and paternal filiation recognized (or, as the doctrine sometimes calls it, the right to status) and in this sense is the holder of the actions to accredit his civil status.

3. The conceived child who is born alive has the right to be compensated for the damages suffered in his or her family situation (due to the death of the father or the mother, as the most illustrative examples). The damage includes both his or her assets and his or her emotional and psychological state (moral damage).

4. The child who is born alive is entitled to compensation for any damage he/she may have suffered to his/her person during the period of gestation[55].

The right to life of the unborn child is, without a doubt, the most controversial aspect in the traditional treatment of its legal protection. This quality of a disputed and debatable right is due, among other reasons, to the variety of positions held in different spheres (political, doctrinal and ideological) in defense or open criticism of the admissibility of such a theoretical construction, as well as the fact that, unlike other rights defended by their current holder (the person after their live birth or their legal representative), there is a vacuum in the ownership of the right if the conceived child is not born alive. The debate is also directly affected by the controversy over abortion (and in fact the extent or restriction of women's rights to dispose of "their own body") and that concerning the application of assisted human reproduction techniques, the cryopreservation of embryos, their manipulation for research or therapeutic purposes, basically.

Recognizing the right of the unborn child to life can be explained on the basis that without this protection it is practically impossible to protect the rest of the child's rights. It is illogical, according to the order of these arguments, to protect certain

---

[55] P. Zatti, 'Diritti dell'embrione e capacità giuridica del nato', Rivista di Diritto Civile, Padua, a. XLIII (enero-febrero, 1997) 109. Arroyo I Amayuelas, p. 106.

interests and expectations and to subject rights to a situation of interim or pendency (subject as we know to the *conditio iuris* of live birth) if no rules are established to guarantee the birth. Thus, the safeguarding of the life of the unborn child would be the first concretization of favorable effects[56].

The recognition of a right to life, beyond the obstacles it will have to overcome in its doctrinal and normative construction and the inevitable confrontation with the interests and rights of other subjects, has a profound ethical component that is rooted in the recognition of the dignity of man and the assumption of life as a value specially protected by the legal system. The recognition of a right to life in favor of the conceived child is, in this sense, the palpable manifestation of the State's recognition that it is in the presence of a new legal interlocutor (subject of law) that must be protected and accepted[57].

The strongest objections made against the admission of a right to life focus on the indeterminacy of the subject — whether the conceived person dies without acquiring a personality — and the attack that the existence of such a right implies on the legitimacy of abortion. Abortion, allowed in some jurisdictions, limited to certain cases specifically regulated by law or absolutely prohibited by others, has generated one of the most complex doctrinal controversies within the field under consideration. The complexity of the controversy is fundamentally due, among other factors, to the variety of subjects or actors involved, the polysemy of some key concepts (person, fetus, pre-embryo,

---

56   Castiella Rodríguez, pp. 37–38.
57   A. Ollero Tassara, 'Derecho a la vida. ¿Derecho a la muerte? La libre autodeterminación Personal y las imprecisas fronteras del Derecho', paper presented at "El libre desarrollo de la personalidad en el ordenamiento jurídica español", Universidad de Alcalá de Henares, mayo de 1993, Servicio de Publicaciones de la Universidad de Alcalá, p. 108. See also, A. Ollero Tassara, 'Todos tienen derecho a la vida. ¿Hacia un concepto constitucional de persona?', in J. Ballesteros, M.E. Fernández, A. Luis Martínez (eds.), *Justicia, Solidaridad, Paz. Estudios en Homenaje al Profesor José María Rojo Sanz*, I, 1st edn (Facultad de Derecho de la Universitat de Valencia, 1995), p. 356.

freedom) depending on who uses them, the different normative solutions, and judicial decisions in this respect[58].

In Cuba, the right to life was not expressly enshrined in the 1976 Constitution, although a systematic interpretation of the Magna Carta and the legal system leads one to affirm that life as a legal right is protected in various ways (maternity protection, punishment of criminal conduct, social security, etc.). Article 46 of the 2019 Constitution states that everyone has the right to life, but the reference to the concept of person makes it difficult to apply it to the legal situation of the unborn child[59]. The Civil Code does not make a special reference to the content of the protection when adopting the principle of *commodum*, so that it cannot be directly stated that the right to life is listed as the content of the favorable effects (although this possibility is not excluded either).

In the face of the debated right to be born, contemporary doctrine, and particularly in the decisions reached by some courts of justice, has submitted that such right exists and should be recognized. Although the doctrine and some legal systems have come to allow compensation for damages for harm a person suffered during gestation or for the aggravation of a condition as a consequence of medical malpractice, the right not to be born has not been accepted[60].

The unborn child's right to damages as a form of legal protection is a topic under constant transformation (mainly through the jurisprudential work of various courts of justice around the world). This connection is based on the admission that the child has the right to be compensated for the harm that it has suffered in its family situation or in its "person" during gestation. The casuistic nature of the decisions adopted and

---

58 R. Dworkin, *El dominio de la vida. Una discusión acerca del aborto, la eutanasia y la libertad individual*, 1st edn (Barcelona: Ariel, 1994).
59 See Article 24 of the Civil Code. E. Torres-Cuevas and R. Suárez Suárez, *El libro de las Constituciones*, I-III (La Habana, Ediciones Imagen Contemporánea, 2018). C.M. Villabella Armengol, *Estudios de Derecho Constitucional* (La Habana: Unijuris, 2020).
60 C. Larroumet, *Derecho Civil. Introducción al estudio del Derecho Privado* (Bogotá: Editorial Legis, 2006) pp. 223–27.

the close connection with other controversial aspects (e.g., the application of insurance contracts, medical malpractice, labor and social security law, the complex controversy over abortion, etc.) determine the advanced nature of the jurisprudential decisions on this issue, as opposed to the reservations found in legal doctrine and legal regulations.

Traditional doctrine prefers *inter vivos* and *mortis causa* acquisitions as a way of enshrining the protection of the future rights of the unborn child in the patrimonial sphere. However, there is nothing to indicate that these are the only manifestations of such protection. The possibility of recognizing a merely conceived being, in spite of the *sui generis* character it presents due to the very conditions in which it is found, has been admitted with notable generality as an effect favorable to its legal status. The recognition of the filiation of a conceived child can be contained in a will — regardless of whether it is common or special — or in another public document. The special features of the recognition of the filiation of the unborn child determine the vicissitudes of the figure in the notarial sphere[61].

The legal protection available to the unborn child in traditional civil law is limited to patrimonial protection, especially based on succession *mortis causa* (inheritance) and *inter vivos* (gifts). Yet, the protection of the unborn child should not be limited to these instruments[62]. An integral protection of the unborn child must start from the consideration of the protective effects of the figure in those sensitive aspects such as its life, its physical integrity, in order to subsequently regulate other effects — still within a sphere that is not eminently patrimonial, such as those related to its identity — and thus give way to the traditional protection that focuses on patrimonial aspects. This comprehensive protection

---

61 In spite of the absence of a specific provision on the matter, there is no obstacle, therefore, to admitting the possibility of recognizing a child in a will in Cuban law. See *per omnia*, by the author of the present investigation: 'Apuntes sobre el reconocimiento filiatorio a favor del concebido no nacido en sede notarial' IUS. Revista del Instituto de Ciencias Jurídicas de Puebla, a. IX (julio-diciembre de 2015).

62 C. del C. Valdés Díaz, *Comentarios al Código Civil cubano*, I, 1, artículo 25 (LA Habana: Editorial Félix Varela, 2014).

will materialize when such protection is approached in an all-encompassing manner, stripped of its primarily economic character, with the doctrine shifting its attention to such protection and laws and the decisions of the courts of justice focusing on the personal aspects of such protection. The absence of regulation, the inertia of dogmatic categories — and even spurious and often unmentionable motives — are not valid reasons for restricting the protection of the conceived person in terms of those spheres that affect his or her condition as a human subject of the law.

MILAGROS KOTEICH[*]

INFLUENCE OF THE ITALIAN EXPERIENCE ON THE NEW NOTION OF NON-PECUNIARY DAMAGES IN LATIN AMERICA

(Colombia, Peru and Venezuela)

Introduction

For more than three decades, in Italy, the Constitution has led the broadening of the scope of the notion of "non-pecuniary damages" beyond the narrow limits of article 2059 of the *Codice Civile*[1], in such a way as to provide (compensatory) civil law protections for a person's fundamental interests.

As result of this process, in 2003, the Italian Court of Cassation, civil section, issued two important decisions (known as the "twin rulings") that provided a new "map" for non-pecuniary damages in Italy. Reference is made to Rulings Nos. 8828 and 8827, both dated May 31, 2003, whose arguments were later adopted by the Constitutional Court in a subsequent ruling that same year[2].

The first ruling contends that, in the then-current state of the legal system (where the Constitution enjoyed a pre-eminent position, and whose article 2 recognizes and guarantees the inviolable rights of a person), non-pecuniary damages pursuant to article 2059 of the *Codice Civile* (the "C.C.") can no longer be considered exclusively (as per the traditional restrictive reading of said article *vis-a-vis* article 185 of the *Codice Penale*) as subjective moral damages, i.e., the contingent suffering and temporary nuisance of the spirit caused by a criminal act. In

---

[*] Professor of Civil Law and Director of the Department of Civil law of the Universidad Externado de Colombia.
[1] E. Navarretta, 'Ripensare il sistema dei danni non patrimoniale', in Resp. Civ. Prev., 2004, p. 3.
[2] No. 233 of July 11, 2003. The "twin rulings" were also be reiterated in decisions Nos. 16525/03, 10482/04 and 15022/05 of the Italian Court of Cassation, civil section.

addition to the traditional subjective moral damages (as per the specific cases provided for by law), the notion of "non-pecuniary damages" — referred to in article 2059 of the C.C. — also encompasses any hypothesis where an "unfair injury to a person's constitutionally protected values is verified, that causes damages not susceptible of economic valuation"; which are not subject to the limits stemming from article 185 of the *Codice Penale*.

With this "constitutional reading" of said provision, the notion of non-pecuniary damages in Italy was significantly upended[3], because said reading leads to overturning the limits under article 2059 of the C.C. in cases where an injury relates to a person's constitutionally protected values.

By virtue of constitutional provisions related to the inviolable values of the person, the foregoing applies in cases against the State and must also be directly enforceable within the field of private law[4]. Injury may result in non-pecuniary damages that must be compensated under article 2059 of the C.C.[5]

---

[3] Prior to the Court of Cassation rulings Nos. 8828 and 8827 of 2003, jurisprudence had equated the concept of moral damages and the concept of non-pecuniary damage referred to in article 2059 of the Civil Code, which resulted in compensation requests for non-pecuniary damages were equivalent to a compensation request for all damages provided for under said article, for the different aspects that the specific case presented. See ruling of the Court of Cassation No. 15022/2005.

[4] "Roughly speaking, it could be said that we are perhaps witnessing a process of 'privatization' of fundamental rights, in the sense that their effectiveness expands beyond the State-citizen relationship. Judges are given the power to reinterpret disciplines of private law whose application could violate fundamental rights of the individual. [T]he logic behind this trend is not to treat 'private' abuses differently from public ones, in cases where the principles of equality, human dignity, freedom of expression, etc. come into play.": G. Comandé, *Diritto privato Europeo e diritti fondamentali*, in AA.VV., *Diritto privato Europeo e diritti fondamentali*, Giappichelli, Torino 2004, pp. 27 ff.

[5] However, the same ruling may yield a different solution-interpretation, and namely that such a limit did not actually exist in the case at hand. This view was based on the fact that the law allows, and even requires, for the reparation of other forms of non-pecuniary damages, incorporated in article 2059 by reference following the entry into force of the Constitution (1948), resulting from the injury to the inviolable rights of the person of a non-

In addition, ruling No. 8827 of the Italian Court of Cassation, also dated May 31, 2003, though it repeats some of the arguments contained in the aforementioned ruling No. 8828, proports that "according to the principles of causal regularity, only in the case of harmful consequences deriving from injury to interests of constitutional rank, *damages other than biological damage and subjective moral damages* are compensated, when said consequences have, like the latter, a non-pecuniary nature" (emphasis mine).

Thus, it must be stressed that this "constitutional reading" makes it possible to argue that non-pecuniary damages under article 2059 of the C.C. include: biological damages (in the strict sense), subjective moral damages (as traditionally conceived), and the different and additional damages that result from an injury to a constitutionally protected interest (despite the fact that, according to the rulings, damages must be considered as a whole).

For its part, the Italian Constitutional Court, in its ruling No. 233 of July 11, 2003, confirmed this new jurisprudential development regarding personal damage by also embracing the three-fold notion of damages that is now understood as covered under article 2059 of the C.C.

In Latin America, too, there is a certain turmoil within the category of non-pecuniary damages. This is partially due to the circulation and influence of European models in the region, including the Italian example.

Having examined the aforementioned influence, it is possible to identify specific elements that reveal where and why Latin American legal science borrowed some categories of non-pecuniary damages. It must, however, be born in mind that these categories (such as "personal damage", "damage to health", "damage to relational quality of life",

---

economic nature — which (even if implicitly) necessarily require protection (compensation). Consequently, harm to Constitutionally protected interests would, in the end, constitute one of the cases *determined by the law itself,* at the highest level, of reparation of non-pecuniary damages. See in a similar sense, Ibid., p. 36.

"biological damage", and even the controversial "existential damage") were originally developed in an environment or reality different from that of Latin America. This would, thus, ultimately explain why said categories have not always permeated or have not found a "comfortable" place within the region's legal systems (for example, the subsequent adoption following rejection by the Colombian Council of State of the notion of "damage to health" or — to use the French terminology — "physiological damage", which was later accepted by this judicial body).

To study the effect the Italian experience has had in Latin America, the following sections will analyze three different experiences corresponding, in turn, to three different "extents of reception" of the elements of non-pecuniary damages. The first is the Colombian case, where case law has primarily advanced the expansion of "non-pecuniary damages" through the recognition — although not always smooth — of categories that developed elsewhere. The second experience discussed will be the Peruvian one, where "personal damage" constitutes a codified reality despite doctrine and jurisprudence discuss their understanding and effective application thirty years after its introduction. And last we'll discuss the Venezuelan experience, where, despite the legal framework (Civil Code and Constitution) offers various tools for an eventual better and greater protection of the person in the field of civil liability, traditional opinions prevail. Therefore, although the doctrine sometimes uses certain categories of non-pecuniary damages developed within the Italian context, this does not entail a leap in quality since, regarding the remedies for harm caused to a person, damages beyond mere pecuniary ones are not actually recognized, except for the *pretium doloris*.

1. *Colombia and its jurisprudence*

Notwithstanding Colombia follows the French mono-normative model on compensable damages (article 1382 of the *Code Civil*) by providing a single provision on "damages" (article 2341 of the Civil Code), which does not distinguish between pecuniary and non-pecuniary damages[6]: the availability of this last type of damages was only established through a ruling of the Colombian Court of Civil Cassation of July 21, 1922[7]. In this decision, the Court, based on a reinterpretation of the article just cited[8]

> established the principle according to which a claim for damages for harm caused to an individual's feelings and affections is equally valid as a claim for the reparation of economic or pecuniary damages and, as such, must be afforded the same legal protections with regard to recognition and extent.[9]

---

6   Unlike what happens in Italy, where there is a rule for pecuniary damages (article 2043 of the *Codice civile*) and another for non-pecuniary damages (article 2059 of the *Codice civile*).
7   Rapporteur Magistrate ("R.M.") Tancredo Nannetti, who resolved the appeal filed by the lawyer Julián Restrepo Hernández, in the case known as Villaveces against the Municipality of Bogotá.
8   In this same sense, the ruling of the Court of Cassation, civil section, dated May 13, 2008, File No. 11001-3103-006-1997-09327-01, R.M. César Julio Valencia Copete, stated: "The general nature of the provisions related to the law of damages grants the judge the possibility of recognizing, of course, in a prudent and reasoned manner, *new classes of compensable damages*, aimed at developing the mentioned principle of comprehensive reparation and to safeguard the rights of the victims, *as is strongly imposed by contemporary law*" (emphasis added).
9   F. Hinestrosa, 'Apreciación del daño moral', in F. Hinestrosa, *Escritos varios*, Bogotá 1983, pp. 719–20. This ruling (Judicial Gazette, T. XXIX, 220) established that "an individual may be harmed by undermining his property, as well as inflicting offense on his honor or personal dignity, or causing pain and discomfort due to malice or negligence of the agent"; and the equally important ruling of August 22, 1924 (Judicial Gazette, T. XXXI, 83), in the same line, held: "And if in many cases it is difficult to determine the amount of the reparation, that circumstance cannot be an obstacle to fix it, even approximately, since otherwise it would be necessary to conclude that rights of high importance were left unprotected by civil laws, whenever their infraction escaped the action of criminal laws. In the case under study, the civil penalty is imposed. Excerpts taken from F. Hinestrosa, 'Devenir del derecho de daños', in *Roma e America. Diritto romano comune*, 10, Rome 2000, pp. 24–5. See also F. Hinestrosa, 'Apreciación del daño moral', 722; and J.C. Henao, *El daño, análisis comparativo de la responsabilidad extracontractual del Estado en derecho colombiano y francés*, Bogotá 1998, pp. 260 ff.

That is, moral or non-pecuniary damages (which were comparable since no subcategories had yet been created) must be considered as on the same footing as economic or pecuniary harm.

In a nutshell, the '40s were a decade marked by a failed attempt — in three rulings dated April 23, 1941[10] — to establish the category of non-pecuniary damages. After that, it is possible to divide the evolution of non-pecuniary damages in Colombia[11] into four periods:

The first, characterized by a Civil Cassation ruling dated April 4, 1968; the second, led by the Council of State of the 1990s, and subsequent years; the third, which begins with a Civil Cassation decision dated May 13, 2008, in which the notion of "*danno alla vita di relazione* (damages to relational quality of life)" was consolidated; and the last one, marked by important decisions, all from the year 2014, both from the Civil Cassation (August 5th) and from the Council of State (August 28th), through which — it could be said — the current "jurisprudence map" of non-pecuniary damages in Colombia was drawn.

1.1. *The Civil Cassation ruling of April 4, 1968*

The Colombian Civil Cassation ruling of April 4, 1968[12] may be considered a pioneer in Colombia in matters of non-economic damages or, more broadly, of a person's civil protections (*rectius*, of the rights of the personality). Indeed, with the aim of establishing a certain order and in this sense following the Italian legal system, it introduced within the Colombian caselaw

---

10 Supreme Court of Justice, General Business Chamber, magistrates presenting: Aníbal Cardoso Gaitán, Juan A. Donado and Arturo Tapias Pilonieta, respectively (G. J., T. LI, Nos. 1971-1972, 424 ff.). Also, ruling of the same body dated November 5, 1942 (G. J., T. LVI, 486).

11 That it is long, complex and was verified "overcoming several obstacles": M.C. M'Causland, *Tipología y reparación del daño no patrimonial*, Bogotá 2008, pp. 59–60.

12 R.M. F. Hinestrosa, in G. J., CXXIV, 63 [Event: death of a minor and bodily injury to his father, due to a traffic accident].

a classification of damages or consequences that may derive from "personal damage", understood as an entity with its own characteristics, "consisting of an immediate detriment to the physical or mental integrity, or an insult to honor, freedom or privacy", which in effect is

> susceptible of being translated into pecuniary consequences, such as expenses for healing or rehabilitation, undisputable profits loss, and whether transitory or definitive, with considerable impact on an individual's relational quality of life, and even affecting their feelings and emotional balance.[13]

Regarding the categorization of damages put forward, in line with the "accident trajectory", the ruling distinguishes between "immediate" and "distant" consequences (which do not allude, by the way, to *causality*) of the injury in relation to the "*derechos personalísimos*".

The first type are determined by the "place" where the "first blow" is received. In the event of an attack on the honor, esteem, intimacy, right to image, or psychophysical integrity, for instance, such immediate injury is constituted by the individual or, more exactly, by the qualities or manifestations of their personality, which delineate "a damage in itself, relevant in itself"[14]. The consequences of the second type, on the other hand, are related to the repercussions that *may* occur in different spheres, such as the victim's net worth, their relational life and, lastly, their feelings[15]. If these *distant consequences* could be grouped into macro-categories of traditional damages, they would be, on the one hand, pecuniary damages (i.e., consequential damages and present and future lost profits) and, on the other hand,

---

13 F. Hinestrosa, 'Devenir del derecho de daños', p. 33.
14 F. Hinestrosa, 'La responsabilidad civil', in F. Hinestrosa, *Escritos varios*, Bogotá 1983, p. 688.
15 F. Hinestrosa, 'La responsabilidad civil', p. 689; F. Hinestrosa, 'Devenir del derecho de daños', p. 33; J.C. Henao, *El daño, análisis comparativo de la responsabilidad extracontractual del Estado en derecho colombiano y francés*, pp. 198–99.

non-pecuniary damage, which may manifest as damage to — temporary or definitive — relational life, or as damage to feelings.

So, for example, affecting a person's psychosomatic integrity may impact three different levels:

In the first place, the victim may incur expenses and eventually acquire loans and increase their debt to pay for medical, hospital and other expenses deriving from the injury. Likewise, a victim may suffer from reduced or lost income due to disability. In short, pecuniary damages in its two manifestations, consequential damages and lost profits. That is not to allude here to "direct and immediate pecuniary damage, but to pecuniary damages as a result or consequence of a 'blow' said victim received to their humanity, to their personal right to integrity"[16] (however, to the extent that such "blow" is considered "a damage in itself", a first damage would already exist, in advance, even without the aforementioned harmful consequences)[17].

Secondly, said injury to a victim's psychophysical integrity may cause her/him to remove her/himself, temporarily or permanently from their normal life, thus altering their lifestyle. One example is when someone who liked to play the piano or play sports — regardless of whether or not they received compensation for it — may no longer continue to do so due to the injury[18].

And lastly, the injury to a person's humanity, constituted for example by their psychophysical integrity, may cause physical pain to the victim and affect their good spirits; in short, moral damage (which, by the way, arises exclusively as a consequence

---

16   F. Hinestrosa, 'La responsabilidad civil', p. 683.
17   In a similar line, J. Tamayo Jaramillo, *De la responsabilidad civil* (t. IV), Bogotá 2017, pp. 144 ff., maintains: "Injury to any of these assets ['non-pecuniary'] constitutes a damage that must be repaired; therefore, it is not strictly necessary for one of these injuries to cause pecuniary or affective damage to the victim to speak of reparable damage. The very fact of the injury to the property is constitutive of the damage. These are ontologically and logically independent damages, which means that, in theory, they may occur with or without the presence of other damages".
18   F. Hinestrosa, 'La responsabilidad civil', p. 689.

of injuries to human qualities (*"derechos de la personalidad"*), and not in an isolated or independent manner)[19].

According to the ruling, all these consequences ultimately constitute "damage to the person, in their various relevant manifestations".

In the Latin American context, speaking of "personal damage" was already in itself, a novelty, since this category only begun to be studied in Italy in 1962 (despite the, almost inadvertent, legal coverage found in article 2057 of the 1942 Civil Code). Moreover, the damage to relational quality of life, which the ruling pointed out as one of consequences of injury, was addressed only by the categories of compensable damages provided within the complex Italian regulatory framework. Thus, it may be argued that this decision was at the forefront of trends and legal developments of the comparative law of its time. It may be further, and above all, said that it was innovative given the Colombian national scene at the time — which could have been, perhaps, the very reason why this thesis was not immediately followed, neither by the civil courts nor, much less, by the contentious-administrative courts (which would, in fact, adopt it only 25 years later, first by the Council of State[20], and more recently, by the Civil Cassation[21]).

The most significant aspect of this ruling is that it constitutes the first step, although not always sustained (in reference to the period that would follow), in the evolution of the Colombian legal system's recognition of the person as the center of the new law of damages (which no longer refers exclusively to the

---

19 "Moral damages are not presented by themselves, but as the repercussion of an injury to the personality, to one's being, in which case its perception and fair value are less complicated or risky for the judge; or of an injury to someone else's personality that impacts ours, due to the said ties of affection and solidarity": F. Hinestrosa, 'Apreciación del daño moral', p. 724.
20 With a ruling of May 6, 1993 (which will be studied later), "'damage to relational quality of life' is assimilated to 'physiological damage' only, and as result, from the outset, the scope of the relevance of those alterations to the hypotheses derived from damage to life and physical integrity is reduced, and therefore, leaving out the damage as a result of aggression to the other assets of the personality": F. Hinestrosa, 'Devenir del derecho de daños', 33 (p. 35).
21 Ruling of the Court of Cassation, civil section, dated May 13, 2008, File No. 11001-3103-006-1997-09327-01, R.M. César Julio Valencia Copete.

pecuniary kind). Indeed, it affirms that individuals are holders of non-pecuniary rights and interests that must be protected, meaning that any harm to such rights must be repaired beyond the traditional *pretium doloris*. And all this was inspired by the legal constructions of the Italian legal system.

1.2. *The Council of State of the 1990s, and after*

At the beginning of the 1990s, the path towards a possible recognition of what is known in the Italian environment as "damage to health", began to be paved in Colombia.

However, the history of the reception by the Colombian Council of State of the notion of "non-pecuniary damages", other than *pretium doloris*, is confusing — to say the least. This is mainly attributable to the fact that the sources on the subject cited in the doctrine (translations of Italian and French texts) were confusing.

Thus, on the basis of the principle of comprehensive reparation, with ruling No. 7428 of May 6, 1993[22], Colombian contentious-administrative jurisprudence gave way for the first time to a category of non-pecuniary damages other than *pretium doloris*. These damages were called *physiological damage or damage to relation quality of life*, understood as the impossibility of the victim to carry on with their normal life in society, as result of an impairment to their health or psychophysical integrity[23].

Said decision was based on the following reasoning:

> In reality, the victim could make the following reflection. My personal integrity granted me three benefits: regular income, emotional stability and pleasant activities. If the first two have been satisfied with compensa-

---

22 Third Section, R.M. Julio César Uribe Acosta [Event: bodily injury, with 100% permanent disability], whose precedent was established by another ruling of the same court, dated February 14, 1992.

23 Regarding the introduction of this concept in Colombian contentious-administrative jurisprudence, see J.C. Henao, *El daño. Análisis comparativo de la responsabilidad extracontractual del Estado en derecho colombiano y francés*, pp. 263 ff.; Javier Tamayo Jaramillo, *De la responsabilidad civil*, pp. 174 ff.

tion, the third remains to be repaired, which is precisely what gives rise to *compensation for physiological damages*. If, for example, the victim is reduced to a wheelchair due to a *total permanent disability*, we cannot say that by having compensated said victim for the material damages and the subjective moral damages, the entire injury has been repaired. What would be the value for the victim to continue receiving wages or obtaining a compensation equivalent to subjective moral damage, if they lack any capacity for the rest of vital activities? Let's continue with the example. Let's suppose that this victim, after compensation for the subjective material and moral damages, is left with money and peace of mind. However, they continue to be far from the privileged situation they were in before the harmful event occurred because they *will no longer be able to continue enjoying the pleasures of life*. This tells us that subjective and physiological moral damages are different. [...] We repeat: compensation for subjective moral damages repairs the psychological satisfaction or physical pain of the victim. On the other hand, *compensation for physiological damage repairs the suppression of vital activities*. We could almost say that the subjective moral damage consists of an attack against the intimate faculties of life, while the physiological damage consists of an *attack on a victim's abilities to do things*, regardless of whether these have a pecuniary yield (emphasis added).

The Council's ruling appears to have merged two separate concepts: the French physiological damage and the "damage to relational quality of life" of Italian origin (the latter, to some extent, equivalent to the French *préjudice d'agrément* or "loss of amenity").

Such amalgamation between the damage to psychophysical integrity and the damage to relational quality of life almost automatically refers us to the beginning of the Italian experience in the matter, where the caselaw had to appeal to the latter in order to compensate damage that, at least apparently, was not envisaged by the legal system. This type of damage would later be called "biological damage" or "damage to health". It is worth noting that once this last concept found its place, that is, an autonomous recognition within the legal system, the need to abandon the "jurisprudential fiction" known as "loss of amenity" was immediately observed and ultimately absorbed (in the 1990s) by the notion of "damage to health".

In other words, the creation or use of the notion of "loss of amenity" was justified in Italy because the availability of non-pecuniary damages (including those derived from injury to psychophysical integrity) was excluded in cases where said injury was not the product of a crime (arts. 2059 of the *Codice civile* and 185 of the *Codice penale*). However, in Colombia this limitation did not exist; on the contrary, part of the doctrine maintains that the resulting concept in the "conjunctural" Italian legal system is a sort of "damage to health", and not "damage to relational quality of life" (or amenity), which would have been created solely to overcome the legal limitations discussed above such that it would not enjoy a truly autonomous ontological character of its own.

> However, this statement does not fully reflect the current reality of the Italian legal system. Although it is true that the creation of "damage to health" was marked by the aforementioned legal limitations, this does not in any way erase its unique virtues. From the moment it was coined, the notion of "injury to psychophysical integrity" has been viewed as an event whose main non-pecuniary consequence may not only be objectively assessed (by means of the legal medical examination), but also appraised — through the tables o *barèmes* — independently from the economic damage (in fact, consequential damages and any lost profits caused by the injury are not part of the definition of this legal category). Before this, the determination of the extent of injury was either based on or reflected economic or salary-based parameters exclusively, with the inequities that this carries.
>
> But even if, for the sake of argument, one were to admit that the Italian notion of "damage to health" was only justified and only has a place in its country of origin; such an affirmation would later be undermined if the notion of "physiological damage" of the French legal system is analyzed (which is substantially equivalent to the Italian "damage to health", from which it was inspired). Indeed, in France — as is the case in Colombia — there is no legal restriction of any kind for the compensation of non-pecuniary damages.

There is, however, a fundamental problem that arises when this notion is not understood in its proper dimension: it ends up being assessed according to parameters that have nothing to do with its nature. Such assessment method, given its "objectivity", is intended to yield an amount that is — at least — equal for all victims afflicted by the same types of injury and percentage of permanent disability.

The inconsistencies of equating "physiological damage" to "loss of amenity", as done by the Colombian contentious-administrative jurisprudence, would become especially evident seven years later, as will be illustrated immediately below.

The Council of State ruling of July 19, 2000 (No. 11842)[24] held that the concept of "damage to relational quality of life" (or loss of amenity) should *replace* that of "physiological damage" (thus finally ceasing to be equivalent), on the basis that "the aforementioned damage does not consist of the injury itself, but of the consequences that arise because of it, in the relational quality of life of the injured person".

This decision establishes that non-pecuniary damage (which the Colombian caselaw has termed "damage to relational quality of life") consists of a *much more comprehensive concept*, for which

> the use of the expression "physiological damage" is certainly inappropriate, because in reality they may not be synonymous, not even in cases where such non-pecuniary damages — other than pain and suffering — are the consequence of a physical or bodily injury. For this reason, the Court must definitively reject its use.

It also states that this greater "amplitude" of "damage to relational quality of life" with respect to physiological damages manifests in different ways: *a) The damage may arise from events other than bodily injury; b) The damage affects not only pleasure activities but also routine activities; and c) It may be suffered by people other than the direct victim.*

It is arguable that, with this ruling, the notion of "loss of amenity" in Colombia was outlined as a central and autonomous legal category from non-pecuniary damages (alongside *pretium doloris*)[25], while the concept of "damage to health" — or

---

24 Third Section, R.M. Alier E. Hernández E. [Event: bodily injuries — paraplegia, with permanent physical deformity and total functional disturbance of the organs].

25 In relation to this distinction between moral damage and damage to relational quality of life, F. Navia, *Del daño moral al daño fisiológico ¿una evolución real?*, Bogotá 2000, p. 41, states: "The important thing is to consider them,

"physiological damage" — embraced in very particular terms for a short period of time, was repealed and replaced precisely by the former.

1.3. The Civil Cassation, 40 years later

After the ruling of April 4, 1968, the Colombian Civil Cassation explained that it would adapt its jurisprudence to the new constitutional order (1991) in a manner that is consistent with the social, economic, and legal changes of recent years. In this spirit, on May 13, 2008[26], the Court issued the first ruling on "damages to relational quality of life" (or loss of amenity), which became a precedent as the matter was either not addressed by the appeal court, or having been addressed, not discussed by any of the parties to the lawsuit before the Court of Cassation (and, given the dispositive character of such recourse, the Court could not *ex officio* deal with the issue).

The wording of this decision reveals that the Court was aware of the difficulties within the Italian legal system surrounding the notion of "loss of amenity", and that Italian jurisprudence was against recognizing "damage to relational quality of life" as an autonomous legal category[27].

However, the ruling additionally points out that

---

because they really are two different aspects of non-pecuniary damages, and, consequently, when establishing the value of the full compensation to which the victim is entitled, must be taken into account as two separate items that must necessarily be quantified independently".

26 File No. 11001-3103-006-1997-09327-01, R.M. César Julio Valencia Copete [Event: bodily injury, with total loss of "capacity to work"]. The ruling begins its analysis by mentioning, and summarizing, the ruling of April 4, 1968, and then expressly states that the Chamber must "retake the path of what was previously determined, to deal again with the study of the damage to the person and, in particular, of one of the consequences that may derive from it, which is the damage to relationship quality of life".

27 Interpreting that, in Italy, the problems that revolve around damages to relational quality life are due to "the different treatments offered to pecuniary and non-pecuniary damages, or due to the emergence of new categories, such as biological damage, damage to health and existential damage, among others".

the truth is that this notion ["damage to relational quality of life"] *responds to the goals pursued in this field by the current Colombian legal system and, at the same time, fits within its own and authentic institutional evolution*. Therefore, it continues to show considerable usefulness in order to extend and deepen the effective guarantees available to people who resort to the administration of justice. [I]t is necessary to state that the recognition by this Chamber of the notion under discussion must be appreciated as a *link in the process of transformation of the legal institutions of a society, which on this occasion, after capitalizing on the study of the various experiences, leads to the adoption of some existing concepts aimed at formulating an approach that meets the needs of the time and the country's own circumstances;* of course, under the consistent understanding that for its practical application, the judicial decisions issued henceforth and the changes in a developing society will warrant that this Collegial Body, acting as the Court of Cassation, be in charge of *preparing and implementing the adjustments, modifications and adaptations that allow this legal institution ["damage to relational quality of life"] to acquire solidity and stability* (emphasis mine).

Yet, the ruling also warns of the latent risk inherent to this type of creation by legal science. That is, that the system might experience an overabundance of civil liability cases due to the persistent broadening of the category of non-pecuniary damages. Therefore, the Court cautions that judges must be mindful of the underlying danger — which lurks over every jurist and judicial decision, whether domestic foreign — and be urged to avoid that a "certain grievance may be wrongfully compensated several times"[28].

1.4. *2014: A crucial year for non-pecuniary damages in Colombia*

Very important jurisprudential decisions were issued in 2014, both within the Colombian Civil Cassation (August 5)[29] and the

---

28 Alluding to the work of the judges in establishing the *quantum* of this type of damage, the Court held: "*[I]t may not respond only to the judge's whim, but a balance must be kept vis-a-vis the alleged and proven circumstances within the controversy, thus ensuring that the teleology that animates the institution of civil liability is not overwhelmed, an issue in which, surely, the jurisprudence will draw a useful frame of reference, in a similar way to what occurs in the case of non-pecuniary damages*" (emphasis mine).

29 Ruling of the Court of Cassation, civil section, August 5, 2014, File SC10297-2014, No. Rad.: 11001-31-03-003-2003-00660-01, R.M. Ariel Salazar

Colombian Council of State (August 28)[30], whose approaches are still followed today.

The aforementioned ruling of the Civil Cassation established that, in addition to pain and suffering damages[31], the "damage to relational quality of life" and the damage to constitutional rights (e.g. freedom, dignity, honor and reputation, deemed fundamental human rights)[32] are separate kinds of non-pecuniary damages[33].

Ramírez [Event: breach of contractual obligations by a credit institution, consisting of the unjustified reporting of the client to the information centers and subjecting the client to constant anxiety, anguish and humiliation due to the insistent collection of an obligation that actually does not exist].

30 Jurisprudential unification rulings of the Council of State, Section 3, August 28, 2014: Exp. 26,251, R.M. Jaime Orlando Santofimio [Event: (escape and subsequent) death of a minor who was in the care of a reeducation center]; File 32,988, R.M. Ramiro Pazos [Event: disappearance and death of four people at the hands of military personnel]; File 27,709, R.M. Carlos Zambrano [Event: death of thirteen police officers at the hands of the guerrillas]; File 31,172, R.M. Olga Mélida Valle de De la Hoz [Event: bodily injury to a soldier from the explosion of a grenade he was carrying in his vest]; File 36,149, R.M. Hernán Andrade [Event: unjust deprivation of liberty]; File 28,804, R.M. Stella Conto Díaz [Event: perinatal death]; File 31,170, R.M. Enrique Gil Botero [Event: bodily injury]; File 28,832, R.M. Danilo Rojas [Event: bodily injury].

31 Damage to health is mentioned only by way of *obiter dictum*. It has never been compensated as such in the ordinary jurisdiction.

32 The ruling goes on to state: "This was recognized by this Chamber in a recent ruling, in which it was said that the following have a non-pecuniary nature: '...relational quality of life, psychosomatic integrity, personal property — i.e., *physical or mental integrity, freedom, name, dignity, intimacy, honor, image, reputation, fame*, etc., — *or to the sentimental and affective sphere...*' (Ruling of cassation of September 18, 2009) [underlined]". "Hence, non-pecuniary damages may be presented in several ways, namely: i) through injury to an inner feeling and, therefore, subjective (non-pecuniary damage); ii) as objective deprivation of the ability to carry out daily activities such as practicing sports, listening to music, attending shows, traveling, reading, hanging out with friends or family, enjoying the landscape, having intimate relationships, etc., (damage to the relational quality of life); or, iii) as a violation of fundamental human rights such as a reputation, one's image, freedom, privacy and dignity, which enjoy special constitutional protection".

33 The ruling points out: "Regarding the impairment of the right to reputation, it must be admitted that the damage is configured when the culpable violation of that legal right is demonstrated, without the presence of any other consequence being required. [...] The compensable damage is identified with

On the other hand, that same year the Council of State issued eight rulings of jurisprudential unification, essentially stating that there are three types of immaterial damages (i.e., non-pecuniary damages, non-pecuniary damages due to injury to constitutional or conventionally protected rights, and damages to health) and incidentally re-introduced the latter to the Colombian legal system. As such, the decision evidences the similarities between this classification of non-pecuniary damages and the Italian one, where, as explained, at least since 2003[34],

> it may be said that the notion of non-pecuniary damages referred to in article 2059 of the C.C. includes: biological damages in the strict sense, subjective moral damages as traditionally conceived, and any additional damage to a constitutionally protected interest resulting from the injury.[35]

2. Peru and its legislation

2.1. The "personal damage", a codified reality, next to moral damages and pecuniary damages

The Italian experience on compensable damages has had a decisive influence on the Peruvian legal system, which, as will be explained below, adopted some of the former's legal

---

the breach suffered by the constitutional right. [...] Regarding the damage to reputation, it is necessary to admit, in the terms of current comparative law, that the reserved sphere of the person is valued based on extrinsic criteria, regardless of the subjective consideration that each one has about his or her own honor, intimacy or image. These external parameters are established by the importance that the legal system grants to very personal essential assets, which enjoy a higher privilege because they are expressly enshrined in the Political Constitution as fundamental guarantees. All of this leads to the conclusion that the aforementioned damage must be appraised in the sum of Col$ 20,000,000 for each of the claimants".

34 Court of Cassation, civil section, Rulings Nos. 8828 and 8827, of May 31, 2003, and of the Constitutional Court No. 233, of July 11, 2003.
35 M. Koteich Khatib, *La reparación del daño como mecanismo de tutela de la persona. Del daño a la salud a los nuevos daños extrapatrimoniales*. Bogotá 2012 (also in: https://bdigital.uexternado.edu.co/server/api/core/bitstreams/2dc142c2-ee52-4a21-b3d9-ec31d1337e1c/content), p. 54.

categories[36]. This is precisely the case of the notion of "personal damage"[37], which the Peruvian legislator expressly enshrined in article 1985 of the 1984 Civil Code[38] as an autonomous category of compensable damages (alongside non-pecuniary and pecuniary damages[39]) and, in doing so, undeniably introduced a true novelty within the Latin American law of non-contractual civil liability[40].

---

36 This is expressly recognized by C. Fernández Sessarego, *El daño a la persona en el Código Civil peruano de 1984 y el Código Civil italiano de 1942*, in *El Código Civil peruano y el sistema jurídico latinoamericano*, Lima 1986, p. 255.

37 This category was expressly mentioned in article 2057 of the Italian Civil Code, however it does not actually have a special systematic value; rather, it has been the doctrine and jurisprudence that have filled it with content, profiling damage to health as its central category. On this point, C. Fernández Sessarego points out in 'Deslinde conceptual entre "daño a la persona", "daño al proyecto de vida" y "daño moral"', in J. Espinoza Espinoza (ed.) *Responsabilidad Civil. Nuevas tendencias, unificación y reforma. Veinte años después*, Lima 2005, pp. 132 ff., that we must recognize that the "biological damage", the "danno alla salute", the "corporal dommage", the "moral damage", "danno esistenziale", "dommage physiologique", "non-pecuniary damage", "extra-economic damage", "non-pecuniary damage", or the more specific ones of "damage to relational quality of life", "aesthetic damage", "damage to the private sexual life", among others in vogue in Italy, France and Spain, are only different denominations to designate specific damages, all of them included in the generic and comprehensive "damage to the person". These denominations were born from the circumstance or times in which the term was coined, or have been motivated by the imagination of the authors or by precise requirements of adaptation to a certain positive legal system in search of a legal basis, among other reasons.

38 Article 1985 of the Peruvian Civil Code, referring to the content of compensation, states: "Compensation includes the consequences arising from the action or omission that caused the injury, including lost profits, damage to the person and moral damage, and there should be an adequate causal relationship between the event and the damage caused. The amount of compensation accrues statutory interest from the date on which the damage occurred".

39 An opinion contrary to the usefulness of the category of personal damage and its entry into the Peruvian legal system, in F. de Trazegnies Granda, *La responsabilidad extracontractual* (II), Lima 2003, p. 110; and also in L. León, 'Funcionalidad del "daño moral" e inutilidad del "daño a la persona" en el derecho civil peruano', Revista Peruana de Jurisprudencia, 2003, pp. I-XXXVIII.I.

40 In this sense, J. Mosset Iturraspe, 'El daño fundado en la dimensión del hombre en su concreta realidad', Revista de Derecho Privado y Comunitario

2.2. The doctrinal systematization refers to "personal damages" and "non-personal damages"

Now, regarding the elements of the notion of "personal damage" there is, however, no absolute consensus[41]. This is mainly because, originally, at least for Fernández Sessarego (architect of this legal category in Peru), said concept encompassed or absorbed the traditional non-pecuniary damages or *pretium doloris*; in such a way that the universe of compensable damages was made up only of "personal damages" and "non-personal damages", with no room for a third category[42].

2.3. "Personal damage" includes "psychosomatic damage" ("biological damage" and "damage to health or well-being") and "damage to the life project"

Accordingly, the author maintains that the concept of the human being should be the very one to guide the system of "personal damage". Moreover, said concept makes it possible to establish the different subcategories of damages in a coherent manner, by anthropologically and philosophically defining the human being as a "psychosomatic unit constituted and sustained in its freedom"[43].

---

(1), Santa Fe 1992, pp. 22 ff., points out that the discussion on the personal damage began in Peru, from where it later spread to other Latin American countries. Thus, for example, it was also expressly provided for in the 1998 Argentine Civil Code project (article 1600).

41 As stated by J.L. Diez Schwerter, 'La resarcibilidad del daño no patrimonial en América Latina: una visión histórico-comparativa', in J. Adame Goddard (ed.), *Derecho civil y derecho romano. Culturas y sistemas jurídicos comparados*, Mexico 2006, pp. 344 ff.

42 C. Fernández Sessarego, 'Hacia una nueva sistematización del daño a la persona', Cuadernos de Derecho (3), Lima 2003, p. 36.

43 That freedom that "radically differentiates humans from the other beings of nature and gives him dignity", and that later allows him "to choose, among many opportunities or possibilities of life, what, precisely, we call a "life project", "vital project" or "existential project". C. Fernández Sessarego, 'Deslinde conceptual entre "daño a la persona", "daño al proyecto de vida" y "daño moral"', p. 150.

So, based on the above definition, an injured party may only recover damages when either her/his psychosomatic unit or freedom — understood as phenomenal in nature which "extroverts or turns to the outside" — has been prejudiced, which equates to a person's "being" as harmed.

The damage affecting a person's psychosomatic unit, that is, the *soma* and/or the *psyche*, translates into "psychosomatic damage", which is then divided into "biological damage" (comprising the static aspect or injury itself), and "damage to health" or "damage to well-being", which encompasses a person's dynamic aspect, understood as the distress of a variable magnitude, that occurs in the daily life of the victim[44]. The second, that is, the damage that affects the freedom of the human being, constitutes the "damage to the life project", defined as the *result of a previous psychosomatic damage*[45], which prevents the human being from achieving their existential fulfillment as per their life project, chosen in exercise of their freedom, taking into account their personal vocation[46]. As explained by the author, the distinction between these two notions is justified and must be maintained, due to the need to specify the respective repair modalities and techniques, which must be different for each case[47].

---

[44] Here you may see a complete transposition of the ideas born and matured on the Italian stage.

[45] C. Fernández Sessarego, 'Deslinde conceptual entre "daño a la persona", "daño al proyecto de vida" y "daño moral"', *passim*, in particular pp. 139 and 165.

[46] C. Fernández Sessarego, 'El daño a la persona en el Código Civil de 1984', in AA.VV., *Libro Homenaje a José León Barandiarán* (Lima: Cultural Cuzco, 1985), p. 202. On the category, see É. Cortés Moncayo, 'L'influenza della dottrina Europea nella formazione del sistema della responsabilità civile in America Latina. L'esempio del danno alla persona', in G. Comandè (ed.), *Persona e tutele giuridiche*, Torino 2003, pp. 383–409; Id., 'El resarcimiento del daño a la persona en el derecho latinoamericano. Elementos para una discusión, traídos de dos modelos europeos', in *Estudios de derecho civil. Libro Homenaje a Fernando Hinestrosa*, I (Bogotá: Universidad Externado de Colombia, 2003), pp. 331–49.

[47] C. Fernández Sessarego, 'Deslinde conceptual entre "daño a la persona", "daño al proyecto de vida" y "daño moral"', p. 138.

To the extent, then, that "non-material damage" is considered a "generally transitory, non-pathological mental disturbance"[48], it is understandable that, according to the thesis put forward by the author, it must be included in the subcategory of damage to the person constituted by psychosomatic damage[49]; something that was not thus reflected in the Civil Code.

This systematization of "personal damage" thus suggests that, although the Italian legal system was undoubtedly taken as a model of inspiration (from which the concept was imported, with the prominence of its central category, i.e., "psychosomatic damage" or "damage to health" as it is called in Italy), an important "local" variant was introduced, i.e. the so-called "damage to the life project",[50] which, compared to the general and comprehensive category of "personal damage", stands in a species-to-genus relationship.

It is worth noting that, the definition of "damage to the life project" — explained above — gives rise to two concerns. First, to the extent that psychosomatic damage alludes (also) to the effects that the injury itself or "biological damage" inflicts on the life of the victim, it is extremely difficult to distinguish the defining features of "damage to the life project" from those of "psychosomatic damage" in its dynamic expression (i.e., "damage to health"). Incidentally, precisely by virtue of this apparent overlap, it is possible to identify a parallel between the Peruvian "damage to the life project" and the Italian so-called

---

48 C. Fernández Sessarego, 'Deslinde conceptual entre "daño a la persona", "daño al proyecto de vida" y "daño moral"', p. 123.
49 C. Fernández Sessarego, 'Daño moral y daño al proyecto de vida', in *Revista de derecho de daños*, Buenos Aires 1999.
50 Which is said to be of Peruvian origin. Indeed, C. Fernández Sessarego, 'Deslinde conceptual entre "daño a la persona", "daño al proyecto de vida" y "daño moral"', p. 115, expressly points out that the notion of "damage to the life project" was publicly explained by first time in the middle of the 1980s of the 20th century in an International Congress gathered in the city of Lima. Also in C. Fernández Sessarego, '¿*Existe el daño al proyecto de vida?*', Persona. Revista electrónica de derechos existenciales, Nov. 2002, No. 11.

"existential damage"[51], since the latter has "invaded" — it is maintained — its space and seeks to indemnify damages that were already recognized under the dynamic aspect of the Italian "damage to health". However, it is possible to draw a distinction since in the Italian system, and this is not a negligible difference, the "existential problem" may arise from hypotheses other than the injury to psychophysical integrity, that is, from the injury to other rights (fundamental and inviolable) of a person. Here, despite the good intentions of aspiring to in some way overcome the Italian approach on the subject (to the extent that its "renewed" version is considered), the doctrinal systematization of the Peruvian "damage to the person" suffers from less conceptual finesse than its Italian counterpart.

On the other hand, it must be emphasized that, in the case of victims without a "defined" life project, the respective damage has been considered "irrelevant or of little magnitude"[52], representing the Achilles heel of this concept. That is, if this category of damages is aimed to preserving the dignity of the human being, then protection should be equal for all aggrieved parties, regardless of whether the person's project is conveyed or evident to society[53].

Second, the assessment and consequent determination of the extent of "damages to the life project" poses the same practical problems as those inherent to other categories of non-pecuniary damages other than damage to health or a person's psychosomatic unit. That is, in both cases it is difficult to establish the magnitude and "adequate" form of reparation (which, in any case, cannot but be based on equity)[54].

---

51 Which, instead, has been expressly rejected by the Peruvian doctrine, which qualifies it as "novel but unnecessary", to the extent that it constitutes nothing but "psychosomatic damage" [?]: C. Fernández Sessarego, '¿Existe el daño al proyecto de vida?', pp. 116, 122.
52 C. Fernández Sessarego, '¿Existe el daño al proyecto de vida?', p. 169.
53 From this perspective, a certain parallel may be identified between the "damage to the life project" and what at some point in Italy was compensated under the name of "damage to relational quality of life".
54 Between both, i.e. difficulty and equity, is what C. Fernández Sessarego argued in 'Deslinde conceptual entre "daño a la persona", "daño al proyecto

Notwithstanding the foregoing, the category of "damage to the life project" has now become part of "living law" (national and supranational); which, coming out of dogma, becomes a concrete reality through the main mediation of jurisprudence. Thus, Peruvian caselaw, albeit incipiently, has received this category in several rulings[55]. The jurisprudence of the Inter-American Court of Human Rights has rather forcefully done the same[56].

---

de vida" y "daño moral"', p. 172, in the sense that "Judges must stay away from harmful extremes such as, on the one hand, leaving the victim without compensation for a clear and ostensible 'damage to the life project' and, on the other hand, granting excessive amounts far removed from reality and the circumstances specific to each case".

[55] Court of Cassation Rulings No. 114-2001 and No. 3063-2001. In this sense, C. Fernández Sessarego, 'El "daño a la libertad fenoménica" o "daño al proyecto de vida" en el escenario jurídico contemporáneo', *Persona,* Revista Electrónica de Derechos Existenciales (dir. Ricardo David Rabinovich-Berkman), June 2008, states: "In Peru, jurisprudence is beginning to discover the damage to the life project. Indeed, there have already been some rulings in this regard, although, unfortunately, their rationale is not sufficiently developed. The same occurs in a certain arbitration case whose content, due to its public implication, has been summarized in a national media outlet. In a specific law, such as the one that creates the National Youth Council, the existence of the life project is explicitly recognized. The Ombudsman of Peru also refers to the existence of damage to the life project. The same occurs in the jurisprudence of the Constitutional Court. An increasingly important sector of the doctrine also accepts it".

[56] Rulings of November 27, 1998 (Loayza Tamayo versus Peru case); of May 26, 2001 (case of "Street Children"-Villagrán Morales *et al.*-versus Guatemala), of December 3, 2001 (case of Cantoral Benavides versus Peru); and of September 12, 2005 (case of Gutiérrez Soler versus Colombia). Other cases in which this "right to a life project" has been invoked before the Court have been, for example, individually: Myrna Mack Chang versus Guatemala (2003), and Hermanos Gómez Paquiyauri versus Peru (2004); on a family basis: Molina Theissen versus Guatemala (2004); and, on a "community" basis: Massacre of Plan de Sánchez versus Guatemala (2004). On the subject, consult, among others, C. Fernández Sessarego, 'El daño al proyecto de vida en una sentencia reciente de la Corte Interamericana de Derechos Humanos', at http://www.derechoycambiosocial.com/RJC/Revista10/LECTURA.htm, and M.C. M'Causland, *Tipología y reparación del daño no patrimonial*, pp. 135 ff.

3. Venezuela: And the doctrine?

3.1. *The persistence of the tradition: "material damage" and "moral damage"*

In Venezuela, the concept of damage is still tied to the 19th-century rulings issued in accordance with tradition, such that the discussion on the new "personal damage" appears not to have found fertile grounds. That is, "damage" strictly refers to material damage and moral damage, with little regard for recent arguments in favor of recognizing "personal damage".

So, despite the most authoritative Venezuelan doctrine[57] nominally discusses this category — personal damage — from an academic perspective, it then relates it to "the quantifiable economic repercussions of the sacrifice suffered by the victim based on the specific use said victim had of their body or the specific part of the body that was harmed".

Hence, by anchoring the notion of "personal damage" to economic parameters, cases to which said parameters are not applicable are left unresolved (as is the case, for example, of a victim who generated no earnings before the injury occurred)[58].

In reality, compensation in case of injury to a person's physical integrity (considered in itself a "supreme good") in Venezuela, beyond material damage (consequential damage and lost profits)[59], only includes the traditional moral damage. This is why the present study focuses on the latter.

Moral damages were recognized for the first time in Venezuela under the current Civil Code of 1942, although their respective reparation had been openly embraced by the doctrine and

---

57 J. Melich-Orsini, *La responsabilidad civil por hechos ilícitos* (Caracas: Biblioteca de la Academia de Ciencias Políticas y Sociales, 2001–2006), p. 213.
58 Although in some cases, in an attempt to alleviate this situation, the doctrine has resorted to the idea of a "generic labor capacity", created and used (once) in the Italian environment (in whose determination the scales elaborated in the insurance world). J. Melich-Orsini, *La responsabilidad civil por hechos ilícitos*, p. 215.
59 In this case, the so-called "specific labor capacity" is used.

jurisprudence before that. Thus, article 1196[60] established that material and moral damages deriving from an illicit act must be compensated. On the other hand, courts had the *authority* to award compensation to the victim, especially in cases of bodily injury, an attack on a victim's honor, their reputation or that of their family, their personal liberty, as well as in the case of the violation of their home or of a secret concerning the injured party. And relatives, partners or spouses and close companions may also be entitled to damages as reparation for pain suffered for a victim's death[61].

To the extent that the provision refers to the judge's (apparent) power[62], it must be understood that it applies only to the effects that impact the moral aspect of a person and not to the potential material consequences that said injury might generate. Moreover, from a comparative law perspective, it could be argued that the cases indicated in the second part of the provision are hypotheses of "personal damage", which may, in fact, produce two simultaneous results (immaterial and material).

The prime example of this type of damage, which triggers both material and moral damages, is "damage to bodily integrity" or "physical damage" (jurisprudence has found that physical damage constitutes an organic material damage which requires medical treatment and medications to be repaired, and causes loss of income). These categories of damage are primarily characterized by physical pain and moral suffering, considered by the legislator in a similar way to an attack on someone's honor

---

60 Which reproduces article 83 of the Franco-Italian draft of the obligations of 1927.
61 The majority doctrine maintains that this list is not exhaustive. E. Maduro Luyando and E. Pittier, *Curso de obligaciones* (t. I), Caracas 2004, pp. 154 ff.; J. Melich-Orsini, *La responsabilidad civil por hechos ilícitos*, p. 51.
62 Part of the doctrine (including J. Melich-Orsini, *La responsabilidad civil por hechos ilícitos*, p. 52) maintains that the term "may" used in article 1196 C.C. refers, rather than a "purely optional power" of the judge, to the fact that the latter is authorized to order compensation for non-pecuniary damages even in cases where the judge is not able to, by virtue of the nature of things, a precise relation between the injury and the established amount.

and reputation or those of their family, or personal freedom[63], for which "it is evident that such bodily harm or physical injury is classified as moral[64] and not material damage"[65].

The doctrine is clearer when stating that this type of damage is characterized by a "damage complex" nature involving both material and moral damages[66], the latter subject to the judge's sovereign assessment[67].

---

[63] On the same topic, see ruling of the Supreme Court of Justice of Venezuela, Civil Cassation Chamber, dated April 6, 2000, R.M. Carlos Oberto Vélez, File No. 99-496.

[64] This definition makes sense only if the expression "non-pecuniary damage" is taken exclusively as *pretium doloris*. In a similar sense, J. Melich-Orsini, *La responsabilidad civil por hechos ilícitos*, p. 43, when he argues that within moral damage, only mental suffering or physical pain cannot be "understood".

[65] However, it is possible to find rulings where it is argued that, if damage to psychophysical integrity or an attack against dignity or privacy exists, these are recognized only to the extent of the economic detriment that their recovery causes. Thus: "Whoever suffered in their intimacy, whoever was the victim of scorn or physical or spiritual pain, has lost nothing materially and has not been deprived of any use, by the mere fact of that pain. Of course, some physical discomfort may lead to a loss, in the event that it is necessary to invest money to 'recover broken or affected physical or mental health', but this is not the case at hand": Ruling of June 25, 1981 of the former Supreme Court of Justice, in Forensic Gazette No. 112, V. II, 3rd stage, 1771.

[66] See in E. Maduro Luyando, *Curso de obligaciones*, p. 146.

[67] "Article 1,196 [...] authorizes Judges to grant *motu proprio* a reparation to the victim for the injuries or wounds that are inflicted, without the need for any proof of their amount in the records, provided that the fact of the wound was duly demonstrated. This last criterion has been upheld by the Chamber in relation to rulings referring to claims for compensation for moral damages, but there is no doubt that it is also applicable to the case of claims for damages resulting from injuries or bodily injuries, first, because that is how it appears from the mentioned legal text and, secondly, because the reason that the Legislator decided to grant said authorization to Judges in relation to Moral Damage itself, also militates to consider that it was also granted in relation to the claim for bodily damage caused by wounds or injuries: The inability to carry out a test of its assessment. The amount of material, non-bodily damage, may be brought to the file through an expertise, but not the amount of moral or bodily damage resulting from wounds or injuries. Hence, so that Justice is not frustrated, it must be understood that the Legislator empowered Judges to decide on compensation, even if the amount of the same was not proven in the records (ruling of October 10, 1973. Forensic Gazette No 82, pp. 391 and 392)": Ruling of the Civil Cassation Chamber of the Supreme Court of Justice of Venezuela, of April 6, 2000, R.M. Carlos Oberto Vélez, File No. 99-496.

Indeed, the judge will infer the existence and *extent* of moral damages, based solely on the evidence of the set of facts that caused the injury being claimed, although the plaintiff's own estimate may be taken into account as a guide[68]. Venezuelan jurisprudence has found that when seeking compensation for non-pecuniary damages, the only thing that must be demonstrated is the *causation*.

On the other hand, there is no guideline for the purposes of setting the *extent* or amount of compensation for non-pecuniary damages; as occurs, instead, in Colombia, where the jurisprudence periodically sets guidelines or limits on compensation of this type of damage.

3.2. The Constitution offers tools to activate a new chapter of civil liability

Finally, the analysis would not be complete without referring to the Venezuelan Constitution,[69] since it contains elements that could serve as a tool to trigger a new chapter of "personal damage" in Venezuela.

The Venezuelan Constitution enshrines the same fundamental principles that allowed Italy to develop the new category of "personal damage" and the idea of affording protection within the framework of civil liability by means of compensation. Reference is made to the principles of dignity, equality and protection of health, which under the Venezuelan Constitution, in reality, are not simple declarations of principle or programmatic norms.

Within the framework of the defense and development of a person, and the respect for a person's dignity (article 3)[70], the

---

68 On this same topic, see ruling of the Criminal Cassation Chamber of the Supreme Court of Justice, dated August 1, 2000, File No. 00-156, R.M. Franklin Arrieche G.; Ruling of the Civil Cassation Chamber of the Supreme Court of Justice, dated April 26, 2000, File No. 99-097, R.M. Carlos Oberto Velez.
69 Enacted on November 17, 1999, and in force since March 24, 2000.
70 Article 3 of the Venezuelan Constitution: "The State essential purposes are the defense and development of the person and respect for their dignity,

text establishes the right to respect for the psychophysical and moral integrity of a person (article 46)[71] and the principle of substantial equality (article 21)[72]. The former are recognized as essential purposes of the State, while the latter implies that the State must remove any obstacles preventing the realization of effective equality between individuals. In addition, some other provisions stand out, including articles 30 and 140[73], which could allow legal science to create a more organic, articulated system of individual protections in accordance with the new demands of damages law.

Final Reflection

The above discussion illustrates how, depending on the legal system in question, the influence of the Italian experience regarding non-pecuniary damages on different Latin American countries has been diverse. However, whatever said experience may be, one could submit that most of the countries in the region are not indifferent to the outcry of the social conscience that calls for comprehensive compensation for damages, and which considers the human-being in all its dimensions way beyond their productive capacity. Thus, one could argue that these countries are, ultimately, on the path of the new law of damages, of the new civil liability, in this "historical moment of the advancement of private law".

---

the democratic exercise of the popular will, the construction of a just and peace-loving society, the promotion of the prosperity and well-being of the people and the guarantee of compliance with the principles, rights and duties enshrined in this Constitution".

71 Article 46 of the Venezuelan Constitution: "Every person has the right to have their physical, mental and moral integrity respected, consequently [...]".

72 Article 21 of the Venezuelan Constitution: "All people are equal before the law [...]. 2. The law shall guarantee the legal and administrative conditions so that equality before the law is real and effective".

73 The first establishes the State's obligation to fully compensate the victims of human rights violations that may be attributed to it, and the second sets forth the liability of the State for the act of public administration.

For Latin America, Italian non-pecuniary damages must be a new, evolved form, consistent with constitutional principles of dignity and equality — protected in both systems — of assessing damages to the values closest to the human person. By adapting and not merely "transplanting" foreign categories of non-pecuniary damages, comparative law offers an invaluable tool (science, art, technique) from which society can benefit; one that not only allows us to know, in the words of Henao, the "state of the art" of our legal system, but also contributes to the understanding of our own identity[74].

To conclude, having shown the value of comparative law, we must always be attentive to its well-known risks.

A first problem relates to the very transposition of the ideas or legal institutions to be imported, which is limited, and in some cases definitively distorted, by linguistic differences — sometimes constituting authentic barriers for the interpreter —, because a simple translation of the selected texts or notions is not sufficient. That is, legal transplants must necessarily be accompanied by an analysis of their meaning or spirit. In this sense, the undifferentiated use of terms, despite constituting apparent synonyms, is not as innocuous in Law as it could be in any other discipline or, more specifically, in literature in general. Here, an imprecise term may give rise to great nonsense and even paradoxical injustices; hence, the inescapable duty of the jurist-translator to be extremely careful and precise in their translation task, which must always be faithful to the genuine meaning of the original text.

Second, even if there are those who maintain, maybe with excessive optimism, that the principle of full compensation should not be negatively influenced by cultural aspects or conditions (for instance because they do not understand how a court, when rendering a decision to solve a case, could ignore aspects such as the standard of living or the socio-economic standard of the environment where the event transpired), reality suggests that

---

[74] J.C. Henao, *El daño, análisis comparativo de la responsabilidad extracontractual del Estado en derecho colombiano y francés*, pp. 333–35.

this is perhaps a natural occurrence. Hence, in the context of diverse countries, it will not always be convenient, or even possible, to apply exactly the same solutions to similar events, to the extent that, we repeat, it is necessary to pay attention to each cultural and socioeconomic reality[75].

When using the comparative law tool, it is also important to bear in mind the context that gave rise to or justified the establishment of the respective institution in its original legal system. This is an important consideration because, otherwise, one runs the risk of the transplanted institution losing (and perhaps becoming devoid) of its intended significance and effect — having lost the connection with the causes that justified its essence in the first place.

Lastly, when employing the precious comparative method or, in short, when drawing inspiration from foreign legal systems, it is necessary to cogitate the latest decisions, discoveries and writings of said legal science, without disdaining in any case the classic texts. In doing so, one thereby elaborates a more mature, more perfect and more valuable instrument over time, increasingly capable of benefiting the society in which it is intended to be introduced. Hence the importance of consulting recent doctrine (and jurisprudence) in order to remain abreast of the evolution of legal institutions and, above all, of the "state of the art" of each matter.

---

[75] In this regard, F. Hinestrosa, 'Devenir del derecho de daños', p. 20, argues that "the vast majority of people, especially in countries other than those of the first world, in the best of cases, barely have basic means of subsistence. That is, at the same time that the need of the victims for comprehensive compensation of the damage is quite precarious, the economic and social weight of the compensation obligation is ominous for the perpetrator and their family".

Luis F. P. Leiva Fernandez[*]
THE ITALIAN CIVIL CODE AND ITS IMPACT ON ARGENTINE CIVIL LAW
(Contracts in General)

1. A Brief History of Argentine Law in 1942.

71 years elapsed between the Civil Code of the Argentine Republic coming into force through Law No. 340 of 1871, the work of the jurist Dalmacio Vélez Sarsfield, and the enactment of the Italian Civil Code of 1942.

However, the incidence of Italian sources was not foreign to this body of law. Indeed, it was influenced by the ancient codes of Naples[1], Sardinia[2] and the Italian code of 1865[3], but not through doctrinal works.

---

[*] Main Consulting Prof. Univ. de Buenos Aires; Main Prof. and Director of the Institute of Civil Law Univ. Nacional de La Plata; Main Prof. U. Austral; Member of the Academy of European Iusprivatists. V. "http://www.leivafernandez.com.ar"www.leivafernandez.com.ar

[1] Cited 395 times among the thousands of explanatory notes to each article contained in the codifier's work, which places it in 6th place by number of citations. In the Chapter on contracts in general, it was cited in the notes to Articles 1168, 1170, 1175, 1193 and 1204 of the Argentine historical code.

[2] Quoted many times in other notes of the same Code, it is not mentioned in the Title "Of contracts in general". It should be highlighted that the notes, originally intended to explain and support the provisions of the legislative text, were not approved by Congress and thus were not recognized. In the note on elevation of the Project, Velez refers specifically to having consulted the writings of Count Portalis in his introduction to the Sardinian Code.

[3] *Codex Civile del Regno di Italia* (Turin: Libreria della Minerva Subalpina di Giacinto Belgrano, 1865). The notes to Articles 1138, 1139, 1168, 1170, 1175, 1193, 1195, all referring to scope of this contribution (i.e., contracts in general), contain references to this Code. There are many more citations in other parts of the Code of Vélez Sarsfield, but no reference to Italian doctrine. I highlight the note to Article 1323, where Vélez Sarsfield expresses: "Having published the Italian Code in 1865, we leave the concordance with the

The original text of the Civil Code of 1871 — enacted before the invention of electric power — underwent scarce modifications over the decades. The most important affected a small number of articles, and even fewer collocated in the general part of contracts (Articles 1137 to 1216) — where only article 1198 introduced the principle of foreseeability or excessive supervening onerousness.

The Italian Civil Code (Article 1467) served as a guide for the application of this institution, which was reformed by Law 17.711, as it was extremely casuistic compared to the Italian precept[4].

That was the panorama from 1871 to 2015 when the Civil and Commercial Code of the Nation (Law 26.994) was promulgated and entered into force, directed by professors Ricardo L. Lorenzetti and Elena Highton de Nolasco (both also Supreme Court justices), as well as Aída Kemelmajer de Carlucci, who summoned one hundred professors for its drafting[5].

However, several attempts were made between 1871 and 2015 to reform the Code of Velez Sarsfield. And despite such developments contributed to the modernization of the doctrine, they did not have the same effect on the law. I bypass the reference of those prior to 1942[6].

Following 1942, reform projects included both partial amendments to the original Code and total substitutions.

Reference to such initiatives is provided below, with analysis limited to the general part of contracts.

    Sardinian Code and we will make them with the new Italian Code, continuing however always with the Code of Naples".
4   See J.J.. Llambias 'Estudio de la reforma del Código Civil. Law 17.711', Jurisprudencia Argentina (1969), p. 311.
5   Including the author of this contribution.
6   These are the Preliminary Draft of Juan Antonio Bibiloni of 1924 and the Draft of reforms of the Civil Code of 1936.

2. Reform projects of the Argentine Civil Code between 1942 and 2015

2.1. The Preliminary Draft of the Civil Code of 1954

In 1954, Dr. Jorge J. Llambías, a very distinguished professor and author, directed the drafting of a comprehensive draft of the Civil Code, with the assistance of Roberto Ponssa, Jorge A. Mazzinghi, Jorge E. Bargalló Cirio and Ricardo Julio Alberdi, in his capacity as Director of the Institute of Civil Law of the National Ministry of Justice. The revolution and consequent rejection of the Executive Power in 1955 hindered the progress of the draft bill, which never reached Congress. The Preliminary Draft[7] was not published until 1968.

In the general part of contracts, the sources cited were Articles 1013[8] to 1349 of the Italian Civil Code; Articles 1020[9] to 1322 and 1339; Articles 1025[10] to 1467 and 1469; Articles 1026[11] to 1453 and 1455; Articles 1048[12] to 1411; Articles 1049[13] to 1412; Articles 1051[14] to 1413.

2.2. The reform by Law 17.711 (1968) of the Civil Code of Vélez Sarsfield.

The year 1968 witnessed a partial reform of very few articles of the Vélez Code that, nonetheless, ostensibly modified and modernized the spirit of the 19th century code[15].

---

7 Preliminary draft of the 1954 Civil Code for the Argentine Republic. National University of Tucumán. Tucumán, 1968, pp. 435-449.
8 On the determination of the subject matter of the contracts.
9 On autonomy of will.
10 On supervening hardship.
11 General rule on termination of contracts
12 On effects of the contract in favor of third parties.
13 On the fate of the performance in case of death of the stipulating party in the contract in favor of a third party
14 On the defense of the promisor in the contract in favor of third parties
15 See P. Lerner, 'The Italian Civil Code of 1942 and the reforms to the Argentine Civil Code', Boletín Mexicano de Derecho Comparado, Universidad Nacional Autónoma de México Distrito Federal, Vol. XXXV,

Among the specific reforms, I will refer to two: the incorporation of the defect of injury, and the then-called principle of unforeseeability[16].

Both institutions display influence of the 1942 code, as well as signs that they were received as independent contributions that improve the source.

Regarding the existence of harm, it is known that some laws establish injury according to the presence of the mere subjective element (exploiting the aggrieved party's need or inexperience), while others require the presence of an objective element (i.e., the objective disproportion in the benefits). Article 1448 of the Italian Code of 1942 requires both conditions, which was considered excessive here[17]. Hence, the rule incorporated in Article 954 only refers to a disproportionate and unjustified pecuniary advantage.

Regarding the principle of unforeseeability, Article 1198 of the Code as amended by Law 17.711 undoubtedly draws on Article 1467 of the Italian Code of 1942. Although Article 1198 did not use the *nomen juris* of the institution — which is currently considered more appropriate than the principle of unforeseeability, which is its first cousin — it made two important contributions. First, it improved the legislative technique by avoiding the word "namely" (*es decir*), which was unnecessary and should not be included[18].

On the other hand, the advisability of legislating on this point was noted, adapting the rule of Article 1467 of the Italian Code

---

103 (January–April, 2002), pp. 517–88. Available at https://www.redalyc.org/pdf/427/42710306.pdf; at pp. 181 ff.

16 Presently better known as "supervening hardship" insofar as it restricts the subjective element. Cfr. Luis F.P. Leiva Fernández, 'Adecuación del contrato por quiebre de sus bases objetivas', Rev. Jurídica Argentina La Ley (September 15, 2022).

17 J.J. Llambias, 'Estudio de la reforma del Código Civil. Ley 17.711', Buenos Aires. Argentine Jurisprudence Ed. 1969, p. 60.

18 Luis F. P. Leiva Fernández, 'Fundamentos de técnica legislativa', Buenos Aires, Ed. La Ley. 1999, No. 275, p. 293.

to include random contracts[19], insofar as the disproportionality of the *alea* of the contract itself[20].

2.3. The 1987 project

This project, developed in the Chamber of Deputies of the Nation, was carried out by distinguished jurists Héctor Alegría, Jorge H. Alterini, Atilio A. Alterini, Miguel C. Araya, Francisco A. de la Vega, Horacio P. Fargosi, Sergio Le Pera and Ana Isabel Piaggi.

Although it was enacted as Law No. 24,032, it was vetoed by President Menem with Dec. 2729/1991.

Despite the project was not intended to integrally substitute the Civil Code of Vélez Sarsfield (since it respected its structure and proposed the modification of only some articles), it was nevertheless the first to envisage the legislative unification of civil and commercial obligations, consequently proposing the repeal of the Code of Commerce.

The report of the Special Commission of Civil and Commercial Legislative Unification to the Chamber of Deputies of the Nation reads: "From the consultation of Comparative Law, a frequent use of the Italian Civil Code resulted, which showed in a greater number of cases proximity with our legal environment and thinking"[21].

2.4. The 1993 projects

Following the veto of the 1987 Bill, the National Executive Power issued Decree No. 468/92 convening a Commission made

---

19 J.J. Llambias, 'Estudio de la reforma del Código Civil. Ley17.711', p. 311.
20 Luis F.P. Leiva Fernández, 'La aplicación de la teoría de la imprevisión a los contratos aleatorios', Revista Jurídica Argentina La Ley (2003-E), p. 1328. Luis F.P. Leiva Fernández, La Ley Revista Juridica Paraguaya. Asunción. 26,11 (December 2003), pp. 1369-1376.
21 Law for the Unification of the Civil and Commercial Legislation of the Nation. Bill approved by the Honorable Chamber of Deputies of the Nation on 15 July 1987. Edition according to the version of the Legislative Gazette No. 8 (Buenos Aires: Abeledo Perrot, 1987), p. 29

up of doctors Augusto César Belluscio, Salvador Darío Bergel, Aída Rosa Kemelmajer de Carlucci, Sergio Le Pera, Julio César Rivera, Federico Videla Escalada and Eduardo A. Zannoni. The text was sent to the Senate of the Nation with Message 1662/93 and appeared in the *Diario de Asuntos Entrados* of August 13, 1993[22].

Simultaneously, on September 5, 1992 (Agenda 503/92), the Chamber of Deputies of the Nation, asserting its authority to pass common law legislation, formed the Federal Commission comprised of doctors Héctor Alegría, Jorge Horacio Alterini, Miguel Carlos Araya, María Artieda de Duré, Alberto Mario Azpeitía, Enrique C. Banchio, Alberto J. Bueres, Osvaldo Camisar, Marcos M. Córdoba, Rafael Manóvil, Luis Moisset de Espanés, Jorge Mosset Iturraspe, Juan Carlos Palmero, Ana Isabel Piaggi, Efraín Hugo Richard, Néstor E. Solari, and Félix Alberto Trigo Represas Ernesto C. Wayar.

Upon finalization, the Bill was submitted to the House of Representatives on April 26, 1993. On November 3, 1993, it was passed by the House of Representatives and submitted to the Senate for review.

Neither of the two projects prospered. They neutralized each other.

My analysis will focus on the Project of the Commission created by Decree No. 468/92, as it is more interesting for the current discussion.

In contract matters, the definition provided by the Vélez Sarsfield Code was excessively broad, as its Article 1137 also included conventions (which, although constituting bilateral legal acts with patrimonial content, are not contracts). Therefore, the Executive Branch's Project followed a more restrictive conception, taken from Article 1321 of the Italian Code. The explanatory annotation inserted in Article 850 of the Draft states:

---

22   Cfr. Luis F.P. Leiva Fernández, *Contratos de Locación*, (Buenos Aires: Abeledo Perrot, 1994), Foreword by A.A. Alterini and R. López Cabana, pp. 17-19.

The current wording of Art. 1137 is modified, which, taken from Savigny, is excessively broad, since it includes all legal conventions. The proposed text follows the orientation of Art. 1321 of the Italian Code and coincides with the position of important national doctrine.[23]

In the same definition, this Project misinterpreted the Italian Code, which in its Article 1321[24] refers to the agreement of two or more parties — a slightly different concept than the one used in the proposed rule which expressed that the contract was a bilateral legal act. The point being that "bilateral" only refers to two parties, which in a narrow interpretation excludes the plurilateral contracts also referenced in Article 1420 of the 1942 Code[25].

Regarding the purpose of the contract, the Executive Branch Bill mimicked Article 1321 of the Italian Code by providing "[the contract's] immediate purpose is to constitute, regulate or extinguish patrimonial legal relationships", an enumeration that is questionable compared to the Vélez text, which simply addressed the "regulation of their rights"[26].

On the elements of contracts, it is worth mentioning that the note to the proposed Article 851 of the Executive Branch Project states: "The enunciation of the essential elements of contracts favors the investigation of their effectiveness. It follows the line of the French Civil Code, Article 1108 and the Italian Civil Code, Article 1325"[27]. However, both foreign sources differ from each other, since the French code includes capacity (which in Argentina is usually admitted as a condition for the validity of the contract, and not as one of its elements) and the Italian code includes the form of the contract.

---

23 *Reformas al Código Civil. Proyecto y notas de la Comisión designada por decreto 468/92* (Buenos Aires: Astrea, 1993), p.164, note to Article 850.
24 Article 1321 "Notion": The contract is the agreement of two or more parties to establish, regulate or terminate between them a legal patrimonial relationship.
25 Cfr. R. Stiglitz and G. Stiglitz, *Contratos. Parte general*, (Buenos Aires: Abeledo Perrot, 1993), p. 46.
26 Cfr. Stiglitz and Stiglitz, p. 51.
27 *Reforms to the Civil Code. Proyecto y notas de la Comisión designada por decreto 468/92*, p. 164, note to art. 851.

In this respect, the Stiglitz & Stiglitz state that

> Messineo considers the parties and consent as constitutive elements. And capacity to act and power to dispose are prerequisites of validity of the contract. Years later, he called these requirements "components of the contract", an expression equivalent to constitutive or legal elements, recalling that in some other provision (e.g., Article 1336-1 on public offers), the term "ends" is used. He affirms that the terminological nuances "complicate things uselessly", but that what must be clear is that the wording of Article 1325 of the Civil Code must be understood in the sense that the contract that does not contain the component elements is not perfected, since the law attributes to them a necessary character, and that this arises from Article 1418 of the Civil Code insofar as it establishes "absence of one of the requirements indicated by Article 1325" as a cause of nullity of the contract
>
> In short, the dominant doctrine equates requirements with elements, in the sense of "entities", whose presence is required for an act to have legal relevance.[28]

The Stiglitz & Stiglitz further add that

> [t]here is a prevailing opinion that Article 1325 of the Civil Code is devoid of normative significance, since it lacks mandatory character (prohibitive or permissive). That is, there is no mandate from the legislator. It seems to be, it is affirmed, a statement more typical of the doctrine than of the law.[29]

The proposal to regulate consent draws from Article 1328 of the Italian Code, "which is considered convenient to include due to the admission of the binding force of the offer"[30].

Article 862 of the Draft, referring to the revocation of the offer already made, also follows Article 1328 of the Italian Code. On

---

28 Stiglitz and Stiglitz, pp. 56 ff.
29 Stiglitz and Stiglitz, p. 57.
30 *Reforms to the Civil Code. Proyecto y notas de la Comisión designada por decreto 468/92*, p. 167, note to art. 858. Art. 1328 of the Italian Code provides: Revocation of proposal and acceptance. The proposal may be revoked until the contract is concluded. However, if the applicant has not completed the execution in good faith before receiving notice of the revocation, the offeror is obliged to indemnify him for the costs and losses incurred by the execution of the contract.
The acceptance may be revoked, provided that the revocation is made known to the proponent prior to acceptance.

the same subject, Article 867 allows the offeror to accept a late acceptance if it is immediately communicated to the accepting party. It is cited in the note to Article 1326 of the Italian Code[31].

Article 933 of the same Project of the Executive Power (insofar as it provides that the contract must be interpreted in a manner that, to the extent possible, will lead to its validity) receives a concept similar to that prescribed in Article 1367 of the Italian Code.

2.5. The 1998 draft Civil Code for the Argentine Republic.

After the frustration of the 1993 projects, with Decree No. 685/95, the National Executive Power appointed an Honorary Commission to prepare a draft Civil Code that also incorporates the Commercial Code.

This was a comprehensive project to replace the two bodies of law.

The project is attributed to professors Héctor Alegría, Atilio Aníbal Alterini, Jorge Horacio Alterini, María Josefa Méndez Costa, Julio César Rivera, and Horacio Roitman[32], despite other members contributed to its elaboration; after 76 meetings between June 1995 and February 11, 1998, when the task was nearly

---

[31] Article 1326 "Conclusion of the contract": The contract is concluded at the moment in which the party who has made the proposal has knowledge of the acceptance of the other party (1335).

The acceptance must be given to the proponent within the term established by him or in the term ordinarily necessary according to the nature of the transaction or according to the uses.

The proposer can effectively terminate the late acceptance, provided that he does not immediately notify the other party.

When the proponent requires a specific form for the acceptance, the acceptance is not effective if it is dated in a different form.

An acceptance not in accordance with the proposal is equivalent to a new proposal.

[32] I served as Secretary of the Commission and prepared the draft of some of its institutions. See Draft of the Civil Code of the Argentine Republic, with note of elevation, Foundations and Complementary Legislation, Ed. Ministry of Justice of the Nation, Argentine Republic, Bs As. 1999. The complete Project can be consulted at www.leivafernandez.com.ar

complete, these other members resigned from the Commission before the project could be submitted to the authorities[33].

In the note, it is emphasized that in the matter of legal persons "The Civil Code of Quebec, the Italian Civil Code, and the fruitful experience in the matter of legal persons developed in our country around foundations, mutual societies, civil associations, cooperatives and commercial companies have been taken into account"[34].

Statement of Reasoning (*Fundamento*) No. 133 reads:

> Firstly, the contract is highlighted as the primary source [of legal obligation]: it is provided that the contract and the other legal relationships and situations to which the law assigns [legal value] are the source of obligations.
>
> The requirements of performance are set out, in accordance with current doctrine. It is established that performance must correspond to an interest of the creditor, even if it is extra-patrimonial, in accordance with Scialoja's formula which was included in Article 1174 of the Italian Civil Code of 1942.[35]

In *Fundamento* No. 161, referring to the requirement of contractual good faith in parity contracting, the authors highlight the enforceability of the requirement at all stages of the contract (i.e., negotiation, conclusion and performance). In particular, it is emphasized that:

> The parties must also act in good faith during the execution of the contract, which generates secondary obligations as it links them to the scope to which a careful and foresighted contracting party would have reasonably bound himself, including the consequences virtually included in it, according to its nature, to the previous negotiations, to the subsequent conduct, to the practices established between the parties, to the usages if they have not been expressly excluded, and to equity, taking into account the purpose of the act and the justified expectations of the other party. This broad wording

---

33   I refer to Professors Aida Kemelmajer de Carlucci and Augusto César Belluscio. Prof. Antonio Boggiano accepted to be a member of the Commission but did not sign the project, nor did he resign to do so.

34   Proyecto de Código Civil de la República Argentina, con nota de elevación, Fundamento y Legislación complementaria. Ed. Ministry of Justice of the Nation. Argentine Republic. Bs As. 1999. Fundamento No. 23, p. 19.

35   Proyecto de Código Civil de al República Argentina, con nota de elevación, Fundamento No. 133, p. 38.

is connected with that of Articles 1374 of the Italian Civil Code of 1942 [...] the conventional exclusion of usages results from Article 1340 of the Italian Civil Code of 1942.[36]

Subsequently in this same *Fundamento* No. 163, it is stated that:

> The death, incapacity or bankruptcy of the offeror or of the acceptor do not prejudice, respectively, the validity of the offer or the effectiveness of the acceptance received subsequently, unless the contrary results from the law, from the nature of the obligation or from the circumstances of the case [...] exclude forfeiture by death or incapacity in cases of simple offer; the Italian Civil Code of 1942, in those of irrevocable offer (Art. 1329) and of offer and acceptance by an entrepreneur (Art. 1330) [...][37]

Regarding the acceptance of the offer, in *Fundamento* No. 166, it is held:

> The acceptance, in turn, can be usefully retracted if the communication of its withdrawal is received by the offeree before or at the same time as the acceptance [...] it is provided that [...] The offeror is entitled to prevail against a late acceptance, if he immediately communicates his decision to the acceptor [...] Italian Civil Code of 1942, Article 1326 [...][38]

As to the form of acceptance, *Fundamento* No. 167 expressly permits:

> that which is produced by means of determined behaviors, such as the *facta concludentia*, or the so-called de facto contractual relations. Tacit acceptance results from certain acts that induce it and, in particular, when, in accordance with the antecedents of the offer, the nature of the business, the practices established between the parties, or customs and usages, the offeror is not required to wait for a communication from the offeree of the offer, unless the offeree wishes to reject it [...] the contract is concluded when performance begins and, depending on the circumstances, it is in-

---

36 Proyecto de Código Civil de la República Argentina, con nota de elevación, Fundamento No. 161, p. 50.
37 Proyecto de Código Civil de la República Argentina, con nota de elevación, Fundamento No. 163, p. 52.
38 Proyecto de Código Civil de la República Argentina, con nota de elevación, Fundamento No. 166, p. 53.

cumbent upon the offeree to give notice to the offeror (...Italian Civil Code of 1942, Article 1326...).[39]

Fundamento No. 174 describes circumstances in which third parties participate in the contract, discerning the various situations. Who contracts on behalf of a third party without the power of representation, the contracting party who promises the act of a third party (further distinguishing between cases when performance is guaranteed and those in which it is not) and the condition precedent that requires a contract for the benefit of an identified or identifiable third party.

> As for the contract for the benefit of a third party nominee, it is envisaged that either party may reserve the right to appoint such party such that the third party assumes its contractual position at a later date, except when the contract cannot be concluded through a representative (cfr. Italian Civil Code of 1942, Article 1401).[40]

With respect to when the third party assumes the qualification of a contractual party, the same *Fundamento* clarifies that the effect is

> retroactive to the date of the contract, when the third party accepts the nomination and its acceptance is communicated to the party that did not make the reservation. This communication must be in the same form as the contract and within the established period or, failing that, within fifteen days of its conclusion. If no valid acceptance by the third party is made, the contract produces effects between the parties (cfr. Italian Civil Code of 1942, article 1402).[41]

This Project, with specific reference only to the general part of contracts, represents a tremendous scientific task that can be appreciated from the aforementioned *Fundamentos*, the development of which is described in the works cited in the footnotes of pages 15 to 147.

---

39 Proyecto de Código Civil de la República Argentina, con nota de elevación, Fundamento No. 167, p. 54.
40 Proyecto de Código Civil de la República Argentina, con nota de elevación, Fundamento No 174, p. 57.
41 Proyecto de Código Civil de la República Argentina, con nota de elevación, Fundamento No 174, p. 57.

Hence, when by Presidential Decree No. 191 of 23 February 2011, the "Commission for the elaboration of the Bill for the reform, updating and unification of the Civil and Commercial Codes of the Nation" was created, composed of professors Ricardo L. Lorenzetti, Elena Highton de Nolasco (both also Supreme Court justices) and Aída Kemelmajer de Carlucci, and one hundred professors were commissioned to write the different parts of the preliminary draft, the 1998 Bill became the primary reference and starting point for the relevant analysis.

3. The doctrine

3.1. The Argentine doctrine

The Thomson Reuters Latam Legal Information database contains 1606 citations of the Italian Civil Code from approximately 2010 to present.

On October 8th, 2014, Decree No. 1795/2014 on the enactment of the new Civil and Commercial Code of the Nation (Law 26,994) was published in the Official Journal. Although Article 7 of Law 2,994 established January 1st, 2016, as the effective date, the Law's entering into force was moved up to August 1st, 2015.

Since then, the Italian Civil Code of 1942 has been cited approximately 370 times.

These numbers clearly merely indicate a trend, because, although La Ley Argentina (Thomson Reuters Latam) is widely published, the abovementioned database only includes periodicals and not the various volumes of the publishing house, nor — of course — those of other Argentine publishers.

3.2. The Italian doctrine in Argentina

The sustained growth of global commerce, the cheapening of communications and the appearance of the e-book facilitated the knowledge by Argentine jurists of the prestigious work of Italian authors.

As a mere reference and in an enunciation that is far from being exhaustive (since any enunciation would be incomplete and, therefore, unfair), I refer to the works of Messineo, Galgano, Roppo, Barassi, Alpa, Fragali, Pajardi, Barbero, Sacco, Scognamiglio, Bianca, Mirabelli, and more recently, with incidence on the analysis of Argentine law in force through books, essays and conferences, Gabrielli, Delfini, Esborraz, Ferrante, etc. Some in their original language in Italian editions, others translated into Spanish.

Not unrelated to all this is the management of the Academy of European Iusprivatists (Pavia Group) which, with the strong impetus of Giuseppe Gandolfi, added a few Argentine jurists to such a prestigious institution.

4. Incidence of the Italian Code in the National Civil and Commercial Code.

4.1. The study of a general part

The Civil and Commercial Code of the Nation has come closer to German law — through Italian law — as evidenced, for instance, by the incorporation of a general part of legal facts and acts (Articles 257 to 400). At the same time, it ignores the theory of the legal transaction (*negocio jurídico*)[42] in favor of the theory of the legal act (*acto jurídico*), coming from the French doctrine, found in the Civil Code of Vélez Sarsfield.

Despite this difference, both concepts "legal act" and "legal transaction" constitute a case of conceptual synonymy. German, Italian, Spanish, and Latin American authors agree on this point[43].

---

42 In Argentine law, it is appropriate to refer to "acto juridico" and not to "negocio juridico". See Luis F.P. Leiva Fernández, *Tratado de los contratos*, I, 9 (Buenos Aires: La Ley, Thomson Reuters, 2017), p. 11.

43 Luis F.P Leiva Fernández, *Ensayos de Derecho Civil y técnica legislativa* (Buenos Aires: La Ley, 2007), pp. 93 ff.; L.F.P Leiva Fernández, 'Acto jurídico o negocio jurídico', Ley & Foro. Rev. del Colegio de Abogados de Puerto Rico, San Juan de Puerto Rico, year 3, n. 3, p. 11; A.G. Spota and Luis F. P. Fernandez (Actualizador), *Instituciones de Derecho Civil. Contratos*, I,

Galgano explains that

> although the Italian civil code has not followed the German one and the legal transaction has not become a legislative category, the Italian civil doctrine — faithful to its German scientific formation — has not ceased to make the legal transaction the object of conceptual elaboration, nor to place it in a dominant position within the theoretical systematics of private law.

And after quoting Stolfi, Betti Cariota Ferrara, Scognamiglio and Calasso, he concludes: "thus the legal transaction remains, despite the contrary legislative choice, among the legal-rational categories of our theoretical and practical jurists, besides being one of the most widespread figures of the legal language"[44].

It should be noted that the Code of Vélez Sársfield of 1869 — repealed in 2015 — did not contain a general part on facts and legal acts with methodological autonomy; however, it did outline the concept in Articles 896–922 and Articles 944–954. Thus, it is not surprising that in 1910 a committee of Professors — Alfredo Colmo, Jesús H. Paz and Eduardo Prayones — from the Law School of the University of Buenos Aires developed a course on the General Part that included this subject, and therefore the general part was organized and taught even though the letter of the law did not yet recognize its scientific autonomy. Hence, the opinions expressed by the aforementioned Italian doctrine were consolidated in university teaching because they already found fertile soil.

4.2. *The unification of the rules on civil and commercial obligations and contracts*

Although this approach was not pioneered by the Italian Civil Code of 1942, it is certainly the most widely disseminated and studied in Argentina and constitutes the most notorious contribution to Argentine private law. For example, the Swiss

---

12 (Buenos Aires, La Ley, 2009), pp. 29 ff. Leiva Fernández, *Tratado de los contratos*, I, 9, p. 11.
44 F. Galgano, *El negocio jurídico* (Valencia: Tirant Lo Blanch, 1992), p. 28.

Code of Obligations - dating from 1881 - was incorporated as Book V of the Civil Code in 1912. It has also been adopted by Tunisia (1906), Morocco (1912), Turkey (1926), Lebanon (1934), Poland (1934), Madagascar (1966), Senegal (1967) and, including civil and commercial matters, by the civil codes of Italy (1942), the Soviet Union (1964), Peru (1984), Paraguay (1987), Cuba (1988), the Netherlands (1992), Mongolia (1994), Vietnam (1995) and the Russian Federation (1994), as well as the Uniform Civil and Commercial Codes of China (Taiwan) and the Kingdom of Thailand and the General Principles of Civil Law of the People's Republic of China of 1987. The Civil Code of Quebec of 1992 follows a similar path, in particular by introducing specific provisions on consumer law[45].

Prior to the promulgation of the Civil and Commercial Code of the Nation, Argentina was subject to two different regimes — one civil and the other commercial — for instance in the case of a deposit agreement, forfeiture agreement, purchase and sale agreement, surety contract, loan, etc. Moreover, for historical reasons, the Commercial Code preceded the Civil Code chronologically, with the result that the rule was subsequent to the exception.

4.3. *The definition of contract. Contract and legal convention*

Italian law had no impact on the Civil Code of Vélez Sársfield. Instead, the Vèlez Code drew on Roman law through the works of Savigny and Maynz, on the work of Augusto Teixeira de Freitas (a brilliant Brazilian jurist), and on the contribution of Aubry and Rau, professors from Strasbourg who commented on the French Code in several successful editions of the Code.

---

[45] Luis F.P. Leiva Fernández. "Tratado de los contratos". Buenos Aires Ed La Ley , Thomson Reuters , 2017, Tomo I, N°34, p. 45. mentioned in "Proyecto de Código Civil de al República Argentina, con nota de elevación, Fundamento y Legislación complementaria. Buenos Aires ,Ed. Ministerio de Justicia de la Nación. República Argentina. 1999, p. 2 , also reproduced in Atilio A., Alterini, "Contratos civiles - comerciales - de consumo. Teoría general", Buenos Aires, Abeledo-Perrot, 1999, p. 109 y ss. The complete Project can be consulted at www.leivafernandez.com.ar.

Article 1137 states: "A contract exists when several persons agree on a common declaration of will, intended to regulate their rights".

Notwithstanding the observations of Gabrielli[46] on the scope of the definition, given its harmony with other provisions of the same Code, the issue did not raise major objections.

However, certain aspects of the Italian Civil Code were criticized and improved in 1942, and Argentine civil law advanced and underpinned this progress.

Take, for instance, the reference to "persons"[47]. Including such term in the definition of contract ignores an essential element for the existence of a contract[48]. The same is true for conflict of interests[49]. Such a conflict — necessary to distinguish the contract from the mere bilateral legal act — involves "parties", not persons[50], as stated in Article 1321 of the Italian Code of 1942[51].

Another issue to consider concerns the effects of the contract.

The Argentine Code repealed in 2015 — the Vélez Code — only states that the contract is intended to regulate the rights of the parties. But what rights? And regulate them how?

Due to its collocation in Book Two, Section Three, entitled "Obligations arising from contracts", there was never any doubt that the provision dealt with economic rights because obligations

---

46   E. Gabrielli, *Doctrina general del contrato*, II, trans. by C. de Cores (Montevideo : Fundación de Cultura Universitaria, 2009) pp. 11 ff.
47   Spota and Leiva Fernández (Actualizador), *Instituciones de Derecho Civil. Contratos*, I, 3, p. 7.
48   Amen that the use of the term "parties" also helps to resolve the recurring issue of self-contracting.
49   Luis F.P. Leiva Fernández. 'Tratado de los contratos' Buenos Aires. Ed La Ley 2017 T. I N.5 p. 5.
50   Spota and Leiva Fernández (Actualizador), *Instituciones de Derecho Civil. Contratos*, I, 3, p. 7. They state on p. 9: "the contract demands as a requirement that there be contradiction, bidding. Hence, in the example given, only when both groups are in conflict — sellers and buyers — we find ourselves before two parties with conflicting interests — the selling party and the buying party — and, therefore, before the contract that requires, not an agreement of several persons, but, as expressed in art. 1321 of the Italian Civil Code, an agreement of two or more parties".
51   See note 18.

are exclusively of that nature. But while the Italian provision expressly stated this, the Vélez provision did not.

Today, the Civil and Commercial Code of the Nation establishes in its Article 957 that "a contract is the legal act by means of which two or more parties express their consent to create, regulate, modify, transfer or extinguish patrimonial legal relationships".

The term "parties" implies the existence of conflicting interests[52].

For this reason, Messineo[53], López de Zavalía[54] and more recently Ibáñez[55], have rightly called the parties "centers of interest".

This is because "party" and "counterparty" are opposing forces that compete to obtain an economic advantage, which is finite by definition.

The Civil and Commercial Code, in using the term "parties", assumes there must be conflicting interests between the parties to the contract.

The Supreme Court of Justice of the Nation (Argentina) established that

> for the configuration of a contract there must be diversity of parties, possibility of deliberation, and differentiation of interests, so that once the relationship of subjection or economic group is proven, all the contractual

---

52 Cfr. E. Betti, 'Teoría general del negocio jurídico', Revista de Derecho Privado (1943), p. 225; J.E. Lavalle Cobo, in A.C. Belluscio, (ed.), *Código Civil y leyes complementarias. Comentado, anotado y concordado*, 5 (Buenos Aires: Astrea, 2002), com. al art. 1137, p. 714; F. Puig Peña, 'Tratado de derecho civil español', Revista de Derecho Privado (1974), IV, 2, p. 7; R. Stiglitz, *Contratos civiles y comerciales*, I (Buenos Aires: Abeledo Perrot, 1998), p. 83; E.Vázquez Bote, *Tratado teórico práctico y crítico de Derecho Privado puertorriqueño*, IX (San Juan: Butterworth, 1992), p. 5.

53 F. Messineo, *Doctrina general del contrato*, I (Buenos Aires: EJEA, 1948), p. 74.

54 F. López de Zavalía, *Teoría de los contratos*, I (Buenos Aires: Zavalía, 1991), p. 13.

55 C.M., Ibáñez, *Derecho de los contratos. Parte general* (Buenos Aires: Ábaco, 2010), p. 68.

appearances with which benefits have been concealed lose their effectiveness.[56]

This is not merely a matter of semantics, but of distinguishing between contract and simple bilateral legal act or legal convention[57].

4.4. The effects of the contract.

The final issue in this regard concerns how such rights are regulated.

Can contracts extinguish obligations? Can they create real or intellectual rights[58]? Can they extinguish or modify such rights?

To "regulate" is comprehensive of any type of incidence — whether to create, modify or extinguish. And property rights — thus *lato sensu* — also include real and intellectual rights. Although in Argentine law — and in all those that include "*traditio*" as a mode of real rights — "*traditio*" is clearly a mode of transfer of real rights.

Indeed:

> The Civil and Commercial Code has chosen to allow that within the field of credit rights can be created, modified, transferred or extinguished by means of a contract. But these five verbs do not all seem necessary, because "to transfer" is to "modify" ownership, that is, to substitute one or both subjects, and both "to modify" and to transfer is "to regulate", so that "to regulate" (i.e., to create, regulate and extinguish patrimonial legal relations) would have sufficed.[59]

---

56 Corte Suprema de Justicia de la Nación *in re* Mellor Goodwin Combustion S.A. c. Gobierno Nacional, 18/10/1973, Fallos: 287:79. TR LALEY AR/JUR/19/197318/10/73 LL152-343.
57 Luis F.P. Leiva Fernández. "Tratado de los contratos" Buenos Aires. Ed La Ley 2017, T. I n. 13, p.17.
58 To make matters worse, at the time of the enactment of the Vélez Code, Edmond Picard had not yet made the tripartite division of property rights that he had only formulated in 1873 at the Brussels Bar. Thus, some of these issues were left to the doctrine. On whether "Contracts can modify or extinguish intellectual rights" see Leiva Fernández, *Tratado de los Contratos*, I, 41, p. 60.
59 Luis F.P. Leiva Fernández, in J.H. Alterini (General Director) and I.E. Alterini (Coord.), *Código Civil y Comercial comentado. Tratado Exegético*, 3rd edn,

The doctrine and positive law (e.g., Article 1351 of the Peruvian Civil Code and the "*in fieri*" regulations)[60] seems to prefer the use of the verbs "to create", "to modify" and "to extinguish"[61].

On the other hand, the less restrictive provision of the Italian Civil Code of 1942 refers to constitute, regulate, or extinguish a patrimonial legal relationship, thus overcoming the criticism of the use of the verbs "transfer" and "modify"; although, I still believe here is a problem with the breadth of the patrimonial rights included, which is not eliminated by the argument that the legal relationship is extraneous to real rights, since it subsists in intangible rights.

4.5. *Contract and inheritance law*

While contracts obviously generate effects within the scope of property law, there are some peculiarities specific to inheritance law that should be highlighted. In fact, deeds in inheritance law are less about creating an enforceable obligation as they are

---

V, 16 (Buenos Aires: La Ley, 2019), p. 26 com. to art. 957.

60 M. Albaladejo, *Derecho civil*, II, 1 (Barcelona: Bosch, 1989), pp. 388 and 389; A.A. Alterini, *Contratos. Teoría general* (Buenos Aires: Abeledo Perrot, 1998), p. 9; E. Betti, 'Teoría general del negocio jurídico', p. 224; L. Díez-Picazo and A. Gullón, *Sistema de derecho civil*, II (Madrid: Tecnos, 1992), p. 29; L. Enneccerus, T. Kipp and M. Wolf, *Tratado de derecho civil. Parte general*, trans. by J. Puig Brutau, I, 2 (Barcelona: Bosch, 1950), p. 142; J. Giorgi, *Teoría de las obligaciones*, III (Madrid: Reus, 1919), p. 22; FLópez de Zavalía, *Teoría de los contratos*, I, p. 12; Federico Puig Peña, 'Tratado de derecho civil español', IV, 2, p. 6; Rubén, Stiglitz, *Contratos civiles y comerciales*, I, p. 85; G. Stolfi, 'Teoría del negocio jurídico', RDP, 195-8, p. 13 in relation to art. 1321 of the Italian Civil Code of 1942; A.Von Tuhr, *Tratado de las obligaciones* (Madrid: Reus, 1934), I, p. 102. For the use of the verb "regular", see F. Galgano, *El negocio jurídico*, p. 58 regarding art. 1321 of the Italian Civil Code of 1942; Spota and Leiva Fernández (Actualizador), *Instituciones de Derecho Civil. Contratos*, I, 15, p. 38.

61 See generally, Article 1 of the Preliminary Draft of the European Code of Contracts of the Academy of European Lawyers (Pavia Group); Article 1 of the Mc Gregor Preliminary Draft (see H. Mc Gregor, *Contract Code*, Draft drawn up on behalf of the English Law Commission (Barcelona: Bosch, 1977).

about establishing different aspects, such as instituting a person as heir or beneficiary of another person's legacy[62].

The three types of succession agreements — namely, the institutional agreement (Articles 1175 and 1176), the waiver (Articles 3311 and 3599), and the disposal of a future inheritance during the lifetime of the deceased[63] — that were expressly prohibited under the repealed Civil Code are still prohibited under Articles 2286[64] and 2449[65] of the Civil and Commercial Code of the Nation. As such, these pacts are considered null and void pursuant to Article 387.

However, the inclusion of commercial matters in the new body of law produced a protective effect on certain business activity, notably the softening of the prohibition.

I refer to Article 1010 of the Argentine Civil and Commercial Code, which provides:

> Future inheritance. Future inheritance cannot be the object of contracts nor can eventual inheritance rights over particular objects, except as provided in the following paragraph or other express legal provision.
>
> Covenants relating to business operations or to corporate ownership interests of any kind, for the purpose of preserving the unity of the business management or preventing or solving conflicts, may include provisions referring to future inheritance rights and establish compensation in favor of other legitimated beneficiaries. These agreements are valid, regardless of whether the future deceased and his spouse are parties, if they do not affect the legitimate inheritance, the rights of the spouse, or the rights of third parties.

Paragraph 2, which aims to maintain the unity of business management, is based on the Civil Code of Catalonia and the

---

62 Spota and Leiva Fernández (Actualizador), *Instituciones de Derecho Civil. Contratos*, I, 69, p. 175.
63 Leiva Fernández, *Tratado de los Contratos*, I, 44, p. 64; Spota and Leiva Fernández (Actualizador), *Instituciones de Derecho Civil. Contratos*, I, 69, pp. 175 ff.
64 Civil and Commercial Code of the Nation Art. 2286 – Time of acceptance and renunciation. Future inheritances cannot be accepted or renounced.
65 Civil and Commercial Code of the Nation Art. 2449 – Unrenounceability. The legitimate portion of a succession not yet opened cannot be renounced.

Italian Civil Code, as amended by Law No. 55 of February 14, 2006, which incorporated the so-called "family pact"[66].

---

[66] See R. Giampetraglia, 'La autonomía de la voluntad en la transmisión de la empresa: El pacto de familia', Anuario de Derecho Civil, ADC, LXVII, 4 (2014), (https://www.boe.es/biblioteca_juridica/anuarios_derecho/abrir_pdf.php?id=ANU-C-2014-40116901197). J.C. Rivera, in J.C. Rivera and G. Medina (eds.), *Código Civil y Comercial de la Nación Comentado*, III (Buenos Aires: La Ley, 2014), com. to art. 1010, p. 515 with citation of Graciela Medina; Leiva Fernández, *Tratado de los Contratos*, I, 44, p. 64. ff.

Leysser León*
THE FATE OF ITALIAN REGULATIONS ON UNJUSTIFIED ENRICHMENT IN THE PERUVIAN CIVIL CODE
The Challenge of Shaping a National Law

I. *Introduction*

The Peruvian Civil Code of 1984 is without a doubt the single most influenced code by the Italian Civil Code of 1942 around the world[1]. When the Peruvian legislators first began their work in 1965, the Italian regulations were practically at their fingertips, given to the broad distribution and popularity of their Spanish translation, published in Buenos Aires, as part of the first volume of Francesco Messineo's renowned handbook on civil and commercial law[2].

Moreover, if compared to other notable Civil Codes, (e.g. the French, Austrian, German, or Swiss[3]), the Italian laws were relatively recent in the context of Peru's codification process. And, thanks to the translations into Spanish of numerous treatises and handbooks authored by Italian scholars, (e.g. Lodovico Barassi, Emilio Betti, Aurelio Candian, Salvatore Pugliatti, Alberto Trabucchi, Luigi Cariota Ferrara, and Domenico Barbero, among

---

*   Sant'Anna School of Advanced Studies (PhD *cum laude*). Principal Professor of Civil Law at Pontifical Catholic University of Peru. Peruvian correspondent of the International Institute for the Unification of Private Law (Unidroit).
1   See L. León Hilario, 'Betti, l'ermeneutica e l'America Latina', in A. Banfi, M. Brutti and E. Stolfi (eds.), *Dall'esegesi giuridica alla teoria dell'interpretazione: Emilio Betti (1890-1968)* (Roma: Roma TrE-Press, 2020), p. 320.
2   F. Messineo, *Manual de derecho civil y comercial*, trans. by S. Sentís Melendo, I (Buenos Aires: Ediciones Jurídicas Europa-América, 1954).
3   Despite being more recent, the Portuguese Civil Code of 1966 was not considered to any significant extent in the last Peruvian codification process.

others[4]), the meaning of those rules could also be reconstructed, albeit basically, by local interpreters.

Take, for instance, the Peruvian provisions on unjustified enrichment. These were just some of the many Italian rules transposed into Peruvian law.

The purpose of this paper is to describe the implications of this legal transplant and illustrate how such has influenced recourse to restitution, a remedy which – being almost entirely precluded in Peruvian legal practice – is largely ignored in favor of others despite its increasing usefulness in unjustified enrichment cases.

However, as with all legal transplants, the success of the unjustified enrichment regime depends on the dominant legal culture of the host country[5].

II. *From natural law to the first Peruvian Civil Code*

Of all the Latin American republics that emerged from the arduous process of emancipation from the Spanish monarchy in the 19th century, Peru stands out for being the first to codify a general rule on unjust enrichment.

In fact, the Peruvian Civil Code of 1852, in its seventh section, regarding the obligations arising from implied consent, provides:

> Art. 2110. – The principles of obligations established without consent are:
> 1. Everyone wants what is useful to him.
> 2. No one may enrich himself to the detriment of another.
> 3. Whoever wishes to take advantage of an event must not fail to submit to its consequences.

---

[4] See L. León Hilario, 'La ricezione nel diritto peruviano delle regole del codice civile italiano sul contratto in genere', in S. Lanni and P. Sirena (eds.), *Il modello giuridico —scientifico e legislativo— italiano fuori dell'Europa* (Napoli: ESI, 2013), pp. 254 ff.

[5] See: H. Scott and D. Visser, 'The Impact of Legal Culture on the Law of Unjustified Enrichment: The Role of Reasons', in E. Bant and M. Harding (eds.), *Exploring Private Law* (Cambridge: Cambridge University Press, 2010), pp. 153 ff.

4. A man is responsible for the damage he causes not only by his own act, but also by his carelessness or imprudence.

Then, in Title One on quasi-contracts, article 2111 establishes "– Quasi-contracts are lawful acts by which people are bound by consent presumed by equity".

Subsequently, a legal framework was provided for the following quasi-contracts: *negotiorum gestio* (articles 2112 to 2118), *indebitum solutum* (articles 2119 and 2127) and, under a separate heading, community and division of inheritance (articles 2128 to 2188).

To the extent that the two rules cited above articulate a group of principles (or, an "equitable presumption"), a correct assessment of the regulation of the First Peruvian Civil Code presupposes an initial consideration of the same.

While the precise origin of these principles is unknown, it is possible they derived from Roman sources, and specifically from a famous maxim of Pomponius included in the *Digesta*: "By the law of nature it is just that no one should become richer by the loss and injury of another"[6]. Alternatively, they could stem from a no less famous passage in Cicero's *De officis*: "For one man to take from another, and to increase his own advantage at the expense of another's, is more contrary to nature than death, than poverty, than pain, and than anything else that may happen to his body or to his external possessions"[7]. Or they may even originate from a precept contained in the *Partidas* of King Alfonso X of Castile,

---

[6] *Digesta* 50.17.206: "*Iure naturae aequum est neminem cum alterius detrimento et iniuria fieri locupletiorem*". The translation quoted in the text is that included in A. Watson (ed.), *The Digest of Justinian* (1985), vol. 4, (Philadelphia: University of Pennsylvania Press, 1989), p. 483. On this maxim see: J.P. Dawson, *Unjust Enrichment. A Comparative Analysis* (Boston: Little, Brown and Company, 1951), pp. 4 ff.; and R. Zimmermann, *The Law of Obligations. Roman Foundations of Civilian Tradition* (Cape Town: Juta & Co, Ltd and Munich: C.H. Beck, 1990, reprint 1992), pp. 851 ff.

[7] Cicero, *On Duties*, ed. by M.T. Griffin and E.M. Atkins (Cambridge: Cambridge University Press, 2003), p. 108.

(aka 'The Wise'): "No one should enrich himself unlawfully at the expense of others[8]".

Regarding equity as the basis of the presumption of consensus, its formulation could be explained by the context in which natural law largely inspired the training of future Peruvian lawyers. Therefore, the Civil Code notion of quasi-contracts could have arisen from an evident moral guideline contained in the handbooks used to teach natural law, which clearly highlighted the lessons of Heineccius[9].

However, neither of the above assumptions is correct.

In fact, article 2110 of the Peruvian Civil Code of 1852 came from a remarkable piece of legislation, which, with all probability, the Peruvian legislators did not know in its original language: the *Codex Maximilianeus Bavaricus Civilis* of 1756, the Civil Code of Bavaria, promulgated by the Elector Maximilian III Joseph.

Indeed, concerning quasi-contracts[10], a French translation of Chapter XIII, Part IV, paragraph 1 of the Bavarian *Codex*,

---

8   See: *Las Siete Partidas del rey don Alfonso El Sabio*, ed. by G. López (Paris: Librería de Rosa Bouret y Cía, 1851), t. V, *Séptima Partida*, tit. XXIII, Ley XIII, *De las reglas derechuderas que son llamadas en latín* de regulis juris, p. 732.

9   Johann Gottlieb Heinecke (Heineccius), *Elementa iuris civilis secundum ordinem Institutionum* (Giessen: Johann Philipp Krieger, 1730), § 778, p. 357: "*Ergo fundamentum quasi contractuum non est consensus tacitus, uti quibusdam visum; (ita enim ignorantes et inviti non obligarentur, § I, Inst. de obl. Quae quasi ex contr.) sed consensus fictus vel praesumtus. Inducitur vero huiusmodi praesumptio, vel ex aequitate, vel ex utilitate, veluti quia nemo debeat cum alterius damno locupletior fieri. L. 14 ff. De condict. indeb.*" One of the many Spanish versions of this book, which made a prestigious appearance in South America during the colonial era and continued to be esteemed after the beginning of the independent period, was the one edited by José Vicente y Caravantes: *Elementos del derecho romano según el orden de las Instituciones* (Madrid: Imprenta de Pedro Sanz y Sanz, 1842), pp. 242–243. On the fortune of Heineccius' works in teaching law in Peru, see: F. de Trazegnies Granda, *La idea del derecho en el Perú republicano del siglo XIX* (Lima: Fondo Editorial de la Pontificia Universidad Católica del Perú, 1992), pp. 77 ff.

10 *Codex Maximilianeus Bavaricus Civilis oder Neu Verbessert – und Ergänzt Chur-Bayrisches Land-Recht* (Munich: Johann Jacob Vötter, 1756), IV, 13, §1, p. 441 (the original wording is maintained): "*In verschiedenen Handlungen wird der Consens offt ohne oder gar wieder Willen deren Interessenten auf einer oder beeder Seiten von dem Gesatz selbst supplirt*

appeared in the *Concordances entre les Codes étrangeres et le Code Napoléon*, written by justice Fortuné Anthoine de Saint-Joseph [1794–1853][11]. This work was subsequently translated into Spanish, where the original rule was reproduced as follows:

> 1.Everyone is presumed to want what seems useful to him. No one should enrich himself to the detriment of another.
> Whoever wishes to take advantage of a fact must also bear its consequences.
> Quasi-contracts are the result of these principles.[12]

No matter the transplanted source, it is interesting to note that the rule contained in the Peruvian Civil Code was devoid of legal consequences; It was nothing more than a prohibitive statute that failed to specify the remedy available to the victim of enrichment, at the expense of his assets.

It is reasonable to assume that this shortcoming determined the provision's practical irrelevance, especially since the Peruvian legal system has always been characterized by the primacy of legislation over other sources of law[13]. Furthermore, the rule's

> *und zwar aus der natürlichen Billichkeits-Regul, nach welcher 1° ein Jeder dasjenige will, was ihm nüsslich scheint, 2° keiner mit des anderen Schaden bereichert werden soll, 3° Niemand das Consequens zuwieder sehn mag, dem das Antecedens gefällig gewest. Dergleichen Handlungen nun werden insgemein Quasi-Contractus gennant, und nich anders beurtheilt, als hätten allerseitige Interessenten ausdrücklich darauf eingewilliget, ob sie schon etwa ein ganz anderes bey sich gedacht oder gewolt haben*". This could be translated as follows: "In various acts the consent is often substituted by the law itself without or even with the will of interested parties on one or both sites, and that from the natural rule of equity, according to which 1° each one wants what seems useful to him, 2° no one is to be enriched to the detriment of the other, 3° no one may object the consequence to whom the antecedent was pleasing. Such acts are called quasi contracts and are judged not differently than if all interested parties had expressly consented to them, even if they had already thought or wanted something quite different".

11 F.A. de Saint-Joseph, *Concordance entre les codes civils étrangeres et le Code Napoléon* (Paris and Leipzig: Charles Hingray and Brockhaus et Avenarius, 1840), p. 75.

12 F.A. de Saint-Joseph, *Concordancia entre el Código Civil francés y los códigos civiles extranjeros*, trans. by F. Verlanga Huerta and J. Muñiz Miranda, 2nd edn (Madrid: Imprenta de don Antonio Yenes, 1847), p. 115.

13 This means that the normative statement of an ambiguous principle or rule is not effective, or not as effective as a detailed precept with unequivocal

ambiguity prompted some scholars to refer to it even as a moral justification for the control of interest rates in loan contracts[14].

The assimilation of Fench law into Peruvian civil law was consolidated in the second half of the 19th century. This phenomenon gave rise to unjust enrichment, which faced the same obstacles that the interpreters of the Napoleonic Code had to overcome to link the French institution to a concrete remedy. In Peru, as in France, references to the *actio de in rem verso*[15], became more frequent, as demonstrated by the following passage by Ricardo Ortiz de Zevallos y Vidaurre [1871–1908], written in the early years of the 20th century:

> Nowhere in the Code is it established as a but in more than one article it presupposes its existence.
> Jurists do not agree on the conditions for the existence of this action.
> Some believe that it is only a kind of extension of the action of *negotiorum gestio*.
> We believe, however, with the majority of authors and with the jurisprudence of the French Court of Cassation, which ruled on June 15, 1892, that the *actio de in rem verso* has as its sole basis this principle of eternal justice by virtue of which no one can enrich himself to the detriment of

---

legal consequences. See: L. León Hilario, 'Desventuras de la doctrina del precedente en el Perú. La experiencia de los Plenos Casatorios Civiles de la Corte Suprema', Gaceta Civil & Procesal Civil, 97 (2021), pp. 57 ff.

14 See: M.A. Fuentes and M.A. de la Lama, *Legislación judicial del Perú*, I, *Código Civil* (Lima: Imprenta del Estado, 1869), p. 408.

15 With regard to the *actio de in rem verso* in 19th-century French law see specially the university dissertations of Georges Raynaud, *De l'action "de in rem verso" en droit français* (Paris: Arthur Rousseau, 1899), pp. 53 f.; T.P. Théodoroff, *De l'enrichissement sans cause* (Toulouse: Imprimerie du "Rapide", 1907), pp. 148 f.; and É. Bouché-Leclercq, *De l'action "de in rem verso" en droit privé* (Paris: Sirey, 1913), p. 33. See also the historical synthesis exposed by J.M. Augustin, 'Introduction historique à l'enrichissement sans cause en droit français', in V. Mannino (ed.), *L'arricchimento senza causa. Atti del Convegno dell'Università degli Studi di Roma Tre. Roma, 24 e 25 ottobre 2003* (Torino: Giappichelli, 2005), pp. 45 ff. In contemporary literature, see: M. Combot, *Quasi-contrat et enrichissement injustifié* (Paris: LGDJ, 2023), pp. 47 ff. For a historical and comparative perspective, see: E. Descheemaeker, 'The New French Law of Unjustified Enrichment', Restitution Law Review, 25 (2017), pp. 86 ff.

another, that it is a kind of restitution action, and that it can therefore be exercised only to the extent of the enrichment.[16]

Ortiz de Zevallos y Vidaurre's reflection sought to incorporate into our culture the progress represented in French jurisprudence by the famous Boudier v. Patureau *affaire*[17].

The plaintiff (Boudier) was a fertilizer dealer who had supplied the lessee of an agricultural property. When the lease was terminated due to the lessee's default, the lessee assigned to the owner of the land (Patureau), as partial payment of his debt, the rights to his outstanding crops. Boudier, who had not been paid in full for the delivery of his produce, claimed regularization directly from Patureau based on the benefit he had received indirectly from the payment for the land. In its judgment based on referred to by Ortiz de Zevallos y Vidaurre, the Court of Cassation, upholding the decision of the Tribunal Civil de Châteauroux, stated:

> Since this action [the *actio de in rem verso*] derives from the principle of equity, which prohibits enrichment to the detriment of another, and since it is not regulated by any of our laws, its exercise is not subject to any particular condition; — and that, in order to be protected, it is sufficient for the plaintiff to allege and offer to prove the existence of an advantage which he has procured by a sacrifice or personal act in favor of the one against whom he is acting; — Therefore, by allowing, in the judgment under appeal, the plaintiffs to prove, through witnesses, that, on the date indicated by the judge, the fertilizer provided by them had been used for

---

16 R. Ortiz de Zevallos y Vidaurre, *Tratado de derecho civil teórico y práctico* (Lima: E. Rosay, 1906), pp. 553–54.

17 On this case see: E.J.H. Schrage and B. Nicholas, 'Unjust Enrichment and the Law of Restitution', in E.J.H. Schrage (ed.), *Unjust Enrichment. The Comparative Legal History of the Law of Restitution*, 2nd edn (Berlin: Duncker & Humblot, 1999), p. 24. In French literature, see the early considerations of G. Baudry-Lacantinerie, *Précis de droit civil*, 5th edn (Paris: Librairie du Recueil Générale des Lois et des Arrêts et du Journal du Palais & L. Larose, 1895), t. II, § 1339*bis*, pp. 942-943. In Peruvian literature, see L. León Hilario, 'Introducción al estudio del enriquecimiento injustificado en el Perú', in *Dogmática y práctica del derecho privado moderno. Estudios jurídicos en homenaje al profesor Gastón Fernández Cruz* (Lima: ARA Editores, 2022), t. II, pp. 307–08.

sowing on the defendant's land and for its benefit, a precise application of the principles of the matter has been made.[18]

However, Ortiz de Zevallos y Vidaurre did not consider the suspicion that the above-mentioned judgment aroused in French doctrine after its publication. It was feared that positive law had come to an end and was in danger of being absorbed by natural law[19]. But against the potential excessive recourse to the newly consecrated *actio de in rem verso*, French law established an exceptional remedy as a defense. That is, a remedy available only when other forms of recourse were inapplicable, taking care not to make it the last resort for those who, for example, had allowed ordinary actions to lapse or to be forfeited. According to the authors who had paved the way for its recognition[20], the so-called rule of "subsidiarity" of the action for unjustified enrichment took root[21].

---

18 Cour de Cassation, 15th June 1892, in *Dalloz Jurisprudence Générale* (1892), I, pp. 596-597. It should be borne in mind, however, that the *actio de in rem verso*, a means of protection against enrichment "without cause," (*sans cause*) had important jurisprudential antecedents. See, in this respect, Théodoroff, *De l'enrichissement sans cause*, pp. 35 ff.
19 See: Augustin, 'Introduction historique à l'enrichissement sans cause en droit français', p. 47.
20 The paternity of subsidiarity as a requirement of the *actio de in rem verso* is unanimously attributed to C. Aubry and C. Rau, *Cours de droit civil français d'après la méthode de Zachariæ*, 4th edn (Paris: Imprimerie et Librairie Générale de Jurisprudence & Marchal, Billard et Cie, 1873), t. VI, § 578, p. 246. See, on this subject, Philippe Remy, 'Le principe de subsidiarité de l'action *de in rem verso* en droit français', in Mannino (ed.), *L'arricchimento senza causa*, pp. 73 ff.
21 See: A. Rouast, 'L'enrichissement sans cause et la jurisprudence civile', Revue Trimestrielle de Droit Civil, 21 (1922), pp. 95–96. See also: H. and L. Mazeaud, J. Mazeaud and F. Chabas, *Leçons de droit civil*, II-1, *Obligations-Théorie générale*, 9th edn (Paris: Montchrestien, 1992), pp. 829 ff. For a comparative perspective, see: B. Nicholas, 'Unjustified Enrichment in Civil Law and Louisiana Law (Part I)', Tulane Law Review, 36 (1962), pp. 633 ff.; A. Posez, 'La subsidiarité de l'enrichissement sans cause: étude de droit français à la lumière du droit comparé', Revue de Droit International et de Droit Comparé (2014), pp. 185 ff.; and C. Jooste and E.J.H. Schrage, 'Subsidiarity of the General Action for Unjust Enrichment (Part I)', Journal of South African Law (2016), pp. 9 ff.

But the idea of subsidiarity did not reach Peru in those years[22]. Only the French notion of general action – including its formula for application – was successfully exported to the Peruvian legal system which could be translated into a restitutionary obligation different from those arising from other sources.

The principle of subsidiarity, conceived to avert the dangers of a new wave of iusnaturalism and principled administration of justice, remained unknown in domestic law, but not for long. Nevertheless, despite its absence, the *actio de in rem verso* remained ineffective in Peruvian legal practice.

III. *Reception of the Swiss Model in the Second Peruvian Civil Code*

The silence on the applicable remedy in unjust enrichment cases did not go unnoticed by the reformers of the Peruvian Civil Code of 1852.

In the new text, enacted in 1936, a rule was introduced to remove all shadow of doubt as to the viability of restitution in such cases: "Article 1149. – Anyone who has unjustly enriched himself at the expense of another shall be obliged to make restitution".

This step was, once again, innovative in Latin America, although it did not have the expected impact.

The president of the reform commission, Manuel Augusto Olaechea [1880–1946], pointed out in an explanatory memorandum that the inclusion of a "general formula" was intended "to specify that whenever there is unlawful enrichment (*enriquecimiento ilícito*), the law imposes the necessity of

---

22 French case law only adopted the criterion of subsidiarity in two 1914 and 1915 famous decisions: *affaire* Vve Clayette, *affaire* Briauhant, respectively. On this major development of French jurisprudence, see: L. Josserand, *Cours de droit civil positif français*, 3rd edn (Paris: Sirey, 1939), t. II, § 574, pp. 361 ff.

restitution"[23]. He also predicted that "undue enrichment" (*enriquecimiento indebido*) — as it was called, in the French style[24], perhaps because of its relation to "undue payment" (*pago indebido*), as well as its relevance to quasi-contracts — would be "the object of judicial applications dominated by the guarantee of the law and by the sense of what is just and equitable"[25].

Thus, apart from the question of terminology, unjust enrichment was confirmed as a source of obligations, albeit not as an autonomous source, as was claimed shortly afterwards. It gave rise to: "the obligation of restitution of what has been obtained contrary to law or equity, to the extent necessary to restore the equilibrium of the patrimony"[26].

The rule was modeled after article 62 of the Swiss Federal Code of Obligations of 1911[27], except for the words "without lawful cause" (*sans cause légitime*), which were excluded. For fear of contradicting the anticausalist postulate of the new Civil Code regarding legal transactions, the expression was replaced by "unjustified" in the singular and placed in Book V, on obligations in general, in Title IX, at the end of the rules on civil liability for unlawful acts.

---

23   Comisión Reformadora del Código Civil Peruano, *Actas de las sesiones* (Lima: Empresa "La Editorial", 1929), t. VII, p. 20.
24   This may have been due to the consultation of the French translation of the German Civil Code edited by Raoul de la Grasserie, *Code Civil allemand et Loi d'introduction* (Paris: A. Pedone, 1897), p. 170, where the German expression *ungerechtfertigte Bereicherung* is rendered as *enrichissement indu*, i.e., "undue enrichment".
25   See: G. Aparicio y Gómez Sánchez, *Código Civil – Concordancias*, III, *La reforma (Motivos)* (Lima: n.p., 1942), p. 407.
26   Á.G. Cornejo, *Código Civil. Exposición sistemática y comentario* (Lima: Librería e Imprenta Gil, 1937), t. I, p. 382.
27   The edition of this Code consulted by Peruvian lawmakers was the one written in the French language. Article 62 states: '*Celui qui, sans cause légitime, s'est enrichi aux dépens d'autrui, est tenu à restitution. La restitution est due, en particulier, de ce qui a été reçu sans cause valable, en vertu d'une cause qui e s'est pas realisée, ou d'une cause qui a cessé d'exister.*' "Cause" can be translated into English also as "legal ground" or "legal basis." See: S. Meier, 'No Basis: A Comparative View', in A. Burrows and Lord Rodger of Earlsferry (eds.), *Mapping the Law. Essays in Memory of Peter Birks* (Oxford: Oxford University Press, 2006), pp. 343–61.

This placement of the new provision, based on the legislator's adherence to the postulates of a segment of French civil doctrine, without excluding its conceptual disputes, created additional problems.

More specifically, this systematic approach was inspired by the doctrine of Marcel Planiol [1853–1931] according to which the *actio de in rem verso* was quasi-delictual in nature: "If enrichment obtained without cause and at the expense of another must be returned", he wrote, "it is because it is not permitted to keep it"[28]. Thus, the injustice of the enrichment determines its illegality. "It would not be permissible", he added, "for the person who possesses it to try to keep it; his obligation is based on a factual situation that is contrary to the law"[29]. Olaechea's commitment to this view was explicit[30].

Accordingly, despite the correct reference to "restitution" in article 1149, it was foreseeable that the expression "indemnification for unjust enrichment" (*indemnización por enriquecimiento indebido*) would be vulgarized in Peruvian law, since all obligations arising from unlawful acts were called "indemnities" (*indemnizaciones*), according to the system of the Civil Code of 1936.

On this point, however, through the studies of José León Barandiarán [1899–1987] the national doctrine allows us to appreciate a small but significant opening towards the German model of unjust enrichment.

The German Civil Code (BGB) states in the first paragraph of its § 812: "Anyone who obtains something as a result of another

---

28 M. Planiol, *Traité élémentaire de droit civil*, 2nd edn (Paris: Librairie Cotillon & F. Pichon, 1902) t. II, p. 291.
29 M. Planiol, 'Classification des sources des obligations', Revue Critique de Législation et de Jurisprudence, 33 (1904), p. 229.
30 See: Aparicio y Gómez Sánchez, *Código Civil*, t. III, p. 407. After completing his law studies in Lima, Olaechea travelled to Paris, where he attended some classes at La Sorbonne, including those of Planiol, who fascinated him. On these biographical details, see: M.P. Olaechea, *Estudio Olaechea 1878-1978*, 3rd ed (Lima: n.p., 1998), p. 67.

person's performance or otherwise at the latter's expense without a legal basis for doing so is obliged to return it to him"[31].

Explaining article 1149 of the former Peruvian Civil Code in light of § 812 BGB, as well the contributions of Friedrich Carl von Savigny [1779–1861], Bernhard Windscheid [1817–1892][32], and the Swiss Code of Obligations, León Barandiarán highlighted:

> Helvetic-Teutonic law has offered the outstanding merit of having made a systematic construction and raised to a general principle that no one may enrich himself to the detriment of others *ex iniusta causa*. In other words, he has correctly established the *condictio generalis*. […]. The system is based on the Roman condictiones. Restitution applies in every case where there has been a transfer of property value without just cause, whether within or outside of a contract. Thus, it is a different regime from that resulting from the *actio de in rem verso*. The fact is that cause, as a necessary integral element of any legal act, is excluded, so that it is necessary, also in the field of conventions, especially those of an abstract nature, and especially here with greater necessity, to introduce the principle of restitution for unjust enrichment.[33]

---

31 Following the English translation included in G. Dannemann and R. Schulze (eds.), *German Civil Code. Bürgerliches Gesetzbuch (BGB)*, (Munich: C. H. Beck & Baden-Baden: Nomos, 2020), v. I, p. 1578.

32 On these foundational contributions see: R. Zimmermann, 'A Road through Enrichment-Forest-Experiences with a General Enrichment Action', Comparative and International Law Journal of Southern Africa, 18 (1985), pp. 1–20; O'Dell Eoin, 'The Principle against Unjust Enrichment', Dublin University Law Journal, 15 (1993), pp. 25–58; R. Zimmermann and J. du Plessis, 'Basic Features of the German Law of Unjustified Enrichment', Restitution Law Review, 2 (1994), pp. 14–43; M.J. Schermaier, 'Performance-Based and Non-Performance Based Enrichment Claims: The German Pattern', European Review of Private Law, 14 (2006), pp. 363–90; and P. Pichonnaz, 'Some Diachronic Reflections on the Scope of Error in Unjustified Enrichment,' in N. Jansen and S. Meier (eds.), *Iurium itinera. Historische Rechtsvergleichung und vergleichende Rechtsgeschichte. Reinhard Zimmermann zum 70. Geburtstag am 10. Oktober 2022* (Tübingen: Mohr Siebeck, 2022), pp. 616 ff.

33 León Barandiarán, *Comentario del Código Civil*, I, p. 286. The source of these remarks, as León Barandiarán himself confesses, is the prestigious comparative work of R. Saleilles, *Étude sur la théorie générale de l'obligation d'après le premier projet de Code civil pour l'Empire allemand* (Paris: Librairie Cotillon & F. Pichon, 1901), § 341, pp. 450–51.
The influence of German legal culture ends here, however. The major systematic studies on the types of unjustified enrichment, such as that of

The above passage indicates that León Barandiarán was familiar with the difference between the French *actio de in rem verso* and the German *condictio generalis* models.

Peruvian scholars also understood that the adverb "unduly," used in the Civil Code, meant: "not only that which is not enforceable by strict law, which should not be interpreted as the non-existence of the contract from which the obligation to perform arises, but that which is contrary to equity, even if it is apparently covered by a right"[34]. Therefore, the "action of unjust enrichment" was based "on the lack of legal basis for the transfer of a value from the assets of the impoverished to the assets of the unjustly enriched, and can operate both in the contractual field and in the non-contractual field"[35].

Finally, as mentioned above, it is necessary to consider an unusual fact in the comparative perspective and experience of legal changes.

With the regulation of the action for restitution of unjust enrichment, which has been carried out with remarkable amplitude, it could be trusted in its development at the

---

W. Wilburg, *Die Lehre von der ungerechtfertigten Bereicherung nach österreichischem und deutschem Recht. Kritik und Aufbau* (Graz: Leuschner & Lubensky, 1932) were not diffused in Peru. Only in very recent times attention has been paid in Peruvian literature to the German taxonomic approaches on this topic, despite the difficulties implied in translating their results into practice, as it has been critically outlined, from a global point of view, by D. Visser, 'Unjustified Enrichment in Comparative Perspective', in M. Reimann and R. Zimmermann, *The Oxford Handbook of Comparative Law* (Oxford: Oxford University Press, 2006, reprint 2008) p. 999. In Peruvian literature, see: León Hilario, 'Introducción al estudio del enriquecimiento injustificado', pp. 326 ff.

On the contrary, in the Spanish literature, which is quite widespread in Peru and accessible for obvious linguistic reasons, there seems to be an optimistic conviction that it is possible to abandon the classical French model and to deal successfully with the complexities of the doctrine of Trennungslehref. See, specially, the numerous works of X. Basozabal Arrue, since *Enriquecimiento injustificado por intromisión* (Madrid: Civitas, 1998), pp. 35 ff.; and the more recent book of R. Fariña Fariña, *La restitución del enriquecimiento sin causa: un reto para el derecho español. Análisis desde una perspectiva comparada con el derecho alemán* (Navarra: Aranzadi, 2022), pp. 73 ff.

34 Cornejo, *Código Civil*, I, pp. 381, 393.
35 Cornejo, *Código Civil*, I, p. 395.

jurisprudential level, by the way, in accordance with the aspiration expressed by the legislator itself. Conversely, from the day after the entry into force of the Peruvian Civil Code of 1936, the doctrine borrowed from the French doctrine[36] (i.e., from a model different from the one that had served as a basis for the drafting of article 1149) to elaborate the characteristic of the subsidiarity of the restitution remedy, which would prove fatal to its acceptance in practice.

It was known, and this was stated by a prominent Peruvian scholar, that "German doctrine and case law do not consider it as a subsidiary remedy. Since a person has actually become poorer, and the thing he has lost has been acquired by another without legal cause, the action for unjust enrichment can intervene to restore the balance between the two estates"[37]. But a residual role was assigned, without further explanation, to the action for unjust enrichment. It was therefore concluded that: "When the law provides the means to restore the balance between the two estates, it is not the action for unjust enrichment that is brought, but that which follows from the corresponding legal provision"[38].

In short, following a model that combined Swiss and German influences, the Peruvian Civil Code of 1936 essentially regulated unjust enrichment as an event giving rise to a restitutionary obligation, without any special conditions for its exercise[39]. In judicial practice, however, the characterization of the action as an ancillary one was consolidated, probably due to the fact that the French legal culture was still quite prevalent[40]. It is enough to

---

36   After the entry into force of the Civil Code of 1936, the context was evidently different from that in which Ortiz de Zevallos wrote his book, anchoring his considerations on unjustified enrichment in the French model of the *actio de in rem verso*.
37   Cornejo, *Código Civil*, I, p. 386.
38   Cornejo, *Código Civil*, I, p. 395.
39   See: J. León Barandiarán, *Manual del acto jurídico* (Lima: Imprenta de la Universidad Nacional Mayor de San Marcos, 1961), p. 81; and by the same author, *Curso del acto jurídico. Con referencia al proyecto del C.C. peruano* (Lima: Imprenta de la Universidad Nacional Mayor de San Marcos, 1983), p. 85.
40   Remarkably, in one of the few papers on unjustified enrichment, published during the 1936 Civil Code, the criterion of subsidiarity was not considered

read the pages of a great historian of Peruvian private law, who, during the first two decades of the Civil Code of 1936, reported only a few judicial decisions on this matter[41], and none of them with a clear basis for the action, to verify what was the result of this unfortunate combination of foreign legal influences.

What can be seen from the scarce case law is that the presence of unjust enrichment in the work of the Peruvian courts was largely limited to disputes between cohabitants. In other words, the general and codified remedy of restitution became an alternative for cases of breakdown of de facto relationships. This impact was probably due to the fact that it was the only legal option, also learned from French law[42], to safeguard the economic stability, above all of the women, in the face of such a situation.

IV. *The arrival of the Italian model in the current Peruvian Civil Code*

The scarce jurisprudence shows that the presence of unjust enrichment in the work of the Peruvian courts was largely limited to disputes between cohabitants. In other words, the general and codified remedy of restitution became an alternative for cases of breakdown of de facto relationships. Therefore, in 1984, the legislator's task was not, of course, to deepen the comparative chaos caused by the blind transplantation of foreign rules, but

---

decisive. See: E. Vásquez Lapeyre, 'El enriquecimiento indebido', Revista del Foro, 34 (1947), pp. 29, 34.

41 C. Ramos Núñez, *Historia del derecho civil peruano* (Lima: Fondo Editorial de la Pontificia Universidad Católica del Perú, 2011), t. VI, vol. 3, pp. 324–25.

42 See, e.g., R. Demogue, *Traité des obligations en général* (Paris: Arthur Rousseau, 1923), t. III, p. 250 s., and M. Carraud, *De la liquidation des biens a la cessation du concubinage* (Université de Dijon, Faculté de Droit & Besançon: Jacques & Demontrond, 1936), pp. 67 f. In Peruvian literature, see: L. León Hilario, "La tutela restitutoria por enriquecimiento injustificado entre convivientes", in S. García Long (ed.), *Estudios sobre los remedios en el derecho privado. Perspectivas desde el derecho contractual nacional y comparado* (Lima: Instituto Pacífico, 2022), pp. 542 ff.

rather to clarify the panorama and remove the wall that hindered the functioning of the restitution remedy.

In fact, if it had been thought that this remedy was useless and that it was right to keep it isolated and ineffective, it should have been noted and the restitution action should not even have been included in the text of the new Civil Code. After all, the maxim that no one may enrich himself at the expense of another could always be derived as a general principle from a multitude of specific rules corresponding to it in all branches of codified civil law: from the general part on legal acts to family law, from the law of succession to property law, and from the general part on obligations.

Instead of proceeding in this way, the legislative technique adopted in 1984 was simply to copy, with minimal nuances[43], the systematic approach of the Italian Civil Code of 1942, reduced to two rules, by the way very much questioned — this is the most serious issue — in its original legal system, where the regulation was even described as a "missed opportunity"[44].

---

[43] In the Italian Civil Code, the regulation of the traditional quasi-contracts (*pagamento dell'indebito, gestione di affari altrui* and *arricchimento senza causa*) is successive, as a reminder of the historical, social, ethical and technical foundations they share. On the other hand, in the current Peruvian Civil Code, the corresponding rules regarding these institutions are scattered and do not allow for a proper integration to be proposed. These methodological deficiencies have been severely criticized. See, e.g., L. Moisset de Espanés, 'Repetición del pago indebido y sus efectos respecto a terceros en Perú y Argentina', Thémis-Revista de Derecho, 23 (1992), pp. 55-68; C. Cárdenas Quirós, 'Hacia la reforma del libro VI del Código Civil', in *Diez años del Código Civil peruano. Balance y perspectivas. Ponencias presentadas en el Congreso Internacional celebrado en Lima del 12 al 16 de septiembre de 1994, organizado por el Centro de Investigación de la Facultad de Derecho y Ciencias Políticas de la Universidad de Lima* (Lima: Universidad de Lima and WG Editor, 1995), t. II, p. 70; and L. León Hilario, 'Presentación', in L. León Hilario (ed.), *Derecho de las relaciones obligatorias. Lecturas seleccionadas y traducidas para uso de los estudiantes universitarios* (Lima: Jurista Editores, 2007), p. 18.

[44] E. Moscati, *Fonti legali e fonti "private" delle obbligazioni* (Padova: CEDAM, 1999), pp. 239 ff. See also the critical considerations of E. Bargelli, *Il sinallagma rovesciato* (Milano: Giuffrè, 2010), pp. 96–98.

The new regime consists of a general clause and a provision on the subsidiarity of the action:

"Art. 1954. – Whoever unjustly enriches himself at the expense of another is bound to compensate him.

Art. 1955. – The action referred to in Article 1954 is inadmissible if the injured party can bring another action to obtain the corresponding compensation"[45].

The regression is clear.

Section IV of Title VII of the current Peruvian Civil Code is entitled "enrichment without cause", a term that corresponds to that used by the Italian codifier: *arricchimento senza causa*. Article 1954, however, retains the adverb "without cause" of the 1936 Civil Code. As shown above, both syntagms, "without cause" and "undue", come from the French and encode the assumption of the legal mandate, the consequence of which is the birth of an obligation. But on this fundamental point, that of the legal consequence, the correct terminology of the Civil Code of 1936, "restitution" (*restitución*), has been replaced by that of "indemnity" (*indemnización*).

The reading of the first doctrinal commentary on the new codified articles, by the members of the Reform Commission and their collaborators, allows us to notice a great contradiction.

On the one hand, the intentionality of the change of words is stated:

> Article 195 has as its immediate previous versions, article 1912 of the Draft of the Revising Commission of 1984; article 2024 of the Draft of

---

[45] The Italian codified rules and which the Peruvian lawmaker tried to adapt are the following:
"2041. *Azione generale di arricchimento.* — *Chi senza una giusta causa si è arricchito a danno di un'altra persona è tenuto, nei limiti dell'arricchimento, a indennizzare quest'ultima della correlativa diminuzione patrimoniale. Qualora l'arricchimento abbia per oggetto una cosa determinata, colui che l'ha ricevuta è tenuta a restituirla in natura, se sussiste al tempo della domanda*".
"2042. *Carattere sussidiario dell'azione.* — *L'azione di arricchimento non è proponibile quando il danneggiato può esercitare un'altra azione per farsi indennizzare del pregiudizio subito*".

the Reforming Commission of 1981, and is equivalent to article 1149 of the Civil Code of 1936, from which it differs only in that it confers on the dispossessed an indemnity right, whereas the previous Code granted him a restitutionary right.[46]

However, only a few paragraphs later, it is stated, divergently:

> Since unjust enrichment disturbs the equilibrium of property without justification or valid legal reason, the law seeks to restore this equilibrium by granting the injured party the right to bring an action.
> We believe that the appropriate action in this sense is the action for restitution — *in rem verso* —; the plaintiff must direct it against the enriched party, and not necessarily against the possible author of the enrichment, and must prove the defendant's benefit and the detriment to his own property. The causal link between the two must also be proved by the plaintiff. [...].
> The INDEMNITY referred to in article 1954 therefore consists, in principle, in the restitution of the enriched property if it is still in the possession of the enriched party, in the value of the property if the enriched party has "causally" disposed of it and, in addition, in the amount of the greater damage caused by any bad faith on the part of the enriched party.[47]

This confusing terminology is open to at least two interpretations, neither of which, as we shall see, is entirely satisfactory.

If "indemnity" is understood as a synonym for "compensation", then the legislator has made the very serious and unprecedented mistake of transforming unjust enrichment into a case of civil liability.

Absurd as it may seem, the text of the provision does not make this thesis unfounded. In fact, in article 1955, the legislator refers to the "person who has suffered the decrease", where it would have been better to mention the situation of "impoverishment".

It is therefore possible, at least literally, to configure the legal relationship that arises between the injured (impoverished) party

---

46 D. Revoredo Marsano, 'Comentario *sub* art. 1954-1955', in Comisión encargada del Estudio y Revisión del Código Civil, *Código Civil*, VI, *Exposición de motivos y comentarios*, 3rd edn (Lima: n.p, 1988), p. 775.
47 Revoredo Marsano, 'Comentario *sub* art. 1954-1955', pp. 777–78. The capital letters highlighting the word "indemnity" appear in the original text quoted.

and the person obliged to compensate him, according to these rules, as a civil liability relationship.

In the Peruvian legal system, on the other hand, there is no trace of the differences between "harm" (*danno*) and "loss" (*pregiudizio*), which in Italian law, from where the model followed in the commented articles originates, are primordial in order to delimit the areas of civil liability and unjust enrichment: while damage denotes the totality of the negative alteration of the subjective integrity, which requires a return to the status quo ante, i.e. to the situation that existed prior to the event that triggers civil liability, loss has the much more limited meaning of a reduction of property, i.e. of an economic loss "as a result of the conduct that violates another's right or protected situation"[48].

This path would also lead to singular compensation for unjust enrichment, consisting of material and non-material damages. In the Peruvian legal and arbitration practice, it is not uncommon to acquit or rule on claims for unjust enrichment, which, without technical rigor, request compensation for "loss of profit"[49].

Finally, this erroneous interpretation would lead to the *a priori* exclusion of the concurrence of claims for damages and for restitution of unjust enrichment.

If, on the other hand, "compensation" is understood as a "legal obligation to compensate", as opposed to "damages", the concept referred to in Articles 2054 and 2055 would become part of the wide repertoire of pecuniary compensation for non-tort losses[50]. This is the path followed, by the way, by part of

---

48 See, in this sense, P. Gallo, *Introduzione al diritto comparato*; II, *Istituti giuridici*, 2nd edn (Torino: Giappichelli, 2003), p. 233.

49 See: E. Palacios Martínez, 'Comentario *sub* art. 1954-1955', in *El Código Civil comentado*, 5th edn (Lima: Gaceta Jurídica), t. IX, p. 698.

50 On the not only theorical, but practical differences between "compensation for damages" and "legal obligation to indemnify," see: L. León Hilario, *Responsabilidad civil contractual y extracontractual. Material autoinstructivo* (Lima: Academia de la Magistratura, 2016), pp. 35–38. The distinction has been recognised in the decision stated in the Third Civil Cassational Plenary of the Peruvian Supreme Court, published in *Sentencias en Casación*, XV, 641 (2011), p. 30182.

the French and Italian doctrines[51], in which the distinction between compensation for damages (*réparation*, *risarcimento*) and indemnity (*indemnité*, *indennizzo*) is unanimous, but not so much the use of the latter term with respect to restitution.

It is undisputed that the use of the term "indemnity" in Articles 1954 and 1955 of the Peruvian Civil Code is the result of a literal translation into Spanish of the word *indennizzo* used in the Italian original[52]. In this imitation, however, no attention was paid to the differences between the Italian words *risarcimento* and *indennizzo* in the original legal language. The Italian doctrine, on the other hand, takes this distinction into account when deciphering the rule: "Whoever has enriched himself without cause and to the detriment of another person is bound, within the limits of the enrichment, to compensate the latter [*a indennizzare quest'ultima*] for the correlative decrease in his patrimony".

In fact, in article 2041 of the Italian Civil Code *indennizzare e non risarcire* is used, because the sum that the impoverished person can claim has a maximum limit, namely that of the enrichment produced. In civil liability, on the other hand, the point of reference for compensation is exclusively the pecuniary or moral damage caused, which may well exceed the enrichment obtained by the liable party[53]. In civil liability, on the other hand, the point of reference for compensation is exclusively the

---

51 See: C. Le Gallou, *La notion d'indemnité en droit privé* (Paris: LGDJ, 2007), pp. 565–67. Among the Italian scholars, see: A. Minozzi, 'Responsabilità e colpa. Esposizione critica di alcune pubblicazioni italiane sulla teorica della responsabilità senza colpa', in *Scritti per il cinquantesimo anno d'insegnamento del professore Francesco Pepere* (Napoli: Società Anonima Cooperativa Tipografica), pp. 394–412; R. Scognamiglio, 'Indennità', in *Novissimo Digesto Italiano* (Torino: Utet, 1962), t. VIII, pp. 594–97; S. Ciccarello, 'Indennità (diritto privato)', in *Enciclopedia del diritto* (Milano: Giuffrè, 1971), t. XXI, pp. 99–106; P. Perlingieri, 'La responsabilità civile tra indennizzo e risarcimento', Rassegna di Diritto Civile (2004), pp. 1061–87; and C. Caricato, *Danno e indennità* (Torino: Giappichelli, 2012), pp. 186–88.
52 See footnote (47).
53 See, among the classical Italian contributions on this topic, those of A. Trabucchi, 'Arricchimento, b) Diritto civile', *Enciclopedia del diritto* (Milano: Giuffrè, 1958), t. III, p. 74; and P. Schlesinger, 'Arricchimento (Azione di)', *Novissimo Digesto Italiano* (Torino: Utet, 1958), t. I-2, p. 1008.

pecuniary or moral damage caused, which may well exceed the enrichment obtained by the liable party.

Even if this philological proposal were to be accepted in order to overcome a dilemma that certainly does not exist in German law or in the common law, two problems would remain unresolved.

Firstly, a monetary compensation, as outlined above, would not exhaust the restitutionary remedies applicable to unjust enrichment. In its imitation, the Peruvian legislator has inexplicably omitted the second paragraph of Article 2041 of the Italian Civil Code, which refers to restitution in kind. This cannot be interpreted as an intentional limitation of the remedies against unjust enrichment, which would leave only the possibility of restitution in value. In order to cover the omission, an appropriate term would have to be found for cases in which restitution in kind operates as restitution.

Secondly, the inclusion of pecuniary restitution in the broader concept of reparation would defeat the purpose of preserving the autonomy of unjust enrichment as a source of obligations. The task imposed on the Peruvian interpreters, due to the imprecision of the legislator, is to outline the applicable remedy in such a way as to distinguish it, and not only by its source, from all other types of obligations. This task was sufficiently and meritoriously carried out by the commentators of the Civil Code of 1936[54]: by its composition and the method of its calculation, by the type of interest it generates, by its limitation periods, by its tax treatment, and so on.

For these reasons, it will always be preferable to refer to "restitution" in the cases about unjustified enrichment.

Obviously, this is not a whimsical choice, nor does it claim to be innovative.

---

54 See: Cornejo, *Código Civil*, I, p. 395, and León Barandiarán, *Comentario del Código Civil*, I, p. 283. In the contemporary literature, see: G. Fernández Cruz, 'Tutela y remedios. La indemnización entre la tutela resarcitoria y el enriquecimiento sin causa,' in R. Vidal Ramos (ed.), *Libro de ponencias al X Congreso Nacional de Derecho Civil* (Lima: Instituto Peruano de Derecho Civil, 2015), p. 124.

The most rigorous historical studies show that the institutional origin of unjustified enrichment is to be found, much more than in the Roman sources, in the theological and medieval doctrine of *restitutio*, which saw in it "a necessary requirement for the sacrament of penitence. No sin could be forgiven, according to what had been taught since Augustine, unless the sinner returned what he had taken from another person"[55]. That doctrine, in the 15th and 16th centuries, was transformed into a "iusnaturalistic theory of corrective justice"[56].

The call for corrective justice — often referred to as "Aristotelian" — is a commonplace in legal scholarship that has sought to ground the remedy of restitution beyond purely civil discourse. In particular, it has been written that restitution should be seen as:

> the law's response to the unjust enrichment of one person at the expense of another. The requirement that the enrichment be "at the plaintiff's expense" reflects the bipolarity of corrective justice by encapsulating the plaintiff's claim to what the defendant must disgorge. Because the defendant's enrichment was at the plaintiff's expense, the plaintiff can be said to have been deprived by the defendant's enrichment. Restitution rectifies this deprivation by compelling the defendant to return the enrichment (or its value) to the plaintiff.[57]

If it is agreed to accept this position, there would be no reason to deny that in relation to unjust enrichment a restitutionary obligation should arise, in a sum of goods or in a value.

> The obligation of restitution and the corresponding right of restitution thus constitute a kind of compensation established by the law for certain

---

[55] N. Jansen, 'Farewell to Unjust Enrichment?', Edinburgh Law Review, 20 (2016), p. 128. With regard to this historical phase, see also: G. Dolezalek, 'The Moral Theologians' Doctrine of Restitution and Its Juridification in the Sixteenth and Seventeenth Centuries', Acta Juridica, 104 (1992), 104–14; and J. Hallebeek, 'Unjust Enrichment as a Source of Obligation: The Genesis of a Legal Concept in the European *Ius Commune*', Restitution Law Review, 10 (2002), 92–99.

[56] Jansen, 'Farewell to Unjust Enrichment?', p. 128.

[57] E.J. Weinrib, *The Idea of Private Law* (Oxford: Oxford University Press, 2012), p. 140.

situations which, although formally in conformity with its rules, lead to results (of unjust enrichment) which are in essence condemned by the law.[58]

With regard to subsidiarity, the Civil Code implied the formalization of the counterweight devised in France, and also legislated in Italy, for the limitation of actions based on unjust enrichment. "Otherwise — it was noted — [this action] would be a panacea for claims in respect of rights that the law does not wish to protect beyond certain limits and conditions"[59].

But, even considering the non-existence of judicial repertories in Peru, it does not seem to have been shared — as it is not now — the idea that that action needed here a normative barrier to neutralise the recourse to a remedy that, clearly, remained largely misunderstood.

A significant number of arbitration awards issued, from the end of the 20th century, in public procurement disputes would demonstrate that subsidiarity, inserted in an ambiguous regulation, unexplored by the domestic scholarship, and suitable for the disfiguring interpretations of certain arbitrators, did not constitute an effective brake on the formulation of debatable claims, and on the protection to the deprivation of the State coffers[60]. In short, many public procurement arbitrations have been the unusual, picturesque laboratory in which the lifeless action for restitution of unjust enrichment came to life, but also the one in which it showed its not so pleasant face as a "catch-all" sanction[61].

---

58 J. de Matos Antunes Varela, *Das obrigações em geral*, 10th edn (Coimbra: Almedina, 2000, reprint 2005), vol. I, pp. 476–77.
59 Revoredo Marsano, 'Comentario *sub* art. 1954-1955', p. 778.
60 See: León Hilario, 'La acción restitutoria por enriquecimiento injustificado en el Perú', pp. 28–30, and footnotes (3)-(7).
61 "*Une sanction attrape-tout*", borrowing a very perceptive statement by J. Carbonnier, *Droit civil. Les biens-Les obligations* (Paris: PUF, 2000, reprint 2004), p. 2435.

V. *Current problems and prospects for solutions (also from Italian law)*

In all legal systems in which the codified regime of unjustified enrichment consists of a general clause, the scholars have taken charge, not only of the systematisation of its codified and jurisprudential casuistry, but also of the projection of its possible applications.

However, the identification of the spaces in which the action established in article 1954 of the current Peruvian Civil Code can be exercised requires, as a prior step, the structural analysis of the premises of the legal protection granted: the enrichment, the absence of title to obtain the enrichment and to keep it, and the impoverishment of the protected party.

Contrary to the structure described above, Peruvian jurisprudence has indicated that the configuration of unjust enrichment requires:

> 1) Enrichment, which means that the defendant must have been enriched by the perception of a material, intellectual or moral benefit; 2) Damage, which is materialized in the impoverishment of the plaintiff; 3) Correlation between the damage and the enrichment; 4) Absence of just cause; and 5) Subsidiarity, which should be understood as an action that can be brought only when the impoverishment has occurred; 6) Subsidiarity, which should be understood as an action that can only be proposed when the impoverished person has no other means of legal protection, that is, no other remedy to obtain satisfaction, which means that the action is residual and inappropriate if the person who suffered the damage can exercise another action to obtain the corresponding compensation.[62]

As will be seen below, in this scheme — which is quite widespread — there is a combination of visions from different legal systems, whose legislation, in some cases, is very different from the Peruvian one. It is always advisable to start from the from the norm itself: to consider the "elasticity" of the general

---

62 Corte Suprema de la República, decision CAS No. 1925-2009-ICA, 28th January 2010, *Sentencias en Casación*, XIV, 634 (2006), p. 29075.

clause, but at the same time "the need for a precise determination of its content and its field of application"[63].

Enrichment consists in the improvement of one's personal position. Such an improvement can be measured in a strictly accounting sense, as the circumstance of having more assets, property, or wealth than before, but then the picture would not be complete. A person is also enriched if he adds attributes that cannot be directly translated into values, such as rights, expectations, and other advantageous legal situations. The same is true of those who avoid costs or expenses that would have burdened them if they had not been enriched, or of those who see their liabilities reduced by the cancellation of a debt thanks to the action of the impoverished person or at the latter's expense.

At this point, the relativization of the ethical imperative is evident. Enrichment is relevant in its objectivity, not in its dimension. It would be wrong to reject the realization of an enrichment simply because the improvement obtained is minimal from a strictly quantitative point of view. Nor does the social repudiation caused by the conduct of the person obliged to make restitution count, no matter how great, small or insignificant. In order to satisfy the requirement, it is sufficient that "something is obtained", that is, that an advantage is obtained[64].

Enrichment can be direct or indirect. In the first case, the enriched party's actions bring him a direct benefit: the craftsman who makes a work with other people's raw materials and incorporates it into his patrimony, for example, and who is obliged to return the value of what he has used to its owner. In the second case, the benefits are obtained by a third party who does not necessarily have a factual or legal relationship with the impoverished party, as happened in the Boudier vs. Patureau case, which inaugurated the history of the institution in French jurisprudence. The Peruvian Civil Code does not make a

---

63 U. Breccia, 'L'arricchimento senza causa', in *Trattato di diritto privato diretto da Pietro Rescigno*, 9, *Obbligazioni e contratti*, 2nd edn (Torino: Utet, 1999), p. 983.
64 In this sense, see H.J. Wieling and T. Finkenauer, *Bereicherungsrecht*, 5th edn (Berlin: Springer, 2020), p. 7.

distinction in this regard, so it must be interpreted as recognizing both modalities.

The burden of proving unjust enrichment rests on the plaintiff, in accordance with the general rule that it is the plaintiff's exclusive responsibility to prove the facts constituting his or her claim[65]. For this purpose, in cases in which an increase in assets is claimed, the means of proof that allow the judge to assess, for example, the accounting and financial situation of the allegedly enriched party will be relevant: the submission of balance sheets and tax returns, if it is a company or a trader, or expert opinions. If the enrichment consists in the possession of an object, the claim for restitution requires proof that the enriched party is exercising or has exercised possession or use, if the object has been consumed, destroyed or lost.

In the case of profits obtained through the unauthorized use of copyrights, such as in the field of software piracy, the Peruvian authority, the National Institute for the Defense of Competition and the Protection of Intellectual Property (INDECOPI) has established the practice of quantifying the due to the affected owner, the payment of which must be imposed on the infringer in accordance with the special regulations in force and taking into account the amount that he would have had to pay according to a hypothetical transaction[66], to the affected owner. Enrichment, in cases such as these, manifests itself as a cost saving.

---

65 According to Peruvian Code of Civil Procedure (1993), article 196: "Unless otherwise provided by law, the burden of proof in on the party who asserts facts that constitute his claim, or on the party who contradicts them by alleging new facts".

66 On this criterion, imported from American law, see: W.J. Gordon, 'Of Harms and Benefits: Torts, Restitution, and Intellectual Property', Journal of Legal Studies, 21 (1992), pp. 449–82; J.C. Jarosz and M.J. Chapman, 'The Hypothetical Negotiation and Reasonable Royalty Damages: The Tail Wagging the Dog', Stanford Technological Law Review, 16 (2013), pp. 769–832; and J.M. Golden and K.E. Sandrik, 'A Restitution Perspective on Reasonable Royalties', Review of Litigation, 36(2) (2017), pp. 335–78. Among the Italian scholars, see: A. Nicolussi, 'Proprietà intellettuale e arricchimento ingiustificato: la restituzione degli utili nell'art. 45 TRIPS', Europa e Diritto Privato (2002), pp. 1003 ff.; and P. Gallo, *Trattato di diritto civile*, VII, *L'arricchimento senza causa, la responsabilità civile* (Torino: Giappichelli, 2018), pp. 60 ff. In Peruvian literature, see: R. Saavedra

Regarding the impoverishment, it is the counterpart of enrichment, i.e., the situation of impairment experienced by the holder of the restitutionary action. The impoverished is someone who has been dispossessed, prevented from exercising a right over a thing, or who, in general, sees his assets reduced, to the benefit of another, as a consequence of the performance of a service, or the removal of an asset or the displacement of his property without obtaining any compensation for his sacrifice.

Like enrichment, impoverishment is determined according to each specific situation, and it is not possible to provide a definition that covers all cases. The proof must be provided by the claimant.

Contrary to an assertion accepted in Peruvian literature[67] and case law, it is not correct to assert that there must be a causal relationship between enrichment and impoverishment in all cases. This assertion is valid only in the case of direct enrichment. In the hypothesis of unjust enrichment, it is clear that the increase in the assets of the recipient is due to the actions of the person who performed them, from whose sphere the sum, the good or the effort made in favor of the enriched party comes. On the other hand, in the case of restitution claimed against the heir of the enriched person or against the shareholders of a company for the profits, the requirement of the interrelation between impoverishment and enrichment comes from France and Italy, as well as from the reading of French and Italian sources received by Spanish scholars, the causal link is not present.

The requirement of the link between impoverishment and enrichment comes from France and Italy, as well as from the reading of French and Italian sources by Spanish scholars[68].

Velazco, 'Configuración del derecho de autor y resarcimiento de daños. ¿Hacia un régimen especial de responsabilidad civil?', in *Análisis económico y comparado del derecho privado – Una introducción* (Lima: Fontana, 2016), pp. 707 ff.; and León Hilario, 'La acción restitutoria por enriquecimiento injustificado en el Perú', pp. 57–60.

67 Revoredo Marsano, 'Comentarios *sub* art. 1954-1955', p. 777.
68 See: J. Puig Brutau, *Fundamentos de derecho civil* (Barcelona: Bosch, 1983), t. II, vol. III, p. 61; J.L. Lacruz Berdejo *et al.*, *Elementos de derecho civil*, II, *Derecho de obligaciones* (Madrid: Dykinson, 1999), vol. 2, p. 437; and L.

In the Italian legal system, such interrelation is postulated on the basis of the dictates of the Civil Code, where article 2041 refers to a "correlative decrease in his patrimony"[69]. Today, Article 1303 of the reformed French Civil Code also states that the impoverishment is verified "by" the benefit obtained by the enriched party[70].

However, the Italian and French rules do not exactly coincide with that of Article 1954 of the Peruvian Civil Code, where it is stated that enrichment occurs "at the expense of another", that is, for the account of another. This simply means that the enrichment represents a cost or expense for someone other than the enriched.

The expression "at the expense of another" is closer to that used in the first part of § 832 BGB, "*auf dessen Kosten*", which German doctrine has always interpreted with the required breadth so as not to prejudice the effectiveness of the protection against unjustified enrichment, or to that which is common in English law: "at the claimant's expense"[71]. In Germany, according to the so-called "doctrine of attribution" (*Zuweisungstheorie*), it is assumed that enrichment occurs at the expense of another when "the advantage gained by the enriched was assigned by the legal system to the creditor [of restitution]"[72]. Only the holder of a right is entitled to enjoy it; only the owner of a thing can dispose of it, in the terms that seem convenient to him; only the one who performs a performance is entitled to obtain the benefit that it brings him, such as the repayment or extinguishment of his debt.

This interpretation clarifies, among many other cases, the picture of the legal protection of the right of personality by means

---

Díez-Picazo y Ponce de León, *Fundamentos de derecho civil patrimonial*, 6th edn (Navarra: Thomson & Civitas, 2007), vol. I, p. 103.

[69] See C.M. Bianca, *Diritto civile*, 5, *La responsabilità*, 3rd edn (Milano: Giuffrè, 2021), p. 792.

[70] On the new French codified rules about unjustified enrichment, after the 2016 reform, see: R. Cabrillac, *Droit des obligations*, 15th edn (Paris: Dalloz, 2022), pp. 216–23.

[71] See: P. Birks, *Unjust Enrichment*, 2nd edn (Oxford: Oxford University Press, 2005), pp. 73 ff. In Peruvian literature, see: S. García Long, '"A expensas de otro". Lo que debemos hacer con el enriquecimiento injustificado en el Perú', Gaceta Civil & Procesal Civil, 103 (2022), pp. 85–116.

[72] See: Wieling and Finkenauer, *Bereicherungsrecht*, p. 55.

of a restitution action for unjust enrichment. It has been rightly emphasized that in the case of economic advantage derived from the exploitation of a person's image, the advantage is not related to impoverishment if the right holder did not intend to commercialize it[73]. From an economic point of view, the actions of the person who is enriched by such exploitation are indifferent to the person concerned: they do not reduce his wealth, but they do not increase it either.

The question of the good faith of the impoverished and that of the enriched is a complex one. Some Peruvian scholars have pointed out that the good faith of the impoverished party is one of the requirements that the restitution action for unjust enrichment must meet, at least in those cases in which the origin of the advantage obtained is a service performed by the party seeking protection. This thesis came from Italy[74] and it has two main bases: on the one hand, a systematic reading of the Italian Civil Code, which in the specific cases of restitution for enrichment, in most cases, includes such a requirement; and on the other hand, knowledge of the jurisprudential standards of restitution in common law countries, whose affordability depends on the conduct of the impoverished party, analysed from the point of view of diligence and reasonableness.

The requirement of good faith prevails in the current Peruvian legal system, even in the absence of a normative framework, in the field of public procurement disputes. For example, in a case involving the execution of a null and void contract, an administrative arbitration panel rejected a contractor's claim for restitution because it was determined that the contractor had submitted inaccurate documentation during the award

---

[73] See: D. Moura Vicente, *Comparative Law of Obligations* (Cheltenham & Northampton: Edward Elgar, 2021), p. 391.

[74] Initially, P. Trimarchi, *L'arricchimento senza causa* (Milano: Giuffrè, 1962), p. 15. See also Breccia, 'L'arricchimento senza causa', p. 998. It is worth remembering that, in the Common Law bibliography, P. Birks, *An Introduction to the Law of Restitution* (Oxford: Clarendon Press, 1985), pp. 402 ff., placed estoppel as the first barrier against restitutionary actions based on unjust enrichment.

process[75]. The case was qualified as a violation of the principle of presumption of good faith. The author was accused of failing to comply with the obligation to verify the authenticity of the information submitted in the tender. This failure had led the State party to declare the contract null and void *ex officio*. It was deemed that the contractor had not acted in good faith, since its conduct had contributed to the invalidity of the contract.

It can therefore be affirmed that, in Peruvian administrative arbitration, equal or greater weight is given to the idea that no one may enrich himself at the expense of another, than to another principle based on equity: that no one may benefit from his own illegal or bad faith actions.

However, the question remains as to whether the requirement of good faith can be generalized and required beyond the administrative field, in all restitution claims for unjust enrichment, and despite the silence of the Civil Code. The doubts are legitimate. It has been pointed out that the requirement of good faith would "arbitrarily" limit the scope of legal protection[76].

In fact, good faith is a determining factor for the validity of the claim for restitution of unjust enrichment only in exceptional cases. First of all, these should be hypotheses in which the enrichment is due to the conduct of the impoverished party, which in itself reduces the scope of the claim in question. On the other hand, legal protection should not be granted if the impoverished party is accused of reckless, immoral, unreasonable or malicious conduct. In this sense, the basis for the requirement can be derived, *sensu contrario*, from the first paragraph of Article 1275 of the Peruvian Civil Code, which excludes the reimbursement of what has been paid to achieve immoral or unlawful scopes[77].

---

75 *Consorcio Chiclayo vs Instituto Peruano del Deporte*, arbitration award issued on April 25th, 2019, available in: http://www.osce.gob.pe/descarga/arbitraje/laudos/EXTERNO/2019/208-2019.pdf.
76 See, in this sense: Bianca, *Diritto civile*, 5, *La responsabilità*, p. 791.
77 French jurisprudence is exemplary in this respect. It has always considered the absence of fault of the impoverished party and his lack of personal interest in the benefit generating the enrichment as a prerequisite for protection against enrichment. Today, with a certain weakening of this historical tendency, art. 1303-2 of the reformed Napoleonic Code gives the judge the power to

Under these conditions, restitutionary claims are rejected due to so-called "imposed enrichment". Therefore, the owner will not be able to recover the value of unauthorized or expressly disallowed expenses. In practice, it is not uncommon for tenants to abuse the right of retention on the grounds that they have not received compensation for improvements made to the property, even close to the end of the contract period. It is the landlord who decides, not always under the strict control of the owner, the necessity or convenience of the improvements and the amount of money required to carry them out. The risks of his abusive or negligent choices cannot be transferred to the owner by means of restitution.

In a Peruvian case, an untitled possessor sued the owner of a property for restitution of the enrichment represented by the value of the buildings constructed on the property over a period of twenty years. The judges considered the actions taken by the owner to recover the property — those of eviction by usurpation and accession — and concluded that the owner had not acted in good faith. The claim was dismissed. The decision stated:

"Since the constructions were carried out on the basis of an act inspired by bad faith, the legal order does not protect such an act, since good faith is precisely the element that allows a claim of this nature to be brought."[78]

---

reduce the compensation if the enrichment "results" from the fault of the impoverished party. On the other hand, according to the same rule, protection is excluded if the impoverished person acted out of his personal interest.

Also in the Italian legal system, as outlined by P. Gallo, "Remedies for Unjust Enrichment in the History of Italian Law and in the Codice Civile", in Schrage (ed.), *Unjust Enrichment*, p. 280, there is no possibility "to recover what has been paid spontaneously in fulfilment of a moral or social obligation".

78   Corte Suprema de la República, decision CAS No. 2683-2011 LA LIBERTAD, May 29th 2012, *Sentencias en Casación*, XVII, 681 (2013), p. 42542.
The Italian legal doctrine is extensive on the subject of imposed enrichment. See, among others: Trimarchi, *L'arricchimento senza causa*, p. 16; L. Barbiera, *L'ingiustificato arricchimento* (Napoli: Jovene, 1964), pp. 292 ff.; Breccia, 'L'arricchimento senza causa', p. 997; A. Nicolussi, Lesione del potere di disposizione e arricchimento (Milano: Giuffrè, 1998, pp. 282, 419), D. Carusi, *Le obbligazioni nascenti dalla legge*, in *Trattato di diritto civile del Consiglio Nazionale del Notariato* (Napoli: ESI, 2004), pp. 363 ff.; A. Albanese, 'Prestazione gratuita, spirito di liberalità e vantaggi indesiderati

Regarding the lack of title, it must be remembered that the Peruvian Civil Code uses the expression "unjust enrichment". However, in unjust enrichment it is necessary to emphasize much more than the absence of a "debt". In fact, what is lacking is a reason, a foundation or a legal basis — in short: a *causa* — that explains the improvement of the enriched party's situation and his right to keep the advantage obtained.

Clearly, there is no justification for the enrichment when one or more performances have been made on the basis of a null and void contract or one that has been annulled. In Peru, in this case, it is inevitable to exercise the action of Article 1954 of the Civil Code, since the restitutionary effects of the nullity of the contract have not been codified[79]. The only way to obtain a judicial decision with a clear mandate in these cases is to combine the declaratory action for nullity of the contract with an accessory action for restitution of unjust enrichment.

Fortunately, the terminology used in the Peruvian Civil Code does not encourage doctrinal disputes about the meaning of "lack of cause" or "injustice" as characteristics of unjust enrichment. These controversies are rather inevitable when the enrichment is legally qualified as "unjust", "without cause" or even "unjustified". If the analysis focuses on causation, the conclusions will depend on the same notion of causation, whose polysemy is notorious. And if the focus is on injustice, the prospects of equity in the institution regain strength, or there is a risk of bringing it too close to the field of civil liability. This risk is greater in a legal system such as the Peruvian one, where judges consider illegality as a condition for obtaining compensation.

(il problema degli scambi imposti', *Contratto e Impresa* (2007), pp. 482 ff.; Gallo, 'Remedies for Unjust Enrichment', pp. 285 ff.; and, *Trattato di diritto civile*, VII, pp. 95 ff.

[79] Peruvian scholarship has had to fill this legislative gap under the Civil Code of 1936 and the current Civil Code. See: León Barandiarán, *Comentario del Código Civil*, t. I, p. 203; and L. León Hilario, *Derecho privado. Parte general. Negocios, actos y hechos jurídicos* (Lima: Fondo Editorial de la Pontificia Universidad Católica del Perú, 2019), p. 86. However, uncertainty remains.

With regard to the problem of the subsidiarity of the action for unjust enrichment, it has been noted that article 1955 of the Peruvian Civil Code reproduces article 2042 of its Italian counterpart. Departing from a more than centennial tendency of the absence of normative limitations to the exercise of the restitutionary protection against unjust enrichment, the Peruvian legislator probably thought that its normative transplantation work would have been incomplete without the two rules regulating the institution in the model followed. Thus, despite not having the problems of Italy — nor those of France, where the criterion comes from — any possibility of developing this legal protection in this part of South America was thwarted.

Extending the criticism, we cannot omit a negative judgment on the regulation finally codified in the Peruvian Civil Code, because from the Italian scholarship itself, even from that translated into Spanish, advice could have been taken — and should have been taken — not only to copy the model but to improve it. An eminent Italian jurist, of undisputed fame even criticized his legislator for using "outdated and inappropriate terminology"[80], having related subsidiarity to the absence of "another action" (*un'altra azione*) to be compensated for the harm suffered.

However, much has changed since the promulgation of the Italian and Peruvian Civil Codes. The Italian law of *arricchimento senza causa* has evolved, especially with regard to the interpretation of the subsidiarity of the remedy. It is important to know its evolution at the present time, even if the purpose of reporting it is not to reaffirm a cultural dependency, but to provide theoretical and practical elements to attenuate the rigidity of a rule limiting tutelage, attributable not only to its explicit mandate of residuality, but to the scarce comparative study of the meaning of subsidiarity in the system from which the Peruvian legislator has taken the model[81].

---

80   E. Betti, *Teoria generale delle obbligazioni*, III, *Fonti e vicende delle obbligazioni* (Milano: Giuffrè, 1954), p. 142.
81   The case of Portuguese law is singular, where the codified regulation on unjustified enrichment, despite having been drafted on the basis of the BGB,

First of all, Italian doctrine distinguishes between subsidiarity *"in abstracto"* and *"in concreto"*[82].

Subsidiarity *in abstracto* refers to the absence of means of protection granted by other legal rules. For its determination, a review of the provisions of the Civil Code as a whole is carried out, in order to establish, residually, the space covered by the remedy of restitution for unjust enrichment. The verification is theoretical, deductive, and, therefore, vulnerable to the biases and restrictive appreciations that usually disturb the interpretation of the laws, and not only those that make up the system of rights protection.

Subsidiarity, *in abstracto*, refers to the absence of means of protection granted by other legal rules. In order for it to be determined it, a review of the provisions of the Civil Code as a whole is carried out in order to determine, residually, the space covered by the remedy of restitution for unjust enrichment. The review is theoretical, deductive and, therefore, susceptible to the biases and restrictive assessments that usually disturb the interpretation of laws, and not only those that make up the system of legal protection.

---

incorporated the criterion on subsidiarity. Portuguese scholars have strongly criticised this legislative choice. See, among others: the classical dissertation of D.J. Paredes Leite de Campos, *A subsidiaridade da obrigação de restituir o enriquecimento* (Coimbra: Almedina, 1974), pp. 333 ff.; and that one of L.M. Teles de Menezes Leitão, *O enriquecimento sem causa no direito civil. Etudo dogmático sobre a viabilidade da configuração unitária do instituto, face à contraposição entre as diferentes categorias de enriquecimento sem causa* (Coimbra: Almedina, 2005), pp. 962–63.

82 See, on this topic: P. Sirena, "La sussidiarietà dell'azione generale di arricchimento senza causa", Rivista di Diritto Civile, LXIV (2018), pp. 379 ff.; B. Cortese, *Indebiti solutio e arricchimento ingiustificato. Modelli storici, tradizione romanistica e modelli attuali* (Napoli: Jovene, 2013), pp. 199 ff.; M. Grondona, 'Arricchimento senza causa', in A. D'Angelo (ed.), *Le obbligazioni restitutorie* (Torino: Giappichelli, 2015), pp. 56 ff; and A. Nicolussi. Le obbligazioni (Milano: Wolters Kluwer, 2021) pp. 370 f. The Italian Cassational Court has recently revisited the question of the subsidiarity, in abstracto and in concreto, of the unjustified enrichment action: Cass. Civ., Sez. Un., 5 dicembre 2023, n. 33954. See: L. León Hilario, "Te di el problema: ¿te doy la solución? La Corte Corte di Cassazione italiana se pronuncia sobre la subsidiariedad de la acción de enriquecimiento injustificado". Actualidad Civil, 114, (2023), pp. 145 ff.

Subsidiarity *in concreto* has to do with the material impossibility for the party seeking redress to have recourse to other remedies in order to repair the damage suffered. For example, if the time limit for bringing an action provided for by the legal system has expired or has lapsed, the question arises as to whether the action for restitution of unjust enrichment would be admissible in any event if it had not expired. And — what is remarkable — there is no lack of those who answer in the affirmative, although the majority of scholars still hold to the contrary[83].

Of course, it would be very risky to affirm that the claim for unjust enrichment can be exercised in Peru in the event of the statute of limitations or the expiration of the "corresponding" action (subsidiarity *in abstracto*), but this possibility cannot be categorically excluded, even more so if one considers that the calculations of the time limits for filing a lawsuit do not usually take into account, as a first term, the moment when the enrichment was known. On the other hand, it does not seem possible to question the rejection of the claim of a person who, through negligence or inertia, has allowed these time limits to expire[84].

On the other hand, in order to clear the way for the principle of subsidiarity in Peruvian law, it can be admitted that, depending on the circumstances of the case, the protection of unjust enrichment can be asserted as a principal claim, cumulative with others, such as damages, or as a subordinate claim.

A judgement of the Italian Cassational Court[85] ruled on the counterclaim of a company against a public entity for restitution of unjust enrichment deriving from two construction contracts, the conclusion of which was tainted by criminal acts, which were proven in criminal proceedings and led to the nullity of the legal transactions, although the counterclaimant had used the work carried out. This request was rejected by the courts,

---

83   Gallo, *Trattato di diritto civile*, VII, pp. 77-78.
84   See, in this sense: Moscati, *Fonti legali e fonti "private" delle obbligazioni*, p. 283; and Carusi, *Le obbligazioni nascenti dalla legge*, p. 369.
85   Cassazione Civile, Sezione III, January 17th 2020, n. 843, *Giurisprudenza Italiana* (2020), pp. 1891 ff.

which considered that the recovery of the amount invested in the work should be channeled through the indemnification of the directors involved in the offense. They thus followed the approach of subsidiarity *in abstracto*. The Italian judges, upheld the construction company's appeal holding that the action for unjust enrichment is admissible even if the impoverished party's claim is also theoretically provided for by general clauses, such as that of non-contractual liability. The Court therefore examined the specific situation of the appellant company, not forgetting that the amount at stake in the dispute was almost 30,000,000.00 Euros.

To reach this conclusion, the Italian scholars worked with rules that are also regulated in Peru. Suffice it to cite, as an example, the case of building in bad faith on someone else's land. In such a case, according to Article 943 of the Peruvian Civil Code, the owner of the land can cumulatively demand the demolition of what has been built, that is, a material restoration, plus the payment of an "indemnity". The nature of this obligation could be restitutionary, where the owner demands payment of the estimated value of the use that the building provided to the person who built it, or compensatory, where the property has been affected in such a way that its market value has been reduced or it has been rendered unusable for the use that its owner could reasonably have given it.

Intuitively, subsidiarity *in concreto* was applied in an important decision of the Peruvian Supreme Court[86].

A commercial company sued a financial institution for restitution (in unjust enrichment) of the pecuniary value of the goods represented by a set of warrants to which the defendant had become the holder through criminal endorsements made by one of its managers. The entirety of the plaintiff's goods, whose value exceeded US$ 800,000.00, was transferred by the defendant to third parties at the same time as the liability

---

86   Corte Suprema de la República, decision CAS N° 215-2005 LIMA, September 20 2005, *Sentencias en Casación*, XI, 552 (2006), p. 16830.

of its agent for forgery and fraud, among other offenses, was established in criminal proceedings.

In the first instance, the claim was declared well-founded; in the second, it was declared inadmissible. The higher court was of the opinion that "the" action corresponding to the case was that of the ineffectiveness of the legal act. When the Supreme Court was called upon to rule, it declared the cassation appeal well-founded and reinstated the original decision.

In doing so, it specifically examined the situation of the plaintiff, who was prevented from pursuing any other remedy to recover the unjust enrichment obtained by the defendant, with whom she had no contractual or other relationship, and who no longer even had dominion over the assets belonging to the plaintiff. Nor, according to the Supreme Court, could it be expected that a direct action against the person directly responsible for the offences would help the appellant to recover from the impoverishment. Therefore, they stated that the term "other action", used in Article 1955 of the Peruvian Civil Code, includes those arising from contractual or other relationships that generate obligations in favor of the plaintiff, and which, in this case, the plaintiff could not bring against the defendant[87].

One last topic is that of the *restitutionary effects* of unjustified enrichment action. As described before, Article 1954 of the Peruvian Civil Code states that the impoverished person must be "indemnified" by the one who enriched himself at his expense.

Indemnity under Article 1954 of the Peruvian Civil Code is quite unique.

On the one hand, the quantification of restitutionary indemnity for unjust enrichment is completely different from that of compensatory damages. Compensation is measured according to the benefit obtained by the enriched party and cannot exceed it. Compensatory damages, are based on an assessment of the material and moral damage to the integrity of the injured party[88].

---

[87] Surprisingly, the bibliographical support used by the judges was the Spanish translation of the treatise of Josserand, mentioned *retro*, footnote (22).

[88] According to the teaching of L. Corsaro, *Tutela del danneggiato e responsabilità civile* (Milano: Giuffrè, 2003), pp. 5 ff.

On the other hand, while legal obligations to compensate are generally expressed in terms of value, compensation for unjust enrichment is expressed in terms of value only when it refers to a pecuniary advantage. This is not the case when the enrichment is embodied in the ownership of an asset, which requires an entirely reintegrative remedy consisting in the material restitution of the asset to its rightful owner, i.e. the impoverished party. To date, this remedy is regulated in the second paragraph of article 2041 of the Italian Civil Code, which the Peruvian legislator has not copied.

It is not possible to reconstruct the reasoning behind the drafting of this provision, except for the preliminary drafts that have survived to this day. Perhaps it was thought that the field of the reinstatement of property deprived of its owners was exclusively dominated by the reivindicatory action provided for in article 927 of the Peruvian Civil Code. Moreover, doubts have been expressed by Italian scholars as to the relevance of the restitution of property to the protection against unjust enrichment, since this remedy, which the Italians have restored to the Civil Code, does not necessarily entail an obligation equal to the benefit obtained by the enriched party[89].

In conclusion, the indemnity of Article 1954 of the Peruvian Civil Code must be redefined as a restitutionary obligation of a value that is different from the many other legal indemnity obligations recognized by the system.

This view is in line with the jurisprudence of the Peruvian Supreme Court, in a decision concerning the restitution of taxes collected by a municipal tax administration.

The plaintiff — the state company responsible for air safety in Peru, which manages several national airports — included the concept of lost profits in its claims. The judges did not grant it: they only ordered the return of the value of what had been collected, plus interest. In their decision, they pointed out that the purpose of compensation for unjust enrichment is to "recover

---

[89] See, about this topic: Barbiera, *L'ingiustificato arricchimento*, p. 63; and Moscati, *Fonti legali e fonti "private" delle obbligazioni*, p. 251.

the value with which the defendant has enriched himself (restitutionary aspect)", the limit of which depends on "the extent of the impoverishment". Therefore, the term "restitution" contained in the rule under analysis "does not consist in seeking compensation for the damage suffered, and as such covers pecuniary damage (consequential damage and loss of profit) and non-pecuniary damage, but rather in seeking the reduction of the defendant's assets, within the limits of the unjust enrichment that he has obtained"[90].

On two last points, which also concern the indemnity for enrichment, it is advisable to adhere to the conclusions reached by the Italian doctrine itself, with uniformity of opinion and on the basis of concepts or rules that, by chance, have also been received in the Peruvian law.

In the first place, this indemnity belongs to the genre of obligations of value. Therefore, it generates interest until the moment of its payment[91].

Secondly, the reference to the person who has suffered a loss in Article 1955 (*il danneggiato*, in the Italian model) allows, for the quantification of the restitution, the application of the criterion of equity enshrined in Article 1332, when a restitution of the precise benefit is impossible[92]. The judge is free to make this assessment. For example, his criterion may be informed by statistical methods such as calculating probabilities.

---

[90] Corte Suprema de la República, decision CAS N° 513-2008 PIURA, July 3rd 2008, *Sentencias en Casación*, XII, 592 (2008), p. 22977.

[91] In accordance with the provisions of article 1236 of the Peruvian Civil Code: "Where the value of a performance is to be refunded, it shall be calculated at the value on the day of payment, unless otherwise provided by law or agreed". On this topic, see: Gallo, *Trattato di diritto civile*, VII, p. 91; and Carusi, *Obbligazioni nascenti dalla legge*, p. 362.

[92] "Article 1332. If it is not possible to prove the exact amount of the damage, it will be determined by the judge on the basis of an equitable assessment". This rule essentially reproduces the text of Article 1226 of the Italian Civil Code: "If the damage cannot be proved in its exact amount, it shall be liquidated by the judge with an equitable valuation". On this topic, see the recent book of F. Mezzanotte, *La valutazione equitativa del danno* (Torino: Giappichelli, 2022), specially, pp. 311 ff.

VI. *Conclusion*

The model received in the current Peruvian Civil Code regarding to the action of unjustified enrichment was that of the Italian Civil Code of 1942. From this legislation came the general clause (Article 1954), but without the regulation of the material restitution of property and the rule of subsidiarity of the restitution action (Article 1955).

The imitation was therefore not perfect. The minimal adjustments made by the Peruvian legislator did not improve the adopted model. For example, the methodological error made in the Italian Code of first regulating the special cases — *indebitum solutum* and *negotiorum gestio* — and then establishing the general clause was not noticed.

Despite the imprecision of the legal framework, the Peruvian jurisprudence has managed to progressively identify the attributes of the restitutionary remedy and has applied the concept of subsidiarity *in abstracto* as a corrective to the practical disadvantages created by this rule, and without falling into the opposite anomaly of the "pan-restitutionary" visions, which could generate the harmful effect of expanding the field of application of unjust enrichment without measure or control.

In this way, the legal and cultural exchange between Italy and Peru takes on a peculiar form, in which it is no longer a mere importation of rules, but a serious learning and imitation of the solutions to the problems created by the rules that both countries have in common.

Juan José Martínez-Mercadal[*]

NORMATIVE NEGOTIATING POWER AND PRIVATE AUTONOMY IN THE FORMATION OF CONTRACT THEORY AND ETHICAL CONTRACT THEORY

Some notes from Italian and Uruguayan Civil Law

1. *Regulatory power in the autonomy of the will of Luigi Ferri*

It was Ferri who inspired the Uruguayan authors Eugenio Cafaro and Santiago Carnelli to develop a theory on contract efficiency based on the notions of normative power and autonomy of will. However, according to the Uruguayan authors, several clarifications about the Italian jurist's perspective make it possible to advance his position.

Ferri points out that the law changes, the law evolves, precisely through the creation of new rules (or the modification or repeal of existing ones), and that legal power is the power to establish new statutes or to modify or repeal existing regulations; that is, through normative acts[1].

According to Ferri, within the positive legal system, power is the ability to establish the Law. It both precedes and is external to the Law. Power, in effect, is not a norm, it is not a duty, it is not a right, but it is before the norm, duty and law[2]. However, the Law is aware of its evolution and therefore confers that power and disciplines its exercise. Therefore, in order to speak of true

---

[*] Lawyer and Master in Tort Law. University of the Republic. Faculty of Law, Montevideo. Professor of Civil Law (Obligations, Contracts and Tort Law) and Postgraduate Professor in the Masters course in Tort Law at University of the Republic, Faculty of Law, Montevideo. Editorial secretary of the Critical Magazine of Private Law, Montevideo. Member of the Research Group "Nucleus of Civil Law", University of the Republic. Aspiring PhD candidate in Civil Law at University of Buenos Aires, Faculty of Law. Email: martinezmercadal@gmail.com.

[1] L. Ferri, *La autonomía privada* (Santiago: Ediciones Olejnik, 2018), p. 190.
[2] Ferri, *La autonomía privada*, p. 191.

mobility of the Law, the changes take place within its scope, that is, by virtue of legal powers[3].

From Ferri's perspective, regulating power implies suitability to modify the legal world, the legal system, through laws that are constructed by abstract and objective will. The former is legal because its source of validity is found in a supra-ordinary rule, that is, in the Law. This attributes or deprives individuals of regulating power and therefore allows or denies them the authority to create legal norms[4].

According to Díez-Picazo y Ponce de León, autonomy is the power to organize one's private affairs, understood as the rights, faculties, entitlements, relationships, etc. held by or attributed to the individual. This does not mean that the individual's control over this personal sphere is total and absolute. There are portions of that sphere for which the law excludes autonomy. For this reason, we speak of rights, situations, relationships, etc. which are "unavailable"; that is, there are aspects of one's personal legal sphere over which s/he cannot exercise power of autonomy[5].

For Ferri, concluding a contract or making a will involve interests that require more, and certainly different, legislative attention compared to activities such as walking or plowing. The law does not simply discipline business activity, as it does with walking or plowing, or merely prohibit actions that restrict free enterprise. Rather, the law intervenes, acting as a "referee" to, above all, confer power on individuals. Take articles 1372 and 457 of the Italian Civil Code, for instance: the former establishes that the contract has the force of law between the parties, while the latter states inheritance is transmitted by law or by will. Thus, both provisions suggest a significant proximity between law and business; whereas in article 1372 business is identified with

---

3   Ferri, *La autonomía privada*, p. 191.
4   E. Cafaro and S. Carnelli, *Metodología de la Eficacia contractual. Anuario de Derecho Civil Uruguayo XI* (Montevideo: Fundación de Cultura Universitaria, 1976), p. 8.
5   L. Díez-Picazo y Ponce de León, 'La autonomía privada y el derecho necesario en la Ley de Arrendamiento Urbanos', Anuario de Derecho Civil, 4 (1956), pp. 1152–53.

the law in terms of "force", in article 457, law and business are placed in an alternative situation of competition to regulate the transmission of inheritance[6].

2. *Regulating power ("Negotiating Normative Power") as an emanation of legal capacity and autonomy of will*

On the theoretical construction of power, as an emanation of the autonomy of the will, Cafaro and Carnelli build in Uruguay the concept of *Negotiating Normative Power* (Regulating power). The expression normative power becomes specific in regulating power when it consists of the possibility of building legal transactions as a rule of law.

Cafaro and Carnelli point out that business is a legal norm because it causes or gives rise to subjective rights and duties. It is an externalization of the normative power that an individual is invested by law[7]. That power cannot be confused with the one inherent to the subjective right, since the former is prior to the latter; the former creates the legal business from which the subjective rights result and these do not contain a power to create legal norms, but rather a power to effect or exercise the content of the right itself. The negotiating normative power leads to the creation of legal relationships solely through the actions of the individuals invested with it. On the other hand, not every legal relationship finds its source in said power and just as the law itself attributes such power, it itself is the cause of legal relationships.

For Ferri, the power of disposition, normative power, and private autonomy are the same theoretical construction, leaving aside any assimilation of power to legal capacity or to act, to a quality of subjective right to any other objective possibility or, in fact. In Ferri's words, "disposal power and private autonomy are the same concept", and "legal business is, by its nature, dispositive and cannot be anything else. And it is [dispositive],

---

6   Ferri, *La autonomía privada*, pp. 202–03.
7   Cafaro and Carnelli, *Metodología de la Eficacia contractual*, p. 8.

for me, precisely because it is an act of exercising the power of disposition, that is, of private autonomy"[8].

The Italian jurist adds that when the legislator wishes to preclude individuals from exercising this normative power, he expressly excludes it from private autonomy, as is the case with article 2969 of the Italian Civil Code. The term "disposition" is used in a broad sense and not linked to persons or legitimacy, notwithstanding that it is also used in a restricted sense.

In Uruguay, and based on Ferri's theory on normative power and power of disposition, Cafaro and Carnelli have stated to prefer the denomination of normative negotiating power to immediately identify a person's power to create legal rules. They understand that the Italian author confuses the possibility of creating a rule with the possibility of it being effective. In the methodology of Cafaro and Carnelli, autonomy of the will, normative negotiating power, and power of disposition are three concepts that respond to three different legal phenomena.

Cafaro and Carnelli understand that private autonomy is the recognition of a legal sphere of its own, exclusive and exclusive of each subject of law. Normative power is the practical instrument which demonstrates the existence of such capacity or authority. It does not, however, establish the way such power is manifested or how it gives rise to rules which, directed to a specific legal sphere, are destined to satisfy one's interests. Finally, the power of disposition supposes linking the normative power with the consequences of its exercise — that is, the effects that its exercise determines via the creation of effective legal rules[9].

In Uruguay, article 1247 of the Civil Code provides:

> The contract is a convention by which one party is obligated to the other or both parties are reciprocally obligated to any provision, that is, to give, do or not do something. Each part can be one or many people.

---

8   Ferri, *La autonomía privada*, p. 203.
9   E. Cafaro and S. Carnelli, *Eficacia contractual* (Fundación de Cultura Universitaria, 1996), p. 8.

In this legal system, following classical Roman law on the binding (not dispositive) effect of contracts, it has been understood that the contract is a convention, i.e., an agreement of the wills of two or more people that produces legal effects. Article 1246 of Uruguayan Civil Code, in establishing the sources of obligations, refers to the contract as "the express concurrence of the wills of two or more people". What distinguishes the contract from other conventions is its function: to produce obligations. The contract, as a convention, requires two or more parties for its existence. Obligations can be agreed for one of the parties or for all of them[10].

According to article 11 of Uruguay Civil Code, "The laws which must be observed in the interest of public order and good customs cannot be repealed by particular agreements". By virtue of private autonomy, one can create rules that derogate general rules to the extent permitted by public order and good customs, i.e., within the limits of legality.

Andrés Mariño points out that contracts occur in the individual sphere of private autonomy, a space where, in accordance with article 11 of the Uruguayan Civil Code, people can exclude the application of general rules within the limits of public order. The contracts contain rules to which the parties must submit "as to the law itself" (article 1291.1). The contract produces effects only between the parties, meaning the legal relationships established under or resulting from the agreement only impact the parties thereto (article 1293). The rights and obligations of the parties extend to the heirs, except when the contract is terminated by the death of one of the contracting parties (article 1292). Contracts must be executed in good faith (article 1291.2). It is expressly prohibited for a single contracting party to determine, at his discretion, the validity or enforceability of a contract (article 1253). The contract can only be modified or terminated by the agreement of the parties thereto (article 1294). One party may be granted the right to terminate the contract by way of declaration

---

10   A. Mariño López, *Código Civil de la República Oriental del Uruguay, anotado y concordado* (Uruguay: La Ley, 2021).

of intent (unilateral withdrawal), but the exercise of such right must be subject to the occurrence of an event external to the will of the assignor or payment by the latter of a penalty, with reasonable notice in good faith[11].

That is to say, the contract creates a legal norm that enters the legal system. The contracting parties, through the normative power, create rules that represent their respective undertakings and which define their legal relationship in the form of a legal obligation. Moreover, articles 1247 and 1291 of Uruguayan Civil Code establish that these rules only apply to the contracting parties and their successors in a universal and particular title. Thus, according to the article 1291 of Civil Code (*pacta sunt servanda*), validly formed contracts constitute a rule to which the parties must submit as to the law itself. Accordingly, all legally recognized agreements must be executed in good faith, in conformity with their provisions, and pursuant to the effects contemplated therein; which, depending on their nature, must be consistent with equity, use or law.

The Negotiating Normative Power, as an expression of party autonomy and the faculty to create legal obligations, is inextricably linked to legal capacity. Moreover, both negotiating normative power and legal capacity constitute essential presuppositions of the contract, without which it is not possible to establish an existing, valid and effective contract.

Negotiating power requires legal capacity, understood as the ability to be the holder of legal relationships and a quality which attributes legal personality to an individual[12]. In this sense, the limits to legal capacity restrict an individual's personality, such that lack of personality (due to incapacity) bars the formation of a legal relationship for the absence of a recognized subject of law, which is the essential structural subjective element for its configuration[13].

---

[11] Mariño López, *Código Civil de la República Oriental del Uruguay, anotado y concordado.*
[12] Cafaro and Carnelli, *Metodología de la Eficacia contractual*, p. 8.
[13] Cafaro and Carnelli, *Metodología de la Eficacia contractual*, p. 8.

It follows that only the individual endowed with generic and abstract legal capacity can be the effective owner of the relationship created through the exercise of regulatory power. Moreover, as the negotiating normative power is conferred by law, it does not depend on the subject's will; legal capacity is a requisite to be the subject of rights and obligations, but is not required to perform subsequent acts. Hence, the capacity to act is not necessary for the attribution of normative power, but it is necessary for the exercise of the right[14].

The problem of lack of capacity to act is solved through the institution of representation of the incapable and must be analyzed together with the expression of will (consent) and not as a premise of the contract.

However, Ferri observes that when the legislator expressly excludes the possibility of exercising the power of disposition in certain relationships or in regard to certain rights, he is essentially establishing that the "matter [is] removed from the availability of the parties" (as expressly provided in article 2969 of the Italian Civil Code). Personality rights, the legitimate and natural filiation relationship, the conjugal bond and, in general, all family law statuses are examples of such categories of "unavailable" affairs over which the power of disposition cannot be exercised. This is a generally accepted affirmation, is equivalent to saying that private autonomy is inapplicable in this field — that it is excluded from it. Take article 5 of the Italian Civil Code, for instance, which prohibits acts that result in a permanent alteration of one's physical integrity (e.g., selling an organ).

3. *Lack of regulatory power and illegal contracts: different prohibited content*

The Uruguayan authors emphasize the importance of keeping in mind *what*, exactly, is prohibited—that is, the matters over which private autonomy has no authority. Lack of regulatory

---

14   Cafaro and Carnelli, *Metodología de la Eficacia contractual*, p. 8.

power does not imply an assessment of behaviors according to morality, public order, or good customs. It does not refer to an act contrary to the legal system, such as the case of a contract with an illegal "object" (or purpose).

Broad restrictions apply to contracts with a lawful object, as only what is prohibited by law and refers generally to the entire population (and not to a particular person) may be considered "illicit." In other words, only that which goes against the relevant legal system, whether generally or a specific rule, irrespective of the transgressor's position or status in relation to the unlawful circumstance, can be considered illegal.

On the other hand, lack of negotiating normative power refers to the individual, considered in relation to his position within the context of a certain contract. We must bear in mind that freedom (of contract) represents both a general principle and a closing clause of modern legal systems — one for which only specific or particular exceptions apply. Whereas a contractual provision that completely strips a party of such freedom is inadmissible, a statute may apply only to a particular circumstance or specific category of individuals. For instance, a law may prohibit certain persons from establishing a business irrespective of any evaluation as to the type of activity pursued; hence, establishing the business regardless of the restriction would result in the commission of an illicit act[15].

When an object is prohibited by law, such restriction refers only to the circumstance identified in the relevant provision and not to a specific person or manner in which one's business is conducted. In short, the prohibition concerns an individual's authority to create legally enforceable rules, preventing the creation of a certain business by way of his mere will (or party autonomy)[16]. The restriction applies to a specific object and relates to one's authority to establish a certain business; the rule does not apply to other matters or, if the same matter, in relation

---

15 Cafaro and Carnelli, *Eficacia contractual*, pp. 22–23.
16 Cafaro and Carnelli, *Eficacia contractual*, pp. 22–23.

to another mode of negotiation, one's business competence, or party autonomy per se[17].

4. The existence category and the effects of the lack of normative negotiating power

Legal capacity and normative negotiating power are essential presuppositions of a binding contract. Moreover, their analysis necessarily precedes considerations as to whether a contract contains the elements necessary for its recognition, or the qualities of these elements (i.e., consent, object and cause).

While legal capacity and normative negotiating power are presuppositions of the contract, they are external to it. They do not compromise or integrate its content, but form its groundwork. They are unrelated to the contract. They precede it. They are outside the elements of consent, object, and cause. Additionally, because they are external and prior to the contract, they allow for the acceptance of the so-called "existence category".

The existence of normative negotiating power must be ascertained prior to concluding the contract. In this sense, it is noteworthy that the subsequent attribution or loss of normative power are potential events that do not per se impact the validity or legitimacy of one's mere expression of intent. The subsistence of a person's normative power must be verified when the declaration of will is made, as this is the critical moment for determining whether the person is legally capable of being bound by any obligations arising therefrom[18].

Put differently, even if a law with retroactive effect were to enter into force such as to subsequently attribute or revoke normative negotiating power, such occurrence cannot affect rights previously acquired by third parties.

Neither Italian Law nor Uruguayan Law regulates the category of existence or non-existence; rather it is a legal fiction

---

17 Cafaro and Carnelli, *Eficacia contractual*, p. 23.
18 Cafaro and Carnelli, *Metodología de la eficacia contractual*, p. 10.

The analysis presented by the Uruguayan Doctrine considers two assumptions of the contract: legal capacity and normative negotiating power.

The Italian Doctrine discusses whether the category of non-existence (of the act, of the matter, or of the contract) is admissible — given it is not envisaged by the Code, by special laws, or by cause — as a fact or matter capable of being ascertained[19].

The null contract does not produce effects, whether between the parties or in relation to third parties. Accordingly, third parties that have acquired rights pursuant to a null contract may challenge such determination as it relates to their interests[20]. Despite laws protecting third-party rights arising from invalid (voidable) agreements, Italian jurist Guido Alpa observes that voidable contracts produce effects to the extent no declaration of invalidity has been issued — that is, as long as the interested party (i.e., the party harmed by the existence of a voidable contract) has not petitioned the court to void the contract. In this case, any effects produced by the voidable contract are eliminated from the moment of the contract's formation (the so-called retroactive effect of voidability), including any rights or benefits acquired by third parties; except when the transaction has been made for consideration and the third-party has acted in good faith. In situations giving rise to a voidable contract, this exception is justified by the understanding that third-party interests must be reconciled with those of the party that requested the annulment. This is not the case, however, in circumstances giving rise to nullity. Consider, for example, a contract entered into by a person lacking legal capacity: since it is possible to verify such condition by consulting public records[21], the law encourages (counter)parties to act diligently by providing that null contacts require restitution *in natura*. The parties must restored to the previous state regardless of any third-party rights acquired in the meantime.

---

19 G. Alpa, *El contrato en general. Principios y Problemas* (Lima: Instituto Pacífico, 2015), p. 223.
20 Alpa, p. 229.
21 Alpa, p. 229.

In Uruguay, professors Eugenio Cafaro and Santiago Carnelli have put forth a different interpretation of the rules on the essential elements of the contract. More specifically, they submit that the absence of the above presumptions gives rise to a situation other than nullity and which protects third-party rights. This notion is predicated on the notion that a contract cannot exist absent the essential elements, and what does not exist cannot be null. That is, to the extent a contract is non-existent for the legal system, it is not subject to the provisions on, for example, legal capacity (suitability to be the holder of rights) or normative negotiating power (this ability to create norms). Accordingly, it cannot be null — because it is nothing, it does not exist.

However, it should be noted that actions taken absent a valid contract are not protected by the traditional contract remedies envisaged by law. For example, if a party's actions have patrimonial consequences, absent good title that justifies such effects, restitution must be carried out through the return of what was unduly received and not via restitution (strictly speaking) pursuant to a null contract. This is because, while the latter presupposes the existence of an existent albeit invalid agreement, the former scenario is based on the absences, or non-existence, of a recognized affair[22]. In this way, third parties that have, acting in good faith, acquired rights through onerous contracts are not obliged to make restitution.

Article 1318 of Uruguayan Civil Code (undue payments) states:

> Whoever has paid what was not due cannot claim restitution of what is held by a third party in good faith and pursuant to valuable consideration; but he is entitled to restitution from the third party who holds the thing without having paid for it, if the thing is returnable and is in the third party's possession.

The action for recovery of undue payments is the instrument through which whoever transferred funds (or other valuable

---

22 Cafaro and Carnelli, *Eficacia contractual*, p. 24.

goods) without a legal basis (e.g., title or justifying cause) can reclaim what was unjustifiably conveyed.

5. *Practical application of the analysis of the presupposition of the contract: the lack of normative negotiating power in sale and donation contracts in the Uruguayan Civil Code*

Under Uruguayan law, some practical consequences of lack of normative negotiating power include the preclusion from making certain donations (or gifts) and/or effecting sales. If those contracts are entered into, they are non-existent, not null or voidable[23].

Article 1657 of the Uruguayan Civil Code establishes, "Any donation from one spouse to another during the marriage will be void. This rule does not include the modest gifts that married people usually give each other on occasions of joy for the family".

The doctrine submits that it is not a matter of nullity or inadequacy of certain essential elements of the contract. Rather, the case concerns the complete absence of normative negotiating power of spouses to make donations (or gifts) in favor of their partners. It is further inappropriate to speak of a void contract, as the contract is technically inexistant. Andrés Mariño highlights that spouses lack the regulatory power to make donations/gifts to each other, except for what is provided in the second part of the provision. Thus, if the donation/gift is made between them, it is non-existent[24].

> Other instances in which the law expressly excludes the power of certain persons to create contractual rules include: Article 1675 of Uruguayan Civil Code: "The contract of sale between spouses who are not [legally] separated is null".

The rule's scope has been broadened to cover legally recognized cohabitants and its violation is understood as not

---

23 Cafaro and Carnelli, *Eficacia contractual*, p. 24.
24 Mariño López, *Código Civil de la República Oriental del Uruguay, anotado y concordado.*

giving rise to a case of nullity; it is merely a case of lack of negotiating normative power. Mariño endorses the contention that spouses not legally separated lack the regulatory power to enter into sales contracts with each other, further purporting that any sale made between them results in a non-existent contract.

Likewise, by preventing guardians, curators and parents from in any way selling their property to those under their guardianship or authority, article 1676 of Uruguayan Civil Code represents a new case of lack of normative negotiating power of certain persons. Regarding parents, this rule it must be coordinated with article 271, which reads:

> Parents are prohibited from: 1st. – Disposing of the children's real estate or the income constituted on the national debt, except for reasons of necessity or evident utility of such children and with prior court approval, with a hearing of the Public Prosecutor's Office.

Article 1678 of Uruguayan Civil Code establishes:

> It is forbidden to purchase, even by public auction, by oneself or through intermediaries: 1. – For parents, the property of the children who are under their authority. 2. – For tutors and curators, the property of the people who are in their care or buy property for them, except in the cases and in the manner set out by law. 3. – For all public employees, the property that is sold by their ministry, whether public or private. 4. – For Judges, clerks, bailiffs and attorneys of the parties, the property involved in the dispute and which is sold as a result of the proceedings.

This provision, too, envisages circumstances in which parties lack negotiating regulatory power.

6. *The power to create contractual rules and an ethical theory for contract*

Normative negotiating power, of which the law is one of its expressions, implies the "suitability to modify the legal world, through norms that are constituted by abstract and objective will"[25].

Professor Arturo Caumont[26] points out that, in Uruguay, the traditional concept of contracting views the parties as opposing forces with conflicting interests and needs. They are in a proverbial battle to subdue and dominate the other in the concomitant search for their individual gain.

The inevitable consequences of such an approach presuppose the division of the contract, that is, the distinction into two segments to the detriment of its integrity as a unit, of its ontologically convergent character, typical of its conventional essence. Every contract is an agreement, as imposed by the Uruguayan Civil Code in its article 1247. It must be considered and understood without ambiguity and in its entirety.

The Uruguayan Civil Code defines a contract as a convention by which one party is obligated towards the other or both reciprocally to comply with any provision to give, perform, or not perform an action (article 1247).

The contract is a form of agreement, and the verb that is conjugated from its essence is highly significant to understand its ethical profile which, it should be reiterated, does not involve a mere illusion of temporary approval and satisfaction of those who empirically observe the phenomenon at the descriptive level[27].

In old French, "*convencion*" means "agreement" and, in Latin, "*convenionem*" means "a meeting, assembly, an agreement". It is an action noun which past-participle stems from *convenire*, meaning "unite, be suitable, agree, assemble", which in turn derives from the assimilated form of *com*, meaning "with, together", plus *venire*, or "to come".

Against this background, it is necessary to develop an Ethical Theory of the Contract. As argued by Caumont, in contractual terms, the respect the contracting parties must have toward

---

25 Ferri, *La autonomía privada*, p. 182.
26 A. Caumont, *Doctrina General del Contrato. Proposiciones Teóricas de innovación* (Montevideo: La Ley, 2014).
27 Caumont, *Doctrina General del Contrato*.

the contract as an autonomous entity of its makers (*pacta sunt servanda*) demonstrates the moral character that underlies the rule of Law.

The contract is essentially an ethical space. The ethical perspective in this regard also covers the phases of pre-contractuality and post-contractuality.

The ethical ontological condition of contractuality is important to recognize in the conceptual substance of the contractual agreement. It is a structural element to which contracting parties must adhere, as if the parties too were "components" of the contract.

Therefore, it is inappropriate to separate the ethical aspect of the legality of the parties' behavior (with regard to the manner in which they conduct negotiations) in the pre-contractual phase from that in the post-contractual dimension. It must also be added that failure to comply with ethical duties is equivalent to breaching legal requirements to behave in accordance with general duties of loyalty, solidarity and respect that are intrinsic to the principle of Good Faith in all its semantic expressions.

In this regard, ethics constitutes a different and transversal dimension. The importance of ethics in the negotiating stage, during the execution of the contract and after the end of the contract is clear if we consider the duty to behave with loyalty, solidarity, and consideration for the other.

Jorge Eduardo Medina Villanueva*

NOTES ON THE INFLUENCE OF THE ITALIAN DOCTRINE ON RIGHTS OF PERSONALITY [*DIRITTI DELLA PERSONALITÀ*] IN MEXICO

Introduction

In Mexico, until relatively few years ago, the protection of the highest values of the human person was considered a matter exclusive to the Fundamental Rights (then called "Individual Guarantees") whose regulation was essentially enshrined in the first 29 articles of the Federal Constitution.

Given this protection — a matter of public law — it was not considered that civil law could and should also include these human values. Thus, the so-called *"rights of personality"*, *"diritti della personalità"* or *"derechos de la personalidad"*, were generally ignored, until relatively recently. Gradually, some civil codes and special laws of different federal states, in a more or less timid way, have begun to include them.

Undoubtedly, in this gradual progress in favor of the legal recognition of the rights of personality, the Italian doctrine of the 20th century has influenced and

> has the merit of studying them in depth — rights of personality — and claiming the category that they have, to extol their enormous transcendence and to achieve the affirmation of the thesis that sustains the existence of true subjective rights.[1]

---

* Professor at the Universidad Panamericana, Campus Guadalajara, Facultad de Derecho.
1 E. Gutiérrez y González, *El Patrimonio. El pecuniario y el moral o derechos de la personalidad*, 6th edn (México: Porrúa, 1999), p. 731.

Outstanding among these learned works is that of Adriano de Cupis, who "has written a beautiful work in which he systematizes the issue"[2].

The subject of this chapter is precisely the analysis of the influence that these Italian ideas have had both on doctrine and on Mexican legislation, primarily in the last third of the 20th century and the first decades of the 21st.

Generalities of the rights of personality

For many years, jurists have written of the existence of certain rights necessary for the integral development of the human being, inherent in their very nature, whose recognition and protection must be one of the basic obligations of the State and the legal order. These are — as Miguel Carbonel defines human rights — the faculties and institutions that specify the demands of dignity, freedom and human equality[3]. Scholasticism and the later Spanish school of natural law had already referred to

> goods found in the person, in his body (*in bonis corporis*), including the following: bodily integrity, tranquility and peace of mind and freedom; including, while remaining distinguished in nature, honor and fame. One and the other can be injured and give rise, in such a case, to the obligation to repair.[4]

Although we find historical manifestations of the protection of the personality, any systematic consideration of what we today call *rights of personality*[5] did not occur until the first half of the 20th century, which reverence is attributed, as we will explain later, to the Italian doctrine of the period, led by Adriano de Cupis.

Notwithstanding the indications of medieval and Renaissance jurists referred to above, the search, study, and reflection of these rights, since the French Revolution, have been addressed

---

2   Gutiérrez y González, *El Patrimonio*, p. 731.
3   M. Carbonel, *Los derechos fundamentales en México* (Mexico: Porrúa), p. 9.
4   F. De Castro, 'Los llamados derechos de la personalidad', ADC, 1959, p. 1241.
5   J. Castán Tobeñas, *Derecho Civil Español, Común y Foral*, (Madrid: Reus, 1987), Voll. 1-2, p. 355.

mainly by public law. This has caused them to be considered only applicable in the relations between ruler and ruled, and not in all legal relations, especially between individuals.

The interest in the study of these rights resurfaced, primarily in the Italian and Spanish legal doctrine, in the final years of the 19th century. Scholars of Civil Law have identified — undoubtedly based on the medieval antecedents noted above — certain subjective rights whose function is to establish the basic criteria of legal personality on a civil level. That is, those necessary and essential rights without which one's personality — the ability to be the holder of rights and obligations — would remain completely unsatisfied, deprived of any concrete value[6]; rights to "goods", such as life, one's name, and honor, that are instrumental in the protection of individual personal interests[7]. These "goods" have been called "rights of personality". Therefore, it is possible to share we can conclude, as Alberto Pacheco does, that the development of the theory of these rights, though not their genesis, is recent[8].

It should also be noted that legal positivism "swept away the idea of those so-called innate or original rights that are born with the person and are the responsibility of the holder for being a person and insofar as he is..."[9]. Thus, the political nuance led scholars

> to see the need to take the idea with another approach and other trappings to private law, admitting the existence of rights that are exercised over the person himself or his qualities or attributes, ensuring the enjoyment of our internal goods, of our physical and spiritual energies.[10]

José Castán emphasizes that the theory of rights of personality belongs, in essence, to civil law. This is because it responds to the need for them to be recognized and proclaimed as a kind of private rights, linked to the concept of person and personality. They are essentially civil, and therefore endowed with protection precisely

---

6 A. De Cupis, *I diritti della personalità*, (Milano: Giuffrè, 1959), Vol. I, pp. 9.
7 J. Castán Tobeñas, 'Los derechos de la personalidad', RGLJ, 1952, p. 6.
8 A. Pacheco, *La persona en el Derecho civil mexicano*, (México: Panorama, 1998), p. 54
9 Castán Tobeñas, *Derecho Civil Español*, Voll. 1-2, p. 357
10 Castán Tobeñas, *Derecho Civil Español*, Voll. 1-2, p. 357.

in the civil sphere. However, nothing prevents other legal bodies from considering some "rights of personality" as human rights, since their scope of protection is within the purview of public law[11]. Thus, we see that their approach is different[12]. While some view them traditionally from the perspective of limits of power and as a guiding principle of the entire legal system, others view them from the civil standpoint, from the norm between persons, between citizens.

An in-depth analysis of the conception of rights of personality reveals an intrinsic correspondence with that of fundamental rights, since they are goods inherent in the person, necessary for his development as a human being. However, the difference is that rights of personality are protected by civil law, and human rights have a greater scope, especially those of the last generation.

The connection between rights of personality and non-pecuniary damage has been the subject of a very interesting note by Francesco Messineo, who asserts that "injury to the rights of personality manifests itself in damage to the person, but assumes the contours of what has been called non-patrimonial damage"[13]. Indeed, as will be seen, such claim is based on the notion of non-pecuniary damage which some Mexican civil codes have allowed as a remedy for injury to one's personality, albeit not necessarily to protect the values of the individual.

Legislative treatment of Rights of Personality in Mexico

In Mexico, rights of personality are not currently governed in a general manner at the Federal level, although they are legislated in some states[14].

---

11 Castán Tobeñas, 'Los derechos de la personalidad', p. 12.
12 Pacheco, *La persona en el Derecho civil mexicano*, p. 54
13 F. Messineo, *Manual de Derecho Civil y Comercial*, (Buenos Aires: EJEA, 1979), Vol. III, p. 4.
14 Given the Mexican conception as a Federal Republic, there are two legislative orders that coexist — in a division by subject made by the Political Constitution of the United Mexican States. Thus, civil matters, as a general

Nonetheless, it is noteworthy that there was an attempt in 1982 to introduce rights of personality into the so-called "Civil Code for the Federal District in Common Matters and for the entire Republic in Federal Matters", although unfortunately it was modified in the legislative process, suppressing the timid allusion made to them.

In the month of December 1982, the recently inaugurated President of the Republic, Miguel de la Madrid Hurtado, presented an initiative to modify, among others, article 1916 of the Civil Code for the Federal District, so that its first paragraph would state as follows:

> Article 1916. Moral damage is understood as the injury that a person suffers in his rights of personality, such as his feelings, affections, beliefs, decorum, honor, reputation, secrecy of his private life and physical integrity, or otherwise in consideration of itself.

The explanatory memorandum of the presidential initiative stated:

> [...] Respect for the rights of personality, guaranteed through the civil liability established for whoever violates them, will contribute to completing the framework that our laws establish to achieve coexistence in which respect for freedoms does not mean the possibility of abuses that threaten the legitimate affections and beliefs of individuals or their honor or reputation.
>
> Under the denomination of rights of personality, a wide range of prerogatives and powers has been designated in contemporary civil doctrine and in some modern laws that guarantee the person the enjoyment of their faculties and respect for the development of their physical and moral personality.
>
> The person possesses attributes inherent in their condition that are qualities or assets of the personality and that positive law must adequately recognize and protect by granting a scope of power and the general duty of respect that is imposed on third parties, which, within civil law, should be translated into the granting of a subjective right to obtain reparation in case of transgression.

Unfortunately, as already mentioned, the text of the initiative was modified throughout the legislative process. It was finally approved, promulgated and published in the Official Gazette of

---

rule, belong to each of the legislatures of the federal entities, which explains the diversity on the subject.

the Federation on December 31, 1982, with the first paragraph of article 1916 reading: "Moral damage is understood as the damage that a person suffers in their feelings, affections, beliefs, decorum, honor, reputation, private life, physical configuration and appearance, or in the consideration that others have of them". In other words, the allusion made to rights of personality was suppressed, leaving only the enumeration of assets and rights specifically protected.

In light of the doctrinal development evolving in the country at the time, as well as the legal and political influence exerted by legislation passed by Congress over the federated states, I believe it would have been more opportune to start with broader national statute on the subject of the rights of personality.

Currently, the issue of rights of personality has witnessed a special legislative development based on its connection with non-pecuniary damage, as we mentioned above, although legislators have not necessarily been concerned with its definition and delimitation.

Comparatively analyzing the laws of the different states, we find three options in the regulation of rights of personality in Mexico:

a) Codes that more or less completely regulate rights of personality. Of these, we can highlight the civil codes of the states of Coahuila, Mexico, Jalisco, Puebla, Querétaro, Quintana Roo and the special law on the subject of Mexico City[15].

I believe the best example of this regulation is provided by the State of Coahuila, where article 88 of its Civil Code defines rights of personality as "the set of attributes inherent in natural persons, whose objective is to guarantee them the enjoyment of their physical psychic, spiritual and relational faculties, in optimal conditions within their own circumstances". It further highlights their characteristics as being "inalienable, imprescriptible,

---

15 The Civil Code of the Federal District does not contemplate them expressly, but it does in the "Civil Liability Law for the protection of the right to private life, honor and one's image in the Federal District", published on May 19, 2006, although this law only specifies the rights indicated in its title.

inalienable, unencumberable and can be opposed to any person, whether authority or individual".

b) Codes that only mention rights of personality, without reference to any other mention or regulation. These are the states of Guerrero, Oaxaca, San Luis Potosí and Zacatecas.

One example of this regulation appears to be found in article 2, third paragraph of the Civil Code of Oaxaca, which states that "[t]he protection granted by the Law to all men and women encompasses all the rights inherent in personality and human dignity," without further regulating or delving into the subject.

c) Codes that do not indicate any rights of personality. The rest of the states (i.e., Aguascalientes, Baja California, Baja California Sur, Campeche, Chiapas, Chihuahua, Colima, Durango, Guanajuato, Hidalgo, Michoacán, Morelos, Nayarit, Nuevo León, Sinaloa, Sonora, Tabasco, Tamaulipas, Tlaxcala, Veracruz and Yucatán) do not make any reference to rights of personality as essential rights and protections afforded to the highest human values. Additionally, there is no mention in relation to moral damage, since these federal entities regulate moral damage according to article 1916 of the Federal Civil Code mentioned above, in its current wording. That is, they do not make any allusion to rights of personality; they only enumerate protected rights.

Doctrinal Treatment of the Rights of Personality in Mexico

At present, within the doctrine, the main Mexican authors who address the issue of non-pecuniary damage are: Ernesto Gutiérrez y González, predominately in his work, "El Patrimonio"; Ignacio Galindo Garfias, principally in his work, "Civil Law"; and finally, Alberto Pacheco, in his work "The person in Mexican Civil Law", which we will detail below.

a) Ernesto Gutiérrez y González

It seems to me that the work "Patrimony. The pecuniary and the moral or rights of personality" by Ernesto Gutiérrez y González provides the most detailed and comprehensive study of rights of personality in Mexico. It is additionally significant that this work has been extensively disseminated, with its first edition having been published by Editorial José Ma. Cajica in 1971 and the current 12th edition published by Editorial Porrúa in 2022.

As the very subtitle of his work suggests, rights of personality are an important part of Gutiérrez y González's theory on patrimony, conceived as "the set of pecuniary and moral assets, obligations and rights of a person, which constitute a universality of law"[16]. Thus, rights of personality play a very important role in Gutiérrez y González's theory, constituting the moral or non-pecuniary part of the patrimony to which the entire Part 6 (Moral or non-pecuniary patrimonial rights. Rights of personality) of his work is devoted (pages 725–1035).

As to the structure, the book comprises 13 chapters, titled as follows:

I.- Rights of personality.

II.- Definition of rights of personality and analysis of the definition.

III.- Moral Patrimony. A. Social-public part. a) Right to honor or reputation. b) Right to title.

IV.- A. Social-public part. c) Right to secrecy or reserve.

V.- A. Social-public part. d) Right to name.

VI.- A. Social-public part. e) Right to aesthetic presence.

VII.- A. Social-public part. f) Rights of coexistence.

VIII.- B. Affective part. g) Rights of affection.

IX.- C. Physical-somatic part. a) Right to life.

X.- C. Physical-somatic part. b) Right to liberty.

XI.- C. Physical-somatic part. c) Right to physical or bodily integrity.

XII.- C. Physical-somatic part. d) Rights related to the human body.

XIII.- C. Physical-somatic part. e) Right over a corpse.

To define rights of personality, the book opens with an analysis of certain definitions (conducted by Francesco Ferrara, Francesco

---

16   Gutiérrez y González, *El Patrimonio*, p. 53.

Degni[17], Mario Rotondi[18], Joaquín Diez Díaz[19] and José Castán Tobeñas[20]) prior to concluding with Gutiérrez y González's own definition, according to which rights of personality "are the goods constituted by certain physical or psychic projections of the human being, related to his physical and mental integrity, attributed to the person himself or to some subjects of law, and which individualized by the legal system".[21]

When discussing the history of rights of personality, the author expressly recognizes Italian legal scholarship:

> And it is precisely the Italian Doctrine that has the merit of studying them in depth — rights of personality — and claiming the category that they have, to extol their enormous transcendence and to achieve the affirmation of the thesis that sustains the existence of true subjective rights[22]

and in a footnote that[23]: "De Cupis Adriano, writes a beautiful work in which he systematizes the issue. It is entitled '*I Diritti della Personalità* and is published as Volume IV, T. I and II of the *Trattato di Diritto Civile e Commerciale* de Cicu-Messineo, 1959".

Thus, the Italian influence on the ideas of the author is not just evident, it is expressly recognized in the terms indicated in the preceding paragraph.

Finally, Gutiérrez y González links non-pecuniary damage to the violation of rights of personality, delving into his work, "Law

---

17 The quotes from Ferrara and Degni are taken from an indirect reference, since as Gutiérrez y González himself points out on page 773, notes 557 and 558, both sources are from the article by José Castán Tobeñas already cited herein. Reviewing this reference, the Spanish master, on page 8, note 4 (reference pointed out by Gutiérrez as the concept of Ferrara) corresponds to the reference to the work of Adriano de Cupis *I diritti della personalità*, and page 8, note 4 does corresponds to Degni's original work *Le persone fisiche e i diritti della personalità*, Torino, 1939, pp. 161 ff.
18 The author takes this reference directly from the work by Rotondi Institutions of Private Law, from Editorial Labor, 1953.
19 This reference is taken directly from the work *Rights of personality or assets of the person?*, RGLJ, June of 1963, Madrid.
20 It is taken directly from the article 'Los derechos de la personalidad'.
21 Gutiérrez y González, *El Patrimonio*, p. 776.
22 Gutiérrez y González, *El Patrimonio*, p. 731
23 Gutiérrez y González, *El Patrimonio*, note 522, p. 731

of obligations", by highlighting: "pecuniary damage affects the economic part of the patrimony, while morality affects the part integrated by the rights of personality..."[24] and it is in this work where he delves into the subject.

b) Ignacio Galindo Garfias[25]

This author, unlike the previous one, frames the issues related to the rights of personality in the rights of the individual, dedicating chapter II (entitled "The rights of personality") to the rights themselves and pages 321 to 340 of the Second Book ("The Right of the Person") to their treatment.

The fact that this author devotes just 19 pages to their study is a clear indication of a superficial treatment of the subject — or in any case that the analysis is much less thorough than what is covered in the 310 pages that Ernesto Gutiérrez y González dedicated to the subject.

Building his chapter based mainly on the works of Francesco Messineo[26], Adriano De Cupis[27], José Castán[28] and Ernesto Gutiérrez[29], Garfias defines the rights of personality as

> those whose purpose is the protection of the essential goods of the person or better, of the personality itself, for the respect due to his category of human being and his dignity, essential qualities for the existence of man and for the development of himself in which his category of subject of law is fully encrypted.[30]

The emphasis that this author places on the link between rights of personality and moral damage is interesting, especially in the part that states:

---

24 E. Gutiérrez y González, *Derecho de las obligaciones* (México: Porrua, 2007), p. 733.
25 I. Galindo, *Derecho Civil. Primer Curso. Parte General. Personas. Familia* (México: Porrúa, 1998).
26 *Manuale di Diritto Civile e Commerciale*, Vol. II, Part I, (Milano: Giuffrè, 1952), cited by Galindo, *Derecho Civil*.
27 de Cupis *I diritti della personalità*.
28 Castán Tobeñas, 'Los derechos de la personalidad'.
29 Gutiérrez y González, *El Patrimonio*.
30 Galindo, pp. 322–23.

The violation of this legal duty to respect such rights of personality compromises the civil liability of the transgressor who violates those rights, and thereby causes damage of a moral, that is to say, not pecuniary nature, to the person who suffers the consequences of that illicit conduct.[31]

He later adds that the liability

is not of a compensatory nature but rather an accused aspect of compensation that in its pecuniary quantification must be freely appreciated by the judge, taking into account the nature of the damage caused, the circumstances and the economic and social position of the agent of the damage.[32]

Undoubtedly, this last idea is found in the Italian doctrine, for instance in the writings of Adriano de Cupis[33], but above all in the works of Francesco Messineo, who very clearly points out: "Injury to the rights of personality is manifested in a damage to the person, but assumes the contours of what has been called non-property damage. The same, as we will see, gives rise to reparation, not compensation […]"[34].

c) Alberto Pacheco Escobedo[35]

In his work, "The person in Mexican civil law", Escobedo dedicates two of the total seven chapters to rights of personality, namely Chapter 3 "The rights of personality. Generalities" (pages 53–75) and Chapter 4 "Rights of personality in particular" (pages 77–133).

The section corresponding to the generalities of rights of personality is based on the works of José Castán, Federico de Castro, Miguel Sancho Izquierdo and Javier Hervada[36], and Jesús García López[37]. In other words, unlike the previous works, it is not based on direct references to Italian doctrine; nonetheless,

---

31 Galindo, p. 336.
32 Galindo, p. 336.
33 de Cupis *I diritti della personalità*, Vol. 1, p. 57
34 F. Messineo, *Manual de Derecho Civil*, Vol. III, p. 4
35 La persona en el Derecho civil mexicano.
36 Compendio de Derecho Natural, EUNSA, 1980. Cited by Galindo, *Derecho Civil*.
37 Los derechos humanos en santo Tomás de Aquino, EUNSA, 1979. Cited by Galindo, *Derecho Civil*.

it is possible to deduce that it indirectly considers Italian ideas, which in turn are included in Spanish doctrine[38].

Finally, it is interesting to point out that this author also links the protection of rights of personality to extracontractual civil liability and, in particular, moral damage[39].

Conclusions

Nowadays, the notion that the consecration and protection of rights inherent to the individual's nature and functional to the enjoyment of his physical, psychic, spiritual, and relationship faculties, is practically accepted as pertaining to Civil law, enshrined in the so-called "rights of personality", irrespective of whether certain of such rights are also considered "human rights".

Mexican law, in one way or another, albeit timidly, recognizes the existence of rights of personality through the legislation of certain states and the contemporary national civil doctrine.

The Italian doctrine on the subject has undoubtedly influenced these formulations, both legislative and doctrinal. This is due to the great systematization achieved predominately by Adriano de Cupis and the diffusion and acceptance of the work of Francesco Messineo in Mexico. It is further due to the influence they had on Spanish doctrine, mainly on José Castán Tobeñas and Federico de Castro.

---

[38] Since an analysis of the influence of the Italian doctrine in Spain would require a much lengthier discussion than suitable for the scope of this contribution, suffice it to say that the works of José Castán and Federico de Castro make frequent and profound references to the Italian doctrine. Thus, albeit indirectly, the Italians did influence Mexican doctrine.

[39] Galindo, pp. 72–75.

Pedro Mendoza Montano[*]

THE DEFINITION OF CONTRACT IN THE PRINCIPLES OF LATIN AMERICAN CONTRACT LAW AND THE INFLUENCE OF THE ITALIAN CIVIL CODE

I. *Importance of including a definition of the contract.*

The opinions regarding whether or not to include a definition of the contract in the normative body that intends to regulate the law of contracts vary and often depends on the legal system from which they come. Some consider that including a definition of the contract does not contribute to the study of the contractual figure nor to its regulation, for which it is sterile; they cling to the Latin expression: *omnis definitio in jure periculosa est*[1]. On the other hand, others attach importance to definitions based on the principle of legal certainty, in the search for legal harmonization and unification, as well as to determine the scope of application of the contract.

In the Anglo-American system, where any type of definition is considered circular, the only thing that could be considered as important to mention would be that it is an agreement that commits at the legal level. In these systems, a single definition of the contract is not contemplated, but several interpretations and conceptions about the contract are abstracted from

---

[*] Lawyer and Notary Public. Professor at Francisco Marroquin University Law, Guatemala City, Guatemala. Master of Laws (LL.M.) Columbia Law School. Licentiate in Juridical and Social Sciences from Francisco Marroquin University Law School. Founding Partner of Iurisconsulti, Abogados y Notarios. pmendoza@iurisconsulti.com.gt. The author would like to thank Domenica Sofía Villeda Ogaldez for her collaboration in the research that was necessary for the preparation of this article.

[1] C. Vattier, J.M. De La Cuesta and J.M. Caballero, *Código Europeo de Contratos. Comentarios en Homenaje al Prof. D. José Luis De Los Mozos Y De Los Mozos*, Vol. I (Madrid: Editorial Dykinson, S.L., 2003), p. 133.

the jurisprudence. Absent the definition of any term in an international or regional harmonizing normative body, it is necessary to analyze the definitions elaborated by the doctrine and jurisprudence of the respective legal systems[2].

On the other hand, most countries whose legal system belongs to the Roman-Germanic tradition define the contract in their respective codes, which, although they may be similar, do not all contain the same characteristics or elements. Such variety of definitions in the different legal systems is the reason why some consider it necessary to include a definition of the concept to be regulated in order to adopt a uniform understanding and ensure the effective application of the norms of the respective regulatory body[3].

However, in international or regional harmonization efforts such as the UNIDROIT Principles and the Principles of European Contract Law (PECL), this same factor was the reason why it was decided not to include a definition of contract. In the case of the UNIDROIT Principles, for example, differences between legal systems did not allow agreement on a unitary definition, and yet it was determined that the absence of a definition should not affect the scope and application of the principles[4].

In the case of Latin America, it is worth noting that Brazil and Paraguay do not include a definition of contract in their civil codes, which most countries do. Consequently, the Principles of Latin American Contract Law (PLDC, by its acronym in Spanish)[5], in accordance with the characteristics of Latin American codes, define contract in an attempt to provide a standard model for

---

[2] D.F. Esborraz, *Contrato y sistema en América Latina* (Santa Fe: Rubinzal Culzoni Editores, 2006), p. 65.

[3] C. Vattier, J.M. De La Cuesta and J.M. Caballero, p. 133.

[4] R. Michaels, 'Purposes and legal nature of the PICC', in S. Vogenauer and J. Kleinheisterkamp (eds.), *Commentary on the Unidroit Principles of International Commercial Contracts (PICC)* (Oxford: Oxford University Press, 2009), p. 32.

[5] R. Momberg, 'Formation of contract under the principles of Latin American contract law', in R. Momberg and S. Vogenauer (eds.), *The future of contract law in Latin America: the principles of Latin American contract law* (Portland: Hart Publishing, 2017), p. 180.

state or international legislators. Such definition also facilitates the uniform application of rules governing the interpretation of international and state laws on contract and related instruments.

II. *Analysis of the definition of Contract in the PLDC*

Article 8 of the PLDC defines contract as "an agreement by which two or more parties create, transfer, modify or terminate a legal contractual relationship of economic content".

Every definition serves to identify what is included in the defined concept and what that is not[6]. To determine the applicability of the regulatory body, it is essential that the premises of the particular case are consistent with the definition; but in order to carry out this analysis, it is necessary to understand each of the elements that comprise the definition itself. Absence of only one of the components would lead to a discrepancy between the definition and the case at hand, and consequently to the non-application of the legal regime on contracts.

The definition of contract provided in the PLDC is made up of the following elements: 1) legal agreement; 2) bilateral or plurilateral agreement; 3) agreement intended to create, terminate, modify or transfer a legal contractual relationship; 4) legal contractual relationship of economic object. Despite the necessary independent explanation of each of the components, it is important to highlight the fact that they should not be considered in isolation, since their value within the meaning of the contract is only perceived if they are considered in connection with each other. Therefore, an agreement that does not contain even one of the components that will be analyzed below will not yield a binding contract under the PLDC.

---

6   V. Roppo, *El Contrato* (Lima: Gaceta Jurídica, S.A., 2009), p. 29.

1. *Legal agreement:*

In most Latin American legal systems, the notion of contract is classified as either a bilateral legal act, convention or legal transaction.

The systems that consider the contract as a bilateral legal act place the concept within the category of legal acts that come from legal facts. Legal acts are defined as lawful voluntary acts whose immediate purpose is to create, modify, transfer or extinguish rights. However, these differ from each other depending on their bilateral (contract) or unilateral (will) character[7]. Most of the Codes elaborated on the basis of the Unpublished Project of 1854 written by A. Bello frame the contract within the genre of lawful voluntary acts with binding effects[8].

On the other hand, the systems that adopt the convention as a genre understand that this concept includes all kinds of agreements between two or more people on an object of legal interest, to create, modify or extinguish obligations. Consequently, the contract is considered as a species that only refers to agreements intended to create obligations, excluding agreements that modify or extinguish obligations (which are considered conventions)[9]. This position had its splendor in France with the 1804 Civil Code and was for a time accepted by a sector of the Argentine doctrine[10]. As a result, the transaction and the transfer of rights were considered as conventions and not as contracts[11]. The Uruguayan Civil Code coincides with this French model and limits the notion of the contract to those conventions through which the parties create an obligatory legal contractual relationship[12]. The Uruguayan legal system also employs the concept of convention to refer to businesses that have

---

7   R.L. Lorenzetti, *Tratado de los contrato. Parte general* (Santa Fe: Rubinzal-Culzoni Editores, 2004), p. 175.
8   Esborraz, p. 73.
9   Lorenzetti, p. 176.
10 Lorenzetti, p. 176.
11 Lorenzetti, p. 177.
12 J. Gamarra, *Tratado de derecho civil uruguayo* (Montevideo: Bianchi, 2012), p. 36.

no legal relevance, such as courtesy relationships and businesses that modify or terminate legal contractual relationships.

Other Latin American systems adhered to the line of thought of the German Pandectist School, which identifies the contract as a subcategory of a broader and higher category: the legal transaction. Legal business is understood as a declaration of explicit will or a conclusive conduct, aimed at producing legal effects[13]. The legal business is differentiated of the contract by dispensing with the elements of bilaterality and patrimonial nature, constituting a much more general figure. The term reduces all the possible manifestations of private autonomy, including those of family law, inheritance law and patrimonial law, to a conceptual unit, i.e., the legal transaction[14].

The PLDC avoided placing the contract within any of the aforementioned categories and opted for a much more neutral and universal terminology: the agreement. This concept is not the one commonly used in Latin American civil codes, but it harmonizes the different positions, assuring and basing the binding nature of contracts on the will of the parties[15]. The term "agreement" implies the existence of a consent between the parties to the contract and is related to the meeting of minds.

A sector of the doctrine understands consent as the meeting of two manifestations of will of diverse, opposite and correlative content that respond to different purposes and interests[16]. It is that contrast and correlativity of the different interests and purposes that, when carried out jointly, lead to the conclusion of a contract. Another sector of the doctrine recognizes that there is consent when the parties coincide in an identical regulation of their interests[17]. Therefore, although the interests are opposed, the expressions of will coincide in identical content. In the end, the use of the term "agreement" manages to indirectly include

---

13 Roppo, p. 85.
14 Esborraz, p. 66.
15 Momberg and Vogenauer, p. 181.
16 J.M. Aparicio, *Contratos. Parte General*, 2nd edn, Vol. I (Buenos Aires: Editorial Hammurabi, 2016), p. 50.
17 Aparicio, p. 51.

in its definition the necessary presence of manifestations of the participants' will, without the need to incur in the discussion of whether it is a meeting of the minds or a coincidence of wills.

This definition also manages to clarify the two meanings in which the word "contract" can be understood: the act that the contracting parties carry out (contract as an act) and the binding normative result that occurs between the contracting parties as a consequence of the act celebrated (contract as a norm)[18].

The contract as an act necessarily implies the existence of expressions of will of the contracting parties[19]. This is because the absence of a party's intrinsic will does not prevent the conclusion of the contract when the parties have performed certain acts directed at reaching an agreement. Under this notion of the contract, the actions of the interested parties to which the legal system attributes certain effects are essential for the formation of a binding contract[20].

On the contrary, when dealing with the contract as a norm, it appears as a precept or rule of conduct to which the contracting parties submit their own behavior[21]. The contract is considered as an autonomous and conventional rule because it derives from the consent of the parties and not from external authoritarian power[22].

The inclusion of the term "agreement" in the definition of the contract in the PLDC prevents the notion of the contract from being categorized according to the typologies of the Latin American systems, achieving a conceptual unification and, at the same time, contemplating the meanings of the contract — contract as an act and as a rule.

---

[18] L. Díez-Picazo, *Fundamentos del derecho civil patrimonial: introducción teoría del contrato*, 6th edn, Vol. I (Pamplona: Editorial Aranzadi, S.A., 2007), p. 139.

[19] C.M. Bianca, *Derecho Civil. 3. El contrato*, trans. by Fernando Hinestrosa and Édgar Cortés (Bogotá: Colombia Universidad Externado de Colombia, 2007), p. 27.

[20] Díez-Picazo, p. 139.

[21] Díez-Picazo, p. 139.

[22] Bianca, p. 28.

2. Bilateral or plurilateral agreement:

The PLDC establish that there can only be a contract if two or more parties participate in the agreement. The definition not only contemplates bilateral contracts, but also recognizes plurilateral contracts between more than two centers of interest, as is usually the case with corporate contracts. This classification comes from the category of legal acts according to the number of parties involved in the conclusion of the contract.

In addition, the use of the term "parties" instead of "persons" is due to the fact that the Principles take into consideration that each of the contracting parties may be made up of one or more natural or legal persons. In a contract, the "party" is not synonymous with a person, but rather is a center of interest that declares its intent[23]. It is recognized then that, in a legal act, several people may tend to the realization of the same interest and act in the same direction; which is why they are considered as a single party in contractual matters. Therefore, a party is a center of interest that manifests the will and to which rights and obligations are conferred[24].

3. Agreement intended to create, terminate, modify or transfer a legal contractual relationship:

The purpose of the contract in the PLDC is both to create a legal contractual relationship and to modify, transfer or terminate it. As previously clarified, because the Principles use the term "agreement", it manages to encompass all the aforementioned purposes and does not exclude them from the contractual scope (as happens, for example, when the contract is categorized as a kind of convention)[25].

It is interesting to note that, unlike the terminology used in some of the Latin American codes (Argentina, Peru, Bolivia), the Principles opted for the term "legal contractual relationship"

---

23   Lorenzetti, p. 179.
24   Aparicio, p. 48.
25   Momberg and Vogenauer, p. 181.

instead of "legal relationship". This draws attention because there are authors who claim that the reason behind the use of the term "legal relationship" is due to the express exclusion of the constitution or transfer of real rights[26]. Following the doctrinal position of Díez-Picazo, the legal relationship is necessarily a relationship between people, and it is not admissible to allude that it also refers to the situation in which a person finds himself with respect to a thing[27].

A) Create a legal contractual relationship

This is the typical function of contracts, the creation or formation of legal relationships that satisfy the needs or interests of the parties. Safeguarding the legal limitations that each legal system observes, the parties are free to determine its content and obligations (regulatory or configuration freedom), being able to use both typical and atypical contracts[28].

B) Modify a legal contractual relationship

It is common for the parties to a contract to wish to alter its substance, without extinguishing it, to suit their interests or for reasons not foreseen at the time the obligation was constituted[29]. The important thing to note under these circumstances is that the mandatory legal bond remains the same, despite the changes made to its content.

C) Transfer a legal contractual relationship

The transfer of a contract implies that one party transfers its contractual position to another party. That is, said party has the rights and obligations over which it has ownership by virtue of a legal contractual relationship. Through the transfer, a new legal relationship is not being extinguished or created, since the link remains the same. However, some authors maintain that the transfer is a type of modification, since, due to the fact that the

---

26 M. De la Puente y Lavalle, *El contrato en general. Comentarios de la Sección Primera del Libro VII del Código Civil*, 2nd edn, Vol. I (Lima: Palestra Editores, S.A.C., 2007), p. 71.
27 Díez-Picazo, p. 73.
28 De la Puente y Lavalle, p. 65.
29 De la Puente y Lavalle, p. 66.

original legal link persists, only one of the parties to said link is being modified.

D) Extinguish a legal contractual relationship

The extinction or termination of a contract occurs when the parties by mutual agreement decide to put an end to it, prior to its fulfillment, either by totally disassociating themselves from it or deciding to bind themselves through a different contractual legal relationship[30]. It is essential to highlight that the process of termination of the contractual relationship contemplated in this point is carried out voluntarily by the parties, as this is their interest, without the need for any judicial pronouncement.

4. *Legal contractual relationship of economic object:*

The PLDC not only consider the link between the parties by way of contract as legal, but also expressly refer to its economic nature. One of the objectives of the Principles is to exclude agreements from the private sphere that only produce moral or social obligations, in which case their forced execution cannot be demanded[31]. The important thing is that the relationships have legal significance, because there are other types of social relationships such as those of courtesy, which, although they have the outward appearance of a contract, their breach does not generate legal consequences[32]; breach of these arrangements may only be sanctioned by social disapproval, for instance.

This characteristic also has the effect of restricting the scope of the contract only to affairs with economic content[33]. In accordance with the Principles, the purpose of the contract is to create, terminate, modify or transfer legal relationships. However, by establishing that the legal bond must necessarily have an economic connotation, said bond must consequently refer to obligations made up of benefits that can be valued economically.

---

30 De la Puente y Lavalle, p. 67.
31 Momberg and Vogenauer, p. 180.
32 Aparicio, p. 53.
33 Momberg and Vogenauer, p. 180.

Other articles of the PLDC make constant reference to the value of the performance, making it necessary for the content of the contract to be susceptible to economic valuation[34]. The aim of most patrimonial theories on contract is, therefore, to exclude from the definition of a binding agreement all types of bilateral legal acts that do not have patrimonial content[35].

III. *Criticism of the patrimonial or economic component of the contract definition*

The necessary patrimonial nature of the contract was identified by Savigny and other jurists as a requirement of Roman law, clarifying that not only the performance should be patrimonial, but also the interest of the creditor[36]. However, the scholars Ihering and Windsheid concluded, on the basis of the same texts of Roman law, that the patrimonial nature of the contract was not an essential requirement of the benefit. According to this theory, the right to benefit from the performance of an obligation does not depend on the fulfillment of a mere economic interest; rather, the performance of an obligation can fulfill all kinds of interests insofar as they are lawful and moral[37]. Ihering and Windsheid purport that even an interest that is not purely economic can have an indirect economic value. In this sense, in the case of legal relationships that lack of patrimonial content, compensatory damages are aimed more at punishing the breaching party than repairing harm[38].

This doctrine can be found in paragraph 241 of the German Civil Code (BGB), which establishes that the performance of an obligation may also consist of an omission. According to some authors, the mention of an interest of a pecuniary nature has been avoided on purpose, since the Code does not require

---

34 For example, articles: 96, 111, 113 and 115 among others.
35 Aparicio, p. 55.
36 A. Hernández-Gil, *Derecho de obligaciones* (Madrid:), p. 109.
37 Hernández-Gil, p. 110.
38 Hernández-Gil, p. 110.

the existence of a pecuniary interest of the creditor, nor for the obligation to deal with a performance that can be acquired with money[39].

Additionally, paragraph 241.2 of the BGB, in defining the content of the duties that derive from the obligation, distinguishes between the so-called "duties of protection" (*Schutzpflichten*) and the "duty of provision" (*Leistungspflicht*). This means that, under German law, the debtor and creditor are mutually obliged to respect the rights, legal assets or interests of the other party. Consequently, paragraph 282 of the BGB provides compensation as a penalty and not as reparation for the violation of these duties[40].

Later, Scialoja discerns between the provision of the obligation and the interest of the creditor. His position is that the creditor's interest does not need to be of a patrimonial nature and could refer to human, scientific or moral reasons; while the provision should be subject to an economic assessment, since, otherwise, it would not be possible to demand its specific performance at the debtor's expense[41]. Article 1174 of the Italian Civil Code adopted this approach by establishing that the obligation must be susceptible to economic valuation and correspond to an interest of the creditor, even when it is not patrimonial[42]. According to this latter approach, a legal relationship is patrimonial when the provision can be subject to economic valuation, regardless of whether or not the interest of the creditor is of an economic nature.

Likewise, this author explains that the responsibility derived from moral damage and the consequent compensation has the rank of a general principle of law. If the patrimonial nature of the provision were upheld as a necessary requirement, it would not

---

39 Hernández-Gil, p. 110.
40 A. Lamarca, *Entra en vigor la ley de modernización del derecho alemán de obligaciones* (Barcelona: Indret, 2002), p. 5. Available at: https://dialnet.unirioja.es/servlet/articulo?codigo=235323.
41 De la Puente y Lavalle, p. 83.
42 P. Allo, *Trattato di Diritto Civile. Il Contratto*, (Torino: Giappichelli, 2017), p. 36.

be possible to compensate for non-pecuniary damage because its original object was devoid of patrimonial value[43]. However, in practice, due compensation is recognized, because legal consequences are recognized for this non-economic provision.

When analyzing the inherent consequences of all obligations, it is identified that the first of them is the susceptibility of its fulfillment through the voluntary conduct of the debtor. Given this situation, there is no problem with the contract being about non-patrimonial legal relations. Now, if the debtor fails to comply, the creditor can request a court order for specific performance or resolution, in addition (in both cases) to compensation for damages[44].

These remedies for breach are not available if the provision lacks patrimonial value. In the first place, it is indisputable that the creditor's right to terminate is not impeded in any way. Second, if the creditor opted for specific performance, it would in any case be possible to make a non-patrimonial performance If the provision is to deliver, steps are taken to cause such performance. If the provision is a *facere*, the judge sets a deadline for the debtor to perform at his expense; and the same happens with provisions requiring omission of an act[45]. As for damages equivalent of performance, there is no problem when they fulfill their punitive function. Consider, for example, the payment of damages for breach of a service or provision of a very personal nature; its very nature suggests that it cannot be measured by a strictly economic criterion[46].

However, Hernández-Gil also recognizes that the only problem with respect to non-economically valuable benefits refers to the assumption that creditors are entitled to pay damages in lieu of performance, and that such payment fulfills a reparatory function[47]. The issue relates directly to creditors' rights, and in this case excludes the availability of certain remedies suitable

---

43 Allo, p. 113.
44 Allo, p. 113.
45 Allo, p. 114.
46 Allo, p. 115.
47 Allo, p. 116.

to satisfy his interests. However, this does not justify failing to recognize obligations without economic value, as unavailability of one remedy should not exclude the availability of all others[48].

Finally, if in any case it is considered that damages are an ill-suited remedy for breach of non-patrimonial obligations, it follows that the latter constitute imperfect obligations — which may in any case arise from a contract.

In conclusion, contracts should not be defined by the economic aspects of the obligations envisaged therein since, as explained, such are not required to give rise to legal effects under the law of obligations.

IV. *Comparative analysis of the definition of contract*

Next, the definition established in the PLDC will be compared with the different definitions of contract contemplated in some Latin American and European Civil Codes, as well as with the prevailing conceptions in Anglo-American Law.

1. *Latin America*

The Civil and Commercial Code of the Nation of Argentina defines the contract at article 957 as "the legal act by which two or more parties express their consent to create, regulate, modify, transfer or extinguish legal patrimonial relations". This definition is very similar to the one contemplated in the PLDC, except that the Argentinian Code considers the contract as a kind of legal act and as such makes express reference to consent[49].

Also categorizing the contract as a legal act, the Chilean Civil Code in its article 1438, as well as the Colombian Civil Code in its article 1495, establish that the "[c]ontract or agreement is an act by which one party is bound to another to give, to do or not to do something. Each party can be one or many people".

---

48 Allo, p. 116.
49 Lorenzetti, p. 532.

This definition refers to the contract as a synonym of convention, since the basis of these codes (i.e., the project prepared by A. Bello from 1841-1845) contains various meanings of the term. However, both the Chilean and Colombian Civil Codes place the contract (or convention) as a kind of lawful legal acts with binding effects[50].

The Peruvian Civil Code establishes, in its article 1351, that "the contract is the agreement of two or more parties to create, regulate, modify or extinguish a legal patrimonial relationship". This definition is similar to the definition adopted by the Italian Civil Code in its article 1321, which defines the contract as an agreement. In addition, Peruvian authors have highlighted the fact that the use of the term "patrimonial legal relationship" instead of "obligation legal relationship" is intended to ensure that the contract only creates obligations and that it does not produce real effects[51]. This definition is the one that bears the greatest similarity to that contemplated in the PLDC, the only differences being that it does not contemplate transmission as the purpose of the contract and that it uses the term legal contractual relationship of an economic nature.

Instead, the Federal District of Mexico Civil Code specifically classifies the contract as a species of the convention[52]. In this sense, article 1792 establishes that "[c]onvention is the agreement of two or more people to create, transfer, modify or extinguish obligations", and article 1793 clarifies that "[a]greements that produce or transfer obligations and rights, take the name of contracts". As previously stated, the PLDC are distinct from the theory of the contract as a kind of agreement, because they also identify as a contract the agreements that extinguish or modify the obligations.

Pursuant to article 1517 of the Guatemalan Civil Code, "[t]here is a contract when two or more people agree to create, modify or extinguish an obligation". In the Guatemalan legal system, the contract is a kind of legal transaction, a figure that is

---

50 Esborraz, p. 73.
51 De la Puente y Lavalle, p. 52.
52 Esborraz, p. 102.

also regulated in said normative body. Additionally, the validity of the contract depends on compliance with the rules specific to the genre of legal transaction contemplated therein.

Unlike the previous Codes, the Brazilian Civil Code intentionally avoided providing a definition of contract. This is because, under the influence of the German doctrine of the late 19th century, it was determined that the formulation of definitions should be left to legal science and not the legislator[53]. However, through the definition of legal transaction contemplated by the Brazilian code, it can be deduced that "contract" is a species of the genus "legal transaction", which is a species of "lawful legal act"[54].

2. *Europe*

In France, in 2016, the law of contracts contemplated in the Civil Code was reformed. The new article 1101 defines the contract as "an agreement between two or several persons intended to create, modify, transmit or extinguish obligations"[55]. The intention of the reform was to reinforce the idea that the contract is a legal act that requires a meeting of minds and distinguish it from the convention as a source of obligation. Consequently, the reform removed the term "convention" disappeared from the text of the code, since the convention (unlike the contract) refers only to acts of generosity and assistance (*gentlemen's agreement*)[56].

As in Brazil, the German BGB does not contemplate a definition of contract. German doctrine, however, defines the contract as the regulation of a legal relationship adopted consensually by the parties in which both consent to the production of a legal result[57]. The inclusion of the expressed consent (or will) of the parties among

---

53 Esborraz, p. 92.
54 Esborraz, p. 93.
55 S. Sánchez Lorenzo, *Derecho Contractual Comparado. Una Perspectiva Europea y Transnacional*, 3rd edn, Vol. I (Navarra: Editorial Aranzadi, S.A.U., 2016), p. 254.
56 Sánchez Lorenzo, p. 254.
57 Sánchez Lorenzo, p. 288.

the essential elements of the contract highlights the fact that, in Germany, the contract is considered as a type of legal transaction[58]. Accordingly, despite there is no section in the BGB dedicated to contracts, the rules relating to the genre of legal affairs are applied and there is a specific section containing rules on contractual relationships in the book dedicated to the law of obligations[59].

3. *Anglo-American Law*

On the other hand, Anglo-American law derives its contract law from Common Law, i.e., the case law of the courts. Despite the fact that there are some normative texts (Statutes), they are not concerned with defining a contract, but rather adopt the general theory of contract developed and established by jurisprudence[60]. English judges in the second half of the 19th century produced contract law of a clearly commercial nature, conceiving the contract as a mechanism designed to facilitate traffic between persons generally capable of asserting their own interests[61].

The following definition of contract can be inferred from common law jurisprudence: "a contract is an agreement that is legally binding because it is supported by consideration or made by deed, it is certain and complete, it is made with the intention to create legal relations and it complies with any formal requirement needed for the existence of the agreement"[62].

On the other hand, in US contract law, a commonly accepted definition of contract is found in the "Restatement (Second) of Contracts". The Restatements prepared by the American Law

---

58 H.S. Moreno, 'Definición de contrato y acto jurídico', in A. Vaquer Alor, E. Bosch Capdevila and M. Paz Sánchez González (eds.), *Derecho Europeo de Contratos: Libros II y IV del Marco Común de Referencia*, Vol. I (Barcelona: Atelier, 2012), p. 78.
59 Sánchez Lorenzo, p. 288.
60 J. Cartwright, *An Introduction to the English Law of Contract for the Civil Lawyer*, 3rd edn, trans. by Juan Pablo Murga Fernández (Universidad de Sevilla: Hart Publishing, 2016), p. 2.
61 Cartwright, p. 2.
62 A. Burrows, *A Restatement of the English Law of Contract* (Oxford: Oxford University Press, 2016), p. 44.

Institute seek to provide a systematic exposition of the jurisprudence of the different States, and contain definitions to avoid the risk of excessive particularism in the law of each State[63]. The Restatement (Second) of Contracts defines the contract as: "a promise or a set of promises for the breach of which the law gives a remedy, or the performance of which the law in some way recognizes as a duty"[64]. Additionally, the respective comments clarify why consideration is a requirement of enforceability, as well as why some cases call for the fulfillment of formal requirements.

Indeed, the Anglo-American legal notion of contract is linked to the doctrine of consideration. In essence, it requires the contract be onerous, implying a necessary exchange of benefits: a bilateral and onerous legal transaction in which each party performs a benefit or promises something in exchange for the promise or benefit of the other party. Consequently, in Anglo-American law, the donation (or the promise of donation) and other gratuitous acts are not considered "contracts"[65].

Additionally, it is important to understand that Roman-Germanic legal systems usually distinguish between a series of general principles applicable to all contracts and a set of special principles and rules applicable to each type of contract. In contrast, in Anglo-American law, all contracts are governed by the same general principles: a general rule for the formation or perfection of all contracts and a general rule for the content of contracts, as well as for derivative remedies for breach[66].

That is why, in Anglo-American law, implied terms (the terms or conditions/implicit clauses of the contract) are used to supplement contracts that are incomplete or imprecise due to the parties' failure to fully discipline all aspects upon signing. Implied terms may appear similar to the legal rules of Roman-German law relating a specific type of contract, insofar as they are contractual clauses or terms established by the courts and

---

63 S. Sánchez Lorenzo, p. 392.
64 Restatement (Second) of the Law of Contract § 1 (Am. Law Inst. 1981).
65 Cartwright, p. 8.
66 Cartwright, p. 4.

which must be integrated in a general and implicit way in certain contractual types[67].

It follows, then, that the notion of contract in Anglo-American law is different from that in Roman-Germanic law: a contract is a legally binding agreement or promise which, when certain formal requirements (including consideration) are met, are recognized by law and give rise to the availability of certain remedies in the event of breach.

V. *Comparative analysis of the definition of contract provided in the Principles of Latin American Contract Law and the Italian Civil Code.*

Article 1321 of the Italian Civil Code defines the contract as the "agreement of two or more parties aimed at establishing, regulating or extinguish a patrimonial legal relationship existing between them", while, as we have already seen, the PLDC define the contract as "an agreement by which two or more parties create, transfer, modify or terminate a legal relationship having economic content".

Next, we proceed to compare the elements of the above legal definitions.

	PLDC	Italian Civil Code
1	Legal agreement.	Legal agreement.
2	Bilateral or plurilateral agreement.	Bilateral or plurilateral agreement.
3	Agreement intended to create, terminate, modify or transfer a legal relationship.	Agreement intended to establish, regulate or terminate a legal relationship.
4	Legal relationship of economic content.	Legal patrimonial relationship.

---

67 Cartwright, p. 4.

1. First component:

As reflected in the comparative table above, both definitions establish a contract is a legal agreement.

The Dictionary of the Spanish Language of the Real Spanish Academy (RAE Dictionary) defines the word "agreement" as "action and effect of agreeing", "agreement between two or more parties", "with agreement or equal opinion"[68]. And the word "legal" is defined as "permitted by or relating to the law"[69]. It follows that the term "legal agreement" is the agreement between two or more parts that is relevant to or may be affected by the law.

In section II, item 1 of this chapter, it was mentioned that the term "agreement" implies the consent between the parties to the contract and relates to the meeting of minds. On the other hand, this definition also manages to clarify the two meanings in which the word "contract" can be understood: the act that the contracting parties carry out (contract as an act) and the binding normative result that occurs between the contracting parties by a celebrated act (contract as a rule)[70].

Unlike some European Civil Codes (e.g., the Italian and French codes), which use the more neutral and universal term "agreement" and thus avoid conflict between legal systems, this terminology is not widespread in Latin American civil codes despite its adoption in the PLDC. One might surmise, then, that the Italian Civil Code has influenced the PLDC regarding this first element of the definition of contract.

2. Second component:

Both the PLDC and the Italian Civil Code define the contract as a bilateral or plurilateral agreement.

---

68 Real Spain Academy Website, available at: https://dle.rae.es/acuerdo?m=form.
69 Real Spain Academy Website, available at: https://dle.rae.es/jur%C3%ADdico%20?m=form.
70 Díez-Picazo, p. 139.

Section II, item 2 of this chapter notes that two or more parties are required to form a contract. It also clarifies that the term "parties" (and not "persons") reflects the fact that natural and legal persons can enter into contract, and that the term represents a center of interest (which is why it is not synonymous with "person") that makes a declaration of will[71].

The contract is used to organize and regulate various (sometimes competing) individual interests. In this regard, it is enough to consider that a regulation of such conflicts could not be solved through private autonomy, but through coordination between the different concerned parties[72].

Some authors submit that the notion of contract as regulated in the manners illustrated above does not support the so-called plurilateral contract (which, either at its formation or subsequently, involves more than two parts). For instance, they observe that the typical plurilateral contract involves multiple parties whose interests are aligned for a common purpose, thus creating (better than a contract) a collective act in a technical sense; instead, in hypotheses where several parties each have their own agenda or position, it is more appropriate to speak of agreement and not about a plurilateral contract[73].

However, this position is contrary to the definitions contained in the PLCD and the Italian Civil Code, which both clearly provide for multiple parties to a contract. Moreover, the Italian Civil Code contains dedicated rules on agreements between more than two parties (e.g. articles 1420, 1446 and 1459, among others) in which several obligations are established to achieve a common purpose. Since these rules expressly refer to contracts (between several parties) and are limited to establishing, in accordance with the general principle of conservation of the contract, that the invalidity or ineffectiveness of the link with regard to one party does not determine the invalidity or ineffectiveness of the

---

71 Lorenzetti, p. 179.
72 R. Scognamiglio, *Teoría General del Contrato*, trans. by Fernando Hinestrosa (Bogotá: Universidad Externado de Colombia, 1991), p. 24.
73 Scognamiglio, p. 24.

contract as a whole[74], it is expected that the PLCDs will adopt this same approach.

3. *Third component:*

The third component of the definitions under analysis differs in that under the PLCD a contract is an "agreement intended to create, extinguish, modify or transfer a legal contractual relationship", whereas the Italian Civil Code establishes a contract is an "agreement destined to constitute, regulate or extinguish a legal relationship".

The following table shows the comparison more clearly regarding the regulation of this component:

Italian Civil Code	PLDC
Agreement	Agreement
Constitute	Create
Regulate	
Extinguish	Extinguish
	Modify
	Transfer
Legal relationship	Legal contractual relationship

a) The term "agreement" was discussed earlier in this chapter, so we will proceed to examine the functions of said agreement in the different contract definitions.

b) In the Italian Civil Code, the word "constitute" is used, while in the PLDC uses the word "create", so the question arises as to whether these terms could be taken as synonyms. The term "constitute", according to the Dictionary of The Real Spain Academy means "Establish, erect, found" or "Form, compose, be"[75] and "create", it can be defined, according to the same dictionary, as "Producing something new" or "Produce

---

74 Scognamiglio, p. 24.
75 Real Spain Academy Website, available at: https://dle.rae.es/constituir.

something from nothing"[76]. There is no substantial difference between these two words, so they could be considered to refer to the same thing.

c) In the two definitions of contract, we see the word "extinguish", a term that has been developed earlier in this chapter, so in terms of this function, the Italian Civil Code and the PLDC coincide.

d) It is noted that the Italian Civil Code refers to a contract as an agreement whose purpose is to regulate legal relationships, which is not established in the PLDC. The word "regulate", according to the Real Spain Academy Dictionary means to "measure, adjust or compute something by comparison or deduction" or "adjust, regulate or put something in order"[77]. However, the PLDCs add several other functions, such as "modify" or "transfer"— terms that have already been analyzed in this chapter. One can surmise that these terms intend to cover the same content, so one definition is not considered broader than the other.

e) As to whether it is a legal relationship or a legal contractual relationship, it is necessary analyze these terms. "Bond" according to the RAE Dictionary, refers to "union or binding of one person or thing with another"[78], while "relation", according to this same dictionary, means the "connection, correspondence of something with another thing"[79].

If the word "legal" is added to these terms, "legal relationship" could be defined as the union or tie of a person or thing with another regulated by the right, and "legal contractual relationship" as the connection or correspondence of something with something else regulated by law. Thus, it is concluded that conceptually these terms could not be separated, since they refer to the same thing.

---

76 Real Spain Academy Website, available at: https://dle.rae.es/crear?m=form.
77 Real Spain Academy Website, available at: https://dle.rae.es/regular?m=form.
78 Real Spain Academy Website, available at: https://dle.rae.es/v%C3%ADnculo.
79 Real Spain Academy Website, available at: https://dle.rae.es/relaci%C3%B3n?m=form.

4. Forth component:

After having concluded that the meaning of legal contractual relationship and legal relationship are similar, it is observed that comparing "legal contractual relationship of economic content" and "patrimonial legal relationship" is pointless, since "economic content" or "patrimonial content" also refer to the same thing.

Adding to what was discussed above in relation to the economic content of the contract, Vicenzo Roppo maintains that an obligation must have economic relevance for the same reason contracts necessarily deal with economic interests. Since both the obligation and the contract are characterized by the legal contractual relationship and are subject to coercibility (meaning the legal commitment cannot be freely disregarded or revoked), non-performance or breach must be met with adequate remedies: specific performance or compensation for equivalent. Non-economic relationships do not give rise to the same remedies, either for policy reasons or due to lack of feasibility. In terms of policy, it is undesirable to subject behaviors and attitudes belonging to the personal sphere to the same rules, e.g., irrevocability or specific performance- governing legal contractual relationships. With regard to feasibility, it is sufficient to consider the difficulty of determining the economic value — for the purpose of establishing equivalent compensation — of commitments which are not subject to economic valuation[80].

These considerations appear to have been incorporated in both the PLDC and the Italian Civil Code.

5. Conclusion of the analysis:

A careful comparative analysis of the elements of the definitions of contract contained in the PLDC and the Italian Civil Code reveals a general similarity. Therefore, one can only infer that the Italian Civil Code undoubtedly influenced the definition of contract under the PLDC.

---

80   Roppo, p. 31.

LORENZO MEZZASOMA[*]

CONTRACT LAW, PANDEMIC AND THE PRINCIPLE OF SOLIDARITY IN THE ITALIAN LEGAL SYSTEM

1. *Foreword: delimitation of the subject of investigation*

The issues of contractual asymmetry[1] and contractual equilibrium[2] — which in recent years have led us to discuss

---

[*] Full Professor of Private Law at Università degli Studi di Perugia.
[1] See, *ex multis*, P. Perlingieri, *Nuovi profili del contratto*, in *Rass. dir. civ.*, 2000, pp. 545 ff.; Id., *La tutela del contraente debole*, in *Riv. giur. Molise e Sannio*, 2011, pp. 101 ff.; V. Roppo, *Contratto di diritto comune, contratto del consumatore, contratto con asimmetria di potere contrattuale: genesi e sviluppi di un nuovo paradigma*, in S. Mazzamuto (ed.), *Il contratto e le tutele. Prospettive di diritto europeo*, Turin, 2002, pp. 83 ff.; V. Rizzo, *Contratti del consumatore e diritto comune dei contratti*, in R. Favale and B. Marucci (*eds.*), *Studi in memoria di Vincenzo Ernesto Cantelmo*, II, Naples, 2003, pp. 620 ff.; F. Romeo, *Contratti asimmetrici, codici di settore e tutela del contraente debole*, in *Obbl. contr.*, 2012, pp. 440 ff.; L. Mezzasoma, *Novità del diritto contrattuale in Italia e tutela del contraente debole*, in *Corti umbre*, 2014, pp. 919 ff.; Id., *Disciplina del contrato, tutela del contrante mas débil y valor Constitucional*, in *Derecho Privado y Constituciòn*, no. 29/2015, pp. 187 ff.
[2] The literature on contractual balance and, more generally, contractual justice is particularly extensive. Among the many, without claiming completeness, see P. Perlingieri, *Equilibrio normativo e principio di proporzionalità nei contratti*, in *Rass. dir. civ.*, 2001, p. 334 ff. and *Il diritto dei contratti fra persona e mercato. Problemi di diritto civile*, Naples, 2003, pp. 441 ff.; P. Perlingieri, *Diritto dei contratti e dei mercati*, in *Rass. dir. civ.*, 2011, pp. 877 ff.; P. Perlingieri, *Il "giusto rimedio" nel diritto civile*, in *Giusto proc. civ.*, 2011, pp. 3 ff.; P. Perlingieri, *Sui contratti iniqui*, in *Rass. dir. civ*, 2013, pp. 480 ff.; L. Ferroni (ed.), *Equilibrio delle posizioni contrattuali ed autonomia privata*, Naples, 2002; F. Volpe, *La rilevanza dello squilibrio contrattuale nel diritto dei contratti*, in *Riv. dir. priv.*, 2002, pp. 303 ff.; F. Volpe, *La giustizia contrattuale tra autonomia e mercato*, Naples, 2004; D. Russo, *Giustizia del contratto e sindacato giudiziale*, in *Rass. dir. civ.*, 2004, pp. 1097 ff.; M. Barcellona, *Sulla giustizia sociale nel diritto europeo dei contratti*, in *Eur. dir. priv.*, 2005, pp. 630 ff.; F. Galgano, *Libertà contrattuale e giustizia del*

so much about consumer protection, the weak contractor and the weak entrepreneur[3] — impose new reflections in light of the consequences of the pandemic and related emergency legislation[4].

And if this debate has concerned the moment of the contract's establishment, we now necessarily move to the phase of its execution and, in particular, to the execution of contracts of duration. Indeed, the pandemic has affected the execution of contracts, giving rise to situations that were certainly unforeseeable and unavoidable, and resulting in either the impossibility of performance or a supervening imbalance of performance[5].

---

contratto, in *Contr. impr./Eur.*, 2005, pp. 509 ff.; U. Perfetti, *L'ingiustizia del contratto*, Milan, 2005, *passim*; Id., *La giustizia contrattuale nel Draft Common Frame of Reference del diritto privato europeo*, in *Riv. dir. civ*, 2009, II, pp. 669 ff.; L.V. Moscarini, *Riflessioni sul tema del "contratto giusto"*, in *Studi in onore di Cesare Maria Bianca*, 2, Milan, 2006, pp. 617 ff.; R. Messinetti, *Il "falso" problema normativo della giustizia contrattuale*, in *Riv. crit. dir. priv*, 2009, pp. 615 ff.; N. Lipari, *Persona e mercato*, in *Riv. trim.*, 2010, pp. 755 ff.; F. Camilletti, *Profili dell'equilibrio contrattuale*, Milan, 2011; A. Di Majo, *Giustizia e materializzazione nel diritto delle obbligazioni e dei contratti tra (regole) di fattispecie e (regole) di procedura*, in *Eur. dir. priv*, 2013, pp. 797 ff.; M. Spinozzi, *Equilibrio contrattuale eterodeterminato*, Naples, 2013; L. Scarano, *Riflessioni sulla giustizia contrattuale fra redistribuzione sociale ed efficienza economica*, in *Riv. dir. priv.*, 2014, pp. 61 ff.; F. Piraino, *Il diritto europeo e la "giustizia contrattuale"*, in *Eur. dir. priv.*, 2015, pp. 233 ff.

3 On the subject, see B. Agostinelli, *L'imprenditore debole*, Turin, 2005; E. Russo, *Imprenditore debole, imprenditore-persona, abuso di dipendenza economica, "terzo contratto"*, in *Contr. impr.*, 2009, pp. 120 ff.; F. Ruscello (ed.), *Contratti tra imprese e tutela dell'imprenditore. Proceedings of the conference*, Roma, 2012 and the contributions therein.

4 In the Italian legal system, the normative recognition of the "state of emergency" occurred with the Resolution of the Council of Ministers January 31, 2020, Declaration of the state of emergency as a result of the health risk related to the outbreak of diseases resulting from transmissible viral agents (*Dichiarazione dello stato di emergenza in conseguenza del rischio sanitario connesso all'insorgenza di patologie derivanti da agenti virali trasmissibili*).

5 Such an issue has been addressed, among others, by F. Piraino, *Osservazioni intorno a sopravvenienze e rimedi nei contratti di durata*, in *Eur. dir. priv.*, 2019, pp. 585 ff.; G. Alpa, *Note in margine agli effetti della pandemia sui contratti di durata*, in *Nuova giur. civ. comm.*, supplement 3/2020, pp. 57 ff.; V. Barba, *I rapporti contrattuali nel periodo di pandemia tra norme*

At the same time, the traditional institutions of civil law, such as contract termination due to supervening impossibility[6] or termination due to supervening excessive onerousness, do not seem adequate to deal with the new emergencies[7]. The dissolution of the contractual bond only in residual cases may be the solution to the unbalanced situation, while the maintenance of the contractual relationship, the overcoming of the emergency, and the recovery of the activity at the end of the pandemic, represent instead the real objective that has been — and must — be pursued to protect economic initiative (constitutionally guaranteed) and the country's economy.

The question that arises and which we must ask ourselves is, then, how to cope with these situations — all within a framework of the relevance of constitutional principles.

Indeed, it cannot be understated that in this context, too, constitutional solidarity[8] (the *fraternité* that was already

---

emergenziali e diritto comune, in *Bilancio comunità persona*, 2020, pp. 14 ff.; N. Cipriani, *L'impatto del lockdown da COVID-19 sui contratti*, in *Riv. dir. banc.*, 2020, I, pp. 655 ff.; C. Masciopinto, *I contratti in corso di esecuzione e l'attuale emergenza sanitaria*, 2020, pp. 449 ff.

6   On supervening impossibility, *ex multis*, see G. Cottino, *L'impossibilità sopravvenuta della prestazione e la responsabilità del debitore*, Milan, 1955; G. Osti, *Impossibilità sopravveniente*, in *Noviss. Dig. it.*, VIII, Turin, 1962, pp. 487 ff.; U. Breccia, *Le obbligazioni*, in G. Iudica and P. Zatti (eds.), *Trattato di diritto privato*, Milan, 1991; L. Cabella Pisu, *La risoluzione per impossibilità sopravvenuta*, in *Tratt. resp. contr.* directed by Visintini, I, *Inadempimento e rimedi*, Padua, 2009, p. 520 ff. With reference to the pandemic situation, see O. Clarizia, *Coronavirus ed esonero da responsabilità per inadempimento ex art. 1218 c.c.: impossibilità sopravvenuta oppure inesigibilità della prestazione?*, in *Actualidad Juridica Iberoamericana*, 2020, no. 12, pp. 352 ff.

7   In these terms, N. Crispino and F. Troncone, *Emergenza Coronavirus: quali possibili effetti sulla locazione a uso commerciale*, in *ilcaso.it*, March 31, 2020.
    Even before the pandemic, he noted the difficulty of such terminating remedies, D. Mantucci, *Il ruolo dell'autonomia negoziale nell'alternativa tra conservazione e risoluzione dei rapporti sinallagmatici inattuati*, in A. Federico and G. Perlingieri (eds.), *Il contratto*. Summer School of the Association of Private Law Doctorates. September 6-9, 2017, University of Salerno, Naples, 2019, pp. 762 ff.

8   For a discussion of the multifaceted meaning of solidarity, see P. Perlingieri in: *Il diritto civile nella legalità costituzionale secondo il sistema italo-comunitario*

established with the French Revolution) must guide the pandemic issue in contract law.

Article 2 of the Italian Constitution enshrines the notion of solidarity, and Article 3 thereof is its corollary. And even the Lisbon Treaty, at the European level, makes numerous references to solidarity; more specifically, some 20 references can be found in the Treaty on European Union and the Treaty on the Functioning of the Union.

As is well known, for the judge — interpreter *par excellence* — hermeneutic activity can no longer rest solely on the literal datum[9]: Article 12 of the precepts (*preleggi*) to the Italian Civil Code on literal interpretation is now implicitly repealed, since

---

delle fonti, 4th edn, Naples, 2020, spec. p. 161 ff.; *"Depatrimonializzazione" e diritto civile*, in P. Perlingieri, *Scuole, tendenze, metodi*, Naples, 1988, pp. 173 ff.; *Mercato, solidarietà e diritti umani*, in *Rass. dir. civ.*, 1995, espec. pp. 82 ff.; *La tutela del consumatore tra liberismo e solidarismo*, in P. Perlingieri, *Il diritto dei contratti tra persona e mercato. Problemi del diritto civile*, Naples, 2003, pp. 305 ff. See also R. Di Raimo, *Date a Cesare (soltanto) quel che è di Cesare. Il valore affermativo dello scopo ideale e i tre volti della solidarietà costituzionale*, in *Rass. dir. civ.*, 2014, pp. 1082 ff.; V. Rizzo, *Contratto e costituzione*, ibid, 2015, pp. 349 ff., spec. p. 351; L. Carlassare, *Solidarietà: un progetto politico*, in *Costituzionalismo*, 2016, pp. 27 ff.; S. Rodotà, *Solidarietà, un'utopia necessaria*, ed. spec, Rome, 2017, p. 42, who observes that "[…] solidarity belongs to those principles or general, flexible clauses that legal technique has prepared so that the legal system can have open windows on society, to keep up with it without the need for an uninterrupted, laborious, almost always late update through new norms".

9 On this subject, see for all, P. Perlingieri in: *L'interpretazione della legge come sistematica ed assiologica. Il broccardo* in claris non fit interpretatio, *il ruolo dell'art. 12 disp. prel. c.c. e la nuova scuola dell'esegesi*, in *Rass. dir. civ.*, 1985, pp. 990 ff.; *Applicazione e controllo nell'interpretazione giuridica*, in *Riv. dir. civ.*, 2010, pp. 317 ff.; *Interpretazione ed evoluzione dell'ordinamento*, pp. 159 ff.; *Interpretazione e controllo di conformità alla Costituzione*, in *Rass. dir. civ.*, 2018, pp. 593 ff.; *Il diritto civile nella legalità costituzionale secondo il sistema italo-comunitario delle fonti*, II, pp. 278 ff., spec. pp. 304 ff. See, also, V. Rizzo, *Interpretazione dei contratti e relatività delle sue regole*, Napoli, 1985; and more recently M. Pennasilico in: *Metodo e valore nell'interpretazione dei contratti*, Naples, 2011; *Interpretazione e integrazione dei contratti nel dialogo tra dottrina e giurisprudenza*, in E. Caterini, L. Di Nella, A. Flamini, L. Mezzasoma and S. Polidori (eds.), *Scritti in onore di Vito Rizzo. Persona, mercato, contratto e rapporti di consumo*, II, Naples, 2017, pp. 1475 ff.; *Contratto e interpretazione. Lineamenti di ermeneutica contrattuale*, 3rd edn., Turin, 2018.

the black letter must be a mere starting point. This provision was written at a time when Constitutional and Community rules were absent from the hierarchy of legal sources; in the Civil Code of 1942, it was the law that took first place. Today, however, this rule must necessarily be subject to both Community principles and Constitutional rules[10].

This is then why the principle of solidarity becomes so important in understanding and reading legal provisions[11].

2. *Pandemic and lease for housing needs*

Having made that premise, let us turn to see how, with reference to pandemic and contract law, this principle has been implemented. And, in the investigation, we must first look at what has happened with reference to a particular term contract: the lease for housing needs.

Here, the need to protect the right to housing (as a fundamental right of the individual under Article 2 of the Constitution[12]) led to

---

10 As the Constitutional Court also points out, in Order No. 322 of July 27, 2001, in *Giur. cost.*, 2001, p. 2595, "the textual tenor of the rule cannot be an obstacle to an interpretation in conformity with the constitutional dictate". In the same sense: Constitutional Court, Jan. 24, 1994, No. 19 in *Giur. cost.*, 1994, pp. 136 ff. Both decisions can be consulted in G. Perlingieri and G. Carapezza Figlia (eds.), *L'interpretazione secondo Costituzione" nella giurisprudenza. Crestomazia di decisioni giuridiche*, II, Naples, 2012, pp. 101 ff, with a note by O. Clarizia, *Efficacia precettiva dei principi costituzionali e inesigibilità della prestazione*.

11 Concerning the need for direct application of constitutional principles to civil law institutions, see P. Perlingieri in: *Scuole civilistiche e dibattito ideologico: introduzione allo studio del diritto privato in Italia*, in *Riv. dir. civ.*, 1978, pp. 414 ff.; as well as in *Scuole tendenze e metodi. Problemi del diritto civile*, Naples, 1989, pp. 73 ff.; *Norme costituzionali e rapporti di diritto civile*, in *Rass. dir. civ.*, 1980, pp. 95 ff.; *Profili del diritto civile*, 3rd edn, Naples, 1994, pp. 18 ff.; *Il diritto civile nella legalità costituzionale secondo il sistema italo-comunitario delle fonti*, II, spec. pp. 247 ff. See, also, M. Pennasilico, *Legalità costituzionale e diritto civile*, in P. Perlingieri and A. Tartaglia Polcini (eds.), *Novecento giuridico: i civilisti*, Naples, 2013, pp. 281.

12 On the right to housing as an existential legal situation, see P. Perlingieri, *Relazione al Convegno Diritto all'abitazione, finanziamento all'impresa,*

a freeze on evictions for default during the most critical time of the pandemic — when many tenants lacked the income to pay rent. This freeze on evictions was an indispensable measure that, while sacrificing landlords' rights, proved essential and appropriate.

Solidarity and protection of the individual were the keys that inspired the legislative intervention to which I refer, and which justified a nearly two-year freeze of evictions for default (i.e., until December 31, 2021)[13].

It is noteworthy that, before an unconditional freeze independent of ownership, the only compensatory measure was to relieve owners from paying municipal property tax (*Imposta municipal propria* or "IMU").

And, here, a first problem arises: can proprietary sacrifice be unlimited? And is it right for such sacrifice to take place *a priori* without any inquiry into the economic condition of the owner himself, tying it to ownership alone? Is the scope of the principle of solidarity unlimited?

The Italian Constitutional Court has intervened on the issue and has, forcefully, introduced a limit to the sacrifice of property rights. In ruling no. 128 of 2021[14] on the suspension of property

---

alla cooperativa, alla persona, in G. Tatarano (ed.), *Diritto all'abitazione, finanziamento all'impresa alla cooperativa alla persona*. Atti del Convegno, tenuto a Selva di Fasano nei giorni 16-18 settembre 1982, Naples-Rome, 1986, pp. 321 ff.; Id., *Il diritto civile nella legalità costituzionale*, III, pp. 177 ff. V., also, L. Mezzasoma, *Il "consumatore" acquirente di immobili da costruzione fra diritto al risparmio e diritto all'abitazione*, Naples, 2008, pp. 215 ff.; M. Ciocia, *Il diritto all'abitazione tra interessi privati e valori costituzionali*, Naples, 2009, p. 43, where we read "by means of art. 47 housing is erected to a public subjective right, representing a substantial element in the formation and development of the human person"; F. Bilancia, *Brevi riflessioni sul diritto all'abitazione*, in *Scritti in onore di Franco Modugno*, Naples, 2011, pp. 347 ff. G.R. Filograno, *Diritto di abitazione, proprietà e impignorabilità della casa*, in *Rass. dir. civ.*, 2020, pp. 552 ff.

13 Thus the so-called Supports Decree (Decree Law No. 41 of 2021), on "*Misure urgenti in materia di sostegno alle imprese e agli operatori economici, di lavoro, salute e servizi territoriali, connesse all'emergenza da COVID-19*", converted with amendments by Law No. 69 of May 22, 2021.

14 Constitutional Court, June 9, 2021, no. 128, in *cortecostituzionale.it* and in *altalex.com*, June 23, 2021, with comment by L. Biarella, *Sospensione sfratti su casa principale del debitore: seconda proroga incostituzionale*.

executions[15], the Court found that the first extension dictated by the emergency from Covid-19 was legitimate to protect the right to housing — a fundamental individual right[16]. Protection of the individual and the principle of solidarity prevail *a priori* over property interests.

At the same time, however, the Court appears to consider a further extension beyond December 31, 2021 to be illegitimate. This opinion is based on the fact that, while it is true that the principle of solidarity exists, the compression of rights, including the right to property, cannot be unlimited[17].

Here, it becomes necessary to perform a "balancing act"[18], which ties in with another constitutional principle: the principle

---

15   More specifically, the suspension of real estate enforcement proceedings concerning the debtor's main home was ordered, in order to contain the negative effects of the epidemiological emergency from Covid-19, by Article *54b* of Decree Law No. 18 of March 17, 2020, introduced by the annex to the conversion law April 24, 2020, No. 27, amended and extended, by Art. 4, Paragraph 1, of Decree-Law No. 137 of October 28, 2020, converted with amendments into Law No. 176 of December 18, 2020, in the term of effectiveness first to December 31, 2020 and, subsequently, to June 30, 2021 *pursuant to* Art. 13, Paragraph 14, of Decree-Law No. 183 of December 31, 2020.
16   This is because since in the face of exceptional circumstances the principle of solidarity makes it possible to justify the temporary sacrifice of creditors in the face of enforced debtors who dwell in the principal dwelling by way of ownership or other real right: see Constitutional Court, June 9, 2021, No. 128, cited above.
17   Insofar as the legislature "extended a generalized measure of *extreme ratio*, [...], while it should have specified the subjective and objective prerequisites of the measure, also possibly delegating the concrete balancing of the interests at stake to the scrutiny of the same presiding judge." Constitutional Court, June 9, 2021, no. 128.
18   "State law - in the presence of other rights deserving protection, such as the fundamental right to housing - may subordinate the satisfaction of the creditor's right to judicial protection, even in the executive branch. However, there must be a reasonable balancing of the conflicting constitutional values, to be assessed by considering the proportionality of the means chosen in relation to the objective needs to be satisfied and the purposes pursued." Constitutional Court, June 9, 2021, no. 128.
    On the fundamental role of "balancing," see P. Perlingieri, *Il diritto civile nella legalità costituzionale secondo il sistema italo-communitario delle fonti*, II, pp. 389 ff.

of reasonableness[19]. The Constitution protects the right to property. And after an initial phase of extraordinary seriousness and emergency that legitimized owner sacrifice (for almost two years), the Court ultimately held that: "state law — in the presence of other rights deserving of protection, such as the fundamental right to housing — may subject the satisfaction of the creditor's right to judicial protection, even in the executive branch. However, there must be a reasonable balancing of the conflicting constitutional values, to be assessed by considering the proportionality of the means chosen in relation to the objective needs to be satisfied and the purposes pursued". Thus, the government may have to identify other types of interventions to protect the tenant; interventions that nevertheless respect the landlord's property right in the long run.

Ergo, "solidarity" on the one hand, but "balance" and "reasonableness" on the other. Our system's founding principles must always be considered within the context of the system as a whole, and not in an autonomous and stand-alone fashion.

3. (Continued): Pandemic and lease for non-housing needs

Legislative interventions have also affected another tenure contract: the lease for non-housing needs[20]. Here, solidarity, on

---

[19] On the current scope of reasonableness, see G. Perlingieri, *Profili applicativi della ragionevolezza nel diritto civile*, Naples, 2015, *passim*; and also, *Ragionevolezza e bilanciamento nell'interpretazione recente della Corte costituzionale*, in *Actualidad juridica iberoamericana*, 2019, I, pp. 10 ff. See also P. Perlingieri and M. Imbrenda, *Autonomia contrattuale, proporzionalità e ragionevolezza*, in P. Perlingieri, *Manuale di diritto civile*, Naples, 2021, p. 459.

Reasonableness as an interpretive criterion for balancing principles is also used by the Court of Justice. See, in this regard, Court of Justice, June 12, 2003, c. 112/00, in *curia.europa.eu* (the "*Schmidberger* case").

[20] On the issue of commercial leases, a great body of literature has appeared in recent months: see G. Carapezza Figlia, *Coronavirus e locazioni commerciali. Un diritto per lo stato di emergenza?*, in *Actualidad Juridica Iberoamericana*, 2020, no. 2, pp. 422 ff.; Id., *Locazioni commerciali e sopravvenienze da Covid-19. Riflessioni a margine delle prime decisioni giurisprudenziali*, in *Danno resp.*, 2020, pp. 698 ff.; Id., *Epidemia e distribuzione del rischio*

one side, and protection of economic initiative under Article 41 of the Constitution, on the other, required further legal reform.

For instance, a tax credit equal to 60% of the rent was granted[21], and the parties could renegotiate[22] the lease agreement to cope

> *contrattuale nelle locazioni commerciali*, in V. Rizzo, L. Mezzasoma, E. Llamas Pombo and G. Berti de Marinis (eds.), *Il consumatore e la normativa emergenziale ai tempi del Covid-19*, Naples, 2021, pp. 149 ff.; N. Crispino and M. Sannino, *L'impatto delle misure di contenimento del coronavirus sulle locazioni commerciali e gli strumenti a disposizione del conduttore*, in *Studium iuris*, 2020, pp. 675 ff.; V. Cuffaro, *Le locazioni commerciali e gli effetti giuridici dell'epidemia*, in giustiziacivile.com, March 31, 2020; A.A. Dolmetta, *Locazione di esercizio commerciale (o di studi professionali) e riduzione del canone per «misure di contenimento» pandemico*, in *ilcaso.it*, April 23, 2020; Id., *Periodo di* lockdown, *locazione di esercizio commerciale*, garantievertrag, in *Bank Exchange tit. cred.*, 2020, pp. 762 ff.; R. Natoli, *L'impatto di Covid-19 sui contratti di locazione commerciale*, in *ilcaso. it*, September 30, 2020, and in U. Malvagna and A. Sciarrone Alibrandi (eds.), *Sistema produttivo e finanziario* post *Covid-19: dall'efficienza alla sostenibilità. Voci dal diritto dell'economia*, Pisa, 2021, pp. 39 ff.; V. Pandolfini, *Epidemia Covid-19 e contratti di locazione commerciale: quali rimedi per i conduttori?*, in *Contratti*, 2020, pp. 308 ff.; V. Ruggiero, *La pandemia e la sorte dei canoni di locazione commerciale*, in *ilcaso.it*, May 1, 2020; U. Salanitro, *La gestione del rischio nella locazione commerciale al tempo del coronavirus*, in giustiziacivile.com, April 21, 2020; U. Salanitro, *Una soluzione strutturale nell'emergenza: locazioni commerciali e impossibilità temporanea*, in *Nuova giur. civ. comm.*, supplement 3/2020, pp. 110 ff.; M. Signorelli, *La locazione commerciale al tempo della pandemia: prime prospettive di sistema e soluzioni resilienti*, in *Resp. civ. prev*, 2020, pp. 1683 ff.; G. Trimarchi, *Le "locazioni commerciali", il Covid-19 e gli equilibri contrattuali dei rapporti di durata*, in *Notariato*, 2020, pp. 235 ff.; C. Boiti, *L'incidenza della pandemia da Covid-19 sulle locazioni ad uso non abitativo*, in V. Rizzo, L. Mezzasoma, E. Llamas Pombo and G. Berti de Marinis (eds.), *Il consumatore e la normativa emergenziale ai tempi del Covid-19*, pp. 83 ff.

21 Article 65 of Decree Law No. 18 of 2020 established that the tenant can obtain a tax credit equal to 60 percent of the rent. This tax incentive is intended to ease the tax burden for landlords, but without relieving them of the obligation to pay the rent. It should be noted that this tax credit was granted for the exclusive benefit of all businesses that were subject to closure (and thus all businesses that do not provide an essential service), provided that the leased properties are in the C/1 cadastral category.

22 Thus, initially, the Supreme Court, July 8, 2020, Office of the Supreme and Role, Thematic Report «*Novità normative sostanziali del diritto "emergenziale" anti-Covid 19 in ambito contrattuale e concorsuale*», available at *cortedicassazione.it*, and later provided for by Article 10 of Decree Law No. 118 of August 24, 2021.

with the tenant's inability to use the property for the intended purposes.

Regarding this latter hypothesis, the pandemic's impact on discos and dance halls is emblematic. Indeed, these businesses were legally required to close for more than a year (in the case of indoor activity) while, perhaps in deference to the principle *pacta sun servanda* now enshrined in Article 1372 c.c., remaining obliged to pay rent for the right to use the premises.

Moreover, because renegotiation was only an *option* and not a requirement, in most cases, landlords (also in crisis due to the pandemic) refused to come to new terms that were more economically advantageous for the tenant — whether on a temporary or permanent basis.

The issue has been addressed in the case law, which has had mixed opinions.

Notably, the Court of Rome[23] affirmed that it is

> not possible to hold that the duty of one party to act in such a way as to preserve the interests of the other contractual party, regardless of the existence of specific contractual obligations or of what is expressly established

---

23 Trib. Rome, Jan. 15, 2021, in *giustiziacivile.com*, with note by V. Nardi, *L'impatto della pandemia sui contratti di locazione commerciale: tra poteri del giudice, obblighi dei contraenti e ruolo del legislatore*. Prior to this decision, a different conclusion was held by Trib. Rome, May 29, 2020, in *DeJure on line* (affirming there was a hypothesis of partial and temporary impossibility of performance which allowed a 70% reduction in rent pursuant to Article 1464 of the Civil Code, albeit only for the period affected by the impossibility); Trib. Rome, (ord.) July 25, 2020, in *Contratti*, 2021, pp. 19 ff.; Trib. Rome, August 27, 2020, in *Giur. it*, 2020, pp. 2433 ff., with note by G. Sicchiero, *Buona fede integrativa o poteri equitativi del giudice ex art. 1374 c.c.?*; and pp. 2439 ff., with note by P. Gallo, *Emergenza Covid e revisione del contratto*, according to which "if there is a contingency in the factual and legal substratum that constitutes the prerequisite of the negotiated agreement, such as that determined by the Covid-19 pandemic, the party who would be disadvantaged by the continuation of the execution of the contract on the same terms as originally agreed upon must be able to have the opportunity to renegotiate its content, based on the general duty of objective good faith (or fairness) in the executive phase of the contract". The Tribunal therefore found it necessary "to have recourse to the general clause of good faith and solidarity enshrined in Art. 2 of the Constitutional Charter in order to bring the contract back within the limits of the normal *alea* of the contract".

by individual rules of law, must be observed even when it entails for the party a sacrifice that is certainly 'appreciable,' as must be considered to be, in the present case, that which the plaintiff seeks to impose on the landlord, having requested a 50% reduction for several months of the rent.

This finding was based on the assumption that

> neither Articles 1374, 1375, 1175, 1366 Civil Code, nor Article 2 Const. allow for the existence in our system of an obligation to renegotiate contracts that have become disadvantageous for some of the parties, nor a power of the judge to modify the contractual regulations freely agreed by the parties.

Thus, this opinion by the Court of Rome highlights an insensitivity to the needs of the tenant who finds himself to be party to a lease agreement for commercial use where the revenues are no longer suitable to support the costs arising from the rent.

Conversely, invoking the principles of solidarity and equity, the Court of Palermo[24] decreed that

> it is [the principle of] good faith, under the different aspects (executive, interpretative) in which it comes into play, that requires the contracting parties to make themselves available to the modification of the contact, when the party interested in maintaining a relationship in a sense adhering to the concrete reality of the market invites the other to renegotiate.

As a result, the party's unjustified refusal to renegotiate is resolved, pursuant to Article 1375 of the Civil Code, "in opportunistic behavior that the law cannot protect and tolerate" in view of the canons of contractual solidarity and good faith (which "prescribe safeguarding the interest of others" albeit "not to the point of suffering an appreciable sacrifice, personal or economic").

On this point, moreover, even our Court of Cassation — referred to in the ruling of the Court of Palermo mentioned above — in its thematic report "Substantive Regulatory Novelties of

---

24 Trib. Palermo, June 9, 2021, no. 2435, in *ilmerito.it*. See also E. Tuccari, *Il Tribunale di Palermo contro l'abuso del processo da Covid-19 nei contratti di locazione ad uso commerciale*, in *Pers. merc.*, 2021, pp. 616 ff.

the 'Emerging' Anti-Covid 19 Law in the Field of Contracts and Bankruptcy"[25] expressly stated that

> renegotiation, in the face of contingencies that alter the reciprocal relationship, becomes an obligatory step to preserve the originally agreed plan of costs and revenues, with the consequence that whoever shirks the obligation to restore it commits a serious violation of contract. And thus the obligation to renegotiate in good faith does not impact, but, on the contrary, respects the bargaining autonomy of the parties who have not manifestly excluded such a duty. In fact, by pandering to the cooperative requirement proper to long-term contracts, the obligation allows for the realization and not the manipulation of the will of the parties.

Consequently, if the landlord refuses to enter negotiations or engages in "mere façade negotiations" without any actual intention to revise the terms of the agreement, one could assume the judges might allow the tenant, in addition to a claim for damages, to bring an action before the court pursuant to Article 2932 of the Civil Code to obtain a constitutive judgment on the obligation to renegotiate.

4. *The renegotiation of contracts*

But the issue of contract renegotiation[26] has also been the subject of a much broader legislative intervention. Here, too,

---

25 V. Supreme Court, July 8, 2020, Office of the Supreme and Role, Thematic Report "*Novità normative sostanziali del diritto 'emergenziale' anti-Covid 19 in ambito contrattuale e concorsuale*", cited.

26 On renegoziation in general, see *ex multis* F. Gambino, *Problemi del rinegoziare*, Milan, 2004; F. Gambino, *Rinegoziazione (dir. civ.)*, in *Enc. giur.* Treccani, XV, 2007, pp. 10 ff.; S. Patti, *Rischio contrattuale e rapporti di durata nel nuovo diritto dei contratti: dalla presupposizione all'obbligo di negoziare*, in *Riv. dir. civ.*, 2002, p. 63; S. Patti, *Obbligo di rinegoziare, tutela in forma specifica e penale giudiziale*, in *Contratti*, 2008, p. 1026; S. Patti, *Regole e prassi della rinegoziazione al tempo della crisi*, in *Giust. civ.*, 2014, pp. 825 ff.; G. Marasco, *La rinegoziazione del contratto*, Padua, 2006; T. Mauceri, *Sopravvenienze perturbative e rinegoziazione del contratto*, in *Eur. dir. priv.*, 2007, pp. 1095 ff.; A. Pisu, *L'adeguamento dei contratti tra ius variandi e rinegoziazione*, Naples, 2017.
With reference to the pandemic, see A.A. Dolmetta, *Il problema della rinegoziazione (ai tempi del coronavirus)*, in giustiziacivile.com, special

intervention must obviously be framed within the issue of the hierarchy of sources and the pivotal principles of the legal system, and especially the constitutional ones. Constitutional solidarity, equality between parties, protection of the enterprise, but also reasonableness and balancing of rights, must form the basis of our discourse[27].

Thus, Article 10(2) of Decree Law No. 118 of 2021[28] (now incorporated into the Code of Business Crisis, in force since July 15 of this year) by introducing the figure of the expert (i.e., a person who must, at the request of the entrepreneur and in the name of specific governing body, intervene at the first signs of

---

no. 3, pp. 319 ff.; D. Marinelli and S. Sabatini, *Rinegoziazione e risoluzione dei contratti in emergenza sanitaria*, Santarcangelo di Romagna, 2020; L. Ruggeri and M. Giobbi, *Vulnerabilità economica tra diritto emergenziale e contrattuale*, in *Actualidad Juridica Iberoamericana*, 2020, no. 12 *bis*, pp. 340 ff.

[27] "Negotiated settlement enhances the value of participation [...]. Participation must be matched by a spirit of solidarity. We are not deluding ourselves by imagining a sweetened reality, but we nonetheless believe that negotiated settlement is a suitable place for smoothing corners, for making a collectivity of subjects perceive that the crisis of the single enterprise often borders on the crisis of the market, and that the crisis of the market can be more dangerous and more harmful than some renunciation. A spirit of solidarity that is not vague could be called the solidarity of compensatory benefits". I. Pagni and M. Fabiani, *La transizione dal codice della crisi alla composizione negoziata (e viceversa)*, in *dirittodellacrisi.it*, November 2, 2021.
See also M. Spiotta, *La solidarietà dei "vantaggi compensativi" alla luce della normativa emergenziale e della l. n. 147/2021*, in *ristrutturazioniaziendali. ilcaso.it*, November 29, 2021, pp. 15 ff.

[28] Decree Law No. 118 of August 24, 2021, on "Urgent measures on business crisis and corporate rehabilitation, as well as further urgent measures on justice," converted with amendments by Law No. 147 of October 21, 2021. For an analysis of the main changes introduced, see *ex multis* S. Leuzzi, *Una rapida lettura dello schema di D.L. recante misure urgenti in materia di crisi d'impresa e di risanamento aziendale*, in *dirittodellacrisi.it*, August 5, 2021; F. Lamanna, *Nuove misure sulla crisi d'impresa del D.L. 118/2021: Penelope disfa il Codice della crisi recitando il "de profundis" per il sistema dell'allerta*, in *ilfallimentarista.it*, August 25, 2021; L. Panzani, *Il D.L. "Pagni" ovvero la lezione (positiva) del covid*, in *dirittodellacrisi.it*, August 25, 2021; A. Farolfi, *Le novità del D.L. 118/2021: considerazioni sparse "a prima lettura"*, in *dirittodellacrisi.it*, September 6, 2021; A. Jorio, *Alcune riflessioni sulle misure urgenti: un forte vento di maestrale soffia sulla riforma!*, October 1, 2021.

company distress to avoid the irreversible crisis of the same), provided that he can renegotiate in good faith the content of contracts (which have become excessively onerous due to the pandemic).

But one must ask why the expert must reconsider contracts that have become excessively onerous. The answer is because there is another founding principle in contracting: the principle of equality between parties (i.e., of contractual balance).

Equality is not — as one often hears — just equality of sex or religion. It is equality in all aspects, including in contract. Hence, when faced with a serious situation of imbalance, one must necessarily renegotiate the content of the contract.

And here, then, is the reference to good faith[29]. Someone might wonder: "but why with reference to contracts of continuous or periodic performance must we worry about renegotiating the contract when our legal system has provided, for so many years, various institutions such as, for example, termination for supervening excessive onerousness?".

But excuse me, what good does it do the struggling entrepreneur to terminate the contract? None. He cannot conduct his business if the contract is terminated[30]. That is why we need to renegotiate the contract. That is why we need to restore the balance. That is why, once again, another underlying constitutional principle of the reform — the principle of contractual balance linked to contractual equality — requires contracts to be renegotiated in good faith[31].

---

[29] On this point, see M. Grondona, *Dall'emergenza sanitaria all'emergenza economica: l'eccessiva onerosità sopravvenuta tra buona fede e obbligo di rinegoziazione*, in *Actualidad Jurídica Iberoamericana*, 2020, no. 12 *bis*, pp. 321 ff.; C. Magli, *Emergenza sanitaria, obbligo di rinegoziazione e buona fede integrativa*, in *Corr. giur.*, 2021, pp. 805 ff.

[30] D. Mantucci, *Il ruolo dell'autonomia negoziale nell'alternativa tra conservazione e risoluzione dei rapporti sinallagmatici inattuati*, in A. Federico and G. Perlingieri (eds.), *Il contratto*. Summer School of the Association of Private Law Doctorates. September 6-9, 2017, University of Salerno, Naples, 2019, pp. 762 ff.

[31] On the subject of contingencies and contract renegotiation, see *ex multis* A. Cinque, *Sopravvenienze contrattuali e rinegoziazione del contratto*, in *Contr. impr*, 2020, pp. 1691 ff.; L. Balestra, *Pandemia, attività d'impresa e*

But beware when the same rule refers to the absence of agreement and indicates that the court can redetermine the terms of the contract equitably. This not because equity is a source of law. It is because, once again, there is the need for contractual balance, the need to comply with the constitutional principles underlying Decree Law No. 118 of 2021.

But even this redetermination is not unlimited. That is, solidarity is not infinite. There must be a balancing act here as well.

And this is where the provision refers to the fact that the court, if it allows the claim, may determine the extent of compensation payable to the other party. The expert must also never forget the rule's founding principles: solidarity (certainly), contractual balance, party equality, but also reasonableness. The expert must always act with regard to the legal system in its entirety and complexity, including the values that exist therein; and, therefore, solidarity and equality, but also reasonableness and balancing of constitutional principles.

It should be noted that Article 10(2) of Decree Law No. 118 of 2021, which has been incorporated into Article 17(5) of the Code of Business Crisis (in force since July 2022) and has seen new life beyond the Covid-19 emergency. Today, the expert,

> in the course of negotiations, [may] invite the parties to renegotiate, in good faith, the content of contracts with continuous, periodic performance

---

solidarietà, in *Riv. trim. dir. proc. civ.*, 2020, pp. 1153 ff.; A.A. Dolmetta, *Il problema della rinegoziazione (ai tempi del coronavirus)*, in *giustiziacivile. com*, 2020, pp. 319 ff.; A. Gemma, *La rinegoziazione nell'emergenza Covid-19 è modalità obbligata di attuazione in buona fede del contratto e l'esecuzione indiretta ex art. 614 bis c.p.c. ne è lo specifico rimedio*, in *Jus civile*, 2020, pp. 724 ff.; S. De Marco, *Clausole di rinegoziazione e stabilità dei rapporti contrattuali*, in *Riv. dir. priv*, 2021, pp. 119 ff.; M. Manelli, *Sopravvenienze e Covid-19: prime applicazioni giurisprudenziali della rinegoziazione secondo la relazione tematica della Cassazione n. 56/2020*, in *Contratti*, 2021, pp. 162 ff.; T.V. Russo, *L'arma letale della buona fede. Riflessioni a margine della "manutenzione" dei contratti in séguito alla sopravvenienza pandemica*, in *Riv. dir. banc.*, 2021, I, pp. 133 ff.; O.T. Scozzafava, *Appunti sulla rinegoziazione*, in *Riv. crit dir. priv.*, 2021, pp. 127 ff.; L. Ambrosini, *L'interesse creditorio nell'emergenza Covid tra rimedi estintivi e tensione conservativa*, in *Resp. civ. prev.*, 2021, pp. 1352 ff.

or deferred performance if the performance has become excessively onerous or if the balance of the relationship is altered due to circumstances that have arisen. The parties are required to cooperate with each other to redetermine the content of the contract or adjust performance to the changed conditions.

The general rule is that, to avoid the crisis of the enterprise, any supervening circumstances are suitable for renegotiation.

However, this represents an increasingly broad application of the principles to which we have referred. And if it is true that Decree Law No. 118 of 2021 sets out the court's authority to intervene in the event of unwillingness to renegotiate disappears, it is also true that creditors subject to protective measures cannot unilaterally refuse to fulfill pending contracts or cause their termination. Nor can they anticipate their expiration or modify them to the detriment of the entrepreneur for the sole fact of non-payment of prior claims (Article 18(5)).

We are in Book IV of the Civil Code, and the worthiness that is so widely discussed[32] with respect to over-indebtedness, in its new meaning (gross negligence, malice, fraud), must become the rule that inspires the entire contractual relationship.

In this context, the Argentine legal system is particularly interesting since, like in France, in reforming the law of contract in the civil code, it included mechanisms for contract adaptation in the case of long-standing relationships, including by obliging counterparties to renegotiate upon request of the other party[33], thereby acting in good faith and not engaging in opportunistic behavior (i.e., abusive exercise of rights).

More specifically, the new Argentine Civil Code (unified with the Commercial Code, the so-called *Código Civil y Comercial de*

---

[32] See L. Mezzasoma, *La tutela del sovraindebitato quale contraente debole*, in E. Caterini, L. Di Nella, A. Flamini, L. Mezzasoma and S. Polidori (eds.), *Scritti in onore di Vito Rizzo. Persona, mercato, contratto e rapporti di consumo*, II, p. 1253 ff.

[33] Thus the new Article 1195 French Civil Code provides that the burdened party "*peut demander une renégociation du contrat à son cocontractant*".

*la Nación*³⁴), which entered into force in 2015 and replaced the previous Civil Code dating back to 1869 (and entered into force on January 1st, 1871), amended the provision on contingencies (the "*imprevisión*" in Article 1.091) and circumscribed its scope to commutative contracts of deferred or permanent performance³⁵ under Article 1.011. By referring to the 'new' category of long-term contracts, it expresses itself in terms of "*oportunidad razonable de renegociar de buena fe, sin incurrir en ejercicio abusivo de los derechos*".

Contract rebalance can now be demanded in its own right, as there is no longer a requirement (as provided under former Article 1.198) for the debtor to be in default.

Thus, in Argentine law, in the case of windfalls, contract adjustment (which preserves the agreement) seems to prevail over the remedy that allows for the contract's termination. The absence of specific parameters for the court to adhere to or otherwise guide its decision may make the adjudicator's task more compressed, but it certainly does not reduce the importance of any judicial review of the original contract.

This Argentine experience clearly evidences the evolution of contract law and the new meaning of the principle *pacta sun servanda*.

---

34 Approved by Act No. 26,994 of Oct. 1, 2014 and entered into force Aug. 1st, 2015.
35 For an in-depth discussion of the issue see, E. Tuccari, *L'eccessiva onerosità sopravvenuta nel nuovo codice civile argentino*, in *Resp. civ. prev.*, 2015, pp. 226 ff.

Roberto Moreno[*]

LEGAL BRICOLAGE

Some Thoughts on the Influence of the *Codice Civile* on the Paraguayan *Código Civil*

> "The life of the law has not been logic and it has not been experience.
> It has been *borrowing*".
>
> Alan Watson

> "Our best and most valued acquisitions have been obtained either from our
> contemporaries or from those who have preceded us in the field of thought and discovery.
> We have all either *begged, borrowed or stolen*".
>
> Frederick Douglass

I Introduction

"Una medesma lingua"

The Italian lawyer who opens the Paraguayan *Código Civil*[1] of 1985[2] at random cannot be faulted for evoking the opening line of *Canto XXXI* of the Divine Comedy. For, although obviously rendered in Spanish, the legal text will many times seem to be, indeed, *una medesma lingua giuridica* with the Italian *Codice Civile* of 1942[3]. Thus, the radically basic conceptual text of

---

[*] Professor of Civil Law at Universidad Nacional de Asunción.
[1] Hereinafter, simply, "*Código Civil*".
[2] The *Código Civil* was enacted by Congress in 1985, but only came into force on January 1st, 1987.
[3] Hereinafter, simply, the "*Codice*".

the law of obligations, Article 419 of the Paraguayan *Código Civil*, is but a literal copy of Article 1174 of the *Codice*; or, to use another example, the entire discipline of interpretation of contracts (Articles 708-715) of the *Código Civil* is but a recitation, in Spanish, of Articles 1362 to 1371 of the *Codice*; or once again: the regulation of the *titoli di credito* contained in Articles 1507–1545 of the *Código Civil* is an almost exact transliteration of Articles 1992–2027 of the *Codice*; and, to give just one more example, the entire discipline of banking contracts, contained in Articles 1404-1430 of the *Código Civil* is, again, a transcription of Articles 1834-1860 of the *Codice*. Last, but not least, Paraguay became the first South American country to unify civil and commercial obligations, and the model borrowed for this was, without a doubt, the *Codice*[4].

However, a closer reading is sufficient to prove not only that there are very significant differences between both codes, but that a genuine gulf exists, in the final balance, between the *Codice* and the *Código Civil*. Whilst there are sections of the *Código Civil* that do indeed copy the *Codice,* and while Paraguay unified civil and commercial obligations with a decisive inspiration from the *Codice* in this point, there are other sections — *recte*, entire Books ("*Libros*") — of the *Código Civil* in which the influence of the *Codice* is next to nil. For instance, the whole of the law of persons and family, of the law of property, and of succession law have almost no traces whatsoever of Italian sources. And, what is more, even the parts of the *Código Civil* that incorporate literal provisions from the *Codice* — such as the general part of obligations or rules for the specific types of contracts — contain at the same time rules that were copied and borrowed freely from other sources, something which often compromises or even mutates the original significance once the Italian *articolo* is placed in its Paraguayan normative context[5].

---

4   See *infra,* especially sections VIII-IX.
5   *Infra*, sections XIII-XVI.

A mixed image emerges, then: at times, there seems to be *a medesma lingua* which approximates the *Codice* to the *Código Civil*; most of the times, however, we are before a different and distinct legal body, a construct that either has no trace of the *Codice* or in which the original Italian text coexists uneasily with other sources.

The *Codice* is thus faraway, yet so close, to the *Código Civil*.

II

The only way to understand the foregoing dialectic of influence/absence of the *Codice* in the *Código Civil* is by looking back and seeing how the Paraguayan code was constructed.

Indeed, the truly defining—and distinguishing—characteristic of the Paraguayan *Código Civil*, which perhaps makes it unique in the landscape of modern civil codes, is that it is a legal corpus that was *intentionally* and *deliberately* constructed by borrowing, copying, and using sources, materials, and legal debris from the most diverse and heterogenous variety of sources. This makes the result a truly *kaleidoscopic, Babelian*, legal code. Once, when reflecting on the famous dictum of Justice Holmes that "the life of the law has not been logic, it has been experience", the roman lawyer Alan Watson considered that it should be reformulated to incorporate what he considered to be the defining feature of law in the Western world: "the life of the law has not been logic and it has not been experience. *It has been borrowing*"[6]. The Paraguayan *Código Civil* is, without a doubt, the quintessential "great legal borrower". The history of the *Código Civil* has, certainly, been one of borrowing. This is its defining characteristic, and it is simply impossible to comprehend its provisions, and to apply them reasonably, without considering this distinguishing feature.

Why was the *Código Civil* constructed on this borrowing principle? The answer is to be found in the firmly entrenched

---

6   A. Watson, *The Spirit of Roman Law* (Athens: The University of Georgia Press, 1995), p. 111 (emphasis added).

idée maîtresse of the great Paraguayan civil lawyer, Luis De Gásperi, who wrote what was to become the original draft of the *Código Civil* — the "*Anteproyecto*"[7]. According to De Gásperi, in law "there is no possible of creation outside what has already been created", and hence no question of "originality" is to be presented. Rather than "inventing" new rules or articles one must be faithful to the available sources[8]. His guiding idea in the codifying effort was to borrow freely from the tradition of the civil law and its modern codes. The Paraguayan jurist would have fully endorsed the judgment of the distinguished African-American public intellectual Frederick Douglass, that "our best and most valued acquisitions have been obtained either from our contemporaries or from those who have preceded us in the field of thought and discovery", and thus, in the end, "we have all either begged, borrowed or stolen"[9]. This same principle of borrowing from foreign sources was also strictly followed by the jurists of the *Comisión Nacional de Codificación*[10] — the institution that was in charge of codifying Paraguayan law which had hitherto been governed by foreign codes — which worked during more than 20 years refining the *Anteproyecto* and delivering the final and definitive version of the *Código Civil* in 1985.

The Paraguayan *Código Civil* was therefore constructed upon the borrowing principle, mining from a great treasury of materials from the three great branches of the civil law tradition: the French, the German, and the Italian[11]. The influence of French law — and this point cannot be sufficiently emphasized — is however *oblique*, as the *Código Civil* does not incorporate gallic sources directly, but indirectly, from the robust Argentinean civilian tradition; crucially, the great Vélez Sarsfield Civil Code

---

7 For a recent reedition of this monumental text, see: L. De Gásperi, *Anteproyecto de Código Civil*, edited with an introduction by R. Moreno Rodríguez Alcalá, (Asunción: La Ley Paraguaya, 2020).
8 See *infra*, section VIII.
9 F. Douglass, "Self-Made Men", in *The Essential Douglass*, edited with an introduction by N. Buccola (Indianapolis: Hackett Publishing Company, 2016), p. 332.
10 Hereinafter, simply, the "*Comisión*".
11 As De Gásperi himself stated: again, see *infra*, section VIII.

of 1867 — which, as will be seen, was in force for 100 years in Paraguay — but also the various reform drafts of this Code, two of which, the Bibiloni draft of 1927 ("*Anteproyecto de Bibiloni*") and the *Draft of 1936* ("*Proyecto de Código Civil de 1936*"), were immensely influential for the *Código Civil*[12]. These two Argentinean drafts also connect the *Código Civil* with the German tradition — particularly, the BGB of 1900 and the Swiss Civil Code and Code of Obligations (and its scholarship) — and this serves to explain why provisions of these Germanic sources are also found scattered in other parts of the *Código Civil*. The Italian branch also had, as mentioned above, a massive influence, especially through the "civilization of mercantile law" with the complete unification of the law of obligations.

Its historical process of elaboration makes the *Código Civil* a unique creature, designed by an endless series of borrowings which compose a multilayered structure of foreign, heterogenous, sources. It is the *great legal borrower*, and an outstanding — though partial — lender was indeed the *Codice* of 1942.

III

Tracing the loans from the *Codice* that made their way to the Paraguayan *Código Civil* is the main purpose of this essay.

---

[12] One of the peculiarities of the Paraguayan *Código Civil* — and one that cannot be underestimated — is the enormous influence that two drafts of reform of the Argentinean Code, the Bibiloni draft of 1927 and the *Draft of 1936* (given the prestige of its authors, such as Bibiloni, Lafaille, Tobal, Repetto, Salvat and others) were to have on the final product. The peculiarity resides not only in the fact that (large parts of) these drafts were finally accepted in a foreign country — i.e., Paraguay — but that since these drafts were in the end disregarded in their home country, no doctrinal scholarship nor case law illuminate its further application. This presents a further source of difficulty for the Paraguayan interpreter of these texts: he must simply work with a blindfold. A brief but lucid note on the drafts for reform of the Vélez Sarsfield code with specific references to the *Anteproyecto de Bibiloni* and the *Proyecto de 1936* is found in: G.A. Borda, *Tratado de Derecho Civil Argentino – Parte General* 2nd edn (Buenos Aires: Editorial Perrot, 1955), vol. 1, pp. 126–129.

This influence, as will be seen, could have been much more profound had the original *Anteproyecto* of De Gásperi had been adopted, since the Paraguayan jurist opted for incorporating the *Libro Quarto* of the *Codice* almost verbatim, attaining *una medesma lingua* in the unification of the law of obligations and contracts. The final *Código Civil*, however, is a more complex and heterogenous body, one in which the Italian influence persists but is less pervasive. More importantly, the jurists of the *Comisión* made matters much harder for the subsequent generations of Paraguayan lawyers, jurists, and judges, since the *Código Civil* incorporates and coalesces solutions from different — sometimes harmonious, sometimes contradictory, sometimes unintelligible — sources. Thus, a provision from the *Codice* may coexist with an Argentinean source, or a Germanic source, and so on and so forth.

The pursuit of the *Codice* and its impact in the *Código Civil* leads directly to a different but inescapable question: how should one read, interpret, and apply a body of law so heterogeneously constructed? In other words, the substantive finding that the *Código Civil* is influenced by the *Codice*, but also by many other sources — even in the sections in which the main source is the *Codice* — necessarily collapses into the methodological question of how is one to make sense of all these borrowings. The Paraguayan lawyer, jurist, or judge cannot remain content in merely noting that these "multinational" sources feed the final text, but precisely because of this defining characteristic, must make sense of his *Babelian* code.

Following these ideas, this essay will not limit itself to outlining the great areas of influence of the *Codice* on the Paraguayan *Código Civil*, but will try to propose, very sketchily and incompletely, a method for understanding this influence and applying it to concrete legal problems which may arise in Paraguay. The task for the Paraguayan civil lawyer is to make the *Código Civil* speak in one voice, as a coherent whole, despite its many underlying tongues and languages. This chapter, after establishing which parts of the *Código Civil* have an Italian inspiration, will then take a further route, ruminating some thoughts on how to solve the methodological problem posed by the *Código Civil*, borrowing — borrowing, again! — a metaphor from the great anthropologist Claude Lévi-Strauss to suggest that a system constructed on borrowing from other legal systems must be analyzed and comprehended by a method which may be called *legal bricolage*. To put it simply, a great legal borrower requires a great legal bricoleur.

The road will be long and — given the limitations of the author — at many times cumbersome. To ease the task of the reader in this journey, the essay will be divided in four parts: (I) Part One will include a brief historical survey that will explain how the *Código Civil* came to be, giving the necessary background for the foreign audience; (II) Part Two will trace the influence of the *Codice* in the first draft of De Gásperi, the *Anteproyecto*; (III) Part Three will turn to the *Código Civil* and will conclude that the influence of the *Codice* was lessened and made to coexist with other diverse sources; finally, (IV) Part Four will seek to provide a methodological solution to the problem posed, submitting that the metaphor of legal bricolage is an apt response. A Conclusion will bring together the many disparate threads woven along the way.

Part One
A (very) brief historical survey

IV

Any inquiry regarding the influence of the *Codice* on the *Código Civil* must be preceded by a cursory historical survey of Paraguayan civil law, since the only way to understand how the *Código Civil* became the quintessential legal borrower is — precisely — knowing how it came into existence[13].

---

13 What follows is a very tight synthesis of the more expanded history of the process of codification of Paraguayan civil and commercial law, the work and personality of Luis De Gásperi, the *Comisión Nacional de Codificación*

Independent since 1811, Paraguay's destiny has always been prisoner of its brute geographical reality: a landlocked country, with no communication to the outside world except for the Paraná River, sitting beside two giants: Brazil — literally, an empire — and Argentina. A paraphrase from Santa Anna's famous maxim may very well sum up Paraguay's history: "So far away from heaven and so near to Brazil and Argentina". The well-known deficiencies of the Spanish crown in establishing the limits of its colonies[14], coupled with the ruthless expansionism of the Brazilian empire and the diplomatic and political blunders of Paraguay's megalomaniac President — the legendary "Mariscal López"[15] — led to the worst war ever fought in South America: the Triple Alliance War of 1864-1870, in which Brazil, Argentina and Uruguay defeated — massacred is a better word — Paraguay[16]. The war has been even called a "genocide"[17], which although may be a bit hyperbolic, is none the less apt to

---

and other related historical incidents, that I have embarked upon elsewhere: R. Moreno Rodríguez Alcalá, 'Estudio Preliminar', in L. De Gásperi, *Anteproyecto de Código Civil* (Asunción: La Ley Paraguaya, 2019), vol. 1, pp. xxv-cccxxx. I refer the reader to those pages for a more nuanced and detailed recounting of this fascinating story.

14 On this important issue see G. Ireland, *Boundaries, Possessions and Conflicts in Central and North American and the Caribbean* (Cambridge: Harvard University Press, 1941), which also contains an excellent recount of the boundary problems that led to Paraguay's other armed conflict, the Chaco War (1932–1935).

15 The literature on López is vast and extraordinarily polemic — as befits its subject. Herein I limit myself to recommending what is arguably (still) the *best written* of his biographies, which although dated and perhaps too benevolent on López is a delight to read: A. Bray, *Solano López - Soldado de la gloria y el infortunio* (Asunción: Ediciones Nizza, 1958); and, for the Italian reader, the very valuable work by M. Cancogni and I. Boris, *Il Napoleone del Plata* (Milano: Rizzoli, 1970).

16 The bibliography on the Triple Alliance War is simply inexhaustible, and at many (most!) times tainted with nationalistic and/or ideological prejudices: I will here only refer the reader to what is in my opinion the most updated, thoroughly researched and — what is more important — impartial survey, which is the three volume history by Thomas Whigham, *La Guerra de la Triple Alianza* (Asunción: Taurus, 2015), a paradigm of historiographical writing and investigation (that also deftly analyzes the causes of the war).

17 By a Brazilian autor, no less: J.J. Chiavenato, *Genocidio Americano – La Guerra del Paraguay* (Asunción: Carlos Schauman, 1985).

describe what legally happened to Paraguay: the war "devastated the country to a degree unknown in American history" and left it "a vast ossuary", a "heap of ruins"[18]. If ever there was a moment were the phrase "*vae victis*" has applied[19], it indeed was with Paraguay in the wake of this devastating conflict.

The "Great War" (*Guerra Guazú*), as it was known by the traumatized survivors for its indelibly deleterious effects, left very few educated Paraguayans standing. The work of reconstruction of the country was therefore marred by extreme poverty, no resources, and fratricide infighting between the few remaining political leaders; reading the history of those post-War years is like reading an extremely tragic, sad and miserable novel — except that it is true[20]. Of course, the rebuilding of a nation such as the decimated Paraguay of the last third of the 19th century implicated the construction of a new legal order from scratch, since the old Spanish colonial laws — many of which were still in force before the Triple Alliance War — were absolutely archaic[21]. Given that there were few, if any, remaining Paraguayans who could take on the complex task of drafting a Constitution and legal codes, the solution of the occupying allied

---

18   E. Cardozo, *Paraguay Independiente* (Asunción: Carlos Schauman Editor, 1987), p. 265. As an Argentinean witness stated: "No ha habido saqueo, lo que ha habido *es robo en la manera más indecente*"; quoted in B. Potthast, ¿*"Paraíso de Mahoma" o "País de las Mujeres"?* (Asunción: Fausto Ediciones, 2011), p. 328 (this excellent book includes truly devastating and heartbreaking stories of suffering by women in those years, which included not only rape, prostitution but even mass suicides).

19   For a colorful rendering of the legendary story of "*vae victis*" as the archetypal abusive position adopted by winners of wars, see S. Kovaliov, *Historia de Roma* (Madrid: Akal Textos, 1992), pp. 135–38.

20   Harris Gaylord Warren, *Paraguay y la Triple Alianza – La Década de la Posguerra: 1869-1878* (Asunción: Intercontinental Editora, 2011), contains a fully documented and extensive study of those sad years, including the fratricide and intestine conflicts, political murders and conspirations which followed the war.

21   The best history of the evolution of the laws applicable to Paraguay as a colony first and as an independent nation then, up to the war (and thereafter), is still the great book by the Paraguayan jurist J.J. Soler, *Introducción al Derecho Paraguayo*, 2nd edn (Asunción: La Colmena, 1959), pp. 181–286.

forces was simple: *we will give you* the laws for your country[22]. Thus, the first Paraguayan formal Constitution, enacted when the ashes of the war were still burning in 1870, was but a copy of Alberdi's Argentinean Constitution of 1853, and the workings of the national convention were scrupulously followed and controlled by the foreign invading armies[23]. The subsequent task of issuing civil and commercial laws was carried on "politically, under the supervision of the Triple Alliance and, intellectually, under the influence of Argentina"[24]. This was a cultural, but also practical, decision; Brazil after all was Portuguese and its laws were — at that moment — less developed in technical terms than the vanguardist Argentinean codes[25].

Thereinafter the process of "reception of Argentinean law in Paraguay"[26] began, a process which transformed Paraguayan legal history into one of bitter irony: one of the first South American country to declare its independence from Spain became, for more than 100 years, *legally dependent on a neighboring country* (i.e., Argentina). The reception of Argentinean law was total and

---

22 As an Argentinean historian — very critical of his own country's conduct — described the matter graphically: *"los ideólogos que en la punta de las bayonetas aliadas impusieron su hegemonía sobre el Paraguay en ruinas tenían que demostrar rápidamente su voluntad de cumplir los compromisos pactados. Para ello, había que darle una envoltura legal al sistema de poder que representaban... sobre la tierra calcinada y baldía había que plasmar un cuerpo ficticio: la caricatura de un Estado"*: G. Mellid, *Proceso a los falsificadores de la historia del Paraguay* (Buenos Aires: Theoria, 1963), vol. II, p. 413.
23 Gaylord Warren, pp. 115–137.
24 Soler, p. 289.
25 It must be immediately added, however, that the extraordinarily prescient work of the great Brazilian jurist Teixeira de Freitas — which *inter alia* composed the first draft of a code to contemplate the general category of the legal act or *Rechtsgeschäft* — was extensively borrowed upon by Vélez Sarsfield when drafting the Argentinean Civil Code: for his influence specifically on the notion of the "legal act" see S. Cifuentes, *Negocio Jurídico*, 2nd edn (Buenos Aires: Astrea, 2004), pp. 5–9; and in general, see the study by E. Martínez Paz, *Freitas y su influencia sobre el Código Civil argentino* (Córdoba: 1927).
26 Soler, unconsciously echoing what has been called the "reception" of Roman law in the late medieval period, uses without a doubt the correct term to convey the extensive, revolutionary and profound modification of the previous legal system by the new one: Soler, p. 289.

transversal: it covered civil, commercial, rural, procedural and criminal laws and confirms the fact of the continued dependence of Paraguay to the allied forces influence during many years after the Great War.

To cut a very long story short[27]: the first legal change involved commercial law, as the (then provisional) Paraguayan government adopted the Acevedo in 1870 and Vélez Sarsfield draft of a commercial code, which was to be in force until 1891, when Congress adopted in its stead the new Commercial Code of Argentina of 1889[28]. Incidentally, one whole book of the Commercial Code — *Libro III*, referred to maritime law — is in fact still in place in Paraguay to this day (!). Subsequently, in 1880 the Criminal Code of the Buenos Aires province was adopted, which was to be in place until 1910, when a notable Paraguayan criminal lawyer, Teodosio González, drafted the first truly Paraguayan Code: the *Código Penal* of 1910. In 1883 the Argentinean Criminal Code of Procedure was adopted *in integrum* and was to be in place until 1998 (!). The Rural Code of Argentinean jurist Valentín Alsina was copied without amendments in 1877. In 1883, the *Law of the Judiciary* ("*Ley Orgánica de Tribunales*"), a transliteration of an Argentinean statute, was adopted, and the Argentinean Code of Civil Procedure was sanctioned in 1883 and was in place until 1989 (!).

Last, but not least — given the extraordinary influence that civil codes had in the liberal bourgeois society of the late nineteenth century — the Argentinean Civil Code, drafted by Vélez Sarsfield, was approved *in totum* in 1876, coming into force in 1877[29]. Thus, in 1877 the civil legal order of Paraguay abandoned the archaic Spanish colonial laws which had been in place for more than 300 years — the *Fuero Juzgo*, the *Siete*

---

27 Once again, full details in Moreno Rodríguez Alcalá, pp. xxx–xxxix.
28 Soler, pp. 291–92.
29 "*(E)l Código Civil del doctor don Dalmacio Vélez Sarsfield, sancionado como ley de la República argentina en 1875, con excepción de aquello que se refiere a las provincias*": as Soler notes, this is a clear clerical error of the enacting law, since the Code was adopted in 1869, not 1875: Soler, p. 295.

Partidas, the *Ordenamiento de Alcalá,* etc.[30] —, and supplanted them with a new quasi-colonial law (Argentinean), changing one set of legal chains for another, to put it dramatically. The Argentinean Civil Code was to rule Paraguayan civil society for 110 years, making Paraguay's absolute legal dependence on a foreign system a cruel fact which was to be remembered by every Paraguayan lawyer, every Paraguayan legislator, every Paraguayan scholar, every time a legal situation arose for over a century[31].

As a one of the most egregious Paraguayan jurists of the first half of the 20th century, Juan José Soler, put it: the most harmful effect of the adoption in block (of foreign laws) was that Paraguay had been "thwarted from having a national legal doctrine, which interprets its own laws and gives it a proper personality", and it accordingly forced "judges, scholars and lawyers" to apply foreign legal rules. That is why, as he remarked in 1951 — making reference to the year of Paraguayan political independence — Paraguay was still waiting for its "legal 1811"[32]. And, as the greatest Paraguayan legal scholar of all time, Luis De Gásperi, remarked in 1962, whilst one had to admit that the "Argentinean codes were among the best in the hemisphere", they were still "here, in Paraguay, foreign", and this fact nullified the birth and consolidation of a Paraguayan legal doctrine — and, henceforth, the development of a truly *Paraguayan* legal system[33].

V

How was the Paraguayan legal order finally made "independent"?

---

30 Some of which were by the time more than 650 years old (!), as noted by José Antonio Moreno Ruffinelli, *Derecho Civil – Parte General,* 4th edn (Asunción: Intercontinental Editora, 1999), p. 31.
31 As rightly insisted upon by Soler, p. 307.
32 Soler, p. 307.
33 As quoted in: Moreno Rodríguez Alcalá, p. xli.

The end of the "argentinization" of Paraguay's legal system was made possible due to two factors: an (i) idiosyncratic, individual cause, and a concomitant (ii) specific political conjuncture[34].

The (i) individual cause was the existence in the middle of the 20th century of something that had been hitherto lacking: a true *rechtshonoratiore,* a jurist comparable to Latin-American luminaries such as Vélez Sarsfield, Andrés Bello or Clóvis Beviláqua, who could undertake the enormous task of drafting a civil code from aught in Paraguay. This jurist, of course, was the aforementioned Luis De Gásperi, who was the only Paraguayan legal scholar to publish his works in the then prestigious and massively influential Argentinean legal publishing companies and, again, the only local author to be well-known outside Paraguayan borders. De Gásperi was not only a highly prolific scholar — 3 weighty and learned tomes on the law of obligations, 5 even weightier and learned volumes on the law of successions, and innumerable other publications — but also a public intellectual and politician of the highest rank[35]. Moreover, he had acquired the status of "undisputed": as one witness of those years said, "no one in the country could challenge his unique position"[36] as the outstanding Paraguayan legal scholar of those times. The scholar who could undertake the construction of the legal order, absent in the calamitous postwar years, was now to be found in him.

The (ii) political conjuncture was the decision to create the *Comisión Nacional de Codificación* ("National Committee for Codification"), established by *Decreto-Ley* No. 200, and whose explicit mission was to "give the Paraguayan nation a legal order in consonance to Paraguayan legal culture". This was an initiative of the authoritarian government of Alfredo Stroessner,

---

34 Once again, I must refer the reader to the full treatment in Moreno Rodríguez Alcalá, pp. li–lxi.
35 The details on De Gásperi's intellectual profile, including his literary side, in Moreno Rodríguez Alcalá, pp. lxxiv–lxxix.
36 J.C. Mendonça, "Luis De Gásperi – Un anecdotario testimonial", in R. Moreno Rodríguez Alcalá (ed.), *Derecho Privado Paraguayo II – Estudios por los 30 años del Código Civil* (Asunción: La Ley Paraguaya, 2017), p. 13.

who governed Paraguay with an iron hand for 34 years (1954-1989) in an alliance with the military but politically with the "Colorado" party[37] — which, incidentally, is still in power[38]. Whatever criticisms this authoritarian regime (rightly) deserves — with its consistent human right violations in the forefront — the fact is that the "paraguayanization" of the legal order was an initiative of this government, which was the only one in the whole of the Paraguayan 20th century that had the necessary stability for even considering such an undertaking[39].

The *Comisión* originally had 10 members, which included De Gásperi, who was of the opposing "Liberal" party, and it represented what is still — and, by far — the best generation of legal scholars the country has had. The first decision of the *Comisión* was to give De Gásperi, individually, the task of drafting what would in time become the first truly Paraguayan civil code. The letter sent by the rest of the *Comisión* communicating this decision not only made it clear that De Gásperi was the leading Paraguayan jurist of the time, but also specifically instructed him to "unify civil and commercial obligations", an instruction which

---

[37] The wounds opened by this regime have not yet been fully healed and thus it is very difficult to find balanced historiographical treatments. A colorful and useful chronicle is found in B. Neri Farina, *El Último Supremo* (Asunción: El Lector, 2019); a short but very intelligent treatment is undertaken by Carlos Martini, in *Crónica Histórica Ilustrada del Paraguay* (Buenos Aires: Quevedo, 1997), vol. 3, pp. 908 ff. Finally, although it misses on the final — and arguably most decadent— decade of the regime, the work by the American historian Paul Lewis still remains the most complete overview of the regime: P. Lewis, *Paraguay bajo Stroessner* (México City: FCE, 1986).

[38] Since 1948, the Colorado Party has been ousted from power only briefly, in 2008–13, when the former bishop of the Catholic Church Fernando Lugo won with a coalition of opposition parties. The Colorado Party subsequently regained power in the 2013 elections.

[39] The first half of the 20th century was one of extreme political instability and recurring coup d'états in the country; the only government to last for more than 4 years — and, it is submitted, this is the minimum time frame for codifying the laws of a country — other than Stroessner was that of another military strong man, Higinio Morínigo (1940–48). The average length of a presidency from 1870 to 1954 in Paraguay was less than two years (!). See the useful summary in Lewis, pp. 16–17.

would lead, as will be seen below, to the subsequent notorious influence of the *Codice* in Paraguay[40].

Given the extremely precarious legal and material environment that existed in Paraguay in those days — no legal libraries, only one law school, no legal journals, *inter alia* — what De Gásperi achieved in a little less than three years can indeed be called a "cyclopean achievement" — as his fellow *Comisión* members would rightly put it years later[41] — culminating in his massive *Anteproyecto de Código Civil* ("draft of the civil code")[42], which was published at the expense of De Gásperi himself (!) in 1964[43]. This monumental work — which a distinguished Argentinean commercial lawyer dubbed "the most important codifying effort in Spanish since the *Siete Partidas*"[44] — has more than 2000 pages, with 3597 articles, each accompanied by erudite and exhaustive notes by the drafter. And, it is not superfluous to add, De Gásperi undertook this colossal task being of the opposition party and without charging one penny.

The "independence" of Paraguayan civil law would have been accomplished earlier had the *Comisión* — after receiving De Gásperi's draft in 1963 — decided to adopt the *Anteproyecto*

---

40   "*Cumplo en comunicar a Ud., que la Comisión Nacional de Codificación, en su sesión de fecha 27 del corriente, ha resuelto encomendarle la redacción del Anteproyecto de Código Civil. En el mismo sentido, se dispuso la unificación de los códigos civil y de comercio en las ramas de contratos y obligaciones, debiendo en consecuencia, adecuar el anteproyecto de referencia, a este plan de unificación. La Comisión Nacional de Codificación, al encomendarle este delicado trabajo, ha tenido en cuenta su vasta versación jurídica y el indudable patriotismo que le ha impulsado siempre en sus determinaciones intelectuales y en sus afanes de ciudadano*": letter from the President of the *Comisión*, J. Eulojio Estigarribia, to De Gásperi, quoted in Moreno Rodríguez Alcalá, p. xc.
41   The expression is found in "*Exposición de Motivos*" of the *Código Civil*, an equivalent to the *Relazione* of the *Codice*, as quoted in M. Pangrazio, *Código Civil Paraguayo Comentado* (Asunción: Intercontinental Editora, 1994), p. 77.
42   Hereinafter, simply, the "*Anteproyecto*".
43   De Gásperi, who as mentioned in the text did not charge for his codifying services, paid for the publication of the *Anteproyecto* himself.
44   Carlos Malagarriga, quoted in Moreno Rodríguez Alcalá, p. xciii.

without further study and consideration[45]. The *Comisión* however opted not to implement the *Anteproyecto* as it was, but to subject it to further scrutiny and analysis. This decision, as the legend goes, infuriated De Gásperi, who thereafter ceased to contribute to the *Comisión*[46]. However, more important than this anecdotical detail is that the profound changes introduced by the *Comisión* to the *Anteproyecto* made the final product, as will be seen below, much more heterogenous and contradictory than it would have been had the original draft been adopted "in block". Moreover, this decision entailed that the erudite notes by De Gásperi — which, crucially, indicate in detail the various sources from which he borrowed each article — were not incorporated in the final text.

The *Anteproyecto* was not however discarded; on the contrary, it was used as the "bedrock" for the final product. The *Código Civil* was literally drafted "over" the *Anteproyecto*: the starting point was the draft, with many changes and additions subsequently incorporated. But, surely not intentionally but without doubt, this decision makes matters much more complicated for the student, lawyer or judge who wants to discern the sources and rationale for each provision. To the various foreign sources that were used, the nitpicking of the original provisions of the *Anteproyecto*, coupled with the additions from other codes,

---

[45] The rationale for not adopting the *Anteproyecto* "libro cerrado" was explained two decades later in the *Exposición de Motivos* of the *Código Civil*: "*Al reflejar el Anteproyecto solo las opiniones y tesis jurídicas del anteproyectista y dada la multiplicación de teorías sustentadas en doctrina y legislación sobre materias de tan trascendental importancia y que afectan intereses de todos los sectores de la población, fue necesario encomendar a diversas subcomisiones el estudio y dictamen sobre los varios libros que abarca el proyecto de Código unificado, con el encargo de buscar fórmulas únicas de conciliación, tratándose de materias controvertidas, para ser consideradas en las reuniones plenarias de la Comisión*": quoted from Pangrazio, pp. 77–78.

[46] Incidentally, De Gásperi died in 1975, without seeing his life's work come to fruition. To put it dramatically: like the first biblical legislator, he died before seeing the promised land (of Paraguayan legal independence). As Prof. Mendonça has said, "it is saddening to think that the father of the *Código Civil* died without the joy of seeing his greatest work converted into law": Mendonça, p. 16.

makes a painstaking study of the antecedents of each provision of the *Código Civil* simply mandatory. Moreover, the *Código Civil* also contains radical departures from the *Anteproyecto* in many places, something that not only requires further and patient inquiry but also brings an internal tension to its normative system. All of these differences will be further studied below[47]. Here it suffices to note that the final draft was sent by the *Comisión* to the Paraguayan congress in 1985, and it was adopted without amendments to come into force from January 1 1987[48].

VI

Thus, in 1987, 110 years of Paraguayan legal colonization came to an end.

However, as I have tried to make clear for the foreign reader, the story of the Paraguayan *Código Civil* has two parts, or "acts": (i) the first act is the *Anteproyecto* and the legislative decisions adopted by a single person, Luis De Gásperi (and explained in each case with his extensive notes); and (ii) the second act is the final *Código Civil*, which took the *Anteproyecto* as starting point but, drafted by more than 20 hands, constitutes a free-standing product, with many significant departures from its originator.

As will be seen next, this two-part story has profound implications for tracing the influence of the *Codice* on the *Código Civil*, since the *Anteproyecto* spoke a *medesma lingua* during almost one-third of its provisions, while the *Código Civil* opted for a more Babelian approach.

---

47 *Infra*, sections XIII-XIX.
48 For the full story, once again, Moreno Rodríguez Alcalá, pp. xciv–xcix.

Part Two
The road not taken: the influence of the *Codice* on the *Anteproyecto*

VII

In effect: the influence of the *Codice* on Paraguayan civil legislation would have been extremely more pervasive had the *Anteproyecto* been adopted "in block", without further changes. This is so because De Gásperi — in my opinion, correctly — considered the *Codice* not only as *the* "state-of the art" code at the time of his drafting, but also followed it strictly in the unification of obligations, in the law of obligations in general, and the law of contracts in particular. In fact, *Libro Quarto* of the *Codice* is translated almost totally into *Libro II* of the *Anteproyecto*. And, although the final *Código Civil* maintained the general provisions for unification of obligations and many specific solutions of the *Codice,* this was done mixing the Italian sources with other sources, such as Argentinean and Germanic, making a general overview much more difficult but undoubtedly less "Italian".

In other words, had the *Anteproyecto* been adopted straightforwardly, the influence of the *Codice* would have been even greater than it is today — although today, it is still important, as it will be seen.

VIII

After finishing his *Anteproyecto*, but before officially publishing the draft, De Gásperi gave a conference at the local bar association (*Colegio de Abogados*) which is extremely valuable, not only because it contains his most explicit and zealous defense of the need for the birth of a truly Paraguayan doctrine and of acquiring "legal independence" from Argentina, but, what is more important: it contains the only printed summary of the guiding ideas and principles that structured his codifying efforts[49].

In this conference, De Gásperi stated that there were three fundamental guiding ideas — which can be called here for analytical purposes as his underlying legislative "policies" — that inspired the *Anteproyecto*:

> 1°. I have not intended to invent any rule or article in order to give originality to my draft, given that in Law, as in Philosophy, there is no possibility of creation outside what has already been created. At most, only subtle amendments to the principles and rules already known is possible.
> 2°. I have sought to retain (as many) provisions of the Argentinean Code (as possible), but as polished by ulterior reform drafts such as the Bibiloni effort and the Draft of 1936.
> 3°. I have retained, out of respect for tradition, the division of the Code in the four classic books of the Argentinean code.[50]

This official list, which was very faithfully followed by De Gásperi when drafting the *Anteproyecto*, contains however one glaring omission. The omission is more than corrected by the title of the conference itself: "Draft for the internal unification of our private law". In fact, the rest of the conference is but an explanation of how the *Anteproyecto* sought a major legal revolution in Paraguay by unifying hitherto separate civil and commercial laws, a process which — as the civilian that he always was — he defined as the "civilization of commercial law"[51]. That is: the incorporation of commercial contracts and rules into the civil code, which becomes indeed a code of "private law" as the title of the conference indicates. In De Gásperi's own words:

---

49   Since De Gásperi wrote no official "*exposé des motifs*" or a "*relazione*" to his *Anteproyecto*, it is submitted that this learned and detailed dissertation is to be considered as the faithful exposition of the ideas and policies that suffused the draft of the Paraguayan jurist. The full text of the conference is now found in: L. De Gásperi, 'Esquema de unificación interna en nuestro derecho privado', in L. De Gásperi, *Anteproyecto de Código Civil*, ed. by R. Moreno Rodríguez Alcalá (Asunción: La Ley Paraguaya, 2019), vol. II, pp. 1161–83.
50   De Gásperi, p. 1166.
51   Many others would submit — particularly, commercial lawyers — and not without reason, that the process actually entailed the "commercialization of the civil law".

> Contractual commercial law has been [here] absorbed by the civil law of obligations, in the manner predicted with much foresight by Vivante in the prologue to his famous treatise on Commercial Law.[52]

Consequently, more than half of the conference contains a detailed enumeration of the many contractual figures which the *Anteproyecto* included but that were absent in the Argentinean Code, and which are direct copies from the *Codice* (e.g., the *estimatorio* contract, the *riporto*, the provisions on legal instruments or *titolo di credito*, etc.).

Put differently, although not included in the "official" list of policies which he followed when drafting the *Anteproyecto*, it is simply impossible to deny that the main substantive policy of his efforts was the unification of civil and commercial law, and — though De Gásperi mentions the Swiss and German examples — it is clear that the *Codice* was the outstanding and exclusive model for this endeavor.

This substantive policy of unification, therefore, must be included in the list of the legislative "policies" that inspired De Gásperi in drafting the *Anteproyecto*.

Thus, the codification effort to be found in the *Anteproyecto* can be seen as having four fundamental legislative policies:

> i. Borrowing as the basic principle: extensive borrowing from other sources with no pretense of originality; that is, a conscious decision of copying rather than inventing the provisions to be found in the draft;
>
> ii. Respect for the Vélez Sarsfield Code and its draft reforms as main source: faithful observance for the tradition of the Vélez Sarsfield Civil Code and its reform drafts which is to be the foremost and by far most important source used in the whole of the *Anteproyecto*, specially in areas other than the law of obligations (family, succession, property, etc.);
>
> iii. Division of the draft following the institutional model: the *Anteproyecto* is divided into four books, inspired by the classical *Institutes* model, rather than the pandectist method of a general and special part; and
>
> iv. Unification based on the *Codice*: the total and comprehensive unification of civil and commercial obligations, using the *Codice* as the exclusive model.

---

52   De Gásperi, p. 1165.

IX

For the purposes of tracing the influence of the *Codice* on the *Anteproyecto*, it goes without saying that the two most important of these underlying policies are: (i) borrowing with no pretense of originality and (ii) the decision to complete unify private law. Both were followed by De Gásperi with persistence and coherence throughout the *Anteproyecto*. When composing *Libro Segundo* of the *Anteproyecto* — which contains 1818 of the total 3597 articles of the draft (i.e., more than 50% of the text) — De Gásperi adopted, almost verbatim, *Libro Quarto* of the *Codice*. The only exception is the first part of the *Libro Segundo* of the *Anteproyecto*, which in respecting principle (ii) — i.e., observance of the Argentinean tradition — incorporated the general category of the "legal act" (the *Rechtsgeschäft* or *negozio giuridico*), which is famously absent in the *Codice*. However, the rest of *Libro Segundo* is almost exclusively an extensive borrowing of *Libro Quarto* in the effort to internally unify the law of obligations in Paraguay[53].

Thus, "general part of obligations" in the *Anteproyecto* is, almost exclusively, a copy of Articles 1174 to 1259 of the *Codice*, establishing the basic theoretical framework for the unifications of obligations. In these matters, the *Anteproyecto* speaks in translated Italian.

The same goes for the general part of contract: the fundamental provisions of the *Codice* regarding the preliminary part of contracts, the requisite of contracts, offer/acceptance, the object of contracts, interpretation and effects — including termination — was followed, with some very minor modifications, by the *Anteproyecto*. An important conceptual difference to be noted is that De Gásperi refused to include the notion of "cause," that the *Codice* incorporates in its Article 1325, a decision that was to

---

53 Which, as seen above, was divided with a Civil Code on the one hand and a Commercial Code on the other in the aftermath of the Triple Alliance War, following the French tradition.

continue in the *Código Civil*[54], which can be considered in this sense as "anti-cause"[55].

Finally, in the substantive part of the unification of obligations, the symmetry between the *Codice* and the *Anteproyecto* is total. The following order — and concomitant provisions — of the *Codice* are thus to be found in the *Anteproyecto*: sale; permutation; the *estimatorio* contract; supply contract; the *riporto*; lease and hire; enterprise contract; mandate; transport agreement; commission; agency contract; intermediation; deposit; bailment; savings account; banking contracts; insurance; guarantee; etc. The regulation of contracts in the *Anteproyecto* is basically identical with the *Codice*, and where it departs it is only in minor methodical departure. For example, the regulation of corporation in the *Anteproyecto* is in the part of contracts, whereas in the *Codice* is to be found in the book dedicated to "*lavoro*". Moreover, the gift (*donación*) is regulated in the contract section, whilst in the *Codice* it is found in the law of succession[56].

Much the same applies to the notion of the "unilateral obligation" (*promesa unilateral*) and its corollary found in the law of negotiable instruments. Thus, the whole section regulating *titolo di credito* in the *Anteproyecto* is a copy of the *Codice*, whilst the regulation of the bill of exchange (*letra de cambio*) follows the *Real Decreto* of 1933. The same occurs with the check (*cheque*), since the *Anteproyecto* extensively copies the provisions of the Italian Law No. 1736.

---

54 Hence, whilst De Gásperi copies Article 1325 of the *Codice* when stating the requisites of contracts in Article 1017 of the *Anteproyecto*, he deliberately omitted clause 2) referred to "causa". I have explained the — not always straightforward — reasons that De Gásperi gave for this decision in Moreno Rodríguez Alcalá, pp. cxcix–ccvi.

55 An erudite monograph defending this decision was written in the first years of the *Código Civil* by J. Moreno Rodríguez, *Teoría de la Causa* (Asunción: Intercontinental Editora, 1995).

56 It must be nonetheless noted that in the case of the gift the regulation contained in the *Anteproyecto* is not entirely based on the Italian model, as De Gásperi also incorporated many provisions from Argentinean sources. Being a matter more related and intertwined with family law and succession, De Gásperi also preferred to follow tradition and custom here.

Hence, as De Gásperi himself stated, "contractual commercial law is to be absorbed by the civil law of obligations."[57] The *Anteproyecto* thus "civilized" commercial law (or "commercialized" civil law), producing a law of obligations which can be considered as the bulk of "private law". As with the Italian legislator, however, the Paraguayan jurist retained the title of "Civil Code", without reference to the commercial side (and hence the *Anteproyecto* is of a *Código Civil,* rather than a *Código Civil y Comercial* or *Código de Derecho Privado,* etc.). In this, De Gásperi once again shows scrupulous respect for his source, but also his formation as an orthodox *civil* lawyer[58].

In sum: it is simply undeniable that the influence of the *Codice* in the unification of private law in the *Anteproyecto* is absolute, and that *Libro Segundo* of the *Anteproyecto* and *Libro Quarto* of the *Codice* do seem to speak in a *medesma lingua.*

X

However, even in the part most faithfully followed by De Gásperi, that of the unification of obligations, some important differences exist between the *Anteproyecto* and the *Codice.*

As mentioned above, a major difference is that the *Anteproyecto* followed the tradition of the Argentinean Civil Code and included the general category of the legal act — "*Rechtsgeschäft*" or "*negozio giuridico*" —[59] departing here from its Italian model. Albeit some scattered provisions of the *Codice* regarding the

---

57 See section IX, *supra.*
58 My defense of the thesis that De Gásperi was a — quite emphatic — orthodox civil lawyer in Moreno Rodríguez Alcalá, pp. clxxxiii–ccxiv.
59 Articles 497–794 of the *Anteproyecto*. Therein the following chapters or headings may be found: of legal facts (*hechos*), vices of consent (error, fraud and violence), the form of legal acts, simulation and fraud (so-called Pauline fraud), modalities of the act (condition, term, etc.), representation, nullity, confirmation of null acts and finally a chapter on the exercise of rights and evidence.

regulation of legal acts made their way to the *Anteproyecto*[60], they are the exception, and De Gásperi here borrowed massively from the Vélez Sarsfield Code and its various reform drafts, the celebrated *Esboço* of Teixeira de Freitas, and the German BGB. The incorporation of the category of the legal act, and its regulation, by itself undoubtedly has a deep impact not only in the conceptual structure of the draft but also in its practical implications.

The elimination of the requisite of "cause" for contracts has also been mentioned, but other important differences remain. The provisions referred to "nullity of contract" of the *Codice* (Articles 1418–1446) were not incorporated, given that De Gásperi had followed his Argentinean sources for regulation annulation of legal acts in general. On the other hand, the provisions for *rescission* of contracts were not incorporated by De Gásperi (Articles 1447-1452 of the *Codice*). The *Anteproyecto* also departs by regulating the services contract independently, borrowing here heavily from the BGB and the Swiss Code of Obligations (Articles 1381-1407 of the *Anteproyecto*). Although the *Anteproyecto* regulates the "perpetual rent" (*renta vitalicia* or *rendita perpetua*), it does not follow the *Codice* in detail but Argentinean sources, and the same occurs with lottery and bet agreements (*juego y apuesta* or *giuoco e scommesse*). For the guarantee agreement (*fianza* or *fideiussione*), De Gásperi mixed provisions from the Argentinean tradition with the provisions of the *Codice*. With the settlement or transaction agreement (*transacción* or *transazione*), De Gásperi also preferred to follow the Argentinean model rather than its Italian counterpart.

Once we reach the other sources of obligations — particularly unjustified enrichment and torts or civil liability — the departures are more radical.

Indeed, instead of following the (French-influenced) formulation of Article 2041 of the *Codice* for unjust enrichment (*arricchimento senza causa*), the *Anteproyecto* copied § 812 *et*

---

60 Some examples: Articles 522–528 refer to Articles 1428-1433 of the *Codice* with regards to error; Articles 571 and 572 refer to Articles 1416–1417 of the *Codice* with regards to simulation; and other minor provisions.

seq. of the German BGB, thus adopting its very different scheme of the modern abstract *condictio*. The differences between both systems, of course, cannot be underestimated.[61]

When regulating torts (*responsabilità civile*), De Gásperi outright ignored the provisions of the *Codice* — starting from its famous *clausola generale* of Article 2043 — opting instead for the closer Argentinean sources, whilst amalgamating them with other heterogenous models, such as the BGB, and — more curiously — the Polish Code of Obligations (of 1936), when incorporating the "risk theory" for objective liability.[62] More to the point, any discussion of the *danno ingiusto* — which so heavily characterizes legal scholarship of torts in Italy — is absolutely foreign to the architecture of the *Anteproyecto*.[63]

XI

In any event, these specific differences, although important, do not negate the fact that the *Libro Quarto* had an outstanding influence in the *Anteproyecto* and that for the most part De Gásperi copied the provisions of the *Codice* and unified the law of obligations. Here the *Anteproyecto* preponderantly speaks in Italian.

Things change dramatically when we focus on the other books the *Anteproyecto,* regarding other aspects of civil law, such as marriage and family, property and the law of succession.

---

61 I have described the main differences in Moreno Rodríguez Alcalá, pp. ccxlviii–ccliii.
62 The book of R. Moreno Rodríguez Alcalá, *Arqueología de la responsabilidad civil en el derecho paraguayo* (Asunción: La Ley Paraguaya, 2009) contains a detailed analysis of the structure of tort liability in the *Anteproyecto* and its differences with the current *Código Civil*.
63 An erudite essay comparing both systems is to be found in G. Fossati, 'Antijuridicidad y tipicidad en el sistema del ilícito civil. Breves notas comparativas entre los sistemas Paraguayo e Italiano, en Suplemento de Responsabilidad Civil', Revista Jurídica La Ley Paraguaya (2008), pp. 203 ff.

For the rest of these matters, the influence of the *Codice* on the *Anteproyecto* wanes to almost zero.

Most obviously, nothing such as *Libro Sesto* of the *Codice*, dedicated to the protection of rights (*tutela dei diritti*), is to be found in the *Anteproyecto*. Albeit some very scattered provisions of this *Libro* eventually found their way (e.g., Articles 2741 and 2745 referred to preference between creditors and privileges), the *Anteproyecto* departed from the Italian model in this point[64]. The same applies to the *Libro Quinto*, dedicated to *lavoro*, except with respect to the discipline of the *società* in general and the specific types of corporations, which was included as mentioned above by De Gásperi in the book on obligations (as he considered that the *società* is a "contract"); however, the rest of the provisions included in this *Libro Sesto* are absent from the *Anteproyecto*.

With regards to the other books of the *Codice* — *Libro Primo*, *Libro Secondo* and *Libro Terzo,* dedicated to persons/family, succession and property, respectively — a wide but safe generalization may be submitted: only very exceptional and scattered provisions of the *Codice* will be found in the *Anteproyecto*. In these matters, more firmly attached to local social tradition, custom and idiosyncrasies, De Gásperi basically limited himself to the Vélez Sarsfield Civil Code provisions, which had been firmly entrenched in Paraguayan society, and its various reform drafts, such as Bibiloni and the *Draft of 1936*. The law of property also has some important influence from the BGB and its followers. The law of succession, in turn, is completely based on the Argentinean tradition.

Consequently, although a specific enumeration of Italian provisions which found their way to the *Anteproyecto* in these

---

64 De Gásperi did include some provisions of this book when regulating the matter of "evidence." For example: Articles 2706, 2709-13 and 2720 of the *Codice* on documentary evidence; Articles 2731-35 regarding judicial confession; Article 2722 regarding witness testimony, or Article 2727 regarding legal presumptions. These are, however, the exception with regards to the Argentinean tradition and in any case the Paraguayan legislator decided later that all questions of evidence were to be regulated by the Civil Procedure Code (enacted in 1989) and not the Civil Code.

matters would be extremely cumbersome[65], it is safe to say that the *Codice* was a very secondary and unimportant influence in these matters of private law.

XII

Admittedly, the painting sketched in the previous pages used a quite broad brush indeed, mainly for reasons of space. And yet, however generic, the painting allows for reaching two firm conclusions regarding the influence of the *Codice* on De Gásperi and his *Anteproyecto*.

The first conclusion is *positive*, in the sense that the *Codice* had a massive — but not exclusive— influence on the *Anteproyecto*. In this sense, De Gásperi's work shows great coherence with the four policies that he adumbrated as underlying his effort: the *Anteproyecto* showed (i) no originality (in the sense of copying the relevant provisions) in (iv) unifying the civil and commercial obligations, respecting by and large the unification undertaken in the *Codice Civile* in its *Libro Quarto*, which finds it mostly Italian based counterpart in *Libro Segundo* of the *Anteproyecto*. There can be thus no discussion that, with minor differences, the regulation of the general part of obligations, the general part of contract, and the particular instances or types of contract the *Anteproyecto* by and large followed the *Codice*. The borrowing was, to use a figure, in block, and talk of a *medesma lingua* is warranted.

The second conclusion, however, is *negative*, in the sense that in other areas of private law — particularly, those with more local or native impact, such as family law, succession and property — the Codice Civile had a very secondary and minor influence for De Gásperi. In this sense, there can be no doubt about the fidelity of the drafter to his main, controlling policy of (ii) respect for the

---

65 Some provisions on the name and its protection (Articles 14–23); on the presumption of death (Articles 37–61); on civil associations (Articles 95–115 and Articles 116–123); and on co-ownership in buildings (Articles 2752–2791) show strong Italian influence.

Argentinean tradition, which so heavily impacted in the daily lives of Paraguayan for almost a century. And, although there are indeed instances of scattered provisions of the *Codice* in these areas, they are exceptional and mostly uneventful.

These two conclusions in turn jointly produce a phenomenon which is typical of the *Anteproyecto* — and which will only grow and grow in the *Código Civil* — as a vast and impenitent borrower of the most heterogenous sources.

Firstly, where the borrowing has been uniform — such as the unification of obligations — the task of the jurist or judge is simpler, in the sense that it can limit itself to the Italian code and its subsequent interpretation by the legal scholarship (*dottrina*) and the *Cassazione* and its case law.

Secondly, where De Gásperi either followed other sources or mixed the Italian source with provisions from other traditions, the task is more complex and arduous: the job of the interpreter is to make each provision cohere with the other sources, and thus, make the work speak with one voice, to the extent possible.

But here, in this problematic second case, is where one can find De Gásperi's perhaps most profound ideal for the future of Paraguayan civil law, his vision for the development of Paraguayan law after the code had been adopted.

For De Gásperi, rather than a problem, the unique situation produced by the extensive borrowing of different legal sources would give Paraguayan civil law a unique flavor, allowing it to become a synthesis of the best from the civil law tradition. The task of the Paraguayan jurists and lawyers would thus precisely be one of contrasting the different sources, finding a new and fresh synthesis which amalgamated the best of the French, German and Italian tradition — this being the last, and thus to that point most authoritative, *aggiornamiento* of the tradition. As the Paraguayan jurist himself eloquently argued in the above-mentioned conference — which constitutes his *Relazione*, so to speak — with his usual clarity:

> If the *Anteproyecto* were to be adopted by Congress, our jurists and lawyers will need to confront the classic Roman-French doctrines of the Vélez Sarsfield Code with those of the German pandectists and the Swiss

Civil Code, as actualized and conformed by the Latin genius of the drafters of the *Codice Civile* of 1942 [...] Paraguayan lawyers and jurists will find it necessary to collect legal works of diverse European origin, most of which are not translated into Spanish. Introducing them and accommodating them to the daily study and analysis will thus be a condition for renewing of the basic and foundational subjects of Civil and Commercial law that play such a large part in the formation of our culture.[66]

De Gásperi thus saw western civil law — in which Paraguay was of course incardinated — as a tradition that, to quote the famous trope of Lord Mansfield, "works itself pure"[67]: it is constantly in the making, with a necessary confrontation of the solutions arrived to by the different branches, to find the best – that is, the most reasonable, sensible, just solution – to the interminable problems of human beings. Law is, to paraphrase Ortega, a *faciendum* and not a *factum*[68], and this *faciendum* would be found, according to De Gásperi, in the constant "confrontation" of the different sources he used — a task in which his erudite notes, included in each article, would no doubt play a major role. He thus constructed the *Anteproyecto* on the borrowing principle not casually, but *intentionally*, and he thought that the coexistence of different sources would be a positive identifying mark of the new Paraguayan civil law, rather than a defect. The need for permanent confrontation, for discussion of the different sources and their interpretation, for reading the French (and Argentinean), German and Italian scholarship and case law, would be the defining mark — and advantage — of Paraguayan civil law.

This confrontation of the different sources and branches of the civil law in the *Anteproyecto* would thus make it necessary for Paraguayan jurists, judges, and lawyers to immerse themselves into this tradition and mine from it in order to make the draft

---

66 De Gásperi, p. 1182 (emphasis added).
67 The phrase was introduced in the famous case Omychund v. Barker (1744) 26 ER 15.
68 I adopted this brilliant quote by the Spanish philosopher José Ortega y Gasset to explain the civil law tradition more generally and its constant evolution in Moreno Rodríguez Alcalá, pp. cclxxxix–cccxxiv (the reference to Ortega's phrase found in his *Historia como Sistema* is on p. cccii).

a coherent whole. And, of this tradition, the "Latin genius" incardinated in the *Codice* was to play an important part — not the least, in the unification of the whole law of obligations. The influence of the *Codice* and Italian law cannot be henceforth put in question not only in the original text of the *Anteproyecto*, but what is more important, in (as its drafter intended) its subsequent application in daily life and practice.

PART THREE

THE (LESS PERVASIVE AND MORE PROBLEMATIC) INFLUENCE OF THE *CODICE* ON THE *CÓDIGO CIVIL*

XIII

"*If the* Anteproyecto *were to be adopted by Congress [...]*".

But, of course, as has already been noted above, this was not the case. The *Anteproyecto* was not sanctioned "in block" or without further review, but rather was subject to a very thorough revision and innumerable amendments by the *Comisión*.

Indeed, after receiving the *Anteproyecto* in 1963, the *Comisión* had two alternatives: to adopt the *Anteproyecto* without modifications, or to use it as a main source but introducing the necessary changes. The latter route was taken, and the *Comisión* chose to use De Gásperi's work as the principal source — to literally build upon it — but also freely introducing modifications, even radical ones, to the original work. This led to more than 20 different jurists working for more than 20 years, and the final *Código Civil* was finished only in 1985.

These 20 years were not at all ineffectual, and the final product presents not only a very different structure from the *Anteproyecto* but is also noticeably much less coherent. The differences are found in the surface and in the substantive regulation. Not only were the original 4 books divided into 5 books but the 3597 articles of the *Anteproyecto* were trimmed down to 2814 of the *Código Civil*. These superficial differences however are far less important than the profound substantive departures that can be found in the *Código Civil*. It is very safe to say that although the *Anteproyecto* was the basic document used by the members of the *Comisión* from which to start their work, the changes they introduced were so radical, that we are facing two absolutely "different legal universes". The substantiation of this claim would of course implicate hundreds of pages; two specific studies regarding torts and unjustified enrichment have been elsewhere undertaken by this author and they are conclusive in adducing that the differences between the draft and the final product are highly significant[69].

Paradoxically, although the *Código Civil* departed from the *Anteproyecto* in many matters, the methodological process of "confrontation" that De Gásperi had adumbrated for his own draft is even more urgent with the actual code. This is so because although the *Código Civil* took the borrowing principle very seriously, it introduced "originality" in an unintended way: by mixing, whilst regulating a single legal institution, varied sources. Hence, in the *Código Civil* one can find a provision which comes from the *Codice* coexisting with one coming from the Vélez Sarsfield Code and one from a Germanic source. And so on and so forth.

Thus, the "confrontation" of sources to make the code "work itself pure" and find the best possible synthesis, is even more necessary in the *Código Civil* than in the *Anteproyecto*.

XIV

The latter conclusion is explained by the fact that even where the subsequent codifiers followed De Gásperi — for example, when copying the bulk of *Libro Quarto* of the *Codice* to unify obligations — they introduced throughout provisions from other

---

69 For torts: R. Moreno Rodríguez Alcalá, *Arqueología de la responsabilidad civil en el derecho paraguayo* (Asunción: La Ley Paraguaya, 2009); for unjustified enrichment, Moreno Rodríguez Alcalá, introduction (see *supra*), pp. ccxlviii–ccliii.

sources, composing a text filled with potential legal irritants. Hence, the interpreter of the *Código Civil* must be extremely careful: he may find a text that clearly comes from the *Codice*, say article 418 which, as noted above, translates article 1174 of *Codice*, that is however followed by a series of provisions which come from the French-Argentinean tradition and which have — at least purportedly — a different structure for the liability of the debtor (*responsabilità contrattuale*), as well as a "concrete" concept of *fault* which is foreign to the *Codice*[70]. This is not an isolated case, but an endemic situation to be found throughout the *Código Civil*.

Therefore, although many provisions of the *Codice* are still found in the *Código Civil* — specially in its *Libros* II and III, which regulate obligations in general and the law of contracts, respectively — they are contaminated, to use a strong word, with sources from other systems.

The following sections will use a broad brush to paint a global painting of the *Código Civil*, with special attention to the influence of the *Codice* on its provisions. The conclusive finding may however be stated simply: even where the Italian influence was undeniable — that is, in following the *Anteproyecto's* decision to unify civil and commercial obligations — the *Código Civil* attenuated this inspiration by mixing it with other sources; whereas, in other areas of the civil law, the influence of the *Codice* is almost nil[71].

---

[70] Articles 420–427 of the *Código Civil*, which regulate what is the nucleus of the liability of the debtor in Paraguayan law (*responsabilidad contractual*), are inspired by the "fault-based" liability system — which, in the orthodox reading, is found in both the French and Argentinean systems — and incorporates the peculiar, and justly famous, definition of negligence that Vélez Sarsfield introduced in his notorious Article 512. This "concrete" definition of negligence is particular to Argentinean law (and thereafter, Paraguayan law) and is distinct from the concept of *bonus pater familiae* which is still found in the *Codice*. I have touched on many of these issues in Moreno Rodríguez Alcalá, *Arqueología*, pp. 79–106 and 268–75.

[71] Hereinafter, I will use the following edition of the legal text: *Código Civil y leyes complementarias* (Asunción: La Ley, 1988), which painstakingly compiles the sources used in each article of the *Código Civil*, in order to determine the sources found in the final text; the work of linking each article

XV

The *Código Civil*, as was already hinted above, broke down the original 4 books of the *Anteproyecto* into 5 books. This difference is explained by the division of the *Libro* on the law of obligations and contracts — contained in the *Anteproyecto* as a single unit, just as in the *Codice* — into two books. Thus, *Libro II* of the *Código Civil* is dedicated in the first part to the regulation of the "legal act" (Articles 277–416) whilst the second part regulates the general part of obligations (Articles 417–668); and *Book III* begins with the general law of contract (Articles 669–736), and then includes the specific types of agreements (Articles 737–1799), finalizing with the "other" sources of obligations: unilateral obligation, *negotiorum gestio*, unjustified enrichment or payment of undue obligation (*ripetizione di indebito*), and finally torts or *responsabilidad civil* (Articles 1800–1871).

This formal rupture is not, however, the most important difference.

While De Gásperi copied *Libro Quarto* of the *Codice* almost as a single block when unifying the civil and commercial obligations and contracts, the drafters of the final *Código Civil* introduced several changes into the Italian model. For example, the "general provisions" on the "effects of obligations" — basically, the responsibility of the debtor (*responsabilidad contractual*)[72] — were supplanted by provisions of the Vélez Sarsfield Code and its reform in 1968 (the so-called "Borda Reform", named after the jurist who drafted it), which seem, at least taken at face value, firmly subjective (i.e., contractual

---

to its sources was undertaken by the following Paraguayan authors: Antonio Tellechea, Enrique A. Sosa, José V. Altamirano, Raúl Andrada Nogués, Hernan Casco Pagano, Joaquín Irún Grau, Mario Paz Castaing and Manuel Riera. It should be clarified that I have not undertaken here the further task of analyzing — on an article-by-article basis — if each source considered by these authors is exactly correct and thus, in some cases, there may be need for further consideration or qualifications.

72 Articles 420–429 of the *Código Civil*. These provisions also include the regulation of *mora creditoris*, which follows the Argentinean rather than Italian model.

liability rests on fault)[73]. This in turn is followed by norms regulating preference in insolvency and privileges, which although containing some Italian elements, are mostly based on the Argentinean models[74]. Thereafter provisions related to damages, both legal and conventional, are found, including the regulation of the *clausola penale* or liquidated damages. All of these provisions mostly follow Argentinean sources, except the important Article 459, which allows for reduction of the clause and is a mutilated copy of Article 1384 of the *Codice* (mutilated, since it omits the important consideration of the creditor's interest)[75]. Thus, although the *Codice* was used as a source, its provisions coexist with rules coming from other systems — rules which are not necessarily coherent.

With regards to the provisions on the general part of obligations, changes are even more pronounced. No reference is made to the rule of *correttezza* of Article 1175 of the *Codice*, which was copied by De Gásperi and eliminated in the *Código Civil*, and the whole part of "*adempimento*" was also, on the one hand, moved to the chapter dedicated to the "extinction of obligations" (as "payment"), and on the other, had many provisions from Argentinean sources added to the original Italian rules. The system for *mora creditoris* of the *Codice* was also directly eliminated, as well as the chapter dedicated to "*inadempimento*" of obligations (Articles 1218–1229) which, as explained above, was supplanted by provisions from Argentinean (and thus more French) model. The rules for monetary obligations were also eliminated and in its stead rules from the Paraguayan tradition were incorporated (Articles 474–475 of the *Código Civil*). The other rules on "various species of obligations" were maintained from the Italian model but, once again, heavily mixed or

---

[73] See the work and pages cited in n. 70, above, for a sketchy study — and some doubts raised — on this interpretation of the system.

[74] Articles 430–444 (except for Article 430 which, as mentioned, follows the wording of Article 2740 of the *Codice*).

[75] With regards to this specific text, see R. Moreno Rodríguez Alcalá, "El derecho comparado en acción: la doctrina de las 'penalty clauses' como guía para la reducción (y comprensión) de las cláusulas penales excesivas"; Revista Jurídica Paraguaya La Ley (Asunción: La Ley, 2008), pp. 769 ff.

fragmented with provisions from the Argentinean sources — in this part, the *Bibiloni Draft and the Draft* of 1936 played an important role, almost as important as the *Codice Civile*[76]. To quote one example of a rule with a completely different impact, the presumption of solidarity of article 1294 of the *Codice* is directly put on its head in the *Código Civil* (Article 510).

While the Italian rules on credit assignment, *expromissio* and debt transfer were largely respected (Articles 524–546 of the *Código Civil*), when turning to the regulation of the extinction of obligations, once again, the Italian original model followed by De Gásperi was heavily mixed and/or fragmented with rules from other source which, once again, are Argentinean based. Particularly important here are, again, the *Bibiloni Draft* and the *Draft of 1936*[77]. On the other hand, the chapter dedicated to statute of limitations or prescription is not only methodologically included in a different part than the *Codice* but once again is heavily dependent on Argentinean sources rather than the Italian model[78].

Libro III of the *Código Civil* is dedicated to the general law of contract, the particular types of contracts, and "other sources of obligations", which include unilateral obligation, *negotiorum gestio*, unjustified enrichment and torts. Although the basis for this book was the *Anteproyecto*, and behind it, the *Codice*, there are once again many differences, as the *Código Civil* adopted once again many solutions which were copied from other sources.

With regards to the general law of contract: all the preliminary provisions of the *Codice* were eliminated (Articles 1321–1324 of the *Codice*), as well as the requirement of *causa* (Articles 1343–1344, ibid). The German variant of *laesio* was adopted, with a great emphasis on the subjective factor, abandoning the

---

76 For example: in Articles 464, 465, 470, 471, 473, 483, 491, 492, 510, 515, 519, or 521, *inter alia* (of the *Código Civil*).
77 See, *ex multis*, Articles 547, 548, 550, 557, 558, 560, 564, 565, 566, 585, 587, 588, 589, 597, 598, 599, 600, 602, 610, 611, 619, 626 (of the *Código Civil*).
78 Once again, *ex multis*: Articles 634, 639, 641, 647, 649, 659, 661, 662, 663, ect. (of the *Código Civil*).

objective Italian version[79]. The doctrine of *eccessiva onerosità* as regulated by the *Codice* was introduced into the *Código Civil*, albeit with some differences which come from Argentinean sources[80]. The articles on "consent" or offer/acceptance were by and large respected, but again, with some important changes[81]. The rule contained in Article 1341 of the *Codice* regarding abusive or unfair clauses was also incorporated (Article 691 of the *Código Civil*), but the first part, which regulates incorporation of the general conditions of contract, was directly eliminated. The provisions on the object of the contract, in turn, were abandoned for norms which came from the Argentinean sources (Articles 692–698, including the prohibition on sale of a future inheritance established in Article 697). With regards to form, some provisions of the *Codice* are to be found, but the meaning of the section has changed completely, mostly due to the incorporation of Argentinean sources[82]. Moreover, no reference is made to "conditional contracts"; the matter is dealt in the general part of the legal act and incorporating Argentinean sources. The provisions of interpretation (Articles 708–714 of the *Código Civil*) are almost *litteris verbis* from the *Codice*, as mentioned in the introduction, and therefore stands as an exception in this landscape (in the sense that no important additions were introduced to the original version). With regards to the "effects" of the contract, the picture is mixed. Thus, the

---

79 On this point, see: J. Moreno Rodríguez, *Curso de Derecho Civil – Hechos y Actos Jurídicos* (Asunción: Intercontinental Editora, 1991), pp. 409–31.

80 For further detailed analysis of this provision: J. Antonio Moreno Ruffinelli, *La Teoría de la Imprevisión y su aplicación a nuestro derecho positivo,* revised edition by R. Moreno Rodríguez Alcalá (Asunción: La Ley Paraguaya, 2020).

81 For example: Article 685 which establishes the "intention to create legal obligations," or Article 687 which refers to the place of celebration or Article 688 which applies the theory of "expedition" instead of the provision of Article 1328 of the *Codice*, which applies the theory of *cognition*, etcetera.

82 Article 700 of the *Código Civil* establishes form but only *ad probationem*, not *ad solemnitatem*, in contradistinction to the Italian source. The — in practical terms — key provisions of Articles 701 and 702 which establish the consequences of not following the provisions for form also come from the Argentinean sources, as well as the article on *contradocumentos* (Article 707).

Código Civil incorporates some very important provisions from the *Codice*, such as Article 1376 (*consensuality* in contracts[83]), as well as provisions found later in the text of the Italian source, that is, on the chapter on *"risoluzione"*: specially, the provisions of Articles 1453–1458 (not, however, Article 1459: the notion of "plurilateral contracts" is foreign to Paraguayan law). Other rules, such as the effects on successors, the *exceptio de non adimpleti contractus*[84], the *arras* and subsequent impossibility[85] of performance all come predominantly from Argentinean sources.

With regards to the specific types of contracts, other important differences arise. Several contracts foreseen by the *Codice* and the *Anteproyecto* were directly eliminated from the *Código Civil*: for example, the *estimatorio* contract, the supply contract; the *riporto*; the enterprise contract (being supplanted by the traditional *locatio operis*); and the agency contract (as well as the subdivisions contained in the hire contract). On the other hand, the type of contracts that were incorporated from the *Anteproyecto* (and thus from the *Codice*) were also heavily integrated and/or fragmented with provisions that came from other sources, most noticeably again, Argentinean sources, but also provisions drafted by the *Comisión* itself. And, to add to the confusion, these texts are many times mixed with the Italian source. To mention just some examples: a) with regards to the sale contract, the following provisions come from sources other than the original Italian model: Articles 738, 741, 742, 747–751, 755, 757, 761, 765, 768, 770, 771, 779, 782, 785, 791, 792 (i.e., almost a third of all articles are not Italian based); b) hire: Articles 803, 804, 805, 807, 809, 810, 822, 824, 825, 826, 830,

---

83 Article 716 of the *Código Civil*.
84 Although this is a patched-up provision: some parts are Argentinean, and others Italian (particularly the good faith requirement to be found in Article 1460 of the *Codice*).
85 Two very important provisions of the *Código Civil* — not yet duly analyzed by Paraguayan scholarship — are Articles 721 and 722, which come from Argentinean draft reforms (and behind them from the Germanic system) and are inspired on the contractual liability system based on impossibility (*Unmöglichkeit*).

833, 834, 835, 836, 841, 842, 844 (almost half are not Italian); c) services contract, all the articles come from the *Comisión* itself or Argentinean sources; d) *locatio operis*: 852, 853, 854, 856, 860, 862 (once again, almost half are from different sources); d) mandate: Articles 880, 881, 882, 883, 884, 885, 886, 890, 891, 892, 893, 895, 896, 897, 898, 899, 901, 905, 909, 910, 911, 913, 917. Etcetera. All of these specific types of contracts contain rules drawn from the *Codice* but mixed with rules from other sources, which of course makes the result completely different.

With regards to corporations and commercial entities, once again, the final system is a patchwork between the Italian original source and Argentinean sources. For example, with regards to the general part of the *società*, Articles 959, 960, 962, 963, 964, 965, 966, 968, 971, 972, 973, 975, 976, 983, 984, 986, 991, 992, 993, 995, 996, 999, 1000, 1002, 1003–1005, etc., are all either from Argentinean sources, or synthesis from various sources — including the *Codice* — drafted by the *Comisión*. In the most important corporation, the *sociedad anónima*, there exists a true clash between the *Codice*, on the one hand, and Argentinean statute *Ley 19.550* of 1972 (with provisions of the old Argentinean Commercial Code), which coexist in tension in the whole chapter, sometimes in the same provision (for example: Articles 1078, 1080, 1084, 1089, 1095, 1098, 1099, 1102, 1108, 1111, 1113, etc.) (!).

In relation to other types of contracts, although the kind of agreement may be found in the *Codice* and the *Código Civil*, the Italian code cannot be even considered a principal source in some cases. This is what happens to the *fianza* or guarantee (*fideiussione*), where the Argentinean sources prevail; the gift (*donazione*), which is mostly a copy of *Draft of 1936*; and the insurance or *assicurazione* contract (which has the Argentinean Statute *Ley 17418* of 1967 as the almost exclusive source). The rules on the old *aedilitian* remedies — *evicción and vicios redhibitorios* — which cover 40 articles, are also based on the Argentinean sources (once again, the *Draft of 1936* is very important here). Finally, the case of the *transacción* or settlement (*transazione*), is once again one of coexistence of different sources. The *Código Civil* incorporates the definition of Article 1965 of the *Codice*, thereby abandoning the French (and Argentinean) position that a transaction cannot give rise to the creation of new obligations. However, although it includes another article coming from the Italian source (Article 1966), the rest of the provisions are inspired by the French/Argentinean connection, and thus leave the matter in a complex pastiche yet to be understood and analyzed[86].

Hence, even in the specific types of contracts that De Gásperi had included in his draft from the *Codice* that made their way to the *Código Civil*, the original Italian provisions were mixed up with sources that come from other traditions and branches, making the result a patchwork of norms.

XVI

It is only when one reaches the concept of unilateral obligation (*promesas unilaterales* or *promesse unilaterali*) that once again the *Codice* is found in almost pure state — although methodologically the matter is regulated *contra natura*, since the *Código Civil* regulates the *titolo di credito* first and the general concept of *promessa unilaterale* 300 articles later. The *negotiorum gestio* also follows the *Codice* for the most part.

A peculiar situation occurs when the drafters of the *Codigo Civil* decided to depart from the *Anteproyecto* when regulating *unjustified enrichment* and *undue payment* (*ripetizione di indebito*), since the usual move throughout the text is to abandon the Italian model for an Argentinean or other source; here, however, the *Anteproyecto*'s choice of the BGB is itself abandoned and in its stead the provisions of the *Codice* are introduced. Thus, the system of the *condictio* coming from the German BGB was discarded for a copy of Article 2041 of the *Codice*, with a major difference: the key term "*giusta*" was

---

[86] The matter is dealt in (a still unpublished) paper: R. Moreno Rodríguez Alcalá, 'Veritade ascosa sotto bella menzogna: cosa juzgada y resolución del contrato de transacción' (on file with the author).

eliminated from the original, leaving an important vacuum for the interpreter[87].

Finally, with regard to *torts*, the *Codice* was once again definitely not followed by the *Código Civil*, but neither was the *Anteproyecto*; most of the provisions either come from Argentinean sources or are original drafts and/or mixes of foreign provisions undertaken by the *Comisión*. The chapter on *responsabilidad civil* is perhaps the most original one in the *Código Civil*, as it was declaredly abandoning the primacy of fault — the *pas responsabilité sans faute* axiom — and expressly introducing a chapter on "liability without fault"[88]. This said, however, there are a some important Italian provisions which made their way to the final product and which thus coexist with the other rules of the (Argentinean-French) system. Noteworthy here are the provisions on legitimate defense (a copy of Article 2044 of the *Codice*) and necessity (ibid., Article 2045), as well as the rule on solidarity (a transcription of Article 2055 of the *Codice*). Finally, the provision of Article 2050 for "dangerous activities" of the *Codice* was also incorporated into the *Código Civil* but, contrary to the original text, any reference to fault was expressly eliminated. Article 1846 of the *Código Civil* thus goes farther than its Italian source and establishes an indisputably objective standard of liability[89].

---

87 See R. Moreno Rodríguez, 'Commentary to Article 1817', in *Código Civil de la República del Paraguay Comentado*, 3rd edn (Asunción: La Ley Paraguaya, 2019), vol. VII, pp. 918–20.
88 Articles 1846 to 1854 of the *Código Civil*.
89 I have written elsewhere more extensively on this system, especially: R. Moreno Rodríguez Alcalá, *Arqueología de la responsabilidad civil*, pp. 231–46 and R. Moreno Rodríguez Alcalá, '¿'Adhocracia'?: El riesgo de la responsabilidad por riesgo en nuestro derecho', in F. Trazegnies, F. Pantaleón Prieto, C. Soto and R. Moreno Rodríguez Alcalá, *Cómo repensar el derecho privado moderno* (Asunción: La Ley Paraguaya, 2010), pp. 185–215.

XVII

The findings on the law of obligations that flow from the foregoing sections can be summarized as follows: the *Codice* is still a major source of the *Código Civil* for unifying civil and commercial obligations, but not as pervasive and coherent as it had been in the *Anteproyecto*. Instead of following the policy of De Gásperi — which is to be commended — of not prizing originality and keeping fidelity to a single source, the members of the *Comisión* introduced a great number of variations and fragments into the original Italian system. This has a major consequence, of course: whilst the influence of the *Codice* is real, profound and undeniable, *Libros* II and III of the *Código Civil* are far from being simple copies of *Libro Quarto*. The need for constant, and extensive, "confrontation" of the sources, and of harmonizing the Italian sources with their Argentinean counterparts, is widespread.

XVIII

The influence of the *Codice* in the *Anteproyecto* in other fields of private law, more directly enmeshed with local values and customs, as has already been mentioned, is radically less important — and in many parts, in fact, inexistent. The main source for family law, property and succession was, without question, the Argentinean (and behind it, French) tradition.

This remains very much the case with the *Código Civil*. The influence of the *Codice* in the law of persons and family, property, and succession, is also almost nil.

Thus, the law of persons and family law is by and large without traces from the *Codice*. There are some minor exceptions. One example in the law of persons is the figure of *"inhabilitación"*, which was a less severe form of incapacity or persons with mental health or substance abuse problems, and which Article 89 of the *Código Civil* incorporates — modulated however with bits from the *Borda Reform* — from Article 415 of the *Codice*[90]. The influence of the *Codice* is also noteworthy in the rules regarding the civil association (*asociación de utilidad pública;* Articles 102–117), but these provisions are the only ones which show strong Italian pedigree in this part of the law. And, although some very faint instances of provisions which are inspired by the *Codice* can be found in family law, in truth its influence was non-existent: herein the Argentinean sources and the statutes which were already in force in Paraguay were crucial[91].

Proceeding to the provisions regulating the legal act (*negozio giuridico*), as explained above, the Argentinean sources — building on the pioneering work of Brazilian jurist Teixeira de Freitas — were here dominant. Some minor exceptions, which lead to awkward problems, may nonetheless be found. For example, when regulating the simulation of legal acts, the *Código Civil* follows Argentinean sources except in two cases: Article 309, which is a copy of Article 1416 of the *Codice* and more importantly, Article 310 which copies Article 1417 of the *Codice* regarding the issue of admissible evidence in case of simulation. The same situation occurs with so called *actio pauliana*, which includes a provision inspired in Article 2902 of the *Codice* that departs, profoundly, from the original Argentinean sources. The potential legal irritation that follows will be further touched upon below[92]. In any case, besides these provisions and some minor traces found in provisions regarding the evidentiary value of certain documents[93], the *Codice* was definitely not the model.

With regards to property law, regulated in *Libro IV* of the *Código Civil*, the *Codice* once again has a very minor role. Only

---

[90] A couple of provisions regarding the name of persons also show Italian echoes: Articles 42, 44 and 47.

[91] The *Ley de Matrimonio Civil* of 1898 and the *Ley de los derechos civiles de la mujer* of 1954 (which was a pioneering law with regards to equality between men and women and which was originally drafted by De Gásperi) were very important sources for the regulation of patrimonial aspects of marriage.

[92] *Infra*, section XXVI.

[93] For example, Articles 414–416 of the *Código Civil* incorporate Articles 2705, 2712 and 2720 of the *Codice*.

some scattered provisions are to be found[94]; the real and massive influence here are the Vélez Sarsfield Code, and the drafts of *Bibiloni* and *Draft of 1936*, which in many cases — such as possession — show a very strong Germanic influence, which is far from the spirit of *Codice*[95]. An exception is the section regarding the administration of buildings, which does follow the *Codice* with quite some consistency (Articles 2146-2162), although even here Argentinean sources were used subsidiarily or in addition[96]. Some Italian sources are also detected in the servitude section, although always accompanied or mixed with Argentinean sources[97]. The rest of the book dedicated to real rights over other property, liens, mortgages and actions for protecting real rights, show almost no trace of the *Codice* and retain a strong influence of the Argentinean sources.

Finally, *Libro V* of the *Código Civil* which regulates the law of successions, is almost entirely inspired in Argentinean sources. The influence of the *Codice* here is also next to zero.

XIX

Broad and general as they are, the brushes sketched above allow for a clear picture to appear, not only with respect to the influence of the *Codice* in the *Código Civil* but also with regards of the consequences of the method of borrowing so extensively used by the drafters of the *Anteproyecto* and of the final product. It may be helpful to recapitulate these main discoveries.

Firstly, there can be no doubt that the *Codice* was the outstanding and principal source of the *Anteproyecto* of Luis De Gásperi for the unification of civil and commercial obligations. *Libro*

---

94 *Ad exemplum*, Articles 946 and 934 of the *Código Civil*.
95 I have studied these influences in R. Moreno Rodríguez Alcalá, 'György Lukács y la posesión en nuestro Código civil: acerca de un leading case de la Sala Civil sobre el problema de la teoría objetiva y la usucapión inmobiliaria', Revista Jurídica Paraguaya La Ley (2019), pp. 3003 ff.
96 See e.g., Articles 2158, 2161, 2162, etc. (of the *Código Civil*).
97 Thus, Articles 2189 or 2190 (of the *Código Civil*).

Quarto of the *Codice* was thus incorporated, for the most part in block, into *Libro II* of the *Anteproyecto*. However, the rest of the *Anteproyecto* — including the bulk of persons and family law, property law and successions — followed other sources, such as the Argentinean Civil Code and its draft reforms and Germanic models. Thus, the situation in the *Anteproyecto* was mixed, so to speak: with regard to the law of obligations, reference to Italian doctrine and case law would have solved most of the interpretive issues had the *Anteproyecto* been adopted *in totum*, whilst for the other areas of law, as De Gásperi himself asserted, the method would have been one of "confronting" the different sources — Argentinean (and behind it French), the German pandectistic efforts, and the "Latin genius" of Italian scholarship — in order to attain a fresh synthesis explaining Paraguayan private law.

Secondly, the fact remains that the *Anteproyecto* was not adopted as such, since the *Comisión* decided to use it as its foundation but freely modifying or departing from it. During the 20 years that it worked on it, the *Comisión* profoundly changed the *Anteproyecto*, and precisely where De Gásperi had denied any pretense to originality copying the *Codice* almost verbatim, the members of the *Comisión* introduced many changes to the general part of obligations, the general part of contract and the specific types of contracts. The result is of a very piecemeal, stitched set — and it is submitted, not always felicitous — of norms: the *Código Civil* fails to speak in a unified or coherent voice. The need for "confrontation" of sources, which in the *Anteproyecto* would have basically limited to Italian material, is now simply endemic.

These findings fully confirm the apodictic assertions found in the Introduction of this essay. The *Código Civil* is an exemplary proof of the above quoted dictum of Watson: *the life of Paraguayan civil law has been borrowing, borrowing and more borrowing*. It is unique in the sense that it borrows from all three basic civil law traditions: the French (in its Argentinean variant), the Germanic, and the Italian. Moreover, inside these sub-traditions, the borrowing has been as extensive as it is fascinating: many provisions of Paraguayan law are drafts from

Argentina that were never implemented in their country of origin, and in most legal figures, traces from the most varied sources are to be found. This entails that there exist tensions not only between the different main branches, but also within each sub-branch of the civil law tradition. The *Código Civil* is, in the strict sense of the term, a *kaleidoscopic* — albeit a learned and conscious one — work, a *Babelian code*, which speaks in many tongues.

But: what is to be done, how is this heterogenous legal body to be interpreted and applied, how can Babel be put back together?

PART FOUR

METHODOLOGICAL MUSINGS: BRICOLAGE AS A WAY OF FINDING A COHERENT VOICE IN THE *CÓDIGO CIVIL*

XX

The conclusion that the *Código Civil* was constructed by using the borrowing principle so extensively has not only proven that the *Codice* was a very important source for many parts of the law of obligations, but also that its influence is never exclusive, since it is almost always accompanied by other languages. The *medesma lingua* has turned into a *Babelian* product. Even where the *Codice* was used, this is always mixed with Argentinean (most cases) or Germanic (the fewer) sources. Thus, an essay tracing the influence of the *Codice* in the *Código Civil* naturally and without effort leads to the methodological problem of how to best understand, interpret and apply such a heterogeneously composed body of law.

The final pages of this essay will sketch a (very) tentative proposal to this methodological problem and will conclude with a reflection on the still important influence of the "Latin genius" in Paraguayan civil law.

XXI

One answer that Paraguayan doctrine post-*Código Civil* applied to the methodological problem posed by its *Babelian* structure was as simple as wrongheaded: to keep quoting and referring to Argentinean doctrine and scholarship, as if nothing had happened and the Vélez Sarsfield Code was still in force (or as if the whole of the *Código Civil* is based on Argentinean sources, something which of course is untrue).

This position, while coherent, is not correct. It fails precisely to consider that kaleidoscopic character that so uniquely constitutes the *Código Civil*. The approach may work in areas of law in which Argentinean influence is outstanding, such as the regulation of the legal act or *negozio giuridico* or of the law of succession. But in those areas in which the main source is Italian, such as the assignment of obligations, the different types of obligations, the termination of contracts, or negotiable instruments, the Argentinean sources are simply analyzing and interpreting a different rule (!).

A couple of examples will suffice.

Consider the institutions of the assignment of a credit or of debt, or the termination of contract, both subjects in which the *Código Civil* is heavily inspired by the *Codice*. A leading treatise on the law of obligations cites Argentinean and Paraguayan authors, but no Italian scholarship or case law[98]. On the other hand, the most comprehensive commentary on termination of contracts — *risoluzione* — cites Argentinean authors, Paraguayan case law, and a commentary on the UNIDROIT Principles[99]. And so on.

This solution in my view ignores the insight of De Gásperi of the need to confront and synthesize the different legal sources and keeps applying Paraguayan law as if no break with Argentinean law has been attained.

---

[98] A.J. Martínez Simón, *Esbozo de las obligaciones civiles* (Asunción: Editora Litocolor 2016), pp. 463–500.

[99] F. Legal Aguilar, 'Commentary to Articles 725-728', in J. Antonio Moreno Rodríguez, *Código Civil de la República del Paraguay Comentado* (Asunción: La Ley Paraguaya, 2019), vol. V, pp. 959–980.

An even more diffused variant of this option may be found in the literature. Instead of limiting oneself to Argentinean authors, other Paraguayan scholars have opted to include in a random manner German, French, Argentinean, and Italian authors, amalgamating their opinions without considering the different sources for each article, that is, without noting if the German or French doctrine can apply to an Italian provision or whether an Italian author can explain the Argentinean source (of course: it cannot). This approach is well illustrated by the analysis of assignment of credit by another leading treatise on obligations: the author cites indiscriminately 12 Argentinean authors, 10 German authors, 4 Italian scholars[100], 1 French and 1 Paraguayan scholar[101]. This approach, once again, is not sensitive to the different sources and does not consider that the German (or Italian, or Argentinean, etc.) author may in fact be commenting a totally different rule. Although, it does show erudtion shows erudition, it is not sufficiently sensitive to the normative reality of the *Código Civil*.

An even more peculiar position has been taken in the leading commentary on the general part of contract, perhaps the most heavily "Italian part" of the *Código Civil*[102]. Although it does cite some Italian scholarship, it mostly promotes an interpretation of these provisions with reference to the UNIDROIT Principles, the Principles of European Contract Law and the Vienna Convention of 1980. The proposed approach rests on the current transnational trends on contract law, but completely disregards the sources and the meaning of the articles of the *Código Civil*. Interpreting a text from 1942 with a text from 1993 or thereafter — and texts which explicitly so are either condensing of various traditions or directly new provisions as the UNIDROIT and PECL mostly are — may be useful de *lege ferenda* but seems *lege lata* as simply

---

100 Two of them refer to De Ruggiero; that is, an author who is pre-*Codice*.
101 M. Gauto Bejarano, *El Acto Jurídico* (Asunción: Editorial Intercontinental, 2012), pp. 750–776.
102 See J.A. Moreno Rodríguez, *Código Civil de la República del Paraguay Comentado*, 3rd edn (Asunción: La Ley Paraguaya, 2019), vol. V, *et passim*.

a flat-out disregard, contempt even, for the normative reality of the *Código Civil*.

XXII

Neither of the foregoing approaches does, in my view, true justice to the *Babelian* code that is the *Código Civil*. Most notably absent is not only the sensitivity required by the fact that even within one institution many sources were used — making the intellectual operation of "confrontation" required by De Gásperi inevitable — but also a recognition of the true importance and impact that the *Codice* has had in many sections of the code. The learned erudition of Italian scholarship — its "Latin genius" — and the rich development it has had in the *Cassazione* case law, is mostly absent in these pages. This has been, in my opinion, most deleterious for the development of Paraguayan civil law.

Perhaps, one could say, this criticism of ignoring Italian scholarship is too harsh. Specially, considering that Argentinean authors were more readily available for historical, geographical and cultural reasons, whilst the erudite Italian scholarship was mostly inaccessible for Paraguayan scholars. This may have been true in the first ten years of the *Código Civil* — i.e., before internet and its great enabling for reaching unbeknownst places — and given that only a handful of Italian books had been translated into Spanish. But even in those days there were Italian authors — and highly distinguished ones — available. Messineo stands head and shoulders above the rest here, given that not only his truly magisterial *Manuale* was already translated (which covers the whole of private law)[103], but also his *Dottrina Generale* which covered the general law of contract[104]. Insofar as the first *oeuvre* contains a holistic treatment of Italian law, at least one authoritative source was available. Brunetti's treatise

---

103 F. Messineo, *Manual de derecho civil y comercial* (Buenos Aires: EJEA, 1971).
104 F. Messineo, *Doctrina General del Contrato* (Buenos Aires: EJEA, 1952).

on the *società* was also available early on[105]. Barbero's complete (if somewhat idiosyncratic) treatise was also translated early on[106], as well as other monographs, particularly Betti's learned volumes on obligations and the *negozio giuridico*[107], and Cariota Ferrara's and Stolfi's efforts[108] on this subject[109].

Some harshness is thus justified when criticizing the traditional doctrinal position that for the most part ignored Italian scholarship.

Recently, a personal accident has tilted the historic balance of either keep citing Argentinean sources, or an indiscriminate citation of multi-sources, introducing a more detailed analysis and use of Italian doctrine and case law. The accident is that a young jurist, son of an Italian immigrant and fluent in Italian, came to occupy the position of clerk to an influential justice in the Supreme Court, Raúl Torres Kirmser. Through these opinions, many of which carried the majority during his tenure in the Civil Section of the Supreme Court (2004–18), Torres Kirmser incorporated learned and more recent Italian scholarship — posterior to the early works of Messineo *et al.* —, and also the case law of the *Cassazione*. This was a much needed fresh of breath air for Paraguayan civil law and put the *Código Civil* in line with its strong Italian roots. Moreover, in 2017, the young former clerk, Giuseppe Fossati López — who, incidentally, obtained his doctorate in Bologna under the reputed Italian

---

105 A. Brunetti, *Tratado del Derecho de las Sociedades* (Buenos Aires: UTEHA, 1960).
106 D. Barbero, *Sistema del Derecho Privado* (Buenos Aires: EJEA, 1967).
107 E. Betti, *Teoría General de las Obligaciones* (Madrid: Editorial Revista de Derecho Privado, 1969) and E. Betti, *Teoría General del Negocio Jurídico* (Madrid: Editorial Revista de Derecho Privado, 1959).
108 L. Cariota Ferrara, *El Negocio Jurídico* (Madrid: Aguilar, 1956) and G. Stolfi, *Teoría del Negocio Jurídico* (Madrid: Editorial Revista de Derecho Privado, 1959).
109 The list of Italian authors that were translated into Spanish early on is not exhaustive of course; this is just an indicative enumeration of (what the author deems as) the most important books that were available in the early years of the *Código Civil*.

jurist Francesco Galgano[110]— assumed as judge in the Civil and Commercial Court of Appeals (4th session) in Asunción, and from there has elaborated a highly distinctive jurisprudential voice. Once again, his erudite judgments as an appellate judge are filled with the most authoritative Italian scholarship and *massime* of the *Cassazione*[111].

The pendulum has thus started to swing, somewhat, due to this accident, and a careful consideration of the "Latin genius" by both (some of our) courts and (some of our) authors may be found today.

However, it is submitted that this approach can also be taken too far, particularly when it concentrates solely on Italian authors and case law in situations in which the solution of the *Codice* was actually not adopted by the *Código Civil*. Some judgments incurring in this position may hence be criticized precisely on this point[112]. That is to say: while the re-introduction of the

---

110 The resulting book was the first Paraguayan legal text published in Italy: G. Fossati, *L'incidenza del titolo cambiario sui rapporti sottostanti alla sua emissione e girata: ricostruzione di un sistema* (Padova: CEDAM, 2011).

111 Three examples of judgments by Torres Kirmser which rely on Italian doctrine and case law are: Ferreira, Rosa I.c. Avalos Fretes, Esteban (Ac. y Sent. N° 853) (published in La Ley Paraguaya as: PY/JUR/312/2008); Vázquez Galeano, Crescencia c. López Vda. de Guerrero, Blanca Nidia s/ Cumplimiento de contrato y obligación de hacer escritura pública. (Ac. y Sent. No. 183) (published in La Ley Paraguaya as: PY/JUR/131/2015); G. B., S.c. M. M., A. y otros s/Indemnización de daños y perjuicios. (Ac. y Sent. No. 1478) (published in La Ley Paraguaya as: PY/JUR/782/2016); three (brilliant) judgments by Fossati López, which are filled with erudite Italian references are: F. A., M. A.c. N., M. T. y otros s/ indemnización de daños y perjuicios (Ac. y Sent. No. 64) (published in La Ley Paraguaya as: PY/JUR/120/2022); M., A. M.c. Itau Py. S.A. s/Indemnización de daños y perjuicios. (Ac. y Sent. No. 44) (published in La Ley Paraguaya as: PY/JUR/400/2018); and A. S., V. L.c. G. V., R. M. s/Indemnización de daños y perjuicios por responsabilidad extracontractual (Ac. y Sent. No. 37) (published in La Ley Paraguaya as: PY/JUR/163/2020).

112 One example of a case in which a judgment went too far, in my opinion, was the position, partly founded on Argentinean authors, but also on Italian authors such as Sacco and Caterina (specifically, their book on the law of possession: R. Sacco and R. Caterina, *Il possesso* (Milano: Giuffrè, 2000) elaborated to maintain that possession under the *Código Civil* requires the traditional *animus domini* subjective requisite. The *Exposición de Motivos* and the specific sources used, however, indicate that the *Código Civil* here

conceptual acuity and solidity of Italian scholarship and case law into Paraguayan civil law which this position has lately championed is a much needed corrective to the historical tendency of Paraguayan jurists and judges of flatly ignoring Italian sources, this option can also be — when taken too far — insensitive to the actual sources of the specific rules in the *Código Civil*, and thus can fail to duly "confront", as De Gásperi intended, the three main streams that form the river of Paraguayan private law: Argentinean/French, Germanic, and Italian.

None of these positions, taken by themselves, seems fully satisfactory.

XXIII

Almost 15 years ago, whilst investigating the system of tort law that De Gásperi had created for the *Anteproyecto*, I clumsily stumbled upon the insight that it is simply impossible to understand the rules of the *Código Civil* without being extremely sensitive to its *Babelian* structure[113]. Even when studying the rules of, for example, strict liability, it is not sufficient to quote Argentinean authors *in toto*, or a ragbag of Argentinean, German, Italian, etc., or solely Italian authors, but a truly specific and highly sensitive approach, which respected the kaleidoscopic structure of the code, was necessary. I then termed my proposed methodological stance as "archaeological", given that the both the *Anteproyecto* and (more so) the *Código Civil* were created from an infinite amount of legal borrowings, even when regulating one single legal institute, such as civil liability, or possession, or simulation, or the gift, or the contract of sale, and so on and so forth. The task

---

explicitly rejected the subjective approach found both in the Vélez Sarsfield Code and the *Codice*, and in its stead opted to follow the "objective" theory, copying provisions of the Brazilian Civil Code (1916) and the Argentinean drafts for reform (i.e., the Bibiloni and *1936 Draft*), which eliminated this requirement. I have criticized the approach held in this specific judgment by Fossati López in the article mentioned in n. 95, *supra*.

113 Once again: Moreno Rodríguez Alcalá, *Arqueología de la responsabilidad civil en el derecho paraguayo*.

of the legal analyst, the jurist, judge, or lawyer, when facing a specific legal question, was, as I concluded, inevitable: she would have to consult the sources first in order to be able to obtain a reasonable interpretation of the norm in question. Only when the specific sources had been identified, it would be possible to continue and proceed to solve a specific case.

Hence, I concluded, the need for an archaeological approach is simply *sine qua non* to understand the *Código Civil*. As a matter of fact, it was precisely this kind of inquiry that has been undertaken in the previous pages, to show where — and where not — the *Codice* has influenced the *Código Civil* and why it is such an important, albeit by no means exclusive, source.

This essay, which started by tracing the influence of the *Codice* on the *Código Civil* — and keeping always in mind the important idea of De Gásperi of the need of "confrontation" of sources —, has further convinced me however that the archaeological analysis by itself is insufficient, in the sense that it needs one further step to be complete. In order to complete the proposed archaeological approach, in the final pages of this paper, I will borrow — borrowing again! — from the ideas of the great French anthropologist Claude Lévi-Strauss to propose a more complete methodological approach, which includes archaeology first, but must go beyond: *legal bricolage*.

XXIV

In his classic, but extremely difficult work, *La pensée sauvage*[114] — whose complexity starts with the untranslatable title itself[115] — Lévi-Strauss proposed a (then) revolutionary

---

114 Hereinafter cited in the new English translation: C. Lévi-Strauss, *Wild Thought: A new translation of "La Pensée Sauvage"* (Chicago: University of Chicago Press, 2021).

115 "Translating the untranslatable" as the new translator of the book graphically calls it ("Translator's Introduction" by John Leavitt in *Wild Thought*, pp. xii–xvii); and, more generally, see P. Wilcken, *Claude Lévi-Strauss: The Father of Modern Anthropology* (New York: Penguin, 2011), pp. 249–75,

thesis: that so-called "primitive" people (better: people "without writing"[116]) also had a method for facing, and successfully coping, with reality, just as we "modern" people have the "scientific" method, which for us seems to be the only possibility. This form of thought, which although some may call it "primitive," in fact "still subsists among us"[117] as a science of the "concrete".

Vividly, Lévi-Strauss compares this mode of thought to that of the *bricoleur*, who "must make use" of the "set of heterogenous elements" it has at hand "no matter what task it is carrying out". The *bricoleur* faces his task "with 'whatever is at hand'", that is, the "heterogenous" "set of tools and materials" it has at her disposal.[118] Just as the common *bricoleur* creates a new work out of the materials that she has at hand, the French anthropologist suggests that this untamed mode of thinking enabled human beings to subsist during centuries in this world without the aid of modern science. These set of materials and tools, as Lévi-Strauss emphasizes, are the "contingent result of all the occasions that have presented themselves", including the "leftovers from previous constructions and destructions"[119]. The "heterogenous objects" that the *bricoleur* has at hand constitute his "treasury" from which he works and constructs upon[120]. By inspecting, assembling and reassembling these heterogenous objects, the *bricoleur* "builds structures by putting together events, or rather the residues of events"[121], and constructs a new — useful — material out of a "debris of events"[122].

In order to more fully explain his metaphor, Lévi-Strauss proposes to "observe [the bricoleur] at work":

---

116 As Lévi-Strauss later said, we usually but "wrongly" call them "primitive", but we better describe them as "without writing", since "this is really the discriminatory factor between them and us": Claude Lévi-Strauss, *Myth and Meaning* (New York: Schocken Books, 1979) p. 15.
117 Lévi-Strauss, *Wild Thought*, p. 19.
118 Lévi-Strauss, p.19.
119 Lévi-Strauss, p. 20.
120 Lévi-Strauss, p. 21.
121 Lévi-Strauss, p. 24.
122 Lévi-Strauss, p. 24.

Excited by his project, his first practical move is retrospective; he must turn back to an already constituted set, consisting of tools and materials; inventory or reinventory it; finally, and above all, engage in a kind of dialogue with it, in order to identify the responses that the set can offer to his problem, before choosing among the possible solutions.[123]

The results attained by a *bricoleur* after embarking in her task, and considering her limited means, are nonetheless often "brilliant and unforeseen"[124]. This science of the concrete — a "first science" — is to be compared with the abstract, "modern" science which chiefly "operates by means of concepts"[125]. However, the form of "wild thinking", the *pensée sauvage* of the primitive mind, has not disappeared and been supplanted by modern science, since in fact "it still subsists among us". As the great anthropologist insists: "make no mistake: it is not a matter of two stages, or two phases, of knowledge, since the two ways of proceeding are equally valid"[126].

XXV

The idea of *bricolage* as a valid mode of thought, of a way of coping with the complexities of the world that has been around for centuries, is of course nested in the dense philosophy of structuralism that Lévi-Strauss borrowed from structural linguistics[127]. Unrooted from this complex foundation, however, it is here submitted that the metaphors of "bricoleur" and "bricolage" work perfectly — precisely as vivid images — in order to describe the task faced by a Paraguayan jurist, lawyer or

---

123 Lévi-Strauss, p. 21.
124 Lévi-Strauss, p. 20.
125 Lévi-Strauss, p. 22.
126 Lévi-Strauss, p. 26.
127 An excellent history of "structuralism", with an account of the influence of structural linguistics, is to be found in François Dosse, *History of Structuralism – The Rising Sign 1945-1966* (Minneapolis: University of Minnesota Press, 1998). It should be forcefully emphasized that the idea of bricolage is in this essay used particularly as a metaphor, rather than as a "structuralist" analysis of the reality behind the *Código Civil*.

judge when confronting the heterogenous, kaleidoscopic *Código Civil*.

Just as the bricoleur, the Paraguayan jurist will find before her a vast "set of heterogenous elements," a "set of tools of materials", which are the innumerable sources, from a vast array of foreign codes and drafts, that were used in patching up the *Código Civil*. These "heterogenous elements" include, of course, the *Codice* and its great influence when unifying the law of obligations, but also the Vélez Sarsfield Code, its reform drafts, the BGB, the Swiss Civil Code and all the innumerable sources which lie behind the code. The Paraguayan legal bricoleur thus has at her disposal a "treasury" of tools and elements, which are the absolutely contingent[128] result of choices made by De Gásperi first, and the members of the *Comisión*, afterwards, and which leave for the interpreter a vast array of "leftovers" to be sorted out. The *Código Civil* is in this sense a structure built from "debris of events"; the debris here are the heterogenous sources, from Argentina, from France, from Germany, from Italy, and so on and so forth, that were used for composing the final product.

To insist on a key point: the existence of this vast array of sources, of this heterogenous amount of legal debris, was not an accidental side-effect of the codifying effort, but was something intentionally envisaged by De Gásperi when drafting the original *Anteproyecto*. Moreover, this heterogenous composition was not a defect in his view, but something extremely valuable for the future development of Paraguayan civil law, since it would make it absolutely necessary for Paraguayan scholars to delve

---

128 In the sense that the almost infinite amounts of borrowings follow no logical or imperative rationale but are the result of chance: this source for this article, that source for that other, these two sources making up these other articles, etc. No specific plan was followed, but the nitpicking was done in an unsystematic fashion. This fact is confirmed by the decision of the *Comisión* to introduce innumerable provisions from other sources into the Italian model that De Gásperi had by and large respected in the *Anteproyecto*. It is submitted here that no precise legislative policy or decision preordained these additions and subtractions which were, in more ways than one, unintended or taken without a fully conscious idea of what the consequences of mixing so many sources would entail.

deep in the different sources, "confront" them, and make sense of the legal materials. The jurists of the *Comisión* amplified this idea, as was seen, by incorporating an even more varied mix of sources to the final product. Paraguayan private law, in this vision, is thus in the extremely advantageous position of mining from the immense wealth of the civil law tradition, but the price to pay would be one of constantly confronting the sources — or as the metaphor herein adopted, of using *legal bricolage* to make sense of the varied heterogenous provisions.

The vision of De Gásperi of "confrontation", I believe, can be expressed in lévi-straussian terms, by adding to the original quote the corresponding parenthetical additions. Hence, the task of the Paraguayan jurist or "legal bricoleur" would be the following:

> *Excited by his project, his first practical move is retrospective* (i.e., it is impossible to even begin to understand the *Código Civil* without constantly looking behind it, to its form of composition, and this is what makes it such a unique legal document); *he must turn back to an already constituted set, consisting of tools and materials* (the various sources used); *inventory or reinventory it* (this is the phase of archaeology); *finally and above all, engage in a kind of dialogue with it, in order to identify the responses that the set can offer to his problem, before choosing among these possible solutions* (this is the part of synthesizing, of "confronting" the sources, of arriving to the "brilliant and unforeseen" result).[129]

It is thus here submitted that the metaphor of *bricolage* fits the *Código Civil* effortlessly, since it is a legal corpus that was built upon residues and debris of the most heterogenous group of sources. The best way to comprehend the *Código Civil* is by using legal bricolage. This method of "legal bricolage" may be described — adapting the analysis proposed in general by Lévi-Strauss to the *Código Civil* itself — as having three phases or stages:

(i) the first phase of the approach is to focus on the text *always* retrospectively; more than a phase, it is an epistemic mandate, a way of facing the code itself: the Paraguayan jurist cannot limit

---

129 Lévi-Strauss, p. 21.

herself to the text and only the text of the *Código Civil,* but must always, as a matter of principle, look behind it to assemble the different sources that make up the blended text;

(ii) the second phase, or strictly "archaeological" stage, is of assembling the inventory of the different sources that make up one legal figure (e.g. the contract of sale or hire or mandate, etc.) and compiling and studying the legal scholarship and case law from each originating system (Italian, German, etc.); and finally,

(iii) the third and last phase is what Lévi-Strauss envisaged as the bricoleur "engaging in a kind of dialogue" with the material, or De Gásperi called the "confrontation" of the various and different sources, which leads to choosing the best possible solution to the task at hand[130].

XXVI

Perhaps the proposed method may be clarified with some practical instances of figures that necessitate legal bricolage in the *Código Civil*.

To use (but) one example of a figure in which the *Código Civil* contains a *Babelian* debris of sources: the so-called Pauline fraud or *actio pauliana*[131]. In the Vélez Sarsfield Code, this remedy was included in the book regulating the general category of the legal act[132]. Albeit the technique used by Vélez was not conceptually polished with respect to the nature of the remedy — something which opened the room for controversy — Article 971 of the Argentinean code literally stated that if there was transfer of property of goods of the (fraudulent) debtor, then this goods would be "restituted by the acquiring party, accomplice

---

130 However, this third stage will be subject to further refinement below: *infra* section XXVII.
131 I took an early stab at this problem in Moreno Rodríguez Alcalá, 'Los Actos Jurídicos Fraudulentos – El Fraude a los Acreedores', Revista Jurídica Universidad Católica 'Nuestra Señora de la Asunción', vol. 2 (1998), pp. 319–37, and I refer the reader to those pages for full bibliographical references on this figure.
132 Articles 961–972 of the Vélez Sarsfield Code.

to the fraud", whilst Article 954 explicitly stated that fraudulent acts were "null". Hence, the earlier scholarship that commented the Argentinean text concluded — including De Gásperi himself in his treatise on the Argentinean system of obligations — that the *actio pauliana* was an action of nullity[133].

On the other hand, the *Codice* regulates the *azione revocatoria* in the *Libro Sesto* regarding the *tutela dei diritti*; specifically, under *Capo V* as a means of "conservation of the patrimonial guarantee" of the debtor. There is peaceful accordance with regards to the nature of the remedy in Italian law: it is of *inefficacia parziale e relativa* (i.e., not nullity). In other words, if the remedy is successful, the action will entail not so much the restitution of the transferred goods but that the creditor — and this is key: only *the* creditor that questioned the act — may pursue his legal rights against the acquiring party as a "*sorta di diritto di seguito*"[134]. To use another term, the effect of the action is of *inopponibilità*, since the act is not juridically eliminated or annulled, and there is no restitutionary award, but the successful creditor will be able to exercise conservative and executive actions regarding the object of the questioned act[135]. The act in question is valid *erga omnes*, with the sole exception of the creditor that impugned the act[136]. This, of course, is the precise meaning of Article 2902 of the *Codice* which regulates the "*effetti*" of the action: "*il creditore, ottenuta la dichiarazione di inefficacia, può promuovere nei confronti dei terzi acquirenti le azione esecutive o conservative sui beni che formano oggetto*

---

133 L. De Gásperi, *Tratado de las Obligaciones en el derecho civil paraguayo y argentino*, (Buenos Aires: Editorial Depalma, 1945), vol. 1, pp. 493–95. And see Moreno Rodríguez Alcalá, 'Los Actos Jurídicos Fraudulentos', pp. 329–31, for more details and bibliographical information.

134 See authors and cases cited in G. Cian and A. Trabucchi, ed. by G. Cian, *Commentario breve al Codice Civile*, 11th edn (Padova: CEDAM, 2014), p. 3805.

135 A. Torrente and P. Schelsinger, *Manuale di diritto privato* (Milano: Giuffrè, Francis Lefebvre, 2019), 24th edition, p. 503 (and case law therein cited).

136 Ugo Natoli, quoted in F. Gazzoni, *Manuale di diritto privato*, 17th edn (Napoli: ESI, 2015), p. 689.

dell'atto impugnato". No question of nullity can thus be raised in the Italian context.

Let us now turn to the Paraguayan code. The *Código Civil* regulates the *actio pauliana* fraud in Articles 311-317, which are contained in the general category of the "legal act." The first five articles follow by and large the Argentinean sources, which may leave some doubt regarding the nature of the "revocatory" action, since to revoke is to leave without effect, presenting the possible interpretation of the action as one of "nullity". However, here there is a particular instance of irruption of a source from a different source, of a mixing of different sources: Article 316 is a copy of Article 2902, first part, of the *Codice*. This would seem to entail that the Italian solution of *inopponibilità*, rather than the original Argentinean one of nullity, should prevail. And yet, another debris, another leftover material is found in this same Article 316: the *Comisión* introduced to the original Italian the following phrase: "the accomplice must *restitute/return* (the object of the act) with its fruits as a bad faith possessor". This phrase, once again, comes not from the *Codice* but from Article 971 of the Vélez Sarsfield Code, which was criticized by Argentinean doctrine precisely for using this term which misleadingly seems to render the action one of nullity[137]. As it has already been stated, the borrowing, Babelian character of the *Código Civil*, many times occurs in the context of a single provision, which copies one part from one source and another part from a different one, as is the case of this Article 316.

What is to be done?

Well, it is submitted that the legal bricoleur not limit himself only to the text but look retrospectively and then proceed to make his inventory: some Argentinean sources, one Italian source but mixed with an Argentinean irritant, are to be found. Thereafter, the legal bricoleur must delve himself into both the Argentinean and Italian scholarship and case law to better understand each

---

[137] See S. Cifuentes, *Commentary to Articles 971-972*, in A. Belluscio and E. Zannoni (eds.), *Código Civil y leyes complementarias – Comentado, anotado y concordado* (Buenos Aires: Astrea, 1982), vol. 4, pp. 453–54.

system and the conclusion there maintained. After engaging in this "kind of dialogue", and of "confronting" the sources and their respective merit, the legal bricoleur chooses the best solution, which is to consider the *action pauliana* in the *Código Civil* as an *inopponibilità* remedy: not only due to the express decision to incorporate the solution from the *Codice*, but also considering that the majority of the Argentinean scholarship made a rectifying interpretation of the original texts in order to understand them in this manner[138].

Another example.

The issue of debt waiver or remittance (*remisión de deudas* or *remissione del debito*) poses similar problems. When regulating this legal figure, De Gásperi had opted in his *Anteproyecto* to copy the definition contained in Article 1236 of the *Codice* (in Article 869 of the *Anteproyecto*), which makes the waiver by the creditor a unilateral act, that does not depend its validity on the acceptance by the debtor. The rest of the articles regulating this figure were also basically inspired on the Italian model. However, when the *Comisión* studied the draft, the definition of the waiver or remittance was outright eliminated, and in its place a definition coming from the Argentinean tradition was incorporated: Article 610 of the Paraguayan *Código Civil* is a copy of Article 740 of the *Draft of 1936*. This draft included in the definition the term "convenes" (*conviene*), which in turn may lead the interpreter to think that what is required is a "convention", that is, an offer by the creditor followed by an acceptance of the debtor. The matter is thus up for grabs: some articles come from an Argentinean tradition which leads to a bilateral act, whilst some come from the Italian source which understands the waiver as a strictly unilateral act. And so on and so forth. The solution will require the same approach: look retrospectively, focus on the solutions and interpretations given

---

138 See, for example, Eduardo Zannoni, *Ineficacia y nulidad de los actos jurídicos* (Buenos Aires: Astrea, 1986), pp. 424 ff.

in each system, engage in a dialogue and confront these views, to achieve the best possible interpretation[139].

Virtually every legal problem that arises in the *Código Civil*, it is here forcefully submitted, will require a similar approach. Only the faces of the sources will change: sometimes it will be the Vélez Sarsfield Code, sometimes the BGB, sometimes the *Codice*, sometimes the Argentinean draft reforms. Sometimes no less than 3 different sources will be found in the same text! The example of Article 2000 of the *Código Civil*, which establishes the so-called action for the *immissio*, suffices: the first paragraph of Article 2000 comes from the Swiss Civil Code; the second paragraph comes from the Brazilian Civil Code of 1916; and the third paragraph comes from the *Borda Reform* of 1968.

Bricolage indeed!

In sum: given that bricolage was used as the way of constructing the *Código Civil*, I believe that *legal bricolage* is the only method for making this legal body speak with a single, coherent voice.

XXVII

It is time to introduce here a couple of important caveats.

However illuminating for understanding the deepest structure of the *Código Civil*, the legal bricolage metaphor — as indeed, any metaphor — should not be taken too far.

By itself, it is at least in two senses highly incomplete for legal science.

Firstly: because as Lévi-Strauss himself rightly emphasizes, bricolage is usually used to solve one specific problem, and is not devised to construct a whole system. This second, conceptual stage is the proper ambit of the other form or mode of thought, the "scientific" approach. And legal science, especially in the civilian tradition, has always had a strong scientific, conceptual,

---

[139] Which in my opinion leads to viewing the act as "unilateral": I have dealt in depth with these problems in a still unpublished paper, which contains profuse reference to the relevant literature: 'Un palique en torno a la remisión de deuda en nuestro derecho' (on file with the author).

constructive side[140]: the system is constructed in a to and fro of concepts-to-problems-and-problems-to-concepts that has been magisterially explained by (*inter alia*) Esser or Canaris in the civil law tradition or MacCormick and Dworkin in the common law tradition[141]. In this sense, it is by no means the ambit or function of bricolage to construct or conceptualize the system. There is thus ample space for conceptual thinking here, and in this sense, the "Latin genius" contained in the sophisticated legal doctrine of Italy may (must!) be used by Paraguayan jurists, lawyers, and judges. As mentioned above and as was emphasized by Lévi-Strauss himself, bricolage, the solution of specific problems, and system-building, are not mutually exclusive but coexist peacefully: they are "two ways of proceeding, equally valid"[142].

---

140 This scientific, conceptual, constructive side has existed in the western legal tradition (especially in the civilian variant) since its birth, as Harold Berman has so persuasively argued in his extraordinary book recounting the origins of the tradition: H. Berman, *Law and revolution: The formation of the Western Legal Tradition* (Cambridge: Harvard University Press, 1983), pp. 121–64.

141 The literature on this subject is vast, and thus, the text refers (arbitrarily) to what the author considers prominent examples: the *mangum opus* of Esser is of fundamental importance: Josef Esser, *Principio y norma en la elaboración jurisprudencial del derecho privado* (Buenos Aires: Olejnik, 2020) (the original German edition is from 1956); as well as the sophisticated work by Claus-Wilhelm Canaris: *El Sistema en la jurisprudencia* (Madrid: Fundación Cultural del Notariado, 1998) (the original German version is from 1969); the writings of MacCormick on the "rational reconstruction" are of inestimable value, and the book of Neil MacCormick, *Rhetoric and the Rule of Law* (Oxford: Oxford University Press, 2005) contains a powerful restatement of his views; and, of course, Ronald Dworkin's view of law as an essentially and constructively interpretive concept is an inevitable — and simply brilliant — reference: R. Dworkin, *Law's Empire* (Cambridge: Harvard University Press, 1986).

142 It should be noted that the work of doctrinal scholarship (the *dottrina*), although conceptual in its essence, has always a practical dimension which approximates it to the value of justice, which here too — as in the concrete application of rules to particular cases — is thus foundational to legal thought. As Simmonds has argued, the doctrinal writer does not take as his central task the resolution of a specific dispute, but "the systematization of a whole area of law", and this systematization by definition leads to a "principled" view of law, of law as a "sophisticated and coherent system of principles": N. Simmonds, *Law as a Moral Idea* (Oxford: Oxford University Press, 2007), pp. 164–66. The idea that the conceptual construction of the system is not a purely abstract endeavor, but is firmly entrenched in the idea

The second sense in which the bricolage metaphor is insufficient or incomplete is in a deafening silence it contains: that is, there is a word that is absent in the third and final phase of the process, that of *"engaging in a kind of dialogue"* as Lévi-Strauss put it, or of *"confronting"* the various sources as De Gásperi envisaged, in order to reach the best possible solution to the problem at hand.

Missing in these two phrases is the defining term of the legal world: *justice*. That is, the "dialogue," the "confronting," is to be made in the specific context of the law not arbitrarily, or based on whim, or based on aesthetic criteria, but based on that old but perennial word: the method, the interpretation, the solution, must always be according to *justice*. As N.E. Simmonds has argued in his magisterial book, *Law as a Moral Idea,* in the legal world "justice *must be relevant to every case*": that is, "judges [or jurists] must, so to speak, read the law *as a body of texts concerning justice*"[143].

The same goes for interpretation of legal texts such as the *Código Civil*: its solutions, the confrontation of sources, the result of legal bricolage, must not be done accordance to political, aesthetic or any other such criteria, but according to *justice*, to what best realizes the requirements of this virtue. The articles of the *Código Civil*, after the various sources are sorted out, must then be read "as a body of texts concerning justice", and the interpretation of the legal bricoleur must always be controlled by this virtue. In the classical tradition, of course, the task of law was left to persons equipped with this particular virtue, *prudentia*, and thus legal science was *juris-prudentia* (rather than *scientia*

---

of justice, has also been convincingly defended on the civil law side of the discussion. As (for example) Canaris has so very ably argued, the system-building or conceptual part of doctrinal writing is not done for theoretical purity only but for morally relevant practical reasons; doctrinal scholarship has as its fundamental seed and core the "generalizing tendency of the idea of justice" (Canaris, especially pp. 24–26). I have reflected on how, at bottom, the conceptual and systematic aspects of legal doctrine are deeply related to justice in a review of Simmonds book: R. Moreno Rodríguez Alcalá, 'Filosofando (realmente) despierto sobre el derecho: Dos reflexiones en torno al magnifico *Law as a Moral Idea* de N.E. Simmonds', UCA Law Review (Asunción: 2015), pp. 867–905.

143 Simmonds, p. 197 (emphasis added).

juris[144]), that is: practical wisdom applied to legal affairs[145]. The last step of the legal bricoleur must thus be subject to this idea: the "*choosing among these possible solutions*" must be carried out in consideration to what is the most just — i.e., reasonable, sensible, fair — interpretation of the different sources enmeshed together in the *Código Civil*. As the great Italian jurist Mengoni once remarked:

> la questione di conformità a giustizia, alla quale il giurista deve rispondere, è di quest'altro tipo: "quale soluzione del caso da decidere, tra quelle giuridicamente possibili nell'ambito del diritto positivo, si approssima maggiormente al valore della giustizia, meglio soddisfa la giustizia".[146]

---

144 This well-known change of paradigm is rightly emphasized, for example, by Zagrebelsky: G. Zagrebelsky, *El derecho dúctil – Ley, derechos, justicia* (Madrid: Trotta, 1995) (the original Italian edition is from 1992), pp. 122–26.

145 This paragraph presupposes a philosophical position which would require another essay (or full book indeed) to be developed and defended. Of course, as is well known, the classical tradition, starting from Aristotle and on forward, emphasized the point that the virtue controlling the entire legal enterprise was *phronesis* (in Latin: *prudentia*). Citing the relevant literature would be an endless task. It suffices to note here that Professor John Finnis has revitalized — to my mind, convincingly — this tradition in the contemporary legal philosophical scene, preferring to use the term "*practical reasonableness*" in order to insist that the whole ordering and regulating of human affairs — i.e., the process of continual positing of law — must be controlled by this idea: J. Finnis, *Natural Law and Natural Rights* (Oxford: Oxford University Press, 1980) (pp. 88–89/100–32 for the general idea; for its specific application to law, pp. 281–90). As is stated in the end of his absolutely magisterial philosophical reflection of the concept of law: "the act of 'positing' law (whether judicially or legislatively or otherwise) is and act which can and should be guided by 'moral' principles and rules" and thus the task of this reflection should be to "determine what the requirements of practical reasonableness really are, so as to afford a rational basis for the activities of legislators, judges, and citizens" (at p. 290). I have for my part defended this position, quoting the relevant literature — to which I refer the forgiving reader — in the introduction to the *Anteproyecto,* quoted above (*supra* n. 7), pp. cclxxxix–cccxxiii.

146 L. Mengoni, 'I problemi del metodo nella ricerca civilistica oggi in Italia', in L. Mengoni, *Scritti I – Metodo e Teoria Giuridica*, ed. by C. Castronovo, A. Albanese and A. Nicolussi (Milano: Giuffrè, 2011), pp. 194–95. These ideas may be complemented by those given some years before by another great teacher of Mengoni's alma mater in Milan, Biondo Biondi, in a (I think unjustly neglected) essay: '*Scienza del diritto come arte del giusto*' as

The metaphor of legal bricolage is then be complemented by two further ideas. Firstly, that it leaves untouched the conceptual task or side of building the system. And secondly, that the "confronting" of sources, the "choosing of a solution," must always have justice as its guiding principle: the vast array of borrowed legal debris found in the *Código Civil* is to be read as a series of texts concerning *justice*.

CONCLUSION

The road for the reader of this pages has been extremely long and at many tedious; perchance, a final summary may serve to bring together the many threads of argument.

Did the *Codice* influence the *Código Civil*?

The brief answer is, of course, *yes*. The *Codice* was an important source of inspiration for the Paraguayan codification effort — for its "legal independence" — particularly in the complex task of unifying civil and commercial obligations, but also in the regulation of the law of contract (in general) and of the specific types of contracts. Yet, this influence is less pervasive, and much more complicated, than it would have been had the original draft of the code, undertaken by Luis De Gásperi in his *Anteproyecto*, had been more strictly followed, since the first draft basically contains a duplicate of *Libro Quarto* of the *Codice*, and thus through various lengths spoke *a medesma lingua* with this source. Less pervasive, given that at many junctures the *Comisión* departed from or abandoned the Italian source; more complicated, given that even where it followed the *Codice* it mixed its provisions with rules coming from other sources, presenting a not altogether coherent picture. In other words, the

---

translated in Biondo Biondi, *Arte y ciencia del derecho* (Barcelona: Editorial Ariel, 1953), pp. 119–60.

Código Civil, constructed so firmly upon the borrowing principle — its life has literally been to borrow freely from the civil law tradition — allows for the *Codice* to be an important influence whilst at the same time departing or even contradicting the Italian source, leaving the interpreter in the conundrum of trying to find one coherent voice in the disparate texts.

This is why an essay retracing the influence of the *Codice* in the *Código Civil* not only concludes that it was a very important source, but must then turn to the inevitable methodological problem that lies at the core of the Paraguayan code: how is a body of law made up of such a complex and vast array of heterogenous sources to be interpreted?

The solution to this methodological puzzle suggested here borrowed a metaphor from Lévi-Strauss's work on anthropological epistemology: the mode of thought of "bricolage". This method precisely starts from a heterogenous set of tools, inventorying and sorting out these materials to construct the best possible work to solve the problem at hand. This metaphor, it was here submitted, may be applied to the *Código Civil* as the method of "legal bricolage", to make the *Babelian* structure of the code speak in a unified and coherent, in *a medesma lingua*. It was also sketchily suggested how this method of legal bricolage would work in practice: (i) its first phase is epistemically retrospectival, since the *Código Civil* can never be understood purely in its literal terms but must always look behind to find its diverse sources; (ii) in the second phase, the "archaeological" one, the different sources are to be interpreted in accordance to the legal scholarship and case law coming from each source (e.g. Italian, German, Argentinean, etc.); and finally (iii) in the third phase, the legal bricoleur must "engage in a kind of dialogue", or "confront" the sources, as De Gásperi himself envisaged, and finally choose among the best possible solution by finding the "best" interpretation — "best" being understood as the one that not only fits the legal materials but also "*meglio soddisfa la giustizia*".

Hence, the Paraguayan legal bricoleur, however far, however distant, returns to the fundamental insight that those most egregious exponents of the "Latin genius" gave two millennia when they "invented" law[147]: legal knowledge is, as they wisely remarked, but the "the knowledge of things divine and human, the science of the just and unjust"[148]. Thus, fundamentally legal bricolage only wants to give justice its due in a legal corpus constructed in such an idiosyncratic way as the Paraguayan *Código Civil* itself was.

Perhaps, this is, in the last instance, the legacy of the *Codice Civile* of 1942 for the Paraguayan *Código Civil,* a body of law to which it contributed so many provisions: as a rich, learned, and genial fount of legal sources that seek to give reasonable, sensible, fair — in short, *just* — answers to the interminable problems of human beings.

---

[147] As Aldo Schiavone aptly calls it in his book: A. Schiavone, *The invention of law in the West* (Cambridge: Belknap Press, 2012).

[148] Or, as the translation by the late Professor Birks (with Grant McLeod) poetically puts it: "Learning in the law entails knowledge of God and man, and mastery of the difference between justice and injustice". See *Justinian's Institutes*, trans. with and introduction by P. Birks and G. McLeod (Ithaca: Cornell University Press, 1987). The unperishable original Latin is: *Iuris prudentia est divinarum atque humanarum rerum notitia, iusti atque iniusti scientia.*

SHERALDINE PINTO OLIVEROS*
THE INFLUENCE OF ITALIAN CIVIL LAW IN VENEZUELAN CIVIL LAW
Succession Law

1. *Introduction*

Venezuela or "Little Venice" was the name given to this country by the Florentine Amerigo Vespucci, when the houses on stilts of the indigenous people on the shores of Lake Maracaibo reminded him of the houses on the water of Venice. Certainly, this name predicted not only the close ties between Italy and Venezuela, but also the Italian influence in Venezuelan culture.

In the legal field, the influence of Italian law in Venezuelan law is particularly notorious in the area of private law. In this area, the Venezuelan legislator has often used Italian legal provisions as a model, especially due to the authority of Italian scholars[1], whose works have also been used to guide the academic and judicial interpretation of Venezuelan law. At the level of civil law, the Italian influence in Venezuelan civil law has been concretized[2], since the third Venezuelan Civil Code of 1873.

---

* Professor of Civil Law at Universidad Central de Venezuela and Universidad Metropolitana.
1 Cfr. L. Lupini Bianchi and A.I. Vidal, 'La influencia del Código de Napoleón en la Codificación Civil y en la Doctrina Venezolana', in I. de Valera (ed.) *El Código Civil venezolano en los inicios del siglo XXI*, (Caracas: Academia de Ciencias Políticas y Sociales, 2005), pp. 47–97 (p. 76).
2 The Italian influence in the Venezuelan Civil law emerges even before the Venezuelan civil codifications through the impact of the Roman law, which played a key role even in the legal studies at the Venezuelan universities. On this subject, see S. Pinto Oliveros, 'L'influenza del modello italiano nel diritto civile venezuelano', in S. Lanni and P. Sirena (eds.), *Il modello giuridico – scientifico e legislativo – italiano fuori dell'Europa. Atti del II Congresso Nazionale della SIRD* (Napoli: Edizioni Scientifiche Italiane, 2013), pp. 225–46 (pp. 228–32).

At that time, this Code was an anomaly in the Latin American civil codifications, because it followed the Italian Civil Code of 1865[3] as a model with some adjustments and additions mainly based on the previous Venezuelan Civil Code of 1862[4].

The Venezuelan Civil Code of 1873 represents the cornerstone of the development of the Venezuelan Civil law. In fact, "the rules on property law, testamentary and intestate inheritance, donations, contracts, and obligations are clearly defined, following the principles established by the jurists of Rome, and truths demonstrated by reason and experience"[5]. Thus, the Venezuelan Civil Code of 1873 defined the main features of Venezuelan Civil law[6] — although some amendments in later Venezuelan civil codes were relevant, especially in the areas of obligations and contracts. In these areas, the most relevant direct source of the Venezuelan Civil Code of 1942, whose key role

---

3   According to Sanojo, member of the Codifying Commission, "That Commission sometimes moved apart from such great model [...] but it always followed its spirit and its general system". Cfr. L. Sanojo, *Instituciones de derecho civil*, I (Caracas: Imprenta Nacional, 1873), p. XI. For a summary of opinions of the members of the Codifying Commission and the Venezuelan Scholars at that time about the significance of the Italian Civil Code of 1865 on the Venezuelan Civil Code of 1873, see G. Parra-Aranguren, 'Las normas de Derecho Internacional Privado en el Código Civil venezolano del veinte de febrero de 1873', in F. Parra Aranguren (ed.), *Temas de Derecho Civil. Libro Homenaje a Andrés Aguilar Mawdsley* (Caracas: Tribunal Supremo de Justicia, 2004), pp. 109–223 (pp. 120–27).

4   N. Posenato, *Autonomia della volontà e scelta della legge applicabile ai contratti nei sistemi giuridici latino-americani* (Padova: CEDAM, 2010), p. 165. In a similar way, A. Guzmán Brito, *Historia de la codificación civil en Iberoamérica* (Pamplona: Editorial Aranzadi, 2006), p. 316; O. Ochoa, *Derecho Civil I: Personas* (Caracas: Universidad Católica "Andrés Bello", 2006), pp. 161–62; and, S. Pinto Oliveros, 'Culture et Droit Civil au Vénézuela', Droit et Culture. Journées Louisianaises (2008), LVIII, Collection des Travaux de l'Association Henri Capitant des Amis de la Culture Juridique Française (Bruxelles: Bruylant, 2010; LB2V: Paris, 2010) pp. 269–82, (p. 272).

5   T.E. Carrillo Batalla, *Historia de la Legislación Venezolana*, II (Caracas: Academia de Ciencias Políticas y Sociales, 1985), p. 217.

6   S. Pinto Oliveros, 'L'influenza del modello italiano nel diritto civile venezuelano', p. 238. In the same way, J.A. Zambrano Velasco, *Teoría general de la obligación. Parte general de las obligaciones: La estructura* (Caracas: Editorial Arte, 1985), p. 86; and Posenato, p. 165.

in the current Venezuelan Civil Code of 1982 is undeniable, is the General Part of the Franco-Italian Project of Obligations and Contracts of 1927[7].

In other areas[8], such as Succession law, "the provisions of the Venezuelan Civil Code of 1982 are directly inspired by the Italian Civil Code of 1865"[9]. Consequently, Venezuelan scholars have always paid attention to the developments on that subject in Italy[10], even later of the enactment of the Italian Civil Code of 1942, due to the affinity of Succession law rules in both the Venezuelan and the Italian Civil Codes. Therefore, the purpose of this article is to provide an overview of Venezuelan Inheritance law, taking into account its affinities with Italian law.

---

[7] See, among others, E. Maduro Luyando, *Curso de obligaciones. Derecho Civil III* (Caracas: Universidad Católica "Andrés Bello", 1979), p. 21; O. Palacios Herrera, *Apuntes de obligaciones* (Caracas: Ediciones Nuevo Mundo, 2000), p. 7, and 'Introducción a la teoría general de las obligaciones,' Revista de la Facultad de Derecho de la Universidad Central de Venezuela, 9 (1956), 9–30, p. 22; E. Maduro Luyando and E. Pittier Sucre, *Curso de obligaciones. Derecho Civil III*, I (Caracas: Universidad Católica "Andrés Bello", 2000), p. 12; and Zambrano Velasco, pp. 88–89.

[8] According to Hung, "Our current Civil Code has as its immediate model the Italian Civil Code of 1865 and, through it, the French Civil Code of 1804". Cfr. F. Hung Vaillant, *Derecho Civil I* (Caracas: Vadell hermanos Editores, 2015), p. 58. On the other hand, Varela remarks: "90% of the current Venezuelan Civil Code comes from the Venezuelan Civil Code of 1942, in which the title III of the third book related to 'Obligations' came from the famous Franco-Italian Project of Obligations and Contracts of 1927, and the other matters found its mediate antecedent in the influence of the Italian Civil Code of 1865". Cfr. E.L. Varela Cáceres, 'La nueva codificación: Aspectos formales', RVLJ, 18 (2022), 133–48 (p. 134).

[9] Cfr. F. López Herrera, *Derecho de sucesiones*, I (Caracas: UCAB, 2003), p. 17. Similarly, J. Esparza Bracho, *Derecho sucesorio*, I: *Ordenamiento Legal de la Transmisión Sucesoria* (Maracaibo: Ediciones Astro Data S.A., 1993), p. 9.

[10] Regarding Succession law is notorious for the attention paid by Venezuelan scholars to Italian scholars, particularly to Roberto De Ruggiero, *Instituciones de Derecho Civil*, II, 1: *Derecho de Obligaciones, Derecho de Familia. Derecho Hereditario* (Madrid: Instituto Editorial Reus, 1997).

2. Mortis Causa Succession: Concept and Types

In a broad legal sense, succession is the substitution of one person for another in the subjective legal situations[11] of economic value and transferable from the former which takes place by agreement (*inter vivos*), due to the special nature of the legal situation[12], or by the death of someone (*mortis causa*)[13]. In a strict legal sense, succession is identified with *mortis causa* succession — that is, the type of succession that occurs by the death of a natural person.

Similarly to the first paragraph of Article 457 of the Italian Civil Code, "successions shall granted by the Law or by a will" in accordance with the first paragraph of Article 807 of the Venezuelan Civil Code. Therefore, the sources of the *mortis causa* succession (hereafter, "succession") and, consequently, of the hereditary vocation are the law and a will. Consequently, under Venezuelan law, there are two types of successions depending on their origin: On the one hand, "intestate succession" (also called *ab intestato*, legal or legitimate succession), that is, succession by law[14] and, on the other hand, the "testamentary succession", that is, the succession by the testator's wishes through a will"[15].

---

11 In López Herrera's opinion, "succession refers to change in the entitlement of a legal relationship of economic value." Cfr. López Herrera, I, p. 19. Similarly, Calvo Baca says, "In general, succession is the change of subjects of a legal relationship". Cfr. E. Calvo Baca, *Manual de derecho civil venezolano* (Caracas: Librerías Destino, 1984), p. 189.

12 This category includes *propter rem* obligations [those that follow the asset] and those called in other legal systems, "real burden" such as emphyteutic rent.

13 Traditionally, succession takes place by an agreement or by someone's death. In this regard, see M.C. Domínguez Guillén, *Manual de derecho sucesorio* (Caracas: Paredes, 2010), pp. 14 and 34–36; and Calvo Baca, p. 189.

14 Cfr. Domínguez Guillén, *Manual de derecho sucesorio*, p. 179; and 'La familia: Su proyección en la sucesión legal y en la sucesión forzosa', in J. Annicchiarico, S. Pinto Oliveros, and P. Saghy (eds.), *Nuevas tendencias en el derecho privado y reforma del Código civil francés*" (Caracas: EJV and Association Henri Capitant, 2015), p. 74.

15 Cfr. Domínguez Guillén, *Manual de derecho sucesorio*, p. 276. Also, R. Sojo Bianco, *Apuntes de derecho de familia y sucesiones* (Caracas: Mobil Libros, 1990), p. 303. Furthermore, Rojas indicates "testamentary succession is that

Testamentary succession can be subdivided into universal succession and particular succession. In contrast, intestate succession is always a universal succession.

As under Italian law[16], the last paragraph of Article 807 of the Venezuelan Civil Code[17] establishes the primacy of testamentary succession over intestate succession and, in addition, allows concurrence between these two types of succession[18]. Consequently, under Venezuelan law[19], succession is governed pursuant to the following order of priority: (i) exclusively by the will of the testator, if there is a will by which the deceased distributed his/her entire estate; (ii) concurrently by the testator's will and the law[20] if, despite the existence of a will, the deceased has not distribute all of his/her estate and/or the will is partially

---

which takes place by the author's express will. In other words, it is based on the testator's private autonomy, which must be respected after his/her death." Cfr. A. Rojas, *Derecho hereditario venezolano* (Caracas: Praxis Jurídica, 1981), p. 170.

16 Cfr. the second paragraph of Article 457 of the Italian Civil Code. About this issue, see M.L. Loi, 'Le successioni a causa di morte', in *Diritto Privato*, Parte Seconda (Torino: UTET, 2005), p. 1063.

17 According to the last paragraph of Article 807 of the Venezuelan Civil Code, "There is no place to an intestate succession except when a testamentary succession lacks in whole or in part". In a similar fashion, the second paragraph of Article 457 of the Italian Civil Code states, "There is no place to a legitimate succession except when a testamentary succession lacks in whole or in part".

18 In Domínguez Guillén's opinion, "A testamentary succession prevails over an intestate succession if the former observes the law's boundaries of the law. However, legitimate or *ab intestato* succession comes into play in the absence of testamentary succession, or may concur with it, if the deceased's provisions (in the will) are insufficient or exceed private autonomy boundaries. Cfr. Domínguez Guillén, *Manual de derecho sucesorio*, p. 181.

19 For a similar approach, under Italian law, see L. Bigliazzi Geri, F.D. Busnelli, U. Breccia, and U. Natoli, *Diritto Civile. 4** Le Successioni a causa di morte* (Torino: UTET, 1997), pp. 18–19.

20 According to Rojas, "Several authors identify a third type of succession when it is partly testamentary and partly intestate. They call it a 'mixed succession' because a portion of the estate must be delivered in accordance with the testamentary provisions and the other follows succession legal order. However, that is not actually a third kind of succession, but rather the conjunction of both successions". Cfr. Rojas, p. 26.

ineffective; or (iii) exclusively by the law if there is no will and/ or the will is ineffective[21].

3. *Elements of Mortis Causa Succession*

Mortis causa succession is the substitution of a natural person, called the deceased (or *de cujus*), by other person(s), called successor(s), in the deceased's subjective legal situations of an economic value and transmissible on account of his/her death. Therefore, the objective element of a succession is the deceased's subjective legal situations of an economic value and transmissible[22], and its subjective element are the parties of a succession — in other words, a deceased and his/her successor(s).

The deceased[23] (*causante*) is a natural person who owns the subjective legal situations of economic value and transmissible, which, by virtue of a succession, are transferred to his/her

---

21 In López Herrera's opinion, "There is no place to legitimate, intestate or *ab intestato* succession except in the absence of the deceased will regarding whole or portion of the estate. In other words, a will prevails over the law. There is absolute absence of a will when a person dies without a will or, even though there is one, the will is ineffective. There is a partial absence of a will when the author of the will does not encompass the whole estate or, although it includes all the assets of the estate, the will is partially ineffective". Cfr. López Herrera, I, pp. 47–48.

22 For more details, see S. Pinto Oliveros, "A propósito de las sucesiones *mortis causa*", in J.G. Salaverría (ed.), *La importancia del Derecho Civil hoy. XI Jornadas Aníbal Dominici en memoria de la Dra. María Candelaria Domínguez Guillén* (Caracas: Abediciones, 2022), pp. 159–80 (pp. 163–166). About the subjective legal situations under Italian law, see F. Giardina, "Le situazioni giuridiche soggettive", in *Diritto Privato*, Parte Prima (Torino: UTET, 2005), pp. 139–68.

23 In general, Domínguez Guillén defines a deceased (*causante*) as "the one who transfers rights or obligations to another person called successor. The person from whom the other derives their right or obligation". Specifically in succession law, the same author states "a deceased (*causante*) or *de cujus* (the one whose succession is being dealt with) is the deceased, who is the essential person whose death makes the *mortis causa* succession possible. In other words, the author of the succession, using an accurate expression of scholars. It is also called "*causante*" because he/she causes the succession". Cfr. M.C. Domínguez Guillén, *Diccionario de Derecho Civil* (Caracas: Liven Editores C.A, 2009), p. 31; and *Manual de derecho sucesorio*, p. 43

successors. In other words, the deceased is a natural person who, by effect of a succession, is substituted in his/her subjective legal situations of economic value and transmissibility by his/her successors. Since his/her death opens (begins) the succession by law, the deceased is also called *de cujus* by abbreviating the Latin expression "*de cujus successione agitur*" (that is, the one whose succession is being dealt with).

The successor[24] (*causahabiente*) is who, by effect of a succession, replaces the deceased in his/her transferable subjective legal situations of economic value. The successor may be a single person or several (natural or legal[25]) persons. If the hereditary vocation of successors is by law, they are universal successors. By contrast, if the hereditary vocation of successors is testamentary, they may be either universal successors or particular successors, depending on whether the succession (or, more specifically, the testamentary provisions) is under universal or under particular title[26].

---

24 On a general level, Domínguez Guillén defines a successor (*causahabiente*) as "the person who acquires rights or obligations by a transfer or succession from another one. A successor may be *mortis causa* (by hereditary succession) or by an agreement (*inter vivos* acts)". In succession law, the same author explains that "the one who receives rights or obligations is a 'successor' since he/she succeeds them. A successor might be universal or a particular successor. Likewise, successors may be singular or plural". Cfr. Domínguez Guillén, *Diccionario de Derecho Civil*, p. 31; and *Manual de derecho sucesorio*, p. 43.
25 For example, entities.
26 Domínguez Guillén asserts that "based on succession object, universal succession is differentiated from particular succession. In the former, a general or universal portion of the deceased's rights and obligations are acquired, while, in the latter, only a specific or singular portion, pursuant to Article 834" of the Venezuelan Civil Code. Cfr. Domínguez Guillén, *Manual de derecho sucesorio*, p. 38. In a similar fashion, Farrera states that "a universal successor or heir actively and passively succeeds its author or deceased (*causante*) in an absolute manner, that is, in all their rights and obligations. Universal successors are a continuation of the author without any interruption or interposition. A particular successor actively and passively acquires the provisions that modify the manner of being of a corporeal or incorporeal asset, that is the transfer object, or that add an accessory thereto". Cfr. C. Farrera, *Sucesiones*, I (Caracas: Ediciones Vegas Rolando, 1917), p. 18.

4. Probate Process in an Universal Succession

Mortis causa succession is a *fattispecie* that is progressively formed both under Italian law and under Venezuelan law. In this regard, the Venezuelan legal framework requires three stages — the opening of the succession, the inheritance proposal (*delación*), and the acquisition of the inheritance — that must be fully complied in order to the succession to take full effect, including the transfer of the estate from the deceased to his/her heirs[27]. Indeed, although the death (of the deceased) opens the succession, the probate process requires other stages to configure or consolidate the acquisition of the inheritance in the heirs' hands. Thence, three phases are distinguished: the opening of the succession, the inheritance proposal, and the acquisition of the inheritance. This process must be completed in order to establish a joint estate among coheirs and acceding to its division.[28]

4.1 *The Opening of a Succession*

Similarly to Article 456 of the Italian Civil Code, according to Article 993 of the Venezuelan Civil Code, "a succession opens at the time of death of and at the place of last domicile of the *de cujus*". Therefore, the opening of the deceased's succession is one of the most relevant legal effects of the death – as a legal event – of a natural person[29]. Indeed, the certain event of the

---

[27] Pinto Oliveros, "A propósito de las sucesiones *mortis causa*", p. 168.
[28] Cfr. Domínguez Guillén, *Manual de derecho sucesorio*, p. 69.
[29] In Esparza Bracho's opinion, "The opening of a succession is the legal event that defines place and time of the transfer by succession of the estate and other assets of a deceased person to one or several living people, or even people who are to live. The opening takes place solely and exclusively by the event of death, as, according to the principle of *viventis non datur haereditas*, it is not possible to initiate the succession of a living person". Cfr. Esparza Bracho, p. 15.

death of the deceased leaves his/her estate without an owner[30] and, at the same time, opens his/her succession by law.

Consequently, the condition of the opening of a succession is the death of deceased[31], which is proved through a certificate of death[32].

Among other aspects, the opening of a succession is relevant to determine:

> (i) the applicable law to the succession, which is the law in effect at the time of the decedent's death at his/her last domicile[33]; and, in principle, the court's jurisdiction (*forum apertae sucessionis*) for any dispute relating to the succession[34];
> (ii) the date at which the absolute incapacities of (potential) successors to succeed[35] and to receive by will[36] must be assessed;
> (iii) the date from which the declaration of a successor as unworthy to inherit takes effect[37];

---

30 Domínguez Guillén, López Herrera, And Sojo Bianco all agree that, with death, the estate is left without a legal owner. Cfr. Domínguez Guillén, *Manual de derecho sucesorio*, p. 70; López Herrera, I, p. 33, and Sojo Bianco, p. 247. In addition to agreeing with these authors, De Ruggiero adds that the opening of a succession "takes place because of the exigency to go on with (legal) relations, a need that requires that another person takes the deceased's place". Cfr. De Ruggiero, p. 324.
31 In this regard, Sojo Bianco remarks, "The essential requirement for the succession to be opened is that the certain event of the deceased's death must have happened. At that moment, the estate is left without a legal owner, and consequently must be transferred to another who exercises the legal ownership". Cfr. Sojo Bianco, p. 247.
32 On proof of death under Venezuelan law, see M.C. Domínguez Guillén, *Inicio y extinción de la personalidad jurídica del ser humano (nacimiento y muerte)* (Caracas: Tribunal Supremo de Justicia, Caracas, 2007), pp. 243–53.
33 According to Article 34 of the Venezuela Private International Law Act, "successions are governed by the law of the deceased's (*causante*) domicile".
34 Cfr. Article 43 of the Venezuelan Code of Civil Procedure.
35 Cfr. Article 809 of the Venezuelan Civil Code.
36 In the same way, Esparza Bracho, p. 15.
37 Among these effects, "the person excluded as unworthy to inherit has the duty of returning the fruits they have enjoyed since the opening of the succession", in accordance with Article 812 of the Venezuelan Civil Code. A similar provision is foreseen in Article 464 of the Italian Civil Code.

(iv) the date from which the statute of limitations[38] runs for accepting the inheritance[39], unless the testamentary provision that establishes the successor as heir is subject to a condition precedent. In this case, the statute of limitations runs from the day on which the condition is met[40];

(v) the date from which creditors' and/or legatees' term to request the separation of the estate is calculated[41];

(vi) the date from which assets must be returned when a condition subsequent (to which the inheritance and/or legacy is subjected) is met, except for fruits, which must be returned from the date of fulfilling that condition.

The effects of the opening of a succession are:

(i) It initiates the probate process, which consists of three stages: the opening of the succession, the proposal of the inheritance (*delación*) and the acquisition of the inheritance;

(ii) It establishes hereditary vocation[42] (also called successional vocation[43]) — that is, the appointment[44] of certain people designated by the will (testamentary vocation) or by law (legal vocation) to succeed the *de cujus*.

---

38 According to Article 1011 of the Venezuela Civil Code, "The power to accept an inheritance does not lapse until ten years have elapsed". In a similar way, the first paragraph of Article 480 of the Italian Civil Code states "The right to accept the inheritance expires in ten years".

39 Similarly, Domínguez Guillén, *Manual de derecho sucesorio*, p. 88.

40 The retroactive effect of complying with the condition does not apply to the statute of limitation.

41 Cfr. Article 1052 of the Venezuela Civil Code. Under Italian law, see Article 516 of the Italian Civil Code.

42 In De Ruggiero's opinion, the hereditary vocation is "the call to a specific person to pick the inheritance up. While a succession is unopened, it is a virtual call by law (legitimate vocation) or by the testator (testamentary vocation). When the succession is opened, the vocation turns from virtual to effective because only then can the person called to inherit make the inheritance his or hers". Cfr. De Ruggiero, p. 324). Likewise, Rojas states, "Hereditary or successional vocation is the virtual call made by law or the will to a person for them to appear to take the inheritance that shall be left behind by another person when they die. It is a virtual call. In other words, it is not effective, since the person called cannot make the inheritance their own while the author lives". Cfr. Rojas, p. 15.

43 In the opinion of Calvo Baca, the successional vocation is the "call made to specific people to receive the inheritance left behind by the deceased". Cfr. Calvo Baca, p. 192.

44 Sojo Bianco argues "the appointment acquires legal value at the time the succession is opened. The vocation is acquired when the succession is opened, and one is called thereto". Cfr. Sojo Bianco, pp. 248–49.

Therefore, the hereditary vocation is the title of the inheritance proposal (*delación*)[45];

(iii) The opening of a particular succession entails the acquisition of the legacy by law[46], unless the legatee waives it, or the legacy is subject to a condition precedent. In the latter case, the legacy is acquired upon the fulfillment of that condition[47] and provided that the legatee has accepted the legacy[48]; and,

(iv) The opening of an universal succession transfers by law the possession of *de cujus*' assets to the successors, without the need to take material possession, pursuant to the heading of Article 995 of the Venezuelan Civil Code. "This anomalous possession[49] is usually called '*posesión civilísima*' or '*possessio fictitia*' because it is a legal fiction"[50].

The source of the so-called "*posesión civilísima*" in Article 995 of the Venezuela Civil Code derives from the fact that "since 1873, the Venezuelan Civil law has always followed the Italian traditional system in Succession law"[51]. Indeed, since the 16th century, Italian law has adopted the criterion according to which the "*le mort saisit le vif*" rule referred exclusively to the possession of inherited assets (as was its original meaning). Consequently, the heir only acquires the ownership — that is, title to — said assets only by accepting inheritance. This criterion was accepted by the Albertine Code of 1838 (Article 967) which

---

45 Cfr. Loi, p. 1064. Analogously, Domínguez Guillén affirms, "vocation is the previous condition to the proposal of the inheritance (*delación*)". Cfr. Domínguez Guillén, *Manual de derecho sucesorio*, p. 80. In the same fashion, Esparza Bracho states that "the materialization of the hereditary vocation causes the so-called *delación* (proposal of the inheritance) on the *vocatus*". Cfr. Esparza Bracho, p. 25.
46 Cfr. Article 927 of the Venezuelan Civil Code.
47 In this way, Domínguez Guillén, *Manual de derecho sucesorio*, pp. 411–12.
48 Of this opinion, López Herrera, I, p. 389. Of a contrary opinion, R. Escovar León, 'Institución de heredero y legatario', Revista de la Facultad de Derecho de la Universidad Católica "Andrés Bello", 30 (1980), 30, 229–64 (p. 258).
49 About the peculiarities of "*posesión civilísima*" from the succession law approach, see López Herrera, II, pp. 27–29; and, from the property and real rights law approach, see G. Kummerow, *Bienes y derechos reales (Derecho Civil II)*, (Caracas: Universidad Central de Venezuela, 1969), pp. 141–42; and L. Certad, *La protección posesoria y el interdicto restitutorio* (Caracas: Graficas León, 1963), pp. 87–97.
50 López Herrera, II, p. 27.
51 Cfr. López Herrera, II, p. 26.

was in force in Piedmont and in Liguria and, later, in Sardinia. The Italian Civil Code of 1865 took it from there (Article 925).[52]

Since a hereditary vocation is just a mere expectation[53], a potential successor — who at this stage of the probate process is called *vocatus* — may only perform preservation acts[54], including taking true possession of inheritance assets[55] and file injunction proceedings to defend his/her "*posesión civilísima*"[56]. However, "the *posesión civilísima*" does not pertain to who has no capacity to succeed the deceased and is automatically lost upon renunciation of the inheritance[57].

4.2 *The Inheritance Proposal (Delación)*

The *delación*[58] is the proposal of the inheritance to those who have hereditary vocation, which grants on said person(s) — who in this stage of the probate process are called: "called to inherit"

---

52 López Herrera, II, p. 26.
53 About this aspect, López Herrera remarks "That virtual call, which is not a vested right (and, therefore, cannot be exercised), is nothing but a simple legal expectation called vocation." Cfr. López Herrera, I, p. 38.
54 According to Aguilar Gorrondona, preservation acts "are those that meet the following conditions of: (i) being necessary to take away one or more elements of the estate from imminent danger; and (ii) involving, at most an *insignificant* expense compared with the possible consequences of the danger. Preservation acts may be of *material preservation* (e.g., repairs of buildings that are threatened by ruin, provided that the cost is insignificant) or of *legal preservation* (e.g., the registration of a document, interrupting the running of the statute of limitations, etc.)". Cfr. J. Luis Aguilar Gorrondona, *Derecho Civil Personas* (Caracas: Universidad Católica "Andrés Bello", 1991), p. 215. In the same way, Hung Vaillant, p. 350.
55 López Herrera, II, p. 28.
56 Cfr. the last paragraph of Article 995 of the Venezuelan Civil Code. About this issue, see Certad, p. 96.
57 López Herrera, II, p. 29.
58 The proposal of the inheritance to the called to inherit has traditionally been understood as the effective calling to whom has hereditary vocation for them to make the inheritance their own. Of this opinion, Sojo Bianco, p. 248; Rojas, p. 29; López Herrera, I, pp. 38–39; and Domínguez Guillén, *Manual de derecho sucesorio*, p. 79.

— the *ius delationis*, that is, the power to acquire the inheritance through acceptance, or to reject it by waiver or repudiation[59].

The condition of a proposal to inherit is the hereditary vocation, which is the title of the proposal to inherit. Indeed, in order to be called upon to accept or reject a proposal of inheritance (or, in other words, to exercise the *ius delationis*), successor(s) must have been previously designated to succeed the decedent by the will (testamentary vocation) or by law (legal vocation).

The requirement of an inheritance proposal – and, therefore to exercise the *ius delationis* – is the capacity to succeed, which, even though it is an expression of legal capacity, is linked to other presuppositions. In fact, "if a successor lacks the specific capacity to succeed, the right to accept or repudiate the inheritance does not exist"[60].

Ius delationis is the effect of an inheritance proposal that grants upon the people called to inherit the power to accept or reject the inheritance, and also allows them to perform acts of preservation[61], as long as (i) they have not rejected the inheritance; (ii) the statute of limitations has not run out[62], or (iii) in the event the interested parties have exercised an *actio interrogatoria*, the period set by the judge[63] has not expired for the person called to inherit to accept or repudiate the inheritance[64].

---

59 About the repudiation of an inheritance, see, among others, B. Sansó, 'La repudiación de la herencia en el derecho venezolano', Revista de la Facultad de Derecho de la Universidad Central de Venezuela, 34 (1966), pp. 133–55.
60 Cfr. Esparza Bracho, p. 29.
61 To Esparza Bracho, the proposal of the inheritance "has been considered a subjective right of the person called to inherit due to it grants the right to accept or repudiate the inheritance, and to perform preservation acts on the remaining assets without it meaning implied acceptance, if in such acts they have not taken on the capacity or ability of heir". Cfr. Esparza Bracho, p. 25.
62 According to Article 1011 of the Venezuelan Civil Code, the right to accept an inheritance does not lapse until ten years have elapsed.
63 Pursuant to the first paragraph of Article 1019 of the Venezuelan Civil Code, the period set by the judge to deliberate shall not exceed six months.
64 If, at the expiration of that period, the called to inherit has not stated whether they accept or repudiate the inheritance, the inheritance shall be deemed repudiated pursuant to the last paragraph of Article 1019 of the Civil Code. However, Esparza Bracho considers that "this presumptive waiver may be

In principle, preservation acts[65] do not indicate an implied acceptance of the inheritance unless the person called to inherit has taken the title or the capacity of the heir to perform such acts, in accordance with Article 1003 of the Venezuelan Civil Code. In any case, it is up to the judge to determine, taking into account the specific circumstances, whether it is a mere act of preservation or an implied acceptance of the estate[66].

4.3 *The Acquisition of the Inheritance.*

The acquisition of the inheritance[67] is the effective substitution of the deceased by his/her heir(s)[68] in the legal entitlement over the deceased's subjective legal situations of economic value and transmissible. Consequently, the acquisition of the estate determines that heirs replace the deceased in his/her legal relations — the deceased's rights and legal actions, as well as his/her obligations[69], liabilities, and defenses. Likewise, the acquisition of the estate transfers the estate from the deceased to

---

rendered ineffective by any express or tacit act of acceptance". Cfr. Esparza Bracho, p. 85.

65 A list of preservation, guardianship, and temporary administration acts on the estate's assets is provided by López Herrera, II, p. 32; and L. Sanojo, 'Instituciones de derecho civil venezolano', in *Sucesiones*, II (Caracas: Ediciones Vegas Rolando, 1977), pp. 7–202 (pp. 52–53).

66 Cfr. Esparza Bracho, p. 42.

67 In Domínguez Guillén's opinion, the acquisition of the inheritance "is not simple, but a rather complex phenomenon, since it entails several events. Therefore, it is referred to as the dynamics of the acquisition". Domínguez Guillén, *Manual de derecho sucesorio*, p. 84.

68 While differentiating the stages of the probate process, Domínguez Guillén remarks that the acquisition of the inheritance entails the substitution of a new owner over the estate, while the opening of the succession only implies the phenomenon of an estate without an owner, and the proposal of the inheritance only constitutes a legal or testamentary calling for the purpose of a simple expectation of acquiring the inheritance. Cfr. Domínguez Guillén, *Manual de derecho sucesorio*, p. 79. In the same fashion, Sojo Bianco, p. 248.

69 According to Domínguez Guillén, "the acquisition of the inheritance is in essence what determines, to a larger or lesser scope, that the heir takes over the debts of the deceased". Cfr. Domínguez Guillén, *Manual de derecho sucesorio*, p. 84.

his/her heir(s). As a result, heirs are obliged to pay the debts and obligations of the estate, even out of their own assets[70] (*ultra vires hereditatis* liability), unless the heir repudiates the inheritance or accepts it subject to the privilege of an inventory of the estate, in which case the heir's liability is *intra vires hereditatis*.

The inheritance — and, consequently, the capacity to be an heir[71] — is only acquired with the acceptance of the inheritance[72], unless the inheritance is subject to a condition precedent. In this case, it is acquired upon the fulfillment of the condition, provided that the person called to inherit accepts it.

Acceptance of the inheritance is the unilateral legal act of consent of the person called to inherit to the proposal of inheritance, through which the inheritance and the capacity of heir[73] is acquired with retroactive effect since the day of the

---

70 In Sanojo's opinion, "the acceptance of the inheritance irrevocably subjects the acceptor to the duty of satisfying the obligations and liabilities of the succession, many times with their own assets". Cfr. Sanojo, 'Instituciones de derecho civil venezolano', p. 48. Similarly, Rojas asserts "The heir succeeds in the rights, the obligations and in the possession. Therefore, the heir must pay even out of their own pocket the liabilities of the inheritance when they receive it unconditionally", Cfr. Rojas, p. 20.

71 According to López Herrera, "A successor acquires the inheritance only when, through acceptance, becomes an heir." Cfr. López Herrera, II, p. 53. The same position is held by Domínguez Guillén, *Manual de derecho sucesorio*, p. 86.

72 Indeed, López Herrera remarks, "Even though estate assets' possession is passed by law from the *de cujus* to heir at the opening of the succession without material seizure (Article 995 of the Civil Code), the acquisition of the ownership of such assets by successors from the deceased only happens with the acceptance of the inheritance, which is a voluntary act of the person called to inherit". Cfr. López Herrera, II, p. 53. In the same fashion, Rojas says, "Although the called to inherit by the will or by law acquire the possession of the inheritance at the opening of the succession, they do not acquire the capacity of heirs neither the ownership of the estate's assets until they accept the inheritance fulfilling formalities required by law". Cfr. Rojas, p. 17.

73 To Sanojo, the acceptance of the inheritance is generally "an act whereby the person called to inherit states his/her intention of becoming the heir". Cfr. Sanojo, 'Instituciones de derecho civil venezolano', p. 47. In the same fashion, Calvo Baca says the acceptance of the inheritance "is the legal act whereby a person manifests his/her will to be held as the heir of another". Calvo Baca, p. 196.

opening of the succession[74]. In Venezuela, like in Italy[75], there are two types of acceptance of the inheritance according to Article 996 of the Venezuelan Civil Code: On the one hand, unconditional acceptance and, on the other hand, acceptance subject to the privilege of an inventory of the estate.

An unconditional acceptance of the inheritance may be an express acceptance or an implied acceptance. Similarly to the Italian law[76], it "is an express acceptance when the title or the capacity of heir is assumed through a public or private document"[77] by the person called to inherit, and it "is an implied acceptance when the heir carries out an act that necessarily supposes the will to accept the inheritance, and that she/he is not entitled to perform otherwise than in an heir capacity" according to Article 1002 of the Venezuelan Civil Code.

In each of these modalities, an unconditional acceptance of the inheritance implies a fusion of the inherited and the heir's (personal) estates. For this reason, on the one hand, the heir is fully liable, even with his/her own assets, for the debts, obligations, and liabilities of the inheritance[78] (*ultra vires hereditatis* liability); and, on the other hand, the heir's personal creditors will be able to satisfy their claims even with the inherited estate.

An acceptance subject to the privilege of an inventory of the estate can only be an express acceptance and, in addition, must comply with all of the legal requirements and formalities in order to be valid and to have legal effects, including the acquisition of the estate, and the heir's limited liability[79] up to the inherited

---

74   Cfr. Article 1001 of the Venezuelan Civil Code.
75   Cfr. Article 470 of the Italian Civil Code.
76   Cfr. Articles 475 and 476 of the Italian Civil Code.
77   However, Sanojo analyzes several cases that should not be deemed as an acceptance and concludes that "the fact of calling him/herself as heir is subject to legal interpretation". Cfr. Sanojo, 'Instituciones de derecho civil venezolano', pp. 49–50.
78   Liabilities, debts, and obligations of the inheritance become liabilities, debts, and obligations of the heir who unconditionally accepts the inheritance. Therefore, the heir is liable for them with all his/her current and future assets, whether or not obtained from the transfer of the deceased's estate.
79   According to Domínguez Guillén, "Despite the fact that the debts pass to the heir, they are liable *non ultra vires* (that is, they become a limited liability

estate (*intra vires hereditatis* liability), as well as the other effects resulting from the absence of a merger of the inherited estate and the (personal) estate of the heir[80].

According to Article 1023 of the Venezuelan Civil Code, the acceptance of the inheritance subject to the privilege of an inventory of the estate requires the following formalities: (i) an explicit writing declaration of the person called to inherit before the Court of First Instance of the place where the succession was opened; (ii) an extract of that declaration must be published in the official newspaper or in another in the absence of one; and (iii) public notices of that declaration must be posted on the door of the court[81]. In the absence of either of the latter two formalities, the judge should "refrain from continuing the proceeding and from initiating the inventory until the irregularity is remedied. Otherwise, the judge's acts are null and void, since they are performed in violation of the legal formalities for the validity of the act"[82].

Moreover, the acceptance of the inheritance subject to the privilege of an inventory of the estate requires a solemn judicial inventory[83] of the inherited estate. Indeed, the declaration of the person called to inherit according to which he/she intends to become an heir subject to the privilege of an inventory "does

---

debtor) by virtue of the privilege of an inventory". Cfr. Domínguez Guillén, *Manual de derecho sucesorio*, p. 129.

80   Other effects resulting from the absence of a merger of the inherited and the heir's (personal) estates are: The option for beneficiary heirs of releasing themselves from liability by abandoning the inherited estate in favor of the creditors and legatees; and the right to get their own credits paid from the inheritance, pursuant to Article 1036 of the Venezuelan Civil Code.

81   Sanojo remarks that "the purpose of these formalities is to make any interested person aware of the acceptance subject to that privilege". Cfr. Sanojo, 'Instituciones de derecho civil venezolano,' p. 66. In a similar fashion, Sojo Bianco asserts that these formalities aim to ensure the greatest possible publicity to the declaration of the person called to inherit according to which they intend to become an heir subject to the privilege of an inventory of the estate. Cfr. Sojo Bianco, p. 267.

82   Cfr. López Herrera, II, p. 85.

83   To Sojo Bianco, "In order to guarantee to third parties that nothing is omitted or hidden in the inventory, rigorous forms are ordered to make it". Cfr. Sojo Bianco, p. 267.

not produce any effect if it is not preceded or followed by the inventory of the assets of the inheritance made with the formalities established in the Venezuelan Civil Procedure Code and the terms set in this paragraph of the Venezuelan Civil Code"[84], according to Article 1025 of the Civil Code. In other words, without the solemn judicial inventory, the mere declaration of acceptance of the inheritance subject to the privilege of an inventory of the estate does not take effect. Consequently, it does not lead to the acquisition of the estate[85] or the effects inherent in the acceptance of the inheritance subject to the privilege of an inventory of the estate.

In any case, the legal situation of the person called to inherit before and after the acceptance of the inheritance subject to the privilege of an inventory of the estate "is different from that of an ordinary heir and is characterized by the limited powers he/she has over the assets of the estate".[86] In fact, while the inventory is being taken, the persons called to inherit are no more than legal guardians of the estate[87]. As a result, they might only carry out preservation acts, in accordance with articles 1032 and 1033 of the Venezuelan Civil Code. However, they may be authorized by the court to sell those assets that cannot be preserved or whose preservation is costly.

After completing the formalities required by Venezuelan law for accepting the inheritance subject to the privilege of an inventory of the estate[88], beneficiary heirs have the duty to administer estate assets and to render an account of that administration to creditors

---

84 That is, Paragraph 3 (on the privilege of an inventory, its effects, and on the duties of the beneficiary heir) of Section II, Title II, Book III of the Venezuelan Civil Code.

85 According to Domínguez Guillén, the heir's benefit "shall take place if following that process there are remaining assets to be acquired in their favor". Domínguez Guillén, *Manual de derecho sucesorio*, p. 121.

86 Sojo Bianco, p. 268.

87 Cfr. the last paragraph of Article 1032 of the Venezuelan Civil Code. In Sojo Bianco's opinion, "Before the acceptance and during the periods to make the inventory and deliberate, the person is not an heir, and is not obligated to assume that capacity. The person is considered a simple guardian". Cfr. Sojo Bianco, p. 268.

88 The situation might change if the privilege of an inventory is lost.

and legatees[89], pursuant to Article 1037[90] of the Venezuelan Civil Code. In this regard, beneficiary heirs should act with diligence of any administrator of the property of another, in accordance with Article 1038 of the Civil Code. Likewise, their powers are also limited, as it follows from articles 1041 to 1044 of the Venezuelan Civil Code[91].

The provisions of the Venezuelan Civil Code regarding the acceptance of the inheritance subject to the privilege of an inventory of the estate, are mandatory rules due to their function[92] and their special effects for the heirs, creditors and legatees of the inheritance93.

---

89 Therefore, in Domínguez Guillén's opinion, a beneficiary heir is a sort of administrator of other people's assets. Cfr. Domínguez Guillén, *Manual de derecho sucesorio*, p. 130.
90 In the case law of Article 1037 of the Venezuelan Civil Code, la Sala Civil, Mercantil y del Trabajo (G.F., N° 4, 2E, pp. 592–593 / 27-04-54) argues, "Nothing authorizes the conclusion according to which, because the portion of one of the heirs is larger, such heir shall be empowered by that sole fact to represent the others. The condition of the heirs is equal before the Law, and, in the event of the acceptance subject to the privilege of an inventory of the estate, the ordinary principles of representation apply, since, as long as the inheritance is not liquidated, the heirs' rights are simply presumptive". Cfr. E. Calvo Baca, *Código civil venezolano. Comentado y Concordado* (Caracas: Ediciones Libra, 1984), p. 462.
91 For that reason, Sojo Bianco states, "Even though the inheritance might be theirs, they administer it on behalf of the creditors and legatees and are liable to them". Cfr. Sojo Bianco, p. 269.
92 According to Sojo Bianco, the function of the acceptance subject to the privilege of an inventory of the estate "is not only led by the interest of those called to inherit, but also has a social utility purpose." Cfr. Sojo Bianco, p. 266.
93 Cfr. Domínguez Guillén, *Manual de derecho sucesorio*, p. 123.

LILIAN C. SAN MARTÍN NEIRA*
REPERCUSSIONS OF ITALIAN LAW IN THE RE-READING OF THE BELLO CODE CONCERNING BREACH OF CONTRACT

1. *Introduction*

The current Chilean Civil Code was drafted by Andrés Bello and dates from 1855. It is, therefore, a 19th-century code, written almost a century before the *Codice Civile* from 1942. Consequently, one cannot speak of a direct influence of the Italian Code on the formulation of the Chilean Code; unlike what happens with other Latin American Codes, such as the Peruvian, the Bolivian and the Argentine. However, as will be seen throughout this work, the Italian civil law doctrine and, therefore, the regulations that it comments on, have influenced recent developments in Chilean doctrine and jurisprudence, specifically concerning breach of contract.

Indeed, unlike what happens with the *Codice Civile*, which reserves a special section for Breach of Contract[1], the Bello Code is quite sparse and unsystematic when regulating this institution and its consequences. Actually, in the traditional Chilean doctrine, there are no studies especially devoted to the topic; rather, this is seen as a basis for the exercise of creditor protection mechanisms, under the title "obligation effects"[2]. This contrasts with the attention that the most recent doctrine

---

* Researcher and Professor of Civil Law at the Center for Regulatory and Business Law (Centro de Derecho Regulatorio y de Empresa), Universidad del Desarrollo, Chile.
1 Book IV, Title I, Chapter III.
2 R. Ramos Pazos, *De las obligaciones*, 3rd edn (LegalPublishing 2008), p. 230; R. Abeliuk Manasevich, *Las obligaciones*, 6th edn (Thomson Reuters 2014), II, pp. 697 ff. An exception is the work of Fueyo, dedicated expressly to the analysis of the compliance and breach of obligations. F. Fueyo Laneri,

has paid to the institution, which has carried out a true re-reading of the Bello Code to modernise its rules' application. As follows, breach of contract and all associated institutions have been subject to review, which has led to a reformulation of the normative interpretations in force until recently, mutating the notion of Breach of Contract and its consequences. Indeed, as Pizarro very well summarises,

> in Chile, a way of understanding the phenomenon of the non-fault breach of contract has been consolidated, at least at the doctrinal level, with the creditor being able to choose between different powers or claims once the breach has taken place. It is an idea whose roots can be identified in the work of Morales Moreno, from the deepening of the practical purpose concept of Federico de Castro y Bravo. It seeks to protect their interest, although moderated with the principle of contractual good faith. Many authors have welcomed the modernisation of contract law understood as a system of remedies for contractual breaches in their writings. Even this has given rise to a new nomenclature about the possibilities that open up to the dissatisfied creditor; this set of alternatives is called "remedies against breach of contract".[3]

Thus, we speak of a new contract or contracting law, whose main characteristics are:

i. The fact that default is defined objectively, as any deviation from the obligation schedule, regardless of the debtor's fault.

ii. An integrated system of remedies or mechanisms for the protection of the creditor's interests from which s/he can freely choose, provided that the assumptions of the origin of the chosen mechanism are met.

iii. A minimum role to the debtor's fault when building the creditor's protection against breach of contract, a role that, as a principle, is limited to constituting a basis of contractual liability,

---

Cumplimiento e incumplimiento de las obligaciones, 3rd edn (Editorial Jurídica de Chile 2004).

[3] Cfr. C. Pizarro Wilson, 'Notas acerca de los límites a la pretensión de cumplimiento del contrato', Revista de derecho Universidad Católica del Norte, 21 (2014), p. 204. For the notion of practical purpose here referred to A.M. Morales Moreno, 'El propósito práctico, y la idea de negocio jurídico en Federico de Castro', Anuario de Derecho Civil, 36 (1983), p. 1529.

ceasing to be a requirement for other remedies such as resolution and enforcement.

iv. Place great emphasis on the integration of the obligation with a series of accessory or secondary duties of conduct intended for the creditor to satisfy the practical purpose that was proposed at the time of contracting, duties that extend even beyond complying with the main obligation.

In general, the Chilean doctrine recognises a direct influence of this new conception of contract law, and in particular of breach of contract, the Spanish doctrine and the private law harmonisation instruments. However, a concentrated reading of the Italian sources and doctrine, as well as Spanish authors, makes it possible for Chileans to appreciate a clear link between these "new" developments and Italian civil law. In particular, authors such as Betti, Messineo, Giorgianni and Bianca are of great relevance: their ideas are clearly identifiable in the arguments put forward by Chilean authors, whether mediated by the Spanish or directly quoted. Indeed, it is no mystery that Spanish doctrine has traditionally paid attention to doctrinal and jurisprudential developments in Italy, so Spanish works referenced by Chilean authors, in turn, tend to cite Italian authors. Also, in the larger monographic works, it is possible to observe a direct revision of the Italian doctrine, which is cited to endorse the conclusions reached. Finally, in jurisprudence as well, it is possible to find direct references to the Italian doctrine[4].

Given the foregoing, in this chapter I will analyse the influence of the *Codice Civile* on the rules for breach of contract in Chile, but always referring to the direct or indirect repercussions of

---

4   In particular, the works of Messineo, *Dottrina Generale del Contratto and Manuale di diritto civile e comerciale*, in their Spanish translations, are often cited in Chilean court rulings. *V. gr.* Supreme Court, 21.01.2022, Case No. 4162-2021; Supreme Court, 28.12.2021, Case No. 33474-2019; Supreme Court 06.01.2019, Case No. 1232-2019; Supreme Court, 07.07.2016, Case No. 20584-2015; Supreme Court, 28.05.2014, Case No. 1859-2013. The same goes for the works *Teoria generale delle obbligazioni* e *Interpretazione giuridica*, from Betti, also in its Spanish translations, *v. gr.* Supreme Court, 22.07.2019, Case No. 35587-2017; Supreme Court, 24.09.2019, Case No. 35722-2017; Supreme Court, 02.05.2022, Case No. 92048-2020.

the comments and analysis of the Italian doctrine. For this, in what follows, I will split the text into three parts: (part 2) The reconceptualisation of breach of contract and its consequences; (part 3) The balance of interests concerning the breaching of contracts; and (part 4) Concluding remarks.

2. *The reconceptualization of breach of contract and its consequences*

2.1 *The arrival of a neutral and comprehensive concept of breach of contract*

As stated, in the traditional Chilean doctrine, no studies are specifically devoted to breach of contract. In turn, in the same doctrine, there is an automatic association between the breach and the debtor's fault or negligence, thus it is always considered a situation derived from reprehensible the debtor's behaviour. This is reflected in the definition provided by Fueyo, who states that breach of contract is

> an unlawful situation that occurs when, due to the guilty act of the person obliged to do or refrain from doing, the legal relationship is not satisfied in the same tenor in which it was contracted, reacting the law against him/her to impose the consequences of his/her conduct.[5]

It is relevant to point out that such a notion responds to the traditional vision of breach of contract in the Ibero-American comparative panorama[6], which does not account for the fact that not

---

5   Fueyo, p. 256. Along the same lines, but with a more complex structure, consisting of the distinction between what should be done or what should refrain from being done and the due conduct, by virtue of which there is breach when what should be done or what should refrain from being done is not executed and due conduct is not observed, that is, the degree of diligence required to the debtor. P. Rodríguez Grez, *Responsabilidad contractual* (Editorial Jurídica de Chile 2015), p. 121.
6   Regarding Spain, as Baraona points out, the traditional vision was "that there can be no breach if it is not attributable, since program and compliance go hand in hand; in order for the injury to the program of what should be done or what should refrain from being done to truly be qualified as breach, it

doing what should be done or doing what should refrain from being done can be due to multiple causes, among which is the debtor's guilty activity. Faced with this problem, voices arose that proposed a change in terminology. In this sense, in Colombia, Hinestrosa proposes to include among the "ordinary dyad of 'compliance-breach of contracts'[7] a third option that of 'non-compliance'", understanding the latter as the non-satisfaction of the creditor's interest, regardless of the debtor's blameworthy conduct. Along the same lines, Llambías, in Argentina, proposes speaking of a material breach of what should be done or refrain from being done, which must then be analysed to determine whether or not the assumptions of contractual liability concur[8]. Likewise, in Spain, trying to use the broadest possible use of the term, Díez-Picazo uses the expression damage to the right to credit, which encompasses all the hypotheses in which the creditor's interest has not been satisfied[9]. This last opinion is the one that prevails in the current Chilean doctrine, which advocates for a unitary, broad and neutral concept of breach

---

is necessary that it responds to the debtor's behavior of which a judgment of legal reproach can be made, without this negative imputation judgment, there is no breach". Cfr. J. Baraona González, *El retraso en el cumplimiento de las obligaciones* (Dykinson 1998), p. 101. This same author warns about the existence, in the Spanish doctrine, of an intermediate current that "maintains a solidly objective position for the configuration of breach and liability, without inquiring into the subjective attribution of the debtor, up to the limit of the impossibility of the supervening of what should be done or what should refrain from being done. From that milestone, for the breach to subsist, an imputation factor must be added: there is no breach, it will be said, if the impossibility has been made unexpectedly for reasons not attributable to the debtor". Cfr. J. Baraona González, *El retraso en el cumplimiento de las obligaciones*, p. 103.

7   F. Hinestrosa, 'Leyendo el digesto', Roma e America, 22, (2006), p. 73.
8   J. Joaquín Llambías, *Tratado de derecho civil. Obligaciones*, 2nd edn, Vol. I (Perrot 1973), p. 123. In Chile, this idea is found in Cárdenas and Reveco, who distinguish between material breach and breach in the strict sense, the latter would be the one qualified by the presence of some factor attributing liability. H. Cárdenas Villarreal and R. Reveco Urzúa, *Remedios contractuales. Cláusulas, acciones y otros mecanismos de tutela del crédito* (Thomson Reuters, 2018), pp. 31 ff.
9   L. Diez-Picazo, *Fundamentos del derecho civil patrimonial*, Vol. II (Civitas 2008), pp. 646 ff.

of contracts[10]. Unitary, insofar as it would cover all the hypotheses of deviation from the obligations, giving them a uniform treatment in terms of the creditor's remedies. Broad, insofar as it includes any disagreement regarding the obligations, including the breach of accessory or secondary duties of conduct. And, neutral, insofar as it does not prejudge the debtor's guilt. As follows, the term breach indicates

> the debtor not doing what s/he should do or doing what s/he should refrain from doing, or what s/he's done is incomplete, defective or overdue. Its meaning includes both the objective lack of what should be done or what should refrain from being done, as well as the fault attributable to the debtor, either of the main obligation or its accessories.[11]

---

10   Above all, A. Vidal Olivares 'Cumplimiento e Incumplimiento Contractual en el Código Civil. Una perspectiva más realista', Revista Chilena de Derecho, 34 (2007), 41–59; C. Mejías Alonzo, 'El incumplimiento contractual y sus modalidades', in A. Guzmán Brito (ed.), *Estudios de Derecho Civil III* (LegalPublishing, 2008), pp. 459–78; A. Vidal Olivares, 'El incumplimiento y los remedios del acreedor en la propuesta de modernización del derecho de las obligaciones y los contratos español', Revista Chilena de Derecho Privado, 16 (2011), 243–302; L.C. San Martín Neira, 'Noción de incumplimiento en la perspectiva de la armonización del derecho latinoamericano', in G.F. Priori Posada and R. Morales Hervias, *De las obligaciones en general. Coloquio de Iusprivatistas Roma y América* (Fondo Editorial Universidad Católica del Perú, 2012), pp. 321-41; A. Vidal Olivares, 'La noción de incumplimiento. Una mirada unitaria desde la idea de vinculación contractual "garantía"', in A. Vidal Olivares (ed.), *Estudios de derecho de contratos en homenaje a Antonio Manuel Morales Moreno* (Thomson Reuters, 2018), pp. 447–74; Cárdenas and Reveco, pp. 59 ff.; F. González Cazorla, 'Hacia una noción de incumplimiento del contrato de consumo por la entrega defectuosa de productos', Justicia y Derecho, 2 (2019), pp. 43–61; J. Oviedo Albán and A. Vidal Olivares, 'El concepto unitario de incumplimiento en el moderno derecho de los contratos', Universitas, 69 (2020). In a critical sense, R. Barcia Lehmann and J. Maximiliano Rivera Restrepo, '¿En qué sentido es objetiva la noción de incumplimiento del soft law?', Opinión Jurídica, 18 (2019), pp. 165–181.

11   J. Javier De los Mozos Touyá, 'En torno a la idea de incumplimiento en el derecho civil español', Roma e América, 22 (2006), pp. 145–62. In similar terms, it has been said that breach is "any deviation from the program of what should be done or what should refrain from being done agreed the program that entails a disharmony with the interest that the parties intended to satisfy at the time of the contract". Cf. Mejías, 'El incumplimiento contractual y sus modalidades', p. 475.

In summary, for the current Chilean doctrine, breach of contract is defined objectively, as any deviation from the obligations, regardless of the debtor's fault[12].

> The concept of breach of contract is objective and initially acts regardless of the debtor's fault or fraud and is the result of the simple verification of the lack of coincidence between the ideal data (what was promised) and the real one (what the debtor executed), with the consequent dissatisfaction of the creditor's interest.[13]

For instance, the Chilean doctrine recognizes a direct influence of the international instruments for the unification and harmonization of private law, all of which consecrate this neutral vision of breach of contract[14]. A consonance is clearly observed with how the Italian doctrine has read Article 1218 of the Civil Code (C.C.) and, in particular, how the notion of breach of contract has been built by authors such as Giorgianni and Bianca. Indeed, the Italian Civil Code in its Article 1218 alludes to the debtor's liability in the following terms:

> the debtor who does not exactly do what s/he should or does what s/he should refrain from doing is obliged to compensate the damage if s/he does not prove that the breach of contract or delay was due to the impossibility of doing what s/he should or doing what s/he should refrain from doing derived from a cause not attributable to her/him.

---

12 Vidal, 'Cumplimiento e Incumplimiento Contractual en el Código Civil', pp- 41–59; San Martín, 'Una noción de incumplimiento en la perspectiva de la armonización del derecho latinoamericano', pp. 321–41; Cárdena and Reveco, p. 31.
13 Vidal, 'Cumplimiento e Incumplimiento Contractual en el Código Civil', p. 48.
14 See European Principles of Contract Law (EPCL), Article 1:301 and UNIDROIT Principles, Article 7.1.1. The same idea emerges from the Latin American Principles of Contract Law, which defines breach in Article 86 in clearly neutral terms, and in which 'it is irrelevant to define whether or not there is a breach, whether it was caused by the own debtor's conduct, the creditor or his/her auxiliaries, of a third party or in an impediment outside the debtor's sphere of control — act of God or force majeure. Whatever the case, the truth is that there is a breach of the contract, pending the elucidation of the effects that it will produce, the protection means that the creditor will have for that specific case.' I. De la Maza, C. Pizarro Wilson and A. Vidal Olivares, *Los Principios Latinoamericanos de Derecho de los Contratos* (Agencia Estatal Boletín Oficial del Estado 2017) 54.

Commenting on this Article, Bianca wonders if the notion of breach of Contract express in itself the imputation to the debtor in terms of the unlawfulness examination or if in a legislative language such a notion coincides with the objective lack of performance of what should be done or what should refrain from doing, regardless of the subsequent assessment of the debtor's imputation. The author replies to this question by pointing out that the rule's wording allows opting for the second alternative since it offers the breaching debtor the possibility of excusing himself by citing a non-attributable cause. Based on this idea, he concludes that

> breach of contract is not in itself the result of a lawfulness examination but the material element of this examination: an element that is precisely identified with the debtor's objective situation who does not do what s/he should or does what s/he should refrain from doing.[15]

Thus, a clear continuity line can be seen between the redefinition of the notion of breach of contract in the Chilean doctrine and that which, from Article 1218 C.C., was developed by the Italian doctrine.

2.2 *The role of fault concerning the exercise of contractual remedies*

An important sector of the Italian doctrine concluded that it was necessary to distinguish between an imputable and non-imputable breach of contract[16], establishing that breach of

---

15 C.M. Bianca, *Inadempimento delle obbligazioni* (Zanichelli, Il Foro Italiano, 1979), p. 11. The same author in another work states that "breach corresponds to the non-performance or inaccurate performance of what should be done or what should refrain from being done due by the debtor". Cf. C.M. Bianca, *Diritto civile 5* (Giuffrè, 2004), p. 2.

16 In this sense, Betti, after having pointed out that breach consists fundamentally of the injury to the creditor's interest or expectation, states that "it is easily understandable that the mere fact of failing to make the exact payment due in due time is not enough to justify the debtor's liability as a defaulter. It is necessary that this objective fact, which injures the creditor's interest and which is contrary to law, in the sense that it is configured as unjust damage caused to the creditor, is also attributable to the debtor, in the sense that it can

contract is a neutral institution, insofar as it dispenses with the lawfulness examination. As early as the 1960s, Italian authors taught that "breach of contract not attributable to the debtor" "can also lead to the application of measures to protect credit standing. These are objective remedies, aimed at preserving the creditor's position against the alteration of the contractual balance"[17]. Therefore, the principle enshrined is that of "the creditor's interest deserving adequate protection also in those cases in which compliance is prevented for reasons beyond the debtor's attribution"[18]. The concrete consequence of this is that non-attributable breach of contract also gives rise to the exercise of those mechanisms that are only intended to preserve or re-establish the contractual balance, such as the enforced contract's performance or the contract's termination, leaving the requirement of fault reserved for the compensation of damages[19].

Giorgianni affirms that the rule in this regard is that "except for compensation damages, all other remedies against a breach — including contract termination — disregard 'imputability'"[20]. Specifically, as regards termination, the author affirms that "the remedy of termination for breach of contract, far from being a sanction for culpable breach, it is a consequence of the impossibility of the contract's performance with correlative obligations"[21].

In Chile, the idea that breach of contract was in itself an unlawful act, associated with the idea of the debtor's "fault",

---

be charged to this fact, according to the rule of Art. 1218". Cf. E. Betti, *Teoría general de las obligaciones*, Vol. I, trans. by J.L. De los Mozos, Editorial Revista de Derecho Privado, 1969, p. 128.

17   Cfr. Bianca, *Diritto civile 5*, p. 2. For the previous doctrine see M. Giorgianni, 'Inadempimento' (diritto privato), *Enciclopedia del diritto XX* (1975) 886; Bianca, *Inadempimento delle obbligazioni*, pp. 11 ff.
18   Giorgianni, p. 861.
19   Giorgianni, pp. 886 ff.
20   Cfr. Giorgianni, p. 886.
21   Giorgianni, p. 888. More recently, regarding the possibility of requesting the resolution in the presence of a supervening impossibility not attributable to the debtor, L. Cabella Pisu, 'La risoluzione per impossibilità sopravvenuta' in G. Visintini (ed.) *Trattato di responsabilità contrattuale*, Vol. I (CEDAM, 2009), p. 487.

until recently unanimous doctrine and jurisprudence demanded this element as a requirement for the exercise of all contractual remedies arising from the breach. To achieve this all the remedies involved the debtor's default, which, in turn [default], is defined as the "culpable delay in performing the obligation". As follows, faced with a non-imputable breach of contract, the creditor was prevented from exercising defense mechanisms. In particular, in cases of obligations arising from bilateral contracts, the creditor could not claim the contract's termination, since this required the debtor's default and, consequently, the breach's guilt or imputability. Thus, Peñailillo affirms that, although the rule does not expressly require it, this

> is deduced because if the breach was due to an unforeseeable circumstance, the termination cannot be requested, since the obligation was extinguished by other ways to terminate the contract, which is the impossibility to perform the obligation [or termination by frustration] (in the Chilean C.C. also known as "owed-thing loss", Articles 1670 et seq.). Additionally, it has been cleared of the fact that Art. 1489 allows requesting compensation, which only proceeds if there are arrears (Art. 1557), which in turn requires fraud or fault.[22]

Currently, however, it is possible to observe a majority tendency[23] that the creditor's interests must be protected even in the presence of the debtor's non-imputable breach of contract. Accordingly, Vidal affirms that

> breach of contract is an objective or neutral fact because it ignores its cause, the assessment of the debtor's conduct; it does not matter whether it was or whether it was not due to an unforeseeable circumstance, it only matters the debtor not performing what was agreed, causing the creditor's dissatisfaction. That breach that was caused by an unforeseeable circumstance also allows the creditor to count with remedies.[24]

Previously, this same author had argued that

---

22 Cf. D. Peñailillo Arévalo, *Obligaciones. Teoría general y clasificaciones. La resolución por incumplimiento* (Editorial Jurídica de Chile, 2003), p. 412.
23 Against, Cárdenas and Reveco, pp. 349 ff.
24 Vidal, 'La noción de incumplimiento. Una mirada unitaria desde la idea de vinculación contractual "garantía"', p. 467.

the mere breach is sufficient to make protection measures available to the creditor which, generically, are called remedies for breach of contract, that is, actions or rights that the law or the contract confers on the creditor in case the debtor breaches the contract, among which s/he can choose, more or less, freely and which aim is the protection of her/his interest in the performance, affected by the infringement.[25]

This does not mean, in any case, that all breaches entail exactly the same consequences, since the reason that causes the breach is not indifferent. Thus, the breach's subjective element affects the configuration of the remedies that the creditor can exercise to protect its interests. Therefore, breach of contract is split into imputable breach and non-imputable breach, noting that the creditor can be protected even in the presence of a non-imputable breach. Accordingly, there are institutions called upon to operate precisely to protect the creditor against the debtor's non-imputable breach of contract, such as the so-called duty of notice that weighs on the debtor who is the victim of an unforeseeable circumstance or force majeure, who must notify the creditor within a reasonable period, under penalty of being held responsible for the damages that the lack of communication causes to the creditor[26]. Likewise, is the so-called *commodum repraesentationis*, that is, the creditor's right to claim from the debtor the assignment of the remedies against the third party causing the breach[27].

More incisively and in agreement with the Italian doctrine, it has been concluded that the fundamental consequence of the non-imputability of the breach lies in the creditor's exclusion

---

25 Cf. Vidal, 'Cumplimiento e Incumplimiento Contractual en el Código Civil', p. 54. Jurisprudence, however, has not openly ruled on this point and it is possible to find sentences that affirm the contrary idea.

26 Regarding this duty and its applicability, even where it has not been expressly established, L.C. San Martín Neira, 'El deber de aviso ante el caso fortuito o fuerza mayor: ¿tiene aplicación en Chile?', in F. Elorriaga de Bonis (ed.), *Estudios de Derecho Civil VII* (Thomson Reuters, 2012), pp. 547–60.

27 In Chile, this situation is expressly contemplated concerning the loss of what is owed, but it has been stated that it is perfectly possible to extend it to other hypotheses of breach. J. Alcalde Silva, 'El "commodum repraesentationis" del artículo 1677 del "código civil' de Chile", Revista de Derecho de la Pontificia Universidad Católica de Valparaíso, 31 (2008), pp. 37–161.

of compensation for damages, but that does not prevent the creditor from exercising other remedies aimed at protecting her/his interests against an alteration of the contractual balance, such as contract termination[28]. In summary, current Chilean doctrine is practically in unison assigning a minimum role to the debtor's fault when building creditor protection against breach of contract, a role that, consistent with the maximum, is limited to constituting a basis of contractual liability, ceasing to be a requirement for other remedies such as termination, enforced performance[29] and the exception for breach of contract[30].

---

28   A. Vidal Olivares, 'El incumplimiento resolutorio en el Código Civil. Condiciones de procedencia de la resolución por incumplimiento', in C. Pizarro Wilson (ed.), *Estudios de derecho civil IV* (LegalPublishing, 2009), p. 363.

29   J. Baraona González, 'Responsabilidad contractual y factores de imputación de daños. Apuntes para una relectura en clave objetiva', Revista Chilena de Derecho, 24 (1997), pp. 151–77; E. Barros Bourie, 'La diferencia entre "estar obligado" y "ser responsable" en el derecho de los contratos', in H. Corral Talciani and M.S. Rodríguez Pinto (eds.), *Estudios de Derecho Civil II* (LegalPublishing, 2007) pp. 721–51; M.G. Brantt Zumarán, 'La culpa del deudor y la procedencia de la pretensión de cumplimiento específico y la indemnización de daños', in C. Domínguez Hidalgo *et alt.* (eds.), *Estudios de Derecho Civil VIII*, (LegalPublishing – Thomson Reuters, 2013), pp. 541–59; J.I. Contardo González, *Indemnización y resolución por incumplimiento* (Thomson Reuters, 2015), pp. 252 ff.

30   C. Pizarro Wilson, 'La Excepción por Incumplimiento Contractual en el Derecho Civil chileno', in J. Andrés Varas Braun and S. Turner Saelzer (eds.), *Estudios de Derecho Civil* (LexisNexis, 2005), pp. 317–42; C. Pizarro Wilson, 'La culpa como elemento constitutivo del incumplimiento en las obligaciones de medio o diligencia', Revista de Derecho de la Pontificia Universidad Católica de Valparaíso, 31 (2008), p. 255; H. Corral Talciani, 'La cláusula penal en la resolución del contrato', in E. Alcalde and H. Fábrega, *Estudios jurídicos en homenaje a Pablo Rodríguez Grez* (Universidad del Desarrollo, 2009), pp. 331–60; A. Vidal Olivares, 'La noción de incumplimiento esencial en el Código Civil', Revista de Derecho de la Pontificia Universidad Católica de Valparaíso, 32 (2009), p. 225; C. Mejías Alonzo, *El incumplimiento resolutorio en el Código Civil* (LegalPublishing, 2011), p. 21; C. Mejías Alonzo, 'La excepción de contrato no cumplido y su consagración en el código civil chileno', Revista Chilena de Derecho 40 (2013), pp. 389–412. This last author explains that the exception of breach of contract is not equivalent to the delay purges the delay, because, although in delay actually requires the debtor's fault, since compensation for damages is derived from it, the exception of breach of contract does not demand it.

From a broader perspective, Chilean doctrine has pointed out that the adequate protection of the creditor's interests requires the configuration of an integrated system of remedies or mechanisms among which the creditor may choose freely as long as their requirements are met[31]. This entails the need to verify case-by-case whether the procedural requirements of the specific remedy that the creditor intends to exercise concur, thus analysing the legal and contractual provisions that govern the contractual relationship.

To avoid confusion, it is important to highlight a noteworthy difference between the Italian and Chilean systems — concerning risk distribution —, which directly affects the possibility of exercising the remedial remedy. Indeed, in the Bello Code, regarding obligations of a certain kind or body, the maximum *res perit creditoris* is enshrined (repeated in matters of sale with the *periculum est emptor*)[32]. Thus, the creditor of a certain species or body, who is a victim of the debtor's non-attributable impossibility of performing the contract, cannot claim the contract's termination, since that would imply an alteration of the distribution of contractual risks[33].

---

[31] E. Barros Bourie, 'Finalidad y alcance de las acciones y los remedios contractuales', in A. Guzmán Brito (ed.), *Estudios de derecho civil III* (LegalPublishing, 2008), pp. 403–28; C. Pizarro Wilson, 'Hacia un sistema de remedios al incumplimiento contractual', in A. Guzmán Brito, *Estudios de derecho civil III* (LegalPublishing, 2008), pp. 395–402; V.P. López Díaz, 'La indemnización compensatoria por incumplimiento de los contratos bilaterales como remedio autónomo en el derecho chileno', Revista Chilena de Derecho Privado, 15 (2010), pp. 65–113; J.I. Contardo González, *Indemnización y resolución por incumplimiento* (Thomson Reuters, 2015), pp. 22 ff.; Cárdenas and Reveco, pp. 13 ff.

[32] Articles 1550 and 1820.

[33] This is recognized by the doctrine, which explains that the contract resolution for non-attributable performance refers, of course, to those obligations in which the risk of breach is not based on the creditor, such as all obligations with fungible object and obligations of doing. See Vidal, 'El incumplimiento resolutorio en el Código Civil', p. 363.

3. The balance of interests to configure and assess the breaching of contracts

Within the field of breach of contract, one aspect in which the influence of the Italian doctrine — based on the *Codice Civile* — has been key is the weighting of the parties' interests for purposes of configuring breach of contract, as well as its assessment for purposes of the admissibility of certain contractual remedies.

3.1 The incorporation of the creditor's interest to configure the breach

When it comes to the configuration of breach of contract, Chilean doctrine and jurisprudence have paid attention to the creditor's interest in performance, understood as the practical purpose pursued in entering into the contract. Indirectly, this idea is the result of the Italian doctrine's strong influence and a clear relationship of continuity is observed with the evolution that the notion of the contract's cause has had in Italy. Indeed, the idea of practical purpose is taken by the Chilean authors from the Spanish doctrine, specifically from Morales Moreno and De Castro[34]. In turn, the latter found inspiration in the Italian doctrine, specifically in Betti who, in his *Teoria generale del negozio giuridico* (1943), had already shown that legal business does not respond to a purely theoretical question, but to the need of individuals to regulate their interests and the creation of the appropriate means to achieve them[35]. In the same work, Betti refers to the "*intento pratico tipico*" to allude to the contract's cause, which would consist precisely in the social-economic

---

[34] I. De la Maza Gazmuri and A. Vidal Olivares, 'Propósito práctico, incumplimiento contractual y remedios del acreedor. Con ocasión de tres sentencias de la Corte Suprema', Revista Ius et Praxis, 20 (2014), 19; A.M. Morales Moreno, 'El 'propósito práctico' y la idea de negocio jurídico en Federico de Castro', Anuario de Derecho Civil, 36 (1983), 1529–46.

[35] See E. Betti, *Teoria generale del negozio giuridico* (Edizioni Scientifiche Italiane, 2002), pp. 44 ff. The influence of Betti in the work of De Castro is also noted by J. Baraona González, *El retraso en el cumplimiento de las obligaciones* (Dikynson, 1998), p. 187.

function that the legal business is called upon to fulfil[36]. The similarity of language: practical purpose vs. *intento pratico*, is quite evident. To the above, it is worth adding Betti's teaching that the obligation is in itself a cooperative relationship, which responds fundamentally to a creditor's interest that is directly related to the *intento pratico* or business cause which originates it[37]. Following Betti, the dissatisfaction with the creditor's interest, that is, the infringement of the *intento pratico* entails a breach of the obligation[38]. The evolution of Betti's teachings is recognisable in current Italian doctrine, which refers to the cause as "the practical reason of the contract, that is, the interest that the contractual operation is aimed at satisfying"[39] and, consequently, it fulfils various functions, such as contract interpretation criteria, contract qualification criteria and adequacy criteria. Thus, issues such as breach of contract can be adequately resolved only if the overall interest pursued by the parties is taken into account, that is, the economics of the business[40]. In obligations of a contractual nature, therefore, a bi-univocal hermeneutic mechanism can take place, in light of which, in each case, the inquiry about the credit interest may be useful to identify the "specific" cause of the contract, but, at the same time, the interpretation of the title (and therefore of the cause) may prove essential to correctly identify the creditor's interest[41].

As stated, the Chilean doctrine adopted the notion of practical purpose as a criterion to highlight the creditor's interest in the

---

36   Betti, *Teoria generale del negozio giuridico*, pp. 56 and 183.
37   Indeed, when referring to the creditor's interest as an integral part of the obligation, Betti refers to paragraph 3 and chapter III of the *Teoria generale del negozio giuridico*, that is, precisely to the points of the text in which he refers to the *intento pratico* and, more generally, to the cause as an element of the legal transaction. Cfr. Betti, *Teoria general de las obligaciones*, p. 46 and Betti, *Teoria generale del negozio giuridico*, pp. 54 ff. and 167 ff.
38   Betti, *Teoría general de las obligaciones*, pp. 122 ff.
39   C.M. Bianca, *Diritto civile 3*, 2nd edn (Giuffrè, 2000), p. 448; F. Procchi, 'I caratteri della prestazione nell'enunciato dell'art. 1174 Cod. Civ.', in L. Garofalo (ed.) *Trattato delle obbligazioni. La struttura e l'adempimento*, Vol. II (Wolters Kluwer – CEDAM, 2014), p. 571.
40   Bianca, *Diritto civile 3*, p. 448.
41   Cfr. Procchi, p. 572.

obligation. Consequently, in line with what is taught in Italy[42], Chilean authors and courts understand that due performance includes the creditor's interest in the performance, so that a transgression to this interest may be enough to configure a breach of contract, particularly an imperfect breach, that is, one in which the debtor displays some activity leading to the fulfilment of the obligation, but insufficient to satisfy the creditor's interest[43]. An issue that becomes especially relevant when it comes to filling contractual gaps, i.e. cases in which the creditor invokes the fulfilment of an interest that has not been specified in the contract, but that arises from aspects such as the nature of the obligation or other similar[44]. In these ideas, the influence of Betti's thought and its subsequent evolutions can be clearly appreciated. As an example, a Supreme Court judgment of May 2, 2022, expressly quoted Betti when mentioning good faith as collaborating and defining element of the obligatory content, in the following terms:

> contractual good faith, it has been said, is an attitude of 'cooperation that binds the debtor to put his/her energies at the service of the interests of others, considering compliance with all his assets' (Emilio Betti, Teoría General de Las Obligaciones, Ed. Rev. de Derecho Privado, Madrid, p. 118). […] Thus, the interpretation of the contract between the parties in the *sub judice* situation, consistent with the mentioned good faith, inevitably leads to the conclusion that its fulfilment requires that the real estate sold to the plaintiff obtain the construction authorisations and permits, on the whole in its length and breadth, to ensure its legitimate use, enjoyment and disposition or in condition at least to accede to such a situation of regularity or legality, which the defendants did not fulfil in the species.[45]

---

42   Above all, Bianca, *Inadempimento delle obbligazioni*, p. 9; A. Nicolussi, *Le obbligazioni* (Wolters Kluwer – CEDAM), pp. 29 ff.

43   I. De la Maza Gazmuri, 'Obligación de entrega, cumplimiento imperfecto y resolución del contrato. Supreme Court, 16 de Abril de 2013, Case No. 3.967-2010', Revista chilena de derecho privado, 20 (2013), pp. 235–40.

44   In this sense, the notion of practical purpose has been resorted to fill description gaps in a construction contract, when it has been entered into by consensus. See A. Erbetta, 'Propósito práctico y buena fe integradora en contratos consensuales de confección de obra material', Derecho público iberoamericano, 10 (2017), pp. 267–74.

45   Cfr. Supreme Court, 02.05.2022, Case No. 92048-2020. In a previous judgement, the Court had held that "Article 1546 of the Civil Code establishes

In short, for the judges, the interest or purpose of the creditor consisting of inhabiting the purchased house must be considered when determining whether the seller's conduct is sufficient for the fulfilment of its obligation, and that does not happen in this case.

At this point, it is worth noting a particularity of Chilean law, which is related to the penetration of anti-causalism, in contrast to the literalness of the Bello Code. Indeed, the Chilean [Civil] Code expressly contemplates the cause as a requisite of the legal act and the obligation. To this end, it states that "there can be no obligation without a real and lawful cause", later defining it as "the reason that induces the act or contract" (Article 1467). Based on these notions, Chilean doctrine have long debated about which is the notion of the cause that the Chilean legal system accepts, and more recently it has even come to propose the uselessness of the cause, under the understanding that the problems that it solves can be covered with the contract's object or content[46]. In this context, the idea of practical purpose appears as a completely "new" notion, severed from the notion of the cause

---

that contracts must be executed in good faith and therefore obligate not only what is expressed in them but also what emanates precisely from the nature of the obligation. In said provision, the theory of contractual integration, supported by modern doctrine, finds support, highlighting the thought of the Italian jurist Emilio Betti, who postulates that the execution of the contract in good faith imposes not only a duty of loyalty and correctness, but also that the need for reciprocal cooperation in which both contracting parties are found, the judge being empowered to find unexpressed obligations in the contractual bond and that have their source in good faith, which allows interpreting and integrating the content of the requirement of the obligation to inform in contracts such as the mandate, according to its nature, which even extends to the procedures subsequent to its execution and in terms of the effects and consequences of the actions carried out during its validity". Cfr. Supreme Court, 24.09.2019, Case No. 35722-2017. In a similar vein, also quoting Betti, the following Supreme Court judgements are pronounced, 26.08.2015, Case No. 26847-2014; Supreme Court, 29.05.2014, Case No. 2073-2013; Supreme Court, 07.06.2011, Case No. 430-2010.

46 In that regard, E. Barros Bourie, 'Riesgos y límites de la causa en el derecho de contratos. Criterios de interpretación de las normas legales vigentes', in M. Gómez de la Torre Vargas *et al.* (eds.), *Estudios de derecho civil XIV* (Thomson Reuters, 2020), pp. 599–619.

that originated it[47]. Anyhow, some authors provide evidence that this is a new reading of the concept of cause and a replacement of its nomenclature, although lacking further development of the argument[48].

Thus, it is noted that the influence of the Italian doctrine in the matter has been limited; however, the definition of cause provided by Bello can certainly be (re)read in light of the teachings of the Italian authors, since, insofar as it alludes to the "motive that induces the act or contract", it is arguable that the "practical purpose" is included in the cause and, therefore, the creditor's interest in entering into the contract would also be included in the cause. The notion of cause would recover functionality and the idea of practical purpose would get normative support. Thus, there is fertile ground for a greater influence of the *Codice Civile* in Chilean law.

3.2 Delimitation of creditor protection remedies as a balance point: the seriousness of the breach as a requisite of contractual resolution

Contemplating the creditor's interests, as the core of the system of remedies, finds its counterpoint in institutions intended precisely to correct any distortions that the new way of understanding the law of contracts can produce to the debtor's detriment. Thus, emphasis is also placed on the expected creditor's behaviour, who is bound by the same good faith requisites that are imposed on the debtor and, likewise, is subject to a series of charges and even real duties in favour of the debtor, which involve the introduction of mechanisms to protect the

---

[47] See I. De la Maza Gazmuri and A. Vidal Olivares, 'Propósito práctico, incumplimiento contractual y remedios del acreedor. Con ocasión de tres recientes sentencias de la Supreme Court', Revista Ius et Praxis, 20 (2014), 15-38; Erbetta, pp. 267–74.

[48] In that regard, R. Momberg Uribe and C. Pizarro Wilson, 'Fisonomía y efectos de los contratos conexos o grupos de contratos', Revista Ius et Praxis, 27 (2021), p. 164.

debtor's interests and, consequently, the contractual balance[49],

---

[49] The relatively recent doctrine in Chile on these matters is copious, so an exhaustive list at this point is not possible. Only as an example, the following can be cited: O. Lagos Villarreal, *Las cargas del acreedor en el seguro de responsabilidad civil* (Fundación Mapfre, 2006); L.C. San Martín Neira, 'Sobre la naturaleza jurídica de la 'cooperación' del acreedor al cumplimiento de la obligación: la posición dinámica del acreedor en la relación obligatoria, como sujeto no sólo de derechos, sino también de cargas y deberes', Revista de Derecho Universidad de Concepción, 21 (2011), pp. 225–26; A. Vidal Olivares, 'La noción de incumplimiento esencial en el Código Civil', Revista de derecho de la Pontificia Universidad Católica de Valparaíso, 32 (2009), pp. 221–58; Vidal, 'El incumplimiento resolutorio en el Código Civil', pp. 347–68; B. Caprile Biermann, 'Algunos problemas ofrecidos por la excepción de contrato no cumplido y, en especial, el de su invocación para atajar la acción resolutoria en el caso de incumplimientos recíprocos', Revista de Derecho de la Pontificia Universidad Católica de Valparaíso, 39 (2012), pp. 53–93; P. Verónica López Díaz, 'El interés del deudor como límite al derecho de opción del acreedor insatisfecho y su incidencia en el procedencia de la pretensión de cumplimiento específico y la indemnización de daños', in F. Elorriaga de Bonis, *Estudios de Derecho Civil VII* (AbeledoPerrot – Thomson Reuters, 2012), pp. 737–55; P. Verónica López Díaz, 'El abuso del derecho de opción del acreedor y su importancia en la construcción de un sistema equilibrado de remedios por un incumplimiento contractual', Revista Chilena de Derecho Privado, 19 (2012), pp. 13–62; Mejías, 'La excepción de contrato no cumplido', pp. 111-156; L.C. San Martín Neira, *La carga del perjudicado evitar o mitigar el daño* (Universidad Externado de Colombia, 2012); P. Prado López, *La colaboración del acreedor en los contratos civiles* (Thomson Reuters, 2015); P. Prado López, 'La colaboración del acreedor: una aplicación concreta de la buena fe', in L.C. San Martín Neira, (ed.), *La buena fe en la jurisprudencia. Comentarios y análisis de sentencias* (Thomson Reuters, 2015), pp. 125-143; L.C. San Martín Neira, 'La posición dinámica del acreedor en la relación obligatoria. A propósito de "Julio Fritz Vidal con Banco Santander Chile". Supreme Court, Case No. 137-2010', in L.C. San Martín Neira (ed.), *La buena fe en la jurisprudencia. Comentarios y análisis de sentencias* (Thomson Reuters, 2015), pp. 145-55; P. Prado López, 'La inobservancia al deber de colaboración del acreedor en el derecho chileno: un caso de incumplimiento contractual', Revista de Derecho – Universidad Austral, 29 (2016), pp. 59–83; J.I. Contardo Gonzalez, 'El derecho del deudor a la subsanación o corrección del incumplimiento no conforme (*right tu cure*). Acercamiento desde los instrumentos del derecho contractual uniforme hacia el derecho chileno de contratos', Revista Ius et Praxis, 23 (2017), pp. 153–94; M.S. Rodríguez Pinto, 'Cargas de colaboración y distribución de riesgos en el contrato de construcción', in J.E. Figueroa Valdés (ed.), *Derecho de construcción. Análisis dogmático y práctico* (Ediciones DER, 2017), pp. 25–45; C. Aedo Barrena, 'La naturaleza jurídica de las conductas exigidas al asegurado a la luz de la ley N° 20.667', Revista Ius et Praxis, 24 (2018), pp.

[and] in whose development great attention has been paid to the Italian doctrine, particularly to Betti and Bianca when referring to the creditor's duty of collaboration[50].

A central aspect in this line of thought has been the delimitation of the creditor's prerogatives to exercise contractual remedies. Specifically, in the request of constraints not expressly provided for by law when exercising the resolution remedy for breach of contract. The rules of the *Codice Civile* have played a crucial role in this development. The Bello Code does not allocate a section to contract resolution for breach of contract but deals with resolution as regards the general theory of conditions, as a sort of (tacit) resolutory condition in Article 1489, which expressly states:

> in bilateral contracts, the resolutory condition for breach of contract by one of the contracting parties with what was agreed is involved. But in such a case, the other contracting party may request at its discretion the resolution or the contract's performance, with indemnity for damages.

From this single provision, doctrine and jurisprudence developed the theory of contractual resolution for breach of contract. Along these lines, with some notable exceptions[51], the traditional doctrine taught that "any imputable breach"[52] was sufficient to give rise to the resolution. As already indicated,

---

51-9; A. Vidal and R. Momberg, (eds.), *Cumplimiento específico y ejecución forzada del contrato. De lo sustantivo a lo procesal* (Ediciones Universitarias de Valparaíso, 2018); C. Bahamondes Oyarzún, *El cumplimiento específico de los contratos* (Ediciones DER, 2018), p. 105.

50   In jurisprudence, the Supreme Court judgment of 07.04.2011, Case No. 137-2010, which expressly pronounces on creditor collaboration and the possibility of configuring its liability for non-observance, can be cited, with a verbatim quote from Betti's work. A commentary to this judgment can be seen at San Martín, 'La posición dinámica del acreedor en la relación obligatoria', pp. 145–55.

51   In this sense, it is worth noting the opinion of Claro Solar, who already in 1936 advocated the opposite solution, and a sentence of the Talca Court of 1920. However, these are isolated opinions in a context that is uniformly marked by the opposite opinion. See L. Claro Solar, *Explicaciones de derecho civil chileno y comparado*, V, No. X (Editorial Jurídica de Chile, 2015) 174, Fueyo, p. 307.

52   Above all, Fueyo, p. 307; Peñailillo, p. 406; Abeliuk, p. 653.

the current reading of the rule states that imputability for breach of contract is not necessary, although the issue is still not completely peaceful. Likewise, for several years, the fact that any breach is sufficient to terminate the contract has been questioned and the answer has been negative. Thus, the current doctrine sustains that

> the legislator protects the creditor's interest against the debtor's breaches, but does so in a balanced way. The principles of contract conservation and objective good faith of Art. 1546 of the *Civil Code* compels the creditor to accept and keep a defective or non-conforming provision as long as the breach is not serious, taking into account its contractual interest. If it is serious, the creditor may resolve the contract or reject the provision and demand its substitution.[53]

Consequently, "the doctrine and jurisprudence reserve the resolution for non-performance to breaches of a qualified severity or entity, thus limiting the resolving power to breaches affecting essential obligations or serious in themselves"[54].

Undoubtedly, in this re-reading of Article 1489 of the Chilean [Civil] Code, the existence of Article 1455 of the *Codice Civile* was of great relevance, according to which "the contract cannot be resolved if one of the parties' breach is of minor importance — considering the other's interest"[55]. This text is fully reproduced in one of the cornerstone Chilean works on breach of contracts, *Compliance and Non-compliance of Obligations*, by Fernando Fueyo Laneri, written in 1991, and is analysed together with some Italian judgments that apply it[56]. Ever since authors and jurisprudence accepted, as a rule, the opinion that

---

53 Vidal, p. 51.
54 Vidal, pp. 51–2. The same idea has been picked up by the Colombian courts, for which breach, to give rise to the contract resolution, must be essential. See Vidal and Oviedo.
55 For Italian doctrine on this Article see M.G. Cubeddu, *L'importanza dell'inadempimento* (Giappichelli, 1995); L. Nanni, 'La risoluzione del contratto per inadempimento', in G. Visintini (ed.), *Trattato della responsabilità contrattuale*, Vol. I (CEDAM, 2009), p. 433.
56 Fueyo, p. 307. This author also alludes to Article 25 of the Vienna Convention on the International Sale of Goods, as it regulates essential breach, as one of his sources of inspiration.

resolution entails a "serious" breach or of a "certain entity"[57]. The jurisprudential path to achieve this was through the general clause of good faith, set forth in Article 1546 of the Chilean [Civil] Code. In turn, the current majority doctrine, in line with what was stated in the previous point, links the breach's seriousness with the creditor's interest[58], as does a sector of the Italian doctrine[59].

4. Concluding remarks

Even though Bello's Civil Code is nearly a century older than the Italian one, Chilean law has acknowledged the *Codice Civile*'s influence. This influence has occurred through the 're-reading' that Chilean authors and courts are carrying out of the Chilean Code, specifically in contractual matters and, more specifically, in breach of contract matters. Indeed, the most recent Chilean doctrine has paid great attention to breach of contracts, trying to build a notion and a system of remedies, at the centre of which is the creditor's interest, as an integral part of the obligation content.

The influence of the *Codice* in this re-reading has occurred in two ways. In the first place, through the attention that Chilean doctrine and jurisprudence have paid to classic authors of Italian Law, such as Betti, Giorgianni and Messineo, who are frequently cited by authors and court rulings. Secondly, through the analysis of specific rules that solve practical problems, which were not addressed by the Chilean coder. This is, for example, the case of *Codice Civile*'s Article 1455 when referring to the "importance of breach of contract" as a requirement for the contract's resolution.

---

57 Peñailillo, p. 406; Mejías, *El incumplimiento resolutorio en el código civil*, p. 7.
58 Above all, see Mejías, *El incumplimiento resolutorio en el código civil*, p. 133.
59 See Cubeddu, p. 127.

However, more detailed attention to the most recent Italian doctrinal and jurisprudential constructions is lacking, which would allow perfecting the arrival of concepts such as the idea of practical purpose concerning the contract's cause.

Renzo E. Saavedra Velazco[*]
THE ITALIAN LEGACY IN PERUVIAN TESTAMENTARY LAW

Introduction

From a historical perspective, the *Code Napoléon* has been the most influential European[1] "legal product"[2] in Latin America[3]. Thus, during the nineteenth century, period in which the first phase of the codification phenomenon[4] took place in this region[5], the *Code Civil* was the mold from which Andrés Bello (1845–1852) and Dalmacio Vélez Sarsfield (1864–1869)

---

[*] Civil Law Professor at Pontificia Universidad Católica del Perú (PUCP) and Universidad de Lima. Senior Associate in Hernández & Cía. Arbitrator at the Lima Chamber of Commerce, *Center for Conflict Analysis and Resolution PUCP*, International Arbitration Center Chamber of Belgium and Luxembourg and Conciliation and Dispute Resolution Chamber of the Peruvian Soccer Federation.

[1] Nevertheless, the most influential legal product of Latin America origin within the region has been the Bello's Code, which was influenced by the *Code Napoléon*. See M.C. Mirow, 'Borrowing Private Law in Latin America: Andrés Bello use of the Code Napoléon in drafting Chilean Civil Code', Lousiana Law Review, 61 (2001), pp. 291–329.

[2] By the term, I refer to laws, jurisprudential maxims, and legal scholarship. See Renzo Saavedra, *Análisis económico y comparado del derecho privado – Una introducción* (Lima: Fogueras, 2016).

[3] M.C. Mirow, 'The Code Napoléon: Buried but ruling in Latin America', Denver Journal of International Law & Policy, 33 (2005), pp. 179–94.

[4] This period coincides with the so-called "first globalization" of the law, see D. Kennedy, 'Three Globalizations of Law and Legal Thought: 1850–2000', in D. Trubek and A. Santos (eds.), *The New Law and Economic Development* (Cambridge: Cambridge University Press, 2006), pp. 19–73.

[5] J. Sánchez, 'The Reception of Legal Systems in the Americas: Diversities and Convergences', Tulane European & Civil Law Forum, 24 (2009), pp. 231–63.

elaborated their own codification proposals[6]. German influence in that period was virtually limited to Brazil, as illustrated[7] by the presence of a general part (*Allgemeiner Teil*)[8] within Augusto Teixeira de Freitas's projects[9], as well as in the Brazilian Civil Code of 1916. This influence is affirmed with the adoption[10] of concepts attributed to the German Pandectist School[11].

If Latin American Civil Codes imitates the French legal model, then why should we conduct a study about the impact of Italian law?[12] Firstly, because the relative youth of the *Codice Civile* compared to the *Code Civil* and the *BGB* explains, in no small measure, its residual impact. Secondly, because we must not limit ourselves to the study of the influence of a single piece of legislation (much less such a valuable one) like the *Codice Civile,* but we should extend our analysis to Italian law as a whole.

---

6   During this period, the codification projects were primarily prepared by a single scholar. Therefore, his personal preferences were easily transferred to the document. In Perú, however, there was no scholar prepared to undertake such an effort. So, from then on, it was always preferred to carry out a collective work.

7   J.P. Schmidt, 'General Part', in J. Basedow, K.J. Hopt, R. Zimmermann with A. Stier (eds.), *The Max Planck Encyclopedia of European Private Law*, vol. I (Oxford: Oxford University Press, 2012), pp. 774–77.

8   Not all Civil Codes are divided in the same way, nor do they face the task of codification applying the same principles. The use of a general part is typical of Germanic systems or systems influenced by the German model. See G. Golding, 'A Critical Comparison of the Schemes of the French and German Civil Code', Irish Jurist, 6 (1971), 305–22; and U. Drobnig, 'Scope and General Rules of a European Civil Code', European Review of Private Law, 5 (1997), pp. 489–96.

9   *Consolidação das Leis Civis* [1857], vol. I – II (Brasilia: Senado Federal, 2003) and the *Esboço do Código Civil* [1860–1865], vol. I – II (Brasilia: Ministério da Justiça, 1983).

10   T. Reis, 'Teixeira de Freitas, lector de Savigny', Revista de Historia del Derecho, 49 (2015), 181–222; R. Fonseca, 'Os juristas e a cultura jurídica brasileira na segunda metade do século XIX', in *Quaderni Fiorentini per la storia del pensiero giuridico moderno*, vol. XXXV – tomo I (Milano: Giuffrè, 2006), pp. 339–71.

11   J.P. Schmidt, 'El origen de la "Parte general" del derecho privado brasileño', Derecho PUCP, 80 (2018), 33–48.

12   S. Schipani, *Nota Introduttiva*, in *Studi sassaresi*, vol. V (Milano: Giuffrè, 1981), pp. XIII-XIV.

I would like to specify the general idea of the first point. The Bello's Civil Code has been in force in Chile since 1857 as well as, with certain adaptations, in Colombia (1887) and Ecuador (1857), while the Vélez Sarsfield's Civil Code (1871) was replaced in Argentina by the "Código Civil y Comercial" only in 2015. Therefore, the vast majority of the South American legal systems did not have the opportunity to emulate the Italian model (the Uruguayan Civil Code and certain versions of the Venezuelan Civil Codes were inspired by García Goyena's project for the Spanish Civil Code [1851][13], the Bello's Code, the Vélez Sarsfield's Code and/or Teixeira de Freitas's *Esboço do Código Civil*).

Regarding the second point, the Peruvian Civil Code of 1984 [PCC] is atypical[14] in the region since the *Codice Civile* was clearly the model from which its sections dedicated to "Negocio jurídico"[15] (*Rechtgeschäft*) and "Contracts" were elaborated (respectively, Books 2 and 7), while Italian law had a notable influence on its section dedicated to "Law of Persons"[16]. The

---

13 A. Parise, 'The place of the Louisiana Civil Code in the Hispanic Civil Codifications: The Comments to the Spanish Civil Code Project of 1851, Lousiana Law Review, 68 (2008), pp. 823–929.

14 Another expression of the atypical nature of the Peruvian Civil Code lies in the fact that each of the members of the commission in charge of elaborating it was responsible for drafting a 'Book'. Thus, Carlos Fernández drafted the Book 1 – Law of Persons, Fernando Vidal Drafted the Book 2 – Legal Transaction, Héctor Cornejo drafted the Book 3 – Family Law, Rómulo Lanatta drafted the Book 4 – Succession Law, Lucrecia Maisch von Humboldt drafted the Book 5 – Property Law, Felipe Osterling drafted the Book 6 – Law of Obligations, and so on.

15 Inappropriately, our legislation entitles this section 'Acto Jurídico' when in fact it regulates the so-called 'legal transaction'. The term 'Rechtgëschaft' is not easily translated into English; the authors of Civil Law and Common Law who dealt with this subject opted to use 'legal relationship', 'jural act', 'juridical act' or 'legal transaction'. In this article, I have opted for the latter.

16 C. Fernández, *Derecho de las personas*, 9 edn (Lima: Grijley, 2004), p. 19, states: "It is up to the legal scholarship, and within it fundamentally to the Italian, to have served as the main reference source for the formulation of the Second Title on the Law of Persons. For this purpose, the most qualified commentaries and criticisms contained in the works of Italian authors over the last forty years were considered to a great extent. This made it possible to avoid, to an extent, some mistakes found in the Italian Civil Code and,

primary reasons why Peruvian law did took a different path compared to the orientation of the legal systems of the rest of the countries in the region (and in our first two civil codes)[17] include, to name a few[18] the following: a) the limited number of Peruvian legal scholars fluent in French (including the codifiers of 1984); b) the conjunctural growth of Italian legal books that were translated into Spanish in the period 1950–1980; and c) the idea that the *Codice Civile* was, in fact, the synthesis of the *Code Civil* and the *BGB*[19]. However, "every cloud has a silver lining". The change of scenery allowed Peruvian law to notice debates which had been traditionally overlooked given the mentioned linguistic limitations, and set the stage for a group of Peruvian scholars (who were already studying Italian law) to provide the theoretical framework that would the rest of the legal professionals.

Now, why testamentary law? The answer lies in our codification and its explanatory statement. The section dedicated to Succession Law (Book 4) is a mixture of several Civil Codes, so its study requires a comparative approach. Additionally, although Italian law is not the source all the articles and/or legal schemes established in Book 4, it is nonetheless possible to infer an Italian influence on testamentary law.

Curiously, our specialists in succession law have not realized two aspects that will be the axis of this research. On the one hand, the influence of Italian legal schemes does not imply absolute synonymy with the *Codice Civile*, which will allow me to explain why certain Italian legal debates do not make sense in Peru. On

---

fundamentally, to fill in its gaps through a creative legislation that does not recognize, in certain cases, precedents in comparative legislation".

17 C. Ramos, *El Código Napoleónico y su recepción en América Latina* (Lima: Fondo Editorial de la Pontificia Universidad Católica del Perú, 1997), pp. 34–35 and 160–179.

18 Other reasons for such influence, albeit limited to comparative law, have been outlined by Elisabetta Grande, Rodrigo Míguez and Pier Giuseppe Monateri, 'The Italian Theory of Comparative Law Goes Abroad', The Italian Review of International and Comparative Law, 1 (2021), pp. 5–28.

19 P. Lerner, 'El Código Civil italiano de 1942 y las reformas al Código Civil argentino', Boletín Mexicano de Derecho Comparado, 35 (2002), pp. 167–95.

the other hand, some of these imported legal products[20] require a comprehensive knowledge of the processes experienced in Italy. Since these are unfamiliar for most legal professionals other than those of Italian origin, I will attempt to outline the route that anyone interested in the matter should follow.

1. The notion of testament: From Antonio Cicu to Giorgio Giampiccolo

Let us begin with the "notion" of testament. I place the term in quotation marks because, as was accurately stated by Cicu, the *Codice Civile* does not actually offer a definition of will[21]; instead, it proposes a description of what can be done with a testament. In other words, the *Codice Civile* does not answer the question what the will is, but rather what it is for.

Consistent with Roman inheritance law[22], article 587 of the *Codice Civile*[23] stresses the purpose of the testament: to regulate the future of the testator's estate. The observance of tradition is not absolute since testamentary succession does not prevail over the intestate succession in current Italian law[24]. However, the conception that the testament is essentially a patrimonial act, which would be condensed in the designation of heirs, the allocation of assets/rights, etc., is preserved.

---

20 A. Watson, *Legal Transplants*, 2nd edn (Athens: University of Georgia Press, 1993).
21 A. Cicu, *Il testamento*, 2nd edn (Milano: Giuffrè, 1951), pp. 13–14.
22 T. Rüfner, 'Testamentary Formalities in Roman Law', in K. Reid, M. de Waal and R. Zimmermann (eds.), *Comparative Succession Law*, vol. I (Oxford: Oxford University Press, 2011), pp. 9–11. This author states the opposite: E. Perego, *Favor legis e testamento* (Milano: Giuffrè, 1970).
23 Article 587 *Codice Civile*.
A testament is a revocable act by which someone disposes of all or part of his assets for the time he or she will have ceased to live.
The non-patrimonial provisions, which the law allows to be contained in a testament, are effective, if they are contained in an act that has the form of a testament, even if patrimonial provisions are missing.
24 P. Rescigno, *Interpretazione del testamento* (Napoli: Jovene, 1952), p. 412.

Although the influence of Roman Law exerted a significant role on our codifiers, the truth is that when the "Commission for the Study and Revision of the Peruvian Civil of 1936"[25] [Commission] formally began its work (1965)[26], the Spanish translation (1959) of the second edition of Cicu's *Il testamento* (1951) was already in circulation in Latin America[27]. This book, together with some civil law handbooks translated shortly after[28], was deemed an example by the *rapporteur* of this PCC section and it guided the legal interpretation of these rules.

It is symptomatic that a prominent expert such as Fernández[29] has asked himself if "an act that has the form of a testament" can be qualified as a will if contains only non-patrimonial provisions. I highlight Fernández's opinion because he was the vice-president of the "Civil Code Revision Commission"[30] and focused his attention in particular on the Succession Book, as he taught succession law for decades at the PUCP Law School. Now, it is clear that the precise formulation of the question is a *réplique* of what is stated in article 587 of the *Codice Civile* and not the text of article 686 of the PCC[31].

---

25 Commission created by Supreme Decree No. 95, dated March 1, 1965.
26 A brief account of the activity and composition of the Commission can be found at F. Osterling, 'El Proyecto del Código Civil y el Derecho de Obligaciones', Themis, 1 (1984), 7–9.
27 A. Cicu, *El testamento*, trans. by Manuel Fairén (Madrid: Editorial Revista de Derecho privado, 1959).
28 F. Messineo, *Manual de Derecho Civil y Comercial*, trans. by Santiago Sentis, vol. I–VIII (Buenos Aires: Ediciones Jurídicas Europa-América, 1954); A. Trabucchi, *Instituciones de Derecho Civil*, trans. by Luis Martínez, vol. I – II (Madrid: Editorial Revista de Derecho Privado, 1967); and D. Barbero, *Sistema del Derecho privado*, trans. by Santiago Sentis, vol. I–V (Buenos Aires: Ediciones Jurídicas Europa-América, 1967).
29 C. Fernández, *Código Civil: Derecho de Sucesiones*, vol. I (Lima: Fondo Editorial de la Pontificia Universidad Católica del Perú, 2003), p. 392.
30 Commission created by Law No. 23403, published on May 28, 1982.
31 Article 686 Peruvian Civil Code
By the testament a person may dispose of his or her property, totally or partially, for the time after his or her death, and order his own succession within the limits of the law and with the formalities indicated therein.
The provisions of a non-patrimonial nature contained in the testament are valid, even if the act is limited to them.

The precision is relevant because the *Codice Civile* does not attribute the quality of testament to such an act, but merely recognizes its enforceability. The Italian legislator, observing tradition[32], was reluctant to qualify this act as a testament, and hence used a different terminology: "act that has the form of a testament"[33]. On the other hand, our civil codifiers were not reluctant[34] to grant the dignity of testament[35] to an act that fulfills its formalities, regardless of whether its content is limited to patrimonial or non-patrimonial provisions (or a combination of both).

As the *Codice Civile* remained rooted in the past, Italian scholars had no choice but to propose a novel distinction between typical and atypical content of the testament.

Giampiccolo suggested that patrimonial provisions would constitute the "typical" content of the will[36] and, therefore, any act that contains said provisions and satisfies the legal formalities tied to a testament must necessarily be qualified as such. On the other hand, acts that only meet the external formalities of the testament would be recognized as enforceable by an explicit rule, but not be considered a testament. Normally, these acts

---

32   E. Nardi, *Codice Civile e diritto romano: Gli articoli vigente del Codice Civile nei loro precedente romanistici* (Milano: Giuffrè, 1997), p. 26.

33   For comments on the draft Succession and Donations book of the *Codice Civile*, in particular article 587, see G. Pandolfelli and others, *Codice Civile: Libro delle Successioni e Donazioni illustrato con i lavori preparatori e con note di commento*, 11th edn (Milano: Giuffrè, 1940), pp. 165–67 (Relazione Commissione Parlamentare), pp. 167–68 (Relazione al Re Imperatore sul testo del Codice Civile).

34   The absence of a definition of will in the Peruvian Civil Code of 1936 favored a broad interpretation of its content. See, for example, G. Lohmann, *Derecho de Sucesiones*, vol. II – first part (Lima: Fondo Editorial de la Pontificia Universidad Católica del Perú, 1996), p. 48.

35   J.E. Castañeda, *Derecho de las Sucesiones* (Lima: Amauta, 1966), pp. 44–45; and R. Lanatta, *Derecho de Sucesiones*, vol. II, 2 edn (Lima: Editorial Desarrollo, 1981), pp. 23–24.
     In the last book, the influence of the *Codice Civile* is already evident, and the volumes of Cicu and Messineo are also mentioned to support the possibility that the testament (as a document) includes other acts and that its content is limited to non-patrimonial provisions.

36   G. Giampiccolo, *Il contenuto atipico del testamento: Contributo ad una teoria dell'atto di ultima volontà* (Milano: Giuffrè, 1954).

would never qualify as testaments because: (i) they do not share their "typical" content, (ii) their effects are not *mortis causa*[37] (although they may have patrimonial content) or (iii) they are autonomous acts even though they are formally included in a testament. In the latter scenario, it is rightly denounced that there is a tendency to confuse the nature of the acts and the document in which they are contained, which has implications for its revocability[38].

In short, Roman tradition and the verbatim of article 587 of the *Codice Civile* explain why the Italian scholars doubted[39] whether "an act that has the form of a testament" could be defined as such. The question becomes trivial in Peru since we have adopted a broader notion of a will. In consequence, the Italian theoretical difference between typical and atypical content of the testament would play only a pedagogical role among not Italian law professionals.

Notwithstanding the above, the only field in which the value of the distinction could be discussed is in the legal efficacy of some non-patrimonial or patrimonial provisions, but always under the condition that these provisions were functionally independent of the will, to the extent however that these provisions are functionally independent of the will (e.g., the recognition of extramarital filiation). These provisions would be legally effective only upon the death of *de cuius*, the instant in which the testament becomes relevant towards third parties and its content becomes knowable. The exception to this rule is when the content of the will has been disclosed by the testator during his lifetime.

It is not difficult to identify the source of inspiration of the national article since the *rapporteur*, Professor Lanatta, explicitly

---

[37] G. Giampiccolo, 'Atto *mortis causa*', in *Enciclopedia del Diritto*, vol. IV (Milano: Giuffrè, 1959), p. 232.

[38] A. Palazzo, *Le successioni*, 2nd edn, vol. II (Milano: Giuffrè, 2000), p. 626.

[39] However, there are authors in the Italian legal system who advocate overcoming these theories in favor of a position that admits that the content of the testament extends beyond the estate, see V. Barba, *Contenuto del testamento e atti di ultima volontà* (Napoli: ESI, 2018), pp. 95–115.

reveals it[40]. Even if such recognition did not exist, the mere reading of the two articles insinuates a relationship between them.

2. The refusal of the testament as a legal transaction: Giovanni Battista Ferri and Nicolò Lipari

From both a historical and logical perspective, wills must be qualified as a "negozio giuridico" by legal scholars. It is worth remembering that the primary aspiration of this theory was to subsume under a single (but a supra) category all the acts of private autonomy (*Privatautonomie*)[41]. Therefore, it was literally impossible to ignore the testament since this act is the prototype of both unilateral acts[42] and acts with *mortis causa* effect[43].

The objective of the theory of legal transaction was achieved without any difficulty during the 19th century, a period in which the will theory (*Willenstheorie*) prevailed[44]. However, the will theory received severe criticism[45] from German and Italian scholars during the 20th century[46]. Indeed, the number of theories

---

40 R. Lanatta, *Exposición de motivos y comentarios al Libro Derecho de Sucesiones*, ed. by Delia Revoredo, 2nd edn, vol. V (Lima: Thomson Reuters, 2015), p. 54.
41 F. von Savigny, *Sistema di diritto romano attuale*, vol. III–IV, trans. by Vittorio Scialoja (Torino: Utet, 1891 and 1899), *passim*; and B. Windscheid, *Diritto delle pandette*, vol. I, trans. by Carlo Fadda e Paolo Bensa (Torino: Utet, 1925), pp. 202–07.
42 B. Biondi, 'Autonomia delle disposizioni testamentarie ed inquadramento del testamento nel sistema giuridico', Foro italiano, 72 (1949), pp. 565–572.
43 G. Stolfi, *Teoria del negozio giuridico* (Padova: CEDAM, 1961), pp. 46–47.
44 R. Saavedra, *El negocio jurídico testamentario* (Lima: Jurista, 2013).
45 For a detailed account of the objections to the will theory, see N. Davrados, 'A Louisiana Theory of Juridical Acts', Louisiana Law Review, 80 (2020), pp. 1119–1284.
46 D. Kennedy, 'From the Will Theory to the Principles of Private Autonomy: Lon Fuller's "Consideration and Form"', Columbia Law Review, 100 (2000), 94–175.
   The 1960's and 1970's gave life to what was known as the period of crisis or decline of the legal transaction, which was overcome by highlighting the practical utility of the category and not through the refutation (at least not

concerning the substance of the legal transactions increased in the last century, but the focus of attention merely shifted between a subjective or objective reading of the institution with each new proposal[47]. This, of course, does not pretend to ignore the considerable differences in terms of the basis that each theory proposed for the description of the phenomenon.

In Peru, as has been recently confirmed by León[48], law students are taught with continuous references to the writings and ideas of Emilio Betti or Giuseppe Stolfi. Although Betti and Stolfi built their personal theories about the legal transactions from opposite bases, each of which could provide a satisfactory explanation to various scenarios and phenomena, the truth is that, at some point, these authors (as well as all Italian and Peruvian scholars who studies this topic) always had to face the problem that testaments imply.

But what is the problem? In brief, I will limit myself to stress the circumstance that the testament does not produce legal effects over third parties until the death of the testator, so it is incapable of engendering their reliance[49] (or *tanquam non esset*). This characteristic explain its permanent revocability, the focus in the true intention of the testator and the impossibility of applying all the legal requirements designed to judge the invalidity of other acts of autonomy.

And why is this a problem? Because the Italian theories of the legal transactions have been built with the focus on offering answers and explanations for contractual scenarios when, in fact, they should be capable of being applied in several

---

all) of the objections raised. See M. Talamanca, *Elementi di diritto private romano* (Milano: Giuffrè, 2001), p. 103.
47 R. Morales, 'Nuevas perspectivas del negocio jurídico', Derecho & Sociedad, 28 (2007), pp. 293–306.
48 L. León, *Derecho privado. Parte General: Negocios, actos y hechos jurídicos* (Lima: Fondo Editorial de la Pontificia Universidad Católica del Perú, 2019), pp. 22–23.
49 R. Sacco, 'Affidamento', in *Enciclopedia del diritto*, vol. I (Milano: Giuffrè, 1958), pp. 661–6; and V. Pietrobon, 'Affidamento', in *Enciclopedia giuridica Treccani*, vol. I (Roma: Istituto della Enciclopedia Italiana, 1988), pp. 1–2.

situations[50], such as those of Family or Succession Law. Given the peculiarities of the testament as an act of private autonomy, it has often become the express exception to what was theorized. This would imply the recognition that: (a) the specific theory did not achieve its goal of unifying the acts of autonomy in a single category[51]; (b) the goal of the general theory is unattainable[52] or, at least, (c) the will should not be considered a legal transaction.

The contributions of Betti and Stolfi are consistent with alternative (a), since the authors, after explaining the peculiarities of their respective theories, recognize that their proposal does not apply to the testament[53] or, at least, that different rules or criteria will be applied — making it "the" exception to everything (from interpretation to effects; and from invalidity to the notion of private autonomy). Thus, according to Betti and Stolfi's thesis, the testament is artificially (but *de facto*) extracted from the theory of legal transaction, due to the difficulties that its explanation would entail[54] within a general theory.

Option (b), in contrast, has rarely been accepted by scholars, who seem to agree on the logical and practical advantages of using a category such as the legal transaction. The situation outlined above is clearly perceived in Peru. The reason: the testamentary provisions of the PCC do not address such prominent problems as interpretation, making it unavoidable to shift the attention to the general rules on legal transaction. Unfortunately, such regime has been elaborated based on the contractual interpretative rules of the *Codice Civile*, so that, instead of offering legal rules applicable to all type of legal transactions, they only deal with

---

50 V. Scalisi, *La revoca non formale del testamento e la teoria del comportamento concludente* (Milano: Giuffrè, 1974), pp. 11 and 35.
51 G. Mirabelli, 'b) Negocio giuridico (teoria del)', in *Enciclopedia del Diritto*, vol. XXVIII (Milano: Giuffrè, 1978), pp. 1–16.
52 P. Rescigno, *L'interpretazione del testamento* (Napoli: Jovene, 1952), p. 205.
53 E. Betti, *Teoria generale del negozio giuridico*, 2edn (Torino: Utet, 1950), now E. Betti, *Teoria generale del negozio giuridico* (Napoli: ESI, 2002), pp. 356–63.
54 In the light of this, it has been accurately argued that the rejection of the will as a legal transaction would imply the denial of the category itself: see Enrico Perego, *Favor legis e testamento* (Milano: Giuffrè, 1970), pp. 121–22.

scenarios of conflicts of interest and protection of the reliance of the receiver of a declaration.

Finally, option (c) is embraced by scholars such as Lipari and Ferri. Lipari denied that the testament is a legal transaction on the grounds that the "classic" definition of private autonomy (an act of self-regulation of private interests) is inapplicable to it and that the hereditary effect (*vocatio hereditatis*) is produced by force of the law and not because of private will[55]. Ferri's opinion was based on the supposed absence of any creative force[56] to the testament (present, for example, in contracts and, in general, in *inter vivos* transactions), which must be redirected to the law[57].

It may be appropriate to explore further the views of the referred authors.

Thus, Lipari makes an extensive assessment of the positions that the Italian legal scholarship has adopted with respect to the qualification of the testament as a legal transaction, criticizing the absence of a critical approach[58]. Thus, he claims that, in respect of tradition[59], it has been automatically concluded that the will is a legal transaction or, in other words, the legal scholars — without having carried out a critical examination of the peculiarities of its perfection and effectiveness, its potential to create legal effects and the ownership of the private interest

---

[55] N. Lipari, *Autonomia privata e testamento* (Milano, Giuffrè, 1970), pp. 50–56; 141, 199.

[56] M. Bin, *La diseredazione: Contributo allo studio del contenuto del testamento* (Torino: Giappichelli, 1966), p. 152, who admits that the denial of the testament as a legal transaction is a logical, but not necessary, corollary of the recognition of the *vocatio hereditatis* as an effect caused by the law.

[57] G.B. Ferri, *Causa e tipo nella teoria del negozio giuridico* (Milano: Giuffrè, 1966), pp. 40 and 52–57.

[58] Lipari (n. 55), pp. 50–62.

[59] Lipari. I am interested in highlighting the following excerpt: "Se si tenta, sia pure in termine di estrema sintesi, di cogliere il momento in cui la dottrina del testamento è stata ricondotta alla teoria generale del negozio, si può dire alternativamente – né sembri un paradosso – sia che tale assimilazione è stata ritenuta, per lo meno da quando è sorta una dogmatica dell'atto negoziale, come del tutto automatica ed evidente, sia che il problema non resulta mai essere stato posto, in termini di sufficiente consapevolezza critica, quasi che esso non importasse conseguenza alcuna di ordine pratico o interpretativo" (p. 50).

affected at the moment in which the legal effect is concretized in reality — assigned a legal nature to the institution, but without knowing how to justify it.

Ferri's position, instead, is much less consistent than the one adopted by Lipari. While Ferri in "Causa e tipo" rejects the qualification of the will as a legal transaction, in "Il negozio giuridico" he concludes exactly the opposite. It is important to mention that the author does not offer a convincing explanation for the change of opinion.[60]

3. From the "anomalous succession" to the "contractual alternatives to the testament": The transition from Francesco Santoro-Passarelli to Rosario Nicolò to Antonio Palazzo.

In 1930, Professor Santoro-Passarelli proposed the concept of "anomalous vocation"[61], which includes those cases characterized by the fact that a bundle of legal prerogatives or assets are transferred outside the general rules on inheritance law of the *Codice Civile* (whether because there is an alteration in the succession order due to certain subjective qualities of the successor, whether because assets are conveyed to those who would not normally be entitled to succeed, or because there is a deviation from the principle of equal treatment of heirs)[62]. Furthermore, these rules could not be derogated by private autonomy. The concept "anomalous vocation" was later expanded[63] to include those operations that arose from private autonomy.

---

60   G.B. Ferri, *Il negozio giuridico*, 2nd edn (Padova: CEDAM, 2004), p. 64.
61   F. Santoro-Passarelli, *Appunti sulle successioni legittime* (Roma: Sampaolesi, 1930), p. 258.
62   M. Ieva and A. Rastello, 'Le successioni anomale', in P. Rescigno (ed.), *Trattato breve delle successioni e donazioni*, vol. I (Padova: CEDAM, 2010), pp. 697–726.
63   G. De Nova, 'Successioni anomale legittime', in *Digesto delle discipline privatistiche - Sezione Civile*, vol. XIX (Torino: Utet, 1999), pp. 182-86.

In practical terms, these hypotheses entailed a rupture of the principle of unity of succession[64] or, in other words, that the entire estate of the decedent will no longer always be disciplined by a unique legal regime.

The term and the phenomena related to it have remained unknown to Peruvian legal scholars until 2006, year in which I defended my law degree thesis. However, I must admit that a paper published in 1990 by Professor Ferrero, entitled precisely "anomalous succession", deals with a completely different topic[65]. The purpose of this precision is to emphasize that the lack of familiarity of our scholars and legal operators with this topic explains, in no small measure, why there has been no controversy about the contractual alternatives to the testament in Peru, nor has there been any debate about the special legal rules applicable to the transfer of certain types of rights and assets.

The absence of debate is obvious from a civil law perspective, although not from the practice of corporate law (e.g., corporate governance) and tax law, especially of family-owned companies[66]. Within this segment of the Peruvian economy a sense of dissatisfaction was incubating for years, which induced the importation of family wealth transfer models[67] based on

---

64   G. Cattaneo, 'Le vocazioni anomale', in P. Rescigno (ed.), *Trattato di Diritto privato*, vol. V (Torino: Utet, 1989), pp. 461-73.
65   A. Ferrero, 'Sucesión anómala', Advocatus, 1 (1990), 15–17. Although Ferrero mentions Ieva, who have developed the topic, the explanation does not fully coincide with the "anomalous legitimate succession", see A. Ferrero, *Tratado de derecho de las Sucesiones*, 7 edn (Lima: Gaceta Jurídica, 2012), pp. 118–23.
66   P. Schlesinger, 'Interessi dell'impresa e interessi familiari nella vicenda successoria', Rivista di diritto civile, 40 (1994), pp. 447–51.
67   Thus, real revolutionaries in the field are virtually unknown in Peru, such as J. Langbein, 'The Nonprobate Revolution and the Future of the Law of Succession', Harvard Law Review, 97 (1984), pp. 1108–41; J. Langbein, 'The Twentieth-Century Revolution in Family Wealth Transmission', Michigan Law Review, 86 (1988), 722–51; and G. McCouch, 'Will Substitutes under the Revised Uniform Probate Code', Brooklyn Law Review, 58 (1993), pp. 1123–94.

"family protocol" in the last twenty years, though without a comprehensive understanding[68] of the imported legal product.

Although the original scheme[69] of the *Codice Civile* and the *Code Civil* was hostile towards the so-called "succession pacts" [patti successori] and "contractual alternatives to the testament",[70] both codes were modified in February and June 2006, respectively. The reforms were focused on the relaxation of the prohibition of succession pacts to allow the incorporation of contractual mechanisms aimed at regulating the intergenerational transfer of the family-owned companies[71]. Thus, the discipline of "patto di famiglia" was included in the *Codice Civile*, but the prohibition of succession pacts was maintained, so a restrictive understanding of the institution was required[72].

Such a restrictive understanding of succession pacts was possible because for decades[73] Italian scholarship[74] and jurisprudence[75] had paved the way for different succession scenarios[76]. The first step was the recognition of the anomalous

---

68 A. Morales, 'Protocolo familiar: ¿Por qué unos funcionan y otros no?', Revista Peruana de Derecho de la Empresa, 73 (2018), 253–74; and L. Pizarro and F. Lanfranco, 'El planeamiento sucesorio como práctica de buen gobierno corporativo de las "empresas familiares"', Ius et veritas, 32 (2006), pp. 148–56.
69 G. Vismara, *Storia dei patti successori* (Milano: Giuffrè, 1986).
70 A. Fusaro, 'Uno sguardo comparatistico sui patti successori e sulla distribuzione negoziata della ricchezza d'impresa', Rivista di Diritto privato, 3 (2013), pp. 355–74.
71 P. Manes, 'Prime considerazioni sul patto di famiglia nella gestione del passaggio generazionale della ricchezza familiare', Contratto e impresa, 22 (2006), 539-78; and S. Delle Monache, 'Il patto di famiglia', Le nuovi leggi civili commentate, 30 (2007), pp. 21–125.
72 C. Cicero, 'Il divieto del patto successorio nel codice civile italiano e le sue motivazioni', Rivista del Notariato, 72 (2018), pp. 699–710.
73 I have reported the process in R. Saavedra, 'Los negocios jurídicos *mortis causa* en el sistema jurídico peruano: Los contratos *mortis causa* y los pactos sucesorios', *Actualidad Jurídica*, 165 (2007), pp. 54–58
74 In addition to the authors cited throughout this article, and specifically in the present section, I would like to mention M.V. De Giorgi, *I patti sulle successioni future* (Napoli: Jovene, 1976).
75 L. Bertino, 'I patti successori nella giurisprudenza', La nuova giurisprudenza civile commentata, 19 (2003), pp. 191–200.
76 Luigi Carraro, *La vocazione legittima alla successione* (Padova: CEDAM, 1979), pp. 221–25.

succession, and the second step was the detailed examination of the legal-economic characteristics of the succession pacts. Once both steps were taken, individuals were authorized to encapsulate assets during their lifetime, so that after the extinction of their ownership there was no legal reason to justify why, upon their death, these assets should be included in their estate. Likewise, the individuals were allowed to establish that third parties (including non-heirs) would receive upon their death, as consideration, benefits or behaviors that had remained unexecuted. A typical example is the money to be paid out from a life insurance policy, where insured's death became a condition of effectiveness.

Both Rosario Nicolò and Antonio Palazzo played a decisive role in this historical process. Even though their respective contributions occurred almost fifty years apart, there is a very close connection between the authors' thoughts and their books. Fortunately, due to what has been related in the preceding section of this paper, the intrinsic link of what is outlined by each author will be easily understood.

Nicolò laid the foundations for contesting[77] the role of the will and the private autonomy of the testator to produce the inheritance effect or *vocatio hereditatis* (although the author did not dispute the characterization of the will as a legal transaction)[78]. Concretely, the author argued that the inheritance

---

[77] R. Nicolò, *La vocazione ereditaria diretta ed indiretta* (Messina: Principato, 1934), now also in R. Nicolò, *Raccolta di Scritti*, vol. I (Milano: Giuffrè, 1980), pp. 3–269. Specifically, he argued: "undoubtedly the law takes into consideration, at least normally, the will of the *de cuius* legitimately manifested, but this will serves to impart a certain direction to the vocation, is intended to designate a specific recipient of it, but cannot have the efficacy of creating the vocation itself, that is, *the legal title to the attribution of the complex legal position of inheritance*" (p. 19).

[78] R. Nicolò, 'Attribuzioni patrimoniali post mortem e *mortis causa*', Vita notarile (1971), pp. 147 and 149, now also in R. Nicolò, *Raccolta di Scritti*, vol. III (Milano: Giuffrè, 1993), p. 199, stating: "I would like to remind you [...] that a recent scholarship has considered it necessary to devalue the character of a legal transaction of the will, but we instead start from the common premise, which it is not the case here to question, that the will is a negotiating act that represents the expression of the private autonomy of the subject destined to regulate after death — as the law says — certain relationships; through those two forms that represent the possible content

effect was always traceable to the law, so that the existence of a private will did not produce an alteration with respect to the ultimate source of the transmissive effect of the decedent's estate. The argument, as we have seen, was used by legal scholars to contend that the testament was not a legal transaction.

For his part, Palazzo carried out the work of identifying the legal and economic characteristics of succession pacts with other acts of private autonomy[79]. In doing so, Palazzo took advantage of the previous contributions not only to delineate when we were truly before a succession pact ("patto successorio") that deserved the sanction of nullity under article 458 of the *Codice Civile*[80], but to differentiate them from those acts in which the death of the author or authors assumed a role of term or condition[81]. Palazzo developed a category of legal transactions related to a person's hereditary succession that could not be considered succession pacts[82]. This impossibility is supported by the fact that these operations do not involve an act of disposition of the quality of heir (the so-called inheritance agreement and inheritance waiver agreement)[83] or even hereditary assets (transfer of inherited assets)[84].

The term "contractual alternatives to the testament" subsumes a variety of legal transactions characterized by the presence of three (3) elements: (a) the cessation or extinction of the link of ownership of the asset (whether a good or a right) to the estate

---

of the testamentary transaction, namely the institution of heir and the dispositions under the title of legatee".
79 A. Palazzo, *Autonomia contrattuale e successione anomale* (Napoli: Jovene, 1983).
80 Article 458 *Codice Civile*.
Any agreement by which someone disposes of their succession is void. Likewise, any act by which someone disposes of or renounces any rights to which he or she may be entitled concerning a succession that has not yet been opened is void.
81 Pandolfelli and others (n. 33), p. 22 (Relazione al Re Imperatore sul testo del Codice Civile).
82 A. Zaccaria, 'Negozi "*mortis causa*" e negozi "*trans mortem*"', Studium Iuris, 20 (2014), 436–39.
83 "Patto successorio istitutivo" and "patto successorio abdicativo", respectively.
84 "Patto successorio dispositivo".

of the transferor from the same instant in which the transaction is carried out, (b) the immediate acquisition of the ownership by another subject (whether the economic or legal beneficiary of the transaction) and (c) the transferor has the prerogative to revoke the patrimonial attribution[85] or eliminate the legal effect at any time prior to his or her death[86].

Thus[87], the category "trans mortem transaction" was coined (for example: the contract in favor of a third party with postmortem effects, the life insurance contract and, finally, the life annuity), for the description of those operations that are alternatives (in a strict sense) to the testament. These transactions require that the assets be immediately segregated or transferred from the estate of the transferor, but the definitive acquisition of the ownership by the beneficiary will only occur upon the death of the former (in this sense, the transferor may modify or revoke his decision until his death has not been verified).

Instead, the category "legal transactions with post-mortem effects" is an alternative, in a broader sense, to the testament. Although their effects are destined to take place after the death of the transferor, these transactions do not require that the assets (whether goods or rights) leave the transferor's estate, nor is there any possibility that the latter may alter his decision after the transaction's conclusion. If such an option were to be maintained in favor of the transferor, it could potentially affect the reliance that the beneficiary or the counterparty placed on the transaction.

Despite the time elapsed, these developments have not been echoed in Peru[88]; on the contrary, a significant number of

---

85 R. Nicolò, 'Attribuzioni patrimoniali *post mortem* e *mortis causa*', Vita notarile (1971), 147–55, now also in R. Nicolò, *Raccolta di Scritti*, vol. III (Milano: Giuffrè, 1993), pp. 195–209.

86 This feature is peculiarly shown in the "inheritance contract" (*Erbvertrag*) of the German legal system. The future decedent can no longer "revoke" his will contained in the particular contract through a will or other inheritance contracts, but asset disposition can be affected by *inter vivos* legal transactions.

87 A. Palazzo, *Istituti alternativi al testamento* (Napoli: ESI, 2003).

88 A. Palazzo, 'Commentario a Luisa Mezzanotte, *La successione anomala del coniuge* (Napoli: ESI, 1989)', Rivista di Diritto Civile, 36 (1990), pp. 315–17.

contract and inheritance law specialists consider nullity to be the ideal sanction for succession pacts. The traditional reasons for such a sanction in these cases have weakened to the point that they currently lack any persuasive force. The attempt to avoid *votum captandae mortis*, or even the proclaimed effort to protect young heirs from their own impulsive or careless acts, seems to be a remnant of a moralistic and paternalistic vision of the Law that hardly fit with the economic and practical demands of our times. All the above without forgetting that they express a prejudice with respect to the capacity of heirs to decide on their own interests, which, even if true, would be better protected with the applicable remedies for cases of error or fraud.

There is only one reasonable argument: The protection of the decedent's complete discretion to determine the content of his or her succession does not consider the comparative experience. Indeed, there are several legal systems that recognize succession contracts without such producing a significant restriction of the decedent's freedom. Consequently, the search for "contractual alternatives to the testament" arises as a need, especially in legal systems with such a traditionalist vision.

The theoretical-practical relevance of "will substitutes", as well as the need to reduce the scope of the sanction of nullity due to succession pacts, led me to suggest two sets of rules in the Preliminary Draft of the PCC Reform[89]. The first set of rules[90]

---

[89] In 2016, the Peruvian Ministry of Justice created a Working Group responsible for reviewing and proposing improvements to the PCC, whose members were Gastón Fernández (Chairman), Juan Espinoza, Luciano Barchi, Carlos Cárdenas, Enrique Varsi and Gustavo Montero. The Group formed subgroups of advisors to propose amendments to specific sections of the PCC. Thus, the coordinator of the Succession Book was Professor Guillermo Lohmann, and the other advisor was the undersigned. Once the work was completed, I was responsible for defending the recommendations of the sub-group.

[90] Regarding succession pacts, I proposed to the subgroup and then to the Working Group the inclusion of an article with the following text:
"Article 663 – Legal transactions *mortis causa*
1. The legal transactions whose effects are conditioned, under any modality, to the death of a person, are valid.
2. However, plurilateral legal transactions or succession pacts concluded prior to the opening of the succession are void if they

was intended to specify the characteristics of the prohibited succession pacts, since the possibility of their abrogation in the Civil Code (the option I would have preferred) was discarded. The second group of rules[91] was intended to incorporate a

---

a) Involve, as a legal consequence, the disposition, in whole or in part, of the future decedent's estate; or the disposition in favor of any person of the title of successor held by the transferor; or
b) Stipulate that the transferor cannot revoke the transaction or its effects.
The voidance claim shall expire ten years after the opening of the succession.
3. The provisions of the preceding paragraphs shall not be applicable to the waiver of collation in favor of forced heirs and in cases of family pact.
4. The rule contained in Article 1622 remains in full force and effect".
In view of this proposal, it was necessary to amend an article of the Book of Contracts (the specific sections to be modified are shown in bold type):
Article 1405 – Nullity of succession pacts
1. The parties may contract with respect to the right to participate in an already caused estate, being the transferor obliged to guarantee his quality of heir.
2. Contracts whose effects are conditioned, under any modality, to the death of a person, are valid.
3. Any contract on the right of succession to the property of a person who has not died or whose death is unknown is void, unless expressly provided by law.

91 Regarding the intergenerational transmission of family-owned companies, I proposed to the subgroup and then to the Working Group the inclusion of two articles with the following text:
Article 663 A.- Family pact.
1. The family pact is the legal transaction by which, subject to the provisions of the General Law of Corporations and other special laws, the future decedent agrees with his or her spouse, member of a *de facto* union and/or descendants the rules applicable to the transfer of his rights of participation in a family-owned legal entity or on the regime of its administration.
2. The purpose of the family pact is to preserve the existence or management of the family-owned legal entity.
3. The entering into the family pact must involve all the relatives who, at the date of its signature, are forced heirs.
4. The family pact must be executed by public deed under sanction of nullity.
5. The forced heirs who will receive rights in the family-owned legal entity will compensate the others for the corresponding value. The parties may agree on the way in which such payment shall be made, which may include the disposition by the beneficiaries of the shares of the remaining assets that they would eventually receive because of the succession of the common decedent or with their own patrimony.
6. The payment received by the forced heirs' non-beneficiaries of the shares is imputed to their legitimate quota.

figure similar to the "patto di famiglia" to provide a legislation to the family protocol that are currently subscribed. This piece of regulation was imperative since currently family-owned companies use the family protocol even though many of its provisions contravene the legislation on inheritance contained in the PCC.

The first proposal was rejected (though the rejection creates an implicit contradiction with the rest of the preliminary draft), while the second was accepted with amendments[92]. Naturally, all the proposals were inspired by the Italian developments described in this section. I am encouraged to provide this clarification because, in my role as second advisor to the succession subgroup, I discussed the theoretical origin of my proposal, as well as the legislative source I used as a model, both with the coordinator (Lohmann) and the supervisor of the Working Group (Varsi)[93]. I do not deny that the approved version partially deviates from the Italian inspiration. Although the lack of full acceptance of the proposal I made in the framework of the PCC Reform largely explains many of the weaknesses and omissions in the final draft, this does not prevent us from glimpsing the influence of Italian Law. This can be perceived in the reference to non-beneficiary heirs's right to compensation for the shares or participations of

---

7. The payment received by the forced heirs' non-beneficiaries of the shares is not subject to the action of reduction or collation.
8. The provisions of Articles 733, 736 and 846 do not extend to the family pact and its term.
Article 663 B.- Forced heirs who do not subscribe the family pact.
At the opening of the succession, the forced heirs who had not entered the family pact may request from those who received the payment described in numeral 5 of Article 663.

92 The Preliminary Draft of the PCC Reform can be consulted on the undersigned's Academia web-site at: https://www.academia.edu/40177706/Anteproyecto_de_Reforma_del_Codigo_Civil_Grupo_de_Trabajo.
93 On the role played by the members of the Working Group and some advisors in the subgroups, see: Grupo de Trabajo de revisión y mejora del Código Civil peruano de 1984, *Anteproyecto de Reforma del Código Civil peruano de 1984* (Lima: Instituto Pacífico, 2019), p. 27.

family-owned legal entity, and also because the Argentine Civil Code has the Italian system as a reference[94].

4. *An ending or a starting point?*

The previous sections demonstrate the enormous influence that the *Codice Civile* and Italian law have had on the genesis and development of Peruvian Testamentary law.

Unfortunately, such influence has caused our scholars to uncritically import certain debates that are pointless in our legal system[95]. In other cases, instead of encouraging research targeted at refreshing legal scholarship and our legislation, the force of tradition (or inertia, if you prefer), and the legitimacy of the original discourses (in addition to the limited number of experts in succession law) has prevented the theoretical study and formulation of contractual alternatives to the testament. Beyond brief remarks on succession law and contract law handbooks, there is no specific research on succession pacts. The undergraduate or master's theses on civil law that have been written on this subject have focused on the prohibition itself and reiterate the classic reasons for the same, without revisiting them[96]. Instead, in the case of undergraduate or master's theses on corporate law, the problem of succession in the ownership of the family-owned

---

[94] M. Cesaretti and O. Cesaretti, 'El pacto sucesorio y la empresa familiar en la unificación', Revista del Notariado, 918 (2014), pp. 56–67.

[95] This *modus operandi* has been denounced, from a comparative perspective, by L. León, *El sentido de la codificación civil: Estudios sobre la circulación de modelos jurídicos y su influencia en el Código Civil peruano* (Lima: Palestra, 2004).

[96] See the research carried out by Professor of Succession Law V. Zambrano, 'Sucesión contractual' (unpublished master's thesis, Pontificia Universidad Católica del Perú, 2002); and G. Merino, 'La inscripción ante SUNARP de testamento otorgado mediante escritura pública de persona con domicilio en el extranjero' (unpublished thesis, Universidad Nacional de Piura – UNP, 2019), available through the Digital Institutional Repository of the UNP: https://repositorio.unp.edu.pe/.

companies is discussed, but no space is dedicated to the impasses that this figure would create with Succession Law[97].

Although the proposals developed within the Succession Law subgroup demonstrate that Italian law and the *Codice Civile* still inspire our legislation, it is no less true that some glimpses of originality can be observed[98].

However, the question that serves as this section's title remains: Is the influence of Italian law and the *Codice Civile* the end point or the starting point of the work of Peruvian Succession Law experts? I would like to believe that the answer to the question will depend essentially on the way we approach the study of Peruvian law. Thus, if the purpose of our research is to understand the meaning of a certain regulation or theoretical concepts that are discussed in our legal system, Italian law becomes an undeniable starting point. If our purpose is to reform the PCC, I believe that Italian law will sometimes become an end point, at least if the regulation is not completely modified and we wish to maintain internal coherence with the state of the art in our legislation and legal scholarship. While in other cases, especially if our purpose is to update our legal discourses, Italian law will again become only a starting point and it will be entirely up to us to determine where we will go from here.

In conclusion, in the short term, it is undeniable that Italian law will have a substantial impact on how we approach certain succession law issues and even on the scope and direction of several of the PCC reform proposals (at least if they are proposed

---

97 See the research carried out by Profesor of Succession Law J. Olavarria, 'Necesidad de regular el protocolo de transmisión sucesoria para las empresas o negocios unipersonales, como una excepción a la legítima y a los herederos forzosos' (unpublished master's thesis, Universidad de Lima, 2021), available through Ulima repository: https://repositorio.ulima.edu.pe/handle/20.500.12724/1409; and T. Cárdenas, 'El protocolo familiar como instrumento jurídico de planificación de la sucesión en el negocio para las sociedades familiares peruanas. Su eficacia jurídica y oponibilidad' (unpublished master's thesis, Pontificia Universidad Católica del Perú – PUCP, 2019), available through the PUCP digital thesis repository: https://tesis.pucp.edu.pe/repositorio/.

98 R. Saavedra, 'El anteproyecto de reforma al Código Civil y los negocios jurídicos *mortis causa*', *Actualidad Civil*, 64(2019), pp. 43–71.

by scholars). However, the demands coming from corporate and tax law, which have not been examined in this research (although they are well known to the experienced European legal professional)[99], have a relevant role to play, which has been avoided in legal research. Nevertheless, corporate and tax lawyers cannot avoid taking a position in their daily work, so the solutions implemented are not always consistent with Civil Law (including of course Succession Law). Consequently, a problem similar to the one denounced by Peter Stein regarding the way in which the Common Law dealt with legal personality[100] will arise in Peru in the field of Succession Law (i.e., succession of family-owned companies). In simple terms, due to more urgent practical needs, theoretical problems attached to a topic were avoided by legal professionals until such practice was no longer possible. And when such a moment arrives and a solution is required, we must turn our attention to those legal systems that have a theoretical explanation of the phenomenon. Whether or not I'm right, time will tell.

---

99 I refer to Commission Recommendation 94/1069/EC on the transfer of small and medium-sized enterprises and its impact on the adaptation and reform in various Civil Law systems.

100 P. Stein, 'Nineteenth century English company law and theories of legal personality', in *Quaderni Fiorentini per la storia del pensiero giuridico moderno*, vol. XII-XIII – tomo 1 (Milano: Giuffrè, 1982/1983), pp. 503–19, stating: "Legal personality is a classic example of the way in which English law manages to avoid theory as long as possible and then turns to contemporary continental doctrine when at last it needs a theoretical explanation of the institutions which it has developed pragmatically" (p. 503).

FÁBIO SIEBENEICHLER DE ANDRADE[*]
THE REGULATION OF CHANGING CIRCUMSTANCES
The Influence of the Italian Civil Code of 1942 on Brazilian Civil Law

1. Introduction

According to the *pacta sunt servanda* principle, once a binding contract has been formed, it must be strictly complied with — the debtor cannot simply rid himself of the obligations established therein[1]. However, this classic premise of the Laws of Obligation has exceptions. One of the greatest examples is provided by the *rebus sic stantibus*[2] clause, a proviso of great historical importance in Private Law. Basically, this caveat allows the debtor to be released from — or entitled to modify — the obligations provided under contract, insofar as the original pact is affected by significant supervening circumstances and the new terms are aimed at respecting the undertakings and/or conditions previously agreed. Thus, a fundamental change of circumstances entitles the debtor to withdraw from, terminate or modify the original agreement.

In essence, change of circumstances is considered a sub-type of the problem of impossibility of performance, and is dealt with as follows: the doctrine considers it a situation of economic

---

[*] Full Professor of Civil Law at the Law School, Pontifícia Universidade Católica do Rio Grande do Sul.
[1] J. Bärmann, 'Pacta Sunt servanda: Considérations sur l'histoire du contrat consensuel', Revue Internationale de Droit, 13 (1961), 18–53 (pp. 36–40); R. Zimmermann, *The Law of Obligations*, (New York: Oxford University Press, 1996), p. 576–77; A. Supiot, *Homo juridicus* (Buenos Aires: Siglo Veintiuno Editores, 2007), pp. 121–22.
[2] R. Köbler, *Die "clausula rebus sic stantibus" als allgemeiner Rechtsgrundsatz* (Tubingen: Mohr Siebeck, 1991), pp. 30–33.

impossibility[3] when performance of the contract would result in a significant burden, which is similar to the notion of hardship, for the debtor. This is why the term "excessive burden" is given to such situations in Italian and Brazilian law.

Within the scope of this contribution, an analysis will be conducted of the subject in Brazilian civil law — an analysis that would not be complete without a discussion on the legislative evolution of the matter. Indeed, after special consideration for its introduction in Brazilian law, it is necessary to examine how the matter has developed more recently, including through important changes reflected in the Civil Code of 2002.

The current regime, which considers the contractual relationship as a system of cooperation and not a mere exchange of benefits, raises some serious issues[4].

This premise is based on the existence of another contemporary position: the connection between constitutional and civil principles. More specifically, with the coming into force of the Federal Constitution of 1988, there has been a view that the principle of solidarity also applies in Brazilian civil law[5].

This issue deserves special consideration in light of the contemporary question regarding the extent the role of solidarity should play in contractual relations. This, in turn, leads to the

---

3   C. do Couto e Silva, *Obrigação como processo*, (São Paulo: Bushatsky 1976), p. 129.
4   A. D'Angelo, P.G..Monateri and A. Somma, *Buona Fede e Giustizia Contrattuale: Modeli Conflittuali a confronto* (Torino: Giappichelli, 2005), p. 86; V. Roppo, *Il contratto del Duemila*, 3rd edn. (Torino: Giappichelli, 2011), p. 86; G.E. Nanni, 'O dever de cooperação nas relações obrigacionais à luz do princípio constitucional da solidariedade', in G.E. Nanni (ed.), *Temas relevantes do Direito Civil contemporâneo: reflexões sobre os cinco anos do Código Civil* (São Paulo: Atlas, 2008), p. 307.
5   C. Jamin, *Plaidoyer pour le solidarisme contractuel*, Études offertes à Jacques Ghestin (Paris: LGDJ, 2001), p. 441; L. Grynbaum, 'La notion de solidarisme contractuel', in L. Grynbaum and M. Nicod (eds.), *Le Solidarisme Contractuel* (Paris: Econômica, 2004), p. 25; S. Rodotà, *Solidarietà un'utopia necessaria* (Bari: Laterza, 2014), pp. 3–10; M. Stolleis, 'Wer Solidarität sagt, will etwas haben', Rechtsgeschichte, 5 (2004), pp. 49–54.

question regarding the influence of fundamental rights in private legal relations[6].

This framing reveals the extraordinary contribution made by the Italian Civil Code of 1942 to Brazilian civil law since the promulgation of the current Brazilian Civil Code in 2002. Before analyzing the relationship between the *pacta sunt servanda* principle and the *rebus sic stantibus* clause, in light of the theory of excessive burden (as the topic is titled both in the Italian Civil Code of 1942 and the current Brazilian Civil Code), it is necessary to outline the historical development of the subject in Brazilian civil law. This contextual foundation highlights the mitigation of the principle in the national order and, later, the process of ascertaining the pertinence of remedies available under contemporary Brazilian law.

Given the scope of this work is to examine the link between the Italian Civil Code of 1942 and the current Brazilian Civil Code of 2002, it should be noted that the provisions related to contractual review contained in the Brazilian Consumer Protection Code of 1990 will not be addressed.

2. The Evolution of Brazilian Civil Law regarding changes to contractual circumstances

Brazilian civil law is unique in having been originally influenced directly by extant Portuguese law; itself nothing more than a subsystem of roman law. Like every legal order, however,

---

6   I.W. Sarlet, 'A Influência dos Direitos Fundamentais no Direito Privado: O Caso Brasileiro', in A. Pinto Monteiro, J. Neuner and I. Wolfgang Sarlet (eds.), *Direitos Fundamentais e Direito Privado: Uma perspectiva de Direito Comparado* (Coimbra: Almedina, 2007), pp. 111–20; L. Maurin, *Contrat et Droits Fondamentaux* (Paris: LGDJ, 2013); M. Barcellona, 'L'Intervento europeo e la sovranità del mercato', in C. Salvi, *Diritto Civile e Principi Costituzionali europei e italiani* (Torino: Giappichelli, 2012), p. 155; J. Rochfeld, 'Du Statut du droit contratuel de protection de la partie faible', in M. Fabre-Magnan and others (eds.), *Liber Amicorum: Études offertes à Geneviéve Vivney* (Paris: LGDJ, 2008), pp. 851–60; C. Jamin, 'Le Droit des contrats saisi par les droits fondamentaux', in G. Lewkowicz and M. Xifaras (eds.), *Repenser le contrat* (Paris: Dalloz, 2009), p. 175.

it has its idiosyncrasies, which allow it to stand out in the context of legal traditions[7].

With this in mind, the distinctive feature of primitive Brazilian law — if it can be deemed as such — consists in the unchanging influence of a systematic body of Portuguese laws, especially the Philippine Ordinances (1603). These bodies of law manifested themselves as Portuguese law as applied in Brazil until the enactment of the Civil Code of 1916.

Especially relevant to our analysis is to bear in mind that the Philippine Ordinances contemplated an appropriate discipline for cases of "enormous harm" (*laesio enormis*). The harm was considered enormous when the damages exceeded half of the market price, and highly enormous when someone had received a third of the value of the good itself (L, IV, ti. XIII).

This particular regulation derived from the ordinances and was included in the first batch of decrees issued in Brazil after independence, as was the case of the Consolidation of Civil Laws of 1850 (arts. 359 and 390).

In this way, solutions markedly influenced by the *favor debitoris* principle were disseminated in Brazilian law, and favored the debtor as opposed to strict provisions that supported the rights of the creditor[8].

The first Brazilian Civil Code (i.e., that of 1916) reveals a strong liberal influence derived from the French Civil Code. Thus, the first Brazilian Civil Code does not acknowledge express exceptions to the *pacta sunt servanda* principle: bound by the parties' agreement, the debtor was charged with fulfilling whatever obligations had been established.

More specifically, no instrument was envisaged to allow the party to modify the contract in the event of supervening and potentially burdensome circumstances. In short, the concept

---

[7] C. do Couto e Silva, 'O Direito Civil brasileiro em perspectiva histórica e visão de futuro', in V.M. Jacob De Fradera (ed.), *O Direito Privado brasileiro na visão de Clóvis do Couto e Silva* (Porto Alegre: Livraria do Advogado Editora, 1997), pp. 11–20.

[8] J.C. Moreira Alves, 'As Normas de Proteção ao Devedor e o Favor Debitoris', Notícia do direito brasileiro, 3 (1997), 109–65 (p. 82).

of *rebus sic stantibus* was not a part of the first Brazilian Civil Code[9].

The primary historical reason for this stems from the strong liberal leanings of the 19th century, when the principle of party autonomy was recognized as a supreme value that infused ideas about politics, society and civics of the period[10]. This was not an isolated characteristic of Brazilian law; Portuguese law, first codified in 1867, also failed to include any mention of *rebus sic stantibus*.

From the 1930s onward, in the midst of major Brazilian economic crises, the liberal premises represented by the aforementioned legislation were seriously upended and challenged. While significantly affecting the Brazilian political landscape, there was no substantial change, however, in terms of the law itself.

The rupturing of the economic status quo, with the Great Depression of 1929, inaugurated a string of profound political changes in Brazil: a revolution in 1930, a series of new constitutions (1934 and 1937), and an 11-year dictatorial period (1934–1945).

A series of early legislative reforms to the Civil Code of 1916 attempted to address the following points: in 1933, legislation was enacted (Decree 22.626) to limit contractual interest rates to the level of 12% per year; in 1934, lessee protections in commercial property leases were put in place, in the face of the urban chaos of the first half of the 20th century; and finally, again by decree, in 1938, a *laesio enormis* remedy was re-established to prevent and punish crimes committed against the common good (Decree-law 869).

Twenty years following the enactment of the 1916 Civil Code, this proliferation of special laws began, eventually giving rise to a kind of legal particularism in Brazilian law. Although certain

---

9 C. do Couto e Silva, 'A teoria da base do negócio jurídico no Direito brasileiro', in V.M. Jacob De Fradera (ed.), *O Direito Privado brasileiro na visão de Clóvis do Couto e Silva* (Porto Alegre: Livraria do Advogado Editora, 1997), p. 89–92.
10 M. Waline, *L'Individualisme et le Droit* (Paris: Dalloz, 1945), pp. 19–25.

regulatory measures aim to mitigate the supremacy the principle of party autonomy, they do not address the problem of changing circumstances as a matter of contract law or establish exceptions to the *pacta sunt servanda* principle in the performance phase.

This scenario gradually changed, starting in the 1940s, on the occasion of the first attempt to reform the 1916 Civil Code[11]; in 1941, a draft of the general part of the code of obligations was prepared, which addressed the possibility of modifying contractual clauses.

However, this attempted reform ultimately failed. Notwithstanding the permanence of the normative framework in Brazilian law up until the 1960s, this period was the effective driving force for the changes in legal thinking regarding subject, insofar as the phenomenon of dramatic inflation plagued the national economy.

This problem was aggravated by the adoption of the nominalist principle, expressed in the Civil Code of 1916 under art. 1061. In the wake of these changes, the expansion in Brazilian law of the so-called "value debts" was progressive. The most expressive example being alimony, in which the necessity to compensate for the monetary value was first recognized. Also, at this moment, monetary correction was introduced in the Brazilian legal system in order to keep the currency adjusted to inflation indices — an arrangement still practiced in Brazil today.

In view of the uncontrolled inflation in Brazil, the courts began allowing for the modification of continuous or deferred execution contracts[12].

In 1963, Caio Mário da Silva Pereira authored[13] a new Draft of the Code of Obligations in a second attempt to reform the Civil

---

11 C.M. da Silva Pereira, 'Cláusula Rebus Sic Stantibus', Revista Forense, 92 (1942), 797–800 (p. 797); N. Azevedo, 'O Dirigismo na vida contratual: Cláusula "rebus sic stantibus"', Revista Forense, (1944), 22–35 (p. 29).
12 Supremo Tribunal Federal: Recurso Extraordinário n. 56.960/SP, 13.11.1964, Rel. Min. Hermes Lima, 2ª Turma.
13 F. Siebeneichler de Andrade, *Da Codificação: crônica de um conceito* (Porto Alegre: Livraria do Advogado Editora, 1997), p. 93.

Code of 1916, which included guidelines regarding changing business circumstances.

This reform of the Civil Code, too, failed. It was not to be until a fresh commission of jurists was established, under the coordination of Professor Miguel Reale, in 1969 that a new draft Civil Code could be developed.

3. The Italian model as the basis for the Brazilian Civil Code of 2002

After a long-drawn-out process, the Civil Code project helmed by Professor Miguel Reale in 1972 was finally adopted in 2002, coming into effect a year later in 2003.

Among the various amendments still in force, considering the scope of this work, it is worth mentioning that article 478 provides for the renegotiation of contractual provisions in cases where extraordinary and unforeseeable circumstances have rendered performance excessively burdensome for one of the parties.

The adoption of this specific legal provision suggests that the Brazilian codification process was clearly influenced by Italian law; this inference is further supported by the similar wording of said article 478 compared to article 1467(1) of the Italian Civil Code.

The authors of the Brazilian code also introduced elements of French and German origin over other prominent facets of traditional Brazilian doctrine. Indeed, an analysis of the doctrine of the first half of the 20th century reveals there was a strong French influence in Brazilian civil law. For instance, during this period, it was common to use the theory of *imprévision* (inspired by French law) as a basis for solving the problem of change of circumstances[14]. In the same way, German influence is

---

14 A. Medeiros da Fonseca, *Caso Fortuito e Teoria da Imprevisão* (Rio de Janeiro: Forense, 1943).

manifest in the theory of the basis of the contract[15]; this doctrine was known in Brazilian civil law from the works of jurist Karl Larenz, which Spanish translations were widely circulated among Brazilian jurists.

It should also be noted that Brazilian law is intimately linked, as stated in the first part of the work, with Portuguese civil law. As such, prior to the work of the Civil Code Commission of 2002, Portuguese tradition influenced the discipline of change in circumstances under article 437 such that it was essentially analogous to the regime contained in the Portuguese Civil Code of 1966.

Therefore, despite the availability of other legal models, by the second half of the 20th century it is discernable that the Brazilian legislator preferred the legal solutions offered by the Italian Civil Code, thus revealing the extent of the influence of Italian law on Brazilian doctrine during the period.

This question of the option of the Brazilian architects of law is connected to the more general debate on the circulation of legal models in Latin America[16]. During the 19th and early 20th centuries, along with the influence of Roman law borrowed from Portugal[17], it is necessary to recognize the influence of French civil law on Brazilian jurists. This tendency came to the fore with the ascendancy of French thought in Latin America in this period, especially since Napoleon's Civil Code came into existence.

The authority of French thought fell into decline only at the end of the 19th century, with the emergence of the German school in Brazilian law — and, later, before the enactment of the German Civil Code in 1900 — due to the studies of the jurist Tobias Barreto of German writers[18]. This movement constituted

---

15 C. do Couto e Silva, *A teoria da base do negócio jurídico no Direito brasileiro*, pp. 89–95.
16 V. Fradera, 'A Circulação dos Modelos Jurídicos Europeus na América Latina', Revista dos Tribunais, 86 (1997), 20-39 (pp. 20–25).
17 do Couto e Silva, 'O direito civil brasileiro em perspectiva histórica e visão de futuro', p. 20.
18 M.G. Losano, 'Tobias Barreto e a recepção de Ihering no Brasil', Revista Brasileira de Filosofia, 41 (1993), 335–56 (pp. 335–40); M. Giuseppe, 'La

what is known as the Recife School[19], which had among its members Clóvis Beviláqua, the author of the 1916 Civil Code, and Pontes de Miranda, considered by many to be the greatest Brazilian jurist of the 20th century.

These two major influences on Brazilian law, the French and German models, have coexisted since the second half of the 20th century, alongside the presence of Italian legal thought in Brazilian private law.

In this regard, it is important to consider the arrival to Brazil of Tulio Ascarelli, an eminent Italian jurist, as fundamental. Ascarelli lived in Brazil from 1940 to 1946, during which time he taught in two Brazilian cities, São Paulo and Porto Alegre, and published several works on private law[20]. He dedicated himself to the studies of Brazilian legal themes, and went on to publish his ideas about Brazil in his book, *Sguardo sul Brasile*.

Equally relevant for the diffusion of Italian legal culture in Brazil was the visit of the important Italian jurist Emilio Betti to Porto Alegre in 1958, an episode reported on by the Italian jurist himself[21]. During the stay, he gave a course in comparative law[22] which provided an opportunity for the jurists of Porto Alegre[23], among them the young Clóvis do Couto e Silva, a future member of the Civil Code Commission of 2002, to engage with Italian legal ideas.

Biblioteca Tedesca di Tobias Barreto a Recife', Quaderni Fiorentini del Pensiero Giuridico Moderno, 21 (1992), 159–76 (pp. 159–62).

19   M.G. Losano, 'La scuola di Recife e l'influenza tedesca sul diritto brasiliano', in G. Tarello (ed.), *Materiali per la storia della cultura giuridica*, IV (Bologna: il Mulino, 1974), pp. 321–412.

20   T. Ascarelli, 'Osservazioni di diritto comparato privado brasiliano', in T. Ascarelli, *Studi di diritto comparato e in tema di interpretazione* (Milano: Giuffrè, 1952).

21   M. Fridolin Sommer Santos, 'Relato de Emilio Betti sobre a visita à Universidade do Rio Grande do Sul', Revista da Faculdade de Direito da UFRGS, 24 (2004), pp. 279–92.

22   M. Grondona, 'Emilio Betti e la comparazione giuridica: premesse per uma discussione', in A. Banfi, M. Brutti and E. Stolfi (eds.), *Dall'esegesi giuridica alla teoria dell'interpretazione: Emilio Betti* (Roma: Roma Tre-Press, 2020), pp. 255–86.

23   S. Gialdroni, *Emilio Betti in Brasile* (Roma: ISEB, 2019).

Finally, it is worth mentioning the presence of Enrico Tulio Liebmann, a professor of civil procedure in Brazil. He stayed in São Paulo from 1939 to 1946, and contributed to the training of several professors of civil procedure. Thanks to one of his students, Professor Alfredo Buzaid, the Civil Procedure Code of 1973 was enacted.

This milieu of legal and cultural influences was ultimately consolidated in the formation of Brazilian jurists in the second half of the 20th century. Here, the presence of Italian legal thought in the members of the 2002 Civil Code Commission coordinated by Professor Miguel Reale[24] was quite natural and to be expected. Coming from the University of São Paulo[25], Reale was closely linked with Tulio Ascarelli and remained so even after his return to Italy.

4. *Key characteristics of the Brazilian Civil Code for the modification of contractual circumstances*

The provision set out in article 478 is especially intended for long-term contracts, excluding, therefore, those of instantaneous execution. In Brazilian civil law, aleatory contracts are not expressly excluded; this constitutes a distinction from Italian civil law, which expressly excludes this species of application[26]. As laid out in article 480, unilateral contracts are covered.

Article 478 of the Civil Code applies to civil and business contracts, as opposed to consumer contracts, which are regulated separately in the 1990 Consumer Protection Code.

It is noteworthy that, in relation to business contracts, they can only be modified if such is required to mitigate the

---

24 F. Siebeneichler de Andrade, 'Miguel Reale', in C.E. do Rêgo Monteiro Filho, M.F. Morsello and N. Rosenvald (eds.), *Protagonistas da Responsabilidade Civil* (São Paulo: Foco, 2022), pp. 213–30.
25 Note that Miguel Reale wrote studies on the work of Tullio Ascarelli; M. Reale, 'A Teoria da Interpretação segundo Ascarelli', Revista da Faculdade de Direito da Universidade de São Paulo, 74 (1979), pp. 195–210.
26 N. Borges, 'A teoria da imprevisão e os contratos aleatórios', Revista dos Tribunais, 782 (2002), 78–89 (p. 81).

adverse consequences of exceptional and unforeseen events. This provision has been officially recognized by Brazilian jurisprudence[27] and was ratified by the so-called Economic Freedom Act of 2019. It is important, however, that the business contracts are of an asymmetric nature, especially when they are constituted by parties in a clear material inequality or asymmetry; a necessity of unbalanced relations recognized by sectors of the contemporary doctrine[28].

Another point of contention concerns whether the debtor in arrears can claim protection from excessive onerousness, given that — unlike, for example, the Argentine Civil Code (art. 1198)[29] and the Portuguese Civil Code (art. 438)[30] — such possibility is not expressly provided in the 2002 Code.

Nor does the Brazilian Civil Code contain a provision similar to article 6.2.3(2) of the UNIDROIT Principles, according to which the request for renegotiation must be made immediately and, furthermore, does not have any effect on performance obligations[31].

---

27 Superior Tribunal de Justiça: Recurso Especial n° 936.741/GO, 03.11.11, Rel. Min. Antonio Carlos Ferreira, 4ª Turma.
28 V. Roppo, 'Ancora su contratto asimmetricco e terzo contratto', in G. Alpa and V. Roppo (eds.), *La Vocazione civile del giurista* (Bari: Laterza, 2013), pp. 178–82; V. Roppo, *Il contratto del Duemila* (Torino: Giappichelli, 2011), p. 65; G. Amadio, 'Il terzo contrato: Il problema', in G. Gitti and G. Villa (eds.), *Il Terzo Contratto* (Bologna: il Mulino, 2008), p. 14; Specifically on the subject covered, see F. Macario, 'Sopravvenienze e gestione del rischio nell'esecuzione del terzo contratto', in G. Gitti and G.Villa (eds.), *Il Terzo Contratto* (Bologna: il Mulino, 2008), pp. 179–85.
29 Art. 1198. "No procederá la resolución, si el perjudicado hubiese obrado con culpa o estuviese en mora" ("There shall be no grounds for termination if the injured party was at fault or in default of payment").
30 Art. 438. "A parte lesada não goza do direito de resolução ou modificação do contrato, se estava em mora no momento em que a alteração das circunstâncias se modificou" ("The injured party is not entitled to terminate or renegotiate the contract if he was in default when the change in circumstances occurred").
31 Art. 6.2.3 (Effects of hardship) (1) In case of hardship the disadvantaged party is entitled to request renegotiations. The request shall be made without undue delay and shall indicate the grounds on which it is based. (2) The request for renegotiation does not in itself entitle the disadvantaged party to withhold performance.

However, it is significant that this provision tends to be applied conservatively. Indeed, in the event of changed circumstances, it is advisable for the affected debtor to notify the creditor of his situation and, should the parties fail to renegotiate the terms of the contract, file the corresponding action immediately[32].

Along with these central assumptions, Brazilian law requires the change of circumstances to be due to a "supervening and extraordinary event". This is a strict requirement: the party seeking protection must demonstrate that the supervening circumstance meets this definition.

Although adhering to, for example, the Portuguese model may have provided more flexibility than what is provided under Brazilian law [33], it is significant that the more rigid requirements under Brazilian law improves legal certainty. Indeed, the requirement of 'abnormal alteration' set out under art. 437(1) of the Portuguese civil code has been criticised for its vagueness as, except with regard to a contract's excessive onerousness[34], it is difficult to establish with any certainty what constitutes 'normal' conditions.

In addition to requiring performance to be excessively onerous, article 478 of the Brazilian Civil Code further requires that the creditor be in a situation of extreme advantage — an implicit added requirement for the party intending to benefit from the provision[35]. In light of this condition, any price fluctuation in favor of one of the parties does not constitute an extreme advantage; despite being contrary to the principle of good faith, or even in contrast to the innovative principle present in the Civil Code of 2002, regarding the social functionality of contracts[36].

---

[32] Superior Tribunal de Justiça: Recurso Especial nº 246.106/SP e Recurso Especial nº 607.961/RJ.

[33] On the topic see M.J. de Almeida Costa, *Direito das Obrigações* (Coimbra: Almedina, 1994), p. 277.

[34] Superior Tribunal de Justiça: Recurso Especial nº 945.166/GO, 28.02.2012, Rel. Min. Luis Felipe Salomão, 4ª Turma.

[35] See R. Rosado de Aguiar Júnior, *Extinção dos Contratos por Incumprimento do Devedor* (Rio de Janeiro: Aide, 1991), p. 152.

[36] Superior Tribunal de Justiça: Recurso Especial nº 803.481-GO, Rel. Min. Nancy Andrighi, 3ª Turma.

5. Termination of contract as a solution to the Civil Code of 2002 for the modification of contractual circumstances

The above considerations, therefore, reveal that the authors of the Brazilian Code embraced, in the aforementioned article 478, significant statutory solutions already provided for in the Italian law tradition: the party who meets all the established requirements may terminate the contract which performance has become excessively burdensome. Furthermore, the Brazilian provision excludes the possibility of judicial adaptation of the contract at the request of the aggrieved party.

Moreover, while article 479 (consistent with what is set out in art. 1467(3) of the Italian Code) allows the creditor to avoid termination, avoidance is only possible to the extent that the defendant proposes, as a defense, an equitable modification of the terms of the contract[37]. In this case, the adaptation will only occur if the plaintiff accepts the offer to renegotiate. This brings up the questions regarding the judge's powers in the analysis of the defendant's proposal[38].

In this regard, the possibility of judicial review[39] of the business relationship is expressly provided for in article 480, also following the paradigm of the 1942 Italian code, in relation to unilateral contracts: in these cases, the party may request that its obligations be reduced or altered[40].

Considering the above, it is clear that Brazilian framers reproduced, almost verbatim, the Italian formula regarding the

---

37   Art. 479. A resolução poderá ser evitada, oferecendo-se o réu a modificar eqüitativamente as condições do contrato (*Termination can be avoided by offering the defendant to equitably modify the terms of the contract*).

38   A. de Assis, R. de Andrade and F. Alves, *Comentários ao Código Civil brasileiro* (Rio de Janeiro: Forense, 2007), pp. 729–33.

39   Article 317 of the Code of 2002: "To preserve the intended benefit the contract, article 317 of the Code of 2002 allows the judge to, at the claimant's request, correct a manifest imbalance between the benefit contemplated at the time of formation and that of effective performance when such imbalance is the result of unforeseeable circumstances".

40   Art. 480. If in the contract the obligations are incumbent upon only one of the parties, that party may claim that its performance be reduced or that the manner of performance be modified so as to avoid excessive burden.

legal assumptions and the development of the invocation of excessive onerousness.

6. The debate regarding the contract review solution in Brazilian private law

The provision in the Civil Code of 2002 of termination as a remedy for excessive onerousness made it necessary to identify other paths for contractual review in national law, which have become matters of major debate in doctrine[41] and jurisprudence[42] ever since.

In sum, it was generally agreed that the Brazilian model was restrictive, as it represents a highly exceptional solution. Although it is possible to point out the existence of guidelines favorable to this possibility[43], there was, *prima facie*, the active, dynamic solution: the sense of unequivocally allowing the continuity of the contract[44].

In this sense, Brazilian private law is in line with studies on the need of contract solvency in both the Italian and wider European legal context[45].

This guideline was reinforced with the impact of the Covid-19 pandemic, insofar as the need to review contractual services in the current Brazilian legal and economic scenario was dramatically

---

41 See, for example, L. Ancona Lopez de Magalhães Dias, 'Onerosidade Excessiva e Revisão Contratual no Direito Privado Brasileiro', in W. Fernandes (ed.), *Fundamentos e Princípios dos Contratos Empresariais* (São Paulo: Saraiva, 2013), pp. 385, 434; J.R. Pereira Lira, 'A Onerosidade Excessiva no Código Civil e a Impossibilidade de Modificação Judicial dos Contratos Comutativos sem Anuência do Credor', Revista de Direito Renovar, 44–45 (2009), pp. 91–117 (p. 91).

42 Recurso Especial nº 977.077-GO, 24.11.2009, Rel. Min. Nancy Andrighi, 3ª Turma.

43 Superior Tribunal de Justiça, *obter dictum* in the Recurso Especial n. 977.077-GO, 24.11.2009, Rel. Min. Nancy Andrighi, 3ª Turma.

44 In view of this circumstance, the Brazilian Congress is considering bill n. 6,960/2002, with the purpose of changing the wording of the aforementioned article 478 of the Civil Code, in order to favor the judicial review of contracts.

45 F. Macario, p. 179, 190; D. Mazeaud, *Renégocier ne rime pas avec réviser* (Paris: Dalloz, 2007), p. 765.

revealed[46]; even more so in light of the legislative interventions that took place, for example, in Italian law during the height of the pandemic[47].

It is true that in some cases hardship clauses can be used, along with arbitration, especially when dealing with business between large companies[48]. These are still relatively few examples in the Brazilian legal system, however, which is why the legislative discipline of the Civil Code is regarded as indispensable for solving the issue.

In this context, contractual review in Brazilian law came to have a broadly linked theme of the already-mentioned solidarity, which is also linked to Italian thought[49], in a way that recognizes the need of contractual review when a party faces significant difficulties to perform the obligations. According to this reasoning, it is possible to extract an intention of efficacy from the constitutional framework; to affect private legal relations and in order to favor the contractual review[50].

It so happens that it is, *prima facie*, preferable to determine the possibility of adapting the contract from the principles of obligation law, as well as from the normative structure established in the broader civil legislation.

Along these lines, Brazilian contractual law is clearly guided by the principle of good faith, provided for in art. 422 of the Civil Code. Consequently, the possibility of contractual review is upheld regardless of the final solution for terminating the contract provided for in article 478 of the Civil Code.

---

46 V. Ferreira, 'Impactos da Pandemia na revisão contratual', Valor Econômico <https://valor.globo.com/legislacao/noticia/2020/04/20/impactos-da-pandemia-na-revisao-contratual.ghtml> [accessed 28 November 2022].

47 A.M. Benedetti, 'Il rapporto obbligatorio al tempo dell'isolamento: brevi note sul Decreto cura Italia', I Contratti, 2 (2020), pp. 213–16.

48 I. Schwenzer, 'Force Majeure and Hardship in International Sales Contracts', VUWLR, 39 (2008), pp. 709–25.

49 S. Rodotà, *Solidarietà um'utopia necessaria* (Bari: Laterza, 2014), pp. 3–10; A.-S. Courdier-Cuisinier, *Le Solidarisme Contractuel* (Paris: Litec, 2006), p. 568.

50 Sarlet, pp. 111–21; Maurin, p. 10; Barcellona, pp. 155–64.; Rochfeld, pp. 851–53; C. Jamin, *Le Droit des contrats saisi par les droits fondamentaux*, p. 175.

However, an alternative legislative solution has been used to support the right to contractual adaptation: art. 317 of the Civil Code provides that, in the face of unforeseeable circumstances, such as the event of a gross disproportion between the value of the benefit due and that at the time of its execution, the judge may offer corrections at the request of the party. These adjustments are meant to ensure, as far as possible, the real value of the service rendered[51].

It should be noted that the main purpose of the aforementioned device was to mitigate the principle of nominalism and the problem, quite commonplace in the Brazilian economy, of currency devaluation — again to ensure the equivalence between the nominal value of the installment and its real value.[52] In essence, this lessens the strain on the debtor since, in principle, he does not suffer disproportionate to the economic facts.

In practice, this mechanism has been used by the Judiciary to allow contractual review of broader situations due to an increase in demands for contractual review, especially in the case of leaseholders[53].

It should also be noted that the so-called "Economic freedom law" (law 13.874/2019), introduced a provision in the Civil Code that both restricts and supports judicial review: article 421-A, III, establishes that the contractual review should take place only exceptionally and in a limited capacity.

This article grants the individual a subjective right to seek contractual review. The new article 421-A, III, however, does not contain any other presupposition for its invocation (other than

---

51 A.C. Costa Machado and S.J. Chinellato, *Código civil interpretado*, 6th edn (Santana de Parnaíba: Manole, 2013), p. 282.
52 do Couto e Silva, *A Obrigação como processo*, pp. 186–90.
53 Tribunal de Justiça de São Paulo: Agravo de Instrumento nº 2081753-47.2020.8.26.0000, 06.05.2020, 36ª Câmara de Direito Privado. Due to the Covid-19 pandemic, the Court ordered a reduction in rent due linked to the ban on opening commercial establishments. Price adjustments were justified by the existence of a force majeure event (i.e., the Covid-19 pandemic) Article 317 of the Civil Code authorizes, in these cases, the readjustment of the amount and a reduction by 50%, considered reasonable as long as the ban persists.

its exceptionality) and, therefore, did not establish integrated regulations. In principle, however, it can be argued that its assumptions are the same as those provided for in the above-mentioned article 478, which requirements mirror those laid out in Italian law.

Therefore, both article 317 and article 421-A, III, of the Civil Code update Brazilian private law and establish the basis for the judicial claim of renegotiation, subject to certain legislative requirements. While there has been no change in the regulatory prerequisites, there has certainly been a change as a solution to the problem of changed contractual circumstances has been introduced.

It ought to be recognized that the decision to grant contractual adjustments occurred during the Covid-19 pandemic due to the interruption of certain business activities. While it may appear that the party may invoke the concept of a sudden disturbance to the equivalence of the benefit, from a formal perspective, the requirement to pay rent remains unchanged. On the other hand, from a material point of view, the essential purpose of the contract is impeded.

Furthermore, it should be noted that the aforementioned article 421-A, III, provides that the judge's interference must be limited, without providing further details on the meaning of this provision. First and foremost, it can be interpreted as guidance for the judge to limit the scope of his intervention to the extent of damage caused to the aggrieved party. For example, the judge would be authorized to readjust the price, but able to adopt other measures, such as changing the object of the contract, the payment method, or even releasing the debtor from a particular installment agreement[54].

---

54 In this sense, cfr. decision of the Court of São Paulo which, for example, denied the tenant's moratorium's claim, on the grounds that Brazilian law does not authorize the debtor to purely and simply suspend the fulfillment of the obligation. However, the reduction of the rent amount by 50% of the amount owed was granted. Agravo de Instrumento n° 2072891-87.2020.8.26.0000, 22.04.2020, 34ª Câmara de Direito Privado.

The simplicity and ambiguity of the existing provision in Brazilian law reveals, however, the need to update this area of Brazilian law. Indeed, similar to French law following the 2016 reform, Brazilian law, too, would benefit from establishing a specific procedure for the renegotiation of contracts under article 1195 of the Civil Code[55].

While this solution is not a magic formula[56] capable of resolving the perennial dialectical tension existing in contract law, it provides the parties and the judge with a mechanism to resolve contractual disputes.

It is also important to enforce this new duty to renegotiate in a manner that does not impair its operational effectiveness[57]. One solution might be to sanction parties for being uncollaborative. For example, if a party refuses to renegotiate or is unreasonably uncompromising, the judge could award the aggrieved party punitive damages in the amount of the court fees and filing costs of the lawsuit.

However, it is important to bear in mind that the contours of the subject are anything but black and white. Even in French law, there is no express provision that defines renegotiation of contract as a matter of public order and, as such, compulsory for the creditor.

Under Brazilian civil law, in view of the reform introduced by the aforementioned Economic Freedom Law (Law 13.874/2019),

---

[55] "Si un changement de circonstances imprévisible lors de la conclusion du contrat rend l'exécution excessivement onéreuse pour une partie qui n'avait pas accepté d'en assumer le risque, celle-ci peut demander une renégociation du contrat à son cocontractant. Elle continue à exécuter ses obligations durant la renégociation. En cas de refus ou d'échec de la renégociation, les parties peuvent convenir de la résolution du contrat, à la date et aux conditions qu'elles déterminent, ou demander d'un commun accord au juge de procéder à son adaptation. A défaut d'accord dans un délai raisonnable, le juge peut, à la demande d'une partie, réviser le contrat ou y mettre fin, à la date et aux conditions qu'il fixe".

[56] G. Chantepie and M. Latina, *Le nouveau droit des obligations*, 2nd edn. (Paris: Dalloz, 2018), pp. 468–72.

[57] D. Mazeaud, 'L'Obligation de renégocier n'emporte pas obligation de parvenir à um accord', Révue trimestrielle de droit civil, 2007, 335–50 (p. 341).

article 421, I, establishes the parties can set their own parameters for the contractual review. This implies the parties are free to restrict, and even exclude, the application of rules on the renegotiation of contracts.

In this sense, an affinity between Brazilian civil law and Italian law is evident; the matter of integration, a theme of idiosyncratic relevance to Italian law in view of the provisions in the Italian Civil Code, also takes on a role of clear importance in Brazilian law[58].

Finally, it must be observed that, in contrast to the Brazilian Code, there is no express provision for contractual review in the Italian Civil Code. This disparity, however, does not overshadow the intimate dialogue between both systems.

The Italian legislator is currently debating a revision of the Italian Civil Code of 1942, through Bill n. 1151 of 2019. One potential amendment regards the rules on excessive onerousness[59].

As of now, the possibility of contractual renegotiation is allowed, representing an updated view of regulations of contract in Italian law and, in short, a rapprochement between the concepts of Italian and Brazilian civil law.

Doctrinal debates in Italy reveal the difficulty of settling clear rules on the matter; the adoption of the remedies that maintain the contract opens up a whole series of questions regarding the way in which this procedure is established and what the economic logic is for this attempt at contract preservation[60].

In this sense, despite potential criticism of the decision not to include a renegotiation procedure in the Brazilian Code, it is nonetheless significant that the guidelines dictate review should be conducted exceptionally and in a limited capacity.

---

58   R. Sacco and G. di Nova, *Il Contratto*, 2nd edn (Torino: UTET, 2004), pp. 417–23.
59   M. Grondona, 'Qualche osservazione sulla (auspicabile, ma non così prossima) riforma italiana del codice civile', Revista da Ajuris, 48 (2021), pp. 319–23.
60   Grondona, 'Qualche osservazione sulla (auspicabile, ma non così prossima) riforma italiana del codice civile', p. 338.

Conclusion

The theme chosen for this text highlights one of the most dynamic subjects of civil law, especially considering its long historical pedigree. The possibility of using the expression "*clausula rebus sic stantibus*" to express its meaning well poignantly demonstrates this astuteness.

Moreover, the topic has a striking contemporary and practical importance, insofar as it is also of interest to both parties involved in a contractual dispute, as well as the judicial sphere more generally. The subject, therefore, goes well beyond the confines of mere academic curiosity.

Specifically, as concerns the scope of this work, the topic illustrates a striking influence of Italian law and the Italian Civil Code of 1942 on contemporary Brazilian civil law.

Acknowledging the significant presence of French and Germanic legal culture as a relevant model in Brazilian law during the 19th and early 20th centuries, this scenario changed dramatically from the second half of the 20th century onwards.

The Civil Code of 2002 is highly representative of this trend. Among many other examples, the issue of changes in circumstances supervening in the contract is one of the most emblematic and, hence, the focus of this text.

As unambiguously affirmed throughout the work, the legislative lynchpin of the matter (i.e., article 1478 of the Civil Code) essentially corresponds to the provisions of the Italian Civil Code — in this case, article 1467.

Not only were the foundational premises for framing of the problem adopted, but also its solution: it was a matter of introducing termination as a remedy for the contract affected by so-called excessive onerousness.

Prior to this introduction, Brazilian law was clearly insufficient to the extent that it lacked mechanisms capable of allowing, in a satisfactory manner, the continuity of the contract.

Some recent changes to Brazilian civil law now allow for contractual review, but do not delineate concise rules for the subject; it remains an unfinished legal project.

The dialectic between the need for legal certainty balanced with contractual justice is essential to fair and functioning private law, but the subject of contractual review still demands refinement in the context of contemporary Brazilian law.

And finally, it should be noted that the acceptance of contractual adjustment in the Brazilian Civil Code did not lead to the suppression of the provisions on excessive onerousness; therefore, the influence of the Italian Civil Code of 1942 remains.

Hopefully the proposed reform of the Italian civil law will allow this constructive dialogue to continue, maintaining the tradition of exchanging ideas between the two countries.

It will be especially interesting to see the long-term effects of the current Italian experiment of reforming the Civil Code and reframing the process of renegotiation and the economic criteria for the preservation of the contract.

Soyla H. León Tovar*

THE VOTING RIGHTS OF THE SHAREHOLDERS OF THE MEXICAN CORPORATION, INFLUENCE OF ITALIAN LAW

1. Reception and Influence of Italian Commercial Law in Mexico

During the Spanish colonization, for almost three centuries (1521-1810), trade in Mexico was regulated by Spanish law and its commercial organizations. For instance, there was the Casa de Contratación de Indias in Seville (founded on January 10, 1503[1]) and its consulate, the Universidad de Cargadores de Indias, created by order of King Charles to resolve disputes arising from commercial operations[2]. After Mexico's independence in 1810, various Spanish legislation remained in force. The Bilbao Ordinances[3] (Ordinances of the Consulate of the University

---

* Professor at the Panamerican University. School of Law. Alvaro del Portillo 49, Zapopan, Jalisco, 45010, Mexico.
1 Called Casa o Audiencia de Indias to promote and regulate commerce and navigation in the New World, it lasted until it was suppressed with decree of June 18, 1790, cfr. S.H. León Tovar and H. González García, *Derecho Mercantil* (México: Oxford University Press, 2007), pp. 39–40.
2 Cfr. R. de San Miguel, *Curia Filípica Mexicana. Obra completa de práctica forense. En la que se trata de los procedimientos de todos los juicios, ya ordinarios, ya extraordinarios y sumarios, y de todos los tribunales existentes en la República, tanto comunes como privativos y privilegiados. Conteniendo además un tratado integro de la jurisprudencia mercantil* (México: Librería General de Eugenio Maillefert y Compañía, 1858), pp. 588–89.
3 A. Fernández, *Ordenanzas de la Ilustre Universidad y Casa de Contratación de la M.N. y M.L. Villa de Bilbao, aprobadas y confirmadas por el Rey Felipe Quinto en el año de 1737* (Madrid: Antonio Fernández, 1975), pp. 72–73; the same that came into force in the so-called East Indies and especially in Mexico by order of April 22, 1801 and that were printed in 1639, 1772 and 1816; M. Dublán, M.and J.M. Lozano, 'The Decree of October 16, 1824. The Suppression of Consulates', *Legislación Mexicana ó colección completa*

of Merchants of New Spain) are particularly relevant, as they were effective until 1854 when Mexico promulgated its first Commercial Code, the "Code of Teodosio Lares"[4]. This was a code of intermittent duration[5], inspired by the Spanish Commercial Codes of 1829[6] and the Italian Code of 1829, in turn inspired by the French Commercial Code of 1807. In 1884, a new Commercial Code came into force. The first of a federal nature, the new code was also influenced by the codes of said European

---

      de las disposiciones legislativas expedidas desde la independencia de la República (México: Dublán y Lozano Hijos, I no 429, 1876), p. 738; Ó. Cruz Barney, 'La codificación mercantil y sus personajes', in Ó. Cruz Barney and others, *Los abogados y la formación del estado mexicano* (México: UNAM, 2013) p. 389.

4   Cfr. El Archivo Mexicano. Colección de leyes, decretos, circulares y otros documentos (Messico. Vicente G. Torres, II, 1856) p. 441; Manuel Dublán y José María Lozano, Legislación mexicana- Colección completa de las disposiciones legislativas (Messico: Dublán y Lozano, VIII, 1856-1859), p. 274.

5   Two years after it was in force, on October 29, 1856, it was abrogated according to the declaration of then President Ignacio Comonfort, by articles 1 and 77 of the law of November 23, 1855, so that in commercial matters the laws prior to 1853, whose application was entrusted to special courts, should govern throughout the Republic. However, in 1863, by imperial decree of July 15, their validity was reestablished, cfr. *El Boletín de las Leyes del Imperio Mexicano, or Código de la Restauración, complete collection of laws and decrees*, p. 133.

6   This Spanish Commercial Code was influenced by the French Commercial Code, although it was not the product of the first project, because according to the order of 1797 to draft a Commercial Code, the general project of Commercial Ordinances had already been drafted, which was also taken into account by the commission that drafted the Spanish Code of 1829 known as the Code of Pedro Sainz de Andino, abrogated by the entry into force of the Code of 1885; cfr. J.L. Soberanes Fernández, (ed.), 'Memoria del Ministerio de Justicia y Negocios Eclesiásticos presentada a las augustas Cámaras del Congreso General de los Estados Unidos Mexicanos por el Secretario del Ramo en febrero de 1850', in J.L. Soberanes Fernández, *Memorias de la Secretaría de Justicia* (México: UNAM, 1997), p.185; Cruz Barney (n 3), p. 389. Likewise, the Albertine Code in Italy was abrogated by the code of 1865, which in turn was abrogated by the code of 1882, which would also be abrogated by the current Civil Code according to J. Barrera Graf, 'Títulos de Crédito', in *El derecho en México, una visión de conjunto* (México: UNAM, II, 1991), p. 569.

countries, which had been studied by the Mexican doctrine[7]. The Italian Commercial Code was especially influential in relation to the qualification of speculative purchases of any kind of goods, "even if they are real estate", as acts of commerce — which was incorporated in our code[8].

This second Mexican law lasted only ephemerally, since on April 10, 1888 the articles relating to corporations were repealed with the publication and entry into force of the Corporations Law, and on January 1, 1890 it was abrogated by a new commercial code published on September 15, 1889. The latter was also inspired by the Italian commercial code of 1882, particularly with respect to the concept of merchant, the list of commercial acts, the classification of the purchase and sale of real estate for the purpose of commercial speculation, the leasing of movable property for the same purpose, and the acts of business[9].

---

[7] Said commission, recognizes that, in order to form the present draft of the Code of Commerce, the Commission has had before it all the mercantile laws and foreign codes, including the most modern ones, such as those of Germany, Buenos Aires and Belgium, cfr. *Proyecto de Código de Comercio del Distrito Federal y Territorio de la Baja California, Con las bases generales de la legislación mercantil que han de regir en toda la República, conforme a la fracción décima del artículo 72 de la Constitución Federal* (México: Tipografía de Gonzalo A. Esteva, 1880), pp. 568–69.

[8] See J. Barrera Graf, 'Codificación en México. Antecedentes. Código de Comercio de 1889, perspectivas', in *Centenario del Código de Comercio* (México: UNAM, 2003), p. 76; which is not strange given that the doctrine was already looking at foreign sources and the Italian, one of them, as is attested in the work of A. de J. Lozano, *Código de comercio de los Estados Unidos Mexicanos. Concordado con el de 1884 (en vigor antes) y con los de su especie vigentes en Guatemala, Chile, Argentina, España, Francia, Bélgica, Alemania, Italia, Holanda y Portugal así como con algunas otras leyes relativas a la materia* (México: J. Buxo, 1899).

[9] J. Barrera Graf, *Temas de Derecho Mercantil* (México: UNAM, 1983), p. 192. This is not surprising given that foreign legislation and doctrine were studied and compared with national legislation, as attested by the work of Antonio de J. Lozano, regarding the Mexican commercial code of 1890, in which he makes a comparative study with European codes, including that of Italy, cfr. A. de Jesús Lozano, *Código de comercio de los Estados unidos mexicanos, que comenzó a regir el 1.° de enero de 1890, concordado literalmente con el que dejó de estar en vigor en la misma fecha, y con los vigentes en España, Francia, Bélgica, Alemania, Italia, Holanda y Portugal. Lleva un supuesto que contiene íntegra la Ley del timbre, y sus aclaraciones, reformas,*

At the end of the 19th century and the beginning of the 20th century, a greater ascendancy of Italian law was observed in Mexico. Such influence was due, among others, to the entry in the National School of Jurisprudence of Mexico of several professors trained in Germany and Spain in accordance with German and Italian doctrines, and to the intense translation of foreign legal works into Spanish[10].

Several works of Italian mercantilists were translated into Spanish and published in Mexico. For instance, 'Los actos de comercio y la noción jurídica del comercio' and 'Teoría General de los títulos de crédito' by Ageo Arcángeli; 'Los Principios de derecho mercantil' by Alfredo Rocco; 'Instituciones de Derecho Mercantil' (with almost sixty editions by 1934, and being reprinted in 2002 by the Tribunal Superior de Justicia del Distrito Federal, Mexico)[11] by César Vivante, an author who has been fundamental in Mexican doctrine and legislation up to the present day. This last author was moreover instrumental in the introduction of the concept of negotiable instruments contained in article 5 of the Mexican Ley General de Títulos y Operaciones de Crédito, and further influenced the formation of the original article 198 of the LGSM on the nullity of the Voting shareholder agreements. Finally, among others, Tullio Ascarelli's *Derecho mercantil*, translated and annotated by Joaquín Rodríguez, had a powerful influence on authors such as Jorge Barrera Graf, one of the leading exponents of Mexican commercial law[12].

---

adiciones, etc., en número de ciento setenta y siete, hasta el 31 de julio del presente año (1890), y las leyes sobre marcas de fábrica y patentes de privilegio (México: Impresión de A. de J. Lozano, 1890).

10   E.E. Martínez Chávez, *España en el Recuerdo México en la esperanza. Juristas* (Madrid: Carlos III University of Madrid, 2020), p. 199.

11   A.O. Piccato Rodríguez, 'Joaquín Rodríguez y Rodríguez: La empresa y el moderno derecho mercantil', in *Los maestros del exilio español en la Facultad de Derecho* (México: Porrúa, 2003), p. 316.

12   Cfr. T. Ascarelli, 'Joaquín Rodríguez y Rodríguez, Tratado de sociedades mercantiles', trans. by Jorge Barrea Graf, Revista de la Escuela Nacional de Jurisprudencia (México: UNAM, XII no 45, 1950), p. 204–207 http://historico.juridicas.unam.mx/publica/librev/rev/indercom/cont/6/bib/bib13.pdf accessed 1 July 2022; J. De Stéfano, 'La influencia del Derecho Civil,

This doctrinal influence was also strengthened by the work of a pleiad of mercantilists in Mexico from the 1930s onwards, from Alberto Vásquez del Mercado[13] and the Spaniard Joaquín Rodríguez Rodríguez[14], Felipe de J. Tena, to Roberto Mantilla Molina, Raúl Cervantes Ahumada and Jorge Barrera Graf.

The splendor of Italian ancestry in Mexican commercial law is recognized by Mantilla Molina and Barrera Graf, who together with Raúl Cervantes Ahumada formed the drafting commission of the Mexican commercial code reorganized in 1951[15]. Molina and Graf acknowledge in the Introduction to the Draft Commercial Code that their objections to previous drafts of the commercial code were based fundamentally on the draft commercial codes of Vivante and D'Amelio, or of the Confederation of Industrial and Commercial Chambers, the Italian Civil Code of 1942 and German corporate law. They also imply that Italy was already "at the forefront of legal science" by the third decade of the 20th century.[16] That is, when projects for a commercial code and the unification of private law were being discussed, in 1942 Italy followed this trend by establishing a civil

---

Mercantil y Penal italiano en el ordenamiento jurídico venezolano', Estudios de derecho público homenaje a Humberto J. Laroche Rincón (Caracas: Tribunal Superior de Justicia, I, no 3, 2001), p. 274.

13 One of the so-called Seven Wise Men of Mexico, of the generation of 1915, noted for his great passion for literature and law. Previously, in 1905 Silvestre Moreno Cora had published his *Tratado de Derecho Mercantil Mexicano*, in which he made constant references to French and Italian authors, such as Supino, and to the commercial codes of Spain, France and Italy.

14 An outstanding Spanish jurist who was exiled by the Spanish War and arrived in Mexico and in ten years wrote, among other great works, one of the most important in commercial law, his treatise on corporations.

15 Although Jorge Barrera Graf resigned in 1954 and was replaced by Salvador Mondragón Guerra, R.L. Mantilla Molina, 'El proyecto de Código de Comercio para la república mejicana', conferencia dictada en el Cuarto Centenario de la Facultad de Derecho, Revista de la Facultad de Derecho de México, UNAM, 15 (1953) 143–170, (p. 143). http://historico.juridicas.unam.mx/publica/librev/rev/facdermx/cont/15/dtr/dtr6.pdf, accessed 10 August 2022. This project was entrusted in 1951 to the mercantilists Mantilla Molina, Barrera Graf and Cervantes Ahumada, after the commission that preceded them had taken too long to draw up the Project.

16 Mantilla Molina, 'El proyecto de Código de Comercio para la república mejicana'.

code that would substitute and repeal its commercial code. This current was even promoted by César Vivante himself, although he retracted support in 1922 in his draft commercial code due to the belief that such unification would be a serious mistake and prejudice commercial law[17]; to date, this has not occurred and, on the contrary, unification has solved many problems and challenges that still affect countries like Mexico that have a commercial code, a federal civil code, and 32 local civil codes and corresponding procedural codes.

Some Italian legislation and projects that influenced Mexican commercial legislation were, among others, the reform projects of Vivante and the counter-project of the General Confederation of Italian Industry, called the D'Amelio project[18], in the General Law of Commercial Companies of 1934 (hereinafter the LGSM), the Project of Lorenzo Mossa, in Insurance Contract Law; the Bankruptcy Law of 1942, in the Bankruptcy and Suspension of Payments Law; and the Civil Code of 1942, in the draft commercial codes of 1950 and 1962. In this sense, Barrera Graf expressed himself in his lectures on the Draft Mexican Commercial Code of 1952, given on July 21 and 23, 1953, on the occasion of the celebration of the fourth centenary of the Law School of the National University of Mexico. On these occasions, he specifically pointed out some figures adopted from Italian law, such as the "checks with guaranteed coverage", the non-competition agreement with a maximum duration of five years in the case of the sale of a company, the regulation of the company, and the substitution of the objective criterion of the act of commerce for the subjective criterion of the company — where

---

[17] After the publication of the Mexican Commercial Code of 1889, several drafts have been elaborated. For instance, in 1929, 1943, 1947–1950, 1980 and 1988, the Barrera Graf project, without success, as referred to in Barrera Graf, Jorge, 'Codificación en México. Antecedentes. Código de Comercio de 1889, perspectivas', in *Centenario del Código de Comercio, México* (México: UNAM, 1991), p. 76.

[18] Cfr. A. Padoa Schioppa, *Saggi di Storia Del Diritto Commerciale*. (Milano: LED Edizione Universitarie, 2009), p. 233.

he constantly and copiously quotes Italian doctrine[19]. Finally, other concepts such as the commercial factor, transportation and insurance, acts of commerce, commercial companies, checks and negotiable instruments[20].

2. *Italian influence on voting rights*

In independent Mexico, the corporation was regulated by the commercial codes of 1854 and 1884 until the entry into force of the Corporations Law published on April 10, 1888, which was of fleeting duration since it was repealed by the Commercial Code of 1889. With the process of mercantile decodification, on August 4, 1934, the current LGSM was published, repealing from the Code of Commerce the chapter related to mercantile corporations[21]. This law was drafted during the economic depression of the United States in 1929 and introduced substantial changes in relation to the Code of Commerce, maintaining the influence of Italian corporate law. This sway can be seen in the Mexican legislator's express and manifest rejection of the Anglo-Saxon doctrine, in spite of its "broad worldwide recognition and acceptance", since in the exposition of motives, he dismisses the bill presented by the Secretary of Industry of 1929, which

---

19   J. Barrera Graf, 'Proyecto del código de comercio mexicano. Normas sobre obligaciones de los comerciantes y sobre derecho industrial y cambiario', Revista de la Facultad de Derecho de México, UNAM, 14 (1953), pp. 9–45 (pp. 21–23). http://historico.juridicas.unam.mx/publica/librev/rev/facdermx/cont/14/dtr/dtr1.pdf. it is one, accessed 15 August 2022.

20   Cfr. Secretaría de Hacienda y Crédito Público, *La crisis económica en México y la nueva legislación sobre Moneda y crédito* (Cultura, México 1933); J. de Stéfano, 'La influencia del Derecho Civil, Mercantil y Penal italiano en el ordenamiento jurídico venezolano', Estudios de derecho público homenaje a Humberto J. Laroche Rincón, Fernando Parra Aranguren (Caracas: Tribunal Supremo de Justicia, 2001), p. 274, argues that the Italian Commercial Code is of essential importance for Venezuela, as it is the main source of its current Commercial Code; and, C. Vivante, *Trattato di diritto commerciale*, 5th edn (Milano: Vallardi, 1929), no 953, 3, p. 124.

21   Cfr. M. Dublán and J.M. Lozano, *Legislación mexicana – Colección completa de las disposiciones legislativas*, XIX, (Mexico: Official edition, 1889), pp. 56–63.

proposed to adopt "a more flexible legal framework of unwritten law and a rapid displacement of companies by shares". Instead, the legislator opted to retain the rigid tradition of the French, Spanish and Italian written law Commercial Codes, as well as the Italian doctrine regarding voting rights, which manifested itself in two apparently opposing currents of thought, postulated in the draft Commercial Codes, championed by César Vivante and Mariano D'Amelio.

This influence of Italian law is even exercised on Mexican judges, as can be seen in a judgment of the Mexican Supreme Court of Justice of the Nation issued in 1937, three years before the publication of the LGSM, during the Second World War, regarding a decree of the President of Mexico that had ordered the blockade of Italian products[22]:

> ITALIAN LEGAL DOCTRINE, APPLICATION OF THE. The decree of the Federal Executive, which in compliance with international treaties ordered the blockade of Italian products, cannot prevent the Judges from invoking in support of their thesis, the opinions of an author of that nationality, because ostensibly that blockade is reduced to economic and commercial purposes and it would be monstrous to understand that its effects extend to the field of scientific or social ideas.

Part of the Italian doctrine, represented by Scialoja and Vivante, considered the right to vote as an absolute, essential and inalienable right of the shareholder, as the greatest of the shareholder's individual rights, as the most important of the rights of realization, proportional and constructive of the governing majority within the general shareholders' meeting where the portion of social sovereignty is concretized and the shareholders' will is manifested. This conception is accepted by Mexican law to the extent of declaring null and void any agreement that restricts or limits this right, as mentioned below[23].

However, following various phenomena (such as shareholder abstentionism, the existence of savings shareholders, the

---

22 T. Perlín de Niembro, *sucesión* [1937]SCJN [AR 3087/35] LII SJF, p. 2409.
23 J. Rodríguez Rodríguez, *Curso de derecho mercantil*, 16th ed (México: Porrúa, 1982), p. 494; R. Illescas Ortiz, *Prologue: Las acciones sin voto en la sociedad anónima* (Madrid: Distribuciones de La Ley, 1991), p. 1.

integration of controlling minorities, the strengthening of control, the need for financing and the recognition of shareholders loyal to the company, among others), in this 21st century, the right to vote has gone from being essential to being a natural right of the shareholder and, therefore, has become a right that can be suppressed, altered, suspended, limited, conditioned or privileged by the company or by the shareholder in exchange for dividends, or without dividends in cases in which for the shareholder this suppression or alteration of his voting right has an indirect economic meaning or value. According to Paz-Ares, the suppression of the vote may be due to the agreement between those interested in corporate control or management and those interested in an income proportional to the privileges, so that such shares that see the vote altered or suppressed are instruments of exchange of control for a price; which implies extracting the right to vote from the shareholder's political rights and taking it to the patrimonial sphere. As the same author maintains, this is possible because voting is a mere contractual technology, an economic approach in which absenteeism must be seen from an economic point of view; that is, the fact that the shareholder abstains from voting, even though he is entitled to do so, does not mean that he loses interest in this right, which, although it lacks use value, has an economic value that can be negotiated for a price, whose particularity, according to Paz-Ares, is that it must be paid through future cash flows, i.e. in the form of preferential dividends[24]. In this sense, the economic value of the share outweighs the power to influence the assembly, which forms the social will; the right to vote becomes effective only when one has control or when someone has to exercise a residual power to act because its agreements are incomplete.

---

24 C. Paz-Arez Rodríguez, ¿Dividendos a cambio de votos?(Contribución al estudio de la conversión de la of voting shares into non-voting shares) (Madrid: McGraw-Hill, 1996), p. 12.

2.1. *The general shareholders' meeting in Mexico*

The Italian Commercial Code of 1865 and the French Commercial Companies Act of 24 July 1867[25] strengthened the structure of the joint-stock company and established the shareholders' meeting as a sovereign body that functions on the basis of the adoption of resolutions by majority vote[26], by establishing with precision the functions of the administrators and the commissioners, "until the organs of the joint-stock company were perfected"[27]. And as Mossa refers, the shareholders' meeting was organized according to the common rules of economic and political meetings and assemblies[28], as an organ of the democratic society, in a parallelism, for some mistakenly[29], of the political structures or organs of democratic states where the general assembly appears as a deliberative and sovereign organ. It is within this body that the fundamental decisions of the corporation are taken under the principles of proportionality, one share one vote and majority, according to which decisions

---

25   According to R. Cervantes Ahumada, *Derecho Mercantil* (México: Porrúa, 16th ed, 1978), p. 84, although French law recognized the right to freely create joint-stock companies under provisions dictated by the State and without prior authorization, there were already laws authorizing the free incorporation of joint-stock companies, such as that of the State of North Carolina, in 1795; the laws of Massachusetts in 1799; New York in 1811 and Connecticut in 1837; the English law of 1844 and the French law of 1867; and the increasing complexity of corporations in the 19th century.

26   F. De Solá Cañizarez, *Tratado de derecho comercial comparado*, III, (Barcelona: Montaner y Simón, 1968), p. 319, argues that "Parallel to the political evolution, the joint-stock company became more democratic and liberalized in the 19th century... the general meeting of shareholders was exalted to the rank of a sovereign body, which operated under the rigorous application of the majority system... in the internal life of the company the principle of equal rights for all shareholders was in force [...]".

27   T. Ascarelli, *Sociedades y Asociaciones*, trans. by Sentís Melendo, (Buenos Aires: Ediar, 1947), p. 253.

28   L. Mossa, *Derecho Mercantil*, trans. by Felipe de J. Tena (Buenos Aires: UTHEA, 1940), p. 140; M. Broseta Pont, *Manual de Derecho Mercantil* (Madrid: Tecnos, 1974), p. 189.

29   A. Menéndez 'Los pactos de sindicación para el órgano administrativo de la S.A.', in *Estudios de Derecho Mercantil en Homenaje a Rodrigo Uría* (Madrid: Civitas, 1978), p. 363.

are binding for all members, even for the minority that voted against, which in turn enjoys a system of protection against possible abuses of the majority. Since then, the general meeting of shareholders has remained, in various countries that adopt the dualist system of administration, as the supreme body of the company to which the administration and supervisory bodies in public limited companies are subordinate.

The LGSM was inspired by two Italian currents of thought, at once contrary and complementary, embodied in the Italian draft commercial code, that of César Vivante and that of Mariano D'Amelio in 1925[30]. The former was fundamental for the consideration of the general meeting of shareholders as the supreme body of the company. Unlike the Corporations Law of 1888 (article 40) and the 1889 commercial code (articles 178, 201, 204), the LGSM expressly recognizes the supremacy of the general shareholders' meeting over the other corporate bodies (articles 144, 178, 185, 189, 199, 201 and 206 of the LGSM), the rights of proportionality, equal value and voting rights of the shares, as well as minority rights and limited voting shares, as postulated by Italian law[31].

This supremacy was expressly recognized in the associations and civil partnerships regulated in the Civil Code of 1928 (article 2674 CFF), in the limited partnerships by shares, limited liability companies, corporations, and, since 2016 in the simplified joint-stock companies or SAS (articles 77, 178, 208 and 266 LGSM). In all of these, it is specified that the general meeting adopts its

---

30 Project formulated by the commission composed of Mariano D'Amelio, Arcangeli, Asquini, Bonelli and Fré; Commisione Reale per la riforma del codici, Sottocommissione B. Codice di Commercio, Vol. I, Progetto (Roma 1925). Thus, A. Martínez Báez, 'Algunas consideraciones sobre las acciones preferentes en las sociedades anónimas', Revista de la Escuela Nacional de Jurisprudencia, 8, no. 30, (1942), pp. 9–26 (p. 21).
31 Cfr. M. Dublán and others, 'Ley de Sociedades Anónimas', in *Legislación mexicana. Colección completa de las disposiciones legislativas* (Mexico: official edition, 1889) http://cdigital.dgb.uanl.mx/la/1080042593_C/1080043033_T19/1080043033_014.pdf. Regarding supremacy, it can be said that these laws only recognized the powers of the assembly to ratify all acts of the corporation, as well as to reform the corporate bylaws as long as the bylaws did not establish otherwise.

resolutions under the principle of simple, absolute or reinforced majority, depending on the matter. Therefore, the general shareholders' meeting becomes, as Donati argued, "the master key of corporate life, directly decisive in internal relations, for the other bodies and for the partners"[32]. In other words, the general shareholders' meeting represents the instrument that allows the owners of the capital to make effective the right to receive, approve or reject the accounts, operations and information to the administrative body, to elect its members, to decide on fundamental issues of the company and of the corporate management.

2.2. Minority protection

As purported by Vivante, the LGSM recognizes rights and protection of minority shareholders as one of the most important matters of corporate law. The explanatory memorandum of the law points out that this is one of the most difficult issues of shareholder democracy because in the latter the decisions of the general meeting are adopted under the majority principle, but there is a need to protect the minority without subjecting the majority to the decisions of the smallest number of shares[33]. According to the original text of the LGSM, the minority representing at least 33% of the capital stock (a percentage that has now been reduced to 25%) is a serious interest group, worthy of protection and therefore grants it the following rights (articles 144, 178, 185, 199, 201, 206 and 198 LGSM); to request a meeting for the matters it freely determines, to oppose the resolutions of the meeting, to demand liability from the administrators even though the meeting has resolved that there is no liability whatsoever; to request the suspension of decision-making when it is not considered sufficiently informed, and to minorities representing

---

[32] A. Donati, *Sociedades anónimas, la invalidez de las deliberaciones de las asambleas*, trans. by Felipe de Jesús Tena Ramírez (México: Porrúa, 1939), p. 6.
[33] C. Vivante, *Derecho mercantil* (México: Tribunal Superior de Justicia del Distrito Federal, 2002), p. 128.

25% of the capital, or 10% in the case of listed companies, the right to appoint a director when there are three or more directors, a rule that also applies to the supervisory board.

2.3 *Limited voting shares*

With respect to voting rights in corporations, the LGSM adopted the general rule established by the prevailing doctrine that each share has the right to one vote and that there are no non-voting shares, which is in accordance with the doctrine of César Vivante, who held that all shareholders have the right to vote in general meetings, and that the bylaws cannot deprive them of this right[34]; and on the other hand, in consensus with the current of the Draft of the 1925 Commercial Code led by D'Amelio, by stating in Article 113 that "each share shall only have the right to one vote", which meant the prohibition of issuing shares without voting rights and plural voting shares, but the possibility of issuing limited voting shares, as provided for in Articles 113 and 195 of the LGSM[35].

One of the most important issues in the LGSM was the admission of limited voting shares, because the original text of the CCo regulating corporations, although it allowed the issuance of shares with different economic rights and even left open the possibility of considering plural voting shares, did not recognize shares with limited, restricted or suppressed voting rights. Furthermore, there was also no consensus in comparative law doctrine regarding shares deprived of voting rights. Nevertheless, the Mexican legislator, in accordance with the D'Amelio Project of 1925, authorized the shareholders' meeting to issue shares with limited voting rights, with the following requirements: grant their holders a preferential dividend of 5% per annum of the nominal

---

34 Vivante, *Derecho mercantil*, p. 128.
35 Project formulated by D'Amelio, Arcangeli, Asquini, Bonelli and Fré, Commissione Reale per la riforma del codici, Sottocommissione B. Codice di Commercio, Vol. I, Progetto, Roma, 1925, Vol. II, Relazione sul progetto, Roma, 1925, citing A. Martínez Báez, 'Algunas consideraciones sobre las acciones preferentes en las sociedades anónimas'.

value to be paid with the profits of the corporate year; if in any year there were no profits, the dividend should be accumulated for the following years; in case of liquidation such shares would be repaid in advance of the ordinary shares; they would enjoy the rights of opposition and balance sheet review, in addition to configuring the special meeting of shareholders holding such shares to previously accept any proposal of the general meeting that could prejudice their rights. Although this class of shares altered in some way the principle of equality of corporate rights enshrined in Mexico, it enshrined the prohibition of issuing non-voting shares and plural voting shares, in accordance with the categorical expression of the LGSM that remains in force to date: "each share shall only have the right to one vote", although it left the door open to issue voting shares limited to certain matters of the meeting; but voting is not suppressed, it simply limits its effectiveness and only reaches certain items of the extraordinary general meeting: extension of the duration of the corporation, early dissolution, change of purpose, change of nationality, transformation and merger[36].

Both the D'Amelio Project and the Mexican LGSM recognize that the admission of limited voting shares is one of the most important problems of the corporate law of the time, because it implies admitting different amounts of equity rights and different voting intensity in the shares, contrary to the postulate of equality of value and rights. However, the reasons for the recognition of this type of shares in our LGSM differ from the reasons for the D'Amelio project. In Mexico, it was due, according to the Explanatory Memorandum, to the abstentionism of the shareholders that prevented or hindered the installation of

---

[36] As of the amendment to the LGSM published in the Official Gazette of the Federation on 13 June 2014, pursuant to Article 91, section VII, subsection c) of the LGSM, corporations may include in their bylaws the possibility of issuing shares without voting rights, restricted voting shares; with non-economic social rights other than the right to vote, exclusively voting rights; with veto and necessary voting rights; which will be counted for determining the quorum required for the installation and voting at shareholders' meetings, exclusively in those matters in respect of which they confer the right to vote to their holders.

the meeting and the adoption of resolutions. But the Mexican legislator did not intend to suppress the right to vote because this was a much debated matter at the time and was only recognized in English and some American legislations; what the legislator wanted was to eliminate the obstacles to the constitution of the meeting by partially suppressing the vote of the investor shareholders, those for whom the acquisition of shares has as its sole purpose an investment:

> For these persons, the vote, with the exceptions mentioned in the law, does not protect any real interest that deserves to be protected. In such cases, what must be protected is precisely the security of the investment within the indispensable limits so that these same persons continue to be partners, that is, continue to be linked to the final fate of the company, and do not become mere mutuants.

According to the D'Amelio project, on the other hand, the so-called "privileged" limited voting shares were an alternative to avoid the change of control in the company and mitigate the danger to the continuity of the company, without having to resort to drastic and controversial solutions such as the plural voting shares, which Vivante defended and which are currently admitted in Italy. For both D'Amelio and the Mexican legislator, the limited voting shares were a powerful instrument to satisfy the interests of the pulverized investor shareholders, without the total deprivation of the right to vote, because they retain it for matters of great importance in the company, and in compensation for the limitation they suffer, they are granted a preferential dividend and other special rights, with the possibility that the management partners can adopt decisions in the assembly without depending on the attendance or the vote of the former. According to Martínez, the issuance of these shares does not cause disorders or obstacles for their placement in the market and instead facilitates the constitution of the meeting, since it allows the common shares to fulfill the same function of the shares on demand[37].

---

37 A. Martínez Báez, 'Algunas consideraciones sobre las acciones preferentes en las sociedades anónimas'. This argument will later be admitted also for

2.4. Prohibition of plural voting shares

Following the D'Amelio project, the LGSM categorically prohibited the issuance of plural voting shares, thus closing the door to the multiple voting shares advocated by César Vivante, who argued that with proper regulation they could be useful to prevent instrumental abuses of minorities, to combat hostile takeovers of shares and to ensure the stable and programmed development of the industry by strengthening the position of the administrators, and to defend the company from its shareholders and avoid the disruptive influence of shareholders' meetings in the management of corporate affairs. One of the most delicate problems faced by the commission was to recognize the issuance of shares with different voting rights, whose repercussions were not only economic, but also in terms of control of the company and, therefore, the direction of its strategic trajectory.

These shares had been introduced in the United States as early as 1836, in the United Kingdom in 1908 and, according to Garrigues, in Germany since 1937. Recognition, however, was not peaceful in Italy, as can be seen from the aforementioned draft of commercial codes. Although Vivante argued in favor of them, he admitted that multiple voting shares could be detrimental to the company and ordinary shareholders in the face of abuse and illicit appetites of other shareholders. Despite multiple voting shares were harshly criticized in Italy and in Europe, in the third decade of the 20th century, several voices demanded their admission — especially in favor of those who have been loyal to the company, and currently the so-called fidelity shares have been admitted especially in the countries of the European Union. In Italy, the Competitiveness Decree of 2014, admitted multiple voting shares and thereby definitively settled the discussion on the one-share-one-vote principle, which had already been greatly

---

issuing shares without voting rights, since, as Giampaolino argues, non-voting shares typically satisfy the expectation of financing, and the suppression of voting rights is the reflection of the character of the rationally apathetic and absent shareholder, C.F. Giampaolino, *Le Azioni Speciali. Saggi di Diritto Commerciale* (Milano: Giuffrè, 2004), p. 3.

weakened by the 2003 corporate reform. But Mexico continues to prohibit their issuance, although probably not for long.

2.5. Prohibition of voting shareholder agreements (pooling agreements)

The consideration of voting as a right to be exercised at the shareholders' meeting to form the will of the Company was the basis for considering the unlawfulness of shareholders' voting arrangements, which were then necessarily clandestine, on the grounds that they seriously undermined public order by preventing the free exercise of the right to vote since the shareholders were prevented from forming their opinion and casting their vote freely after joint deliberation; this meant that the vote cast under a share syndication was a sham because the vote was already preformed (the company's will was not formed at the meeting but beforehand) and the functioning of the meeting was distorted[38]. According to this school of thought, one of the most valuable conditions of the right to vote was its complete freedom of emission, while the pact obliged the shareholder to vote according to the will of others, or to cede to others his right to vote by means of the precarious delivery of his shares with the danger of exercising the vote in a different sense and without the prudence with which the holder of the shares would do it. Finally, although the voting right could not be assimilated to a subjective public right like the electoral voting right, it was nevertheless a personal right with patrimonial consequences, in any case outside of commerce. Therefore, shareholder agreements between voting shareholders were illicit.

Although another sector of the doctrine argued in favor of voting pacts, Vivante's position permeated not only his project, but also to a certain extent the Italian Civil Code and court decisions. For the Italian courts, these agreements violated the prohibition of splitting the ownership of shares and votes, the

---

38 C. Vivante, *Tratado de derecho mercantil*, trans. by César Silió Belena, 5th. edn Italian (Madrid: Reus, 1932), p. 248.

principle of the free formation of the will in the meeting, the rules of mandatory or statutory law, and implied a usurpation of the powers of the administrative body, in violation of the public corporate order and fundamentally undermined the entire legislative regime established for the protection of the regular function of the company, whose rules and activities in the national economy were of public order. The Italian Court of Cassation has repeatedly upheld the unlawfulness of these agreements on the grounds that they undermined the entire legislative regime established for the protection of the regular function of the general meeting of partners.

Mexico, influenced by Italian doctrine and jurisprudence[39], did not escape these considerations and included the nullity of voting agreements in Article 198 of the LGSM. According to this provision, our 20th century doctrine categorically denied the validity of voting agreements since, following Scialoja, Lalumia and Vivante, among others, it considered that such agreements were unlawful as they obliged the shareholders to cast their vote in a certain sense before the constitution of the meeting, whereas each shareholder must cast his vote freely, at the meeting and after they have deliberated together on the corporate business, in order to form the corporate will, while the syndication of shares violated this principle.

The doctrine, which even referred to Vivante as "the illustrious Italian jurist", outlawed share syndication agreements. Thus, Mantilla Molina, in relation to his review of Antonio Pedrol's book on share syndication, argued that considering the voting commitment valid was a valid thesis in pure dogmatic speculation and in accordance with other legal systems, but that it was not in accordance with our positive Mexican law[40]. This

---

39 J. Barrera Graf, 'Influence of the Italian Commercial Code of 1882 on the Mexican Commercial Code of 1890', Communication presented at the Colloquium on the Centenary of the Codice di Commercio of 1882, held in Taormina, Sicily, on November 4, 5, 6, 1982, *Temas de Derecho Mercantil* (México: UNAM, 1983), p. 189.
40 R.L. Mantilla Molina 'La sindicación de acciones. – Antonio Pedrol – Editorial de Derecho Privado – 206 págs, 1951. Madrid', *Boletín del Instituto de Derecho Comparado de México*, 13 (1960), pp. 184–195 (p. 184).

view was based on the consideration that the LGSM (article 198) expressly declared null and void "any agreement that restricts the shareholders' freedom to vote"[41]. Likewise, Barrera Graf held that agreements were null and void, although not the votes cast to comply with them; furthermore, he held that the agreements were null and void, although not the votes cast to enforce them. In the same sense, Barrera Graf also pointed out that the voting agreement lacked force and effectiveness against both the company and the shareholder; however, unlike Mantilla, he held that nullity could be applied to the vote only when it was decisive in obtaining the majority (principles of resistance) and if the requirements of the challenge actions were met[42].

Finally, in accordance with current Italian doctrine and legislation, Mexico has recognized the legality of share syndication and has shown a strong inclination towards US law, as is the case in Europe[43]. The reform of the LGSM of 13 June 2014 recognizes the supremacy of the autonomy of the shareholders' will and allows them, among other rights, to enter into the following shareholders' agreements (which are not enforceable against the company, except in the case of a judicial decision): 1. Put or call options, whereby one or more shareholders: (a) may only dispose of all or part of their shareholding, where the acquirer also undertakes to acquire a proportion or all of the shares of one or more other shareholders, (b) may require another shareholder to dispose of all or part of their shareholding, where they accept a takeover offer, on the same terms; (c) have the right to dispose of or acquire from another shareholder, who must be obliged to dispose of or acquire, as the case may be, all or part of the shareholding which is the subject of the transaction, at a specified or determinable price; (d) are obliged to subscribe and pay for a certain number of shares representing the company's share capital, at a specified or determinable price; and (e) other

---

41 R.L. Mantilla Molina, *Derecho mercantil* (México: Porrúa, 1996), p. 410.
42 J. Barrera Graf, *Instituciones de Derecho Mercantil* (México, Porrúa 1989), p. 538.
43 W. Wiegand, 'The Reception of the American Law in Europe', American Journal of Comparative Law, 39 (1991), pp. 229–48.

rights and obligations of a similar nature; 2. Disposals and other legal acts relating to the ownership, disposal or exercise of pre-emptive rights to subscribe shares, regardless of whether such legal acts are carried out with other shareholders or with third parties; 3. Agreements to exercise voting rights at shareholders' meetings; 4. Agreements for the disposal of its shares in public offerings; and 5. Others of a similar nature.

3. *Conclusion*

Mexican commercial law, and in particular the voting rights of the shareholders of the corporation, was initially configured according to French, Spanish and Italian law. However, since the end of the 19th century, the influence of Italian law began to take hold in Mexican legislation, doctrine and jurisprudence until it became the dominant doctrine of the 20th century. At the same time, with globalization, the financial scandals occurring in the dawn of 2021 and the access to new information technologies, both Mexican and Italian law — directly and through the Directives of the European Commission and the European Parliament — have taken a look at the law of the United States and assimilated some of its corporate figures and systems of issuance of new classes of shares in which the right to vote is suppressed, limited, restricted or suspended. Nevertheless, the Italian doctrine is still in force in Mexico and Mexican jurists continue to draw from it.

ACKNOWLEDGMENTS

We would like to express our deepest and sincerest gratitude to Edison S.p.a. for generously contributing to the publication of this volume.

MIMESIS GROUP
www.mimesis-group.com

MIMESIS INTERNATIONAL
www.mimesisinternational.com
info@mimesisinternational.com

MIMESIS EDIZIONI
www.mimesisedizioni.it
mimesis@mimesisedizioni.it

ÉDITIONS MIMÉSIS
www.editionsmimesis.fr
info@editionsmimesis.fr

MIMESIS COMMUNICATION
www.mim-c.net

MIMESIS EU
www.mim-eu.com

Printed by
Rotomail Italia S.p.A.
February 2024

www.ingramcontent.com/pod-product-compliance
Lightning Source LLC
Chambersburg PA
CBHW020602300426
44113CB00007B/477